FOOD & WINE

Annual Cookbook 2015

FOOD & WINE ANNUAL COOKBOOK 2015

EDITOR IN CHIEF **Dana Cowin**

EXECUTIVE EDITOR **Kate Heddings**

EDITOR **Susan Choung**

DESIGNER **Phoebe Flynn Rich**

DEPUTY WINE EDITOR **Megan Krigbaum**

COPY EDITOR **Lisa Leventer**

PRODUCTION ASSOCIATE
Stephanie Thompson

EDITORIAL ASSISTANT **Manon Cooper**

FRONT COVER

Belgian Beef Stew (recipe, p. 78)

PHOTOGRAPHER **Christina Holmes**

FOOD STYLIST **Kay Chun**

PROP STYLIST **Carla Gonzalez-Hart**

BACK COVER

PHOTOGRAPHER (SOUP AND FISH)
Con Poulos

PHOTOGRAPHER (TARTS) **Johnny Miller**

FOOD & WINE MAGAZINE

SVP/EDITOR IN CHIEF **Dana Cowin**

CREATIVE DIRECTOR **Fredrika Stjärne**

EXECUTIVE MANAGING EDITOR **Mary Ellen Ward**

EXECUTIVE EDITOR **Pamela Kaufman**

DEPUTY EDITOR **Christine Quinlan**

EXECUTIVE FOOD EDITOR **Tina Ujlaki**

EXECUTIVE WINE EDITOR **Ray Isle**

DIGITAL DIRECTOR **Alex Vallis**

FEATURES

RESTAURANT EDITOR **Kate Krader**

DEPUTY WINE EDITOR **Megan Krigbaum**

STYLE EDITOR **Suzie Myers**

ASSOCIATE EDITORS **Chelsea Morse,
M. Elizabeth Sheldon**

ASSISTANT EDITOR **Maren Ellingboe**

FOOD

DEPUTY EDITOR **Kate Heddings**

SENIOR EDITOR **Sarah DiGregorio**

TEST KITCHEN SENIOR EDITORS **Justin Chapple,
Kay Chun, Chris Morocco**

ASSOCIATE EDITOR **Ben Mims**

EDITORIAL ASSISTANT **Julia Heffelfinger**

TEST KITCHEN ASSISTANT **Emily Tylman**

ART

ART DIRECTOR **James Maikowski**

SENIOR DESIGNER **Angelica Domingo**

DESIGNER **Bianca Jackson**

PHOTO

PHOTO EDITOR **Sara Parks**

ASSOCIATE PHOTO EDITOR **Samantha Bolton**

PHOTO ASSISTANT **Olivia Weiner**

COPY & RESEARCH

COPY CHIEF **Elizabeth Herr**

SENIOR EDITOR **Amanda Woytus**

ASSOCIATE RESEARCH EDITOR **Erin Laverty Healy**

PRODUCTION

PRODUCTION DIRECTOR **Joseph Colucci**

DIGITAL MEDIA

DEPUTY DIGITAL EDITOR **Lawrence Marcus**

ASSOCIATE DIGITAL EDITORS **Noah Kaufman,
Justine Sterling**

EDITORIAL ASSISTANT **Brianna Wippman**

SENIOR PRODUCER **Caitlin Drexler**

PHOTO COORDINATOR **Erin Fagerland**

ASSOCIATE MANAGING EDITOR **Kerianne Hansen**

ASSISTANT TO THE EDITOR IN CHIEF **Annie P. Quigley**

TIME HOME ENTERTAINMENT INC.

PUBLISHER **Margot Schupf**

VICE PRESIDENT, FINANCE **Vandana Patel**

EXECUTIVE DIRECTOR, MARKETING SERVICES
Carol Pittard

PUBLISHING DIRECTOR **Megan Pearlman**

ASSISTANT GENERAL COUNSEL **Simone Procas**

SENIOR PRODUCTION MANAGER **Susan Chodakiewicz**

ASSISTANT PROJECT MANAGER **Allyson Angle**

FOOD & WINE

Annual Cookbook

AN ENTIRE YEAR OF RECIPES

2015

FOOD & WINE
BOOKS
Time Inc. Affluent Media Group

JAPANESE PIZZA
Recipe, page 256

Contents

BUCATINI ALL'AMATRICIANA WITH PARMIGIANO
Recipe, page 88

Foreword

WITH THE RISE OF INFOGRAPHICS to explain everything from science to pop culture, we thought it would be appropriate to give an overview of this year's annual cookbook with numbers:

670
RECIPES
This cookbook is a megadose of inspiration, with ideas for breakfast, lunch, din ner, holidays, snacks and even afternoon tea. There are over 50 chicken recipes, more than 75 desserts and nearly 100 salads.

300
CONTRIBUTORS
The recipes here come from people all over the world: chefs and bakers and, increasingly, bloggers and food artisans. All are innovators who are shaping the way we cook today and whose recipes reflect exactly what we want to eat right now.

320
WINES
Peppered throughout this book are accessible, delicious pairings for every kind of dish, suggested by *Food & Wine*'s wine editors.

We hope that you'll love this book as much as we do. Please let us know what you think of the recipes on Twitter (tweet @foodandwine) and share photos of your proudest successes on Instagram (tag @foodandwine), using the hashtag #FWCookbook.

Dana Cowin
Editor in Chief
FOOD & WINE

Kate Heddings
Executive Editor
FOOD & WINE Cookbooks

FROM TOP:
CHARRED EGGPLANT AND YOGURT DIP;
BUTTERNUT SQUASH AND TANGELO
DIP WITH SAGE; GREEN OLIVE, WALNUT
AND POMEGRANATE DIP
Recipes, pages 10 and 14

Starters

PAGE NUMBERS IN RED INDICATE F&W STAFF FAVORITES

Spinach-Yogurt Dip
Total **1 hr**; Makes **4 cups**

- 2 **Tbsp. unsalted butter**
- 2 **Tbsp. extra-virgin olive oil**
- 1 **large onion, finely chopped**
- 5 **garlic cloves, minced**
  Salt and pepper
- 3 **lbs. curly spinach,
  thick stems discarded**
- 2 **cups plain Persian or Greek yogurt**
  Pita chips and za'atar, for serving

1. In a large saucepan, melt the butter in the olive oil. Add the onion, garlic and a generous pinch each of salt and pepper and cook over moderate heat, stirring, until softened and caramelized, 20 minutes.

2. Add the spinach to the saucepan in large handfuls, allowing it to wilt slightly before adding more. Cook over moderate heat, stirring occasionally, until wilted and very tender, about 20 minutes. Scrape the spinach into a medium bowl, season with salt and pepper and let cool completely.

3. Add the yogurt to the spinach and mix well. Season with salt and pepper and refrigerate until slightly chilled, about 15 minutes. Serve with pita chips and za'atar. —*Goshtasb and Homa Dashtaki*

MAKE AHEAD The dip can be refrigerated for up to 3 days. Let stand at room temperature for 15 minutes before serving.

Charred Eggplant and Yogurt Dip
📷 PAGE 8
Active **25 min**; Total **1 hr 30 min**
Makes **1½ cups**

- One **1¼-lb. eggplant**
- 2 **large shallots, halved lengthwise**
- 3 **large garlic cloves**
- 1 **Tbsp. extra-virgin olive oil**
  Salt and pepper
- ½ **cup plain Greek yogurt**
- 2 **Tbsp. fresh lemon juice**
- 2 **Tbsp. each of finely chopped parsley,
  cilantro and mint**

1. Preheat the oven to 375°. Roast the eggplant over an open flame or under a broiler until softened and charred, 12 minutes. Transfer to a baking dish. Add the shallots and garlic to the eggplant, drizzle with the oil and season with salt and pepper; roast for 35 minutes, until very tender. Let cool completely. Scrape the eggplant flesh into a colander to drain for 15 minutes; discard the skin.

2. Mince the eggplant, garlic and shallots; transfer to a bowl. Stir in the yogurt, lemon juice and herbs. Season the dip with salt and pepper. —*Serge Madikians*

SERVE WITH Pita chips and crudités.

NOTE For a pretty presentation, drizzle the dip with pomegranate molasses and sprinkle with pomegranate seeds.

MAKE AHEAD The dip can be refrigerated overnight. Serve at room temperature.

Green Olive, Walnut and Pomegranate Dip
📷 PAGE 8
🕐 Total **25 min**; Makes **2¼ cups**

This chunky dip, a specialty in the Gilan province of northern Iran, is from chef Serge Madikians of Serevan Restaurant in Amenia, New York. Madikians, who left Iran in the 1980s to come to the US, makes his version with pomegranate in two forms: seeds and molasses.

- ½ **cup walnuts**
- 2 **cups pitted briny green olives,
  finely chopped**
- ½ **cup pomegranate seeds**
- 3 **Tbsp. pomegranate molasses**
- 3 **Tbsp. finely chopped tarragon**
- 3 **Tbsp. extra-virgin olive oil**
- 1 **Tbsp. red wine vinegar**
  Salt and pepper

Preheat the oven to 375°. Spread the walnuts in a pie plate and bake until toasted, 10 minutes. Let cool, then finely chop. In a bowl, mix the walnuts with the remaining ingredients and season with salt and pepper. —*Serge Madikians*

SERVE WITH Pita chips and crudités.

MAKE AHEAD The dip can be refrigerated for up to 2 days. Bring to room temperature before serving.

Hummus with Spiced Beef and Pine Nuts
Active **35 min**; Total **1 hr 15 min plus overnight soaking**; Makes **2 cups**

The unexpected topping of sautéed ground beef and pine nuts adds texture and deep flavor to this extra-creamy chickpea spread.

- 1 **cup dried chickpeas—soaked
  overnight with ½ tsp. baking soda,
  drained and rinsed**
  Kosher salt
- 2 **Tbsp. tahini**
- 2 **Tbsp. fresh lemon juice**
- 1 **garlic clove, crushed**
  Freshly ground pepper
- 2 **Tbsp. extra-virgin olive oil,
  plus more for drizzling**
- 1 **Tbsp. pine nuts**
- 3 **oz. lean ground beef**
  Pinch of ground allspice
  Paprika, for dusting

1. In a medium saucepan, cover the chickpeas with water and bring to a boil. Add a generous pinch of salt and simmer over moderately low heat until the chickpeas are tender, 45 minutes; add more water as needed to keep them covered; drain, reserving ⅓ cup of the cooking liquid.

2. In a food processor, puree the chickpeas with the reserved cooking liquid, tahini, lemon juice and garlic until very smooth. Season the hummus with salt and pepper, then scrape it into a shallow bowl.

3. In a small skillet, heat the 2 tablespoons of olive oil until shimmering. Add the pine nuts and cook over moderate heat, stirring, until golden, 3 minutes. Using a slotted spoon, transfer the pine nuts to paper towels.

4. Add the ground beef to the skillet and season with salt, pepper and the allspice. Cook over moderately high heat, breaking up the meat with a wooden spoon, until browned and cooked through, 5 minutes. Using a slotted spoon, transfer the meat to paper towels. Spoon the meat and pine nuts onto the hummus, drizzle with olive oil and dust with paprika. —*Reem Acra*

WINE Juicy Spanish Garnacha blend: 2012 Celler de Capçanes Mas Donís.

HUMMUS WITH SPICED BEEF
AND PINE NUTS

Pumpkin and Chickpea Hummus with Jalapeño Oil

Total **30 min**; Serves **8**

Sara Kate Gillingham, founding editor of The Kitchn food blog, blends pumpkin puree into her hummus, then tops the dip with crunchy candied pumpkin seeds and a fragrant, fiery jalapeño-and-cilantro oil.

JALAPEÑO OIL

¼ cup grapeseed or canola oil
2 Tbsp. minced cilantro
1 Tbsp. minced seeded jalapeño
Salt

PUMPKIN SEEDS

¼ cup pumpkin seeds
2 tsp. grapeseed or canola oil
1 Tbsp. sugar
Pinch of cayenne pepper
Salt

HUMMUS

One 15-oz. can chickpeas, rinsed and drained
1 cup pumpkin puree
¼ cup tahini
3 Tbsp. fresh lemon juice
3 Tbsp. water
2 small garlic cloves, finely chopped
½ tsp. ground cumin
Salt

1. Make the jalapeño oil In a small saucepan, heat the oil over moderate heat until hot but not shimmering, about 3 minutes. Transfer to a small bowl and stir in the cilantro and jalapeño. Let cool completely, then season with salt.

2. Meanwhile, make the pumpkin seeds In a small skillet, toast the seeds in the oil over moderate heat, stirring occasionally, until just starting to brown, about 5 minutes. Add the sugar, cayenne and a generous pinch of salt and cook, tossing, until the sugar melts and the seeds are browned, about 2 minutes longer. Transfer to a plate to cool completely, then break the candied pumpkin seeds into small pieces.

3. Make the hummus In a food processor, combine all of the ingredients except the salt and puree until smooth, then season generously with salt. Scrape the hummus into a serving bowl. Drizzle some of the jalapeño oil on top, garnish with the candied pumpkin seeds and serve.
—Sara Kate Gillingham

SERVE WITH Tortilla chips or pita chips.

MAKE AHEAD The candied pumpkin seeds can be stored in an airtight container for up to 3 days. The jalapeño oil and hummus can be refrigerated separately overnight. Bring to room temperature before serving.

Charred Eggplant Spread

Total **35 min**; Makes **3 cups**

A very quick marinade and just a few minutes on the grill turn eggplant into the perfect base for this must-make spread from Chicago chef Jimmy Bannos, Jr. It's smoky, incredibly flavorful and fresh-tasting, thanks to all the chopped herbs.

¾ cup extra-virgin olive oil
½ cup red wine vinegar
1 cup coarsely chopped flat-leaf parsley
½ cup coarsely chopped basil
½ cup coarsely chopped cilantro
6 garlic cloves, minced
1 large eggplant, sliced lengthwise ¼ inch thick
¼ cup mayonnaise
1 Tbsp. fresh lemon juice
Kosher salt and pepper
Crackers, for serving

1. In a large bowl, whisk ½ cup of the olive oil with the vinegar, parsley, basil, cilantro and two-thirds of the garlic. Add the eggplant slices and coat well. Marinate for 15 minutes.

2. Light a grill. Grill the eggplant over moderate heat, turning and basting occasionally with the marinade, until nicely charred and tender, about 10 minutes. Chop the eggplant.

3. In a large bowl, combine the remaining garlic with the mayonnaise and lemon juice. Gradually whisk in the remaining ¼ cup of olive oil. Fold in the chopped eggplant and season with salt and pepper. Serve with crackers. —Jimmy Bannos, Jr.

Fava Bean Puree

Active **15 min**; Total **1 hr 30 min**; Serves **6**

You'll find this hearty puree all over Italy's Puglia region, where it's commonly served with cooked bitter greens dressed with olive oil. Potato gives the puree a light and fluffy texture.

½ lb. dried split fava beans
1 yellow onion, chopped
½ medium baking potato, peeled and diced
2 tsp. kosher salt
Extra-virgin olive oil
Fleur de sel and pepper

1. In a small saucepan, bring the favas, onion, potato and 4 cups of water to a boil over high heat, skimming any foam that rises to the surface as needed. Add the salt, cover loosely and cook over low heat until the favas are very tender, 1 hour. Let cool for 10 minutes.

2. Pour the contents of the saucepan into a food processor and pulse until almost smooth. Scrape into a serving bowl, drizzle with olive oil and sprinkle with fleur de sel and pepper. Serve warm. —Ylenia Sambati

SERVE WITH Crusty bread.

Petty Cash Guacamole

Total **15 min**; Makes **about 2 cups**

The salty crunch of *pepitas* (hulled pumpkin seeds) makes this creamy, spicy guacamole from L.A.'s Petty Cash taqueria especially good.

2 small ripe Hass avocados, peeled and pitted
2 Tbsp. fresh lime juice
2 Tbsp. finely chopped cilantro
1 Tbsp. roasted *pepitas*, chopped
1 Tbsp. chopped tomato
½ serrano chile, minced
1 tsp. finely chopped red onion
Kosher salt

In a blender, combine the avocados and lime juice and puree until smooth. Transfer the puree to a small bowl. Stir in the remaining ingredients, season with salt and serve. —Walter Manzke

Market Math: Avocados

1 Avocado-Hummus Dip

In a food processor, puree 2 chopped **avocados** with one 15-ounce can drained **chickpeas**, ¼ cup **lemon juice**, 1½ Tbsp. **tahini** and ½ cup **olive oil**; season with **salt** and **pepper**. Serve drizzled with olive oil, alongside **crudités**.

2 Avocado Hollandaise

In a blender, puree ½ chopped ripe **avocado** with 2 tsp. **lemon juice** and ⅓ cup **hot water** until smooth, 2 minutes. With the machine on, drizzle in 2 Tbsp. **olive oil** until combined. Season with **salt** and **pepper** and serve over **poached eggs**.

3 Avocado Tartare

Stir 2 Tbsp. each of **olive oil** and minced **red onion** with 1 Tbsp. each of **Dijon mustard**, **lemon juice**, drained **capers** and chopped **parsley**. Stir in ½ small minced **jalapeño** and 3 drops **Worcestershire sauce**; season with **salt** and **pepper**. Fold in 2 diced **avocados** and serve with **toasts**.

4 Carrot-Avocado Salad

Whisk 6 Tbsp. **olive oil** with 3 Tbsp. fresh **grapefruit juice** and 1½ tsp. **ground coriander**. On a baking sheet, toss 3 Tbsp. of the vinaigrette with 1½ lbs. medium **carrots** cut into ¼-inch coins; season with **salt** and **pepper**. Roast at 450° for 20 minutes. In a small bowl, mix ¼ cup roasted chopped **almonds** with ⅓ cup chopped **parsley** and 2 tsp. finely grated **grapefruit zest**. Put the carrots on a platter along with 2 **avocados** cut into wedges. Top with the vinaigrette and gremolata; serve.
–Kay Chun

Herb-Marinated Goat Cheese in a Jar

Active **10 min**; Total **3 days**; Serves **8**

You can save the flavorful oil after you marinate the goat cheese; it's terrific drizzled over salads, pastas and grilled meats.

- 1 small bunch each of rosemary, thyme, oregano, basil, dill and mint sprigs
  One 11-oz. goat cheese log, cut crosswise into 4 pieces
  2½ to 3 cups extra-virgin olive oil
  Toasted sliced baguette or sourdough bread, for serving

Spread half of the herbs in an 8-cup canning jar or a bowl at least 3 inches deep. Set the cheese rounds on top and cover with the remaining herbs. Add enough of the olive oil to completely submerge the cheese and herbs. Cover with the lid or plastic wrap and marinate in the refrigerator for at least 3 days and up to 5 days. Remove the cheese from the oil and serve with baguette slices. Strain the herb oil and reserve for other uses. —*Patricia Wells*

WINE Tangy, minerally Sancerre: 2012 Lucien Crochet.

Honey Citronette with Crudités

Total **20 min**; Serves **8**

Winery chef Kristofer Kalas created this sweet and tangy dip to showcase organic fruits and vegetables from the greenhouse at Wölffer Estate Vineyard on Long Island, New York. Serve it with a platter of sliced radicchio, radishes, baby carrots, cucumbers, pears and apple.

- ¼ cup orange blossom or wildflower honey
- ¼ cup fresh lime juice
- ¼ tsp. finely grated orange zest
- ½ cup plus 2 Tbsp. extra-virgin olive oil
  Kosher salt and pepper
  Assorted seasonal crudités, for serving

In a medium bowl, whisk the honey with the lime juice and orange zest. Gradually whisk in the oil and season the citronette with salt and pepper. Serve with crudités for dipping. —*Kristofer Kalas*

WINE Crisp rosé: 2013 Wölffer Estate.

Ratatouille and Goat Cheese Dip

Active **1 hr**; Total **1 hr 30 min**; Serves **8 to 10**

- ½ cup plus 2 Tbsp. extra-virgin olive oil
- 2 medium onions, cut into ½-inch dice
- 4 large garlic cloves, minced
  Kosher salt
  One 1¾-lb. eggplant, cut into ½-inch dice
- 1 tsp. finely chopped thyme
- 2 large red bell peppers, cut into ½-inch dice
- 1 zucchini, cut into ½-inch dice
- 1 medium yellow squash, cut into ½-inch dice
- 1 lb. medium tomatoes, cut into ½-inch dice
- ¼ cup chopped basil, plus more for garnish
- 1 Tbsp. fresh lemon juice
  Freshly ground pepper
- ¾ lb. fresh goat cheese

1. In a large skillet, heat 2 tablespoons of the olive oil. Add the onions, garlic and a generous pinch of salt and cook over moderate heat, stirring occasionally, until just softened and starting to brown, about 8 minutes. Scrape the onions and garlic into a large bowl.

2. Wipe out the skillet and heat ¼ cup of the oil in it. Add the eggplant and thyme and cook over moderate heat, stirring occasionally, until the eggplant is tender and lightly browned, 8 to 10 minutes. Scrape the eggplant into the bowl with the onions. Repeat with the red pepper, zucchini, yellow squash and tomatoes, cooking each vegetable separately in 1 tablespoon of oil with a generous pinch of salt until just tender and lightly browned, 5 to 7 minutes per vegetable. As they are cooked, add the vegetables to the bowl of onions and eggplant. Stir in the chopped basil and lemon juice; season with salt and pepper.

3. Preheat the oven to 350°. Spread the goat cheese in the bottoms of 2 small baking dishes (about 1 quart each). Spoon the ratatouille on top, cover with foil and bake for about 25 minutes, until hot. Top with more basil. —*Joey Wölffer*

SERVE WITH Assorted chips and crackers.

WINE Herbal, cassis-scented Cabernet Franc: 2011 Wölffer Caya.

Butternut Squash and Tangelo Dip with Sage

PAGE 8

Active **25 min**; Total **1 hr 35 min**
Makes **2½ cups**

- One 2½-lb. butternut squash—peeled, seeded and cut into 1-inch pieces
- 1 tsp. finely grated tangelo or mandarin zest
- 1 tangelo or 2 mandarin oranges, peeled and separated into sections
- 2 Tbsp. unsalted butter, cubed
- 2 Tbsp. honey
- 1 small cinnamon stick
- 2 cardamom pods, cracked
- 1 star anise pod
  Small pinch of saffron threads
  Salt and pepper
- 2 Tbsp. fresh tangelo or mandarin orange juice
- 3 Tbsp. extra-virgin olive oil, plus more for drizzling
- 2 Tbsp. minced sage
  Hot paprika, for sprinkling

1. Preheat the oven to 400°. In a large baking dish, toss the squash with the tangelo zest and sections, butter, honey, cinnamon stick, cardamom, star anise and saffron and season with salt and pepper. Pour ½ cup of water into the dish and bake for about 1 hour, until the squash is very tender and browned in spots; discard the spices.

2. Transfer the squash, tangelo sections and any pan juices to a food processor and let cool completely. Add the tangelo juice and 3 tablespoons of olive oil and pulse until nearly smooth. Stir in the sage and season with salt and pepper. Scrape the dip into a bowl, drizzle with olive oil and garnish with hot paprika. —*Serge Madikians*

SERVE WITH Pita chips and crudités.

MAKE AHEAD The dip can be refrigerated for up to 3 days. Stir in the sage just before serving at room temperature.

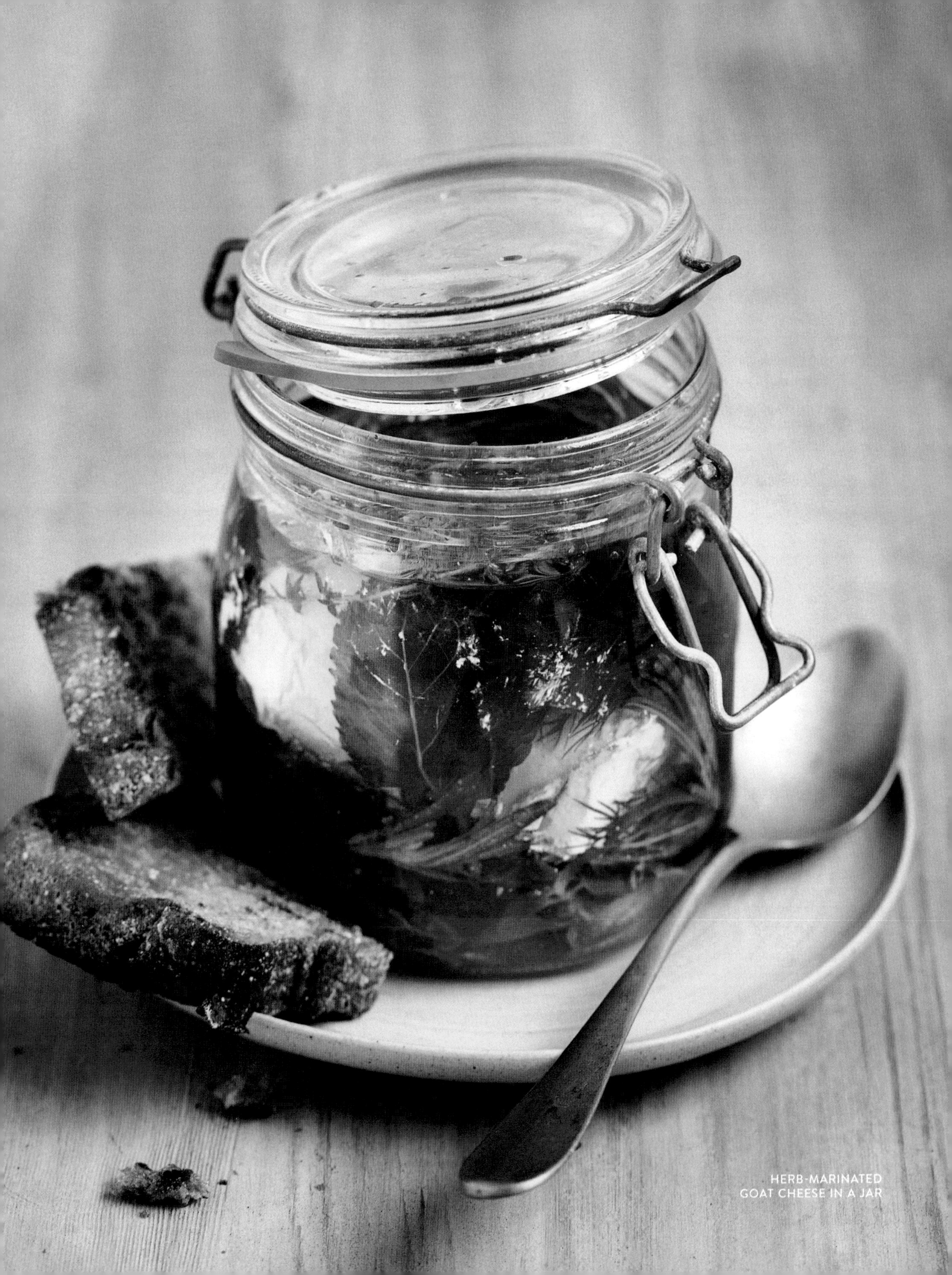

HERB-MARINATED
GOAT CHEESE IN A JAR

Curried Kabocha Squash Dip

Active **25 min**; Total **45 min plus cooling**
Makes **3 cups**

- 1 kabocha squash (2½ lbs.)—halved, seeded, peeled and cut into 1-inch pieces (6 cups)
- ¼ cup extra-virgin olive oil
- 2 tsp. hot curry powder
- Kosher salt and pepper
- 1 jalapeño, minced
- 2 Tbsp. finely chopped red onion
- 2 Tbsp. fresh lime juice
- ⅓ cup chopped cilantro

1. Preheat the oven to 450°. On a large baking sheet, toss the squash with 2 table-spoons of the olive oil and the curry pow-der and season with salt and pepper. Roast for about 20 minutes, stirring occasionally, until the squash is lightly golden and tender. Let cool to room temperature.

2. Scrape the squash into a medium bowl. Fold in the jalapeño, onion, lime juice, cilan-tro and the remaining 2 tablespoons of olive oil and season with salt and pepper. —*Kay Chun*

SERVE WITH Thick-cut tortilla chips or pita chips.

Pumpkin Seed and Tomatillo Dip

Total **30 min**; Makes **2 cups**

- 1 lb. tomatillos—husked, rinsed and halved
- 7 garlic cloves, crushed and peeled
- 5 Tbsp. extra-virgin olive oil
- Kosher salt and pepper
- 2 dried chiles, such as New Mexico or guajillo, stemmed and cut into 1-inch pieces
- 1 cup salted roasted pumpkin seeds, coarsely chopped
- ⅛ tsp. sugar

1. Preheat the oven to 450°. On a large bak-ing sheet, toss the tomatillos and garlic with 2 tablespoons of the olive oil and sea-son with salt and pepper. Roast for about 15 minutes, stirring occasionally, until the tomatillos are tender. Add the dried chiles and roast for 3 minutes longer, until the chiles are toasted.

2. Scrape the tomatillo mixture into a food processor and pulse until smooth. Trans-fer the dip to a medium bowl and stir in the pumpkin seeds, sugar and remaining 3 tablespoons of olive oil. Season with salt and pepper. —*Kay Chun*

SERVE WITH Chips or roasted vegetables.

MAKE AHEAD The dip can be refrigerated for up to 3 days.

Provoleta with Oregano and Tomatoes

Total **15 min**; Serves **4**

Francis Mallmann serves this crisp, melty grilled provolone to accompany all the beef at his restaurant Siete Fuegos at The Vines resort in Argentina's Uco Valley. The suc-cess of this dish, he says, depends on the quality of the cheese. "You want a sharp, mature cheese that's about eight or nine months old."

- One 1-inch-thick slice of provolone cheese (½ lb.)
- 2 Tbsp. small oregano leaves
- ½ tsp. crushed red pepper
- 6 grape tomatoes, halved
- Sea salt
- Basil leaves, for garnish
- Crusty bread, for serving

Preheat the oven to 450°. Heat a small cast-iron skillet until hot. Add the cheese and sprinkle with 1 tablespoon of the oreg-ano and ¼ teaspoon of the crushed red pepper. Cook over moderate heat until the cheese begins to melt and brown on the bottom, about 2 minutes. Flip the cheese and cook until the bottom begins to melt and brown, about 2 minutes. Sprinkle with the remaining 1 tablespoon of oregano and ¼ teaspoon of crushed red pepper and top with the grape tomatoes. Bake until the cheese is melted and the tomatoes are warmed through, about 4 minutes. Season with sea salt and garnish with basil. Serve with bread. —*Francis Mallmann*

WINE Argentinean sparkling wine: NV Regi-nato Rosé of Malbec.

Chicken Liver Mousse with Mascarpone

Active **45 min**; Total **3 hr**; Makes **2 cups**

- ¼ lb. bacon, finely chopped
- 1 cup finely chopped onion
- ½ tart apple—peeled, cored and finely chopped
- Salt
- ½ tsp. minced thyme
- ¼ tsp. white pepper
- ¼ tsp. sweet paprika
- Pinch of grated nutmeg
- Pinch of cinnamon
- 1 stick plus 2 Tbsp. unsalted butter, softened
- 1 lb. chicken livers, trimmed and patted dry
- 2 Tbsp. bourbon
- ½ cup mascarpone cheese

1. In a large cast-iron skillet, cook the bacon over moderate heat, stirring, until the fat is rendered and the bacon is crisp, 7 minutes. Using a slotted spoon, transfer to a bowl; reserve for another use.

2. Add the onion, apple and a generous pinch of salt to the skillet and cook over moderate heat, stirring, until starting to brown, 8 minutes. Stir in the thyme, pep-per, paprika, nutmeg and cinnamon and cook until fragrant, 1 minute; transfer to a food processor.

3. In the skillet, melt 2 tablespoons of the butter. Season the livers with salt and cook over moderately high heat, turn-ing, until barely pink inside, 4 minutes. Add the bourbon and simmer for 1 minute. Scrape the livers and any juices into the processor; let cool.

4. Add the mascarpone and remaining stick of butter to the processor and puree. Press the mousse through a fine sieve and season with salt; spread in a serving bowl. Press a sheet of plastic wrap onto the surface and refrigerate for at least 2 hours or up to 2 days. Serve at room temperature. —*Camas Davis*

SERVE WITH Baguette toasts, mustard and jam.

WINE Earthy red Burgundy: 2012 Domaine Faiveley Mercurey Clos Rochette.

PROVOLETA WITH OREGANO
AND TOMATOES

Three-Cheese Fondue with Pickles

⏱ Total **30 min**; Serves **8**

Actress and cookbook author Ali Larter is a fondue expert: Her mother made it regularly, and it was her favorite dish when she went skiing in Switzerland. She prepares an excellent rendition with Gruyère and, more unexpectedly, sparkling wine and Brie, which makes the fondue especially creamy.

½ lb. Gruyère cheese, shredded

½ lb. Emmentaler cheese, shredded

2 oz. Brie, rind discarded, cheese cut into small chunks

1½ Tbsp. all-purpose flour

1 garlic clove, halved

1¼ cups dry sparkling wine

2 tsp. kirsch

½ tsp. freshly grated nutmeg

Kosher salt and freshly ground pepper

Cornichons, cubed bread and sliced fennel, for serving

In a medium bowl, toss the cheeses and flour. Rub the inside of a fondue pot or an enameled cast-iron casserole with the cut sides of the garlic. Add the sparkling wine and simmer over moderately low heat for 3 minutes. Add the cheese in small handfuls, stirring constantly until melted before adding the next handful. Stir in the kirsch and nutmeg. Remove from the heat and season with salt and pepper. Serve hot with cornichons, bread and fennel. —*Ali Larter*

MAKE AHEAD The fondue can stand at room temperature for 4 hours. Let cool slightly, then press plastic wrap directly onto the surface. Remove the plastic before reheating.

WINE Creamy, splurge-worthy sparkling wine: 2006 Perrier-Jouët Belle Epoque Brut Champagne.

Smoked Trout Dip with Sweet Onion Vinaigrette

⏱ Total **45 min**; Serves **6 to 8**

"When my wife, Nicole, and I lived in the Midwest, smoked fish was a big part of the holidays," says chef Stuart Brioza of The Progress in San Francisco. He uses smoked trout to make a creamy, caper-studded dip that he drizzles with a tangy, oniony dressing. Serve with sturdy, thick-cut potato chips for scooping.

DIP

2 large egg yolks

2 Tbsp. sherry vinegar

1 Tbsp. Dijon mustard

1 small garlic clove, finely grated

1 lb. boneless smoked trout fillets, skin discarded, trout broken up into large flakes (2½ cups)

1 cup extra-virgin olive oil

Kosher salt and pepper

VINAIGRETTE

2 Tbsp. minced sweet onion

2 Tbsp. minced red onion

2 Tbsp. capers—rinsed, drained and minced

2 Tbsp. minced parsley

2 Tbsp. sherry vinegar

6 Tbsp. extra-virgin olive oil

Kosher salt and pepper

Thick-cut potato chips, for serving

1. Make the dip In a food processor, combine the egg yolks with the vinegar, mustard, garlic, 2 tablespoons of water and ½ cup of the trout and puree until smooth. With the machine on, gradually drizzle in the olive oil until emulsified. Scrape the puree into a medium bowl and fold in the remaining 2 cups of trout. Season the dip with salt and pepper.

2. Make the vinaigrette In a medium bowl, whisk together all of the ingredients except the salt, pepper and potato chips. Season the vinaigrette with salt and pepper and spoon a little on the trout dip. Serve with potato chips, passing the remaining vinaigrette at the table. —*Stuart Brioza*

WINE Crisp, fruit-driven sparkling wine: NV Domaine de la Taille aux Loups Triple Zéro.

Tuna Pâté

Total **10 min** plus 8 hr chilling
Serves **10 to 12**

Inspired by the cured-meat trend, chefs are transforming seafood into gorgeous terrines and rillettes. Chef Cathy Whims of Nostrana in Portland, Oregon, purees olive oil–packed tuna with butter, cream, capers and lemon to create a pâté that she says is "luscious but not heavy."

Two 10-oz. cans solid albacore tuna packed in olive oil, drained

2 sticks unsalted butter, at room temperature

¼ cup heavy cream

Finely grated zest of 1 lemon

¼ cup fresh lemon juice

¼ tsp. cayenne pepper

6 anchovy fillets, drained

3 Tbsp. capers, rinsed and drained, plus 2 Tbsp. minced capers

Kosher salt and pepper

¼ cup finely chopped parsley

¼ cup finely chopped celery

Toast or crackers, for serving

1. Line a 7½-by-3½-inch loaf pan with plastic wrap, leaving plenty of overhang. In a food processor, combine the tuna, butter, cream, lemon zest, lemon juice, cayenne, anchovies and the 3 tablespoons of capers. Season with salt and pepper and process until smooth. Scrape the puree into the loaf pan and smooth the top. Cover with the overhanging plastic wrap and refrigerate until firm, at least 8 hours or overnight.

2. In a small bowl, stir the 2 tablespoons of minced capers with the parsley and celery and set aside. Unwrap and unmold the pâté onto a serving dish and sprinkle the parsley mixture on top. Serve chilled with toast or crackers. —*Cathy Whims*

WINE Bright, citrusy sparkling wine: NV Bisol Jeio Prosecco.

THREE-CHEESE FONDUE
WITH PICKLES

Tomato-Thyme Shortbreads with Olive Gremolata

Active **40 min**; Total **2 hr**
Makes **32 shortbreads**

While shortbread is most often served as a sweet, here it's cleverly transformed into a savory biscuit richly flavored with tomato paste, Parmigiano-Reggiano cheese and fresh thyme. The shortbreads are fantastic with the olive gremolata or on their own.

SHORTBREADS

- 1 **cup all-purpose flour**
- ¼ **cup tomato paste**
- 1 **Tbsp. sugar**
- 1 **Tbsp. freshly grated Parmigiano-Reggiano cheese**
- 1 **Tbsp. fresh thyme leaves**
- ½ **tsp. kosher salt**
- ¼ **tsp. cayenne pepper**
   Pinch of freshly ground black pepper
- 1 **stick cold unsalted butter, cubed**

GREMOLATA

- ½ **cup finely chopped pitted green olives, such as Castelvetrano**
- ½ **cup finely chopped pitted kalamata olives**
- 3 **Tbsp. extra-virgin olive oil**
- 2 **Tbsp. finely chopped flat-leaf parsley**
- 1½ **tsp. finely grated lemon zest**
- 1 **tsp. fresh lemon juice**
- 1 **small garlic clove, minced**
   Kosher salt and freshly ground black pepper

1. **Make the shortbreads** In a food processor, pulse the flour, tomato paste, sugar, cheese, thyme, salt, cayenne and black pepper until the tomato paste is evenly distributed. Add the butter and pulse until the dough starts to come together. Scrape the dough onto a large sheet of plastic wrap and roll it into an 8-inch log, 1½ inches in diameter. Wrap the dough in the plastic and refrigerate until well chilled, at least 1 hour.

2. **Meanwhile, make the gremolata** In a medium bowl, combine all of the ingredients and season with salt and black pepper.

3. Preheat the oven to 350° and line 2 baking sheets with parchment paper. Slice the shortbread log into ¼-inch-thick rounds and arrange on the prepared baking sheets.

Bake the shortbreads in the upper third and center of the oven for about 18 minutes, until the edges are lightly browned; rotate the baking sheets from top to bottom and front to back halfway through baking. Transfer the shortbreads to a wire rack to cool completely. Serve with the olive gremolata. —*Melia Marden*

MAKE AHEAD The shortbread-dough log can be frozen for up to 2 weeks; thaw slightly before slicing. The baked shortbreads can be stored in an airtight container for up to 2 days. The gremolata can be refrigerated for up to 2 days; bring to room temperature before serving.

WINE Dry, berry-rich Lambrusco: NV Venturini Baldini.

Garlicky Mushroom-Onion Toasts

⏲ Total **30 min**; Serves **4**

- ¼ **cup plus 2 Tbsp. extra-virgin olive oil**
   Four ¾-inch-thick slices of country bread
- 1 **small onion, chopped**
- 3 **garlic cloves, thinly sliced**
- 1 **lb. cremini mushrooms, sliced ¼ inch thick**
   Kosher salt and pepper
- ¼ **cup dry white wine**
- 2 **Tbsp. chopped parsley**
- ½ **tsp. chopped thyme**

1. In a large cast-iron skillet, heat 2 tablespoons of the olive oil. Add the bread and toast over moderately high heat, turning once, until golden and crisp on both sides, 3 minutes. Transfer the toasts to a platter.

2. Add 2 tablespoons of the olive oil to the skillet along with the onion and garlic and cook over moderately high heat, stirring, until golden, about 2 minutes. Add the remaining 2 tablespoons of olive oil and the mushrooms and season with salt and pepper. Cook, stirring frequently, until the mushrooms are well browned, 7 to 8 minutes. Stir in the wine and cook until evaporated, 1 minute. Stir in the parsley and thyme. Top the toasts with the mushrooms and serve. —*Francis Mallmann*

Smoked Salmon on Rye with Brined Herb Stems

Active **10 min**; Total **2 hr 10 min**
Makes **4 open-face sandwiches**

Herb stems have a ton of flavor but usually end up in the trash. Instead of wasting them, however, Icelandic chef Gunnar Karl Gíslason pickles them, a technique he details in his book, *North*. The tart dill or basil stems are delicious on this classic open-face smoked salmon sandwich.

- ½ **cup apple cider vinegar**
- ¼ **cup superfine sugar**
- 20 **dill or basil stems, cut into ½-inch pieces**
- 4 **slices of rye bread**
- ½ **cup goat cheese**
- 4 **oz. smoked salmon**

1. In a bowl, whisk the vinegar with the sugar until the sugar dissolves. Add the herb stems and let stand at room temperature for 2 hours. Drain.

2. Spread the slices of rye bread with the goat cheese and top with the smoked salmon. Sprinkle with the brined herb stems and serve. —*Gunnar Karl Gíslason*

Roasted Pepper and Garlic Puree Toasts

Active **25 min**; Total **1 hr 30 min**
Makes **8 large toasts**

- 5 **red, orange or yellow bell peppers**
- 4 **garlic cloves, unpeeled**
- ½ **cup plus 2 Tbsp. extra-virgin olive oil**
   Kosher salt
   Four ¾-inch-thick slices of rustic or sourdough boule (12 oz.), halved on the diagonal and toasted
   Finely chopped flat-leaf parsley, for garnish

1. Preheat the oven to 425°. On a large rimmed baking sheet, brush the peppers and garlic all over with 2 tablespoons of the olive oil and season with salt. Roast for about 30 minutes, until softened and browned in spots. Transfer the peppers and garlic to a large bowl, cover with plastic wrap and let steam until cooled, about 30 minutes. Peel the garlic. Peel, stem and seed the peppers.

2. In a food processor, combine the roasted peppers with the roasted garlic and puree until smooth. With the machine on, gradually add the remaining ½ cup of olive oil until incorporated. Season with salt. Spread the pepper puree on the toasts, garnish with parsley and serve. —*Melia Marden*

Ricotta and Roasted Grape Crostini

Total **30 min**; Makes **12 crostini**

Roasting the grapes concentrates and deepens their sweetness in this striking appetizer.

- **1 lb. seedless mixed green and black grapes, stems discarded**
- **1 Tbsp. aged balsamic vinegar**
- **2 rosemary sprigs, plus chopped fresh rosemary for garnish**
- **3 Tbsp. extra-virgin olive oil**
   Flaky sea salt and pepper
- **3 Tbsp. pine nuts**
   Twelve ½-inch-thick baguette slices
- **¾ cup fresh ricotta cheese**
   Honey and finely grated lemon zest, for serving

1. Preheat the oven to 400°. On a parchment paper–lined baking sheet, toss the grapes with the vinegar, rosemary sprigs and 2 tablespoons of the olive oil. Season with salt and pepper and toss to coat. Roast for about 15 minutes, stirring occasionally, until the grapes are softened and the skins start to pop.

2. Meanwhile, spread the pine nuts in a pie plate and roast in the oven for 6 to 8 minutes, until golden. Brush the baguette slices with the remaining 1 tablespoon of olive oil. Arrange on a baking sheet and toast for about 8 minutes, until golden and crisp.

3. To assemble the crostini, dollop 1 tablespoon of the ricotta onto each toast. Spoon the warm grapes on top and sprinkle with the pine nuts. Arrange on a platter and top with a drizzle of honey and some lemon zest. Sprinkle the crostini with salt and garnish with chopped rosemary. —*Athena Calderone*

WINE Fresh, fruit-forward Champagne: NV Delamotte Brut.

Avocado Toasts with Oaxacan Sesame Sauce

Total **30 min**; Makes **12 toasts**

- **1 cup sesame seeds (4 oz.)**
- **⅓ cup raw slivered almonds**
- **⅓ cup raw peanuts**
- **1 tsp. crushed red pepper**
- **1 cup peanut oil**
   Salt
- **2 Hass avocados, cut into ½-inch chunks**
- **1 Tbsp. fresh lime juice**
   Twelve ½-inch-thick baguette slices, toasted
   Chopped cilantro, for garnish

1. In a medium skillet, toast the sesame seeds, almonds and peanuts over moderate heat, stirring occasionally, until golden and fragrant, 7 minutes. Transfer to a food processor and let cool completely.

2. Add the crushed red pepper and peanut oil to the processor and pulse until a chunky sauce forms. Scrape the sesame sauce into a small bowl and season with salt.

3. In a medium bowl, toss the avocados with the lime juice and season with salt. Mash the avocado onto the toasts and transfer to a platter. Spoon some of the sesame sauce on top, garnish with chopped cilantro and serve, passing additional sesame sauce at the table. —*Karen Gillingham*

Fiery Thai Tomato Romesco

Active **20 min**; Total **1 hr**; Makes **1⅓ cups**

Spicy and sweet, this roasted-tomato *romesco* (a Spanish sauce traditionally made with red peppers) is great as a dip for raw vegetables or spread on a sandwich.

- **¼ cup slivered almonds**
- **1 lb. cherry or baby plum tomatoes, halved**
- **3 large garlic cloves, crushed**
- **¼ cup plus 2 Tbsp. extra-virgin olive oil**
   Kosher salt and pepper
- **1 oz. country bread, torn into small pieces (½ cup loosely packed)**
- **2 Tbsp. fresh lime juice**
- **5 small Thai chiles, chopped**

1. Preheat the oven to 475°. Spread the almonds in a pie plate and roast for 3 to 4 minutes, until golden.

2. On a rimmed baking sheet, toss the tomatoes and garlic and drizzle with ¼ cup of the olive oil; season with salt and pepper. Roast for 10 minutes, until lightly browned. Reduce the oven temperature to 325° and roast the tomatoes for 30 minutes longer, until very tender and shriveled. Scrape the tomatoes and almonds into a food processor. Meanwhile, in a small bowl, stir the bread with the lime juice and let stand for 10 minutes.

3. Add the bread, chiles, the remaining 2 tablespoons of olive oil and ¼ cup of water to the processor and pulse until the dip is slightly chunky. Season the *romesco* with salt and pepper. —*Kay Chun*

SERVE WITH Crudités.

Endive and Apricot Tartines

Total **30 min**; Serves **4**

- **Four ¾-inch-thick slices of a rustic or sourdough boule**
- **¼ cup pecans**
   Extra-virgin olive oil, for brushing and drizzling
- **2 endives—halved lengthwise, cored and thinly sliced**
- **2 tsp. fresh lemon juice**
   Salt
- **2 fresh apricots—halved, pitted and thinly sliced**
   Shaved sheep-milk cheese, such as Manchego, and chopped marjoram, for garnish

1. Preheat the oven to 375°. Arrange the bread and pecans on a baking sheet. Brush the bread with some olive oil. Toast until the bread and pecans are golden, 8 to 10 minutes. Chop the pecans.

2. In a medium bowl, toss the endives with the lemon juice and season with salt. Let stand until slightly wilted, about 3 minutes. Add the apricots and pecans and toss. Top the toasts with the endive salad and garnish with cheese and marjoram. Drizzle with olive oil and serve. —*Heidi Swanson*

WINE Lively Spanish sparkling wine: NV Castellroig Brut Cava.

Ricotta and Roasted Tomato Bruschetta with Pancetta

⏱ Active **15 min**; Total **40 min**; Serves **8**

Roasting tomatoes on the same baking sheet as pancetta flavors them with luscious cured pork.

- 10 oz. multicolored cherry tomatoes
- 2 garlic cloves, thickly sliced
- 5 Tbsp. extra-virgin olive oil, plus more for drizzling
  Kosher salt and pepper
- 4 thin slices of pancetta
- 32 sage leaves
- 1 lb. fresh ricotta cheese
- 8 slices of country bread, cut ¾ inch thick and toasted
  Flaky sea salt, for serving

1. Preheat the oven to 325°. In a bowl, toss the tomatoes with the garlic and 1 tablespoon of the olive oil; season with kosher salt and pepper. Transfer the tomatoes to one side of a parchment-lined baking sheet and lay the pancetta slices out on the other side. Bake for 25 minutes, until the pancetta is crisp. Transfer the pancetta to paper towels to drain, then crumble.

2. Roast the tomatoes for about 10 more minutes, until bursting and lightly caramelized. Transfer the tomatoes and any rendered fat from the pancetta to a bowl.

3. Meanwhile, in a small skillet, heat the remaining ¼ cup of olive oil over moderately high heat. Add the sage and fry until bright green and crisp, 30 to 45 seconds. Drain the sage on paper towels; reserve the oil for another use.

4. Spread the ricotta on the toasts and top with the tomatoes and crumbled pancetta. Drizzle with olive oil, sprinkle with sea salt and pepper and top the toasts with the sage leaves. Serve immediately. —*Susan Spungen*

WINE Berry-scented Provençal rosé: 2013 Château Montaud.

Pecorino Crisps with Rhubarb-Cherry Chutney

Active **40 min**; Total **1 hr 20 min** plus cooling; Serves **6 to 8**

CHUTNEY

- 1 Tbsp. extra-virgin olive oil
- ¼ cup finely chopped red onion
- 1 Tbsp. minced peeled fresh ginger
- ¼ tsp. ground coriander
- ¼ tsp. crushed red pepper
- ½ lb. rhubarb, cut into ½-inch pieces
- ¼ cup fresh or frozen cherries, pitted and halved
- ½ cup apple cider vinegar
- ¼ cup sugar
  Kosher salt

PECORINO CRISPS

- ¾ cup freshly grated Pecorino Romano cheese
- ¾ cup freshly grated Parmigiano-Reggiano cheese
  Freshly ground black pepper

1. Make the chutney In a medium saucepan, heat the olive oil until shimmering. Add the onion, ginger, coriander and crushed red pepper and cook over moderately high heat, stirring, until softened, about 3 minutes. Stir in the rhubarb, cherries, vinegar and sugar and bring to a boil. Simmer over moderately high heat, stirring occasionally, until the rhubarb starts to break down and the chutney thickens slightly, about 8 minutes. Season the chutney with salt and let cool completely.

2. Make the crisps Preheat the oven to 350° and line a baking sheet with a silicone mat or parchment paper. In a medium bowl, whisk together the Pecorino and Parmigiano cheeses. Working in batches, spoon 1-tablespoon mounds of the cheese onto the prepared baking sheet, spacing them 2½ inches apart. Use your fingers to flatten the mounds slightly, then season each one with pepper. Bake for about 13 minutes, until the crisps are golden brown and lacy. Using a spatula, transfer the crisps to a rack to cool and harden. Serve the crisps with the rhubarb-cherry chutney. —*Melia Marden*

Smoked Sturgeon Spread with Grilled Bread

Active **20 min**; Total **1 hr 15 min**; Serves **10**

The smoked sturgeon here is baked with maple syrup, crushed red pepper and garlic, making it sweet and spicy. Mixing it with crème fraîche creates a luxurious spread.

- ½ cup extra-virgin olive oil
- 1 cup thinly sliced shallots (from 2 large shallots)
- 6 garlic cloves, crushed
- 1 lb. smoked sturgeon, broken into large chunks
- 4 thyme sprigs
- 2 tsp. pure maple syrup
- ¼ tsp. crushed red pepper
- ¾ cup crème fraîche
- 1 tsp. finely grated lemon zest
  Kosher salt and black pepper
  Grilled country bread, watercress and pickled onions, for serving

1. Preheat the oven to 300°. In a large ovenproof skillet, heat the olive oil. Add the shallots and garlic and cook over moderate heat, stirring occasionally, until softened, about 5 minutes. Fold in the sturgeon, thyme, maple syrup and crushed red pepper and bake until the fish is heated through, about 10 minutes. Discard the thyme sprigs.

2. Scrape the contents of the skillet into a food processor and let cool completely. Pulse until very coarsely chopped. Scrape the mixture into a bowl, fold in the crème fraîche and lemon zest and season with salt and black pepper. Cover and refrigerate until chilled, about 30 minutes. Serve the smoked sturgeon spread with grilled bread, watercress and pickled onions. —*Mehdi Brunet-Benkritly and Gabriel Stulman*

MAKE AHEAD The smoked sturgeon spread can be refrigerated overnight.

CIDER Dry, lively hard cider: Eve's Cidery Autumn's Gold.

RICOTTA AND ROASTED TOMATO
BRUSCHETTA WITH PANCETTA

Mussel Toasts with Pickled-Carrot-and-Coriander Butter
Active **40 min**; Total **1 hr 20 min**; Serves **6**

¼ tsp. coriander seeds

¼ cup apple cider vinegar

¼ cup sugar

Kosher salt

1 medium carrot, very thinly sliced

1 stick unsalted butter,
at room temperature

¼ cup cilantro leaves

24 large mussels, scrubbed
and debearded

1 Tbsp. extra-virgin olive oil

1 Tbsp. minced chives

Six 2-by-3-inch rectangles
of country bread, toasted

6 paper-thin slices of lardo (optional)

1. In a small saucepan, toast the coriander seeds over low heat, stirring, until fragrant, 2 minutes. Add the vinegar, sugar, ½ teaspoon of salt and ¼ cup of water and cook, stirring, until the sugar dissolves and the brine is warm. Stir in the carrot slices and let stand for 1 hour.

2. Drain the carrot, reserving the pickling liquid. Transfer the carrot and 1 tablespoon of the pickling liquid to a blender. Add the butter and cilantro and puree. Pass the butter through a fine sieve into a small bowl and season with salt.

3. In a medium saucepan, bring 1 inch of water to a boil. Add the mussels, cover and cook just until they open. Drain and remove the mussels from their shells. In a small bowl, toss the mussels with the olive oil and chives.

4. Spread some of the carrot butter on the toasts. Top with the mussels, drape the lardo on top and serve. —*Viet Pham*

WINE Zippy Muscadet: 2012 Domaine du Haut Bourg Côtes de Grandlieu.

Oysters on the Half Shell with Ceviche Topping
Total **30 min**; Makes **1 dozen oysters**

Dylan Fultineer, the chef at Rappahannock in Richmond, Virginia, is always dreaming up new ways to show off Chesapeake Bay oysters. This is one of his favorites: The combination of raw seafood and a tangy cilantro-chile topping evokes ceviche.

1 tsp. coriander seeds

¼ cup finely diced peeled Asian pear

¼ cup peeled, seeded and finely
diced cucumber

1 serrano chile, seeded and minced

1 Tbsp. minced cilantro

1 Tbsp. fresh lime juice

1 tsp. minced candied ginger

1 tsp. Asian fish sauce

1 tsp. extra-virgin olive oil

Kosher salt and pepper

12 freshly shucked oysters on the half
shell, such as Rappahannocks

1. In a small skillet, toast the coriander seeds over moderate heat until fragrant, about 2 minutes. Let cool, then coarsely crush the seeds in a mortar. In a small bowl, mix the crushed coriander with all of the remaining ingredients except the oysters.

2. Arrange the oysters on crushed ice. Spoon some of the topping on each one and serve right away, passing additional topping at the table. —*Dylan Fultineer*

WINE Crisp, melony Loire white: 2012 Sauvion Muscadet Sèvre-et-Maine.

Citrus-Pickled Oysters on Toast
Active **30 min**; Total **2 hr**; Serves **6**

Gently pickling oysters in warm Champagne vinegar, lime and lemon just barely cooks them while they retain their creamy texture. They're a spectacular make-ahead appetizer on grilled bread, topped with bitter greens like radicchio.

2½ Tbsp. extra-virgin olive oil

½ cup finely chopped red onion

4 garlic cloves, minced

2 dried árbol chile peppers

1 bay leaf

Kosher salt and pepper

½ cup dry sherry

¼ cup Champagne vinegar

1 Tbsp. honey

½ tsp. finely grated lime zest,
plus 2 Tbsp. fresh lime juice

½ tsp. finely grated lemon zest,
plus 3½ Tbsp. fresh lemon juice

12 freshly shucked oysters
with their liquor

1 cup lightly packed frisée, white
and light green leaves only

1 cup chopped radicchio

Grilled rustic bread, for serving

1. In a medium saucepan, heat 2 tablespoons of the olive oil. Add the onion, garlic, chiles, bay leaf and a generous pinch each of salt and pepper and cook over moderate heat, stirring occasionally, until softened, about 5 minutes. Add the sherry, vinegar, honey, lime zest and juice, lemon zest and 3 tablespoons of the lemon juice. Bring to a boil. Transfer to a medium heatproof bowl and immediately add the oysters along with their liquor. Let the oysters cool completely at room temperature, then refrigerate until chilled, about 1 hour.

2. In a medium bowl, toss the frisée and radicchio with the remaining ½ tablespoon each of olive oil and lemon juice and season with salt and pepper. Serve the oysters with a little of their pickling liquid on grilled bread, topped with the frisée and radicchio. —*Dylan Fultineer*

MAKE AHEAD The oysters can be refrigerated in the brine for up to 3 days.

WINE Lively California Pinot Grigio: 2013 Palmina.

OYSTERS ON THE HALF SHELL
WITH CEVICHE TOPPING

Miso-Pickled Eggs

Total **40 min** plus **4 hr** pickling
Serves **6 as part of a multicourse meal**

Traditional Japanese eggs pickled in soy sauce were the inspiration for this very simple version. Nancy Singleton Hachisu, author of *Japanese Farm Food*, coats shelled hard-cooked eggs in miso for four hours, then wipes them off. These pickled eggs are tasty on their own, or try them as a topping for ramen noodles.

    Ice water
  6 large eggs
 ¾ cup brown rice miso

1. Fill a bowl with ice water. Bring a saucepan of water to a boil. Using a slotted spoon, lower the eggs into the water. Simmer the eggs over moderately high heat for 9 minutes. Transfer the eggs to the ice bath to cool completely. Drain and peel the eggs.

2. Working with 1 egg at a time and with lightly dampened hands, spread 2 tablespoons of the miso in the palm of one hand and set the egg in the middle. Fold the miso around the egg, spreading it to cover the egg entirely. Carefully transfer the egg to a large, sturdy resealable plastic bag. Repeat with the remaining miso and eggs. Refrigerate the eggs for 4 hours.

3. Wipe the miso off the eggs; save the miso for another pickling. Serve the eggs or refrigerate for up to 3 days.
—*Nancy Singleton Hachisu*

INGREDIENT TIP

Get Creative with Deviled Eggs
In addition to pickled shrimp or spicy candied bacon (as in the recipes at right), try topping deviled eggs with crushed wasabi peas or sliced pickled okra.

Deviled Eggs with Pickled Shrimp

Total **1 hr 15 min** plus overnight pickling
Makes **24 deviled eggs**

SHRIMP
 ¾ cup fresh lemon juice
 ½ cup water
 ¼ cup plus 2 Tbsp. white wine vinegar
 ½ small Spanish onion, chopped
  1 garlic clove, crushed
 ½ Tbsp. pickling spice
  1 small dried red chile
 12 shelled and deveined
     medium shrimp

EGGS
  1 dozen large eggs
 ½ cup mayonnaise
  1 Tbsp. whole-grain mustard
  4 cornichons, finely chopped
  2 Tbsp. finely chopped dill,
     plus dill sprigs for garnish
  1 Tbsp. finely chopped chives
     Salt and pepper
     Hot sauce, for serving

1. Brine the shrimp In a medium saucepan, combine all of the ingredients except the shrimp and bring to a boil. Simmer over moderately low heat for 5 minutes; let cool completely.

2. In a saucepan of salted boiling water, blanch the shrimp until nearly cooked through, 2 minutes. Drain and cool under running water. Add the shrimp to the cooled brine, cover and refrigerate overnight. Drain and cut in half lengthwise.

3. Make the eggs In a large saucepan, cover the eggs with water and bring to a boil. Simmer over moderately high heat for 8 minutes. Drain the water and shake the pan gently to crack the eggs. Chill the eggs slightly under cold running water, then peel them under running water. Pat dry.

4. Cut the eggs in half lengthwise and remove the yolks; transfer the yolks to a bowl and mash well with a fork. Fold in the mayonnaise, mustard, cornichons and chopped dill and chives; season with salt and pepper. Mound the filling in the egg-white halves and top with the shrimp. Garnish with dill sprigs and serve lightly chilled with hot sauce. —*Bobby Flay*

Deviled Eggs with Ancho Chile Candied Bacon

Active **15 min**; Total **1 hr**
Makes **24 deviled eggs**

Thick-cut bacon baked with sugar and chile powder comes out of the oven caramelized, crispy and utterly irresistible. It's fabulous on deviled eggs.

 ¼ cup packed light brown sugar
 ¼ cup granulated sugar
  1 Tbsp. ancho chile powder
  1 lb. thick-cut meaty bacon
 24 Deviled Eggs (recipe follows)

Preheat the oven to 400° and line 2 large rimmed baking sheets with heavy-duty foil. In a small bowl, whisk both sugars with the chile powder. Arrange the bacon strips on the foil and coat the tops with the chile sugar. Bake for 10 minutes, until sizzling and lightly browned. Spoon off the excess bacon fat from the baking sheets. Bake for 5 to 7 minutes longer, until crisp; transfer to a rack set over a sheet of foil to cool completely. Break the bacon into 1-inch pieces and serve one piece on each deviled egg. —*Chris Carter and James Peisker*

DEVILED EGGS
Total **30 min**; Makes **24 deviled eggs**

  1 dozen large eggs
 ½ cup mayonnaise
1½ tsp. Dijon mustard
1½ tsp. yellow mustard
  3 dashes of Worcestershire sauce
     Salt

1. In a saucepan, cover the eggs with cold water; bring to a rolling boil. Cover, remove from the heat and let stand for 12 minutes.

2. Immediately drain the eggs and gently shake the pan to lightly crack the shells. Fill the pan with cold water and shake lightly to loosen the shells. Let stand until the eggs are cool. Drain and peel the eggs; pat dry.

3. Cut the eggs in half lengthwise. Transfer the yolks to a bowl. Add the mayonnaise, Dijon and yellow mustards and Worcestershire sauce and mash with a fork until smooth and creamy; season with salt.

4. Using a pastry bag fitted with a star tip or a teaspoon, fill the egg whites with the yolk mixture. Arrange the eggs on a platter.
—*F&W Test Kitchen*

DEVILED EGGS TOPPED WITH ANCHO CHILE CANDIED BACON, PICKLED OKRA AND WASABI PEAS

Twice-Cooked Latkes with Shallot Cream

Total **1 hr 30 min**; Serves **4**

½ cup sour cream

1 Tbsp. minced shallot

Kosher salt and freshly ground pepper

Two 10-oz. baking potatoes, peeled and cut into wedges

1 small onion, quartered

1 large egg, lightly beaten

1 large egg yolk

2 Tbsp. unsalted butter, melted

2½ Tbsp. cornstarch

Vegetable oil, for frying

1 large sweet onion, halved and thinly sliced

Snipped chives, for garnish

1. In a small bowl, whisk the sour cream with the shallot and season with salt and pepper. Cover and refrigerate the shallot cream until chilled, about 30 minutes.

2. Preheat the oven to 325°. In a food processor, shred the potatoes and the small onion. Transfer to a strainer set over a bowl and season with 1 tablespoon of salt. Let stand for 5 minutes, then squeeze dry in a kitchen towel. Pour off the liquid in the bowl and add the potatoes and onion. Stir in the egg, egg yolk, butter and cornstarch.

3. Scoop ⅓-cup mounds of the potatoes onto a parchment paper–lined baking sheet and flatten them to ¼ inch thick. Bake for about 15 minutes, until just set. Let cool. Reduce the oven temperature to 200°.

4. In a large saucepan, heat 1½ inches of oil to 350°. Working in batches, fry the sweet onion slices until golden, about 4 minutes. Using a slotted spoon, transfer the onions to a paper towel–lined baking sheet to drain; keep warm in the oven.

5. Reheat the oil to 350°. Working in batches, fry the latkes, turning occasionally, until browned and crisp, about 4 minutes. Transfer the latkes to a platter and garnish with snipped chives. Serve with the fried onions and shallot cream. —*Marc Forgione*

WINE Fresh American sparkling wine: NV Domaine Carneros Brut.

Mini Pea Pancakes with Herbed Yogurt

Total **30 min**; Makes **18 mini pancakes**

¾ cup plain whole-milk yogurt

2 Tbsp. each of finely chopped parsley, tarragon and chervil, plus sprigs for garnish

Kosher salt and freshly ground black pepper

1½ cups frozen peas (8 oz.), thawed, plus more for garnish

1 large egg

1 large egg yolk

½ cup heavy cream

¼ cup all-purpose flour

1 tsp. finely grated lemon zest

½ tsp. baking powder

¼ tsp. ground cardamom

¼ tsp. cayenne pepper

Unsalted butter, for greasing

1. In a medium bowl, mix the yogurt with the chopped parsley, tarragon and chervil and season with salt and black pepper. Cover with plastic wrap and refrigerate the herbed yogurt until chilled, at least 15 minutes.

2. Meanwhile, in a medium saucepan of salted boiling water, blanch the peas until crisp-tender, about 1 minute. Drain well and let cool.

3. In a food processor, pulse the 1½ cups of peas with the egg and egg yolk until the peas are finely chopped. Add the cream, flour, lemon zest, baking powder, cardamom and cayenne and a generous pinch each of salt and black pepper; pulse until the batter is nearly smooth.

4. Heat a large cast-iron skillet or griddle. Generously grease the skillet with butter. Spoon 1-tablespoon mounds of batter into the skillet and cook over moderate heat until lightly browned on the bottom, about 2 minutes. Flip the pancakes and cook for 1 to 2 minutes longer, until lightly browned and cooked through. Transfer the pancakes to a platter and keep warm. Brush the skillet with butter as needed and repeat with the remaining batter. Serve the warm pancakes topped with the herbed yogurt and garnished with peas and herb sprigs. —*Georgia Pellegrini*

WINE Crisp, apple-scented sparkling wine: NV Adami Garbèl Brut Prosecco.

Kimchi Pancake

Total **20 min**; Serves **4**

SOY-SESAME DIPPING SAUCE

2 tsp. sugar

¼ cup soy sauce

2 Tbsp. black vinegar

2 tsp. jarred kimchi liquid

1 tsp. toasted sesame seeds

PANCAKE

3 Tbsp. jarred kimchi liquid

1 tsp. black bean sauce

1½ tsp. kosher salt

2 Tbsp. plus 1 tsp. canola oil

¾ cup all-purpose flour

½ cup chopped drained kimchi

4 scallions, cut into 1-inch lengths (½ cup)

1. Make the soy-sesame dipping sauce In a medium bowl, whisk 1 tablespoon of warm water with the sugar until dissolved; whisk in the remaining ingredients.

2. Make the pancake In a large bowl, whisk ½ cup plus 1 tablespoon of water with the kimchi liquid, black bean sauce, salt and 1 teaspoon of the canola oil. Add the flour and stir just until a batter forms. Fold in the kimchi and scallions.

3. In a large nonstick skillet, heat the remaining 2 tablespoons of canola oil. Scrape the batter into the skillet and gently spread it into a round, evenly distributing the kimchi and scallions. Cook over moderately high heat until golden brown and crisp on the bottom, 4 minutes. Carefully flip the pancake; cook over moderate heat until crisp and cooked through, 3 minutes longer. Transfer the pancake to a paper towel–lined plate to drain. Cut into wedges and serve with the soy-sesame dipping sauce. —*Joshua Walker*

WINE Green-apple-inflected Spanish sparkling wine: NV Jaume Serra Cristalino Brut Cava.

MINI PEA PANCAKES
WITH HERBED YOGURT

Pork-Kimchi Dumpling Pancakes

Total **1 hr**; Serves **6 to 8**

In a brilliant twist, chef Corey Lee of Benu in San Francisco reinvents pan-fried dumplings as a single round, crisp pancake.

DIPPING SAUCE

- ¼ **cup soy sauce**
- 1 **Tbsp. white vinegar**
- ½ **Tbsp. *gochugaru* (Korean chile powder) or ½ Tbsp. crushed red pepper**
- 1 **Tbsp. sesame seeds**
- 1 **Tbsp. sugar**

DUMPLINGS

- 10 **oz. ground pork**
- 2 **scallions, minced**
- ⅓ **cup finely chopped drained kimchi**
- 2 **garlic cloves, minced**
- 1 **Tbsp. minced peeled ginger**
- 1 **large egg, lightly beaten**
- 1 **Tbsp. soy sauce**
- 1 **tsp. kosher salt**
- ¼ **cup firm tofu, finely chopped**
- 30 **round wonton wrappers**
- 1½ **Tbsp. cornstarch**
- 3 **Tbsp. canola oil**

1. Make the dipping sauce In a small bowl, mix all of the ingredients until the sugar dissolves.

2. Make the dumplings In a large bowl, mix all of the ingredients except the wrappers, cornstarch and oil. Arrange 4 wrappers on a work surface; keep the rest covered with a damp paper towel. Brush the edges of the wrappers with water and drop 1 tablespoon of the filling in the centers. Fold over one side of the wrapper to form a half-moon, pressing the edges together. Transfer to a parchment-lined baking sheet and cover with plastic wrap; assemble the remaining dumplings.

3. In a small bowl, stir the cornstarch with 1 cup plus 2 tablespoons of water to make a slurry.

4. Heat 1 tablespoon of the oil in an 8-inch nonstick skillet. Arrange 10 dumplings around the edge of the skillet, overlapping them slightly (there should be almost no empty space). Cook over moderate heat until golden on the bottom. Drizzle one-third of the slurry over and around the dumplings, cover the skillet and cook for 1 minute. Uncover and cook until the dumplings are cooked through and the slurry forms a thin crust, 4 minutes. Carefully invert the dumpling pancake onto a plate. Repeat to make 2 more pancakes. Serve with the dipping sauce —*Corey Lee*

WINE Crisp, tangy Grüner Veltliner: 2013 Berger Kremstal.

Fried Shrimp Toasts

⏱ Total **40 min**; Makes **24 toasts**

Joshua Walker, the chef at Xiao Bao Biscuit in Charleston, South Carolina, shallow-fries his shrimp toasts instead of deep-frying them, so they're less greasy than traditional Vietnamese toasts. He likes to spread the shrimp mousse unevenly over the toasts before cooking them. "If the mousse is higher on one side, it gets crisper and more browned than the other side, which is more lightly cooked," he says. "That's the perfect contrast."

NUOC CHAM

- 1 **Tbsp. sugar**
- 2 **Tbsp. fresh lime juice**
- 2 **Tbsp. Asian fish sauce**
- 1 **small Thai chile, stemmed and thinly sliced**
- ½ **small garlic clove, minced**

SHRIMP TOASTS

- 1 **lb. shelled and deveined large shrimp**
- 1 **large egg**
- 1 **Tbsp. tapioca flour**
- 3 **small Thai chiles, stemmed and chopped**
- 2 **tsp. Asian fish sauce**
- 1 **Tbsp. sliced scallions, plus more for garnish**
- 2 **tsp. minced garlic**
- 2 **tsp. finely grated peeled fresh ginger**
- 1½ **tsp. kosher salt**
- 24 **baguette slices, cut ⅓ inch thick**
- 6 **Tbsp. canola oil**
   Cilantro, for garnish

1. Make the *nuoc cham* In a small bowl, whisk the sugar with ½ cup of warm water until dissolved. Whisk in all of the remaining ingredients.

2. Make the shrimp toasts In a food processor, combine all of the ingredients except the baguette slices, canola oil and garnishes and puree until nearly smooth. Spread the mousse on the baguette slices.

3. In a large nonstick skillet, heat 3 tablespoons of the oil. Add half of the toasts, mousse side down, and cook over moderate heat until golden, 2 minutes. Flip the toasts and cook until browned on the bottom, 1 minute. Transfer the toasts to paper towels to drain. Repeat with the remaining oil and shrimp toasts. Transfer the toasts to a platter, garnish with cilantro and scallions and serve with the *nuoc cham*. —*Joshua Walker*

WINE Zesty, light Vinho Verde: 2013 Quinta da Aveleda.

Quick Korean Egg Custards with Shrimp

⏱ Total **20 min**; Serves **4**

- 8 **large eggs**
- 2 **cups chicken stock**
- 2 **tsp. Asian fish sauce**
- ½ **tsp. kosher salt**
- 8 **small shelled and deveined shrimp (5 oz.)**
- 1 **scallion, thinly sliced**
   Toasted sesame seeds and toasted sesame oil, for garnish

1. In a large bowl, whisk the eggs with the stock, fish sauce and salt. Pour the mixture into four 10-ounce heatproof bowls or ramekins. Arrange the bowls in 2 large, wide pots with lids. Add enough boiling water to the pots to reach two-thirds of the way up the sides of the bowls. Bring the water to a simmer, cover and simmer gently until the custards are slightly wobbly in the center, 6 to 7 minutes.

2. Divide the shrimp and scallion among the bowls, cover and steam until the shrimp are cooked through and the custards are set, 3 minutes longer. Garnish the custards with sesame seeds and sesame oil and serve warm. —*Judy Joo*

WINE Zesty, briny Albariño: 2012 Do Ferreiro.

PORK-KIMCHI DUMPLING PANCAKE

Spring Rolls with Pork and Glass Noodles

Total **1 hr**; Makes **12 rolls**

- **2** oz. glass (cellophane) noodles
- **¾** lb. ground pork
- **2** Tbsp. oyster sauce
- **1** tsp. sugar
- **1½** tsp. kosher salt
- **½** tsp. freshly ground pepper
- **½** cup julienned carrots (about 1 small)
- **½** cup finely shredded green cabbage
- **½** cup thinly sliced yellow onion (½ small)
- **½** cup julienned taro or potato
  Vegetable oil, for frying
  Twelve 7-inch square spring roll wrappers
- **1** large egg, lightly beaten
  Chinese hot mustard and/or sweet chile sauce, for dipping

1. In a small saucepan of boiling water, cook the noodles until al dente, 4 to 5 minutes. Drain and transfer to a bowl of ice water to cool. Drain the noodles well and chop into 3-inch pieces.

2. Transfer the noodles to a large bowl and add the pork, oyster sauce, sugar, salt, pepper and vegetables; mix well.

3. In a large enameled cast-iron casserole, heat 2 inches of oil to 350°. Place 1 wrapper on a work surface with a corner facing you; keep the remaining wrappers covered with a damp clean kitchen towel. Spoon ¼ cup of the filling in the lower third of the wrapper. Bring the corner up and over the filling and roll up, folding in the sides as you roll. Dab the top corner with the beaten egg and press to seal the spring roll. Repeat with the remaining wrappers and filling.

4. Fry the spring rolls in the hot oil, turning occasionally, until golden and crispy and the pork is cooked through, about 5 minutes. Drain on a paper towel–lined baking sheet and serve with hot mustard and/or sweet chile sauce. —*Danny Bowien*

MAKE AHEAD The uncooked spring rolls can be refrigerated for up to 4 hours; keep covered with a damp cloth.

WINE Off-dry German Riesling: 2013 Leitz Rüdesheimer Klosterlay Kabinett.

Bacon-Wrapped Shrimp with Cocktail Sauce

Active **45 min**; Total **1 hr 30 min**
Serves **6 to 8**

SHRIMP
- **½** cup extra-virgin olive oil, plus more for brushing
- **2** tsp. finely grated lemon zest
- **¼** cup fresh lemon juice
- **6** garlic cloves, thinly sliced
- **6** small jarred or dried Calabrian chiles, minced
- **20** jumbo shrimp, shelled, with tails intact
- **10** slices of bacon, halved crosswise

COCKTAIL SAUCE
- **1** cup ketchup
- **⅓** cup prepared white horseradish, drained
- **1** small shallot, minced
- **1** Tbsp. red wine vinegar
- **1** tsp. finely grated lemon zest
- **1½** Tbsp. fresh lemon juice
  Kosher salt and freshly ground pepper
  Lemon wedges, for serving

1. Prepare the shrimp In a large baking dish, whisk the ½ cup of oil with the lemon zest, lemon juice, garlic and chiles. Wrap each shrimp with a piece of bacon and add to the marinade. Cover and refrigerate for 1 hour; turn the shrimp halfway through marinating.

2. Make the cocktail sauce In a bowl, whisk the ketchup, horseradish, shallot, vinegar, lemon zest and lemon juice. Season with salt and pepper.

3. Light a grill or heat a grill pan; brush with oil. Season the shrimp lightly with salt and pepper. Grill over high heat, turning once, until the bacon is browned and the shrimp is just cooked through, 4 to 6 minutes. Transfer the shrimp to a platter and serve with the cocktail sauce and lemon wedges. —*John Gorham*

WINE Zesty cava from Spain: NV Segura Viudas Brut Reserva.

Bacon-Wrapped Peaches

Total **30 min**; Serves **4**

- **6** scallions, white and light green parts only
  Vegetable oil, for brushing
  Kosher salt
- **4** large peaches, halved and pitted
- **16** thin strips of bacon (about ½ lb.)
- **16** toothpicks, soaked in water for 30 minutes

1. Light a gas grill. Brush the scallions with oil and season lightly with salt. Grill them over moderate heat, turning, until softened and lightly charred, about 3 minutes total. Let cool and cut into ¾-inch lengths. Leave the grill on.

2. Fill the peach pit cavities with the scallion pieces and season with salt. Wrap 2 strips of bacon around each peach half and secure them with toothpicks.

3. Lightly brush the stuffed peaches with oil and grill them cut side down over moderately high heat until lightly charred, 1 to 2 minutes. Carefully flip the peaches and grill them over moderately low heat, turning occasionally, until they just start to soften and the bacon is crisp at the edges, 7 minutes. Transfer to a platter and serve. —*Tom Mylan*

Grilled Cantaloupe with Prosciutto and Mozzarella

Total **30 min**; Serves **6 to 8**

  Extra-virgin olive oil, for brushing and drizzling
  One 2-lb. cantaloupe—halved, seeded, cut into 1-inch wedges and peeled
  Kosher salt and pepper
- **4** oz. thinly sliced prosciutto
- **¾** lb. fresh mozzarella, thinly sliced
  Finely chopped parsley, for garnish

Light a grill and brush with oil. Brush the melon wedges with oil and season generously with salt and pepper. Grill the melon over high heat, turning once, until lightly charred, about 5 minutes. Transfer the wedges to a platter and top with the prosciutto and mozzarella. Garnish with parsley, a large pinch of pepper and a drizzle of oil and serve. —*Gabrielle Quiñónez Denton and Greg Denton*

Cauliflower and Cumin Fritters

Total **1 hr**; Serves **4 to 6**

LIME SAUCE

1⅓ cups plain whole-milk Greek yogurt

2 Tbsp. finely chopped cilantro

1 tsp. finely grated lime zest

2 Tbsp. fresh lime juice

2 Tbsp. extra-virgin olive oil

   Kosher salt and ground pepper

FRITTERS

1 small cauliflower, about ¾ lb.,
   cut into little florets

   Scant 1 cup all-purpose flour

3 Tbsp. finely chopped parsley, plus
   whole parsley leaves for garnish

2 shallots, finely chopped (¼ cup)

1 garlic clove, minced

4 large eggs, preferably organic

1½ tsp. ground cumin

1 tsp. ground cinnamon

½ tsp. turmeric

1½ tsp. kosher salt

1 tsp. freshly ground pepper

   About 2 cups sunflower oil, for frying

1. Make the lime sauce In a medium bowl, whisk all of the ingredients well. Taste—it should be vibrant, tart and citrusy; adjust the seasoning as necessary. Chill or leave at room temperature for up to 1 hour.

2. Prepare the fritters In a saucepan of salted boiling water, simmer the florets until very soft, 15 minutes; drain.

3. Meanwhile, in a large bowl, whisk the flour, chopped parsley, shallots, garlic, eggs, spices, salt and pepper to make a smooth batter. Add the warm cauliflower and mix, smashing the cauliflower into the batter with the back of a wooden spoon.

4. In a wide skillet, heat ⅔ inch of oil over high heat until very hot. Working in small batches, add 3-tablespoon mounds of the cauliflower mixture. Separate the fritters and fry them, adjusting the heat so they don't burn, 3 to 4 minutes per side.

5. Drain the fritters on paper towels. Garnish with parsley leaves; serve hot or warm with the sauce. —*Yotam Ottolenghi*

WINE Fruity, full-bodied white: 2013 Ferraton Samorëns Côtes du Rhône Blanc.

Mini Kale-Mushroom Calzones with Smoked Mozzarella

Total **1 hr 15 min**; Makes **18 mini calzones**

3 Tbsp. unsalted butter

3 Tbsp. extra-virgin olive oil,
   plus more for brushing

¾ lb. mixed oyster and cremini
   mushrooms, cut into ¾-inch pieces

   Kosher salt and pepper

   One ¾-lb. bunch of curly kale,
   stemmed and leaves finely chopped

1 cup jarred tomato or marinara
   sauce, plus more for serving

2 Tbsp. black olive tapenade

¼ cup finely chopped basil

3 oz. each of Fontina and smoked
   mozzarella cheese, shredded
   (¾ cup each)

1½ lbs. store-bought pizza dough

   All-purpose flour, for dusting

1. In a large nonstick skillet, melt 2 tablespoons of the butter in 2 tablespoons of the olive oil. Add the mushrooms and cook over high heat, stirring occasionally, until browned and tender, about 5 minutes. Season with salt and pepper and transfer to a medium bowl.

2. In the same skillet, melt the remaining 1 tablespoon of butter in the remaining 1 tablespoon of olive oil. Add the kale and a generous pinch of salt and cook over moderately high heat, stirring occasionally, until just tender, about 5 minutes. Season with salt and pepper.

3. In a bowl, mix the 1 cup of tomato sauce with the tapenade and basil. In another bowl, toss the Fontina with the mozzarella.

4. Preheat the oven to 450° and lightly brush 2 large rimmed baking sheets with olive oil. Cut the pizza dough into 18 pieces and roll into balls. On a lightly floured work surface, roll out 1 ball to a 5-inch round, a scant ⅛ inch thick. Spoon 1 tablespoon of the olive-tomato sauce on one half of the round, then top with 1 tablespoon each of the mushrooms, kale and cheese. Fold the dough over to form a half-moon and press the edge to seal tightly. Crimp the edge with a fork or pinch at intervals to make pleats. Transfer the calzone to a baking sheet and brush lightly with olive oil. Repeat with the remaining dough and fillings.

5. Bake the calzones in the upper and lower thirds of the oven until golden and puffed, shifting the pans halfway through baking, 12 to 14 minutes. Serve hot, with tomato sauce for dipping. —*Joey Wölffer*

WINE Berry-rich California Pinot Noir: 2012 Buena Vista Sonoma County.

Stuffed Kale with Bulgur Tabbouleh and Lime Yogurt Dip

Total **1 hr**; Serves **4**

1 cup plain Greek yogurt

2 Tbsp. finely grated lime zest

1 Tbsp. fresh lime juice

   Kosher salt

½ cup medium-grade bulgur

1 tsp. baking soda

16 large Tuscan kale leaves (1 lb.)

1 small shallot, minced

1 garlic clove, minced

1 cup chopped flat-leaf parsley

½ European cucumber—peeled, halved,
   seeded and finely chopped

½ cup dried sour cherries, chopped

¼ cup chopped mint

¼ cup extra-virgin olive oil

2 Tbsp. fresh lemon juice

   Freshly ground pepper

1. In a small bowl, mix the yogurt, lime zest and lime juice. Season with salt. Cover and refrigerate the dip.

2. In a small saucepan, bring the bulgur and 1½ cups of water to a boil and simmer for 2 minutes. Cover and let stand off the heat until tender, about 15 minutes. Drain.

3. Meanwhile, in a large pot, boil 16 cups of water with ½ cup of salt and the baking soda. Add the kale and boil until tender, 3 minutes. Drain and cool the kale in an ice bath. Drain well, squeeze dry and blot thoroughly with paper towels. Cut out and discard the tough kale stems.

4. Transfer the bulgur to a large bowl and mix with the shallot, garlic, parsley, cucumber, sour cherries, mint, olive oil and lemon juice. Season with salt and pepper.

5. Spread 1 kale leaf at a time on a work surface. Spoon ¼ cup of the bulgur onto each leaf 1 inch from the bottom; roll up, tucking in the sides as you roll. Serve with the dip. —*Jean-Georges Vongerichten*

Pickled Fried Fish with Danish Rye Bread and Crème Fraîche

Total **40 min plus overnight pickling**
Serves **10**

This robust make-ahead dish is from Paul Berglund, chef at the Nordic-inspired Bachelor Farmer in Minneapolis. He matches Scandinavian technique—pickling fish—with the Midwest's freshwater catch.

BRINE

- **3 cups water**
- **2 cups distilled white vinegar**
- **¼ cup sugar**
- **2 medium red onions, halved and thinly sliced**
- **2 celery ribs, thinly sliced**
- **1 medium carrot, thinly sliced**
- **5 garlic cloves, thinly sliced**
- **½ Tbsp. allspice berries**
- **3 bay leaves**
- **¼ cup kosher salt**

FISH

- **¼ cup grapeseed oil**
- **2 lbs. skinless walleye, fluke or flounder fillets, ½ to ¾ inch thick, cut into 10 equal pieces**
- **Kosher salt**
- **All-purpose flour, for dusting**
- **Dill sprigs, for garnish**
- **Danish rye bread, crème fraîche and minced red onion, for serving**

1. Make the brine In a large saucepan, combine all of the ingredients and bring to a boil. Simmer over moderately low heat until the vegetables are just softened, about 12 minutes. Let cool completely.

2. Prepare the fish Meanwhile, in a large skillet, heat 2 tablespoons of the oil until shimmering. Working with half of the fish at a time, season with salt and dust with flour; pat off the excess. Add the floured fish to the skillet; cook over moderate heat, turning once, until golden and just cooked through, 5 to 6 minutes. Transfer to a plate. Repeat with the remaining oil and fish.

3. Spoon half of the brine and vegetables into a large bowl or baking dish. Add the fish and pour the remaining brine and vegetables over the top. Cover with plastic wrap and refrigerate overnight. Bring the fish to room temperature before serving.

4. Transfer the pickled fish and vegetables to a platter. Garnish with dill sprigs and serve with rye bread, crème fraîche and minced red onion. —*Paul Berglund*

WINE Zesty Napa Valley Sauvignon Blanc: 2013 Frog's Leap.

Beef and Onion Empanadas

Active **1 hr 30 min; Total 2 hr 30 min**
Makes **30 empanadas**

DOUGH

- **Kosher salt**
- **¼ cup lard**
- **4¾ cups all-purpose flour, plus more for dusting**

FILLING

- **1 lb. well-marbled beef, such as tri-tip or sirloin tip, very finely chopped**
- **Kosher salt and black pepper**
- **¼ cup lard**
- **6 Tbsp. unsalted butter—4 Tbsp. cut into tablespoons, 2 Tbsp. cut into small cubes**
- **3 medium onions, quartered and thinly sliced**
- **2 tsp. crushed red pepper**
- **1 Tbsp. ground cumin**
- **1 Tbsp. sweet smoked Spanish paprika**
- **4 scallions, white and green parts minced separately**
- **2 Tbsp. extra-virgin olive oil**
- **¼ cup chopped oregano**
- **2 large hard-cooked eggs, chopped**
- **½ cup chopped pitted green olives**

1. Make the dough In a small saucepan, combine 2 cups of water and 1 tablespoon of salt and bring to a simmer. Add the lard and stir until melted. Pour the liquid into a large bowl and let cool to room temperature.

2. Using a wooden spoon, stir in 4 cups of the flour, 1 cup at a time, until the dough begins to form a ball. Turn the dough out onto a lightly floured work surface and knead, adding the remaining flour as necessary, 2 tablespoons at a time, until a stiff, dry dough forms. Divide the dough into 4 equal pieces, pat them into 1-inch-thick disks and cover with plastic wrap. Chill for at least 1 hour and up to 24 hours.

3. Meanwhile, make the filling In a medium bowl, season the meat well with salt and black pepper. In a large nonstick skillet, melt 1 tablespoon of the lard in the 4 tablespoons of butter. Add the onions and cook over moderately low heat, stirring, until translucent, 8 minutes. Stir in the crushed red pepper, cumin, paprika and the scallion whites and cook, stirring, for 2 minutes. Off the heat, stir in the scallion greens. Season with salt and black pepper and transfer the onions to a large bowl.

4. Wipe out the skillet and heat 1 tablespoon of the oil in it. Add half of the meat and cook over moderately high heat, stirring, until well browned, about 2 minutes. Using a slotted spoon, transfer the meat to the onions. Wipe out the skillet and repeat with the remaining 1 tablespoon of oil and meat; transfer to the bowl. Add the oregano and remaining 3 tablespoons of lard to the meat and mix well. Season with salt and black pepper. Cover and chill until firm.

5. Line 2 baking sheets with parchment paper. On a lightly floured work surface, using a lightly floured rolling pin, roll out 1 piece of dough to a 7-by-14-inch rectangle, about ⅛ inch thick. Using a 3½-inch round cookie cutter, stamp out 6 rounds of dough and transfer them to the prepared baking sheets; save the scraps. Repeat with the remaining 3 pieces of dough. Combine all of the scraps and knead them into a disk. Roll out and stamp out 6 more rounds; transfer to the baking sheets.

6. Preheat the oven to 350°. Place 1 tablespoon of the meat filling in the center of each dough round. Top with the chopped eggs, olives and small cubes of butter. Using your finger, moisten the rim of each dough round with water and fold the dough in half over the filling to form half-moons. Pinch the edges together to seal and crimp decoratively. Bake the empanadas for 20 to 25 minutes, flipping them halfway through baking, until golden. Serve hot. —*Francis Mallmann*

WINE Bold, fruit-forward Malbec from Argentina's Uco Valley: 2012 Los Nevados.

Avgolemono Custards with Crispy Chicken Skin
Active **40 min**; Total **1 hr**; Serves **8**

In this riff on classic Greek egg-and-lemon soup, lemony custard is enriched with a tiny bit of luscious rendered chicken fat.

- ¼ lb. chicken skin (from 4 whole legs)
- 3 cups chicken stock
- 1 cup heavy cream
- 2 tsp. kosher salt
- ¼ tsp. pepper
- 4 large eggs
- 4 large egg yolks
- 6 Tbsp. fresh lemon juice
- Parsley, extra-virgin olive oil, Maldon salt and shaved white onion and radish, for garnish

1. Spread the chicken skin in a large non-stick skillet and cook over moderate heat, turning once, until golden and crisp, about 7 minutes. Transfer to paper towels to drain; reserve 2 tablespoons of the fat. Let the skin cool, then break into shards.

2. Preheat the oven to 350°. In a medium saucepan, bring the stock, cream, salt, pepper and reserved chicken fat just to a simmer. In a large bowl, beat the whole eggs and yolks. Gradually whisk in the stock mixture, then the lemon juice.

3. Pour the custard base into eight 8-ounce ramekins and set them in a large roasting pan. Pour enough hot water into the roasting pan to reach halfway up the sides of the ramekins. Cover the pan tightly with foil and poke holes in the foil. Bake the custards for 20 minutes, until just set but still slightly jiggly in the center. Uncover; let stand in the water for 5 minutes.

4. Remove the custards from the water. Garnish with parsley, olive oil, Maldon salt, onion and radish and the shards of chicken skin. Serve right away. —*Erik Anderson*

MAKE AHEAD The crispy chicken skin can be stored in an airtight container overnight. Recrisp in a warm oven if necessary.

WINE Lemony, medium-bodied Greek white: 2013 Boutari Moschofilero.

A SCALLOP CRUDO LESSON FROM ERIC RIPERT

Tender, sweet scallops are fantastic in raw dishes. Seafood master Eric Ripert of New York City's Le Bernardin shares three fast flavorings. Each of the toppings below makes enough for six thinly sliced large scallops.

Wasabi-Ginger Sauce Whisk together 2 Tbsp. canola oil, 1½ Tbsp. fresh lime juice, 1 Tbsp. wasabi paste and ½ tsp. finely grated fresh ginger; season with fleur de sel. Drizzle on the scallops and serve.

Lemon and Piment d'Espelette Drizzle extra-virgin olive oil and fresh lemon juice on the scallops and season with fleur de sel and piment d'Espelette (red pepper powder from Basque Country; available at lepicerie.com) and serve.

Pecans and Ponzu Sauce Drizzle the sliced scallops very lightly with ponzu sauce and dot each slice with a small drop of aged balsamic vinegar. Sprinkle 2 Tbsp. finely chopped toasted pecans on top and serve right away.

Filipino-Style Ceviche with Coconut Milk

⏱ Total **45 min**; Serves **4 to 6**

This creamy, fresh *kinilaw* (a Filipino dish of raw ingredients) is Manila-born chef Paul Qui's go-to raw seafood starter.

- ¾ **cup unsweetened coconut milk**
- ¼ **cup raw coconut vinegar (see Note)**
- ½ **small red onion—thinly sliced, rinsed under cold water and patted dry**
- 3 **Thai chiles, thinly sliced**
- 4 **tsp. grated peeled ginger**
- 1 **Tbsp. minced cilantro stems and leaves, plus small leaves for garnish**
- 1 **tsp. kosher salt, plus more for seasoning**
- ¼ **tsp. pepper, plus more for seasoning**
- ¾ **lb. sashimi-grade tuna or hamachi, cut into ½-inch dice**
- 3 **Tbsp. extra-virgin olive oil**
  Lime wedges, for serving

1. In a medium bowl, combine all of the ingredients except the olive oil and lime wedges. Stir in 2 tablespoons of the olive oil. Cover the bowl with plastic wrap and refrigerate for 20 minutes.

2. Stir in the remaining 1 tablespoon of olive oil and season with salt and pepper. Transfer the ceviche to a serving bowl, garnish with cilantro leaves and serve with lime wedges. —*Paul Qui*

NOTE Raw coconut vinegar is available at health food shops and from amazon.com.

WINE Brisk, zesty Spanish white: 2012 Lagar de Costa Albariño.

Golden Shallot Custards

Active **30 min**; Total **1 hr 30 min**; Serves **4**

- 4 **large shallots, peeled**
- 1 **Tbsp. unsalted butter**
  Kosher salt and white pepper
- 1 **tsp. sugar**
  Freshly grated nutmeg
- 2 **large eggs**
- 1½ **cups heavy cream**

1. Preheat the oven to 275°. Using a sharp paring knife, very thinly slice the shallots lengthwise, leaving the slices attached at the root ends. Using your palm, gently flatten the shallots, fanning out the slices.

2. In a medium skillet, melt the butter. Add the shallots and season with salt and white pepper. Sprinkle the sugar and a pinch of nutmeg on top and cook over moderate heat, turning once, until nicely browned and very soft, about 15 minutes; let cool slightly.

3. Fan out the shallots in the center of four 10-ounce ramekins. In a bowl, beat the eggs, cream, ½ teaspoon of salt, ¼ teaspoon of white pepper and a pinch of nutmeg; pour into the ramekins, cover with plastic wrap and set in a glass or ceramic baking dish.

4. Pour enough hot water into the baking dish to reach halfway up the sides of the ramekins. Transfer the baking dish to the middle of the oven and bake until a toothpick inserted in the center of the custards comes out clean, 40 minutes. Remove the baking dish from the oven and let the custards stand in the water for 5 minutes, then carefully remove the ramekins and let cool slightly. Serve warm or at room temperature. —*Ludo Lefebvre*

Poached Shrimp with Coconut Water and Lime

Active **30 min**; Total **1 hr**; Serves **4**

- ½ **lb. shelled and deveined medium shrimp**
- ¼ **cup coconut water**
- ¼ **cup unseasoned rice vinegar**
- 3 **Tbsp. fresh lime juice**
- 1 **scallion, finely chopped**
- 2 **garlic cloves, minced**
- 1 **Tbsp. finely grated ginger**
  Pinch of sugar
  Kosher salt and pepper
- ½ **English cucumber, peeled and cut into ½-inch dice**
- 1 **small red bell pepper, cut into ½-inch dice**
- ½ **small red onion, sliced**
- 1 **serrano chile, thinly sliced**

1. Fill a bowl with ice water. In a medium saucepan of salted boiling water, poach the shrimp until just cooked through, 2 to 3 minutes. Drain, then transfer the shrimp to the ice bath to cool. Drain and pat dry.

2. In a medium bowl, whisk the coconut water with the rice vinegar, lime juice, scallion, garlic, ginger and sugar. Season the marinade with salt and pepper. Add the poached shrimp and all of the remaining ingredients and toss to combine. Cover and refrigerate for 30 minutes before serving. —*Edward Lee*

WINE Juicy, aromatic Loire Valley Chenin Blanc: 2012 Champalou Vouvray.

Snails in Parsley Butter

Active **20 min**; Total **4 hr 30 min** Serves **4 to 6**

L.A. chef Ludo Lefebvre has a clever way to bake snails in garlicky herb butter so they don't tip over: He nestles the shells in a bed of rock salt. Snail shells are sold at many specialty markets; alternatively, you can use an escargot baking dish or sauté the escargots in the infused butter in a small pan.

- 2 **sticks unsalted butter, softened**
- ¼ **cup minced parsley**
- 2 **Tbsp. minced shallot**
- 1 **Tbsp. dry white wine**
- 1 **Tbsp. minced garlic**
- 1½ **tsp. kosher salt**
- 1 **tsp. Cognac**
- ½ **tsp. freshly ground pepper**
  Pinch of freshly grated nutmeg
  Rock salt, for baking
- 24 **snail shells, rinsed and dried**
- 24 **canned giant snails, drained and rinsed**
  Crusty bread, for serving

1. In a medium bowl, blend the butter, parsley, shallot, wine, garlic, salt, Cognac, pepper and nutmeg. Cover and refrigerate for at least 4 hours or overnight. Let return to room temperature before using.

2. Preheat the oven to 400°. Spread a ¼-inch-thick layer of rock salt on a rimmed baking sheet. Pack ½ teaspoon of the parsley butter into each escargot shell and stuff a snail inside. Fill with the remaining butter. Nestle the shells in the salt, butter side up.

3. Bake the snails for about 10 minutes, until the butter is bubbling. Serve hot with crusty bread. —*Ludo Lefebvre*

WINE Crisp Chablis: 2012 Gilbert Picq.

POACHED SHRIMP WITH
COCONUT WATER AND LIME

ESCAROLE AND BRUSSELS
SPROUT SALAD
Recipe, page 48

Salads

Summer Market Salad with Jalapeño Dressing

⏱ Total **45 min**; Serves **4**

Grilled corn and jalapeño add smoky flavor and heat to the dressing for this terrific salad. The recipe is excerpted from *The Portlandia Cookbook*, based on the food-obsessed satirical TV show starring Fred Armisen and Carrie Brownstein.

- 2 Tbsp. canola oil, plus more for brushing
- 1 large jalapeño
- 1 ear of corn, shucked
- 2 Tbsp. extra-virgin olive oil
- 2 Tbsp. fresh lime juice
- 1 scallion, white and green parts thinly sliced separately
- 2 Tbsp. chopped cilantro, plus leaves for garnish
  Kosher salt
- ¾ lb. mixed heirloom tomatoes—halved, quartered or sliced, depending on size
- 2 oz. sugar snap peas, thinly sliced on the diagonal

1. Light a grill or preheat a grill pan and brush the grate or pan with canola oil. Lightly brush the jalapeño and corn with canola oil and grill over moderate heat, turning occasionally, until lightly charred all over, about 15 minutes. Transfer to a plate to cool. Peel, seed and chop the jalapeño. Cut the corn kernels off the cob; discard the cob.

2. In a mini processor, combine the 2 tablespoons of canola oil with the olive oil, lime juice, scallion whites, chopped cilantro, jalapeño and half of the grilled corn kernels. Pulse until a chunky dressing forms. Season with salt.

3. In a large bowl, toss the tomatoes with the snap peas, scallion greens, the remaining corn and half of the dressing. Toss to coat and transfer to a serving platter. Spoon the remaining dressing over the salad and garnish with cilantro leaves. —*Grace Parisi*

MAKE AHEAD The jalapeño dressing can be refrigerated overnight.

Butter Lettuce Salad with Tomato Vinaigrette

Active **50 min**; Total **1 hr 20 min**
Serves **8**

- 2 plum tomatoes, halved
- 2 medium shallots, quartered lengthwise
- ⅓ cup canola oil, plus more for brushing
- 1 Tbsp. plus 2 tsp. sherry vinegar
- 2 tsp. Dijon mustard
- ⅔ cup crumbled blue cheese (2½ oz.)
- ⅓ cup plus 1 Tbsp. extra-virgin olive oil
  Kosher salt and freshly ground pepper
- ½ cup pumpkin seeds
- 1½ tsp. pure chile powder, preferably guajillo
- ¼ lb. slab bacon, cut into ¼-inch dice
- 2 medium heads of butter lettuce, quartered through the cores
  Thinly sliced onion and diced tomato, for serving

1. Preheat the oven to 425°. Brush the tomatoes and shallots with canola oil. Roast on a rimmed baking sheet for about 30 minutes, until softened and browned in spots. Transfer to a blender and let cool completely. Add the vinegar and mustard and puree until nearly smooth. Add the blue cheese and puree until smooth. With the machine on, gradually add the ⅓ cup of canola oil and ⅓ cup of olive oil until incorporated. Season the tomato vinaigrette with salt and pepper.

2. Meanwhile, in a pie plate, toss the pumpkin seeds with the remaining 1 tablespoon of olive oil and the chile powder and season with salt and pepper. Bake for about 10 minutes, until the seeds are lightly browned; let cool completely.

3. In a small skillet, cook the bacon over moderate heat, stirring occasionally, until browned and crisp, about 7 minutes. Using a slotted spoon, transfer the bacon to paper towels to drain.

4. Arrange the lettuce wedges on plates and top with the pumpkin seeds, bacon, sliced onion and diced tomato. Serve with the roasted tomato vinaigrette. —*Tim Love*

MAKE AHEAD The tomato vinaigrette can be refrigerated for up to 3 days.

Bibb Lettuce Salad with Vinegar-Roasted Beets

Active **30 min**; Total **1 hr 15 min**
Serves **6 to 8**

Beets roasted in vinegar have a superb tang that's delicious in this fresh, healthy, yogurt-dressed salad from F&W's Justin Chapple. His inspiration: a recipe from Minneapolis chef Jamie Malone.

- 1¼ cups plus 3 Tbsp. unseasoned rice vinegar
- 1 Tbsp. sugar
  Kosher salt
- 1½ lbs. small beets
- 2 thyme sprigs
- 2 garlic cloves, crushed
- 1 bay leaf
- ¾ cup plain yogurt
- 3 Tbsp. minced shallot
  Pepper
  Two 8-oz. heads of Bibb lettuce, light green leaves only, large leaves torn
  Cilantro leaves and small dill sprigs, for garnish

1. Preheat the oven to 425°. In a large, deep ovenproof skillet, whisk 1¼ cups of the vinegar with 1¼ cups of water, the sugar and 1 tablespoon of salt. Add the beets, thyme, garlic and bay leaf. Cover the skillet and roast the beets for about 45 minutes, until tender, turning them halfway through. Remove the beets from the skillet and let cool completely, then peel and cut into wedges; discard the cooking liquid.

2. In a medium bowl, whisk the yogurt with the shallot and the remaining 3 tablespoons of vinegar. Season the dressing with salt and pepper.

3. Arrange the lettuce on a platter and top with the beets. Drizzle with half of the dressing and garnish with cilantro leaves and dill sprigs. Serve right away, passing the remaining dressing at the table. —*Justin Chapple*

MAKE AHEAD The drained roasted beets can be refrigerated for up to 3 days.

BIBB LETTUCE SALAD
WITH VINEGAR-ROASTED BEETS

Harvest Salad with Gorgonzola, Bacon and Concord Grapes

Total **35 min**; Serves **4**

Star chef Nancy Silverton doesn't toss her salads; instead, she layers the ingredients. "I guess it's part of my controlling nature," she laughs. "With every bite, you get the proper amount of stuff."

- 6 slices of thick-cut applewood-smoked bacon
- ½ cup hazelnuts
- 1 Tbsp. hazelnut or canola oil
  Kosher salt and pepper
- ¼ cup sherry vinegar
- ¼ cup minced shallots
- 2 Tbsp. fresh lemon juice
- 1 tsp. sugar
- ½ cup extra-virgin olive oil
  Light green leaves from 2 small heads of Bibb lettuce
- ½ cup Concord grapes, halved and seeded
- 4 oz. Gorgonzola dolce, crumbled
  Snipped chives, for garnish

1. Preheat the oven to 325°. On a foil-lined rimmed baking sheet, bake the bacon for about 17 minutes, turning once, until browned but still chewy. Transfer the bacon to paper towels to drain, then cut into 1-inch pieces. Leave the oven on.

2. Meanwhile, spread the hazelnuts in a pie plate and bake for about 12 minutes, until lightly browned and the skins start to crack. Transfer the hazelnuts to a clean kitchen towel and rub them together to remove the skins; let cool. Coarsely chop the hazelnuts and transfer to a small bowl. Stir in the hazelnut oil and season with salt and pepper.

3. In a medium bowl, whisk the sherry vinegar with the minced shallots, lemon juice and sugar. Gradually whisk in the olive oil until incorporated. Season the shallot vinaigrette with salt and pepper.

4. In a large bowl, dress the lettuce leaves with ¼ cup of the shallot vinaigrette and season lightly with salt and pepper.

5. On a serving platter or plates, layer the lettuce leaves with the bacon pieces, chopped hazelnuts, Concord grapes and Gorgonzola dolce. Garnish with snipped chives and serve, passing the remaining shallot vinaigrette at the table.
—*Nancy Silverton*

WINE Fragrant, medium-bodied Piedmontese white: 2013 Vietti Roero Arneis.

Romaine and Charred Corn Salad with Avocado Dressing

Total **35 min**; Serves **6**

Smashing ripe avocado with olive oil, lemon juice, honey and garlic creates a creamy dressing without cream for this hearty salad. The recipe is from Molly Chester of the biodynamic Apricot Lane Farms in Moorpark, California.

- 2½ cups fresh corn kernels (from 3 to 4 large ears)
- ⅓ cup extra-virgin olive oil
- 3 Tbsp. fresh lemon juice
- 2 tsp. honey
- ½ tsp. minced garlic
- ½ Hass avocado, peeled and cut into ¼-inch dice
  Kosher salt and pepper
  Three 6- to 8-oz. romaine hearts, torn into bite-size pieces
- ½ cup very thinly sliced red onion
- ½ cup shredded pecorino cheese, plus more for garnish

1. Preheat the broiler. Spread the corn kernels on a large rimmed baking sheet and broil 6 inches from the heat for about 5 minutes, until lightly charred. Let the corn kernels cool completely.

2. In a medium bowl, whisk the olive oil with the lemon juice, honey and garlic. Add the avocado and, using a fork, lightly smash it against the side of the bowl and mix it in to form a chunky dressing. Season with salt and pepper.

3. In a large bowl, toss the cooled corn with the romaine pieces, sliced onion and the ½ cup of pecorino cheese. Add the dressing, season with salt and pepper and toss well. Garnish the salad with shredded cheese and serve right away.
—*Molly Chester*

Iceberg Wedges with Roasted Tomato Dressing

Active **30 min**; Total **1 hr**; Serves **10**

This not-so-heavy take on the classic iceberg wedge salad features a French-style dressing made with roasted tomatoes and Dijon mustard.

- 1 lb. medium tomatoes, halved crosswise
- ¾ cup extra-virgin olive oil, plus more for brushing
  Kosher salt and pepper
- ¼ cup sherry vinegar
- 2 Tbsp. fresh lemon juice
- 2 Tbsp. Dijon mustard
- 1 small shallot, quartered
- 1 large egg yolk
- 2 garlic cloves
  Two 1-lb. heads of iceberg lettuce, each cut into 6 wedges through the core
- ½ lb. baby carrots, preferably multicolored, thinly shaved lengthwise on a mandoline or with a vegetable peeler
- 8 radishes, very thinly sliced
  Salted roasted pumpkin seeds and small dill sprigs, for garnish

1. Preheat the oven to 425°. On a rimmed baking sheet, brush the tomatoes with olive oil and season with salt and pepper. Roast the tomatoes for 20 to 25 minutes, until lightly browned in spots and softened. Let cool, then squeeze out and discard the seeds. Transfer the tomatoes to a blender. Add the sherry vinegar, lemon juice, mustard, shallot, egg yolk and garlic and puree until nearly smooth. With the blender on, gradually add the ¾ cup of olive oil until incorporated. Season the dressing with salt and pepper.

2. Arrange the lettuce wedges on a platter. Scatter the carrot ribbons and sliced radishes over the lettuce and drizzle some of the dressing on top. Garnish with pumpkin seeds and dill sprigs and season the salad with salt and pepper. Serve right away, passing additional dressing at the table.
—*Mehdi Brunet-Benkritly and Gabriel Stulman*

HARVEST SALAD WITH GORGONZOLA,
BACON AND CONCORD GRAPES

Arugula Salad with Mandarin Vinaigrette

Total **15 min**; Serves **4**

- ¼ cup extra-virgin olive oil
- ¼ cup fresh mandarin orange or tangerine juice
- 2 Tbsp. apple cider vinegar
- 1 garlic clove, minced

  Kosher salt and freshly ground pepper
- 5 oz. baby arugula (8 cups)
- 5 oz. bean sprouts (2 cups)
- 4 mandarin oranges, peeled and sectioned
- ¼ cup sliced almonds

In a large bowl, whisk the olive oil with the mandarin juice, apple cider vinegar and garlic and season with salt and pepper. Add the arugula and bean sprouts and toss to coat. Transfer the salad to a large platter, top with the oranges and almonds and serve. —*Diane Cu and Todd Porter*

Autumn Salad with Figs and Blue Cheese

Total **30 min**; Serves **4**

- ¼ cup extra-virgin olive oil
- 2 Tbsp. apple cider vinegar
- ½ Tbsp. whole-grain mustard

  Sea salt and pepper
- 6 slices of bacon (5 oz.)
- 1½ Tbsp. salted butter
- 1 crisp apple, such as Honeycrisp or Fuji—halved, cored and thinly sliced
- ⅓ cup toasted hazelnuts, chopped
- 2 cups mesclun greens
- 3 oz. Roquefort cheese, crumbled
- ½ lb. small seedless dark grapes, halved
- 4 fresh figs, cut into wedges

1. In a small bowl, whisk the olive oil with the apple cider vinegar and whole-grain mustard. Season with salt and pepper.

2. In a large nonstick skillet, cook the bacon slices over moderate heat, turning, until golden and crisp, about 5 minutes. Transfer to a paper towel–lined plate to drain. Break the bacon into pieces.

3. In the same skillet, melt the butter. Add the apple and cook over moderate heat until lightly golden, 3 to 4 minutes. Stir in the hazelnuts and cook until deep golden, 1 to 2 minutes. Let cool slightly.

4. Arrange the greens on a platter. Top with the apple, hazelnuts, cheese, grapes, figs and bacon. Drizzle with the vinaigrette and serve. —*Mimi Thorisson*

WINE Ripe, fruit-forward Chardonnay: 2013 Terres Dorées Beaujolais Blanc.

Mizuna Salad with Kumquats

Total **20 min**; Serves **6** as part of a multicourse meal

- 1 lb. mizuna greens—leaves cut into 2-inch pieces, stems cut into 1-inch lengths (10 cups)
- 6 kumquats—halved lengthwise, seeded and very thinly sliced lengthwise
- 2 Tbsp. canola oil, preferably cold-pressed
- 1½ Tbsp. yuzu juice or Meyer lemon juice

  Salt

In a large bowl, toss the mizuna with the kumquats, oil and yuzu juice. Season with salt and serve right away. —*Nancy Singleton Hachisu*

Romesco Vinaigrette

Total **10 min**; Makes **1** cup

- ¼ cup roasted almonds
- ¼ cup basil leaves
- ¼ cup tarragon leaves
- 3 drained piquillo peppers
- 2 Tbsp. sherry vinegar
- ½ garlic clove
- ¼ cup extra-virgin olive oil

  Kosher salt

In a food processor, puree the almonds with the basil, tarragon, piquillo peppers, vinegar and garlic until a paste forms. With the machine on, gradually add ⅓ cup of water and the olive oil. Season with salt. —*Geoffrey Zakarian*

SERVE WITH Chicory.

Winter Lettuces with Pomegranate Seeds

Total **20 min**; Serves **8**

- ½ shallot, minced
- 2 Tbsp. fresh lemon juice
- 1 Tbsp. red wine vinegar
- 1 Tbsp. Dijon mustard
- ½ cup extra-virgin olive oil

  Kosher salt and ground pepper
- 1½ lbs. mixed greens, such as escarole, frisée, endive and watercress, torn into bite-size pieces (about 20 loosely packed cups)
- ¾ cup pomegranate seeds

In a large bowl, combine the shallot with the lemon juice, vinegar, mustard and 1 tablespoon of water. Whisk in the olive oil until emulsified and season the vinaigrette with salt and pepper. Add the mixed greens and toss to coat. Transfer the salad to a platter, garnish with the pomegranate seeds and serve. —*Ali Larter*

Mâche Salad with Curry Vinaigrette

Total **20 min**; Serves **4**

Chef Eric Ripert of Manhattan's Le Bernardin combines mâche (a.k.a. lamb's lettuce), spiced croutons and a curry vinaigrette in this lovely, unexpected salad.

- 5 Tbsp. extra-virgin olive oil
- ¾ tsp. Madras curry powder
- 3 oz. peasant or country bread, torn into ½-inch pieces (2½ cups)
- 2 Tbsp. fresh lemon juice

  Kosher salt
- 2 oz. mâche
- ¼ cup chopped chives (¼-inch pieces)

1. In a large nonstick skillet, heat 2 tablespoons of the olive oil. Whisk in ¼ teaspoon of the curry powder and add the bread. Toast over moderate heat, stirring frequently, until golden and crisp, about 8 minutes. Transfer the croutons to a plate.

2. In a large bowl, whisk the remaining 3 tablespoons of oil and ½ teaspoon of curry powder with the lemon juice; season with salt. Add the mâche and chives and toss gently. Transfer to plates and top with the croutons. —*Eric Ripert*

Grapefruit and Escarole Salad
⏱ Total **45 min**; Serves **6 to 8**

- 2 Tbsp. fennel seeds, lightly crushed
- ½ cup fresh lemon juice
- ¼ cup honey
- 1 cup extra-virgin olive oil
- ¼ cup minced shallots
- 2 tsp. minced rosemary
  Kosher salt and pepper
- 3 Ruby Red grapefruits
- 1 fennel bulb—cored, halved lengthwise and very thinly sliced
- 1 head of escarole, white and light green leaves only, chopped
- 1 cup basil leaves, chopped
- ½ cup pomegranate seeds
- 6 oz. bloomy rind goat cheese, cut into small pieces
- ¾ cup walnuts, toasted and coarsely chopped

1. In a medium skillet, toast the fennel seeds over moderate heat, stirring, for 2 minutes. Add the lemon juice and cook over moderate heat until reduced by half, 5 minutes. Whisk in the honey. Remove from the heat. Slowly whisk in the oil until combined. Stir in the shallots and rosemary and season the dressing with salt and pepper.

2. Using a sharp knife, remove the skin and white pith from the grapefruits. Working over a large bowl, cut in between the membranes to release the sections; discard the membranes. Add the sliced fennel, escarole, basil and 1 cup of the fennel dressing, season with salt and pepper and toss. Mound the salad on plates and top with the pomegranate seeds, goat cheese and walnuts. Serve the remaining dressing on the side. —*Jennifer Jasinski*

Endive and Grapefruit Salad with Pistachio Vinaigrette
Active **35 min**; Total **1 hr**; Serves **4**

- ½ cup unseasoned rice vinegar
- ½ tsp. sugar
- 1 small red onion, halved and thinly sliced
- 2 Tbsp. grapeseed oil
- 1 Tbsp. pistachio oil
- 1 Tbsp. apple cider vinegar
- 1 tsp. Dijon mustard
- 1 Tbsp. finely crushed pistachios, plus more for garnish
- 1 tsp. minced chives
  Kosher salt and ground pepper
- 1 large Ruby Red grapefruit
- 2 Belgian endives—halved lengthwise, cored and thinly sliced lengthwise
- ½ cup lightly packed parsley leaves
- 1 tsp. finely chopped tarragon

1. In a small saucepan, combine the rice vinegar with ½ cup of water and the sugar and bring just to a boil. Add the onion and let cool completely, about 1 hour. Drain.

2. In a large bowl, whisk both oils with the cider vinegar and mustard. Stir in the 1 tablespoon of crushed pistachios and the chives, then season with salt and pepper.

3. Using a sharp knife, remove the skin and bitter white pith from the grapefruit. Cut in between the membranes to release the grapefruit sections into the large bowl. Add the endives, parsley, tarragon and ½ cup of the pickled onion and toss well. (Reserve the remaining pickled onion for another use.) Season the salad with salt and pepper. Pile the salad on plates, garnish with crushed pistachios and serve right away. —*Hugh Acheson*

WINE Lively, citrusy, light-bodied white: 2013 Vidigal Vinho Verde.

Bitter Greens Salad with Asian Pears, Avocado and Tahini Dressing
⏱ Total **45 min**; Serves **8 to 10**

TAHINI DRESSING
- ¼ cup tahini
- 3 Tbsp. apple cider vinegar
- 2 Tbsp. tamari or soy sauce
- 1 garlic clove, crushed
- 2 tsp. minced peeled fresh ginger
- 1 tsp. *sambal oelek* or Sriracha
- ½ cup canola oil
- 1 Tbsp. Asian chile oil
  Kosher salt and pepper

SALAD
- 3 mandarin oranges
- 1 fennel bulb—halved, cored and thinly sliced on a mandoline
- 1 lb. mixed chicory lettuces, such as frisée, escarole, endives and radicchio, chopped (16 cups)
- ½ cup each cilantro and small mint leaves
- 2 Asian pears—peeled, cored and thinly sliced
- 1 Hass avocado, thinly sliced
- 2 Tbsp. toasted sesame seeds
  Flaky sea salt and pepper, for seasoning
  Extra-virgin olive oil, for drizzling

1. **Make the tahini dressing** In a food processor, combine the tahini, vinegar, soy sauce, garlic, ginger and *sambal oelek* and puree until blended. With the machine on, slowly drizzle in the canola oil and chile oil until incorporated. Transfer to a small bowl and season with kosher salt and pepper.

2. **Make the salad** Using a sharp knife and working over a bowl, remove the skin and white pith from the mandarins. Cut between the membranes to release the sections.

3. Arrange the fennel, lettuces, cilantro and mint on a platter and top with the pears, avocado and mandarin sections. Sprinkle with the sesame seeds and season with sea salt and pepper. Drizzle some of the tahini dressing and a little olive oil on the salad and serve the remaining dressing on the side. —*Stuart Brioza*

Kale Salad with Root Vegetables and Apple

Active **20 min**; Total **50 min**; Serves **8 to 10**

This refreshing, superhealthy salad is adapted from a recipe in *Marcus Off Duty* by Marcus Samuelsson, the visionary chef at New York's Red Rooster in Harlem. The dish is one of his favorite ways to showcase kale. To make the fibrous green tender, he massages it with vinegar, salt and olive oil.

- 2 **lbs. curly kale, stemmed and leaves thinly sliced**
- 2 **Tbsp. apple cider vinegar**
- ¼ **cup plus 2 Tbsp. extra-virgin olive oil**
  Kosher salt
- 1 **tsp. finely grated lemon zest**
- ¼ **cup fresh lemon juice**
- 1 **Tbsp. soy sauce**
- 1 **Tbsp. agave syrup**
  Pepper
- 1 **medium carrot, julienned**
- 1 **Granny Smith apple, peeled and julienned**
- 1 **cup peeled and julienned rutabaga**
- 2 **scallions, thinly sliced**

1. In a large bowl, massage the kale with the vinegar, 2 tablespoons of the olive oil and 1 teaspoon of salt. Let stand at room temperature for 30 minutes.

2. Meanwhile, in a medium bowl, whisk the lemon zest and juice, soy sauce, agave syrup and remaining ¼ cup of olive oil. Season the dressing with salt and pepper.

3. Toss the carrot, apple, rutabaga and scallions with the kale. Add the dressing and toss again. Season with salt and pepper and serve. —*Marcus Samuelsson*

MAKE AHEAD The salad can be refrigerated overnight.

Tuscan Kale in Ginger-Sesame Vinaigrette

Total **15 min**; Serves **4**

F&W's Kay Chun created this recipe for blanched, chilled kale in a gingery soy dressing. She took inspiration from *oshitashi*, the Japanese dish of cold cooked spinach in a light soy vinaigrette.

- 3 **Tbsp. low-sodium soy sauce**
- 2 **Tbsp. distilled white vinegar**
- 1 **tsp. grated peeled fresh ginger**
- 1 **small garlic clove, minced**
- 1 **tsp. sesame seeds**
- 2 **lbs. Tuscan kale, stems discarded and leaves chopped**
  Kosher salt

Fill a large bowl with ice water. In a medium bowl, stir together the soy sauce, vinegar, ginger, garlic and sesame seeds. In a large pot of salted boiling water, blanch the kale until tender, about 3 minutes. Drain and cool the kale in the ice bath. Drain well, squeeze dry and add the kale to the vinaigrette. Toss to coat, season with salt and serve. —*Kay Chun*

MAKE AHEAD The blanched and drained kale can be refrigerated overnight.

Parsley-Mint Tabbouleh

Total **30 min**; Serves **6 to 8**

Manhattan-based fashion designer Reem Acra's tabbouleh recipe reflects her childhood in Beirut: The herb-heavy Lebanese version of the Middle Eastern classic swaps the usual ratio of bulgur to herbs, making it brighter, leafier and less grainy.

- ¼ **cup medium-grade bulgur**
  Boiling water
  Three 12-oz. bunches of flat-leaf parsley, stems discarded
- 2 **cups lightly packed mint leaves**
- 5 **medium tomatoes, finely diced**
- ½ **medium onion, finely diced**
- ½ **cup extra-virgin olive oil**
- ½ **tsp. finely grated lemon zest**
- ¼ **cup fresh lemon juice**
- ½ **tsp. paprika**
- ⅛ **tsp. ground allspice**
- ⅛ **tsp. ground cinnamon**
  Kosher salt

1. In a small heatproof bowl, cover the bulgur with boiling water and let stand until tender, 20 minutes; drain very well.

2. In a food processor, pulse the parsley and mint until finely chopped. In a large bowl, toss the herbs, bulgur and the remaining ingredients except the salt. Season with salt, toss again and serve at once. —*Reem Acra*

Chopped Kale Salad with Prosciutto and Figs

Total **25 min plus freezing**
Serves **8 to 10**

Food Network star Giada De Laurentiis tops her fantastic chopped salad with Gorgonzola. She freezes the cheese first so it's firm enough to shave, but you could also crumble it.

- 1 **cup walnuts, chopped**
- ½ **cup mascarpone cheese**
- ¼ **cup plus 2 Tbsp. apple cider vinegar**
- ¼ **cup extra-virgin olive oil**
- 1 **Tbsp. walnut oil**
  Salt and pepper
- 10 **oz. Tuscan kale, stems discarded and leaves thinly sliced**
- 3 **Belgian endives—halved, cored and thinly sliced**
  One 6-oz. head of radicchio—halved, cored and thinly sliced
- 8 **fresh or dried figs, cut into wedges**
- 4 **oz. sliced prosciutto, chopped**
  One 4-oz. wedge of Gorgonzola cheese, frozen until solid, for serving

1. Preheat the oven to 400°. Spread the walnuts in a pie plate and bake for 8 minutes, until golden. Let cool.

2. In a very large bowl, whisk the mascarpone, vinegar and both oils; season with salt and pepper. Add the toasted walnuts, kale, endives, radicchio, figs and prosciutto and toss well. Season the salad with salt and pepper. Using a vegetable peeler, shave half of the frozen Gorgonzola over the salad and serve right away, shaving the remaining cheese at the table. —*Giada De Laurentiis*

KALE SALAD WITH ROOT VEGETABLES AND APPLE

Shaved Cabbage Salad with Paprika Vinaigrette

⏱ Total **30 min**; Serves **6 to 8**

Chef Tim Wiechmann serves this *kraüter salat* at Bronwyn, his Central and Eastern European spot in Somerville, Massachusetts. It's a colorful mix of red and green cabbage, radishes, herbs and apple in a lightly smoky paprika dressing.

- 1 **small shallot, minced**
- 2 **Tbsp. Dijon mustard**
- ¼ **cup fresh lemon juice**
- ¼ **cup distilled white vinegar**
- 1 **tsp. honey**
- 1½ **Tbsp. sweet paprika, plus more for garnish**
- 1 **cup extra-virgin olive oil**
  Kosher salt and pepper
  One ¾-lb. head each of green and red cabbage—halved, cored and shredded
- 1 **large apple—peeled, cored and julienned**
- 1 **cup chopped parsley**
- 1 **cup chopped cilantro**
- ½ **cup snipped chives**
- ½ **cup julienned baby turnips**
- ½ **cup salted roasted *pepitas* (hulled pumpkin seeds)**
- 6 **red radishes, thinly sliced**

1. In a medium bowl, whisk the shallot with the mustard, lemon juice, vinegar, honey and the 1½ tablespoons of paprika. Gradually whisk in the olive oil, then season with salt and pepper.

2. In a large bowl, toss the cabbages with the apple, parsley, cilantro, chives, turnips, *pepitas* and radishes. Add ½ cup of the dressing and toss well. Season the salad with salt and pepper and garnish with paprika. Serve the extra dressing at the table. —*Tim Wiechmann*

Red Cabbage Slaw

Total **20 min plus 4 hr macerating**
Serves **6**

Crunchy, fresh and slightly sweet, this Burmese-Thai slaw from chef Dennis Lee of Namu Gaji in San Francisco is the perfect accompaniment to rich meats.

- ¼ **cup fresh lime juice**
- ¼ **cup white wine vinegar**
- 2 **Tbsp. Asian fish sauce**
- 2 **Tbsp. sugar**
- 1¾ **lbs. red cabbage, cored and very thinly sliced**
- 1 **cup finely chopped parsley**
  Salt

In a large bowl, whisk the lime juice with the vinegar, fish sauce and sugar. Add the cabbage, parsley and a generous pinch of salt and toss well. Cover and refrigerate for at least 4 hours. Season with salt and serve. —*Dennis Lee*

MAKE AHEAD The cabbage slaw can be refrigerated overnight.

Red-and-Green Coleslaw

⏱ Active **15 min**; Total **45 min**; Serves **8**

This classic coleslaw is excellent piled onto pulled pork sandwiches (p. 282) or served on its own.

- ½ **cup sour cream**
- ½ **cup mayonnaise**
- ¼ **cup distilled white vinegar**
- 2 **tsp. turbinado sugar**
- 1 **tsp. dry mustard powder**
  Kosher salt and pepper
- 1 **lb. green cabbage (½ medium head), cored and very thinly sliced**
- 1 **lb. red cabbage (½ medium head), cored and very thinly sliced**

In a large bowl, whisk the sour cream, mayonnaise, vinegar, sugar and mustard powder; season with salt and pepper. Add both cabbages and toss. Cover and refrigerate for 30 minutes. Season with salt and pepper and toss once more before serving. —*Ruby Duke*

MAKE AHEAD The coleslaw can be refrigerated overnight.

Escarole and Brussels Sprout Salad

📷 PAGE 38
⏱ Total **45 min**; Serves **10 to 12**

Instead of roasting her brussels sprouts, F&W editor in chief Dana Cowin shreds them raw and tosses them with escarole and almonds in a tangy buttermilk dressing.

- ½ **cup plus 2 Tbsp. Champagne vinegar**
- 1 **Tbsp. sugar**
  Kosher salt
- 1 **medium red onion, halved lengthwise and very thinly sliced crosswise**
- ½ **cup buttermilk**
- 2 **Tbsp. extra-virgin olive oil**
- 1 **tsp. coarsely ground black pepper**
- ½ **small garlic clove, minced**
  Two ¾-lb. heads of escarole, white and light green leaves only, torn into bite-size pieces
- 1 **lb. brussels sprouts, shredded**
- 1 **cup marcona almonds, chopped**

1. In a medium bowl, whisk ½ cup of the vinegar with the sugar and ½ teaspoon of salt until the sugar dissolves. Add the onion and toss. Let stand at room temperature, tossing occasionally, until the onion is bright pink and crisp-tender, about 30 minutes. Drain well.

2. In a serving bowl, whisk the buttermilk with the olive oil, pepper, garlic and the remaining 2 tablespoons of vinegar. Season the dressing with salt. Add the escarole, brussels sprouts, almonds and pickled onion and toss. Season with salt, toss again and serve. —*Dana Cowin*

MAKE AHEAD The undressed salad can be refrigerated for up to 6 hours. The dressing can be refrigerated overnight.

Market Math: Cabbage

1 Potted Ham and Cabbage

In a small saucepan, melt 2 **oil-packed anchovy fillets** in ¼ cup **olive oil**. Scrape into a bowl. Stir in ½ lb. shredded **smoked ham**, 1 cup finely chopped **green cabbage**, 1 small chopped **dill pickle** and 2 Tbsp. chopped **dill**; season with **salt** and **pepper**. Pack into a 3-cup ramekin and serve.

2 Chicken-Cabbage Salad

In a large bowl, whisk 5 Tbsp. **canola oil** with 3 Tbsp. **lime juice**, 1½ Tbsp. **fish sauce** and 1 minced **Thai chile**; season with **salt** and **pepper**. Toss in 6 cups finely shredded **Savoy** and **red cabbage**, 2 shredded **carrots**, 2 cups shredded **chicken**, 2 oz. crushed **ramen noodles** and ½ cup chopped **basil** and **cilantro** and serve.

3 Fresh Cabbage Kimchi

In a saucepan, heat ⅓ cup **kosher salt** and ¼ cup **sugar** with 2 quarts **water**. Pour over 1 lb. each of chopped **napa cabbage** and quartered **bok choy** in a bowl; let stand 30 minutes. Rinse and drain. Add 2 Tbsp. **fish sauce**, 2 tsp. grated **garlic**, 1 tsp. grated fresh **ginger**, 1 tsp. **sugar** and 1 Tbsp. each of **Korean red pepper flakes** and **toasted sesame oil**; let stand 30 minutes; serve.

4 Cabbage Slaw

In a bowl, toss supremes from 1 **grapefruit** and 2 **clementines** with ¼ cup of **grapefruit juice**. Add 4 sliced **kumquats**, ½ lb. shredded **brussels sprouts**, ⅓ cup chopped **green olives**, 4 thinly sliced **dates** and 3 Tbsp. **olive oil**. Season with **salt** and **pepper** and serve. –*Kay Chun*

Tomato Salad with Camembert Fondue

Active **30 min**; Total **1 hr 10 min**; Serves **4**

This salad is from Wesley and Chloe Genovart of SoLo Farm & Table in South Londonderry, Vermont. With its warm cheese sauce, both fresh and roasted tomatoes and garlic croutons, it's like a deconstructed pizza.

- **8 small Italian plum tomatoes or large cherry tomatoes**
- **¼ cup extra-virgin olive oil**
- **1 tsp. thyme leaves**
- **⅛ tsp. sugar**
- **Kosher salt**
- **Two ¾-inch-thick slices of rustic country bread**
- **1 garlic clove, halved**
- **¼ cup mushroom or vegetable stock**
- **3 oz. Brie or Camembert with the rind, chopped and at room temperature**
- **2 large heirloom tomatoes—1 chopped, 1 thinly sliced**
- **Basil leaves and flaky sea salt, for garnish**

1. Preheat the oven to 300°. Bring a large pot of water to a boil and fill a large bowl with ice water. Using a sharp knife, score an X on the bottom of each plum tomato. Blanch just until the skins start to peel back, 30 seconds. Using a slotted spoon, transfer the tomatoes to the ice bath to cool, then peel them.

2. Set the peeled tomatoes on a rimmed baking sheet. Drizzle with 2 tablespoons of the oil, sprinkle with the thyme and sugar and season with salt. Toss to coat. Roast the tomatoes for 1 hour, until very soft but not too shriveled. Let cool.

3. Meanwhile, in a skillet, heat the remaining 2 tablespoons of oil. Add the bread and toast over moderate heat until golden on both sides, about 3 minutes. Transfer to a plate and rub both sides with the garlic clove. Tear into bite-size croutons.

4. In a small saucepan, bring the stock to a light simmer. Place the cheese in a blender, add the stock and puree until completely smooth.

5. Spoon some of the warm cheese fondue onto plates. Top with the heirloom tomatoes, roasted tomatoes and croutons. Garnish with basil and sea salt and serve. *—Chloe and Wesley Genovart*

WINE Fruity Italian rosé: 2013 Proprietà Sperino Rosa del Rosa.

Heirloom Tomato Salad with Tuna Confit

Active **20 min**; Total **1 hr 20 min**; Serves **6**

George Mendes, the chef at Aldea in Manhattan, slowly poaches fresh tuna in olive oil for his version of the tomato salads common in southern Portugal. For a shortcut, use best-quality canned tuna packed in olive oil.

- **4½ cups extra-virgin olive oil**
- **3 thyme sprigs**
- **1 bay leaf**
- **1 small fennel bulb, thinly sliced**
- **½ small carrot, thinly sliced**
- **1½ tsp. coriander seeds**
- **1½ tsp. black peppercorns**
- **1 tsp. white peppercorns**
- **2 small yellow onions, thinly sliced**
- **1 lb. tuna steak**
- **2 beefsteak tomatoes, sliced ¼ inch thick**
- **2 ripe green heirloom tomatoes, such as Green Zebra, sliced ¼ inch thick**
- **¼ cup sherry vinegar**
- **1½ tsp. fresh oregano, large leaves torn**
- **1½ tsp. lemon thyme**
- **6 large basil leaves, torn**
- **6 large mint leaves, torn**
- **Kosher salt and pepper**

1. In a medium saucepan, combine the olive oil, thyme, bay leaf, fennel, carrot, coriander seeds, black and white peppercorns and half of the sliced onion. Add the tuna, submerging it in the oil. Attach a candy or deep-fry thermometer to the pan and warm the oil over moderate heat to 160°. Remove the saucepan from the heat and let the tuna cool at room temperature until slightly warm, 30 minutes. Remove the tuna from the oil, break it into 1-inch pieces and transfer to a large bowl. Strain the poaching oil; reserve ¾ cup of the oil and discard the solids and remaining oil.

2. Add the tomato slices and remaining onion to the bowl with the tuna. In a small bowl, whisk ½ cup of the reserved poaching oil with the sherry vinegar, oregano, lemon thyme, basil and mint. Pour the mixture over the tuna and tomatoes. Season with salt and pepper and toss gently.

3. Arrange the salad on a serving platter and top with any dressing left in the bowl. Drizzle the salad with the remaining ¼ cup of reserved poaching oil and serve. *—George Mendes*

MAKE AHEAD The tuna confit can be refrigerated for up to 1 day.

WINE Lively, berry-scented Portuguese rosé: 2013 Esporão Vinha da Defesa.

Tomato, Onion and Green Pepper Salad with Shiso

Total **20 min**; Serves **6 as part of a multicourse meal**

Although this mix of raw tomatoes, paper-thin onion and mild green peppers seems Italian, it's also typical of rural Japan, according to Nancy Singleton Hachisu, author of *Japanese Farm Food*. Japanese cooks often serve it with a squirt of mayonnaise, but Hachisu prefers drizzling with soy sauce, oil and rice vinegar.

- **1 lb. cherry or grape tomatoes, halved**
- **¼ lb. small mild green peppers, such as Italian frying peppers, halved lengthwise and thinly sliced crosswise**
- **½ small onion, very thinly sliced**
- **2 Tbsp. canola oil, preferably cold-pressed**
- **1½ Tbsp. organic soy sauce**
- **1½ Tbsp. brown rice vinegar**
- **6 shiso leaves, thinly sliced (see Note)**

In a large bowl, gently toss the tomatoes, peppers and onion. Drizzle with the oil, soy sauce and vinegar. Scatter the shiso on top and serve right away. *—Nancy Singleton Hachisu*

NOTE Shiso is a pungent, aromatic herb with large, serrated, slightly sweet and peppery leaves. It's available at Japanese and other East Asian groceries.

TOMATO, ONION AND GREEN
PEPPER SALAD WITH SHISO

Sugar Snap Peas with Mint and Warm Coconut Dressing

⏱ Total **25 min**; Serves **4**

Chef Edward Lee of 610 Magnolia in Louisville, Kentucky, is brilliant at infusing Southern cooking with Asian flavors. Here he creates an unusual warm dressing of coconut milk and lemon juice for a salad of orange slices and charred snap peas.

- **1** blood or navel orange
- **2** tsp. toasted sesame oil
- **½** lb. sugar snap peas
- Salt
- **¾** cup unsweetened coconut milk
- **2** tsp. fresh lemon juice
- Pinch of sugar
- Chopped mint and freshly cracked pepper, for garnish

1. Using a very sharp knife, peel the navel orange, making sure to remove all of the bitter white pith. Halve the orange lengthwise and slice it crosswise into ⅛-inch-thick slices. Transfer the slices to a small bowl.

2. In a medium skillet, heat the sesame oil. Add the sugar snap peas in a single layer and cook over moderately high heat, without stirring, until they are nicely charred, 2 to 3 minutes. Transfer the peas to a medium bowl and season them lightly with salt.

3. Add the coconut milk, lemon juice and sugar to the skillet and cook over moderately low heat, whisking frequently, until the dressing is thickened, about 5 minutes. Spoon the dressing onto plates and top with the sugar snaps and orange slices. Garnish with chopped mint and freshly cracked pepper and serve warm.
—*Edward Lee*

Herbed Pea Puree and Ricotta Salad with Black Garlic and Lemon Confiture

Active **1 hr 30 min**; Total **2 hr 30 min**
Serves **6**

This wonderful, complex-tasting warm salad by F&W Best New Chef 2014 Matthew Accarrino combines three types of peas with a creamy ricotta-pea puree, sweet-tart lemon confiture and almonds.

LEMON CONFITURE

- **¾** cup sugar
- **½** tsp. kosher salt
- **2** firm lemons, very thinly sliced crosswise on a mandoline and seeded

PEA PUREE

- **¼** cup extra-virgin olive oil
- **½** medium onion, minced
- Kosher salt
- **1** cup fresh or thawed frozen peas
- **2** Tbsp. finely chopped mint
- **2** Tbsp. finely chopped parsley
- **½** cup fresh ricotta
- **2** Tbsp. freshly grated Parmigiano-Reggiano cheese

SALAD

- **1½** Tbsp. extra-virgin olive oil, plus more for brushing
- **12** small peeled black garlic cloves (see Note)
- **1** cup freshly shelled English peas (¼ lb.)
- **¼** lb. sugar snap peas, trimmed
- **¼** lb. snow peas, trimmed
- Kosher salt
- Pea shoots, thinly sliced radishes, small mint leaves, finely chopped chives, chopped marcona almonds and edible flowers, for garnish

1. Make the lemon confiture Preheat the oven to 350°. In a small saucepan, combine the sugar and salt with ¾ cup of water and bring to a boil, stirring to dissolve the sugar. Transfer to a small baking dish and add the lemon slices in an even layer. Bake for 20 to 25 minutes, until the rinds are translucent and the lemons are tender. Let cool completely.

2. Meanwhile, make the pea puree In a medium skillet, heat the olive oil. Add the onion, season with salt and cook over moderate heat, stirring occasionally, until just starting to brown, about 7 minutes. Add the peas and cook, stirring, until warmed through, about 3 minutes. Stir in the mint and parsley until just wilted, 1 minute. Transfer the mixture to a mini food processor and let cool completely, then puree until smooth. Scrape the pea puree into a medium bowl and fold in the ricotta and Parmigiano-Reggiano. Season with salt.

3. Prepare the salad Lightly brush a large square of wax paper with olive oil. Arrange the black garlic cloves on the wax paper 3 inches apart and put another piece of wax paper on top. Using a rolling pin, gently roll the cloves until very flat. Slide the paper onto a plate and freeze until slightly firm, about 15 minutes.

4. Meanwhile, in a large saucepan of salted boiling water, blanch the English peas, sugar snaps and snow peas until they are crisp-tender, about 3 minutes. Drain, transfer to a large bowl and stir in the 1½ tablespoons of olive oil. Coarsely chop 8 of the lemon slices and fold them in. Season with salt.

5. Scoop ⅓-cup mounds of the pea puree onto plates and spoon the warm peas alongside. Peel the top sheet of wax paper off the smashed black garlic and, using a small offset spatula, lay 2 garlic cloves on each mound of pea puree. Arrange 1 slice of lemon confiture on the garlic and garnish the salads with pea shoots, radishes, mint, chives, marcona almonds and edible flowers. Serve right away.
—*Matthew Accarrino*

NOTE Black garlic is fermented and has a sweet, molasses-like flavor. It's available at specialty food shops and blackgarlic.com.

MAKE AHEAD The ricotta-pea puree can be refrigerated overnight. The lemon confiture can be refrigerated for up to 1 week.

WINE Zippy, green apple–scented northern Italian Pinot Grigio: 2013 Erste + Neue.

HERBED PEA PUREE AND RICOTTA SALAD
WITH BLACK GARLIC AND LEMON CONFITURE

Fennel and Fava Bean Salad

Total **1 hr**; Serves **8**

Winemaker Jayson Woodbridge uses wild fennel from the St. Helena Farmers' Market in Napa Valley for this refreshing salad, but regular supermarket fennel works perfectly well, too.

DRESSING

- **2 Tbsp. honey**
- **1 Tbsp. fresh lime juice**
- **1 small garlic clove, minced**
- **2 tsp. pumpkin seed oil**
- **2 tsp. walnut oil**
- **3 Tbsp. olive oil**

SALAD

- **4 lbs. fresh fava beans, shelled (3 cups)**
- **1 Tbsp. olive oil**
- **½ cup pine nuts**
- **½ cup shelled pistachios**
  Kosher salt and freshly ground black pepper
- **2 lemons**
- **5 medium fennel bulbs—trimmed, halved lengthwise, cored and very thinly sliced crosswise**
- **1 medium jalapeño, seeded and minced**
  Pinch of cayenne pepper

1. Make the dressing In a very large bowl, whisk the honey with the lime juice, garlic and pumpkin seed, walnut and olive oils.

2. Make the salad In a large saucepan of salted boiling water, blanch the fava beans until just tender, 3 to 5 minutes. Drain and rinse under cold water. Squeeze the favas from their skins; discard the skins.

3. In a medium skillet, heat the olive oil until shimmering. Add the pine nuts and pistachios and cook over moderate heat, shaking the pan frequently, until the nuts are golden, about 5 minutes. Season the nuts with salt and black pepper and transfer them to paper towels to drain and cool completely.

4. Using a very sharp knife, peel the lemons, being sure to remove all of the bitter white pith. Thinly slice the lemons crosswise. Pick out and discard any seeds, then cut the lemon slices into thin strips.

5. Stir the lemon strips into the dressing. Add the fava beans, fennel, jalapeño, cayenne and toasted pine nuts and pistachios and toss. Season the salad with salt and black pepper and toss again. Serve the salad right away. —*Jayson Woodbridge*

WINE Zesty, unoaked California Chardonnay: 2012 Layer Cake.

Celery, Fennel and Apple Salad with Pecorino and Walnuts

Total **30 min**; Serves **4 to 6**

- **¾ cup walnuts**
- **3 Tbsp. extra-virgin olive oil, plus more for drizzling**
- **2 Tbsp. fresh lemon juice**
  Kosher salt and pepper
- **3 celery ribs, sliced diagonally ¼ inch thick**
- **2 fennel bulbs—trimmed, halved, cored and thinly sliced on a mandoline**
- **2 Honeycrisp apples—halved, cored and sliced**
- **½ cup basil leaves, torn if large**
  Pecorino cheese shavings, for garnish

1. Preheat the oven to 375°. Spread the walnuts in a pie plate and toast for 7 to 8 minutes, until they are golden. Coarsely chop the nuts.

2. In a large bowl, whisk the 3 tablespoons of olive oil with the lemon juice and season with salt and pepper. Add the celery, fennel, apples and basil and toss to coat. Transfer the salad to a platter. Season with pepper and drizzle with olive oil, then top with the walnuts and garnish with cheese shavings. —*Athena Calderone*

Haricots Verts and Artichoke Salad with Hazelnut Vinaigrette

Total **1 hr**; Serves **4**

At Lazare, his brasserie in the Saint-Lazare train station in Paris, Eric Frechon (also the chef at the Michelin three-star Epicure) turns out impeccable French classics like this updated nouvelle cuisine *salade gourmande*. He dresses crisp-tender haricots verts and artichokes in a sherry vinegar, hazelnut and shallot vinaigrette.

- **2 large artichokes**
- **1 lb. haricots verts**
- **3 Tbsp. hazelnut oil**
- **1 Tbsp. peanut oil**
- **1 Tbsp. sherry vinegar**
  Kosher salt and freshly ground pepper
- **2 Tbsp. finely chopped shallot**
- **3 Tbsp. chopped toasted hazelnuts**

1. Fill a medium bowl with water. Working with 1 artichoke at a time, snap off the tough outer leaves and trim the stem. Cut off all the remaining leaves. Peel and trim the bottom and stem; add the trimmed artichoke to the water. Repeat with the remaining artichoke.

2. In a medium saucepan of salted boiling water, cook the artichokes over moderate heat until tender, 18 to 20 minutes. Using a slotted spoon, transfer them to a cutting board; let cool slightly. Scoop out the furry chokes with a melon baller or spoon. Cut each artichoke into quarters.

3. Prepare a medium bowl of ice water. In the medium saucepan, cook the haricots verts over moderate heat for 3 minutes. Drain and transfer to the ice water to cool; drain. Dry on paper towels, then cut in half.

4. In a large bowl, whisk the hazelnut oil, peanut oil and sherry vinegar and season with salt and pepper. Add the haricots verts, artichokes and shallot and toss. Sprinkle with the hazelnuts and serve. —*Eric Frechon*

FENNEL AND FAVA BEAN SALAD

Tomato and Peach Salad with Crisp Tofu

Total **30 min**; Serves **6**

Georgia chef Hugh Acheson combines sweet, salty, spicy and tangy flavors in this exceptional summer tomato salad, tossing peaches, pickled serranos and fried tofu with a zippy ginger-lime dressing.

- **2 serrano chiles, thinly sliced**
- **½ cup unseasoned rice vinegar**
- **1 tsp. sugar**
  Kosher salt
- **1 Tbsp. low-sodium soy sauce**
- **1 Tbsp. fresh lime juice**
- **1 Tbsp. minced peeled fresh ginger**
- **1 tsp. Dijon mustard**
- **½ cup plus 3 Tbsp. canola oil**
- **6 oz. extra-firm tofu, drained well and cubed**
- **2 heirloom tomatoes, sliced**
- **2 peaches, cut into wedges**
- **1 cup arugula or mizuna**
- **½ cup basil leaves**

1. Put the serranos in a small heatproof bowl. In a small saucepan, bring ½ cup of water to a boil with the vinegar, sugar and ½ teaspoon of salt, stirring to dissolve the sugar. Pour the brine over the serranos and let stand for 15 minutes, until cooled to room temperature.

2. Meanwhile, in a small bowl, whisk the soy sauce, lime juice, ginger, mustard and 3 tablespoons of the oil.

3. In a large cast-iron skillet, heat the remaining ½ cup of oil until shimmering. Add the tofu and cook over moderate heat, turning, until crisp, 5 minutes. Using a slotted spoon, transfer to a paper towel–lined plate. Season with salt.

4. Arrange the tomatoes, peaches, arugula and serranos on a platter. Drizzle with the soy-lime dressing, scatter the tofu and basil on top and serve. —*Hugh Acheson*

WINE Juicy Pinot Noir–based rosé: 2013 Stoller Family Estate.

Laotian Bean and Tomato Salad

Active **40 min**; Total **1 hr 40 min**; Serves **6**

A mix of charred haricots verts, blanched wax beans and raw cherry tomatoes gives this salad terrific texture. The spicy dressing includes roasted garlic and, less conventionally, roasted ginger (roasting mellows out the flavor).

- **1 head of garlic, halved crosswise**
- **2 Tbsp. canola oil, plus more for brushing**
  Kosher salt
  One 1-inch piece of unpeeled fresh ginger
- **2 Tbsp. Asian fish sauce**
- **2 Tbsp. soy sauce**
- **4 small Thai chiles, stemmed**
- **1½ tsp. palm sugar or light brown sugar**
- **1 lb. green and yellow wax beans, trimmed**
- **1 lb. haricots verts, trimmed**
- **2 cups mixed cherry tomatoes, halved**

1. Preheat the oven to 350°. Brush the cut sides of the garlic with oil and season with salt. Wrap the garlic in foil, cut side up, and roast for about 1 hour, until very soft. Let cool, then squeeze the garlic cloves from the skins into a blender.

2. Meanwhile, roast the ginger directly over an open flame until charred all over and slightly softened, 7 minutes. Peel and chop the ginger. Add to the blender along with the fish sauce, soy sauce, chiles, sugar and 2 tablespoons of water and puree until smooth. Season the dressing with salt.

3. In a saucepan of salted boiling water, cook the wax beans until crisp-tender, 2 minutes. Drain and cool under running water. Drain again and pat dry, then transfer to a large bowl.

4. In a very large wok or skillet, heat the 2 tablespoons of oil. Spread the haricots verts in the wok in a single layer and season well with salt. Cook over high heat until the beans are charred on the bottom and crisp-tender, 3 to 4 minutes. Add the haricots verts to the wax beans, then add the tomatoes and one-third of the dressing; toss well. Season the salad with salt and serve with the remaining dressing. —*Joshua Walker*

Raw Asparagus Salad with Tomatoes and Hard-Boiled Eggs

Active **25 min**; Total **50 min**; Serves **4**

The key to this simple salad is slicing the raw asparagus thinly, so it takes on the flavor of the lemony marinade.

- **⅓ cup fresh lemon juice**
- **⅓ cup chopped scallions**
  One 2-oz. can anchovy fillets, drained
- **2 small garlic cloves**
- **¾ cup extra-virgin olive oil**
  Kosher salt and pepper
- **1 lb. asparagus, woody ends discarded and stalks thinly sliced diagonally**
- **4 large eggs**
- **2 cups mixed cherry tomatoes, halved**

1. In a blender, combine the lemon juice with the scallions, anchovies and garlic and puree until nearly smooth. With the machine on, gradually add the olive oil until emulsified. Season the dressing with salt and pepper. Transfer one-third of the dressing to a serving bowl and toss with the asparagus. Refrigerate for 30 minutes.

2. Meanwhile, in a medium saucepan, cover the eggs with water and bring to a boil. Remove from the heat, cover and let stand for 10 minutes. Drain and cool the eggs under cold running water. Peel the eggs and pat dry, then quarter lengthwise and season with salt and pepper.

3. Fold the tomatoes into the asparagus; season with salt and pepper. Arrange the eggs on top and serve, passing the remaining dressing at the table. —*Molly Chester*

MAKE AHEAD The dressing can be refrigerated overnight.

Charred Broccoli and Red Onion Salad

⊙ Total **45 min**; Serves **6**

In Raleigh, North Carolina, local-hero chef Ashley Christensen cuts broccoli into thick slices, then grills it with sweet red onion. Broccoli with large, very tight heads make the best "steaks."

- 2 large, tight heads of broccoli (2½ lbs.), cut lengthwise into ¾-inch-thick steaks (reserve any extra florets for another use)
- 2 Tbsp. extra-virgin olive oil, plus more for brushing

  Kosher salt and pepper
- 2 medium red onions, sliced crosswise ½ inch thick
- 3 medium tomatoes, cut into 1-inch pieces
- 2½ Tbsp. red wine vinegar

  Freshly shaved *ricotta salata*, for serving

1. Light a grill or heat a grill pan. Brush the broccoli steaks with oil and season with salt and pepper. Grill over moderately high heat, turning once, until lightly charred and crisp-tender, about 7 minutes. Transfer to a baking sheet and let cool.

2. Meanwhile, brush the red onions with oil and season with salt and pepper. Grill over moderately high heat, turning once, until lightly charred and softened, about 5 minutes. Transfer to a work surface and let cool, then cut into ¾-inch pieces.

3. In a large bowl, toss the tomatoes with the 2 tablespoons of olive oil, the vinegar and a generous pinch of salt and let stand for 5 minutes. Add the grilled onions; season with salt and pepper. Arrange the broccoli on plates or a platter and spoon the tomato–red onion salad on top. Garnish with shaved *ricotta salata* and serve right away. —*Ashley Christensen*

12
Minutes

- -

BROCCOLINI, MUSHROOM AND SESAME SALAD

- -

Blanch 12 oz. **Broccolini** until bright green, 2 minutes. Drain and transfer to a large bowl with 2 cups sliced **button mushrooms,** 2 Tbsp. **toasted sesame seeds,** ¼ tsp. **crushed red pepper,** 1 minced **garlic clove,** 1 thinly sliced **scallion** and 1½ Tbsp. each of **apple cider vinegar, toasted sesame oil** and **soy sauce.** Season with **salt** and **black pepper,** toss and serve. –*Judy Joo*

Hazelnut-Zucchini Salad

⏱ Total **30 min**; Serves **4**

- ¼ cup hazelnuts
- 3 small zucchini (¾ lb.), very thinly sliced lengthwise on a mandoline
- ½ tsp. finely grated lemon zest
- 3 Tbsp. fresh lemon juice
- 3 Tbsp. extra-virgin olive oil
  Sea salt and pepper
  Mint leaves and shaved Parmigiano-Reggiano cheese, for garnish

1. Preheat the oven to 375°. Spread the hazelnuts in a pie plate and toast for 12 minutes, until fragrant; transfer to a clean kitchen towel and let cool slightly, then rub together to remove the skins. Coarsely chop the hazelnuts.

2. Arrange the zucchini strips on a platter and sprinkle with the lemon zest and lemon juice. Drizzle with the oil; season with sea salt and pepper. Scatter the hazelnuts over the zucchini and garnish with mint and Parmigiano-Reggiano cheese.
—*Francis Mallmann*

WINE Crisp Argentinean Sauvignon Blanc: 2013 Zorzal Terroir Único.

Summer Squash Salad with Pickled Currants

⏱ Total **15 min**; Serves **4**

- 2 Tbsp. red wine vinegar
- ¼ tsp. kosher salt
- ¼ tsp. sugar
- 2 Tbsp. dried currants
- 1 lb. baby summer squash, thinly sliced, preferably on a mandoline
- 2 cups mixed baby greens
- ¾ cup chopped basil
- 2 Tbsp. extra-virgin olive oil
- ¼ cup roasted hazelnuts, chopped
  Freshly shaved *ricotta salata,* for garnish

1. In a small saucepan, combine the vinegar, salt, sugar and currants and warm over moderate heat just until the sugar dissolves. Remove from the heat and let cool slightly. Drain the currants, reserving 2 teaspoons of the pickling liquid.

2. In a large bowl, toss the squash with the greens, basil, olive oil, currants and the reserved pickling liquid. Transfer to a platter. Top with the hazelnuts, garnish with cheese and serve. —*Jimmy Bannos, Jr.*

Greek Salad with Oregano-Roasted Salmon

⏱ Total **30 min**; Serves **4**

- 7 oregano sprigs, plus 1 Tbsp. chopped oregano
  One 1½-lb. salmon fillet
- ½ cup plus 2 Tbsp. extra-virgin olive oil
  Kosher salt and freshly ground black pepper
- 3 Tbsp. fresh lemon juice
- ¾ cup pitted kalamata olives, chopped
- 1 head of romaine lettuce, coarsely chopped
- 2 small tomatoes, cut into wedges or large chunks
- 1 Kirby cucumber, cut into ½-inch dice
- ½ small red onion, thinly sliced
- 2 Tbsp. chopped chives
- 6 oz. feta cheese, sliced

1. Preheat the oven to 450°. Set a rack over a baking sheet and arrange the oregano sprigs in the center.

2. Rub the salmon all over with 2 tablespoons of the olive oil and season with salt and pepper. Place the salmon skin side up on top of the oregano sprigs and roast for 12 to 15 minutes, until the salmon is just cooked through. Let cool slightly, then discard the oregano sprigs and salmon skin; break the salmon into large pieces.

3. Meanwhile, in a large bowl, combine the chopped oregano and lemon juice. Gradually whisk in the remaining ½ cup of olive oil, then whisk in the olives and season with salt and pepper. Reserve 2 tablespoons of the olive vinaigrette. Add the lettuce, tomatoes, cucumber, red onion and chives to the large bowl and season with salt and pepper. Toss to coat.

4. Transfer the salad to a platter. Top with the salmon and feta. Spoon the reserved olive vinaigrette over the salmon and serve. —*Kay Chun*

WINE Lively, fruit-forward Greek rosé: 2013 Kir-Yianni Akakies.

Roasted Cauliflower Salad with Lentils and Dates

⏱ Total **45 min**; Serves **4**

- ½ cup raw almonds
- 1 cup beluga or green lentils, rinsed
- 1 head of cauliflower, cut into 1- to 1½-inch florets
- ¼ cup plus 1 Tbsp. extra-virgin olive oil
- ¼ tsp. ground cumin
- ¼ tsp. ground cinnamon
- ¼ tsp. ground ginger
  Pinch of cayenne pepper
  Kosher salt and freshly ground pepper
- 2 Tbsp. tahini
- 3 Tbsp. fresh lemon juice
- 1 tsp. honey
- 10 dates, pitted and chopped
- ½ small red onion, sliced
- 4 cups loosely packed spinach or arugula

1. Preheat the oven to 350°. Spread the almonds in a pie plate and toast for 10 to 12 minutes, until golden. Let cool, then coarsely chop. Increase the oven temperature to 425°.

2. Meanwhile, in a saucepan, combine the lentils with 2 cups of water and bring to a boil. Simmer over moderate heat until tender, 20 minutes. Drain well and let cool.

3. On a large rimmed baking sheet, toss the cauliflower with ¼ cup of the olive oil and the cumin, cinnamon, ginger and cayenne; season with salt and ground pepper. Roast for 20 minutes, turning, until the cauliflower is tender and golden brown.

4. In a large bowl, whisk the tahini with the lemon juice, honey, the remaining 1 tablespoon of olive oil and 2 tablespoons of water until smooth. Add the lentils and season with salt and ground pepper; toss to coat. Scrape the roasted cauliflower into the bowl and add the toasted almonds, dates, onion and spinach. Toss the salad, transfer to a platter and serve.
—*David Frenkiel and Luise Vindahl*

Warm Chicory Salad with Mushrooms

⏱ Total **35 min**; Serves **6**

This hearty salad is from Marjorie Taylor, co-owner of the Cook's Atelier, a culinary center in Beaune, in the Burgundy region of France. Here Taylor sautés fresh wild mushrooms, but occasionally she substitutes sliced pears.

- 2 **Tbsp. minced shallot**
- 2 **Tbsp. sherry vinegar**
  Salt and freshly ground pepper
- ½ **cup extra-virgin olive oil**
- ¼ **lb. shiitake mushrooms, stems discarded and caps thickly sliced**
- ¼ **lb. oyster mushrooms, sliced**
- 2 **thyme sprigs**
- 1 **Belgian endive, cut into 1-inch pieces**
- 1 **small head of radicchio, cut into 1-inch pieces**
- 1 **small head of escarole, inner pale leaves only, cut into 1-inch pieces**
- ¼ **cup flat-leaf parsley leaves**
- 1 **oz. Parmigiano-Reggiano, shaved (½ cup)**

1. In a small bowl, combine the shallot with the vinegar and season with salt and pepper. Let stand for 10 minutes, then whisk in ¼ cup plus 2 tablespoons of the olive oil.

2. Meanwhile, in a large skillet, heat the remaining 2 tablespoons of olive oil. Add the mushrooms and thyme sprigs and season with salt and pepper. Cook over moderately high heat, stirring occasionally, until the mushrooms are golden and tender, about 8 minutes. Discard the thyme sprigs. Remove the skillet from the heat, add the dressing and toss to coat.

3. In a large bowl, combine the endive, radicchio, escarole and parsley. Using a slotted spoon, add the mushrooms. Drizzle with some of the dressing from the skillet, season with salt and pepper and toss. Add the shaved cheese and gently toss. Serve right away, passing any remaining dressing at the table. —*Marjorie Taylor*

WINE Crisp white Burgundy: 2011 Louis Jadot Saint-Aubin.

Grilled Fig Salad with Spiced Cashews

⏱ Total **45 min**; Serves **4 to 6**

A vibrant, Asian-style sesame, ginger and scallion dressing brings together the soft, sweet figs and buttery cashews in this salad. The recipe is from Ratha Chaupoly and Ben Daitz of New York City's Num Pang sandwich shops.

- ½ **cup sugar**
- ½ **Tbsp. unsalted butter**
- ¼ **tsp. Chinese five-spice powder**
- 1 **cup raw cashews**
  Kosher salt
- ¼ **cup canola oil, plus more for brushing**
- 2 **Tbsp. toasted sesame oil**
- 2 **Tbsp. unseasoned rice vinegar**
- 3 **Tbsp. finely grated peeled fresh ginger**
- 3 **scallions, green parts only, finely chopped (⅓ cup)**
- 1 **Tbsp. toasted black sesame seeds**
- 12 **fresh figs, halved**
  Pepper
- 2 **heads of Bibb or oak leaf lettuce (10 oz.), leaves torn**

1. Line a baking sheet with parchment paper. In a medium saucepan, bring the sugar and 2 tablespoons of water to a boil. Boil over moderately low heat, undisturbed, until a light amber caramel forms, about 5 minutes. Using a wet pastry brush, wash down any sugar crystals on the side of the pan. Remove from the heat and whisk in the butter and five-spice powder. Stir in the cashews until evenly coated. Scrape the cashews onto the prepared baking sheet and spread in an even layer; season with salt and cool. Break up the glazed cashews into individual pieces.

2. Meanwhile, in a small bowl, whisk the ¼ cup of canola oil with the sesame oil, rice vinegar, ginger, scallions and sesame seeds.

3. Light a grill and oil the grate. Brush the cut sides of the figs with canola oil and season with salt and pepper. Grill over moderate heat just until lightly charred and barely juicy, about 2 minutes per side; transfer to a plate.

4. In a large bowl, toss the lettuce with two-thirds of the dressing and season with salt and pepper. Arrange the lettuce on plates and top with the figs. Drizzle more dressing over the figs, sprinkle with the candied cashews and serve. —*Ratha Chaupoly and Ben Daitz*

WINE Bright, lightly floral Italian white: 2013 Prà Soave Classico.

Jicama and Citrus Salad

⏱ Total **25 min**; Serves **4 to 6**

On a trip to Valladolid, Mexico, private chef and world traveler Jane Coxwell picked up the fixings for this bright jicama salad at the market and made the simplest of seasonings with citrus juices, salt and pepper.

- 2 **Ruby Red grapefruits**
- 2 **navel oranges**
  One 1-lb. jicama, peeled and cut into ½-inch dice
- 4 **radishes, thinly sliced**
- 2 **Tbsp. fresh lime juice**
- ¾ **cup lightly packed cilantro, chopped**
  Salt and pepper

Using a very sharp knife, peel the grapefruits and oranges, being sure to remove any bitter white pith. Working over a large bowl to catch the juices, cut in between the membranes to release the sections into the bowl. Cut the citrus into pieces. Add all of the remaining ingredients to the bowl and toss well. Serve the salad right away. —*Jane Coxwell*

Watermelon, Feta and Charred Pepper Salad

Total **30 min**; Serves **4 to 6**

F&W Best New Chefs 2014 Joe Ogrodnek and Walker Stern update the classic combination of watermelon, feta and olives with smoky charred shishito peppers, fresh herbs and spicy Korean red chile powder.

- 1 lb. seedless watermelon, cut into 1-inch cubes (from one 3¼-lb. watermelon)
- 2 Kirby cucumbers, peeled and cut into ¾-inch dice
- ¼ cup very thinly sliced red onion
- 1½ Tbsp. sherry vinegar
- ½ tsp. *gochugaru* (Korean chile powder) or Aleppo pepper
- 6 Tbsp. extra-virgin olive oil
  Kosher salt and pepper
- 20 medium shishito peppers (4 oz.)
- 20 pitted kalamata olives, halved
- 4 oz. feta, crumbled
- 1 cup lightly packed watercress leaves
- 2 Tbsp. minced cilantro
- 2 Tbsp. finely chopped dill

GENIUS TIP

Chefs' Secret to Crisp Salads

There's a reason the salads at very good restaurants are so crisp and fresh: The vegetables were soaked in an ice-water bath. Every kind of vegetable–paper-thin carrot slices, whole French breakfast radishes, even wilted greens–can get a zap of vitality from an icy dunk.

1. In a large glass or ceramic baking dish, gently toss the watermelon, cucumbers, red onion, vinegar, *gochugaru* and ¼ cup of the olive oil. Spread in an even layer and season with salt and pepper.

2. In a large skillet, heat the remaining 2 tablespoons of olive oil until shimmering. Add the shishitos and cook over high heat, tossing, until charred in spots and crisp-tender, about 2 minutes. Transfer the shishitos to the baking dish and toss.

3. Transfer the salad to plates and garnish with the olives, feta, watercress, cilantro and dill. Serve right away.
—*Joe Ogrodnek and Walker Stern*

WINE Robust, berry-scented rosé: 2013 Mulderbosch.

Peppered Herb-Yogurt Dressing

Total **15 min**; Makes **about ¾ cup**

This creamy and tart dressing with cracked black peppercorns is fantastic on an iceberg wedge or cooked, chilled green beans.

- ½ cup plus 1 Tbsp. plain whole-milk yogurt
- 1 tsp. coarsely cracked black peppercorns
- ½ tsp. very finely chopped garlic
- 3 Tbsp. extra-virgin olive oil
- ¼ cup chopped mixed herbs, such as chives, dill and tarragon
  Kosher salt

In a medium bowl, whisk together the yogurt, peppercorns, garlic and 2 tablespoons of water. Gradually whisk in the olive oil until emulsified. Stir in the herbs and season with salt. —*Kay Chun*

Tomato-Shallot Dressing

Total **10 min**; Makes **about 1 cup**

F&W's Kay Chun steals a technique from Spanish kitchens for this easy dressing: grating a whole tomato for perfect skin-free pulp. Use the dressing on salads, pasta, fish or grilled chicken.

- 1 large heirloom tomato
- 2 Tbsp. minced shallot
- 2 Tbsp. fresh lemon juice
- ¼ cup extra-virgin olive oil
- 1 Tbsp. chopped chives
  Kosher salt

Working over a medium bowl, grate the tomato on the large holes of a box grater until only the skin remains in your hand; discard the skin. Whisk in the shallot, lemon juice, olive oil and chives. Season with salt. —*Kay Chun*

Miso, Ginger and Sesame Dressing

Total **10 min**; Makes **about 1 cup**

Fabulous with spinach salad, steamed broccoli, roasted carrots or grilled zucchini, this simple dressing gets zing from fresh ginger and a toasty flavor from sesame seeds.

- 3 Tbsp. *shiro* (white) miso
- 2 Tbsp. finely grated peeled fresh ginger
- 1 Tbsp. distilled white vinegar
- ½ cup canola oil
- 1 Tbsp. toasted sesame seeds

In a medium bowl, whisk the miso with the ginger, vinegar and 6 tablespoons of water until smooth, then whisk in the oil and sesame seeds. —*Kay Chun*

Avocado-Tarragon Dressing

Total **10 min**; Makes **about 1 cup**

This multipurpose dressing makes a perfect dip for crudités and a great go-with for grilled steak. Or swap it for the mayonnaise in chicken salad.

- 1 medium Hass avocado, halved and pitted
- 2 Tbsp. fresh lime juice
- 1 garlic clove, minced
- ¼ cup plus 2 Tbsp. extra-virgin olive oil
- 2 Tbsp. chopped tarragon
  Kosher salt

Scoop the avocado into a blender. Add the lime juice, garlic and ¼ cup of water and pulse to blend. With the machine on, slowly drizzle in the olive oil until incorporated. Transfer the dressing to a bowl, stir in the tarragon and season with salt. —*Kay Chun*

WATERMELON, FETA AND
CHARRED PEPPER SALAD

CURRIED CARROT AND APPLE SOUP
Recipe, page 68

Soups & Stews

PAGE NUMBERS IN RED INDICATE F&W STAFF FAVORITES

Golden Gazpacho with Avocado

Active **15 min**; Total **45 min**; Serves **4**

Based on a salsa recipe, this eye-catching gazpacho is made with yellow tomatoes, which are less acidic than red ones. Jalapeño gives it subtle heat.

- **2 lbs. yellow or orange cherry tomatoes, halved**
- **1 small garlic clove, crushed**
- **¼ cup extra-virgin olive oil**
- **1 jalapeño, seeded and minced**
- **Kosher salt and pepper**
- **Diced avocado and tortilla chips, for serving**

In a blender, puree the halved tomatoes and crushed garlic with ¼ cup of water. With the machine on, gradually add the olive oil until incorporated. Transfer to a bowl, stir in the jalapeño and season with salt and pepper. Refrigerate until chilled, about 30 minutes. Ladle the gazpacho into bowls and top with diced avocado. Serve with tortilla chips. —*Justin Chapple*

MAKE AHEAD The gazpacho can be refrigerated overnight.

Tangy Cucumber Soup

Active **10 min**; Total **40 min**; Serves **4**

To turn this refreshing yogurt-based soup into a terrific light meal, simply add poached shrimp.

- **2 lbs. Persian or English cucumbers— halved lengthwise, seeded and chopped**
- **½ cup plain fat-free Greek yogurt**
- **3 Tbsp. fresh lemon juice**
- **2 small garlic cloves**
- **½ cup extra-virgin olive oil, plus more for garnish**
- **1 Tbsp. chopped dill, plus dill sprigs for garnish**
- **Kosher salt and pepper**

In a blender, puree the cucumbers, yogurt, lemon juice and garlic. With the machine on, gradually add the ½ cup of oil until incorporated. Transfer to a bowl, stir in the chopped dill and season with salt and pepper. Cover and refrigerate until chilled, 30 minutes. Ladle the soup into bowls and garnish with a drizzle of olive oil and dill sprigs. —*Justin Chapple*

Chilled English Pea Soup with Prosciutto Crisps

Active **45 min**; Total **2 hr 10 min**; Serves **4**

Back in 2003, chef Grant Achatz served Nick Kokonas (his future business partner in the Chicago restaurants Alinea and Next) an English pea soup with dehydrated prosciutto. "The soup was silky, absolutely delicious," Kokonas remembers. He called Achatz for the recipe, and the chef revealed it was just peas, salt and water. This utter simplicity, Achatz told him, is the secret to the pure flavor. The recipe here is Kokonas's version. He adds a few tablespoons of simple syrup, but you may need much less, depending on the sweetness of your peas.

- **4 thin slices of prosciutto (2 oz.)**
- **4 cups shelled English peas (3½ lbs. in the pod)**
- **Simple syrup (see Notes)**
- **Kosher salt and pepper**
- **Extra-virgin olive oil, for drizzling**

1. Preheat the oven to 250°. Line a baking sheet with a silicone baking mat and arrange the prosciutto in an even layer on top. Bake for about 2 hours in the center of the oven, flipping once, until dehydrated and very crisp. Transfer to paper towels to drain and cool, then break into pieces.

2. Meanwhile, fill a large bowl with ice water. In a large saucepan of salted boiling water, blanch the peas until just tender, about 2 minutes. Using a slotted spoon, transfer the peas to the ice water to cool. Reserve 1¾ cups of the cooking water.

3. Drain the peas and add to a blender. With the machine on, add the reserved cooking water in a thin stream and puree until very smooth. (You may not need all of the reserved water.) Blend in simple syrup to taste. Strain the soup through a fine sieve and season with salt and pepper. Refrigerate until chilled, about 30 minutes. Ladle the soup into bowls, top with the prosciutto crisps and a drizzle of olive oil and serve. —*Nick Kokonas*

NOTES For faster prosciutto crisps: Preheat the oven to 350°. On a parchment paper–lined baking sheet, arrange the slices of prosciutto in a single layer and bake until crisp, about 17 minutes. Transfer to paper towels to drain and cool, then break into large pieces.

To make simple syrup: In a small saucepan, simmer ½ cup of water with ½ cup of sugar over moderate heat, stirring, until the sugar dissolves, about 4 minutes; let cool. Refrigerate for up to 1 month. Makes about ½ cup.

MAKE AHEAD The soup and prosciutto crisps can be refrigerated in separate containers overnight.

WINE Unoaked, full-bodied Piedmontese white: 2012 Vietti Roero Arneis.

Silky Zucchini Soup

Total **45 min**; Serves **4**

Visionary chef Grant Achatz of Alinea in Chicago makes this simple, creamy, sublimely smooth zucchini soup without any cream at all.

- **1 Tbsp. unsalted butter**
- **2 Tbsp. extra-virgin olive oil**
- **1 small onion, finely chopped**
- **1 garlic clove, thinly sliced**
- **Kosher salt and pepper**
- **1½ lbs. zucchini, halved lengthwise and sliced ¼ inch thick**
- **⅔ cup vegetable stock or low-sodium broth**
- **Julienned raw zucchini, for garnish**

1. In a large saucepan, melt the butter in the olive oil. Add the onion and garlic, season with salt and pepper and cook over moderately low heat, stirring frequently, until softened, 7 to 8 minutes. Add the zucchini and cook, stirring frequently, until softened, about 10 minutes. Add the stock and 1½ cups of water and bring to a simmer; cook until the zucchini is very soft, about 10 minutes.

2. Working in 2 batches, puree the soup in a blender until it's silky-smooth. Return the soup to the saucepan and season with salt and pepper. Serve it either hot or chilled, garnished with julienned zucchini. —*Grant Achatz*

MAKE AHEAD The soup can be refrigerated overnight. Reheat gently.

GOLDEN GAZPACHO WITH AVOCADO

Tomato Soup with Feta, Olives and Cucumbers

⏱ Total **40 min**; Serves **4**

This pretty, fresh-tasting chilled tomato soup is Momofuku chef David Chang's reinvention of Greek salad.

- **6 Tbsp. extra-virgin olive oil, plus more for drizzling**
- **1 small red onion, thinly sliced**
- **¾ cup pitted Niçoise olives**
- **2 Tbsp. oregano leaves**
- **3 Tbsp. red wine vinegar**
- **1 Tbsp. sherry vinegar**
- **Kosher salt**
- **1 small Kirby cucumber, thinly sliced**
- **1 Tbsp. honey**
- **5 tomatoes, chopped**
- **Freshly ground black pepper**
- **4 oz. cherry tomatoes, halved**
- **2 oz. feta cheese, preferably Greek, crumbled (½ cup)**
- **Baby greens, for garnish**

1. In a medium saucepan, heat the 6 tablespoons of oil. Add the onion, olives and oregano and cook over moderately low heat, stirring, until the onion is softened, about 7 minutes. Remove from the heat and stir in both vinegars. Season with salt. Let cool to room temperature.

2. Meanwhile, in a bowl, toss the cucumber slices with ½ tablespoon of the honey and season with salt.

3. In a blender, puree the chopped tomatoes with the remaining ½ tablespoon of honey and season the soup generously with salt and pepper.

4. Pour the soup into shallow bowls. Top with the onion-olive mixture, cherry tomatoes, cucumber slices and feta. Drizzle with olive oil, garnish with baby greens and serve. —*David Chang*

WINE Tangy, vibrant Provençal rosé: 2013 Commanderie de Peyrassol.

Two-Tomato Soup with Fennel

Total **1 hr 15 min**; Serves **8**

- **2 Tbsp. canola oil**
- **12 medium plum tomatoes, cored**
- **1 Tbsp. sugar**
- **Kosher salt**
- **¼ cup Pernod**
- **¾ cup extra-virgin olive oil**
- **3 medium fennel bulbs—halved lengthwise, cored and thinly sliced; fronds coarsely chopped for garnish**
- **3 large shallots, thinly sliced**
- **¼ cup thinly sliced garlic**
- **1 tsp. fennel seeds**
- **1 tsp. dried oregano**
- **¼ tsp. crushed red pepper**
- **Freshly ground white pepper**
- **One 28-oz. can whole Italian peeled tomatoes, crushed by hand**
- **1 Tbsp. red wine vinegar**
- **Freshly shaved Parmigiano-Reggiano cheese, for serving**

1. In a large cast-iron skillet, heat the canola oil until nearly smoking. Add the plum tomatoes and sugar and season with salt. Cook over moderately high heat, turning, until the tomatoes are lightly charred and starting to burst, about 10 minutes. Add the Pernod and cook over moderately low heat, breaking up the tomatoes, until a chunky sauce forms, about 20 minutes.

2. In a saucepan, heat ¼ cup of the olive oil. Add the fennel, shallots, garlic, fennel seeds, oregano, crushed red pepper and a generous pinch each of salt and white pepper. Cook over moderate heat, stirring, until the fennel starts to soften, 5 minutes. Add the canned tomatoes with their juices and 4 cups of water and bring to a boil. Simmer over moderately low heat, stirring, until the fennel is very tender, 20 to 25 minutes.

3. Ladle half of the fennel mixture into a blender and puree until nearly smooth; return the puree to the saucepan. Transfer the chunky tomato sauce to the blender and puree until smooth. With the machine on, gradually add the remaining ½ cup of oil until incorporated. Stir the tomato sauce into the saucepan along with the vinegar. Cook over moderately low heat until heated through; season with salt and white pepper. Garnish with fennel fronds and serve, passing cheese at the table. —*Alex Guarnaschelli*

Corn Soup with Vadouvan

Active **1 hr 15 min**; Total **3 hr 30 min** Serves **4**

F&W Best New Chef 2014 Ari Taymor doesn't let a single bit of corn go to waste in this soup, combining corn cob broth with corn juice and fresh corn kernels seasoned with *vadouvan*, a French spice blend inspired by Indian curry (available at specialty food shops and from amazon.com).

- **12 ears of corn, shucked**
- **2 Tbsp. unsalted butter**
- **1 large onion, thinly sliced (2 cups)**
- **2 Tbsp. *vadouvan***
- **Kosher salt**
- **2 Tbsp. fresh lime juice**

1. Cut the kernels from the cobs (you should have about 8 cups); reserve the cobs. Set aside ⅓ cup of the raw kernels for garnish.

2. In a juicer, juice 3 cups of the corn kernels. Reserve the juice.

3. In a large pot, combine the corn cobs and 4 quarts of water and bring to a boil. Simmer over moderate heat, skimming the foam occasionally, until the broth is reduced to 6 cups, about 1 hour. Strain the corn broth through a sieve into a large bowl; discard the cobs.

4. In a large saucepan, melt the butter. Add the onion and cook over moderately low heat, stirring occasionally, until softened, 10 minutes. Add the remaining corn kernels and the *vadouvan* and season with salt. Cook, stirring, until very fragrant and the kernels are well coated in the spices, 2 minutes. Add the corn broth and simmer over moderate heat until the liquid is reduced by half, about 1 hour. Stir in the reserved corn juice.

5. In a blender, and working in 2 batches, puree the soup until smooth; add water if a thinner consistency is desired. Strain the soup through a sieve into a large bowl. Stir in the lime juice and season with salt. Serve warm, garnished with the reserved raw corn kernels. —*Ari Taymor*

TOMATO SOUP WITH FETA, OLIVES
AND CUCUMBERS

Summer Vegetable Soup with Carrot Top–Pumpkin Seed Pistou

Active **1 hr**; Total **1 hr 45 min plus overnight soaking**; Serves **8**

SOUP

- 1 cup dried cranberry beans, soaked overnight and drained
- 1 garlic clove
  Kosher salt
- 2 Tbsp. olive oil
- 1 yellow onion, finely chopped
- 5 medium carrots with leafy tops—carrots sliced ¼ inch thick, 2 cups of the tops reserved
- 1 medium leek, halved lengthwise and sliced crosswise ¼ inch thick
- 1 small bulb fennel—halved lengthwise, cored and finely chopped
- 1 celery rib, thinly sliced
- 1 quart chicken stock
- 3 plum tomatoes, seeded and finely chopped
- 1 thyme sprig
- 1 bay leaf
- 4 oz. green beans, cut into 1-inch lengths
- 1 medium zucchini, cut into ½-inch dice
- ¾ cup dried ditalini pasta, cooked until just al dente
  Pepper

PISTOU

- ½ cup extra-virgin olive oil
- ½ cup pumpkin seeds
- 2 garlic cloves, chopped
  Reserved 2 cups of carrot tops
- ½ cup packed parsley leaves
- ½ cup freshly grated Parmigiano-Reggiano cheese
  Kosher salt and pepper

1. Make the soup In a medium saucepan, cover the beans with 4 cups of water, add the garlic and bring to a boil. Reduce the heat, cover partially and simmer the beans until tender, about 45 minutes. Add 1 teaspoon of salt and let the beans cool in their liquid; discard the garlic.

2. Meanwhile, in a large saucepan, heat the olive oil. Add the onion and cook over moderate heat until translucent, about 8 minutes. Add the carrots, leek, fennel and celery and cook until softened, about 6 minutes. Add the chicken stock, tomatoes, thyme, bay leaf and 3 cups of water and bring to a boil. Reduce the heat, cover partially and simmer until vegetables are tender, about 25 minutes.

3. Make the *pistou* In a small skillet, heat ¼ cup of the olive oil. Add the pumpkin seeds and garlic and cook over moderately high heat until the seeds turn light brown, 2 to 3 minutes. Scrape the contents of the skillet into a food processor and let cool. Add the carrot tops, parsley, cheese and remaining ¼ cup of olive oil and process until smooth. Season the *pistou* with salt and pepper.

4. Add the green beans and zucchini to the soup and simmer until crisp-tender. Stir in the ditalini and cooked cranberry beans with their liquid and bring to a simmer. Season the soup with salt and pepper and serve with the *pistou*. —*Susan Spungen*

Miso Soup with Turmeric and Tofu

Total **40 min**; Serves **4**

- 2 Tbsp. extra-virgin olive oil
- 1 medium fennel bulb, trimmed and quartered
- 1 large carrot, chopped
- 1 small yellow onion, quartered
- 4 garlic cloves, halved
- 1 Tbsp. whole black peppercorns
- 2 tsp. ground turmeric
- 3 Tbsp. white miso
  Kosher salt
- 6 oz. firm tofu, cubed
  Minced chives, for garnish

1. In a large saucepan, heat the olive oil. Add the fennel, carrot, onion, garlic, peppercorns and turmeric and stir over moderate heat until evenly coated with oil. Add 6 cups of water and bring to a boil. Gently simmer until the liquid is slightly reduced and the vegetables are soft, 15 to 20 minutes. Strain the soup into a large bowl; discard the solids.

2. Wipe out the saucepan and return the broth to it. Whisk the miso into the broth and cook over low heat, whisking, until hot. Season with salt. Stir in the tofu and simmer until the tofu is warm, about 2 minutes. Serve the soup garnished with chives. —*Heidi Swanson*

Curried Carrot and Apple Soup

PAGE 62

Active **30 min**; Total **1 hr**; Serves **12**

This recipe makes ingenious use of gingersnap cookies to sweeten the fragrant soup.

- 4 Tbsp. unsalted butter
- 1 medium onion, chopped
- 1 medium leek, halved lengthwise and thinly sliced crosswise
- 1 medium fennel bulb, cored and chopped
  Salt and pepper
- 2 lbs. carrots, cut into ¼-inch rounds
- 1¼ lbs. celery root, peeled and chopped
- 1 Granny Smith apple—peeled, cored and chopped
- 7 gingersnap cookies
- 1 Tbsp. Madras curry powder
- 2 garlic cloves, crushed
- 1 tsp. finely grated peeled fresh ginger
- 2 thyme sprigs
- 2 quarts chicken stock
- 1 cup sour cream
- 1 tsp. apple cider vinegar
  Toasted pumpkin seeds and chopped mint and cilantro, for garnish

1. In a large saucepan, melt the butter. Add the onion, leek, fennel and a generous pinch each of salt and pepper and cook over moderately high heat, stirring occasionally, until softened and just starting to brown, 9 minutes. Add the carrots, celery root, apple, gingersnaps, curry powder, garlic, ginger and thyme and cook, stirring, until the carrots and celery root soften slightly, 10 minutes. Add the stock and bring to a boil. Simmer over moderate heat, stirring, until the vegetables are very tender, 25 minutes. Discard the thyme sprigs.

2. Working in batches, puree the soup in a blender with the sour cream and vinegar until smooth. Reheat the soup if necessary and season with salt and pepper. Ladle the soup into bowls, top with toasted pumpkin seeds and chopped mint and cilantro and serve. —*Tamalpais Star Roth-McCormick and Mark Slawson*

MAKE AHEAD The soup can be refrigerated overnight. Reheat gently before serving.

WINE Ripe California Chardonnay: 2012 Copain Tous Ensemble.

SUMMER VEGETABLE SOUP WITH
CARROT TOP–PUMPKIN SEED PISTOU

Mexican Chicken Soup

Active **30 min**; Total **1 hr 40 min**
Serves **4 to 6**

Cookbook author Jane Coxwell improvised this chicken soup recipe during a trip to Valladolid, Mexico. She adds cinnamon to the broth and garnishes with crisp flour tortillas instead of the usual corn tortillas.

   One 3½-lb. chicken
3 medium tomatoes, cored and quartered
1 medium carrot, sliced ½ inch thick
1 small red onion, cut into 1-inch pieces
2 garlic cloves, crushed
½ tsp. ground coriander
½ tsp. ground cumin
1 small cinnamon stick
½ cup chopped cilantro, plus more for garnish
   Salt and pepper
2 small flour tortillas, halved
6 Tbsp. fresh lime juice

1. In a large saucepan, combine the chicken, tomatoes, carrot, onion, garlic, coriander, cumin, cinnamon and the ½ cup of cilantro with 10 cups of water. Add a generous pinch each of salt and pepper and bring to a boil. Cover partially and simmer over moderately low heat for 30 minutes, skimming as necessary. Discard the cinnamon stick and continue simmering until the chicken is cooked through, 30 minutes longer.

2. Meanwhile, in a large skillet, toast the tortillas over moderate heat, turning once, until crisp in spots, 3 minutes. Cut the tortillas into thin strips.

3. Transfer the chicken to a plate and let cool slightly. Shred the meat; discard the skin and bones. Return the chicken to the saucepan and reheat the soup. Stir in the lime juice and season with salt and pepper. Ladle the soup into bowls. Garnish with the tortilla strips and cilantro and serve. —*Jane Coxwell*

Thai Chicken Soup

Active **25 min**; Total **45 min**; Serves **8**

"My wife, Amy, has celiac disease, so at home I cook things you can have with rice instead of high-gluten carbs like pasta," says Spike Gjerde, the chef at Woodberry Kitchen in Baltimore. He makes the light, tangy broth here with ginger, lime and lemongrass that Amy grows in their garden.

3 quarts chicken stock or low-sodium broth
1 lemongrass stalk, cut into 4-inch lengths
   One 2-inch piece of fresh ginger, sliced
4 Thai bird chiles
   Four 1-inch-wide strips of lime zest
1 large head of cauliflower, broken into small florets
½ lb. shiitake mushrooms, stemmed and caps sliced ½ inch thick
   One 13½-oz. can unsweetened coconut milk
4 cups shredded cooked chicken
1 cup frozen shelled edamame, thawed
¾ cup fresh lime juice (from about 5 limes)
½ cup Asian fish sauce
   Kosher salt
½ cup chopped cilantro

1. In a large saucepan, combine the chicken stock with the lemongrass, ginger, chiles and lime zest and bring to a boil. Simmer over moderately low heat for 10 minutes. Strain and return to the saucepan. Discard the solids.

2. Add the cauliflower, shiitake and coconut milk to the stock and bring to a boil, then simmer over moderate heat until the cauliflower is crisp-tender, about 5 minutes. Add the chicken and edamame and simmer just until heated through, about 2 minutes. Stir in the lime juice and fish sauce and season with salt. Garnish with the cilantro and serve. —*Spike Gjerde*

Chicken and Wild Rice Soup

Active **20 min**; Total **1 hr 15 min**; Serves **8**

At Our Town Bakery in Hillsboro, North Dakota, Amanda Johnson uses leftover chicken or turkey and wild rice harvested nearby to make this soup.

4 Tbsp. unsalted butter
3 celery ribs, cut into ½-inch pieces
2 carrots, cut into ½-inch pieces
1 medium onion, chopped
2 garlic cloves, minced
1½ tsp. finely chopped thyme
   Salt and pepper
¼ cup all-purpose flour
1 cup wild rice (5 oz.)
2 quarts chicken stock or low-sodium broth
4 cups bite-size pieces of roasted chicken or turkey
1 cup heavy cream

1. In a large saucepan, melt the butter. Add the celery, carrots, onion, garlic, thyme and a generous pinch each of salt and pepper and cook over moderate heat, stirring occasionally, until the vegetables just start to soften, about 10 minutes. Sprinkle the flour over the vegetables and cook, stirring, until evenly coated and lightly browned, about 3 minutes.

2. Add the wild rice to the saucepan and gradually stir in the stock and 2 cups of water. Bring to a boil, then simmer over moderately low heat, stirring occasionally, until the vegetables are tender, about 30 minutes. Add the chicken and simmer, stirring occasionally, until the wild rice is tender, 10 to 15 minutes longer. Stir in the cream and season with salt and pepper. Ladle the soup into bowls and serve. —*Amanda Johnson*

MAKE AHEAD The chicken soup can be refrigerated for up to 2 days. Reheat gently before serving.

WINE Fresh-fruit-scented, full-bodied South African Chenin Blanc: 2013 Indaba.

CHICKEN AND
WILD RICE SOUP

Curried Kabocha Squash Soup

Active **35 min**; Total **1 hr**; Serves **6**

- 3 Tbsp. extra-virgin olive oil
- 2 large shallots, finely chopped
- 2 large garlic cloves, thinly sliced
  Kosher salt
  One 4-lb. kabocha squash—peeled, seeded and cut into ¾-inch cubes
- 1 Tbsp. hot curry powder
- ½ tsp. ground cumin
- ¼ tsp. ground cinnamon
- ¼ tsp. crushed red pepper
- 1 quart chicken stock
- 3 Tbsp. fresh lemon juice
- 2 Tbsp. apple cider vinegar
- ½ cup heavy cream
- 1 Tbsp. Asian fish sauce
  Chopped cilantro, for garnish

1. In a large saucepan, heat the oil until shimmering. Add the shallots, garlic and a generous pinch of salt and cook over moderately high heat, stirring, until the shallots start to brown, 3 minutes. Add the squash and spices and cook, stirring occasionally, for 3 minutes. Add the stock, lemon juice, vinegar and 3 cups of water and bring to a boil; reduce the heat to moderately low and simmer, stirring occasionally, until the squash is very tender, about 20 minutes.

2. Working in batches, puree the soup in a blender until smooth. Return the soup to the saucepan, add the cream and fish sauce and stir over moderately low heat until hot, about 5 minutes. Season with salt. Ladle the soup into bowls, garnish with cilantro and serve. —*Beth Kirby*

Red Lentil Soup with Cumin and Fried Onions

Total **1 hr**; Serves **6**

- 2 cups red lentils (12 oz.), rinsed
- ¼ cup short-grain rice, rinsed
- 3 medium onions—1 thinly sliced, 2 finely chopped
- 6 cups chicken stock
- 2 tsp. ground cumin
- ¼ tsp. ground allspice
  Kosher salt
- ¼ cup vegetable oil
- 4 oz. rustic bread, torn into bite-size pieces

1. Preheat the oven to 375°. In a large saucepan, bring the red lentils, rice, sliced onion, chicken stock, cumin, allspice and 2 cups of water to a boil. Add a generous pinch of salt, cover and simmer over moderately low heat, stirring, until the lentils and rice are tender, about 20 minutes.

2. In a blender, puree the soup in batches until very smooth. Return the soup to the saucepan and season with salt. Add more water for a thinner consistency, if desired.

3. Meanwhile, in a large skillet, heat the oil until shimmering. Add the chopped onions and a generous pinch of salt and cook over moderate heat, stirring occasionally, until golden, 15 minutes. Remove from the heat.

4. Spread the bread on a rimmed baking sheet and bake for 10 minutes, until nearly crisp; let cool slightly. Reheat the soup, if necessary, then ladle into shallow bowls. Top with the fried onions and croutons and serve. —*Reem Acra*

Roasted Cauliflower Soup with Cumin

Active **25 min**; Total **1 hr**; Serves **4 to 6**

- 1 medium head of cauliflower (1½ lbs.)—halved, cored and cut into 1½-inch florets
- 1 tsp. cumin seeds
- 1 tsp. curry powder
- ¼ cup sunflower or grapeseed oil
  Kosher salt and ground pepper
- 1 small onion, diced (1 cup)
- 3 Tbsp. unsalted butter
- 1 bay leaf
- ¼ cup whole milk

1. Preheat the oven to 375°. On a large rimmed baking sheet, toss the cauliflower with the cumin seeds, curry powder and 3 tablespoons of the oil. Season with salt and pepper and roast for about 25 minutes, turning occasionally, until just tender.

2. In a large saucepan, heat the remaining 1 tablespoon of oil. Add the onion and cook over moderate heat, stirring occasionally, until softened but not browned, about 5 minutes. Add the roasted cauliflower, butter, bay leaf and 4 cups of water and bring to a simmer. Cook over moderate heat until the liquid is reduced and the cauliflower is very soft, about 15 minutes. Pick out and discard the bay leaf.

3. In a blender, puree the soup in 2 batches until very smooth. Return the soup to the saucepan and stir in the milk. Rewarm over moderate heat, adding more water for a thinner consistency, if desired. Season the soup with salt and pepper and serve hot. —*Alice Quillet and Anna Trattles*

Beef and Farro Soup

Active **30 min**; Total **2 hr 40 min**; Serves **6**

- 2 Tbsp. canola oil
- 1½ lbs. beef chuck, cut into 1-inch pieces
  Kosher salt and pepper
- 9 cups chicken stock
- 1 head of garlic, pierced all over with a knife
- 3 thyme sprigs
- 3 bay leaves
- 1 cup farro
- 2 medium tomatoes, chopped
- 1 leek, light green and white parts only, thinly sliced
- 2 celery ribs, thinly sliced
- 3 small carrots, chopped
- 1 small bunch of Tuscan kale, chopped (3 cups)
- 2 Tbsp. white miso
- 1 tsp. smoked paprika
  Freshly shaved Parmigiano-Reggiano cheese, for garnish

1. In a large enameled cast-iron casserole, heat the oil. Season the meat with salt and pepper, add half to the casserole and cook over moderate heat, turning, until browned, about 5 minutes; transfer to a large plate. Repeat with the remaining meat.

2. Pour off all of the oil from the casserole. Add 1 cup of the stock and stir, scraping up any browned bits. Add the remaining 8 cups of stock along with the meat, garlic, thyme and bay leaves and bring to a simmer. Cover and cook over low heat, stirring occasionally, until the meat is tender, 1½ hours.

3. Stir in the farro and bring to a simmer; cover and cook over moderate heat until almost tender, 20 minutes. Stir in the vegetables, miso and paprika. Cover and cook until the vegetables are tender, about 10 minutes. Discard the garlic, thyme sprigs and bay leaves. Season with salt and pepper. Ladle the soup into bowls, garnish with cheese and serve. —*Hugh Acheson*

BEEF AND FARRO SOUP

Garden Vegetable Stew

Active **45 min**; Total **2 hr 30 min**
Serves **4 to 6**

- 2 Tbsp. unsalted butter
- 2 small fennel bulbs, chopped
- 3 celery ribs, chopped
- 6 medium shallots, thinly sliced
- 1 small lemongrass stalk, tender inner bulb only, chopped
- 8 garlic cloves, crushed
- ½ lemon
- 6 thyme sprigs
- 1 Tbsp. fennel seeds
- 1 tsp. crushed red pepper, plus more for garnish
- 1 cup fresh orange juice
  Kosher salt and black pepper
- 1 Parmigiano-Reggiano rind (3 oz.)
- 2 medium carrots, cut into 1-inch pieces
- 2 small turnips, cut into 1-inch pieces
- 10 radishes, halved, or quartered if large
- ½ lb. green cabbage, cut into 1-inch pieces
- ½ lb. shiitake mushrooms, stems discarded and caps quartered
  Extra-virgin olive oil, for garnish
  Crusty bread, for serving

1. In a large saucepan, melt the butter. Add the chopped fennel, celery, shallots, lemongrass, garlic, lemon, thyme, fennel seeds and the 1 teaspoon of crushed red pepper. Cook over moderate heat, stirring occasionally, until the vegetables are softened, 8 minutes. Add the orange juice and 8 cups of water and bring to a boil. Cover partially and simmer over moderately low heat, stirring occasionally, until slightly reduced and the vegetables are very tender, 1 hour and 30 minutes. Strain through a fine sieve into a heatproof bowl, pressing on the vegetables with a wooden spoon; discard the solids.

2. Wipe out the saucepan. Add the fennel broth to the saucepan, bring to a boil and season with salt and black pepper. Add the cheese rind, carrots, turnips, radishes, cabbage and shiitake and simmer over moderate heat, stirring occasionally, until the vegetables are tender, about 25 minutes. Discard the cheese rind.

3. Ladle the stew into shallow bowls. Garnish each bowl with crushed red pepper and olive oil and serve with crusty bread.
—*Georgia Pellegrini*

WINE Tangy Austrian Grüner Veltliner: 2012 Domäne Wachau Terrassen Federspiel.

Lentil and Smoky Eggplant Stew

Active **20 min**; Total **1 hr 30 min**
Serves **12**

- ¼ cup extra-virgin olive oil, plus more for drizzling
- 1 medium onion, finely chopped
- 1 celery rib, finely chopped
- 5 garlic cloves, finely chopped
- 1 bay leaf
- 3 cups green Puy lentils (20 oz.), rinsed and picked over
- 1 can (14.5 oz.) chopped tomatoes
- 2 quarts vegetable stock
- 2 medium eggplants (1½ lbs.)
- 2 Tbsp. harissa
- ⅓ cup chopped parsley
  Salt and pepper
  Greek yogurt, chopped walnuts and parsley, small mint leaves and pomegranate molasses, for serving

1. Preheat the broiler. In a large saucepan, heat 2 tablespoons of the oil. Add the onion, celery, garlic and bay leaf and cook over moderate heat until softened. Add the lentils, tomatoes and stock; bring to a simmer over moderately high heat. Cover, reduce the heat and simmer, stirring occasionally, until the lentils are tender but still hold their shape, about 45 minutes.

2. Meanwhile, set the eggplants on a foil-lined baking sheet and rub with the remaining 2 tablespoons of olive oil. Broil 6 inches from the heat, turning occasionally, until completely blackened and tender, about 20 minutes. Let cool.

3. Cut the eggplants in half lengthwise and scoop the flesh into a colander set over a bowl; discard the skins. Let the eggplant drain for 5 minutes, then transfer to a bowl and mash until smooth.

4. Stir the harissa and half the eggplant into the lentils until warmed through. Stir in the ⅓ cup of chopped parsley and season with salt and pepper. Ladle the stew into bowls; top with the remaining eggplant. Garnish with yogurt, chopped walnuts and parsley, mint leaves and a drizzle of pomegranate molasses and olive oil and serve. —*Fernanda Milanezi*

WINE Medium-bodied Pinot Noir: 2012 Chehalem Three Vineyard.

Chickpea-Vegetable Stew

Total **35 min**; Serves **4**

- 2 Tbsp. extra-virgin olive oil
- 1 cup frozen pearl onions (about 4 oz.), thawed and halved
- 1 red bell pepper, diced
- ½ lb. fingerling potatoes, halved lengthwise
- 2 garlic cloves, minced
- 1 Tbsp. finely chopped peeled fresh ginger
- 1 Tbsp. harissa
- 3 cups chicken stock or low-sodium broth
  One 15-oz. can chickpeas, drained and rinsed
- ¾ cup unsweetened coconut milk
- 2 Tbsp. fresh lemon juice
  Kosher salt and pepper
- 1 Tbsp. minced cilantro
  Toasted bread, for serving

1. In a large saucepan, heat the olive oil. Add the onions and bell pepper and cook over moderately high heat, stirring, until browned, about 5 minutes. Add the potatoes, garlic, ginger and harissa and cook, stirring, until the harissa darkens, about 2 minutes. Add the stock and chickpeas and bring to a boil. Cover and simmer over moderately low heat until the potatoes are tender, 12 to 14 minutes.

2. Add the coconut milk and bring to a simmer. Stir in the lemon juice and season with salt and pepper. Sprinkle the stew with the cilantro and serve with toasted bread.
—*Cathal Armstrong*

WINE Juicy, unoaked Spanish white: 2013 Zestos Blanco.

CHICKPEA-VEGETABLE STEW

Slow-Cooker Vegetable-Farro Stew with Figs and Pine Nuts

Active **30 min**; Total **6 hr 30 min**; Serves **6**

- 2 **rosemary sprigs**
- 5 **oregano sprigs**
- 5 **thyme sprigs**
- 2 **small artichokes**
- 1 **cup farro**
- ¼ **cup extra-virgin olive oil, plus more for drizzling**
- 1½ **cups tomato juice**
- ½ **cup water**
- 2 **tsp. kosher salt, plus more for seasoning**
- 1 **tsp. crushed red pepper**
- 2 **heads of garlic, ¼ inch cut off the tops**
- 1 **lemon, sliced ⅛ inch thick**
- 1 **Cubanelle pepper, sliced ⅓ inch thick**
- ½ **red bell pepper, sliced ⅓ inch thick**
- ½ **yellow bell pepper, sliced ⅓ inch thick**
- 1 **medium onion, quartered**
- 1 **large Japanese eggplant, cut into 6 wedges**
- 1 **cup dried Black Mission figs (5 oz.), stemmed**
- ½ **cup golden raisins**
- 1 **fennel bulb, trimmed and cut into 6 wedges**
- ½ **lb. large cherry tomatoes, halved**
- 1 **small zucchini, cut into 2-inch pieces**
- 1 **small yellow squash, cut into 2-inch pieces**
- 1 **bunch of kale (6 oz.), stemmed and leaves quartered**

  Toasted pine nuts, chopped fresh oregano, lemon wedges, freshly grated Parmigiano-Reggiano and sherry vinegar, for garnish

1. Using kitchen twine, tie the rosemary, oregano and thyme sprigs into a bundle. With a serrated knife, cut off the top third of the artichokes. Snap off the small leaves from around the artichoke stem. Cut the artichokes in half lengthwise. With a spoon, scrape out the hairy chokes and discard them.

2. Turn a 6- to 6½-quart slow cooker to high and set the timer for 6 hours. Add the artichokes and the next 17 ingredients, up to and including the cherry tomatoes, then add the herb bundle; spread the ingredients in even layers. Cover the slow cooker and cook for 4 hours.

3. Stir the stew gently and add the zucchini, yellow squash and kale, stirring to submerge them in the liquid. Cover and cook for 2 hours longer.

4. Discard the herb bundle, season the farro stew with salt and serve with the garnishes at the table. —*Grant Achatz*

WINE Herb-scented, light-bodied Italian red: 2012 Allegrini Valpolicella.

Lamb and Apricot Tagine with Almond Couscous

Active **45 min**; Total **2 hr 45 min** Serves **6 to 8**

TAGINE
- 2 **lbs. tomatoes**
- 2 **Tbsp. extra-virgin olive oil**
- 5 **lbs. lamb shanks, cut in half crosswise**

  Kosher salt and pepper
- 1 **large onion, finely chopped**
- 2 **carrots, finely chopped**
- 6 **garlic cloves, finely chopped**
- 1 **tsp. ground ginger**
- 1 **tsp. ground cumin**
- 1 **tsp. ground turmeric**

  Two 3-inch cinnamon sticks
- 2 **cups dry red wine**
- 4 **cups chicken stock or low-sodium broth**
- ½ **cup chopped parsley**
- ½ **cup chopped cilantro, plus cilantro leaves for garnish**
- ¾ **lb. dried apricots**
- ¼ **cup honey**

  One 19-oz. can chickpeas, drained

COUSCOUS
- 2 **cups couscous**
- 4 **cups chicken stock or low-sodium broth**

  Kosher salt and pepper
- ⅔ **cup chopped roasted almonds**
- 2 **Tbsp. chopped parsley**

1. Make the tagine Score an X on the bottom of each tomato. In a large pot of boiling water, blanch the tomatoes just until the skins shrivel, about 30 seconds. Remove the tomatoes and let cool slightly, then peel and finely chop them.

2. In a large enameled cast-iron casserole, heat the olive oil. Season the lamb shanks with salt and pepper and cook over moderately high heat, turning, until golden brown all over, about 5 minutes. Transfer the lamb to a baking sheet.

3. Add the onion, carrots, garlic, ginger, cumin, turmeric and cinnamon sticks to the pot and cook over moderate heat, stirring, until the onion is golden and softened, about 8 minutes. Add the lamb shanks and wine. Bring to a simmer and cook for 3 minutes. Add the tomatoes, stock, parsley and ½ cup of cilantro and return to a simmer. Cover and cook gently until the lamb is almost tender, about 1½ hours. Add the apricots and honey to the tagine and cook until the lamb is very tender, about 30 minutes longer. Discard the cinnamon sticks. Stir in the chickpeas and season with salt and pepper.

4. Meanwhile, make the couscous Put the couscous in a large heatproof bowl. In a medium saucepan, bring the stock to a simmer and season with salt and pepper. Pour the hot stock over the couscous and stir well. Cover with plastic wrap and let stand until all the stock has been absorbed and the couscous is tender, about 30 minutes. Fluff the couscous with a fork and stir in the almonds and parsley.

5. Garnish the lamb tagine with cilantro and serve with the couscous. —*Fernanda Milanezi*

MAKE AHEAD The lamb tagine and couscous can be refrigerated separately for up to 3 days. Stir the almonds and parsley into the couscous just before serving.

WINE Bright, red-berry-inflected Beaujolais: 2012 Guy Breton Régnié.

Slow-Cooker Seafood and Chicken Gumbo

Active **30 min**; Total **4 hr 30 min**; Serves **8**

- 5   oregano sprigs
- 5   thyme sprigs
- 1½ sticks unsalted butter
- 1½ cups all-purpose flour
- ½ lb. andouille sausage, cut into 1-inch pieces
- 16 cipollini onions, peeled
- 6   garlic cloves, minced
- 1   leek, white and light green parts only, chopped
- 1   red bell pepper, diced
- 1   green bell pepper, diced
- 3   celery ribs, sliced
- 3   carrots, cut into ½-inch-thick rounds
- 2   Tbsp. smoked paprika
- 1   lb. okra, thickly sliced
- 2   tsp. kosher salt, plus more for seasoning
- 4   bay leaves
- 2   quarts chicken stock or low-sodium broth
- ½ cup long-grain rice
- 1   lb. boneless, skinless chicken thighs, cut into 1½-inch pieces
- 16 shelled and deveined jumbo shrimp
- 8   snow crab legs
     Chopped parsley and hot sauce, for serving

1. Using kitchen twine, tie the oregano and thyme sprigs into a bundle. Turn a 6- to 6½-quart slow cooker to high and set the timer for 4 hours. Add the butter and cover until the butter melts. Stir in the flour and mix with a wooden spoon until well incorporated and a paste forms. Add the herbs and the next 13 ingredients, up to and including the stock, and stir. Cover and cook for 3 hours.

2. Stir in the rice and chicken, cover and cook for 45 minutes. Add the shrimp and crab, cover and cook for 15 minutes longer.

3. Discard the herb bundle and bay leaves and season with salt. Garnish the gumbo with parsley and serve in bowls with hot sauce and shell crackers for breaking the crab legs. —*Grant Achatz*

BEER Crisp, hoppy ale: Shipyard Brewing Co. Export Ale.

Pork and Cider Stew

Active **35 min**; Total **3 hr 30 min**
Serves **10 to 12**

- 3   Tbsp. unsalted butter
- 3   Tbsp. extra-virgin olive oil
- 5   lbs. trimmed boneless pork shoulder, cut into 1½-inch cubes
     Kosher salt and pepper
- 10 oz. skinless, meaty slab bacon, cut into ½-inch dice
- 1   large onion, thinly sliced
- 5   garlic cloves, finely chopped
     One 750-ml bottle sparkling dry apple cider
- 1   quart chicken stock or low-sodium broth
- 2   bay leaves
- ¼ cup cornstarch
- 1   cup heavy cream
- 3   Tbsp. grainy mustard
- 2   tsp. finely chopped sage leaves

1. In a large enameled cast-iron casserole, melt 1 tablespoon of the butter in 1 table-spoon of the oil. Season the pork with salt and pepper, add one-third of it to the casse-role and cook over moderately high heat, stirring occasionally, until well browned, about 8 minutes. Transfer the pork to a bak-ing sheet. Repeat twice more with the remaining butter, oil and pork.

2. Add the bacon to the casserole and cook until golden; add to the pork. Add the onion and garlic to the casserole; cook over mod-erate heat, stirring, until golden and soft-ened, 5 minutes. Add the pork, bacon, cider, stock and bay leaves to the casserole and bring to a simmer. Cover and simmer gently until the pork is tender, 2½ hours. Discard the bay leaves.

3. In a small bowl, whisk the cornstarch with ¼ cup of water. Add the cornstarch mixture and the cream to the stew and simmer until the liquid is thickened, 5 min-utes. Stir in the mustard and sage, season with salt and pepper and serve.
—*Fernanda Milanezi*

MAKE AHEAD The stew can be refrigerated for up to 3 days.

CIDER Earthy artisanal hard cider: Farnum Hill Semi-Dry.

SLOW-COOKER HISTORY

1958

Inspired by his grandma, Irving Naxon patents the Naxon Beanery All-Purpose Cooker.

1970

Rival Company buys out Naxon, relaunching his machine as the Crock-Pot slow cooker.

1975

Mable Hoffman writes the first-ever slow-cooker cookbook, *Crockery Cookery*—an instant best seller.

2013

A study reveals that 19 percent of all US households use a slow cooker in any two-week period.

2014

Crock-Pot introduces the first WiFi-enabled slow cooker, which can be controlled via smartphone.

Belgian Beef Stew

Active **45 min**; Total **2 hr 45 min**; Serves **6**

Chef Andrew Zimmern calls this recipe "a one-pot rock star beef stew that will warm you from the inside out."

- 3 lbs. trimmed beef chuck, cut into 1½-inch pieces
- Salt and white pepper
- 1½ cups all-purpose flour
- 6 Tbsp. canola oil
- 3 onions, thinly sliced
- 4 garlic cloves, minced
- One 12-oz. bottle Duvel or other Belgian golden ale
- 1 quart beef stock
- 3 thyme sprigs, 3 parsley sprigs and 1 bay leaf, tied in cheesecloth
- 10 new potatoes, halved
- 2 large carrots, cut into ½-inch pieces
- 1 Tbsp. Dijon mustard
- 2 Tbsp. red wine vinegar
- Chopped parsley, for garnish

1. Preheat the oven to 325°. Season the beef with salt and pepper. In a large resealable plastic bag, combine the beef and flour and shake well; remove from the bag, shaking off excess flour. In a large enameled cast-iron casserole, heat 2 tablespoons of the oil. Add one-third of the beef and cook over moderate heat until browned all over, 5 minutes; transfer to a plate. Repeat with the remaining oil and beef.

2. Pour off all but 2 tablespoons of the fat from the casserole. Add the onions, season with salt and pepper and cook over moderate heat, stirring, until softened and browned, 8 minutes. Add the garlic and cook until fragrant, 1 minute. Add the beer and cook, scraping up any browned bits. Return the meat to the casserole and add the stock and herb bundle. Bring to a boil, then cover and braise in the oven for 1½ hours, until the meat is very tender.

3. Add the potatoes and carrots, cover and braise for 25 minutes longer, until tender. Discard the herb bundle. Stir in the mustard and vinegar; season with salt and pepper. Garnish with parsley and serve. —*Andrew Zimmern*

WINE Dark-fruited Italian red: 2011 Di Majo Norante Ramitello.

Creamy Parsnip Soup with Pear and Walnuts

Active **45 min**; Total **1 hr**; Serves **8 to 10**

SOUP

- 2 Tbsp. extra-virgin olive oil
- 1¾ lbs. parsnips, peeled and chopped (6 cups)
- ¾ lb. sunchokes, peeled and chopped (2 cups)
- 4 garlic cloves, chopped
- 4 tsp. garam masala
- 2 tsp. ground cumin
- 1 tsp. ground turmeric
- Kosher salt
- 3 cups chicken stock or low-sodium chicken broth
- 1½ cups heavy cream
- 1 Tbsp. fresh lemon juice
- Pepper

TOPPING

- 1 tsp. extra-virgin olive oil
- ½ cup walnuts, chopped
- 1 garlic clove, minced
- 1 Tbsp. fresh lemon juice
- ½ Tbsp. walnut oil
- 1 small Bosc or d'Anjou pear, finely chopped
- 1 Tbsp. chopped parsley
- 1 Tbsp. chopped tarragon
- Kosher salt and pepper

1. Make the soup In a large saucepan, heat the olive oil. Add the parsnips, sunchokes and garlic and cook over moderate heat, stirring, until lightly golden, 5 minutes. Stir in the garam masala, cumin, turmeric and 1 teaspoon of salt. Cook, stirring, until fragrant, 2 minutes. Add the chicken stock, cream and 4 cups of water. Bring to a simmer and cook until the vegetables are soft, about 25 minutes.

2. Working in batches, puree the soup in a blender until very smooth. Pour the soup into a clean saucepan and stir in the lemon juice. Season with salt and pepper.

3. Make the topping In a medium skillet, heat the olive oil. Add the walnuts and cook over moderately low heat, stirring, until golden, 3 minutes. Remove from the heat and stir in the garlic and lemon juice. Scrape the mixture into a small bowl and

toss with the walnut oil. Cool to room temperature, then stir in the pear, parsley and tarragon; season with salt and pepper. Serve the soup sprinkled with the topping. —*Marcus Samuelsson*

MAKE AHEAD The soup (without the topping) can be refrigerated for up to 3 days. Reheat gently before serving.

WINE Lively, pear-scented Oregon Pinot Gris: 2012 Benton-Lane.

Squash Soup with Pumpkin Seeds

Total **45 min**; Serves **6**

Jeni Britton Bauer of Jeni's Splendid Ice Creams uses pumpkin ice cream (made from fresh pumpkins) to flavor her terrific winter squash soup.

- ¼ cup vegetable oil
- 2 large onions, finely chopped
- 2 garlic cloves, minced
- Kosher salt
- 4 cups chicken stock or low-sodium broth
- 2 lbs. thawed frozen squash puree
- Pinch of freshly grated nutmeg
- 1 cup pumpkin ice cream
- White pepper
- Unsweetened whipped cream and toasted shelled pumpkin seeds, for serving

1. In a large saucepan, heat the oil until shimmering. Add the onions, garlic and a generous pinch of salt and cook over moderate heat, stirring occasionally, until softened and just starting to brown, about 10 minutes. Add the stock, squash and nutmeg and bring to a boil. Simmer over moderate heat, stirring, until the onion is very soft, about 5 minutes. Stir in the pumpkin ice cream until melted.

2. Working in batches, puree the soup in a blender until smooth. Return the soup to the saucepan and reheat. Season with salt and white pepper. Ladle the soup into bowls and swirl in dollops of whipped cream. Top with toasted pumpkin seeds and serve. —*Jeni Britton Bauer*

CREAMY PARSNIP SOUP WITH
PEAR AND WALNUTS

TAGLIATELLE WITH GARLICKY
TOMATO SAUCE
Recipe, page 84

Pasta & Noodles

PAGE NUMBERS IN RED INDICATE F&W STAFF FAVORITES

Rigatoni with Lemony Kale-and-Pecorino Pesto

Total **30 min**; Serves **4 to 6**

This hearty pesto is particularly great in the fall and winter, when basil isn't flourishing in gardens. Chef Chris Cosentino of Porcellino in San Francisco adds Pecorino Toscano, a hard sheep-milk cheese that's nuttier and milder than Pecorino Romano.

1½ lbs. Tuscan kale, stemmed

1 lb. rigatoni

3 large garlic cloves

¼ cup pine nuts, toasted

⅔ cup extra-virgin olive oil

1½ oz. Pecorino Toscano cheese, coarsely grated (½ cup), plus more for serving

1 Tbsp. finely grated lemon zest (from 1 lemon)

Pinch of Aleppo pepper, plus more for seasoning

Kosher salt and black pepper

1. Bring 2 large pots of generously salted water to a boil. Fill a large bowl with ice water. Add the kale to one of the pots and cook for 1 minute, until bright green and just tender. Drain and immediately transfer to the ice water. When cool, drain again. Transfer the kale to a work surface with some water clinging to the leaves and chop.

2. Meanwhile, add the rigatoni to the other pot of boiling water. Cook until almost al dente. Reserve ½ cup of the cooking water, then drain the pasta.

3. Transfer the kale to a blender. Add the garlic and pine nuts and pulse until coarsely chopped. Add the oil and process until smooth. Transfer the pesto to a large bowl and stir in the ½ cup of Pecorino and the lemon zest. Season to taste with the Aleppo pepper, salt and black pepper.

4. Return the pasta to the pot. Add the pesto and cook over moderate heat, stirring constantly, for 2 minutes, adding some of the pasta water if it seems dry. Spoon the pasta into bowls, top with additional cheese and Aleppo pepper and serve. —*Chris Cosentino*

WINE Fresh Italian white: 2013 Giovanni Almondo Roero Arneis.

Spaghetti with Sunday Sauce

Active **50 min**; Total **5 hr**; Serves **8 to 10**

When butcher Pat LaFrieda was growing up, the meat in the family's weekly spaghetti sauce varied based on what his dad brought home from the butcher shop—one weekend, it might be spicy Italian sausage; the next, it might be spareribs. The slow-cooked beef short ribs that Pat uses in this recipe from his cookbook, *Meat*, give the dish a lovely richness.

2 Tbsp. extra-virgin olive oil

3 lbs. bone-in, English-cut beef short ribs, cut into 2-inch pieces (see Note)

Kosher salt and pepper

2 medium onions, finely chopped

2 Tbsp. tomato paste

3 garlic cloves, minced

1 tsp. dried oregano

Two 28-oz. cans whole peeled Italian tomatoes, crushed by hand

1 medium carrot, peeled

2 lbs. spaghetti

1. In a large enameled cast-iron casserole, heat the olive oil until shimmering. Season the short ribs with salt and pepper and add them to the casserole in a single layer. Cook over moderately high heat, turning occasionally, until browned, 10 minutes. With tongs, transfer the short ribs to a plate.

2. Pour off all but 1 tablespoon of fat from the casserole. Add the onions and a generous pinch of salt; cook over moderate heat, stirring occasionally, until browned, 12 to 15 minutes. Add the tomato paste, garlic and oregano and cook, stirring, until fragrant, about 2 minutes. Add the crushed tomatoes with their juices and the carrot and bring to a boil.

3. Return the short ribs and their juices to the casserole, cover partially and simmer over low heat, turning the short ribs occasionally, until the meat is very tender and the sauce is thick, about 4 hours.

4. Transfer the short ribs to a plate; discard the carrot. Discard the bones and cut the meat into 1½-inch chunks. Return the meat to the sauce and season with salt and pepper; keep warm over low heat.

5. In a large saucepan of salted boiling water, cook the spaghetti until al dente. Drain the pasta, reserving ½ cup of the cooking water. Transfer the spaghetti to the pot with the sauce, toss well and cook for 1 to 2 minutes. Add a splash of the reserved pasta water if the sauce is too thick. Serve the pasta immediately. —*Pat LaFrieda*

NOTE Ask your butcher to cut the short ribs as specified.

WINE Spicy, vibrant Sangiovese: 2012 Fattoria Le Pupille Morellino di Scansano.

Orecchiette with Broccoli Rabe

Total **25 min**; Serves **6 to 8**

Ear-shaped orecchiette are typical of the far southern Italian region of Puglia. Locals cook the pasta with bitter greens called *cime di rape*, known in the US as broccoli rabe.

2 lbs. broccoli rabe, trimmed

1 lb. orecchiette

6 Tbsp. extra-virgin olive oil

4 garlic cloves, minced

2 tsp. crushed red pepper

6 anchovies in oil, drained and finely chopped

Kosher salt and black pepper

1. In a large pot of salted boiling water, cook the broccoli rabe until just tender, about 6 minutes. Using tongs, transfer the broccoli rabe to a work surface and let cool slightly, then coarsely chop.

2. Add the pasta to the boiling water and cook until al dente. Drain the pasta, reserving 1 cup of the cooking water.

3. In the same pot, heat the olive oil. Add the garlic, crushed red pepper and anchovies and cook until fragrant, about 2 minutes. Add the chopped broccoli rabe, pasta and reserved cooking water, season with salt and black pepper and cook, stirring, until hot, about 2 minutes. Serve right away. —*Ylenia Sambati*

WINE Crisp Puglian white: 2012 Alticelli Fiano Salento.

RIGATONI WITH LEMONY
KALE-AND-PECORINO PESTO

Tagliatelle with Garlicky Tomato Sauce

📷 PAGE 80
🕐 Total **30 min;** Serves **2 to 4**

Known as *tagliatelle all'aglione* in Tuscany, this dish is named for the generous amount of garlic (*aglio*) in the sauce. This version from chef Paolo Coluccio of Monteverdi, a boutique hotel in the Tuscan hilltop village Castiglioncello del Trinoro, is simple to prepare and full of Mediterranean flavor.

⅓ cup extra-virgin olive oil

4 large garlic cloves, thinly sliced

1¼ lbs. plum tomatoes, cored and chopped

¼ tsp. crushed red pepper

Salt

½ lb. dried tagliatelle

1. In a large, deep skillet, heat the olive oil. Add the garlic and cook over moderate heat, stirring, until softened and fragrant, about 2 minutes. Add the tomatoes, crushed red pepper and a generous pinch of salt and cook, stirring occasionally, until the tomatoes break down and form a sauce, 20 minutes. Season the sauce with salt; keep warm.

2. Meanwhile, in a large saucepan of salted boiling water, cook the tagliatelle until al dente. Reserve ½ cup of the cooking water, then drain the pasta well.

COOKBOOK TIP

How to Boil Pasta

The perfect pot of pasta water: 4 quarts of water, ¼ cup of kosher salt and a handful of semolina flour. When adding reserved pasta water to sauces, the starch in the semolina helps bind the sauce.

Flour + Water
Thomas McNaughton

---

3. Add the pasta and half of the cooking water to the sauce and toss over moderately low heat until coated, 2 minutes; add more of the cooking water if the pasta seems dry. Transfer the pasta to shallow bowls and serve. —*Paolo Coluccio*

WINE Bright, red cherry–inflected Chianti: 2012 Coltibuono Cetamura.

Pasta with Fresh Puttanesca Sauce

🕐 Total **30 min;** Serves **6**

This no-cook spicy tomato sauce from F&W's Kay Chun is flavor-packed, with anchovies, capers, green olives and crushed red pepper. The puttanesca sauce can also be spooned over fish, grilled vegetables or fresh mozzarella.

¼ cup drained capers

3 anchovy fillets, minced

2 large heirloom tomatoes (1¼ lbs.), chopped

¾ cup chopped pitted green olives (5 oz.)

½ cup extra-virgin olive oil

1 tsp. crushed red pepper

¾ lb. short pasta

⅓ cup chopped basil

Kosher salt and black pepper

In a large bowl, mash the capers with the anchovies, heirloom tomatoes, green olives, olive oil and crushed red pepper until a chunky sauce forms. In a pot of salted boiling water, cook the pasta until al dente; drain. Add the pasta and chopped basil to the sauce, season generously with salt and black pepper and toss to coat. —*Kay Chun*

WINE Spicy Sicilian red: 2012 Colosi Nero d'Avola.

Linguine with Kale, Lemon and Walnuts

🕐 Total **45 min;** Serves **6**

Either Tuscan or curly kale is great in this lemony pasta from Curtis Stone, the chef at Maude in Los Angeles.

½ cup walnuts (2 oz.)

1 lb. kale, stems discarded and leaves thinly sliced (10 cups)

1 lb. linguine

⅔ cup extra-virgin olive oil

6 garlic cloves, minced

2 Tbsp. finely grated lemon zest

2 Tbsp. fresh lemon juice

½ cup lightly packed basil leaves, torn

½ cup freshly grated Parmigiano-Reggiano cheese, plus more for serving

Kosher salt and freshly ground pepper

1. Preheat the oven to 375°. Spread the walnuts in a pie plate and bake for about 10 minutes, until golden and fragrant. Let cool, then coarsely chop.

2. Meanwhile, in a large saucepan of salted boiling water, blanch the kale until bright green and just tender, 3 to 5 minutes. Transfer the kale to a colander to drain.

3. Return the water in the saucepan to a boil. Add the linguine and cook until al dente. Reserve 1 cup of the cooking water and drain the pasta.

4. Wipe out the saucepan and add ⅓ cup of the oil; heat until shimmering. Add the garlic and cook over moderate heat, stirring, until fragrant, about 30 seconds. Add the drained kale and lemon zest and cook, tossing, until hot, about 2 minutes. Add the linguine, lemon juice and the remaining ⅓ cup of oil and toss to coat. Add the basil, toasted walnuts, ½ cup of cheese and half of the reserved cooking water and simmer over moderate heat, tossing, until the pasta is lightly coated; add more cooking water if the sauce is too thick. Season the pasta with salt and pepper, transfer to bowls and serve, passing additional cheese at the table. —*Curtis Stone*

WINE Bright, full-bodied Chenin Blanc from South Africa: 2012 Raats Family.

Black-and-White Pici Pasta with Squid and Shellfish

Active **40 min**; Total **1 hr 10 min**; Serves **4**

For this dramatic dish, fresh, toothsome black-and-white noodles are tossed with a big, briny seafood sauce and spicy pickled cherry peppers.

- ¼ cup extra-virgin olive oil
- 2 large garlic cloves, thinly sliced
- 1¼ cups finely chopped flat-leaf parsley
- ¼ tsp. crushed red pepper
  Kosher salt
- ⅓ cup dry white wine
- ½ lb. cleaned small squid—tentacles halved, bodies cut into ¼-inch rings
- 1 lb. Black-and-White Pici Pasta (recipe follows), or fresh store-bought pici pasta, preferably black-and-white
- 20 littleneck clams, scrubbed
- 20 mussels, scrubbed and debearded
- ½ lb. bay scallops
- 4 small pickled hot cherry peppers, seeded and thinly sliced
- 1 Tbsp. fresh lemon juice

1. In a large saucepan, heat the olive oil. Add the garlic and cook over moderately low heat, stirring, until it just starts to brown, 2 minutes. Add 1 cup of the parsley, the crushed red pepper and a generous pinch of salt and cook until fragrant. Add the wine and bring to a boil. Stir in the squid, cover and braise over low heat, stirring, until tender, 30 minutes.

2. In a large saucepan of salted boiling water, cook the pasta until al dente, about 5 minutes, then drain well.

3. While the pasta cooks, add the clams, mussels and scallops to the squid. Cover and cook over high heat until the clams and mussels just start to open, 3 minutes. Uncover and cook until the clams and mussels open fully and the broth is slightly reduced, 4 minutes. Add the pasta, pickled peppers, lemon juice and the remaining ¼ cup of parsley and cook over moderate heat, tossing, until the pasta is hot and coated in a light sauce, 3 minutes. Season lightly with salt. Transfer the pasta to shallow bowls and serve right away. —*Eli Kulp*

WINE Crisp, minerally Sicilian white: 2013 Planeta Carricante.

BLACK-AND-WHITE PICI PASTA

Active **1 hr 15 min**; Total **2 hr 15 min**
Makes **1 pound**

Chewy, tender plain pasta and squid ink pasta are rolled together for a visually striking black-and-white effect.

PLAIN PASTA

- 1 cup all-purpose flour
- ½ tsp. kosher salt
- 2 tsp. extra-virgin olive oil

SQUID INK PASTA

- 1 cup all-purpose flour, plus more for dusting
- ½ tsp. kosher salt
- 1 Tbsp. squid or cuttlefish ink (see Note)
- 2 tsp. extra-virgin olive oil

1. Make the plain pasta In a medium bowl, whisk the flour with the salt. Stir in ½ cup of water and the olive oil until the dough is shaggy. Scrape the dough out onto an unfloured work surface and knead until very smooth and elastic, about 5 minutes. Wrap the dough in plastic and let rest at room temperature for 1 hour.

2. Make the squid ink pasta In a medium bowl, whisk the 1 cup of flour with the salt. In a small bowl, whisk ⅓ cup plus 1 tablespoon of water with the squid ink and olive oil. Stir the wet ingredients into the flour until a shaggy dough forms. Scrape the dough out onto an unfloured work surface and knead until very smooth and elastic, about 5 minutes. Wrap the dough in plastic and let rest at room temperature for 1 hour.

3. On an unfloured work surface, roll out each piece of dough to an 8-by-4-inch rectangle, about ½ inch thick. Lightly brush the top of 1 piece of dough with water and lay the other piece of dough on top, pressing lightly to help them adhere. Roll out the dough to a 14-by-4-inch rectangle, a scant ¼ inch thick. Using a sharp knife, cut the dough crosswise into ¼-inch-wide strips.

4. Generously dust a baking sheet with flour. Work with 1 strip at a time and keep the rest covered with plastic: On an unfloured work surface, roll the strip into an ⅛-inch-thick rope and transfer to the baking sheet, tossing it in flour to prevent sticking. Repeat with the remaining strips. Let the pasta dry for 10 minutes.

5. To serve, cook the pasta in a large pot of salted boiling water until al dente, about 5 minutes, then drain. —*EK*

NOTE Squid ink is available at specialty food stores and from amazon.com.

MAKE AHEAD The pasta can be prepared through Step 4 and refrigerated overnight or frozen for up to 1 month. To freeze, toss with cornmeal and store in a sturdy plastic bag.

INGREDIENT TIP

Squid Ink Pasta
Filotea's dried squid ink spaghetti alla chitarra from Italy has the tender texture of fresh-made pasta.
$19; marxfoods.com.

Spaghetti with Smoky Eggplant Sauce

Total **30 min**; Serves **6**

Chickpeas and prepared baba ghanoush, the smoky Middle Eastern eggplant spread, season this easy no-cook pasta sauce. You can give the dish more Middle Eastern flavor by adding tomatoes, olives, parsley and mint.

- **2 cups baba ghanoush (16 oz.)**
- **2 Tbsp. extra-virgin olive oil**
- **¼ cup fresh lemon juice**
- **One 15-oz. can chickpeas, rinsed and drained**
- **3 scallions, thinly sliced**
- **1 lb. spaghetti**
- **Kosher salt and pepper**
- **Salted toasted sunflower seeds, for garnish**

1. In a large bowl, mix the baba ghanoush with the olive oil, lemon juice, chickpeas and scallions.

2. In a large pot of salted boiling water, cook the spaghetti until al dente. Drain, reserving 1 cup of the pasta cooking water.

3. Add the spaghetti and the reserved pasta water to the sauce, season generously with salt and pepper and toss to coat. Sprinkle with sunflower seeds and serve. —*Kay Chun*

WINE Fresh, lemony Chilean Sauvignon Blanc: 2013 Tololo.

Lemon Spaghetti with Shrimp

Total **45 min**; Serves **6**

TV star chef Giada De Laurentiis serves this lovely pasta at her restaurant, Giada, inside The Cromwell hotel in Las Vegas. The sauce that coats the spaghetti is a simple mix of olive oil, Parmesan and lemon; crisp fried capers give the dish a pungent kick.

- **Vegetable oil, for frying**
- **¼ cup capers—rinsed, drained and patted dry**
- **1 lb. spaghetti**
- **⅔ cup plus 1 Tbsp. extra-virgin olive oil**
- **1 cup freshly grated Parmigiano-Reggiano cheese**
- **1 Tbsp. finely grated lemon zest**
- **½ cup fresh lemon juice (from 3 lemons)**
- **1 lb. large shrimp, shelled and deveined**
- **Salt and pepper**
- **½ cup chopped basil, plus more for garnish**

1. In a small skillet, heat ¼ inch of vegetable oil until shimmering. Add the capers and fry over moderately high heat, stirring, until browned and crisp, 3 minutes. Using a slotted spoon, transfer the capers to paper towels to drain.

2. In a saucepan of salted boiling water, cook the spaghetti until al dente. Drain, reserving 1 cup of the cooking water.

3. Meanwhile, in a medium bowl, whisk ⅔ cup of the olive oil with the grated cheese, lemon zest and lemon juice.

4. In a very large skillet, heat the remaining 1 tablespoon of olive oil until shimmering. Season the shrimp with salt and pepper, add to the skillet and cook over moderately high heat, turning once, until just opaque, 4 minutes. Reduce the heat to moderate and add the pasta, lemon sauce, half of the reserved pasta water and the ½ cup of basil. Cook, tossing, until the pasta and shrimp are coated, 2 minutes, adding more of the pasta water if the spaghetti is dry. Transfer to shallow bowls, garnish with basil and the fried capers and serve. —*Giada De Laurentiis*

WINE Bright Sicilian white: 2012 Feudo Principi di Butera Insolia.

No-Cook Green Harissa Pasta with Shrimp and Feta

Total **15 min**; Serves **4**

Ashley Rodriguez, creator of the blog Not Without Salt, uses a blender to make quick work of this clever harissa sauce. Laced with fragrant spices, it's excellent tossed with pasta and shrimp.

SAUCE

- **1 cup lightly packed mint leaves**
- **1 cup lightly packed cilantro leaves and stems**
- **3 jalapeños, seeded and coarsely chopped**
- **1 garlic clove**
- **½ tsp. ground cumin**
- **½ tsp. ground fennel**
- **½ cup extra-virgin olive oil**
- **1 Tbsp. fresh lemon juice**
- **½ tsp. kosher salt**

PASTA

- **12 oz. gemelli or other noodles, cooked al dente and drained**
- **1 lb. shelled cooked medium shrimp**
- **½ cup crumbled feta cheese**

In a food processor, combine all of the sauce ingredients and pulse until a sauce forms. Toss with the hot pasta and shrimp, top with the feta and serve. —*Ashley Rodriguez*

WINE Herbal, zesty New Zealand Sauvignon Blanc: 2013 Matua.

SPAGHETTI WITH SMOKY EGGPLANT SAUCE

Bucatini all'Amatriciana with Parmigiano

📷 PAGE 6

⏱ Active **15 min**; Total **45 min**
Serves **4 to 6**

Chef Jenn Louis of Lincoln Restaurant in Portland, Oregon, makes this riff on pasta all'amatriciana with just a few powerhouse ingredients. For the *salumi,* she provides options on a spectrum of porkiness, from robust *guanciale* (cured pork jowl) to milder pancetta.

- **4 oz. pancetta or *guanciale*, sliced ½ inch thick and cut into ½-inch dice**
- **1 medium red onion, finely diced**
- **¼ tsp. crushed red pepper**
- **One 28-oz. can whole peeled Italian tomatoes, drained, then tomatoes crushed by hand**
- **Kosher salt and black pepper**
- **1 lb. bucatini**
- **Extra-virgin olive oil, for drizzling**
- **Freshly grated Parmigiano-Reggiano cheese, for serving**

1. In a large skillet, cook the pancetta over moderate heat, stirring occasionally, until golden brown and the fat is rendered, about 12 minutes. Add the onion and cook until softened, about 8 minutes. Stir in the crushed red pepper and tomatoes, season with salt and black pepper and bring to a boil, then simmer over moderately low heat until the tomato sauce is slightly reduced, about 10 minutes.

2. Meanwhile, in a large pot of salted boiling water, cook the bucatini until al dente.

3. Drain the bucatini and add it to the skillet. Toss over low heat until coated in the sauce, about 2 minutes. Transfer to bowls, drizzle with olive oil and serve with grated cheese. —*Jenn Louis*

WINE Fragrant Piedmontese red: 2012 Matteo Correggia Barbera d'Alba.

Creamy One-Pot Spaghetti with Leeks

⏱ Total **30 min**; Serves **4**

Instead of boiling pasta in water, food blogger Ashley Rodriguez cooks it in a super-flavorful combination of chicken stock, cream, leeks, scallion, garlic and chives.

- **1 Tbsp. extra-virgin olive oil**
- **5 garlic cloves, minced**
- **3 scallions, thinly sliced**
- **2 leeks, white and light green parts only, trimmed and thinly sliced**
- **1 medium shallot, chopped**
- **1 anchovy fillet, drained**
- **Pinch of crushed red pepper**
- **1 lb. spaghetti, noodles broken in half**
- **3¾ cups chicken stock or low-sodium broth**
- **¾ cup heavy cream**
- **Kosher salt**
- **2 Tbsp. chopped chives**
- **¼ cup freshly grated Parmigiano-Reggiano cheese, plus more for serving**

In a large pot, heat the olive oil. Add the garlic, scallions, leeks and shallot and cook over moderate heat, stirring occasionally, until the leeks are softened, 6 minutes. Add the anchovy, crushed red pepper, spaghetti, stock, cream and ½ teaspoon of salt and bring to a boil. Reduce the heat to low and cook, stirring, until the pasta is tender and a sauce forms, about 11 minutes. Stir in the chives and ¼ cup of cheese; season with salt. Serve the pasta with extra cheese on the side. —*Ashley Rodriguez*

WINE Floral, juicy Italian white: 2012 Inama Soave Classico.

Salami Carbonara

⏱ Total **35 min**; Serves **8**

Charles Wekselbaum of Charlito's Cocina in New York City uses his amazing small-batch salami as an alternative to the usual pancetta in this inventive take on pasta carbonara.

- **¼ cup extra-virgin olive oil**
- **¾ lb. good-quality salami, sliced ¼ inch thick and finely diced**
- **1½ lbs. bucatini**
- **6 large egg yolks**
- **½ cup freshly grated pecorino cheese, plus more for serving**
- **Salt and coarsely ground black pepper**

1. In a large, deep skillet, heat 2 tablespoons of the olive oil. Add the salami and cook over moderately low heat, stirring occasionally, until the fat is rendered and the salami is tender, about 20 minutes.

2. Meanwhile, in a large pot of salted boiling water, cook the pasta until al dente. Drain, reserving 1½ cups of the cooking water.

3. In a medium bowl, whisk the egg yolks with the ½ cup of cheese and the remaining 2 tablespoons of olive oil.

4. Add the pasta and ½ cup of the reserved pasta water to the salami and cook over moderate heat, tossing, until the bucatini is coated and hot, about 2 minutes. Remove the skillet from the heat and immediately add the egg mixture and remaining 1 cup of cooking water. Using tongs, toss the pasta until it's creamy, about 1 minute. Season with salt and black pepper. Serve the pasta in shallow bowls, passing more cheese at the table. —*Charles Wekselbaum*

WINE Robust southern Italian red: 2011 Terredora di Paolo Aglianico.

Tagliatelle with Braised Chicken and Figs

Active **1 hr**; Total **2 hr**; Serves **4**

This Spanish-inflected pasta is from chef Kyle Bailey of Bluejacket brewery's Arsenal restaurant in Washington, DC. It's rich and complex-tasting thanks to a sauce made from chicken braising liquid that's reduced until silky and luscious. Finishing touches of dried figs and marcona almonds add sweetness and crunch.

- 2 Tbsp. canola oil
- 2 lbs. skinless, bone-in chicken thighs
  Kosher salt and pepper
- 1 carrot, chopped
- 1 onion, chopped
- 2 celery ribs, chopped
- ½ small tomato, chopped
- 2 Tbsp. Madeira
- 1 quart chicken stock or low-sodium broth
- 2 garlic cloves
- 1 Tbsp. black peppercorns
- 2 Tbsp. unsalted butter
- ½ cup dried figs, stemmed and chopped
- 8 oz. dried tagliatelle
- 2 Tbsp. freshly grated Parmigiano-Reggiano cheese
- 2 Tbsp. chopped tarragon
- ¼ cup marcona almonds, chopped
  Freshly shaved Manchego cheese, for garnish

1. Preheat the oven to 350°. In a large enameled cast-iron casserole, heat the oil. Season the chicken thighs with salt and pepper and cook over moderately high heat, turning, until browned, about 5 minutes. Transfer the chicken to a plate.

2. Add the carrot, onion and celery to the casserole and cook over moderate heat, stirring occasionally, until golden, about 5 minutes. Stir in the tomato and cook until it breaks down and is lightly caramelized, about 5 minutes. Add the Madeira and cook until evaporated, then add the chicken stock, garlic and peppercorns. Return the chicken to the pot and bring to a simmer. Cover and braise in the oven for 1 hour, until the chicken is tender.

3. Using tongs, transfer the chicken to a plate to cool. Shred the meat; discard the bones. Strain the cooking liquid into a bowl, pressing on the solids. Return the liquid to the casserole and bring to a boil. Simmer briskly until thickened to a saucy consistency, 5 to 7 minutes. Add the butter, shredded chicken and figs and cook just to warm through.

4. Meanwhile, in a pot of salted boiling water, cook the pasta until al dente. Drain, reserving ½ cup of the pasta water. Add the pasta and reserved pasta water to the casserole and toss. Remove from the heat and stir in the Parmigiano and tarragon. Serve in bowls topped with the almonds and Manchego shavings. —*Kyle Bailey*

MAKE AHEAD The braised chicken can be refrigerated for up to 2 days.

BEER Rich and malty sour beer: New Belgium La Folie.

Pappardelle with Duck Ragù

Active **1 hr 15 min**; Total **2 hr 45 min** Serves **6**

Inspired by his grandmother, who always served her stews with potatoes or noodles to sop up the sauce, chef and TV host Curtis Stone serves this sumptuous duck ragù with wide pappardelle noodles and a dollop of creamy ricotta.

- 2 Tbsp. extra-virgin olive oil
  Three 1-lb. duck legs, skin and excess fat removed
  Kosher salt and freshly ground pepper
- 6 large shallots, finely chopped
- 1 large carrot, chopped
- 2 celery stalks, chopped
- 3 oz. prosciutto, finely chopped
- 2 rosemary sprigs
- 2 Tbsp. thyme leaves
- 4 garlic cloves, very finely chopped
- ¼ oz. dried porcini mushrooms, ground to a powder in a spice grinder
- 1½ cups dry white wine
- 3 cups chicken stock or low-sodium broth
- 8 oz. dried pappardelle
- ½ cup fresh ricotta cheese
- 2 Tbsp. freshly grated pecorino cheese, plus more for serving

1. Preheat the oven to 350°. In a large enameled cast-iron casserole, heat the olive oil until shimmering. Season the duck legs with salt and pepper and add to the casserole. Cook over moderately high heat, turning once, until browned, about 8 minutes; transfer to a plate.

2. Pour off all but 2 tablespoons of fat from the casserole. Add the shallots, carrot, celery, prosciutto, rosemary, thyme and garlic. Cook over moderately high heat, stirring occasionally, until the vegetables are softened and just starting to brown, about 5 minutes. Stir in the porcini powder and wine. Simmer, scraping up any browned bits from the bottom of the casserole, until slightly reduced, about 3 minutes. Add the chicken stock and bring to a boil. Return the duck legs to the casserole, cover and braise in the oven until the legs are very tender, about 1 hour and 30 minutes; turn the duck legs halfway through braising.

3. Transfer the duck legs to a plate and let them cool slightly. Remove the duck meat from the bones and shred into bite-size pieces. Return the duck to the ragù and season with salt and pepper; keep warm. Discard the rosemary stems.

4. In a large saucepan of salted boiling water, cook the pappardelle until al dente. Drain, reserving 2 cups of the cooking water. In a small bowl, whisk the ricotta with 2 tablespoons of the cooking water until smooth.

5. Add the pasta to the ragù along with ¾ cup of the reserved cooking water and the 2 tablespoons of pecorino. Cook over moderate heat, stirring gently, until the pasta is hot and coated with sauce; add more cooking water if the sauce is too thick. Transfer the pasta to shallow bowls, top with the ricotta and serve, passing additional pecorino at the table. —*Curtis Stone*

WINE Smooth, juicy Nero d'Avola from Sicily: 2012 Ceuso Scurati.

Lasagna Puttanesca

Active **45 min**; Total **2 hr 30 min**
Serves **10 to 12**

Puttanesca is a classic southern Italian pasta sauce made with tomatoes, capers, anchovies and olives. Here, it lends a ton of flavor to a hearty but not heavy eggplant lasagna layered with ricotta and mozzarella.

- **5 Tbsp. extra-virgin olive oil, plus more for tossing and greasing**
- **1 lb. dry lasagna noodles**
- **1 medium onion, finely chopped**
- **1 medium eggplant, diced (½ inch)**
- **Kosher salt and freshly ground pepper**
- **7 anchovy fillets in oil, chopped**
- **7 garlic cloves, finely chopped**
- **1 cup pitted olives, chopped**
- **3 Tbsp. drained capers**
- **Two 28-oz. cans whole peeled tomatoes and juices, crushed**
- **3 cups fresh ricotta cheese**
- **3 large eggs, lightly beaten**
- **1 lb. mozzarella, thinly sliced**

1. Preheat the oven to 450°. Lightly grease a 9-by-13-inch ceramic baking dish with oil.

2. In a large pot of salted boiling water, cook the lasagna noodles until they just start to soften, 4 to 5 minutes. Drain, transfer to a baking sheet and toss with olive oil.

3. In a large saucepan, heat 2 tablespoons of the oil. Add the onion and cook over moderate heat until lightly golden, 5 minutes. Add the eggplant and the remaining 3 tablespoons of oil; season with salt and pepper. Cook, stirring, for 3 minutes. Add the anchovies and garlic and cook for 1 minute. Stir in the olives, capers and crushed tomatoes. Bring to a boil and cook until the sauce is thickened, about 10 minutes. Season the puttanesca sauce with salt and pepper.

4. Meanwhile, in a bowl, stir the ricotta with the eggs and season with salt and pepper.

5. Spread 1½ cups of the puttanesca sauce in the baking dish. Top with 5 lasagna noodles and spread with half of the ricotta. Top with another layer of noodles and half of the remaining sauce. Arrange another layer of noodles on top and spread with the remaining ricotta. Repeat with a final layer of noodles and the remaining sauce.

6. Cover with foil and bake the lasagna for 40 minutes. Uncover and bake for 15 minutes. Arrange the mozzarella slices over the top and bake for 15 minutes longer, until most of the liquid has been absorbed. Let stand for 15 minutes before serving.
—*Kay Chun*

WINE Bright Barbera d'Alba: 2011 G.D. Vajra.

MAD GENIUS TIP

No-Mess Garlic Paste

For perfect garlic paste, place peeled garlic cloves in a resealable plastic sandwich bag, add a generous pinch of kosher salt, then pound the bag with a meat mallet. Using a rolling pin, roll over the bag to further crush the garlic. Push the garlic down to the bottom of the bag and continue rolling until you have a spoonable paste.

LogHouse Macaroni and Cheese

Active **30 min**; Total **1 hr 10 min**; Serves **6**

At Kurtwood Farms on Vashon Island in Washington state, Kurt Timmermeister makes his own LogHouse cheese, an intensely flavorful take on tomme, a type of small, round cheese from the Alps. He shreds it into a sauce for this superbly creamy mac and cheese.

- **1 lb. penne**
- **3 Tbsp. rendered lard or unsalted butter**
- **3 Tbsp. all-purpose flour**
- **2 bay leaves, preferably fresh**
- **3¼ cups whole milk**
- **1 lb. LogHouse, Tomme de Savoie or other semisoft tomme-style cheese, rind discarded and cheese shredded (12 oz.); see Note**
- **Salt and pepper**

1. Preheat the oven to 400°. In a large saucepan of salted boiling water, cook the pasta until al dente; drain well.

2. Meanwhile, in a medium saucepan, melt the lard. Whisk in the flour and cook over moderate heat, whisking, until bubbling but not browned, about 2 minutes. Add the bay leaves and cook, stirring, until the roux is golden, 3 to 5 minutes. Gradually whisk in the milk until smooth, then bring to a boil and simmer over moderate heat, whisking, until the sauce is thickened and no floury taste remains, about 5 minutes. Remove from the heat and stir in the shredded cheese until melted. Season the sauce generously with salt and pepper; discard the bay leaves.

3. In a large bowl, toss the penne with the hot cheese sauce and season with salt and pepper. Transfer to a 9-by-13-inch oval baking dish. Bake for about 35 minutes, until bubbling and lightly browned on top. Let the macaroni and cheese stand for 5 minutes before serving.
—*Kurt Timmermeister*

NOTE Tomme de Savoie is a mild, semisoft cow-milk cheese.

MAKE AHEAD The unbaked macaroni and cheese can be made earlier in the day and refrigerated. Bring to room temperature before baking.

WINE Bright Barbera d'Asti: 2012 Damilano.

LASAGNA PUTTANESCA

DIY White Lasagna

ACTIVE: 1 HR 30 MIN; TOTAL: 3 HR 30 MIN; SERVES 10

Chef **GERARD CRAFT** of Pastaria in St. Louis creates a luxurious version with fresh pasta, béchamel and two types of cheese—plus three kinds of toppings.

THE ULTIMATE INDULGENT LASAGNA
This creamy white version, without meat or tomatoes, is for true pasta lovers.

STEP 1 MAKE THE PASTA

**3½ cups all-purpose flour,
   plus more for dusting**
1½ tsp. kosher salt
3 large eggs, lightly beaten

In a food processor, pulse the 3½ cups of flour with the salt. Add the eggs and ½ cup of water and pulse until the dough starts to come together. Turn the dough out onto a work surface and knead by hand until smooth and elastic, about 10 minutes. If the dough is too sticky to work with, lightly dust it with flour. Wrap the dough in plastic and let rest at room temperature for 1 hour.

STEP 2 MAKE THE BÉCHAMEL

2 sticks unsalted butter
1 medium onion, finely chopped
2 rosemary sprigs
2 thyme sprigs
3 garlic cloves, crushed
   Kosher salt
1 cup all-purpose flour
2 quarts whole milk

Meanwhile, in a large saucepan, melt the butter. Add the onion, herbs, garlic and a pinch of salt; cook over moderate heat, stirring occasionally, until the onion is softened but not browned, 8 minutes. Add the flour and cook, stirring constantly, until the roux is light golden, 3 to 5 minutes. Gradually whisk in the milk and bring to a boil, then simmer over moderately low heat, stirring frequently, until no floury taste remains, about 20 minutes. Press the béchamel through a fine sieve into a bowl; discard the solids. Season with salt and let cool.

STEP 3 ASSEMBLE THE LASAGNA

   Extra-virgin olive oil
**½ lb. imported Fontina cheese,
   shredded (2½ cups)**
**5 oz. Grana Padano cheese,
   freshly grated (1¼ cups)**

1. Cut the dough into 8 equal pieces; work with 1 piece at a time, keeping the rest covered with a towel. Flatten the dough slightly. Run it through a pasta machine a total of 6 times: Start at the widest setting, then run through successively narrower settings. Dust the sheet with flour and lay it on a parchment paper–lined baking sheet. Repeat with the remaining dough, separating the pasta sheets with parchment.

2. In a large pot of salted boiling water, cook the pasta sheets until just al dente, 1 to 2 minutes. Drain in a colander and cool under running water, then drain again. Return the pasta to the baking sheet and toss with olive oil to prevent the sheets from sticking together.

3. Preheat the oven to 350°. Brush a deep 9-by-13-inch baking dish with oil; spread with ½ cup of the béchamel. Arrange a layer of pasta over the béchamel, trimming to fit. Spread one-fifth of the remaining béchamel over the pasta; sprinkle with ½ cup of the Fontina and ¼ cup of the Grana Padano. Repeat the layering 4 more times, ending with the cheeses.

4. Tightly cover the baking dish with foil and bake the lasagna for 45 minutes, until bubbling. Remove from the oven and uncover. Preheat the broiler. Broil the lasagna 6 inches from the heat until lightly browned on top, 2 to 4 minutes. Let rest for 15 minutes, then cut into squares and serve with one of the toppings at right.

MAKE AHEAD The assembled, unbaked lasagna can be refrigerated for 1 day.

WINE Spiced, dark-fruited Chianti Classico: 2010 Querciabella.

HOW TO MAKE PERFECT LASAGNA

1 PULSE THE FLOUR, salt, eggs and water in a food processor until the dough just comes together.

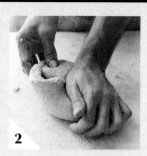

2 KNEAD THE DOUGH by hand until smooth and supple, about 10 minutes.

3 WRAP THE DOUGH in plastic to prevent it from drying out. Let sit at room temperature for 1 hour.

4 RUN THE DOUGH through a pasta machine six times, using a successively narrower setting each time.

5 CHECK THE TEXTURE The pasta sheets should be so thin and delicate that they're almost see-through.

6 PLACE THE PASTA between sheets of parchment paper and dust them with flour.

7 PARCOOK THE PASTA in a large pot of salted boiling water until just al dente.

8 DRAIN THE PASTA in a colander, rinse under cold running water and then drain again. Toss with oil.

9 LAYER PASTA over some of the béchamel in a baking dish, cutting to fit as necessary.

10 SPREAD BÉCHAMEL on the pasta, followed by an even layer of the cheeses.

11 REPEAT THE LAYERS four more times, ending with the béchamel and cheeses. Bake for 45 minutes.

12 BROIL THE LASAGNA until it's browned and bubbly. Let rest for 15 minutes before cutting.

THREE GREAT TOPPINGS

Roasted Wild Mushrooms

Preheat the oven to 450°. In a large bowl, toss 2 lbs. **mixed chopped mushrooms** (such as maitake, stemmed shiitake, oyster and cremini) with ½ cup **extra-virgin olive oil** and season with **salt.** Spread the mushrooms on 2 large rimmed baking sheets and roast for about 30 minutes, stirring once, until golden. Season with **fresh lemon juice.**

Salsa Verde

In a large bowl, whisk ¾ cup **extra-virgin olive oil** with 1½ Tbsp. **fresh lemon juice,** 1 minced **garlic clove** and 3 Tbsp. each of finely chopped **parsley, tarragon, dill, mint** and **chives.** Season with **salt.** *Makes 1 cup.*

Roasted Carrot Puree

Preheat the oven to 350°. In a large ovenproof skillet, heat 2 Tbsp. **vegetable oil.** Add 3 cups chopped **carrots** (1½ lbs.) and 2 **thyme sprigs;** cook over moderate heat, stirring, until the carrots are browned, 10 minutes. Transfer to the oven and roast for 10 minutes, until the carrots are tender. Pulse in a food processor until chopped. With the machine on, drizzle in 1 cup **extra-virgin olive oil** and ¾ cup **water;** puree until smooth, about 30 seconds. Season with **salt.** *Makes 2¼ cups.*

MAKE AHEAD The toppings can be refrigerated overnight. Gently reheat the mushrooms and carrot puree.

Baked Rigatoni with Broccoli, Green Olives and Pancetta

Total **1 hr 20 min**; Serves **6**

As an alternative to standard baked ziti, Georgia chef Hugh Acheson makes his version with intensely sweet roasted tomatoes, loads of broccoli and briny green olives. It comes out of the oven with a crispy Parmesan crust.

- **2 Tbsp. unsalted butter, plus more for greasing**
- **1½ lbs. plum tomatoes, halved lengthwise**
- **3 garlic cloves, crushed**
- **2 thyme sprigs**
- **1 basil sprig, plus ½ cup torn basil leaves**
- **3 Tbsp. extra-virgin olive oil**
- **Kosher salt and freshly ground black pepper**
- **1½ lbs. broccoli, cut into small florets and stems reserved for another use**
- **One 4-oz. slice of pancetta, finely diced**
- **1 large onion, very finely chopped**
- **1 cup pitted green olives, such as Castelvetrano, halved**
- **1 lb. rigatoni**
- **2 cups fresh ricotta cheese**
- **¾ cup freshly grated Parmigiano-Reggiano cheese**

1. Preheat the oven to 425° and butter a 9-by-13-inch ceramic or glass baking dish. On a rimmed baking sheet, toss the tomatoes, garlic and thyme and basil sprigs with 1 tablespoon of the olive oil and season with salt and pepper. Roast for about 20 minutes, until softened and browned in spots; let cool. Discard the thyme and basil sprigs and coarsely chop the tomatoes and garlic, reserving any juices.

2. Meanwhile, on another rimmed baking sheet, toss the broccoli florets with 1 tablespoon of the olive oil and season with salt and pepper. Roast for 15 minutes, or until crisp-tender. Leave the oven on.

3. Meanwhile, in a large, deep skillet, heat the remaining 1 tablespoon of olive oil. Add the pancetta and cook over moderately high heat, stirring occasionally, until browned and nearly crisp, about 5 minutes. Add the onion and cook, stirring occasionally, until softened, about 5 minutes. Stir in the olives, tomatoes and garlic and the 2 tablespoons of butter; keep warm.

4. In a pot of salted boiling water, cook the rigatoni until al dente. Drain, reserving 1¼ cups of the cooking water. Stir the pasta into the skillet along with the reserved cooking water, broccoli, ricotta, torn basil and ½ cup of the Parmigiano. Season with salt and pepper. Transfer the pasta to the prepared baking dish. Sprinkle the remaining ¼ cup of Parmigiano on top and bake for 15 minutes, until bubbling and browned on top. Let stand for 5 minutes before serving. —*Hugh Acheson*

MAKE AHEAD The baked pasta can be refrigerated overnight.

WINE Juicy, medium-bodied Provençal red: 2011 Domaine Le Galantin Bandol Rouge.

Baked Macaroni with Mortadella and Mozzarella

Active **45 min**; Total **2 hr**
Serves **4 to 6**

Chef Paul Kahan of The Publican in Chicago ramps up his Italian take on mac and cheese with fresh mozzarella, mortadella, eggs and a rich pork ragù.

- **¼ cup extra-virgin olive oil**
- **1 onion, finely chopped**
- **1 garlic clove, minced**
- **1 lb. ground pork**
- **1 cup dry white wine**
- **One 28-oz. can crushed tomatoes**
- **Generous pinch of crushed red pepper**
- **Kosher salt**
- **2 large eggs**
- **12 oz. elbow macaroni**
- **2 Tbsp. finely chopped basil**
- **2 Tbsp. finely chopped parsley**
- **One ¼-lb. piece of mortadella, cut into small dice**
- **1 lb. fresh mozzarella, cut into bite-size pieces**
- **1 cup freshly grated Parmigiano-Reggiano cheese**

1. In a large saucepan, heat the oil until shimmering. Add the onion and garlic and cook over moderately high heat, stirring, until softened, 4 minutes. Add the ground pork and cook, breaking up the meat, until browned, 10 minutes. Stir in the wine and cook until evaporated, 3 minutes. Add the tomatoes, crushed red pepper and a generous pinch of salt and bring to a boil. Cook over moderately low heat, stirring, until thickened, 1 hour.

2. Meanwhile, in a small saucepan, cover the eggs with water and bring to a boil. Cook over moderately high heat for 8 minutes. Drain the eggs and cool under running water, then peel and finely chop.

3. Preheat the oven to 425°. In a large saucepan of salted boiling water, cook the macaroni until al dente; drain well and stir into the sauce with the basil, parsley, chopped eggs, mortadella, three-fourths of the mozzarella and ¾ cup of the Parmigiano-Reggiano.

COOKWARE TIP

Baking Dish

The unexpected use of color on Riess's 8-by-13-inch enamel pan reimagines the look of a kitchen basic.
$75; potagernyc.com.

4. Transfer the macaroni to a 3-quart ceramic baking dish and scatter the remaining mozzarella and Parmigiano-Reggiano on top. Bake for 25 minutes, until hot. Let stand for 5 minutes before serving. —*Paul Kahan*

WINE Robustly fruity Zinfandel: 2011 Healdsburg Ranches California Coastal Series.

Peruvian-Style Pasta Bolognese
⏲ Total **35 min**; Serves **4**

This pasta from L.A. chef Ricardo Zarate is based on *tallarín saltado,* a classic Bolognese-like comfort food in Zarate's native Peru. Unlike the Italian version, this recipe calls for *lomo saltado* sauce—a garlicky puree of red wine vinegar, chile paste and soy sauce.

- **One 1-inch piece of fresh ginger, peeled and chopped**
- **7 garlic cloves, chopped**
- **3 Tbsp. red wine vinegar**
- **1 Tbsp. ají amarillo paste (see Note)**
- **¼ tsp. freshly ground black pepper**
- **3 Tbsp. soy sauce**
- **1 lb. dried tagliatelle**
- **2 Tbsp. canola oil**
- **¾ lb. ground beef sirloin (90 percent lean)**
- **1 medium red onion, finely diced**
- **2 plum tomatoes—halved, seeded and finely diced**
- **1 cup chicken stock or low-sodium broth**
- **½ cup freshly grated Parmesan cheese, plus shavings for garnish**
- **2 Tbsp. minced cilantro**
- **Kosher salt**

1. In a blender or mini processor, combine the ginger, garlic, vinegar, ají amarillo paste, black pepper and 1 tablespoon of the soy sauce and puree until smooth. Reserve the ginger-garlic sauce.

2. In a large pot of salted boiling water, cook the pasta until al dente. Drain well.

3. Meanwhile, in a large skillet, heat the oil. Add the ground beef and cook over high heat, stirring to break up the meat, until browned, 3 to 4 minutes. Using a slotted spoon, transfer the meat to a bowl.

4. Add the onion to the skillet and cook over moderate heat, stirring occasionally, until softened, about 5 minutes. Add the meat and tomatoes and cook over high heat for 1 minute, then add the remaining 2 tablespoons of soy sauce and boil for 1 minute. Stir in the chicken stock and the ginger-garlic sauce and bring to a boil.

5. Add the pasta and grated Parmesan to the sauce and toss to coat. Fold in the cilantro and season with salt. Transfer to a bowl, garnish with Parmesan shavings and serve. —*Ricardo Zarate*

NOTE Ají amarillo paste is a spicy Peruvian yellow chile paste. It's available in many supermarkets and from amazon.com.

WINE Blackberry-rich Washington state Syrah: 2010 àMaurice Estate Fred.

Cumin Lamb Noodles with Eggplant
⏲ Total **30 min**; Serves **4 to 6**

Food blogger Ashley Rodriguez creates a luxurious lamb ragù with delicious Greek flavors; it's a total crowd-pleaser and a nice alternative to more common Italian pasta dishes.

- **3 Tbsp. extra-virgin olive oil**
- **1 onion, thinly sliced**
- **1 medium eggplant (1 lb.), peeled and cut into ¾-inch cubes**
- **2 garlic cloves, minced**
- **1 tsp. dried oregano**
- **1 tsp. ground cumin**
- **½ tsp. smoked paprika, preferably hot**
- **Pinch of crushed red pepper**
- **Kosher salt**
- **¾ lb. ground lamb**
- **¼ cup tomato paste**
- **¾ cup chicken stock or broth**
- **8 oz. gemelli**
- **½ cup plain whole-milk Greek yogurt**
- **⅓ cup chopped mint**

1. In a large skillet, heat the oil. Add the onion and cook over moderate heat, stirring occasionally, until softened, 5 minutes. Add the eggplant, garlic, oregano, cumin, paprika and crushed red pepper and season with salt. Cook, stirring, until fragrant, 1 minute. Add the lamb and cook, breaking up the meat with a wooden spoon. Add the tomato paste and cook, stirring, for 2 minutes. Stir in the stock and bring to a boil. Cover and cook over low heat until the sauce is thickened, 12 minutes.

2. Cook the pasta in a pot of salted boiling water until al dente, 8 minutes. Drain, reserving ½ cup of the pasta cooking water. Stir the pasta and ¼ cup of the reserved cooking water into the sauce; add more water if a thinner sauce is desired. Remove the skillet from the heat and stir in the yogurt and mint. Season with salt and serve hot. —*Ashley Rodriguez*

WINE Dark-berried Barbera d'Alba: 2012 Andrea Oberto.

INGREDIENT TIP

Using Tomatoes Year-Round

Mark Ladner, chef at New York City's Del Posto, shares his best tips for getting sun-ripened tomato flavor beyond the summer months.

DEHYDRATED TOMATOES Toss whole cherry tomatoes in olive oil and bake them in the oven at its lowest setting until they're wrinkled but still plump. "The flesh is tanned and dried," says Ladner, "but they're whole so you still get that juicy burst when you eat them."

CANNED TOMATOES "I think people underestimate the quality of really good canned or jarred tomatoes," says Ladner. His highest praise goes to the piennolo tomatoes from Mount Vesuvius.

TOMATO POWDER "It's not a primary ingredient, but it's so concentrated it can elevate fresh tomatoes that aren't at their peak–kind of like doubling down on them." Sprinkle the powder on top of fresh tomatoes in dishes.

Fennel Frond Orzo

⏲ Total **30 min**; Serves **4 to 6**

Capers, almonds, fennel, scallions and olives are pounded along with vinegar-soaked bread to create the tasty vegetarian sauce for this elegant orzo salad.

- **8 oz. orzo (1½ cups), preferably whole-wheat**
- **One 4-by-4-inch, 1-inch-thick slice of country bread, crust removed and bread cubed**
- **3 Tbsp. white wine vinegar**
- **1 tsp. coriander seeds**
- **1 garlic clove**
- **Kosher salt**
- **3 Tbsp. capers, drained and rinsed**
- **½ cup roasted almonds, chopped**
- **2 scallions, chopped**
- **Fronds from 1 leafy fennel bulb (½ cup), finely chopped (see Note)**
- **10 pitted black olives, such as kalamata, chopped**
- **½ cup extra-virgin olive oil**
- **1 small head of radicchio—halved, cored and shredded (4 cups)**

1. In a large saucepan of salted boiling water, cook the orzo until al dente; drain and transfer to a large bowl.

2. Meanwhile, in a small bowl, soak the bread in the vinegar. In a small skillet, toast the coriander seeds, stirring, until fragrant, 2 minutes. Transfer the seeds to a mortar. Add the garlic and ½ teaspoon of salt and pound with a pestle until a paste forms. One ingredient at a time, pound in the capers, almonds, scallions, fennel fronds and olives until the mixture is chunky. Pound in the soaked bread, then pound in the olive oil, 2 tablespoons at a time.

3. Add the dressing and radicchio to the orzo, season with salt and toss well.
—*Heidi Swanson*

NOTE You can finely chop the fennel bulb and add it to the orzo as well, if desired.

Orzo with Caramelized Onions and Raisins

⏲ Total **30 min**; Serves **6 to 8**

Danny Seo, an eco-lifestyle expert, makes this simple orzo salad with ingredients he always has in his kitchen. It's a great fast lunch or weeknight meal.

- **12 oz. orzo (2 cups)**
- **½ cup raisins**
- **¼ cup extra-virgin olive oil**
- **1 medium yellow onion, thinly sliced lengthwise**
- **Kosher salt**
- **3 garlic cloves, minced**
- **½ cup pitted kalamata olives, thinly sliced lengthwise**
- **½ cup freshly grated Parmigiano-Reggiano cheese**
- **¼ cup finely chopped parsley**
- **Freshly ground pepper**

1. In a large pot of salted boiling water, cook the orzo until al dente, about 8 minutes. Meanwhile, in a small bowl, cover the raisins with warm water and let stand until softened, 10 minutes. Drain the orzo and rinse under cold water. Drain the raisins and transfer them to a large bowl with the orzo.

2. In a medium skillet, heat the olive oil. Add the onion, season with salt and cook over moderately high heat, stirring, until lightly browned, about 10 minutes. Add the garlic and cook until fragrant, about 2 minutes. Add the onion to the orzo along with the olives, cheese and parsley and stir. Season with salt and pepper and serve.
—*Danny Seo*

WINE Full-bodied organic white Rhône blend: 2012 M. Chapoutier Belleruche Blanc.

Cherry Couscous Salad

⏲ Total **25 min**; Serves **4**

- **3 Tbsp. extra-virgin olive oil**
- **1½ cups Israeli couscous**
- **1 Tbsp. fresh lemon juice**
- **1½ cups chopped pitted cherries**
- **½ cup oil-cured black olives, pitted and chopped**
- **¼ cup chopped tarragon**
- **Kosher salt and pepper**

In a medium saucepan, heat 1 tablespoon of the olive oil. Add the couscous and cook over moderate heat, stirring, until lightly golden, about 3 minutes. Add 2 cups of water, cover and cook over low heat until the couscous is tender and all the liquid is absorbed, about 10 minutes. Transfer the couscous to a bowl. Stir in the remaining ingredients and serve.
—*Kay Chun*

Four-Citrus Couscous

⏲ Active **20 min**; Total **40 min**
Serves **8 to 10**

Star chef Marcus Samuelsson uses the juice and zest of lemon, lime, grapefruit and orange in his aromatic couscous.

- **2 cups couscous**
- **⅓ cup plus 2 Tbsp. extra-virgin olive oil**
- **½ cup minced shallots**
- **1 tsp. finely chopped sage**
- **Kosher salt and pepper**
- **2 Tbsp. fresh grapefruit juice**
- **2 Tbsp. fresh orange juice**
- **2 Tbsp. fresh lime juice**
- **¼ cup plus 2 Tbsp. fresh lemon juice**
- **½ tsp. finely grated grapefruit zest**
- **½ tsp. finely grated orange zest**
- **½ tsp. finely grated lemon zest**
- **½ tsp. finely grated lime zest**

Put the couscous in a large heatproof bowl. In a medium saucepan, heat 2 tablespoons of the olive oil until shimmering. Add the shallots, sage and a generous pinch each of salt and pepper. Cook over moderate heat, stirring, until softened, 5 minutes. Add 1¾ cups of water, the grapefruit, orange and lime juices and 2 tablespoons of the lemon juice. Season with salt. Bring to a boil and stir in the citrus zests. Pour the liquid over the couscous, cover with plastic wrap and let stand at room temperature until the liquid is absorbed, 20 minutes. Fluff with a fork. Fold in the remaining ⅓ cup of olive oil and ¼ cup of lemon juice. Season with salt and pepper and serve.
—*Marcus Samuelsson*

FENNEL FROND ORZO

Sesame-Paprika Fregola

⏱ Total **30 min**; Serves **4**

Fregola, a toasted Sardinian pasta with an appealing chewy texture, is combined in this tasty dish with sweet and smoked paprika, sesame seeds, coriander and feta. It can be served as a side or topped with fried or poached eggs for a satisfying vegetarian main course.

1¼ cups fregola or Israeli couscous (7½ oz.)
1½ tsp. coriander seeds
1 small garlic clove
Fine sea salt
1 Tbsp. toasted sesame seeds, plus more for garnish
½ tsp. sweet paprika
⅛ tsp. smoked paprika
1 tsp. honey
½ cup extra-virgin olive oil
4 oz. feta cheese, cubed or crumbled
1 cup arugula, chopped

1. In a saucepan of salted boiling water, cook the fregola until tender, about 20 minutes. Drain well, then transfer the fregola to a medium bowl to cool.

2. Meanwhile, in a nonstick skillet, toast the coriander seeds over moderately low heat until fragrant, 2 minutes. In a mortar or mini processor, puree the garlic with ½ teaspoon of fine sea salt. Add the toasted coriander, 1 tablespoon of sesame seeds and both paprikas; process to a paste. Add the honey and olive oil until a chunky sauce forms.

3. Add the sesame-paprika sauce to the fregola, stir well and season with salt. Transfer to a serving bowl and top with the feta and arugula. Garnish with sesame seeds and serve. —*Heidi Swanson*

Gnocchi with Creamy Crab Pan Sauce

Total **2 hr**; Serves **8**

The key ingredients of the creamy pan sauce that coats star chef John Besh's tender potato gnocchi are a rich crab stock, a splash of vermouth and a pinch of crushed red pepper. In a nod to his hometown of New Orleans, Besh adds lump crabmeat to the sauce, too.

GNOCCHI
1½ lbs. Yukon Gold potatoes, peeled and quartered
6 large egg yolks
1⅓ cups all-purpose flour, plus more for dusting
½ tsp. kosher salt
Pinch of freshly grated nutmeg

CRAB SAUCE
1 quart fish stock
2 fresh blue crabs
1 Tbsp. extra-virgin olive oil
1 small onion, finely chopped
¼ small fennel bulb, finely chopped
2 garlic cloves, minced
1 tsp. crushed red pepper
¾ cup heavy cream
¾ cup dry vermouth
½ tsp. thyme leaves, chopped
1 tarragon sprig
1 bay leaf
¾ lb. jumbo lump crabmeat
3 Tbsp. unsalted butter
Kosher salt
Freshly shaved Parmigiano-Reggiano cheese, for garnish

1. Make the gnocchi In a saucepan, cover the potatoes with 1 inch of water and cook over moderate heat until tender, 15 minutes; drain and pass through a food mill or ricer into a bowl. Add the egg yolks, 1⅓ cups of flour, salt and nutmeg; gently mix until the dough starts to come together. Gently knead on a floured work surface, dusting with flour if sticky. Divide the dough into 4 equal pieces.

2. Roll out one piece of dough into a ¾-inch-thick rope; keep the remaining dough covered with a damp kitchen towel. Cut the rope into 1-inch pieces and lightly dust with flour. Roll each piece against the tines of a fork or a gnocchi paddle to make ridges. Transfer the gnocchi to a lightly floured baking sheet. Repeat with the remaining dough.

3. Working in 2 batches, cook the gnocchi in a large pot of salted boiling water until they rise to the surface, about 2 minutes, then simmer until just cooked through, 1 to 2 minutes longer. Transfer to an ice bath and let cool. Drain well and let dry on paper towels.

4. Make the crab sauce In a large saucepan, bring the stock to a simmer. Add the crabs, cover partially and simmer over high heat until the liquid is reduced to 2 cups, 15 minutes. Strain into a bowl; discard the crabs.

5. In the same saucepan, heat the olive oil. Add the onion, fennel, garlic and crushed red pepper and cook over moderate heat, stirring, until tender, 5 minutes. Add the reduced crab stock, cream, vermouth, thyme, tarragon and bay leaf and bring to a boil. Simmer over moderately high heat until reduced to 2 cups, 15 minutes. Discard the tarragon and bay leaf.

6. In a medium skillet, heat half of the pan sauce. Add half of the gnocchi and cook over moderate heat until hot, 2 minutes. Add half of the crabmeat and 1½ tablespoons of the butter; cook until warmed through and the sauce is slightly thickened, 2 minutes. Season with salt and transfer to a platter. Repeat with the remaining pan sauce, gnocchi, crabmeat and butter. Garnish with the cheese and serve at once. —*John Besh*

WINE Fragrant, minerally Chardonnay: 2013 Joseph Drouhin Vaudon Chablis.

SESAME-PAPRIKA FREGOLA

DIY Pad Thai

Pad Thai may be a favorite takeout dish, but chefs **ANN REDDING** and **MATT DANZER** of the Thai restaurant Uncle Boons in New York City show how to make a much, much better version at home. The key: Prepare one portion at a time in a large skillet so the noodles absorb the sauce as quickly as possible without becoming gummy.

Shrimp Pad Thai

Total **35 min plus 2 hr soaking;** Serves **1**

Thai ingredients are available at specialty food stores and online from templeofthai.com. If you can't get head-on shrimp, regular shrimp will still be delicious here.

- 2 oz. flat rice noodles
- 1½ Tbsp. peanuts
- 3 Tbsp. canola oil
- 2 Tbsp. dried shrimp
- 7 head-on shrimp, peeled and deveined
- 2 Tbsp. diced extra-firm tofu (1 oz.)
- 1 Tbsp. minced garlic
- 1 Tbsp. finely chopped shallot
- 1 Tbsp. minced Thai preserved sweet radish
- 3 Tbsp. Pad Thai Sauce (recipe follows)
- 1 large egg, beaten
- 2 Tbsp. 1-inch pieces of garlic chives
  Bean sprouts and lime wedges, for serving

1. In a large bowl, cover the noodles with cold water and let stand for 2 hours. Drain well.

2. Meanwhile, preheat the oven to 375°. Spread the peanuts on a baking sheet and toast for 10 minutes, until fragrant. Let cool, then coarsely chop.

3. In a large nonstick skillet, heat 1 tablespoon of the oil. Add the dried shrimp and stir-fry over high heat for 1 minute. Using a slotted spoon, transfer the shrimp to a paper towel–lined plate. Let cool slightly, then coarsely chop the dried shrimp.

4. In the same skillet, cook the fresh shrimp over moderately high heat, turning once, until just white throughout, 2 minutes. Transfer the shrimp to a plate.

5. Add the remaining 2 tablespoons of oil to the skillet and heat until shimmering. Add the tofu, garlic, shallot and radish and stir-fry until the garlic and shallot are golden, 1 minute. Add the noodles and Pad Thai Sauce and stir-fry until most of the sauce is absorbed, 2 minutes. Add the egg and chives and cook, stirring, until the egg is cooked, 1 minute. Off the heat, stir in the peanuts and dried shrimp. Transfer to a plate, top with the fresh shrimp and serve with bean sprouts and lime wedges.

WINE Zesty, fragrant Riesling: 2012 Bründlmayer Kamptaler Terrassen.

Pad Thai Sauce

Makes **¾ cup**

In a medium saucepan, bring ¼ cup **tamarind concentrate**, ¼ cup **Asian fish sauce**, 1½ oz. coarsely grated **palm sugar**, 1 Tbsp. **distilled white vinegar**, ½ tsp. **shrimp paste in oil** and ¼ tsp. **Thai chile powder** to a boil, stirring to dissolve the sugar. Let cool. The sauce can be refrigerated for up to 1 week.

FOUR KEY STIR-FRY STEPS

COOK SHRIMP Sauté the head-on shrimp over moderately high heat, turning, until white throughout.

STIR-FRY AROMATICS Add the tofu, garlic, shallot and preserved radish and cook until golden.

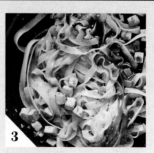

ADD NOODLES AND SAUCE Toss the noodles and Pad Thai Sauce in the pan until the liquid is absorbed.

SCRAMBLE EGG Quickly stir in the beaten egg, along with the chives, until cooked through.

BALANCING ACT
A good pad Thai balances sweet and salty, fresh and rich, chewy and crunchy.

Kitchen-Sink Soba Noodles

Total **50 min**; Serves **4**

Chef Susan Feniger of Mud Hen Tavern in Los Angeles also calls this recipe "clean out the refrigerator soba": Tossed in a spicy citrus-soy dressing, the noodle salad is adaptable to whatever vegetables you happen to have in your crisper.

NOODLES

- 1 **cup fresh orange juice**
- 2 **Tbsp. fresh lime juice**
- 3 **Tbsp. low-sodium soy sauce**
- 2 **Tbsp. hot sesame oil**
- 1 **Tbsp. unseasoned rice vinegar**
- 1 **tsp. sugar**
  Kosher salt
- 12 **oz. dried soba noodles**
- 1 **bunch of scallions, sliced**
- 2 **Tbsp. black sesame seeds**
- 7 **oz. drained extra-firm tofu, cut into ½-inch dice**

VEGETABLES

- 3 **Tbsp. vegetable oil**
- ½ **small onion, thinly sliced**
- ⅓ **head of broccoli, cut into florets**
- ⅓ **head of cauliflower, florets sliced**
- ½ **small fennel bulb—halved, cored and thinly sliced**
- 1 **carrot, thinly sliced**
- 1 **Tbsp. finely grated fresh ginger**
- 1 **Tbsp. unseasoned rice vinegar**
- 1 **bunch of Swiss chard, stems removed and leaves sliced**
  Sriracha, for serving

1. Prepare the noodles In a small skillet, simmer the orange juice over moderate heat until syrupy, 15 minutes. Scrape into a small bowl. Whisk in the lime juice, soy sauce, sesame oil, vinegar and sugar; season the vinaigrette with salt.

2. Meanwhile, in a large pot of salted boiling water, cook the soba noodles until al dente, about 4 minutes. Drain and rinse under cold water; shake off any water and blot dry. Transfer the noodles to a large bowl. Add the scallions and sesame seeds and toss with three-fourths of the vinaigrette. Add the tofu to the remaining vinaigrette.

3. Cook the vegetables In a large skillet or wok, heat the vegetable oil. Add the onion and stir-fry over high heat until starting to brown, about 3 minutes. Add the broccoli, cauliflower, fennel, carrot and ginger and stir-fry until the vegetables are tender, about 5 minutes. Add the vinegar and chard leaves and cook until wilted, about 2 minutes. Add the vegetables to the bowl with the soba, top with the tofu and serve with Sriracha. —*Susan Feniger*

WINE Ripe, juicy Oregon Pinot Gris: 2012 Erath.

Eggplant Noodle Salad

Total **20 min**; Serves **2**

To maximize Chinese eggplant's texture and flavor, F&W's Kay Chun steams thin slices, then tosses them with chilled glass noodles in a soy-ginger dressing.

- 4 **oz. glass noodles**
- 3 **Chinese eggplants (1 lb.), thinly sliced crosswise**
- 1 **Kirby cucumber, thinly sliced**
- 2 **Tbsp. canola oil**
- 1 **tsp. finely grated peeled fresh ginger**
- ½ **cup chopped basil**
- ¼ **cup soy sauce**
- ¼ **cup distilled white vinegar**
  Kosher salt and freshly ground pepper

1. In a medium saucepan of boiling water, cook the noodles until al dente, about 8 minutes. Drain, rinse under cold water until cool, then drain well. Transfer the noodles to bowls.

2. In a steamer basket set over a pot of boiling water, steam the eggplants until tender, about 8 minutes. Transfer to a medium bowl. Add the cucumber, oil, ginger, basil, soy sauce and vinegar; season with salt and pepper and toss. Serve over the noodles. —*Kay Chun*

Soba Noodles with Miso-Roasted Tomatoes

Total **30 min**; Serves **4**

Roasting cherry tomatoes in a mix of miso, ginger, sesame, lime juice and honey creates a tangy, bright sauce for soba noodles; try adding shrimp for an even more substantial dish.

- ⅓ **cup canola oil**
- 3 **Tbsp. unseasoned rice vinegar**
- 2 **Tbsp. light yellow miso**
- 1 **Tbsp. minced peeled fresh ginger**
- 1 **Tbsp. toasted sesame oil**
- 1 **Tbsp. honey**
- 2 **tsp. finely grated lime zest**
- 2 **Tbsp. fresh lime juice**
  Kosher salt
- 2 **pints cherry tomatoes**
- 8 **oz. dried soba noodles**
- 4 **scallions, thinly sliced**
- 1 **Tbsp. toasted sesame seeds**

1. Preheat the oven to 425°. In a small bowl, whisk the canola oil, vinegar, miso, ginger, sesame oil, honey, lime zest and lime juice until smooth. Season the miso dressing with salt.

2. On a rimmed baking sheet, toss the tomatoes with 3 tablespoons of the miso dressing and season with salt. Roast for 20 minutes, stirring, until the tomatoes are charred in spots. Scrape into a large bowl.

3. Cook the soba in a pot of boiling water just until al dente, about 4 minutes. Drain and cool under cold running water. Add the soba, scallions and half of the remaining dressing to the tomatoes and toss well. Season with salt, transfer to a platter and garnish with the sesame seeds. Serve with the remaining dressing. —*Ashley Rodriguez*

WINE Brisk Australian Riesling: 2013 Yalumba Y Series.

SOBA NOODLES WITH
MISO-ROASTED TOMATOES

MUSSELS WITH PANCETTA
AND CRÈME FRAÎCHE
Recipe, page 135

Seafood

PAGE NUMBERS IN RED INDICATE F&W STAFF FAVORITES

Salmon with Mashed Peas and Tarragon Butter

◔ Total **45 min**; Serves **4**

At the Casa Marín winery in Chile's San Antonio Valley, peas mashed with cream make a luscious base for grilled salmon.

- **1 lb. frozen peas (about 3 cups)**
- **7 Tbsp. cold unsalted butter, 6 Tbsp. cubed**
- **½ cup heavy cream**
- **Kosher salt and freshly ground pepper**
- **1 cup dry white wine**
- **2 tsp. fresh lemon juice**
- **2 Tbsp. slivered tarragon**
- **Four 6-oz. salmon fillets with skin**
- **2 Tbsp. extra-virgin olive oil**

1. In a large saucepan of boiling water, cook the peas until tender, 3 to 4 minutes; drain. In the same saucepan, melt 1 tablespoon of the butter in the cream. Add the peas and mash with a potato masher until chunky. Season with salt and pepper and keep warm.

2. In a small saucepan, simmer the wine with the lemon juice over moderate heat until reduced to 1 tablespoon, 8 to 10 minutes. Reduce the heat to low and whisk in the remaining 6 tablespoons of butter, one cube at a time, until the sauce is thickened. Whisk in the tarragon and season with salt and pepper. Transfer the sauce to a small bowl and keep warm.

3. Heat a grill pan. Rub the salmon with the olive oil; season with salt and pepper. Grill skin side down over moderate heat, turning once, until browned and just cooked through, 10 to 12 minutes. Spoon the mashed peas onto plates and top with the salmon, skin side up. Spoon the tarragon-butter sauce over the salmon and serve. —*Gerardo Valenzuela*

WINE Wild berry–scented Pinot Noir: 2009 Casa Marín Lo Abarca Hills Vineyard.

Mustard Salmon with Cannellini Bean Ragù

Total **50 min**; Serves **4**

RAGÙ

- **3 Tbsp. extra-virgin olive oil**
- **1 large shallot, minced**
- **2 garlic cloves, minced**
- **2 tomatoes, chopped**
- **2 tsp. finely chopped thyme**
- **Salt and pepper**
- **Two 15-oz. cans cannellini beans, rinsed and drained**
- **¾ cup chicken stock or low-sodium broth**
- **One ¾-lb. head of escarole, dark green leaves discarded and remaining leaves torn**
- **2 oz. prosciutto, chopped**
- **½ tsp. finely grated lemon zest**

SALMON

- **Extra-virgin olive oil**
- **Four 6-oz. skinless salmon fillets**
- **Salt and pepper**
- **1½ Tbsp. Dijon mustard**
- **1½ Tbsp. whole-grain mustard**
- **2 tsp. dry white wine**
- **2 garlic cloves, minced**
- **1 tsp. finely chopped thyme**

1. **Make the ragù** In a large, deep skillet, combine the oil, shallot and garlic and cook over moderate heat, stirring, until softened, 3 minutes. Add the tomatoes, thyme and a pinch each of salt and pepper. Cook, stirring, until the tomatoes start to break down, 4 minutes. Add the beans and stock and simmer until the beans are hot, 2 minutes. Add the escarole, prosciutto and lemon zest and cook over moderately high heat, stirring, until the escarole is just wilted, 4 minutes; if the bean ragù is too thick, add a little water.

2. **Prepare the salmon** Preheat the broiler. Line a rimmed baking sheet with foil and brush it with oil. Season the fish with salt and pepper and set on the baking sheet. In a small bowl, whisk both mustards with the wine, 2 teaspoons of oil, the garlic, thyme and a pinch each of salt and pepper. Broil the salmon 6 inches from the heat for 2 minutes, until the top just starts to brown. Spoon the mustard on the salmon and broil for 5 minutes, until the fish is nearly cooked through and the top is browned. Spoon the bean ragù into bowls, top with the fish and serve. —*Giada De Laurentiis*

WINE Full-bodied Chardonnay from Sonoma: 2012 La Crema Sonoma Coast.

Arctic Char with Charmoula

◔ Total **40 min**; Serves **4**

Roasted garlic *charmoula*—a classic North African marinade and sauce made with fresh herbs and spices—is excellent with a rich fish like arctic char or salmon.

- **3 unpeeled garlic cloves**
- **⅓ cup plus 2 Tbsp. extra-virgin olive oil**
- **¼ cup flat-leaf parsley leaves**
- **¼ cup cilantro leaves**
- **2 Tbsp. chopped green olives**
- **1 Tbsp. fresh lemon juice**
- **¼ tsp. ground cumin**
- **¼ tsp. paprika**
- **Kosher salt**
- **Four 5-oz. arctic char or salmon fillets with skin**
- **Pepper**

1. In a small skillet, toast the garlic over moderate heat, stirring occasionally, until the skins blacken, 7 to 8 minutes. Let cool slightly, then discard the skins.

2. In a food processor, puree ⅓ cup of the oil with the garlic, parsley, cilantro, olives, lemon juice, cumin and paprika until smooth. Transfer the *charmoula* to a bowl and season with salt.

3. In a large nonstick skillet, heat the remaining 2 tablespoons of oil. Season the fish with salt and pepper, place it skin side down in the skillet and cook over moderately high heat until the skin is golden, about 3 minutes. Flip the fish and cook just until it flakes easily, 2 to 3 minutes longer. Drain briefly on paper towels and serve with the *charmoula*. —*Jessica Koslow*

WINE Citrusy New Zealand Sauvignon Blanc: 2013 Dog Point.

ARCTIC CHAR WITH CHARMOULA

Salmon with Pickled Carrots and Bacon-Fried Potatoes

Total **1 hr** plus overnight marinating
Serves **4**

- ⅓ cup Dijon mustard
- 3 Tbsp. whole-grain mustard
- 3 Tbsp. honey
- 3 Tbsp. white miso
- ¼ cup plus 1 Tbsp. red wine vinegar
- Four 6-oz. salmon fillets with skin
- 1 tsp. pickling spice
- ½ tsp. sugar
- Salt
- ½ lb. medium carrots, shaved lengthwise with a vegetable peeler
- ¼ lb. bacon, finely chopped
- 1¼ lbs. baking potatoes, peeled and cut into ¾-inch dice
- Pepper
- 2 Tbsp. chopped chives
- 1 Tbsp. canola oil

1. In a small baking dish, whisk both mustards with the honey, miso, 1 tablespoon of the vinegar and 1 tablespoon of water. Add the salmon fillets and turn to coat. Cover and refrigerate overnight.

2. Meanwhile, in a small saucepan, combine ¼ cup of water and the remaining ¼ cup of vinegar with the pickling spice, sugar and 1 teaspoon of salt. Bring just to a simmer. Let cool completely, then transfer to a bowl. Add the carrot ribbons and toss to coat. Cover and refrigerate for at least 4 hours or overnight; toss occasionally.

3. Preheat the oven to 350°. In a large ovenproof skillet, cook the bacon over moderate heat until browned, about 7 minutes. Using a slotted spoon, transfer the bacon to paper towels to drain. Add the potatoes to the skillet and cook over moderately high heat until browned on the bottom, about 3 minutes. Toss the potatoes, season with salt and pepper and bake in the oven for about 15 minutes, until tender. Stir in the bacon and chives and transfer to a plate; keep warm. Leave the oven on; wipe out the skillet.

4. Remove the salmon fillets from the baking dish; scrape off any excess marinade. In the skillet, heat the oil until shimmering. Add the fillets skin side down and cook over moderate heat until browned and crisp, about 4 minutes. Turn and cook until browned on the bottom, 2 to 3 minutes. Transfer the skillet to the oven and bake for 5 minutes, until the salmon is medium. Serve the salmon with the carrots and the potatoes. —*Akiko Moorman*

WINE Fragrant California Pinot Noir: 2012 Sandhi Sta. Rita Hills.

Crispy Salmon with Fennel Slaw

Active **30 min**; Total **1 hr**; Serves **4**

The skin on this fish is as crisp as a potato chip. The secret: cooking the salmon fillets entirely skin side down—no flipping necessary.

- 1 large fennel bulb—halved lengthwise, cored and very thinly sliced crosswise
- ¼ cup very thinly sliced red onion
- 3 Tbsp. fresh lemon juice
- 2 Tbsp. finely chopped dill
- 2½ Tbsp. extra-virgin olive oil
- Kosher salt
- Four 6-oz. salmon fillets with skin

1. In a large bowl, toss the fennel with the onion, lemon juice, dill and 2 tablespoons of the oil; season with salt. Let the slaw stand at room temperature for 45 minutes.

2. Preheat the oven to 350°. Season the salmon with salt. In an ovenproof skillet, heat the remaining 1½ teaspoons of oil until shimmering. Add the salmon fillets skin side down and, using a spatula, gently press the fillets to flatten. Cook over moderately high heat until the skin is crisp and the salmon is rare within, 5 minutes. Transfer the skillet to the oven and bake until the salmon is nearly cooked through, 2 minutes; transfer to plates, skin side up. Serve with the fennel slaw. —*Hugh Acheson*

WINE Lively, citrusy Pinot Grigio: 2012 Marco Felluga Collio Mongris.

Grape Leaf–Wrapped Salmon with Serrano-Scallion Sauce

⏱ Total **45 min**; Serves **4**

- 16 large jarred grape leaves, drained and patted dry
- 1 cup orange or yellow grape tomatoes, halved
- 5 scallions, julienned, plus 2 Tbsp. minced scallion
- 3 serranos with seeds, halved and thinly sliced
- Salt and pepper
- Four 6-oz. skinless salmon fillets
- 2 Tbsp. unsalted butter
- ¼ cup Champagne vinegar
- ½ cup heavy cream

1. Preheat the oven to 450° and line a large rimmed baking sheet with parchment paper. Arrange the grape leaves in groups of 4 on a work surface, overlapping them slightly. Mound the tomatoes, three-fourths of the julienned scallions and one-third of the sliced serranos in the center of the grape leaves and season lightly with salt and pepper. Season the salmon fillets with salt and pepper and place them on top, then wrap the grape leaves around the fish. Carefully turn the packets seam side down on the prepared baking sheet and roast for 10 to 12 minutes, until the salmon is medium within. Transfer the packets to plates.

2. Meanwhile, in a small saucepan, melt the butter. Add the minced scallion and cook over moderate heat, stirring, until softened, about 2 minutes. Add the vinegar and bring to a boil. Simmer over moderately high heat until reduced by half, about 3 minutes. Whisk in the cream and bring just to a simmer, then cook over moderately high heat, whisking occasionally, until slightly thickened, about 2 minutes. Stir in the remaining serranos and season the sauce with salt and pepper.

3. Cut open the salmon packets and drizzle the sauce over the fish. Garnish with the remaining julienned scallions and serve right away. —*Justin Chapple*

WINE Vivid, crisp Austrian Riesling: 2012 Domäne Wachau Federspiel Terrassen.

Smoky Salmon with Miso-Dressed Vegetables

Total **1 hr**; Serves **4**

This skillet-smoking method from chef Michael Cimarusti of Connie & Ted's in Los Angeles is amazingly quick. Wood chips can be found at many supermarkets and some Whole Foods stores.

- ¼ cup white miso
- ¼ cup chicken stock
- 3 Tbsp. mirin
- 2 Tbsp. unseasoned rice vinegar
- ¾ tsp. finely grated peeled ginger
- ¼ tsp. finely grated garlic
- 2 tsp. soy sauce
- 3 Tbsp. canola oil
- Four 6-oz. skinless center-cut salmon fillets, about 1 inch thick
- Kosher salt
- Piment d'Espelette (see Note)
- ¼ cup small hardwood chips, such as hickory or applewood
- ¼ lb. shiitake mushrooms, stems discarded and caps thinly sliced
- ½ small onion, thinly sliced
- ½ small fennel bulb—halved, cored and thinly sliced
- 4 medium carrots, thinly sliced on the diagonal
- 4 baby turnips or large radishes, thinly sliced
- 2 cups lightly packed baby spinach

1. In a saucepan, cook the miso, stock, mirin, vinegar, ginger and garlic over moderate heat, whisking, until hot, 3 minutes. Whisk in the soy; remove from the heat.

2. In a large cast-iron skillet, heat 1 tablespoon of the oil. Season the salmon with salt and piment d'Espelette; add to the skillet and cook over high heat, turning once, until lightly browned, 2 minutes total. Transfer to a plate.

3. Working in a well-ventilated kitchen, wipe out the skillet and add the hardwood chips. Cook the chips over high heat until they start to smoke, 5 minutes. Place a wire rack over the skillet and set the salmon on it. Tent the salmon with a large sheet of heavy-duty foil and smoke for 5 minutes, until the salmon is medium within. Transfer the salmon to a plate.

4. Meanwhile, in another large skillet, heat the remaining 2 tablespoons of oil. Add the shiitake and onion and cook over moderately high heat, tossing, until browned in spots and just starting to soften, 4 minutes. Add the fennel and carrots and cook, tossing, until crisp-tender, 2 minutes. Add the turnips and spinach and cook, tossing, until the spinach is just wilted, 1 minute. Season with salt and sprinkle lightly with piment d'Espelette; add 1 tablespoon of the miso dressing and toss well. Transfer to plates. Flake the salmon, scatter it over the salad and serve, passing the remaining dressing at the table. —*Michael Cimarusti*

NOTE Piment d'Espelette, a mildly spicy red pepper, is available at specialty food shops and lepicerie.com.

WINE Ripe, dry German Riesling: 2012 Dr. Bürklin-Wolf.

Deviled Salmon

Active **15 min**; Total **1 hr 30 min**; Serves **4**

Hot sauce, chile and pickled pepper all add heat to the sauce that chef Eli Kulp brushes on the salmon fillets he serves at a.kitchen in Philadelphia. The sauce caramelizes as it cooks, so be sure to grill the fish over a not-too-hot fire to avoid overcharring.

- 1 ancho chile, stemmed and seeded
- 2 Tbsp. Sriracha
- 1 Tbsp. *sambal oelek* or other Asian chile sauce
- 1 Tbsp. extra-virgin olive oil
- 1 Tbsp. fresh lemon juice
- 2 garlic cloves, minced
- 1 hot pickled cherry pepper— stemmed, seeded and minced, plus 1 Tbsp. brine from the jar
- Four 6-oz. skinless salmon fillets, about 1 inch thick

1. In a small bowl, cover the ancho chile with hot water and let stand until softened, about 20 minutes. Drain and mince the ancho. In the same bowl, whisk the ancho with all of the remaining ingredients except the salmon.

2. Add all but ¼ cup of the marinade to a baking dish. Add the salmon fillets and turn to coat. Cover and refrigerate the salmon for at least 1 hour and up to 4 hours.

3. Light a grill. Grill the salmon over moderate heat, turning once, until lightly charred and nearly cooked through, 6 to 8 minutes. Transfer the salmon to plates and serve with the reserved marinade. —*Eli Kulp*

WINE Lively, full-bodied South African rosé: 2013 Mulderbosch.

Maple-Dijon Salmon Skewers

Total **30 min**; Serves **8**

When it's in season, from early spring to late fall, wild Alaskan king salmon from the Pacific is ideal for these simple, delicious, party-perfect skewers.

- 2 Tbsp. pure maple syrup
- 2 Tbsp. fresh lemon juice
- 1 Tbsp. Dijon mustard
- 1 Tbsp. whole-grain mustard
- 3 Tbsp. grapeseed or vegetable oil
- 2¼ lbs. skinless salmon fillet, cut into 1½-inch pieces
- 16 six-inch metal skewers, or wooden skewers soaked in water for 1 hour
- Salt and pepper

1. In a small bowl, whisk the maple syrup with the lemon juice, both mustards and 1 tablespoon of the grapeseed oil.

2. Thread the salmon onto skewers and season all over with salt and pepper. In a large cast-iron skillet, heat 1 tablespoon of oil until shimmering. Add half of the skewers and cook over moderate heat until browned on the bottom, 1 to 2 minutes. Flip the skewers and cook, basting with the mustard glaze and turning occasionally, until glazed and nearly cooked through, about 5 minutes total. Repeat with the remaining oil and skewers. Transfer to a platter and serve right away. —*Ali Banks*

WINE Juicy, light-bodied Beaujolais: 2013 Château Thivin Côte de Brouilly.

Salsa Verde Swordfish Skewers

Active **45 min**; Total **1 hr 45 min**
Serves **4**

Fresh bay leaves impart a lovely fragrance to these grilled skewers from chef Chad Colby of Chi Spacca in Los Angeles. You can find fresh bay leaves in South Asian markets or specialty food shops.

- 1 **cup flat-leaf parsley leaves**
- 10 **garlic cloves, crushed**
- 1 **tsp. crushed red pepper**
- ½ **cup extra-virgin olive oil**
  Salt and freshly ground black pepper
- 28 **fresh bay leaves (1 cup)**
- 1½ **lbs. swordfish, cut into 1½-inch pieces**
- 1 **medium zucchini, very thinly sliced lengthwise on a mandoline**
- 2 **lemons, halved crosswise**

1. In a blender or mini food processor, pulse the parsley, garlic, crushed red pepper and olive oil to a thick puree. Season with salt and black pepper and transfer the sauce to a bowl.

2. Onto each of 4 long skewers, alternately thread a bay leaf, a piece of fish, another bay leaf and a slice of zucchini, repeating until each skewer has 3 pieces of fish, 3 slices of zucchini and 7 bay leaves. Season the skewers with salt and black pepper and brush all over with the parsley sauce. Cover and refrigerate for 1 hour.

3. Light a grill or heat a grill pan. Grill the skewers over moderate heat, turning, until the fish is lightly browned and cooked through, about 6 minutes. Transfer to a platter. Meanwhile, grill the lemon halves cut side down until charred, about 2 minutes. Serve the skewers with the grilled lemons. Discard the bay leaves. —*Chad Colby*

WINE Herby, citrusy Vermentino: 2012 Bisson Vignaerta.

Grilled Swordfish with Miso Sauce

⏱ Total **45 min**; Serves **4**

MISO SAUCE

- 2 **oz. curly spinach, thick stems discarded (2 packed cups)**
- 1 **Tbsp. drained pickled ginger**
- ⅓ **cup white miso**
- 1½ **Tbsp. mirin**
- ½ **Tbsp. sansho powder (see Note)**

SWORDFISH

- ¼ **cup plus 2 Tbsp. soy sauce**
- 3 **Tbsp. sake**
- 3 **Tbsp. mirin**
  Two 1-inch-thick swordfish steaks (1½ lbs.)
  Canola oil, for oiling the grate
  Kosher salt and pepper
  Sesame seeds, for garnish

1. Make the sauce Fill a bowl with ice water. In a large saucepan of salted boiling water, blanch the spinach until tender and bright green, 1 minute. Drain, then transfer to the ice bath. Drain the spinach and squeeze dry.

2. In a blender, puree the spinach, pickled ginger, miso, mirin and sansho powder with 2 tablespoons of water until smooth and spreadable.

3. Prepare the swordfish In a small bowl, whisk the soy, sake and mirin. Place the fish in a resealable plastic bag and pour in half of the marinade. Seal and let marinate at room temperature for 15 minutes.

4. Meanwhile, in a small saucepan, simmer the remaining marinade over moderate heat until reduced to a glaze.

5. Light a grill and oil the grate. Season the swordfish with salt and pepper and grill over moderate heat, turning once, until just white throughout; baste with the glaze during the last minute or two of grilling. Cut each swordfish steak in half.

6. Dollop the miso sauce on plates and top with the swordfish steaks. Garnish with sesame seeds and serve. —*Masa Miyake*

NOTE Sansho powder, or Japanese pepper, has a citrusy, minty aroma and flavor. It's available at Japanese markets and online at amazon.com.

BEER Crisp, fragrant Japanese craft beer: Ozeno Yukidoke IPA.

Grilled Swordfish with Cilantro-Chile Vinaigrette

⏱ Total **30 min**; Serves **4**

Eli Sussman, cookbook author and the chef at Brooklyn's Mile End Delicatessen, tops meaty grilled swordfish steaks with a smoky Moroccan herb sauce.

- **Four 8-oz. swordfish steaks, about ½ inch thick**
- ½ **cup plus 2 Tbsp. extra-virgin olive oil**
  Kosher salt and black pepper
- 2 **Tbsp. unsalted butter**
- 1½ **cups coarsely chopped cilantro leaves and stems**
- ¾ **cup coarsely chopped parsley leaves and stems**
- 2 **garlic cloves, minced**
- 2 **Tbsp. fresh lemon juice**
- 2 **small Fresno or red jalapeño chiles, minced**
  Pinch of saffron threads
- ¼ **tsp. crushed red pepper**
- ¾ **tsp. pimentón de la Vera (smoked paprika)**
- ¼ **tsp. cayenne pepper**

1. Heat a grill pan. Brush the fish with 2 tablespoons of the olive oil and season with salt and black pepper. In 2 batches, cook the fish over moderate heat until browned on one side, about 3 minutes. Flip the swordfish steaks and top each with ½ tablespoon of butter. Grill until the fish is just cooked through, about 2 minutes longer. Transfer to plates.

2. Meanwhile, in a medium bowl, mix the remaining ½ cup of olive oil with the remaining ingredients and season the vinaigrette with salt and black pepper.

3. Spoon the vinaigrette over the swordfish and serve. —*Eli Sussman*

WINE Aromatic white blend: 2012 Domaine de la Becassonne Côtes du Rhône Blanc.

SALSA VERDE SWORDFISH SKEWERS

Tuna Steaks with Mustard Dressing and Mashed Taro

Active **30 min**; Total **1 hr**; Serves **4**

Jose Enrique, chef at his eponymous restaurant in San Juan, Puerto Rico, created this dish with bonito, a tuna-like fish he often catches. Fresh tuna steaks are a great substitute. The phenomenal dressing requires only three ingredients: mustard, cilantro and oil.

- ¼ cup plus 2 Tbsp. Dijon mustard
- ¼ cup plus 2 Tbsp. extra-virgin olive oil
- Kosher salt and pepper
- ½ cup finely chopped cilantro, plus more for garnish
- Four 6-oz. tuna steaks, about 1 inch thick
- 1½ lbs. fresh taro, peeled and cut into 1-inch pieces
- ½ cup heavy cream
- ¼ cup milk
- 3 Tbsp. unsalted butter

1. In a baking dish, whisk ¼ cup of the mustard with 2 tablespoons of the oil and a pinch each of salt and pepper. Stir in ¼ cup of the cilantro. Add the tuna and turn to coat. Cover and refrigerate for 30 minutes.

2. Meanwhile, in a large saucepan, cover the taro with water and bring to a boil. Add a large pinch of salt and simmer over moderate heat until very tender, about 25 minutes. Drain well and return to the saucepan. Add the cream, milk and butter and mash. Season generously with salt and pepper; keep warm.

3. In a small bowl, whisk the remaining ¼ cup of oil and 2 tablespoons of mustard with 2 tablespoons of water. Stir in the remaining ¼ cup of cilantro and season the dressing with salt and pepper.

4. Light a grill or heat a grill pan. Scrape the marinade off the tuna and season the steaks with salt and pepper. Grill over high heat, turning once, until lightly charred outside and rare within, 2 to 3 minutes per side. Transfer the tuna to a platter and garnish with cilantro. Serve the tuna with the mashed taro, passing the mustard dressing at the table. —*Jose Enrique*

WINE Unoaked California Chardonnay: 2013 Chamisal Stainless.

Poached Tuna with Kumquats and Jalapeño

Total **20 min**; Serves **2**

This incredibly quick and easy dish from New Orleans chef Donald Link features tuna steaks poached until rare in a bright, buttery sauce infused with lime, kumquats, jalapeños and mint. Doubled or tripled, it would make an excellent dinner-party dish.

- Two 6-oz. tuna steaks, about 1¼ inches thick
- Kosher salt
- 4 Tbsp. unsalted butter
- ¼ cup extra-virgin olive oil
- 2 Tbsp. fresh lime juice
- 1 small jalapeño—stemmed, seeded and minced
- 4 kumquats, thinly sliced
- ¼ cup mint leaves, torn

1. Season the tuna steaks with salt. In a medium saucepan, melt the butter in the olive oil and lime juice. Stir in the minced jalapeño and sliced kumquats. Add the tuna steaks and cook them over moderate heat, turning once, until they're rare, about 4 minutes.

2. Transfer the tuna steaks to a carving board and slice them ⅓ inch thick, then arrange them on plates. Stir the torn mint into the sauce, spoon over the tuna and serve. —*Donald Link*

WINE Zippy New Zealand Sauvignon Blanc: 2013 Yealands.

Cod Tempura with Cape Malay Curry Sauce

Active **1 hr**; Total **1 hr 30 min**
Serves **4**

At Tokara in Stellenbosch, South Africa, chef Richard Carstens blends the clever spicing of South Africa's Cape Malay cooking and the Dutch affection for dried fruits with Asian and French influences. This crisp, sweet and tangy fish tempura with two sauces is a perfect example.

CAPE MALAY CURRY SAUCE

- 2 tsp. canola oil
- ¼ tsp. curry powder
- ¼ tsp. black peppercorns
- ⅛ tsp. ground turmeric
- 1 small shallot, thinly sliced
- 1½ tsp. chopped peeled fresh ginger
- ½ cup clam juice
- 3 Tbsp. white wine vinegar
- 1 small bay leaf
- 1½ tsp. sugar
- 4 Tbsp. cold unsalted butter, cubed

APRICOT-SAKE PUREE

- ¼ cup dry sake
- 4 dried apricots, chopped
- 1½ Tbsp. unseasoned rice vinegar
- 1½ tsp. sugar
- Pinch of kosher salt

COD TEMPURA

- Vegetable oil, for frying
- ½ cup all-purpose flour
- ¾ cup tempura flour (see Note)
- ¾ cup cold sparkling water
- 3 ice cubes
- Four 4-oz. skinless cod fillets
- Kosher salt
- Cubed fresh pineapple, small cilantro leaves and steamed basmati rice, for serving

1. Make the Cape Malay curry sauce
In a small saucepan, heat the canola oil. Add the curry powder, peppercorns and turmeric and cook over moderately low heat, stirring, until fragrant, about 2 minutes. Add the shallot and ginger and cook, stirring, until softened, about 3 minutes. Add the clam juice, vinegar, bay leaf and sugar and bring to a simmer. Cook over moderate heat until the sauce is reduced by half, 8 to 10 minutes. Discard the bay leaf. Transfer the sauce to a blender and, with the machine on, add the butter one cube at a time until incorporated and the sauce is thickened. Transfer the sauce to a small bowl and keep warm.

2. Make the apricot-sake puree In a small saucepan, heat the sake until warm. Add the apricots and let stand at room temperature until softened, about 30 minutes. In a mini food processor, puree the apricots, sake, vinegar, sugar, salt and 1½ teaspoons of water. Strain the puree through a sieve.

3. Make the tempura In a medium enameled cast-iron casserole or heavy saucepan, heat 2 inches of oil to 400°. Set a rack over a baking sheet. Spread the all-purpose flour in a shallow bowl. In a large bowl, combine the tempura flour, sparkling water and ice cubes and whisk until barely blended, with some small lumps remaining. Season the fish with salt, then dredge in the all-purpose flour, dusting off the excess. Dip the fish in the tempura batter, letting the excess drip off. Fry the fish, turning occasionally, until golden, crisp and cooked through, 5 to 7 minutes. Transfer the fish to the rack to drain briefly.

4. Spoon some of the Cape Malay sauce in the center of each plate and top with the cod tempura. Spoon the apricot puree on one side of the fish and arrange some pineapple on the other. Garnish with cilantro and serve with rice. —*Richard Carstens*

NOTE Tempura flour is a specially blended coating mix based on soft wheat flour and potato starch or cornstarch. It's available at supermarkets and Asian specialty shops.

WINE Passion fruit–inflected South African Chardonnay: 2012 Tokara.

Grilled Black Cod Lettuce Wraps with Pickled Cucumber
⏱ Total **45 min**; Serves **4 as a first course**

Los Angeles chef and Peru native Ricardo Zarate uses paiche (pronounced pie-chay), a firm, white freshwater fish from South America, in these tasty, healthy lettuce wraps. Black cod is a fine substitute.

- ¼ **cup unseasoned rice vinegar**
- ¼ **cup sugar**
- ⅓ **cup peeled and finely chopped cucumber**
- 3 **Tbsp. *shiro* (white) miso**
- 2 **chipotle chiles in adobo**
- 1 **Tbsp. honey**
- 1 **Tbsp. fresh lime juice**
- 1 **Tbsp. red wine vinegar**
- ½ **tsp. ground cumin**
- ½ **tsp. dried oregano**
- 1 **Tbsp. canola oil**
- 1 **lb. skinless paiche or black cod, cut into 8 equal pieces**
  Salt
- 8 **butter lettuce leaf cups**
  Sweet potato chips, for garnish

1. In a small saucepan, combine the rice vinegar and sugar with ¼ cup of water and warm over moderate heat, stirring, just until the sugar dissolves. Transfer the pickling liquid to a small bowl and add the cucumber. Refrigerate for 30 minutes, then drain and discard the brine.

2. Meanwhile, in a food processor or blender, combine the *shiro* miso, chipotles, honey, lime juice, red wine vinegar, cumin and oregano and puree until a smooth sauce forms.

3. Heat a grill pan and brush with the canola oil. Lightly season the fish with salt. Grill over moderate heat, basting the fish liberally with the sauce and turning once, until the fish is golden and cooked through, 10 to 12 minutes.

4. Arrange the lettuce cups on a platter. Set the fish in the lettuce cups. Top with the pickled cucumber, garnish with sweet potato chips and serve immediately. —*Ricardo Zarate*

WINE Bright, medium-bodied Sauvignon Blanc from Chile: 2012 Casas del Bosque.

Olive Oil–Poached Hake on Sautéed Zucchini with Tomatoes
⏱ Total **40 min**; Serves **4**

Top Chef Season 11 winner Nicholas Elmi grew up in New England, and he's always loved every member of the cod family. That includes haddock, pollock and especially hake, which is a little firmer than the others. "Whenever you see nice, fresh hake, buy it!" he says. Gently poaching the fillets in extra-virgin olive oil makes them silky.

- 2 **tomatoes (¾ lb.)**
- 2 **cups plus 2 Tbsp. extra-virgin olive oil**
- 2 **zucchini—quartered lengthwise, seeded and cut into ¼-inch dice**
- ¼ **tsp. finely grated lemon zest**
- 2 **tsp. fresh lemon juice**
- ¼ **tsp. sherry vinegar**
  Salt
  Four 6-oz. skinless hake fillets

1. Bring a saucepan of water to a boil. Score an X in the bottom of each tomato and blanch them in the boiling water for 30 seconds. Drain and cool the tomatoes under cold running water. Peel, seed and cut the tomatoes into ¼-inch dice; transfer to a medium bowl.

2. In a small skillet, heat 2 tablespoons of the olive oil. Add the zucchini and cook over moderate heat, stirring occasionally, until just tender, 3 to 4 minutes. Add the zucchini to the tomatoes. Stir in the lemon zest, lemon juice and sherry vinegar and season with salt. Mix gently and keep warm.

3. In a large, heavy saucepan, heat the remaining 2 cups of olive oil over moderate heat to 180°. Season the hake with salt and poach in the olive oil until just white throughout, 10 to 12 minutes. Remove the fish with a slotted spatula and drain briefly on paper towels. Season with salt. Spoon the zucchini mixture into shallow bowls, set the fish on top and serve. —*Nicholas Elmi*

WINE Juicy, fruit-forward Spanish rosé: 2012 Edetària Vinya d'Irto Rosat.

Pimentón-Roasted Red Snapper with Herb Salad

Active **40 min**; Total **1 hr 15 min**; Serves **4**

¼ cup plus 1 Tbsp. extra-virgin olive oil

2 tsp. pimentón de la Vera (sweet smoked Spanish paprika)

1 tsp. finely grated lemon zest, plus ½ lemon, sliced

6 cups kosher salt (30 oz.), plus more for seasoning

3 large egg whites, beaten

One 2-lb. cleaned and scaled red snapper

Ground black pepper

3 large bay leaves

5 medium celery ribs, thinly sliced on the diagonal

1 cup celery leaves

1 cup parsley leaves

½ cup tarragon leaves

2 Tbsp. fresh lemon juice

1. Preheat the oven to 425°. In a small bowl, whisk 3 tablespoons of the olive oil with the pimentón and lemon zest. In a large bowl, mix the 6 cups of kosher salt with the egg whites and ½ cup of water until it resembles moist sand.

2. Spread a ¼-inch-thick layer of the salt mixture in the center of a large rimmed baking sheet. Season the fish inside and out with black pepper and brush all over with the pimentón oil. Stuff the cavity with the lemon slices and bay leaves and lay the snapper on the salt. Mound the remaining salt mixture on top, lightly packing it to completely cover the fish.

3. Bake the fish for about 30 minutes, until an instant-read thermometer inserted into the fish through the salt registers 135°. Remove from the oven and let stand for 10 minutes. Crack the salt crust and discard it. Brush off any excess salt and transfer the fish to a platter.

4. In a large bowl, toss the celery with the celery leaves, parsley, tarragon, lemon juice and the remaining 2 tablespoons of olive oil. Season the salad with salt and pepper and serve alongside the fish. —*Justin Chapple*

WINE Herb-scented Loire Sauvignon Blanc: 2012 Patient Cottat Le Grand Caillou.

Whole Red Snapper with Roasted Tomato Sauce

Total **35 min**; Serves **4**

Chef Joshua Walker of Xiao Bao Biscuit in Charleston, South Carolina, serves his gingery steamed snapper with a roasted tomato sauce called *jeow*. "It's like a Laotian salsa," he says.

ROASTED TOMATO SAUCE

3 large unpeeled garlic cloves

5 small Thai chiles

One 1-lb. tomato, cored and quartered

2 tsp. Asian fish sauce

Kosher salt

STEAMED FISH

One 1¾- to 2-lb. cleaned and scaled red snapper

Kosher salt

2 oz. fresh ginger, peeled and julienned (½ cup)

One 4-inch piece of lemongrass, tender inner bulb only, julienned

2 fresh kaffir lime leaves

3 Tbsp. Asian fish sauce

3 Tbsp. fresh lime juice

2 tsp. sugar

4 small Thai chiles, sliced

Basil leaves, for garnish

White rice, for serving

1. Make the tomato sauce In a medium skillet, toast the garlic, chiles and three-quarters of the tomato over moderately high heat, turning, until lightly charred all over, 3 minutes for the garlic and chiles and 7 minutes for the tomato; let cool and discard the garlic peels. Transfer to a blender, add the fish sauce and remaining tomato and puree until nearly smooth. Season the tomato sauce with salt.

2. Steam the fish Fill a flameproof medium roasting pan with 1 inch of water and set a rack in the pan. Make 5 parallel slashes to the bone on each side of the snapper. Lightly season the fish inside and out with salt. Stuff the ginger in the slashes, then stuff any remaining ginger inside the cavity along with the lemongrass and lime leaves. Set the fish on a large rimmed heatproof plate and set it on the rack; the water should not touch the plate.

3. In a bowl, whisk the fish sauce, lime juice, sugar and chiles. Pour the sauce over the fish. Cover the pan tightly with foil and bring the water to a boil. Steam the fish until opaque throughout and the meat flakes easily, 10 to 12 minutes. Carefully remove the foil and transfer the fish and its juices to a platter. Garnish with basil; serve with the tomato sauce and rice. —*Joshua Walker*

WINE Berry-rich French rosé: 2013 Bieler Père et Fils Sabine.

Red Snapper with Asparagus and Chorizo

Total **30 min**; Serves **4**

Two 12-oz. red snapper fillets with skin, halved crosswise

Kosher salt

¼ cup extra-virgin olive oil

4 oz. dry Spanish chorizo, thinly sliced (1 cup)

2 Tbsp. minced shallots

2 lbs. asparagus, trimmed and halved crosswise

5 garlic cloves, thinly sliced

2 Tbsp. fresh lemon juice

4 anchovy fillets, minced

½ tsp. finely grated lemon zest

¼ cup chopped parsley

1 Tbsp. unsalted butter

1. Season the fish with salt and rub with 1 tablespoon of olive oil. In a large skillet, heat the remaining 3 tablespoons of olive oil over moderately high heat. Add the fish skin side down and cook for 4 minutes, until golden brown. Turn and cook until the fish is almost white throughout. Transfer to a large plate; keep warm.

2. Pour off the excess fat from the skillet. Add the chorizo and cook over moderate heat, stirring, until the the slices curl. Add the shallots, asparagus and a pinch of salt and cook, stirring, until the shallots are translucent, 2 minutes. Add ¼ cup of water and cook until evaporated, 2 minutes. Add the garlic and cook, stirring, until golden brown. Add the lemon juice and cook, stirring, until evaporated. Stir in the anchovies, zest, parsley and butter. Spoon onto plates, top with the fish and serve. —*Tim Byres*

WINE Perfumed, zesty Spanish white: 2012 Ontañon Vetiver Blanco.

PIMENTÓN-ROASTED RED SNAPPER
WITH HERB SALAD

Pan-Seared Halibut with Braised Swiss Chard
⏱ Total **45 min**; Serves **4**

¼ lb. thick-cut bacon, cut into 1-inch pieces

1¼ lbs. Swiss chard, stems cut into ¾-inch pieces and leaves chopped

3 small shallots—2 halved and thinly sliced, 1 minced

1 garlic clove, minced

½ cup dry white wine

   Kosher salt and ground pepper

6 Tbsp. unsalted butter

1 Tbsp. pine nuts

2 tsp. thyme leaves

1 tsp. finely grated lemon zest

¼ cup fresh lemon juice

   Four 5- to 6-oz. halibut fillets, about ¾ inch thick

2 Tbsp. extra-virgin olive oil

1. In a large, deep skillet, cook the bacon over moderate heat, stirring, until golden; using a slotted spoon, transfer to paper towels. Pour off all but 2 tablespoons of fat from the skillet. Add the chard stems, sliced shallots and garlic and cook over moderately high heat, stirring, until crisp-tender, 4 minutes. Add the wine and simmer until reduced by half, 3 minutes. Add the chard leaves in handfuls, letting each batch wilt slightly before adding more. Add ⅓ cup of water, cover and braise over moderately low heat until the chard is tender, 5 minutes. Stir in the bacon, season with salt and pepper and keep warm.

2. In a small skillet, cook the butter and pine nuts over moderately high heat, stirring, until the milk solids are golden, 5 minutes. Stir in the minced shallot and thyme and cook for 30 seconds. Whisk in the lemon zest and juice, then season with salt and pepper and keep warm.

3. Season the fish with salt and pepper. In a large nonstick skillet, heat the oil. Add the fish and cook over moderately high heat, turning once, until golden and just white throughout, 6 minutes. Transfer the chard to plates and set the fish on top. Spoon the brown butter dressing over the fish and serve. —*Curtis Stone*

WINE Vivid northern Italian Pinot Bianco: 2012 Erste + Neue Weissburgunder.

Pan-Fried Flounder with Lemon-Butter Sauce
⏱ Total **30 min**; Serves **4**

"Flounder is an amazing fish," says Jonathan Waxman, the chef at Manhattan's Barbuto. "It's firm yet delicate, flavorful and sweet." The breading he uses on the fillets is simple and versatile; it works just as well on chicken, pork, veal and other fish.

2 large egg yolks

½ cup whole milk

½ cup all-purpose flour

1 cup plain dry bread crumbs

   Kosher salt

   Four 5-oz. flounder or sole fillets

1 stick unsalted butter, cut into tablespoons

¼ cup extra-virgin olive oil

2 Tbsp. lemon or Meyer lemon juice, plus wedges for serving

   Parsley leaves, for garnish

1. In a medium bowl, whisk the egg yolks with the milk. Spread the flour and bread crumbs in 2 separate shallow bowls and season with salt.

2. Dredge the fish in the flour, dusting off the excess. Dip the fish in the egg mixture, then dredge in the bread crumbs. Transfer to a large plate.

3. In a 12-inch cast-iron skillet, melt 2 tablespoons of the butter in 2 tablespoons of the olive oil. Add 2 fish fillets and cook over moderate heat, turning once, until golden and white throughout, about 6 minutes. Transfer the fish to plates. Wipe out the skillet and repeat with another 2 tablespoons of butter and the remaining 2 tablespoons of oil and fish.

4. Wipe out the skillet. Whisk in the remaining 4 tablespoons of butter and the 2 tablespoons of lemon juice; season with salt. Spoon the sauce over the fish, garnish with parsley and serve with lemon wedges. —*Jonathan Waxman*

WINE Fresh, citrusy Sauvignon Blanc: 2013 Clotilde Davenne Saint-Bris.

Roast Sea Bass with Chickpea Puree and Parsley Sauce
Total **1 hr**; Serves **4**

In this easy Tuscan dish, sea bass fillets are marinated with herbs and rolled up before roasting to help keep them extra-juicy.

1 cup extra-virgin olive oil

1½ tsp. finely grated lemon zest

½ tsp. hot paprika

   Four 6-oz. skinless sea bass fillets, ½ to ¾ inch thick

   Salt and pepper

4 fresh bay leaves

4 small rosemary sprigs, plus ½ tsp. minced rosemary

2 cups lightly packed parsley leaves

2 Tbsp. fresh lemon juice

   Two 15-oz. cans chickpeas, rinsed and drained

½ small garlic clove

1. Preheat the oven to 400° and line a rimmed baking sheet with parchment paper. In a medium baking dish, mix ¼ cup of the olive oil with ½ teaspoon of the lemon zest and the paprika. Season the fish with salt and pepper, add to the marinade and turn to coat. Nestle the bay leaves and rosemary sprigs between the fillets. Cover and refrigerate for 30 minutes.

2. Meanwhile, in a blender, combine the parsley with 1 tablespoon each of the lemon juice and water and puree until nearly smooth. With the machine on, gradually add ½ cup of the oil until incorporated. Season the sauce with salt and pepper.

3. In a food processor, combine the chickpeas with the garlic, minced rosemary, 1 cup of water and the remaining ¼ cup of oil, 1 teaspoon of lemon zest and 1 tablespoon of lemon juice; puree until smooth. Scrape the puree into a medium saucepan and season with salt and pepper. Stir over moderately low heat until hot, about 5 minutes; keep warm over very low heat.

4. Remove the fish from the marinade. Gently roll up the fillets and set them seam side down on the prepared baking sheet. Roast for about 12 minutes, until just cooked through. Spoon the chickpea puree onto plates and top with the fish. Drizzle on the parsley sauce and serve. —*Francesco Ferretti*

MAKE AHEAD The chickpea puree and parsley sauce can be refrigerated separately overnight. Reheat the chickpea puree gently, adding water if it is too thick. Let the parsley sauce come to room temperature before serving.

WINE Herb-scented coastal Italian white: 2013 Aia Vecchia Vermentino.

Whole Roast Fish with Lemon and Herbs
Active **30 min**; Total **1 hr**; Serves **4**

FISH

One 2½-lb. whole fish, such as red snapper, cleaned and scaled

2 Tbsp. extra-virgin olive oil

Kosher salt and pepper

1 lemon, thinly sliced

¼ cup chopped mixed herbs, such as thyme, oregano, parsley and rosemary

1 shallot, thinly sliced

¼ fennel bulb, thinly sliced

3 garlic cloves, crushed

SALSA VERDE

½ cup minced parsley

¼ cup minced basil

¼ cup minced mint

1 Tbsp. minced capers

1 tsp. red wine vinegar

1 garlic clove, minced

½ jalapeño (optional)

1 cup extra-virgin olive oil

2 Tbsp. fresh lemon juice

Kosher salt and pepper

1. Make the fish Preheat the oven to 450°. Put the fish on a parchment paper–lined baking sheet. Make 3 crosswise slashes down to the bone on each side of the fish. Rub with the olive oil and season with salt and pepper. Stuff each slash with 1 lemon slice and some herbs. Stuff the cavity with the shallot, fennel, garlic and remaining lemon slices and herbs. Roast for about 20 minutes, until the flesh is opaque.

2. Make the salsa verde In a medium bowl, mix all of the ingredients. Serve the fish with the salsa verde.
—*Athena Calderone*

WINE Citrusy Sicilian white: 2013 Tasca d'Almerita Leone.

Sea Bass with Lemongrass, Peas and Mint
⏱ Total **45 min**; Serves **4**

Chef José Manuel Miguel of Goust restaurant in Paris has worked with the top chefs in the city, but some of his best dishes are extraordinarily simple. This elegant restaurant dish is easy to replicate at home.

½ cup frozen peas

4 Tbsp. unsalted butter

2 small shallots, finely chopped (½ cup)

2 Tbsp. chopped lemongrass (from 2 stalks of fresh lemongrass, tender white inner bulbs only)

1 garlic clove, finely chopped

1 cup dry white wine

1 cup clam juice

½ cup heavy cream

Salt and freshly ground pepper

2 Tbsp. extra-virgin olive oil

Four 5-oz. sea bass fillets with skin

Thinly sliced mint leaves, for garnish

1. In a medium saucepan of boiling water, cook the peas for 1 minute. Drain and rinse under cold water. Wipe out the saucepan.

2. In the same saucepan, melt 2 tablespoons of the butter. Add the shallots, lemongrass and garlic and cook over moderate heat, stirring occasionally, until softened but not browned, about 5 minutes. Add the wine and cook over moderately high heat until almost evaporated, about 5 minutes. Add the clam juice and ½ cup of water and cook until reduced to ½ cup, 10 to 12 minutes. Add the cream and cook until slightly thickened, 2 to 3 minutes. Transfer the sauce to a blender and puree until smooth. Strain the sauce into a small saucepan, pressing hard on the solids, and season with salt and pepper.

3. In a large nonstick skillet, heat the olive oil. Season the fish with salt, add to the skillet skin side down and cook over moderately high heat until golden, about 3 minutes. Flip the fish and cook until just white throughout, 2 to 3 minutes longer.

4. In a small saucepan, melt the remaining 2 tablespoons of butter. Add the peas and warm over low heat; season with salt and pepper. Gently reheat the sauce. Spoon the sauce into plates or shallow bowls. Top with the peas and fish, sprinkle with mint and serve. —*José Manuel Miguel*

MAKE AHEAD The sauce can be refrigerated overnight.

WINE Fragrant Loire Valley Sauvignon Blanc: 2011 Lucien Crochet Sancerre.

GENIUS TIPS

For Supermoist Roast Fish

SALT-CRUST IT Mixed with egg whites and patted on whole fish, kosher salt hardens in the oven to become a crust that protects food from dry heat. Other options for salt-crust roasting include potatoes, beets–anything, really, with a removable skin or peel.

WRAP IT Chefs use all sorts of wraps for fish, from seaweed and grape leaves to banana leaves and cabbage. There are two benefits–the fish takes on the delicate flavor of the wrap and also comes out of the oven fantastically moist, almost as if it has been steamed.

Striped Bass en Papillote with Lebanese Salad

Active **45 min**; Total **1 hr**; Serves **4**

Lightly sautéed onions and garlic stirred into a spicy chopped tomato and chile salad make a fantastic accompaniment for mild fish.

- ½ cup extra-virgin olive oil
- 1 medium onion, minced
- 4 garlic cloves, minced
- 3 medium tomatoes, cut into ¼-inch dice
- 2 cups lightly packed cilantro leaves, chopped
- 1 cup lightly packed parsley leaves, chopped, plus sprigs for garnish
- 2 jalapeños, minced
- 1 fresh hot red chile, seeded and minced, plus sliced chile for garnish
- 1 Tbsp. ground coriander
  Kosher salt
  Four 6- to 7-oz. skinless striped bass fillets, about ¾ inch thick
- 8 thin slices of lemon
- 4 fresh bay leaves

1. Preheat the oven to 375°. In a medium skillet, heat ¼ cup of the olive oil. Add the onion and garlic and cook over moderate heat, stirring, for 7 minutes. Off the heat, stir in the tomatoes, cilantro, chopped parsley, jalapeños, minced red chile and coriander. Season the salad with salt; let cool.

2. Arrange 4 large sheets of parchment paper on a work surface. Season the fillets with salt and set one in the center of each sheet. Top each fillet with 2 lemon slices and 1 bay leaf; drizzle each with 1 tablespoon of the remaining olive oil. Bring up 2 opposite sides of the parchment over the fish and fold to seal. Fold up the edges to create a packet.

3. Transfer the papillotes to a large rimmed baking sheet. Bake for 15 minutes, until slightly puffed.

4. Mound the tomato salad on plates. Carefully open the packets and set the fish on the salad. Garnish with the parsley sprigs and sliced chile and serve. —*Reem Acra*

WINE Green apple–scented Oregon Pinot Gris: 2013 Willamette Valley Vineyards.

Rainbow Trout with Brown Butter and Salt-Roasted Beets

Active **40 min**; Total **1 hr 30 min**
Serves **4**

While most recipes call for boiling or baking beets, chef Ashley Christensen of Poole's in Raleigh, North Carolina, says this salt-roasting method is her favorite. It requires a lot of kosher salt, but the beets don't taste salty: Instead, they pop with flavor. This dish is also delicious with plain roasted beets.

- 8 small beets with their greens (about 3 lbs.)
- 3 lbs. kosher salt (about 8 cups)
- 2 Tbsp. fresh orange juice
- ¼ tsp. finely grated orange zest
- 3 Tbsp. extra-virgin olive oil
  Sea salt and freshly ground pepper
  Four 6-oz. rainbow trout fillets, pin bones removed and skin scored on the diagonal at 1-inch intervals
- ¼ cup canola oil
- 4 thyme sprigs
- 4 Tbsp. unsalted butter
- 1 tsp. fresh lemon juice
- 4 Tbsp. crème fraîche

1. Preheat the oven to 375°. Cut off the beet greens. Discard the stems; tear the leaves and reserve. In a large baking dish, arrange the beets in a single layer and cover with the kosher salt. Roast for 1 hour, until tender; let cool slightly, then peel and quarter.

2. In a medium bowl, toss the beets with the orange juice, zest and 1 tablespoon of the olive oil. Season with sea salt and pepper.

3. Season the trout with sea salt and pepper. In a large cast-iron skillet, heat 2 tablespoons of the canola oil until shimmering. Cook 2 trout fillets skin side down over moderately high heat until golden, 3 minutes. Add 2 thyme sprigs and cook until the trout skin is crispy. Add 2 tablespoons of the butter and flip the fillets; cook over moderate heat, basting, until just cooked through, 2 minutes longer; transfer to a plate. Discard the thyme. Repeat with the remaining canola oil, trout, thyme and butter.

4. Wipe out the skillet. Add the remaining 2 tablespoons of olive oil and the beet greens and cook, tossing, until just wilted, 2 minutes. Stir in the lemon juice and season with sea salt and pepper.

5. Serve the trout with the beets and greens, spooning a tablespoon of crème fraîche on each plate.
—*Ashley Christensen*

WINE Round, intensely concentrated Chenin Blanc: 2012 Champalou Vouvray.

Trout with Preserved Lemon Vinaigrette

Total **30 min**; Serves **6**

- 3 Tbsp. apple cider vinegar
- 2 Tbsp. fresh lemon juice
- 2 Tbsp. minced preserved lemon peel
- 1 Tbsp. minced shallot
- 1½ tsp. Asian fish sauce
- 1 tsp. sugar
- ½ cup grapeseed oil
- 1 Tbsp. finely chopped parsley
  Kosher salt and freshly ground pepper
  Six 6-oz. trout fillets
- 2 cups watercress sprigs

1. In a medium bowl, whisk the vinegar, lemon juice, preserved lemon, minced shallot, fish sauce and sugar. Whisk in ¼ cup of the oil. Stir in the chopped parsley and season the vinaigrette with salt and pepper.

2. Season the trout with salt and pepper. In a large skillet, heat 2 tablespoons of the oil until shimmering. Add 3 trout fillets skin side down and press with a spatula to flatten. Cook over high heat until the skin is crisp, 3 minutes. Flip the fillets and cook until the fish is just white throughout, about 30 seconds; drain on paper towels. Wipe out the skillet. Repeat with the remaining 2 tablespoons of oil and 3 trout fillets.

3. Set the trout on plates, skin side up, and top with the watercress. Spoon some of the vinaigrette over the fish and watercress. Pass the remaining vinaigrette at the table. —*Viet Pham*

WINE Juicy New Zealand Sauvignon Blanc: 2013 Babich Marlborough.

TROUT WITH PRESERVED
LEMON VINAIGRETTE

DIY Fish Stew

Aromatic and oceanic, homemade fish stock is essential for great seafood stew. San Francisco chef **MARK SULLIVAN** shares his master recipe and three ways to use it. The first step for all three is asking a fishmonger for the freshest head and bones from a white-fleshed, nonoily fish like snapper or cod.

PROVENÇAL FISH STEW
(BOURRIDE)

STEP 1 MAKE THE MASTER FISH STOCK

Master Fish Stock
Active **30 min**; Total **3 hr**; Makes **3½ quarts**

- 1 **lb. fish head and bones, gills removed**
- ¼ **cup olive oil**
- 1 **onion, chopped**
- 1 **fennel bulb, chopped**
- 4 **celery ribs, chopped**
- 4 **garlic cloves, halved**
- ½ **lb. mussels, scrubbed**
- ½ **lb. littleneck clams, scrubbed**
- One 750-ml bottle dry white wine
- 4 **quarts chicken stock**
- 1 **lemon, sliced**
- 6 **sprigs each of thyme and parsley**
- 1 **bay leaf**
- 1 **tsp. white peppercorns**

1. Soak the fish head and bones in ice water for 1 hour. Drain well.

2. In a stockpot, heat the olive oil. Add the onion, fennel, celery and garlic. Cook over low heat, stirring, until soft, 15 minutes. Add the fish head and bones, mussels, clams, wine and stock. Simmer over low heat for 1 hour, skimming the foam.

3. Off the heat, add the lemon, thyme, parsley, bay leaf and peppercorns. Steep for 30 minutes. Strain through a fine sieve and refrigerate until ready to use.

MAKE AHEAD The fish stock can be refrigerated for 1 day or frozen for 3 months.

Aioli for Provençal Fish Stew
Makes **about 1¼ cups**

In a mini food processor, combine 1 **garlic clove** with 1 large **egg yolk**, 2 Tbsp. **fresh lemon juice** and 1 tablespoon **water.** With the machine on, slowly drizzle in 1 cup **extra-virgin olive oil.** Season with **kosher salt.**

STEP 2 PICK YOUR STEW

Sicilian
⏱ Total **45 min**; Serves **4**

AROMATICS

- **2 Tbsp. extra-virgin olive oil**
- **¼ cup minced shallot**
- **2 Tbsp. minced seeded tomato**
- **2 Tbsp. golden raisins**
- **1 Tbsp. minced garlic**
- **1 Tbsp. drained capers**
- **½ tsp. ground coriander**

LIQUIDS

- **3 cups Master Fish Stock (opposite)**
- **¼ cup dry vermouth**

SEAFOOD

- **Four 4-oz. skinless halibut fillets**
- **3 lbs. colossal head-on shrimp**
- **1 lb. littleneck clams, scrubbed**
- **½ lb. mussels, scrubbed**

GARNISHES

- **⅓ cup thinly sliced pitted Sicilian green olives**
- **Chopped mint**
- **Fennel pollen**

Provençal (Bourride)
⏱ Total **45 min**; Serves **4**

AROMATICS

- **2 Tbsp. extra-virgin olive oil**
- **¼ cup minced shallot**
- **2 Tbsp. minced seeded tomato**
- **Pinch of saffron threads**

LIQUIDS

- **4 cups Master Fish Stock (opposite)**
- **¼ cup Pernod**

SEAFOOD

- **Four 4-oz. skinless halibut fillets**
- **3 lbs. colossal head-on shrimp**
- **1 lb. littleneck clams, scrubbed**
- **½ lb. mussels, scrubbed**
- **4 large sea scallops**

GARNISHES

- **Aioli (opposite)**
- **Chopped tarragon**

Catalan
⏱ Total **45 min**; Serves **4**

AROMATICS

- **2 Tbsp. extra-virgin olive oil**
- **¼ lb. dry Spanish chorizo, finely diced**
- **¼ cup minced shallots**
- **2 Tbsp. minced seeded tomato**
- **2 Tbsp. minced piquillo pepper**
- **Pinch of pimentón de la Vera**

LIQUIDS

- **3 cups Master Fish Stock (opposite)**
- **¼ cup dry sherry**

SEAFOOD

- **3 lbs. colossal head-on shrimp**
- **1 lb. littleneck clams, scrubbed**
- **1 lb. mussels, scrubbed**
- **½ lb. cleaned squid, bodies sliced**

GARNISHES

- **¼ cup unsalted roasted almonds, chopped**
- **Chopped flat-leaf parsley**

STEP 3 FINISH THE STEW

1. In a large pot, heat the olive oil. Add the remaining aromatics and sauté over moderately high heat until fragrant, about 1 minute.

2. Add the liquids and bring to a simmer. Add the seafood in stages, in order of cook time: Cook the halibut and shrimp until opaque, flipping once, 8 minutes; the clams and mussels until they open, 3 to 4 minutes; and the scallops and squid until just cooked through, 2 to 3 minutes. Discard clams or mussels that don't open.

3. For the Provençal only Transfer the seafood to 4 serving bowls. Pour half of the stock into a large bowl and vigorously whisk in ½ cup of the aioli until smooth. Pour the aioli-enriched broth back into the pot and whisk again, then pour over the seafood.

4. Serve the stew topped with the garnishes. For the Provençal, pass the remaining aioli at the table.

SERVE WITH Olive oil–rubbed toasts.

Grilled Sardines with Herbed Fennel-and-Olive Salad

Total **30 min**; Serves **4**

Sardines are a great fish to grill: They're quick to prepare, and because they're oily, they're harder to overcook than delicate white fish. Here, they're topped with a crisp and tangy fennel-and-olive salad.

- 12 large fresh sardines, cleaned
- 2 Tbsp. extra-virgin olive oil, plus more for brushing
  Kosher salt and pepper
- ½ medium fennel bulb—halved, cored and very thinly sliced lengthwise
- 1 cup parsley leaves
- ½ cup tarragon leaves
- ½ cup snipped chives
- ¼ cup chopped pitted oil-cured olives
- 2 Tbsp. fresh lemon juice

1. Light a grill or heat a grill pan and brush with olive oil. Brush the sardines with olive oil and season with salt and pepper. Grill over moderately high heat, turning once, until lightly charred outside and just cooked through, about 5 minutes. Transfer the grilled sardines to a platter.

2. In a large bowl, toss the fennel with the parsley, tarragon, chives, olives, lemon juice and 2 tablespoons of olive oil and season with salt and pepper. Pile the fennel-and-olive salad on the grilled sardines and serve right away. —Charlie Hallowell

WINE Minerally, lime-scented Albariño: 2012 Granbazán Etiqueta Verde.

Glazed Mackerel with Fried Eggplant and Mojo

Total **1 hr 30 min**; Serves **4 to 6**

This terrific mackerel dish has a great array of textures and flavors: flaky fish fillets, airy fried eggplant and a superspicy garlic-and-citrus *mojo* sauce.

MOJO

- 6 garlic cloves, minced
- 1 habanero chile, seeded and minced
- 1 Tbsp. cumin seeds
  Kosher salt
- 2 Tbsp. extra-virgin olive oil
- ½ cup each of fresh orange and lime juices
- 1 Tbsp. each of minced cilantro and mint
  Freshly ground pepper

EGGPLANT AND FISH

- 1½ lbs. eggplant, cut into ½-inch dice
  Kosher salt
- 1 cup fresh orange juice
- 2 Tbsp. fresh lime juice
- 1 Tbsp. finely chopped peeled fresh ginger
- 1 Fresno or jalapeño chile, seeded and thinly sliced
- 1 tsp. soy sauce
- 2 Tbsp. extra-virgin olive oil, plus more for brushing
  Canola oil, for frying
- 1 cup cornstarch
- ½ cup chopped cilantro
  Four 6-oz. Spanish mackerel fillets
  Freshly ground pepper

1. Make the *mojo* In a mortar, smash the garlic to a paste with the habanero, cumin seeds and ½ teaspoon of salt. In a small saucepan, heat the olive oil until shimmering. Add the garlic-chile paste and whisk over moderately high heat for 30 seconds. Let stand off the heat for 10 minutes. Whisk in the citrus juices and let cool, then stir in the cilantro and mint and season with salt and pepper.

2. Prepare the eggplant and fish In a large bowl, cover the eggplant with water and add a small handful of salt. Let soak for 45 minutes.

3. Meanwhile, in a small saucepan, bring the citrus juices, ginger, chile, soy sauce and 2 tablespoons of olive oil to a boil. Simmer over moderate heat, stirring, until reduced to ⅔ cup, about 12 minutes. Season the orange glaze with salt and let cool.

4. In a large saucepan, heat 1 inch of canola oil to 375°. Drain the eggplant and pat dry. In a colander set over a large bowl, toss the eggplant with the cornstarch, shaking off the excess. Working in 2 batches, fry the eggplant over moderately high heat, turning occasionally, until lightly browned and crisp, 5 minutes per batch. Using a slotted spoon, transfer the eggplant to a paper towel–lined baking sheet to drain.

5. Light a grill or heat a grill pan. In a large skillet, heat half of the orange glaze. Add the fried eggplant and toss over high heat until hot, 3 minutes. Fold in the cilantro and season with salt; keep warm.

6. Brush the mackerel with olive oil and season with salt and pepper. Oil the grill grate or grill pan. Grill the fish skin side down until lightly charred on the bottom, 4 minutes. Brush the fish with the remaining orange glaze, flip and grill, brushing with the orange glaze, until just cooked through, about 3 minutes longer. Transfer to a platter and serve right away, with the fried eggplant and *mojo*. —Jose Enrique

MAKE AHEAD The *mojo* can be refrigerated for up to 1 week.

WINE Zesty Albariño from Spain's Galicia region: 2013 Condes de Albarei Salneval.

GRILLED SARDINES WITH
HERBED FENNEL-AND-OLIVE SALAD

Pan-Seared Rockfish with Oyster Cream Sauce

◔ Total **30 min**; Serves **4**

- **3** Tbsp. extra-virgin olive oil
- **Four 5- to 6-oz. rockfish fillets with skin**
- **Kosher salt and pepper**
- **1** medium shallot, minced
- **½** cup dry white wine
- **½** cup heavy cream
- **12** freshly shucked oysters with their liquor
- **1** Tbsp. snipped chives, plus more for garnish
- **1** Tbsp. chopped tarragon, plus more for garnish

1. In a large nonstick skillet, heat 2 tablespoons of the olive oil until shimmering. Season the rockfish with salt and pepper and add to the skillet, skin side down. Cook over moderately high heat, pressing gently with a spatula, until the skin is crisp, about 3 minutes. Flip the fillets and cook until flaky, 3 to 4 minutes longer; transfer to a plate and keep warm.

2. In a medium saucepan, heat the remaining 1 tablespoon of olive oil. Add the shallot and cook over moderate heat, stirring, until softened, 1 minute. Add the wine and simmer until nearly evaporated, 3 minutes. Reduce the heat to moderately low, add the cream and simmer until thickened, 3 minutes. Add the oysters along with their liquor and simmer over moderately low heat until the oysters are just cooked, 2 minutes. Stir in the 1 tablespoon each of chives and tarragon and season with salt and pepper.

3. Transfer the rockfish to shallow bowls and spoon the oyster sauce on top. Garnish with chives and tarragon and serve. —*Dylan Fultineer*

SERVE WITH Braised kale.

WINE Ripe Chardonnay from Burgundy: 2013 Mâcon-Lugny Les Charmes.

Grilled Shrimp with Black-Eyed Peas and Chimichurri

Active **45 min**; Total **1 hr 10 min**; Serves **4**

At his forthcoming Ovenbird restaurant in Birmingham, Alabama, chef Chris Hastings will focus on the open-fire cooking of Argentina, Spain, Portugal and Uruguay. Here he uses the vibrant South American herb sauce chimichurri as a marinade for grilled shrimp and as a dressing for the black-eyed pea salad that's served alongside.

- **1** cup packed parsley leaves, finely chopped
- **½** cup extra-virgin olive oil
- **¼** cup fresh lemon juice
- **2** Tbsp. finely chopped oregano
- **2** small garlic cloves, minced
- **¼** tsp. crushed red pepper
- **Kosher salt and black pepper**
- **20** large shrimp, shelled and deveined
- **2** cups cooked or thawed frozen black-eyed peas
- **2** cups yellow cherry tomatoes, halved
- **2** cups baby arugula

1. In a medium bowl, whisk the parsley with the olive oil, lemon juice, oregano, garlic and crushed red pepper. Season the chimichurri generously with salt and black pepper. In a large bowl, toss the shrimp with ¼ cup of the chimichurri and refrigerate for 30 minutes.

2. Light a grill or heat a grill pan. Season the shrimp lightly with salt and black pepper and grill over high heat, turning once, until lightly charred and just cooked through, 3 to 4 minutes. Transfer to a plate.

3. In a large bowl, toss the black-eyed peas with the tomatoes, arugula and ¼ cup of the chimichurri; season with salt and black pepper. Pile the salad on plates, top with the shrimp and serve, passing the remaining chimichurri at the table. —*Chris Hastings*

MAKE AHEAD The chimichurri can be refrigerated overnight. Bring to room temperature before serving.

WINE Juicy, bold Chilean rosé: 2013 Montes Cherub.

Peel-and-Eat Grilled Shrimp with Harissa

Active **30 min**; Total **1 hr 15 min**; Serves **6**

These sauce-coated shrimp from chef Daniel Bojorquez of La Brasa, outside Boston, are messy and delicious. You can split the shells before grilling to make the shrimp a little easier to peel, or keep the shells intact for juicier shrimp.

- **2** lbs. large shrimp, shells intact or split
- **3** Tbsp. fresh lime juice
- **½** cup extra-virgin olive oil
- **1** Tbsp. caraway seeds
- **1** Tbsp. coriander seeds
- **1** Tbsp. cumin seeds
- **1** Tbsp. crushed red pepper
- **¼** cup sweet paprika
- **2** small garlic cloves, finely grated
- **Kosher salt**
- **Lime wedges, for serving**

1. In a large bowl, toss the shrimp with the lime juice and ¼ cup of the olive oil. Cover and refrigerate for 1 hour.

2. Meanwhile, in a small skillet, toast the caraway, coriander and cumin seeds over moderate heat until fragrant, about 2 to 4 minutes. Transfer to a spice grinder and let cool, then add the crushed red pepper and grind into a powder. In a large bowl, whisk the ground spices with the remaining ¼ cup of olive oil, the paprika, garlic and ¼ cup of water. Season the harissa with salt.

3. Light a grill. Season the shrimp lightly with salt and grill over high heat, turning, until lightly charred and just cooked through, about 4 minutes. Add the shrimp to the harissa and toss to coat. Transfer the shrimp to a platter and serve with lime wedges. —*Daniel Bojorquez*

MAKE AHEAD The harissa can be refrigerated for up to 3 days.

BEER Hoppy, grassy, low-alcohol session beer: Founders All Day IPA.

GRILLED SHRIMP WITH BLACK-EYED
PEAS AND CHIMICHURRI

Grilled Cilantro-Lime Shrimp with Yuca

Active **50 min**; Total **1 hr 15 min**; Serves **6**

Jose Enrique, an F&W Best New Chef 2013 (the first ever from Puerto Rico), tosses shrimp with a citrus-and-herb dressing before grilling. He then serves them alongside honey-sauced yuca (a.k.a. cassava or manioc).

- **2** lbs. fresh yuca, peeled and cut into 1-inch pieces
  Salt
- **¼** cup canola oil
- **½** large onion, very thinly sliced
- **1** medium red bell pepper, cut into julienne
- **2** bay leaves
- **¼** cup unseasoned rice vinegar
- **¼** cup distilled white vinegar
- **2** Tbsp. honey
- **½** cup extra-virgin olive oil
- **3** Tbsp. fresh lime juice
- **2** Tbsp. minced cilantro, plus more for garnish
- **24** large shell-on shrimp (1½ lbs.)

1. In a large saucepan, cover the yuca with water and bring to a boil. Add a generous pinch of salt and cook over moderate heat until tender, 25 minutes. Drain well and spread on a baking sheet to cool slightly; discard any stringy bits of yuca.

2. In a large skillet, heat the canola oil. Add the onion, red pepper and bay leaves and cook over moderate heat until the onion is just softened, 3 minutes. Add the rice vinegar, white vinegar and honey and bring just to a simmer. Add the yuca and toss. Discard the bay leaves and season the yuca escabeche with salt; keep warm.

3. Light a grill or heat a grill pan. In a large bowl, whisk the olive oil with the lime juice and 2 tablespoons of cilantro and season with salt. Transfer half of the dressing to a small bowl and reserve. Using small, sharp scissors, slit the backs of the shrimp shells and devein the shrimp; keep the shells attached. Add the shrimp to the dressing in the large bowl, season with salt and toss to coat.

4. Grill the shrimp over high heat, turning and brushing with any remaining dressing from the large bowl, until just cooked through, 5 minutes. Transfer the shrimp to a platter, garnish with cilantro and serve with the yuca escabeche and reserved dressing. —*Jose Enrique*

BEER Easy, refreshing Dominican Republic lager: Presidente.

Jumbo Shrimp with Garlic and Chile Butter

Total **20 min**; Serves **4**

"Jumbo shrimp make any dish more luxurious," says chef Aarón Sánchez of Mestizo in Leawood, Kansas. Here, he cooks the shrimp in a punchy Latin-style sauce.

- **¼** cup olive oil
- **20** jumbo shrimp (about 2 lbs.), shelled and deveined
  Kosher salt and pepper
- **4** garlic cloves, thinly sliced
- **2** dried árbol chile peppers, stemmed and chopped
- **1** cup clam juice
- **4** Tbsp. cold unsalted butter, cut into cubes
- **1** cup cherry tomatoes, halved
- **3** Tbsp. fresh lemon juice
- **¼** cup coarsely chopped cilantro leaves
- **2** Tbsp. snipped chives

1. In a large skillet, heat 3 tablespoons of the olive oil. Season the shrimp with salt and pepper. Add the shrimp to the skillet and cook over moderately high heat until lightly browned, about 3 minutes per side. Transfer to a plate.

2. In the same skillet, heat the remaining 1 tablespoon of olive oil. Add the garlic and chopped chiles and cook over moderately low heat, stirring, until softened, about 1 minute. Add the clam juice and bring to a boil. Simmer over moderate heat until the broth has reduced by one-fourth. Whisk in the butter a few cubes at a time until incorporated. Add the tomatoes and shrimp and simmer until the shrimp are just cooked through, about 2 minutes longer. Stir in the lemon juice, cilantro and chives and serve. —*Aarón Sánchez*

WINE Bright Australian Chardonnay: 2012 Shadow Chaser White.

Garlicky Grilled Shrimp

Total **45 min**; Serves **4**

- **1** Tbsp. extra-virgin olive oil, plus more for oiling the grate
- **¼** cup minced onion
- **8** garlic cloves, minced
- **3** Tbsp. dry white wine
- **1** Tbsp. fresh lime juice
- **2** Tbsp. chopped parsley
- **1** lb. extra-large shrimp, shelled and deveined, tails left on
  Kosher salt and pepper
- **2** Tbsp. unsalted butter, at room temperature
  Steamed rice, for serving

1. Light a grill. In a large bowl, mix the 1 tablespoon of olive oil with the onion, garlic, wine, lime juice and parsley. Season the shrimp with salt and pepper and add to the bowl; rub the shrimp with the marinade and let stand for 15 minutes.

2. Thread the shrimp onto 4 skewers and rub the butter all over the shrimp. Oil the grate. Grill the shrimp over moderate heat, basting with the marinade and turning, until just cooked through, 7 minutes. Serve with steamed rice. —*Marcela Valladolid*

WINE Berry-scented rosé: 2013 Bonny Doon Vin Gris de Cigare.

Orange-Glazed Shrimp

Total **30 min**; Serves **4 to 6**

White on Rice bloggers Diane Cu and Todd Porter lighten this classic Chinese restaurant dish, making it more flavorful and not so sticky-sweet.

- **1½** cups fresh orange juice
- **3** Tbsp. light brown sugar
- **2** Tbsp. soy sauce
- **2** Tbsp. finely grated orange zest
- **¼** cup extra-virgin olive oil
- **2** lbs. large shrimp, shelled and deveined
  Kosher salt and freshly ground pepper
  Chopped parsley, for garnish
  Steamed rice, for serving

1. In a saucepan, bring the orange juice, sugar and soy sauce to a boil. Simmer over moderately high heat until reduced to ½ cup, 20 minutes. Stir in the zest.

2. In a large skillet, heat 2 tablespoons of the oil. Season the shrimp with salt and pepper. Cook half of the shrimp over moderate heat, turning once, until white throughout, 3 to 4 minutes. Transfer the shrimp to a plate. Repeat with the remaining oil and shrimp. Return all of the shrimp to the skillet, add the orange glaze, season with salt and pepper and toss to coat. Transfer the shrimp to a platter, garnish with parsley and serve with rice. —*Diane Cu and Todd Porter*

WINE Floral, zesty Argentinean white: 2012 Dominio del Plata Crios Torrontes.

Shrimp Pan-Roast with Citrus
Total **40 min**; Serves **4**

This pan-roast from chef Alon Shaya of Domenica in New Orleans is an easy one-skillet dish. If you can find head-on shrimp, use them here to add deep flavor.

- 1 **Anaheim or poblano pepper—halved, cored and thinly sliced crosswise**
- 2 **garlic cloves, thinly sliced**
- ¼ **red onion, thinly sliced**
- ½ **cup mixed pitted olives, chopped**
- **Two ¼-inch-thick slices of lemon, halved**
- **Two ¼-inch-thick slices of orange, halved**
- ½ **tsp. crushed red pepper**
- 1 **rosemary sprig**
- 4 **Tbsp. unsalted butter, melted**
- ½ **cup extra-virgin olive oil**
- 1½ **tsp. kosher salt**
- 1½ **lbs. large head-on shrimp—heads and tails left on, bodies shelled and deveined**
- **Grilled country bread, for serving**

Preheat the oven to 450°. In a large bowl, combine all of the ingredients except the shrimp and bread. Add the shrimp and toss to coat. Scrape the shrimp into a large ovenproof skillet and roast for 20 minutes, stirring once, until just cooked through. Serve with grilled bread. —*Alon Shaya*

WINE Ripe, full-bodied California white: 2012 Calera Viognier.

Masala Fried Shrimp
Total **20 min**; Serves **4**

New Delhi–born Suvir Saran, chef at American Masala in San Francisco, is a master of Indian flavors. His tasty shrimp are nicely spiced, with an appealing heat that lingers.

- 2 **tsp. fresh lemon juice, plus lemon wedges for serving**
- 1 **serrano chile, minced**
- 1 **tsp. garam masala**
- ½ **tsp. cayenne pepper**
- ¼ **tsp. ground turmeric**
- ¼ **tsp. dry mustard powder**
- ¼ **tsp. ground coriander**
- 1 **lb. shelled and deveined medium shrimp**
- 1 **Tbsp. canola oil**
- ½ **tsp. cumin seeds**
- **Kosher salt**
- 2 **scallions, chopped**
- ¼ **cup chopped cilantro**

1. In a large bowl, combine the lemon juice, serrano, garam masala, cayenne, turmeric, mustard powder and coriander. Add the shrimp and toss to coat.

2. In a large nonstick skillet, heat the oil. Add the cumin seeds and cook over moderate heat, stirring, until deeply golden, 1 to 2 minutes. Add the shrimp, season with salt and cook, stirring occasionally, until curled and white throughout, about 2 minutes. Stir in the scallions and cilantro. Transfer the shrimp to plates and serve with lemon wedges. —*Suvir Saran*

WINE Zesty, tropical New Zealand Sauvignon Blanc: 2013 Villa Maria Private Bin.

Shrimp and Avocado Salad with Red Goddess Dressing
Total **30 min**; Serves **4 to 6**

Chef Jonathan Waxman of Barbuto in New York City makes his tangy goddess dressing red instead of the classic green, using red bell peppers for color and flavor.

- 1 **roasted red bell pepper, chopped**
- 1 **shallot, minced**
- 1 **garlic clove, minced**
- 1 **tsp. minced jalapeño**
- 3 **Tbsp. plain yogurt**
- 1 **Tbsp. apple cider vinegar**
- 1 **tsp. fresh lemon juice**
- ¼ **cup plus 1 Tbsp. extra-virgin olive oil**
- **Kosher salt**
- 1 **head of lettuce, torn into large pieces**
- ¼ **cup cilantro leaves**
- 1 **tsp. fresh lime juice**
- 2 **Hass avocados, cut into wedges**
- 1 **lb. cooked shrimp**

1. In a blender, combine the roasted pepper, shallot, garlic, jalapeño, yogurt, vinegar and lemon juice and puree until smooth. Scrape the puree into a medium bowl and whisk in ¼ cup of the olive oil. Season with salt.

2. In a large bowl, toss the lettuce with the cilantro leaves, lime juice and the remaining 1 tablespoon of olive oil; season with salt. Arrange the dressed lettuce, avocado wedges and shrimp on plates and drizzle with some of the dressing. Serve the remaining dressing on the side. —*Jonathan Waxman*

MAKE AHEAD The dressing can be refrigerated overnight.

WINE Lively Provençal rosé: 2013 Commanderie de la Bargemone.

Seared Scallops with Caper-Raisin Sauce

Total **1 hr**; Serves **4 as a first course**

For this elegant starter, Jean-Georges Vongerichten ingeniously combines caramelized scallops with a fruity, buttery caper-raisin sauce. The legendary chef came up with this intriguing sauce by accident: "I was walking through the kitchen, grabbed a caper and ate it. A few moments later, I did the same thing with a raisin. The sharp sweet-and-sour combination created an explosion of flavor in my mouth; I knew I had to base a dish around this," he says.

- ⅓ **cup capers, drained**
- ¼ **cup golden raisins**
- 10 **Tbsp. unsalted butter, at room temperature**
- 1 **tsp. sherry vinegar**
  Kosher salt and ground pepper
- ¼ **cup canola oil**
  Eight 1½-inch cauliflower florets, sliced lengthwise ¼ inch thick (24 slices)
- 2 **Tbsp. minced parsley**
- 12 **large sea scallops, halved crosswise**
- ¼ **tsp. freshly grated nutmeg**

1. In a small saucepan, combine the capers, raisins and ¾ cup of water. Simmer over moderately low heat until the raisins are plump, 10 to 15 minutes; do not boil. Transfer to a blender and puree. With the blender on, add 6 tablespoons of the butter, 1 tablespoon at a time, until incorporated. Add the sherry vinegar to the caper-raisin sauce and season with salt and pepper.

2. In a large skillet, melt 1 tablespoon of the butter in 1 tablespoon of the oil. Add half of the cauliflower and cook over moderately high heat, turning, until crisp-tender, 5 minutes. Transfer to a rimmed plate, then repeat with 1 tablespoon each of the butter and oil and the remaining cauliflower. Let the skillet cool for 2 minutes. Add ½ cup of water and cook over moderate heat, scraping up any browned bits, 2 minutes. Stir in the parsley and pour the pan sauce over the cauliflower; keep warm.

3. In a nonstick skillet, melt 1 tablespoon of the butter in 1 tablespoon of the oil. Season the scallops with salt and pepper and add half to the skillet. Cook over moderately high heat, without turning, until the scallops are golden brown on the bottom, 3 minutes; transfer to a plate. Repeat with the remaining butter, oil and scallops. Rewarm the caper-raisin sauce.

4. Spoon the caper-raisin sauce onto 4 plates. Top with the scallops, browned side up. Arrange a cauliflower slice on each scallop, spoon a little of the pan sauce over and garnish with the nutmeg. Serve at once.
—*Jean-Georges Vongerichten*

WINE Ripe, full-bodied Loire Valley Chenin Blanc: 2012 François Chidaine Montlouis Clos du Breuil.

Scallops in Yellow Curry with Spicy Grapefruit Salad

Total **1 hr**; Serves **8**

This crowd-pleasing dish is from chef Andrea Reusing of Lantern in Chapel Hill, North Carolina. Her from-scratch curry sauce is so flavorful, it seems like hours of work must go into it. In reality, it's ready in under an hour and can be made in advance.

CURRY

- 2 **green cardamom pods**
- 1 **whole star anise pod**
- ½ **Tbsp. coriander seeds**
- 1 **tsp. cumin seeds**
- 1 **tsp. canola oil**
- 4 **garlic cloves, peeled and crushed**
  Two ¼-inch pieces of unpeeled ginger
- ½ **Tbsp. ground turmeric**
- ½ **Tbsp. sugar**
  Kosher salt
- 2½ **cups unsweetened coconut milk**
- 2 **Tbsp. Asian fish sauce**
  Pinch of saffron threads
- 2 **Tbsp. fresh lime juice**
- 1 **cup Thai basil leaves, torn**

GRAPEFRUIT SALAD

- 1 **small red onion, thinly sliced**
- 2 **lemongrass stalks, tender inner bulbs only, finely chopped**
- 3 **Tbsp. fresh lime juice**
- 2 **Thai chiles, minced**
- 2 **Tbsp. Asian fish sauce**
- 2 **tsp. sugar**
- 3 **large Ruby Red grapefruits**
- ¼ **cup mint leaves, torn**

SCALLOPS

- ¼ **cup canola oil**
- 24 **large sea scallops (2 lbs.)**
  Kosher salt
- ¾ **cup salted roasted cashews**

1. Make the curry In a skillet, toast the cardamom, star anise, coriander and cumin over moderately low heat, stirring, until fragrant, 2 minutes; transfer to a spice grinder and let cool completely, then coarsely grind.

2. In a saucepan, heat the canola oil. Add the garlic and ginger and cook over moderate heat, stirring, until lightly golden, 3 minutes. Add the ground spices, turmeric, sugar and ½ teaspoon of salt and cook, stirring, for 30 seconds. Add the coconut milk, fish sauce and saffron, bring to a boil and simmer for 5 minutes. Cover and let stand for 15 minutes. Strain the curry sauce and return it to the pot. Stir in the lime juice and basil; keep warm.

3. Meanwhile, make the salad In a bowl, combine all of the ingredients except the grapefruit and mint; let stand for 15 minutes. Carefully peel the grapefruits, removing all of the bitter white pith. Working over the bowl, cut in between the membranes to release the sections. Stir in the mint.

4. Cook the scallops In a large nonstick skillet, heat 2 tablespoons of the canola oil. Season the scallops with salt, add half to the skillet and cook over moderately high heat, turning once, until just barely cooked through, 5 minutes; transfer to a plate. Repeat with the remaining oil and scallops.

5. Arrange the scallops and grapefruit salad on plates; drizzle with some of the curry sauce, garnish with the cashews and serve. —*Andrea Reusing*

WINE Lively Oregon Pinot Gris: 2012 Milbrandt Vineyards.

SCALLOPS IN YELLOW CURRY WITH
SPICY GRAPEFRUIT SALAD

DIY Clambake at Home

The Seattle-based cooks' collective **CHEFSTEPS** staged an authentic clambake on the shores of Puget Sound, and then hacked it for a home kitchen. To capture the flavors of a beach clambake, ChefSteps created a recipe using a cast-iron casserole, Japanese kombu, charred wood chips and hefty rocks.

Ultimate Oven Clambake

Active **1 hr;** Total **2 hr 30 min plus overnight baking;** Serves **4**

The first step is thoroughly drying out the rocks. Set them on a baking sheet and leave them in a 200° oven for 10 hours.

- **5 lbs. large rocks**
- **6 oz. dried kombu**
- **Two 2-lb. live lobsters**
- **⅔ cup small wood chips**
- **2 lemons, halved crosswise and seeded**
- **24 littleneck clams, scrubbed**
- **24 mussels, scrubbed and debearded**
- **½ lb. fresh chorizo, cut into 1-inch pieces**
- **4 medium spring onions, bulbs only, cut into wedges**
- **½ lb. maitake mushrooms, broken into large clusters**
- **¼ cup finely chopped garlic chives**
- **Salmon Roe, Garlic Chive and Chorizo Oil (below right), for serving**
- **Steamed new potatoes and corn on the cob, for serving**

STEP 1 PREP THE POT

1. Preheat the oven to 450°. Set the dried-out rocks in the center of a large enameled cast-iron casserole and bake for 1 hour, until the rocks are very hot.

2. Meanwhile, in a large saucepan, soak the kombu in 8 cups of hot water, turning occasionally, until rehydrated and pliable, about 30 minutes. Lift out the kombu; reserve 2 cups of the soaking water.

3. Fill a large bowl with ice and water. In a large pot of boiling water, blanch the lobsters head-first for 1 minute. Transfer the lobsters to the ice-water bath and let soak until chilled, about 10 minutes. Drain well. Twist off the arms and claws. Twist the lobster bodies to detach the heads from the tails. Discard the lobster heads.

4. Spread the wood chips in a heavy skillet and toast over high heat, without stirring, until they begin to smoke, 3 minutes. Transfer to a small heatproof bowl to cool.

5. Wipe out the skillet. Add the lemons cut side down and cook over moderately high heat until almost blackened, about 5 minutes. Transfer the lemons to a plate.

STEP 2 BAKE

6. Sprinkle the wood chips around the hot rocks in the casserole. Line the casserole with the kombu, overlapping it slightly, to cover the rocks; allow the ends to hang over the edge. Arrange the lobster tails, arms and claws around the casserole along with the clams, mussels and chorizo. Add the spring onions and mushrooms and sprinkle with 2 tablespoons of the garlic chives. Pour in the reserved 2 cups of kombu soaking water and fold the overhanging kombu over everything in the casserole.

7. Cover with the lid and cook in the center of the oven for 20 minutes; the lobster should be bright red and the clams and mussels should be open. Remove from the oven and let stand, covered, for 5 minutes.

STEP 3 TOP AND SERVE

8. Sprinkle the remaining 2 tablespoons of garlic chives over the clambake and serve with the charred lemon halves, Salmon Roe, Garlic Chive and Chorizo Oil, steamed new potatoes and corn on the cob.
—Grant Lee Crilly and Chris Young

For serving: Salmon Roe, Garlic Chive and Chorizo Oil
Makes **about 1¼ cups**

In a blender, combine 4 oz. chopped **dry Spanish chorizo** and 1 cup **extra-virgin olive oil** and blend until the chorizo is minced; scrape into a small saucepan and bring to a simmer over low heat. Remove from the heat and let stand for 20 minutes, until the oil is bright red and infused with chorizo flavor. Strain the oil into a bowl and stir in 2 Tbsp. minced **garlic chives,** then fold in 2 oz. **salmon roe.**

CLAMBAKE HOW-TO, STEP-BY-STEP

Once you've rounded up all of the ingredients—from rocks and kombu to wood chips and a good casserole—assembling this clambake is easy compared to one at the beach.

1
HEAT Dry rocks thoroughly in the oven, then bake them until hot.

2
SOAK In a large pot of hot water, soak kombu until rehydrated and pliable.

3
TOAST Roast small wood chips in a heavy skillet over high heat until smoking.

4
SET UP In a casserole, scatter the wood chips around the rocks, then top with kombu.

5
ASSEMBLE Add the seafood, chorizo, onions and mushrooms and bake.

6
FINISH For extra flavor, squeeze charred lemon over the clambake.

Scallops with Spinach and Orange-Saffron Sauce
Total **45 min**; Serves **4**

- 3 Tbsp. plus 1 tsp. extra-virgin olive oil
- 1 shallot, finely chopped
- ¼ cup dry vermouth
- ½ cup bottled clam juice
- ¼ tsp. finely grated orange zest
- 3 Tbsp. fresh orange juice
- ½ cup heavy cream
- Pinch of saffron threads
- 4 Tbsp. unsalted butter
- Kosher salt and freshly ground pepper
- 1 lb. spinach, thick stems discarded
- 20 large sea scallops
- Fleur de sel, for sprinkling
- 2 Tbsp. chopped roasted almonds, for garnish

1. In a small saucepan, heat 1 teaspoon of the olive oil. Add the shallot and cook over moderate heat until softened, about 2 minutes. Add the vermouth and cook until reduced to 1 tablespoon, about 5 minutes. Stir in the clam juice, orange zest, orange juice and ¼ cup of water and simmer until reduced to ½ cup, about 10 minutes. Add the cream and saffron and cook over moderately low heat until slightly thickened, 7 to 8 minutes. Whisk in 2 tablespoons of the butter, 1 tablespoon at a time, until incorporated. Remove from the heat and season the sauce with kosher salt and pepper; keep warm.

2. In a large nonstick skillet, heat 1 tablespoon of the olive oil. Add the spinach and cook over moderately high heat, tossing, until just wilted, about 2 minutes. Season with kosher salt. Drain thoroughly in a colander and keep warm. Wipe out the skillet.

3. In the same skillet, melt 1 tablespoon of the butter in 1 tablespoon of the olive oil. Season the scallops with kosher salt. Add half of the scallops to the skillet and cook over moderately high heat, turning once, until lightly browned and just cooked through, 2 to 3 minutes per side. Transfer the scallops to a large plate. Repeat with the remaining butter, olive oil and scallops.

4. Mound the spinach on plates and surround with the scallops. Sprinkle with fleur de sel and garnish with the almonds. Spoon the sauce around the scallops and serve. —*Stéphane Rossillon*

WINE Complex, focused Blanc de Blancs Champagne: Jacques Selosse Substance.

Charred Squid Salad with Mustard Greens and Roasted Garlic Dressing
Active **45 min**; Total **1 hr 30 min**; Serves **4**

To get a good char on the squid, work in batches to avoid crowding the griddle.

- 3 heads of garlic
- ½ cup plus 1 Tbsp. extra-virgin olive oil
- 3 Tbsp. fresh lemon juice
- Kosher salt
- 1 pink or Ruby Red grapefruit
- 1 lb. cleaned small squid, bodies quartered lengthwise and tentacles trimmed
- 1 large avocado, halved and pitted
- 4 cups baby mustard greens
- ¼ cup thinly sliced radishes
- ¼ cup roasted almonds, chopped

1. Preheat the oven to 350°. On a sheet of aluminum foil, drizzle the garlic heads with 2 tablespoons of the olive oil. Wrap tightly and roast for about 1 hour, until the garlic is very soft; let cool. Halve the garlic crosswise and squeeze the garlic cloves out of the skins into a small bowl. Add 3 tablespoons of the olive oil and mash to a paste; whisk in 2 tablespoons of the lemon juice and season the dressing with salt.

2. Meanwhile, finely grate 1 teaspoon of grapefruit zest. Using a sharp knife, cut the skin and all of the bitter white pith off of the grapefruit. Working over a medium bowl, cut in between the membranes to release the sections; discard the membranes and stir in the zest.

3. Heat a large cast-iron griddle with 1 tablespoon of the olive oil. Add half of the squid and cook over high heat, turning once, until golden in spots and just white throughout, about 1 minute. Transfer the squid to a large bowl. Repeat with 1 more tablespoon of the olive oil and the remaining squid.

4. Wipe off the griddle and add 1 tablespoon of olive oil. Add the avocado, cut side down, and cook over high heat until nicely charred, about 1 minute. Scoop out the avocado and thinly slice it.

5. Add the avocado, mustard greens and ½ cup of the roasted garlic dressing to the squid and toss; reserve the remaining garlic dressing for another use. Season with salt. Transfer to plates.

6. In a small bowl, toss the grapefruit, radishes and almonds with the remaining 1 tablespoon each of lemon juice and olive oil; season with salt. Mound onto the salads and serve. —*Yoni Levy*

WINE Zippy Sauvignon Blanc: 2012 Philippe Raimbault Sancerre Apud Sariacum.

Seafood-Chorizo Tacos
Total **45 min**; Serves **4 to 6**

- 2 Tbsp. extra-virgin olive oil
- ½ lb. fresh chorizo, casings removed and meat crumbled
- Salt and pepper
- 1 small red onion, minced
- 1 garlic clove, minced
- Pinch of ground cumin
- ½ lb. medium shrimp—shelled, deveined and chopped
- ½ lb. cleaned small squid, cut into thin rings
- 2 Tbsp. Mexican lager
- 2 Tbsp. fresh lime juice
- Warm corn tortillas, diced avocado, cilantro leaves, sour cream and lime wedges, for serving

In a large skillet, heat the olive oil. Add the chorizo and a pinch each of salt and pepper and cook over moderately high heat, breaking up the meat, until browned and nearly cooked through, about 4 minutes. Add the onion, garlic and cumin and cook, stirring occasionally, until the onion is just softened. Add the shrimp, squid and beer and cook over moderately high heat until the seafood is just cooked through, 3 minutes. Stir in the lime juice and season with salt and pepper. Serve with tortillas, avocado, cilantro, sour cream and lime wedges. —*Jane Coxwell*

BEER Refreshing Mexican lager: Sol.

SEAFOOD-CHORIZO TACOS

Seared Scallop Stew with Winter Vegetables

Active **1 hr 30 min**; Total **2 hr 30 min**
Serves **6**

San Francisco chef Corey Lee learned to make the French farmhouse stew *potée* from New York City chefs Daniel Boulud and Christian Delouvrier. Lee tops his *potée* with seared scallops; he likes the sweetness they add to the rich broth.

STEW

- ¼ cup rendered duck fat or bacon fat
- 1 smoked ham hock
- 1 medium onion, chopped
- 2 small carrots, coarsely chopped
- 1 small turnip, thickly sliced
- ¼ small head of Savoy cabbage, shredded, plus ¼ head cut into 2-inch pieces
- 4 oz. mushrooms, thickly sliced
- 6 garlic cloves, crushed
- 1 cup dry white wine
- 3 thyme sprigs
- 2 bay leaves
- 10 whole black peppercorns
- 6 cups chicken stock
- 12 baby turnips, peeled
- 12 baby carrots, peeled
- 18 pearl onions, peeled
- ¼ small head Romanesco broccoli or cauliflower, cut into 1-inch florets
- One 15-oz. can of cannellini beans, rinsed and drained
- 2 tsp. Banyuls vinegar or red wine vinegar
- Kosher salt

SCALLOPS

- 1 Tbsp. rendered duck fat (optional) or canola oil
- 6 oz. slab bacon, sliced ½ thick and cut into ½-inch pieces
- 1½ lbs. medium sea scallops
- Kosher salt
- 2 Tbsp. unsalted butter
- 1 Tbsp. thinly sliced parsley

1. Make the stew In a large pot, heat the duck fat. Add the ham hock and cook over moderate heat, turning, until browned, 5 minutes. Add the chopped onion and carrots, sliced turnip, shredded cabbage, mushrooms and garlic and cook, stirring, until lightly golden, 5 minutes. Add the wine and cook until absorbed. Stir in the thyme, bay leaves, peppercorns and stock; simmer until reduced to 4 cups, 1 hour. Strain into a bowl and wipe out the pot. Return the broth to the pot and bring to a low simmer. Add the baby turnips and carrots and pearl onions, cover and simmer until almost tender, 15 minutes. Add the cabbage pieces and Romanesco, cover and cook until tender, 10 minutes. Stir in the beans and vinegar and season with salt; keep warm.

2. Cook the scallops In a large nonstick skillet, heat the duck fat. Add the bacon and cook over moderate heat until browned; transfer to paper towels. Strain the fat into a bowl. Wipe out the skillet.

3. Heat half of the reserved bacon fat in the skillet. Season the scallops with salt, add half of them to the skillet and cook over moderately high heat until golden on the bottom, 3 minutes. Turn the scallops over and add 1 tablespoon of the butter. Cook, basting the scallops, until just opaque; transfer to a plate. Repeat with the remaining fat, scallops and butter. Stir the parsley into the stew, ladle into bowls and top with the scallops and bacon. —*Corey Lee*

WINE Weighty white Burgundy with lithe acidity: 2011 Domaine Henri Germain.

Scallops with Lemon-Butter Sauce

Total **30 min**; Serves **6**

- ¼ cup lemon sorbet, melted
- 1½ Tbsp. distilled white vinegar
- 1 Tbsp. minced shallots
- 1 stick cold unsalted butter, cubed
- Kosher salt
- 2 Tbsp. extra-virgin olive oil
- 18 large sea scallops
- Pepper
- Snipped chives, for garnish

1. In a small skillet, combine the sorbet, vinegar and shallots and bring to a boil. Cook over moderate heat, stirring occasionally, until reduced to 2½ tablespoons, 7 minutes. Remove from the heat and swirl in the butter 1 piece at a time, briefly returning the skillet to the heat once or twice as necessary. Season the sauce with salt and keep warm over very low heat.

2. In a large skillet, heat the oil until shimmering. Working in batches if necessary, season the scallops with salt and pepper and cook over moderately high heat, turning once, until nearly white throughout, about 5 minutes. Transfer the scallops to plates, drizzle with the beurre blanc and garnish with snipped chives.
—*Jeni Britton Bauer*

WINE Zesty Loire Valley Sauvignon Blanc: 2013 Joseph Mellot Sincérité.

Seared Scallops with Pine Nut Agrodolce

Total **20 min**; Serves **4 as a first course**

- 2 Tbsp. canola oil
- 5 garlic cloves, thinly sliced
- ¼ cup pine nuts
- ½ cup sherry, preferably amontillado
- 2 Tbsp. sherry vinegar
- 6 Tbsp. fresh blood orange juice or plain orange juice
- ½ tsp. finely grated blood orange zest or plain orange zest
- 1 Tbsp. unsalted butter
- 2 Tbsp. chopped tarragon
- Kosher salt and pepper
- 8 sea scallops

1. In a medium skillet, heat 1 tablespoon of the oil. Add the garlic and pine nuts and cook over moderate heat, stirring, until golden, 2 minutes. Stir in the sherry, vinegar and blood orange juice and cook over high heat until reduced by half, 5 minutes. Remove the saucepan from the heat and whisk in the orange zest, butter and tarragon. Season with salt and pepper and keep warm.

2. In a large skillet, heat the remaining 1 tablespoon of oil until shimmering. Season the scallops with salt and pepper and cook over moderately high heat, turning once, until nearly white throughout, about 5 minutes. Transfer the scallops to plates, top with the *agrodolce* and serve.
—*Jennifer Jasinski*

WINE Fruit-forward, full-bodied Loire Valley Chenin Blanc: 2011 Pithon-Paillé Mozaïk.

Red Coconut Curry with Seafood and Mixed Vegetables

⏱ Total **25 min**; Serves **4**

- 1 Tbsp. extra-virgin olive oil
  Four 3-oz. cod fillets
- 12 oz. large shrimp, shelled and deveined
  Kosher salt and pepper
- 3 Tbsp. raw coconut palm sugar
- 1 Tbsp. red curry paste
- 4 oz. green beans, cut into 1-inch pieces
- 1 small carrot, thinly sliced
- 3 cups low-sodium chicken broth
- ¼ cup unsweetened coconut milk
- 20 mussels, scrubbed and debearded
- 1½ tsp. arrowroot or cornstarch
- 1 cup frozen peas
- ¼ cup coarsely chopped cilantro
- 1 lime, cut into wedges, for serving

1. In a large nonstick skillet, heat the olive oil. Season the cod fillets and shrimp with salt and pepper and cook over moderately high heat until browned and cooked through, about 3 minutes per side. Transfer the seafood to 4 bowls and keep warm.

2. Add the sugar to the skillet and cook, stirring frequently, until the sugar starts to melt, about 1 minute. Add the curry paste and cook, stirring, until the paste is fragrant and bright red, about 1 minute. Add the green beans, carrot, 2 cups of the chicken broth and the coconut milk and bring to a simmer. Add the mussels and cook over moderately high heat until the mussels open, 1 to 2 minutes. With a slotted spoon, transfer the mussels to the bowls with the cod and shrimp.

3. In a small bowl, whisk the arrowroot with the remaining 1 cup of chicken broth, add to the skillet and bring to a simmer over moderately high heat. Add the peas and cook until they are heated through, about 3 minutes. Season the sauce with salt and pepper and stir in the cilantro. Pour the sauce and vegetables into the bowls and serve with lime wedges.
—*Rocco DiSpirito*

WINE Lively, juicy Portuguese rosé: 2013 Periquita.

Cilantro Scallops

⏱ Total **15 min**; Serves **4**

- 1 lb. large sea scallops
  Kosher salt and black pepper
- ¼ cup extra-virgin olive oil, plus more for oiling the grate
- ¼ cup chopped cilantro
- 2 garlic cloves, minced
- 2 Tbsp. fresh lime juice
- 1½ tsp. low-sodium soy sauce
- 1½ tsp. crushed red pepper
  Lime wedges, chopped avocado and tortilla chips, for serving

Light a grill. In a medium bowl, season the scallops with salt and black pepper. Add the ¼ cup each of olive oil and cilantro along with the garlic, lime juice, soy sauce and crushed red pepper and toss to coat. Oil the grate and grill the scallops over moderate heat, basting with the marinade, until golden and just cooked through, 2 minutes per side. Serve the scallops with lime wedges, chopped avocado and tortilla chips. —*Marcela Valladolid*

WINE Australian Riesling: 2013 Thomas Goss.

Steamed Mussels with Lemon and Bay Leaves

⏱ Total **25 min**; Serves **4 to 6**

- 4 lbs. mussels, scrubbed and debearded
- 1 stick unsalted butter, cubed, at room temperature
- ½ cup fresh lemon juice
- 4 shallots, minced
- 4 fresh bay leaves
  Salt and freshly ground pepper
  Crusty bread, for serving

Heat a large pot. Add all of the ingredients except the salt, pepper and bread. Cover and cook over high heat, shaking the pan and stirring occasionally, until the mussels open, about 7 minutes. Season lightly with salt and pepper. Discard the bay leaves and any mussels that don't open and serve right away, with crusty bread.
—*Cathal Armstrong*

WINE Light-bodied French white: 2012 Domaine Julie Benau Picpoul de Pinet.

Mussels with Pancetta and Crème Fraîche

📷 PAGE 104

⏱ Total **45 min**; Serves **2**

The luscious broth for these plump mussels from chef Jimmy Bannos, Jr., of The Purple Pig in Chicago is creamy, tangy and lightly scented with fresh marjoram.

- 2 Tbsp. extra-virgin olive oil
- 4 oz. pancetta or bacon, finely chopped
- ½ red onion, finely chopped
- 1 celery rib, finely chopped
- ½ fennel bulb, chopped
- 4 garlic cloves, thinly sliced
- ¾ cup dry white wine
- 4 dozen mussels, scrubbed and debearded
- 1¼ cups fish stock, or ¾ cup clam juice plus ½ cup of water
- ½ cup crème fraîche
- 2 Tbsp. fresh lemon juice
- ½ cup packed parsley leaves
- 2 Tbsp. marjoram leaves
  Pinch of crushed red pepper
  Kosher salt
  Crusty bread, for serving

1. In a large enameled cast-iron casserole, heat the oil. Add the pancetta and cook over moderately low heat until crisp, 5 minutes. Add the onion, celery, fennel and garlic and cook, stirring, until softened, 7 minutes. Stir in the wine and simmer over moderately high heat until almost all of the liquid is evaporated, 3 minutes. Add the mussels and stock and bring to a simmer; cover and cook until the mussels open, 4 minutes. Discard any that don't open. Stir in the crème fraîche.

2. Off the heat, stir in the lemon juice, parsley, marjoram and crushed red pepper. Season with salt and transfer to bowls. Serve with crusty bread. —*Jimmy Bannos, Jr.*

WINE Brisk Italian white: 2013 Fattoria Laila Verdicchio dei Castelli di Jesi Classico.

Mussels with Merguez Sausage
◷ Total **30 min**; Serves **4**

Merguez is a North African sausage generously seasoned with cumin and chiles. It gives these mussels a fast hit of flavor.

- **2 Tbsp. unsalted butter**
- **¼ lb. merguez sausage, casing removed and sausage crumbled (see Note)**
- **4 medium shallots, minced**
  Kosher salt
- **1 cup full-bodied white wine, such as Chardonnay**
- **1 large tomato, finely diced**
- **2 Tbsp. fresh lime juice**
- **1 tsp. Urfa or Aleppo chile pepper flakes (see Note)**
- **¼ cup chopped cilantro plus 1 tsp. minced cilantro stems**
- **2 lbs. mussels, scrubbed and debearded**
  Crusty bread, for serving

In a large pot, melt 1 tablespoon of the butter. Add the merguez and cook over moderately high heat, breaking it up with a spoon, until the fat is rendered and the sausage is starting to brown, 3 minutes. Add the shallots and a pinch of salt and cook, stirring occasionally, until softened, 2 minutes. Add the wine, tomato, lime juice, chile and cilantro stems and cook until the wine is slightly reduced, 2 minutes. Stir in the mussels, cover and steam until the mussels open, 7 to 10 minutes; discard any mussels that do not open. Stir in the chopped cilantro and the remaining 1 tablespoon of butter. Ladle the mussels and broth into bowls and serve with crusty bread. —*Hugh Acheson*

NOTE Merguez sausage and Urfa chile flakes are available at specialty food markets and from penzeys.com.

WINE Salty, fresh fino sherry: NV César Florido.

Mussels in a Saffron-Citrus Cream Sauce
◷ Total **40 min**; Serves **4 to 6**

Chef Mourad Lahlou of Aziza in San Francisco simmers mussels in a lovely saffron cream sauce. Lahlou prefers Mediterranean mussels, which he sources from the Pacific Northwest. "They're plump and juicy, and they don't toughen up as much as other varieties when you cook them," he says.

- **1¼ cups Riesling**
- **4 thyme sprigs**
- **2 garlic cloves, smashed**
- **4 lbs. mussels, scrubbed and debearded**
- **½ cup heavy cream**
- **½ tsp. saffron threads**
- **1½ tsp. finely grated orange zest**
- **1½ tsp. finely grated lemon zest**
- **2½ Tbsp. cold unsalted butter**
  Kosher salt and pepper
  Grilled bread, for serving

1. In a large, wide saucepan, combine the wine, thyme and garlic with 1¼ cups of water and bring to a boil. Add the mussels, cover and cook over moderately high heat, shaking the pan a few times, until the mussels open, about 3 minutes. Using a slotted spoon, transfer the mussels to a large bowl. Discard any mussels that don't open.

2. Pour the cooking liquid through a fine-mesh strainer into a large heatproof measuring cup. Wash the pan and pour in the cooking liquid, leaving behind any grit. Boil the cooking liquid until reduced to 1½ cups, about 10 minutes.

3. Add the cream, saffron and citrus zests and bring to a boil. Reduce the heat and simmer until thickened slightly, about 3 minutes. Stir in the butter until melted, then stir in the mussels until heated through. Season with salt and pepper and serve with grilled bread. —*Mourad Lahlou*

WINE Brisk, vibrant Pinot Grigio: 2013 Kris.

Clams Broiled with Lemon, Thyme and Parmesan
◷ Total **25 min**; Serves **4 as a first course**

At Chile's Casa Marín winery, these clams from the nearby coast are steamed just long enough for them to open, then dressed simply and broiled.

- **24 littleneck clams, scrubbed**
  Kosher salt
- **¼ cup heavy cream**
- **2 Tbsp. dry white wine**
- **2 Tbsp. fresh lemon juice**
  Freshly ground pepper
- **2 Tbsp. freshly grated Parmigiano-Reggiano cheese**
- **2 tsp. chopped thyme**
- **1 tsp. finely grated lemon zest**

1. In a large pot, bring ½ cup of water to a boil. Add the clams, cover and steam over high heat until they open, 5 to 7 minutes. Transfer the clams to a platter to cool. Discard any clams that don't open.

2. Preheat the broiler and position a rack 6 inches from the heat. Spread ¼ inch of kosher salt in an even layer on a small rimmed baking sheet. Remove and discard the top shells of the clams. Carefully loosen the clams in the bottom shells and set them on the salt.

3. In a small bowl, whisk the cream with the wine and lemon juice and season with salt and pepper. Top each clam with 1 teaspoon of the cream mixture and sprinkle with the cheese and thyme. Broil for about 3 minutes, until the cheese is melted. Garnish with the lemon zest and serve. —*Gerardo Valenzuela*

WINE Citrusy Chilean Sauvignon Blanc: 2011 Casa Marín Cipreses Vineyard.

MUSSELS WITH MERGUEZ SAUSAGE

COQ AU VIN
Recipe, page 162

Poultry

Chicken Saltimbocca with Asparagus

○ Total **45 min**; Serves **4**

Star chef Mario Batali makes his version of the Italian classic saltimbocca with vin santo, a sweet Tuscan dessert wine.

- 1 **lb. thick asparagus**
  Eight 3-oz. chicken cutlets, pounded ⅛ inch thick
  Salt and ground pepper
- 16 **sage leaves**
- 8 **slices of prosciutto**
  All-purpose flour, for dusting
- ¼ **cup extra-virgin olive oil**
- 1 **cup vin santo**
- ½ **cup chicken stock or low-sodium broth**
- 4 **Tbsp. unsalted butter**
- 2 **Tbsp. chopped parsley**

1. Cook the asparagus in a large saucepan of salted boiling water until crisp-tender, 3 minutes. Drain and cool under cold running water; drain and pat dry.

2. Season the cutlets with salt and pepper and place 2 sage leaves on each cutlet. Wrap each cutlet in a slice of prosciutto, pressing to help it adhere. Spread the flour in a shallow dish. Dredge the chicken in flour, dusting off the excess; transfer to a baking sheet.

3. Set a rack over a baking sheet. Heat 2 tablespoons of the olive oil in a large skillet. Add half of the chicken and cook over moderately high heat, turning once, until golden and just cooked through, about 3 minutes. Transfer the chicken to the rack. Repeat with the remaining olive oil and chicken.

4. Add the vin santo and stock to the skillet and boil over moderately high heat until the liquid is reduced by half, 4 minutes. Whisk in the butter. Pour half of the sauce into a bowl. Add half of the chicken and asparagus to the skillet and cook over moderate heat until hot, 2 minutes. Season with salt; stir in half of the parsley. Transfer the chicken and asparagus to plates and pour the sauce on top. Repeat with the remaining sauce, chicken, asparagus and parsley. —*Mario Batali*

WINE Aromatic northern Italian Pinot Grigio: 2012 Venica & Venica Jesera.

Chicken Braciole with Spinach

Active **1 hr**; Total **2 hr**; Serves **8**

These chicken thighs are pounded thin and folded around a spinach stuffing, then served with a white wine pan gravy.

- ¼ **cup pine nuts**
- 6 **Tbsp. extra-virgin olive oil**
- 2 **medium shallots, finely chopped**
- 1½ **lbs. curly leaf spinach, stemmed and chopped**
  Kosher salt and ground pepper
- ¼ **cup golden raisins**
- 2 **cups low-sodium chicken broth**
- ½ **cup fine fresh bread crumbs**
- ½ **cup grated Pecorino-Romano cheese**
  Eight 7-oz. skinless, boneless chicken thighs, pounded ½ inch thick
- 8 **thin slices of prosciutto (4 oz.)**
- ½ **cup dry white wine**
- 2 **Tbsp. unsalted butter**
- 1 **Tbsp. fresh lemon juice**

1. In a small skillet, toast the pine nuts over moderately low heat, shaking the pan occasionally, until golden, 5 to 7 minutes.

2. In a large enameled cast-iron casserole, heat 2 tablespoons of the oil. Add the shallots and cook over moderate heat, stirring, until golden, 5 minutes. Add the spinach and cook, stirring, until wilted; season with salt and pepper. Add the raisins and ½ cup of the broth; bring to a boil, then simmer over moderately high heat until almost all of the liquid has evaporated, 3 minutes. Transfer the spinach to a bowl and stir in the pine nuts, bread crumbs and cheese; let cool slightly. Wipe out the casserole.

3. Arrange the chicken thighs on a work surface. Top each thigh with a prosciutto slice and the spinach mixture, spreading it evenly and leaving a ½-inch border all around. Tightly roll up each thigh and tie at 1-inch intervals with kitchen string.

4. Heat 2 tablespoons of the oil in the casserole. Season the chicken with salt and pepper and add half of the bundles to the casserole, seam side down. Cook over moderately high heat, turning, until browned all over, 5 minutes. Transfer the chicken to a platter; scrape up any cheese from the bottom of the casserole. Repeat with the remaining oil and chicken bundles.

5. Add the wine and remaining 1½ cups of broth to the casserole. Bring to a simmer over moderate heat, scraping up any browned bits. Add the chicken bundles and bring to a boil. Cover and cook over low heat, turning, until the chicken is cooked through, 45 minutes. Transfer to a cutting board; cover with foil.

6. Strain the liquid and wipe out the casserole. Add the liquid and boil until reduced to 1½ cups, 10 minutes. Whisk in the butter and lemon juice; season with salt and pepper. Discard the strings from the rolls, slice 1 inch thick and serve with the sauce. —*Ali Larter*

WINE Floral, balanced Italian red: 2012 Grosjean Pinot Noir.

Lemony Chicken Stir-Fry

○ Total **30 min**; Serves **4**

- 2 **Tbsp. extra-virgin olive oil**
- ½ **onion, finely chopped**
- 3 **garlic cloves, minced**
- 2 **lbs. skinless, boneless chicken breasts or trimmed thighs, cut into ¾-inch pieces**
- 1 **Tbsp. soy sauce, plus more for seasoning**
- ¼ **tsp. toasted sesame oil**
  Kosher salt and ground pepper
- 1 **Tbsp. plus 1 tsp. finely grated lemon zest**
- 2 **Tbsp. fresh lemon juice**
- 1 **scallion, thinly sliced**
  Steamed rice, for serving

In a large skillet, heat the olive oil. Add the onion and cook over moderate heat, stirring, until softened, 4 minutes. Add the garlic and cook for 1 minute. Add the chicken and cook over moderately high heat, stirring occasionally, until browned all over, 3 minutes. Stir in the soy sauce and sesame oil, season with salt and pepper and stir-fry until the chicken is cooked through, 3 minutes longer. Remove from the heat and stir in the lemon zest and lemon juice. Season with salt, pepper and soy sauce. Transfer the chicken to a platter, top with the sliced scallion and serve with rice. —*Diane Cu and Todd Porter*

WINE Medium-bodied California Sauvignon Blanc: 2013 Joel Gott.

LEMONY CHICKEN STIR-FRY

Chinese-Style Poached Chicken with Pear and Orange

Total **1 hr**; Serves **4**

This fun, updated take on retro Chinese-American flavors features amazingly juicy chicken breast alongside a mandarin-orange-and-pear salad.

Kosher salt

¼ lb. fresh ginger, thinly sliced and crushed, plus ½ tsp. finely grated ginger

8 scallions, halved, plus ⅓ cup thinly sliced scallions, white and light green parts only

Four 12-oz. bone-in chicken breast halves with skin

3 Tbsp. vegetable oil

3 large garlic cloves, minced

1 tsp. crushed red pepper

¼ tsp. Chinese five-spice powder

1¼ cups chicken stock or broth

2 Tbsp. Chinese black-bean-garlic sauce

1 Tbsp. soy sauce

1 Tbsp. cornstarch mixed with 1 Tbsp. of water

2 tsp. toasted sesame oil

1 Tbsp. plus 1 tsp. unseasoned rice vinegar

1 firm, ripe Bartlett pear, cut into ¼-inch wedges

4 mandarin oranges, separated into sections

1 cup lightly packed basil leaves, torn

¼ cup roasted cashews, chopped

1. In a large pot, bring 16 cups of water and ½ cup of salt to a boil with the crushed ginger and halved scallions. Add the chicken and remove from the heat. Cover and let stand until cooked through, 35 minutes.

2. Meanwhile, in a medium saucepan, heat 2 tablespoons of the oil until shimmering. Add the garlic and cook over moderately high heat, stirring, until golden, 2 minutes. Add the red pepper, five-spice powder and sliced scallions and cook, stirring, until softened, 3 minutes. Add the stock and black-bean and soy sauces and bring just to a boil. Whisk in the cornstarch mixture and cook until the sauce is thickened, 2 minutes. Stir in the grated ginger, sesame oil and 1 teaspoon of vinegar; keep warm.

3. In a large bowl, toss the pear wedges, mandarin sections, basil and cashews with the remaining 1 tablespoon each of oil and vinegar and season with salt.

4. Transfer the chicken to a carving board and discard the skin and bones. Slice the breasts crosswise, transfer to plates and drizzle with some of the sauce. Serve with the salad, passing additional sauce at the table. —*Mark Fuller*

WINE Fruit-forward Loire Valley Chenin Blanc: 2012 Marc Brédif Vouvray.

Curried Maple-Mustard Chicken Breasts

Active **30 min**; Total **1 hr 25 min**; Serves **4**

Molly Chester of California's Apricot Lane Farms uses bold ingredients—curry powder, maple syrup, cayenne and Dijon mustard—to create a spicy-sweet glaze for chicken.

1 stick unsalted butter, cut into pieces

½ cup pure maple syrup

½ cup Dijon mustard

1 Tbsp. mild or hot curry powder

¼ tsp. cayenne pepper

Kosher salt and ground pepper

Four 12-oz. bone-in chicken breast halves with skin

1. Preheat the oven to 350°. In a 9-by-13-inch ceramic baking dish, combine the butter with the maple syrup, mustard, curry powder and cayenne. Bake for about 5 minutes, until the butter is melted. Whisk in a generous pinch each of salt and pepper and let cool slightly, 5 to 10 minutes.

2. Season the chicken with salt and pepper, add to the baking dish and turn to coat with the sauce. Carefully spoon some of the sauce under the chicken skin. Turn the chicken breast side up and bake for about 45 minutes, basting occasionally, until the chicken is glazed and an instant-read thermometer inserted in the thickest part registers 165°. Transfer the chicken to a work surface and let rest for 10 minutes.

3. Cut the chicken off the bones and transfer to plates. Whisk the pan sauce and spoon over the chicken. Serve, passing additional sauce at the table.
—*Molly Chester*

WINE Berry-rich French rosé: 2013 Domaine de la Bastide Figue.

Grilled Chicken with Asian Marinated Tomatoes

Active **1 hr 30 min**; Total **2 hr plus 6 hr marinating**; Serves **4**

TOMATOES

2 Tbsp. grapeseed or vegetable oil

One 2-inch piece of fresh lemongrass with the bulb, thinly sliced

1 Tbsp. finely chopped peeled fresh ginger

2 garlic cloves, thinly sliced

One ½-inch piece of cinnamon stick

½ cup white wine vinegar

1 Tbsp. *sambal oelek* or other Asian chile paste

2 cups cherry or grape tomatoes, halved

Kosher salt

COCONUT BROTH

1 Tbsp. grapeseed or vegetable oil

½ large white onion, thinly sliced

2 garlic cloves

Kosher salt

½ cup finely chopped cilantro

One 1-inch piece of peeled fresh ginger

1 tsp. Thai green curry paste

2 cups chicken stock or low-sodium broth

1 cup unsweetened coconut milk

¼ cup heavy cream

¼ cup fresh lime juice

2 Tbsp. Asian fish sauce

1 Tbsp. sugar

2 kaffir lime leaves, chopped, or ½ tsp. finely grated lime zest

CHICKEN

Eight 6- to 8-oz. boneless chicken thighs with skin, pounded ¾ inch thick

Grapeseed or vegetable oil, for brushing

Kosher salt

Small basil leaves, for garnish

1. **Marinate the tomatoes** In a medium saucepan, heat the oil. Add the lemongrass, ginger, garlic and cinnamon stick and cook over moderate heat, stirring occasionally, until the garlic is golden, about 3 minutes. Transfer to a heatproof bowl, add the vinegar and *sambal oelek* and let cool completely. Fold in the tomatoes and 2 teaspoons of salt and marinate at room temperature for at least 6 hours. Remove the cinnamon stick before serving.

2. **Make the broth** In a medium saucepan, heat the oil. Add the onion and garlic, season with salt and cook over moderate heat, stirring occasionally, until softened and just starting to brown, about 10 minutes. Add the cilantro, ginger and curry paste and cook, stirring occasionally, until the ginger is softened, about 5 minutes. Add the stock, coconut milk and cream and bring to a boil. Reduce the heat to moderately low and simmer, stirring occasionally, until reduced to 2 cups, about 25 minutes.

3. Stir the lime juice, fish sauce, sugar and kaffir lime into the broth and remove from the heat. Let stand at room temperature for 20 minutes.

4. **Meanwhile, cook the chicken** Light a grill or heat a grill pan. Brush the chicken with oil and season with salt. Grill skin side down over moderate heat until the skin is lightly charred and crisp, about 7 minutes. Flip the chicken and grill until just cooked through, about 7 minutes longer. Transfer to a carving board and let rest for 5 minutes.

5. Strain the broth through a fine sieve and return it to the saucepan; discard the solids. Bring to a simmer and season with salt. Slice the chicken crosswise ½ inch thick and transfer to shallow bowls. Ladle the coconut broth around it and spoon some of the tomatoes and their marinade on top. Garnish with small basil leaves and serve. —*Matt McCallister*

MAKE AHEAD The marinated tomatoes and strained coconut broth can be refrigerated separately for up to 3 days. Bring the tomatoes to room temperature and reheat the broth gently before serving.

WINE Lively, tropical fruit–inflected Spanish white: 2013 Cune Blanco.

12
Minutes

SPICY CHICKEN MILANESE

2 large eggs
3 Tbsp. Dijon mustard
1½ tsp. cayenne pepper
   Kosher salt and ground pepper
1½ cups panko
   Four 3-oz. thin-sliced chicken cutlets (¼ inch thick)
⅓ cup plus 1 Tbsp. olive oil
2 cups grape tomatoes, halved
1 Tbsp. fresh lemon juice
¼ cup chopped parsley
   Shaved Parmigiano-Reggiano cheese, for garnish

1. In a pie plate, beat the eggs with the mustard and cayenne and season with salt and pepper. Spread the panko in another pie plate. Dip the chicken in the egg mixture, then dredge in the panko; press to help it adhere.
2. In a large skillet, heat ⅓ cup of the olive oil until shimmering. Add the chicken and cook over moderately high heat, turning once, until browned and white throughout, 4 to 6 minutes. Transfer the chicken to plates.
3. Meanwhile, in a bowl, toss the tomatoes, lemon juice and parsley with the remaining 1 tablespoon of oil; season with salt and pepper. Spoon the tomatoes over the chicken, garnish with the cheese and serve. —*Justin Chapple*

Crisp Chicken Thighs with Peas and Carrots

Total **1 hr plus 2 hr marinating;** Serves **4**

Georgia chef Hugh Acheson likes to fry chicken in vegetable shortening. "It creates a crispier chicken than oil," he says. "The kind I use is low in trans fats, so unless you eat fried chicken every day, your doctor should be happy." He serves the chicken with a quick buttery hot sauce.

Four ½-lb. bone-in chicken thighs with skin

1 **cup buttermilk**

1 **cup all-purpose flour**

Kosher salt

Pinch of cayenne pepper

Pinch of mustard powder

½ **cup vegetable shortening**

1 **cup frozen peas**

¾ **lb. bunch of carrots with tops, tops reserved and carrots thinly sliced on the bias**

1 **Tbsp. fresh lemon juice**

1 **Tbsp. extra-virgin olive oil**

¼ **cup small mint leaves**

2 **Tbsp. apple cider vinegar**

4 **Tbsp. cold unsalted butter, cut into ½-inch cubes**

2 **Tbsp. Louisiana-style hot sauce, such as Tabasco**

1. In a sturdy resealable plastic bag, combine the chicken and buttermilk and refrigerate for 2 hours.

2. Preheat the oven to 425°. Pour the flour in a large bowl. In a small bowl, stir 1 teaspoon of salt with the cayenne and mustard powder. Remove the chicken from the marinade, letting the excess drip off, and transfer to a large plate. Season the chicken all over with the salt mixture.

3. Set a rack over a baking sheet. In a large cast-iron skillet, heat the shortening until it shimmers. Dredge the chicken in the flour, then fry over moderately high heat, turning, until deep golden, 7 to 8 minutes. Transfer the chicken to the rack and bake for about 25 minutes, until crispy and the juices run clear when a thigh is pierced.

4. Meanwhile, in a small saucepan of boiling water, blanch the peas for 1 minute. Drain and cool under cold water. Drain well and transfer to a medium bowl. Add the carrots, lemon juice, olive oil and mint. Chop enough carrot tops to make ⅓ cup and add to the bowl. Season with salt and toss to coat.

5. In the saucepan, bring the vinegar to a simmer. Reduce the heat to low and whisk in the butter, one cube at a time, until incorporated. Whisk in the hot sauce and remove from the heat. Transfer the vegetables to a platter, top with the chicken and serve the buttery hot sauce on the side. —*Hugh Acheson*

WINE Minerally Sauvignon Blanc: 2012 Domaine de Reuilly Les Pierres Plates.

Chicken Thigh Kebabs with Chile-Yogurt Sauce

⏲ Total **40 min;** Serves **4**

½ **cup plus 1 Tbsp. extra-virgin olive oil**

2 **Tbsp. sweet paprika**

8 **boneless chicken thighs with skin (1¾ lbs.), each thigh trimmed of excess fat and cut into 3 pieces**

1 **cup plain Greek yogurt**

1 **Tbsp. fresh lemon juice**

½ **tsp. cayenne pepper**

¼ **tsp. crushed red pepper**

Kosher salt and black pepper

Lemon wedges, for serving

1. In a large bowl, whisk ½ cup of the olive oil with the paprika. Add the chicken and toss to coat; let stand at room temperature for 15 minutes.

2. Meanwhile, in a small bowl, mix the yogurt, lemon juice, cayenne, crushed red pepper and the remaining 1 tablespoon of olive oil. Season with salt and black pepper and mix well.

3. Light a grill. Season the chicken with salt and black pepper and thread 3 pieces onto each of 8 skewers. Oil the grate and grill the chicken over moderate heat, turning occasionally, until golden brown and cooked through, about 10 minutes. Transfer the skewers to a serving platter and serve with the yogurt sauce and lemon wedges. —*Jimmy Bannos, Jr.*

WINE Juicy, light-bodied Beaujolais: 2013 Domaine du Vissoux Pierre-Marie Chermette.

Chicken Breasts with Brown Butter–Chicken Vinaigrette

Active **30 min;** Total **2 hr;** Serves **6**

Chef Viet Pham doesn't serve gravy with roast chicken because he thinks it's heavy and lacking in acidity. Instead, he sauces chicken with a sprightly vinaigrette of reduced stock or poultry drippings, lemon juice and fresh herbs.

5 **Tbsp. grapeseed oil**

1 **Tbsp. Asian fish sauce**

1 **tsp. fresh black pepper**

1 **tsp. smoked paprika**

Kosher salt

Six 10-oz. bone-in chicken breast halves with skin

2 **quarts chicken stock or low-sodium broth**

1½ **sticks unsalted butter**

¼ **cup fresh lemon juice**

2 **Tbsp. minced parsley**

1 **Tbsp. chopped chives**

1 **tsp. thyme leaves**

Lemon wedges, for serving

1. In a large bowl, whisk 3 tablespoons of the oil with the fish sauce, pepper and paprika; season with salt. Add the chicken breasts and turn to coat. Let marinate at room temperature for 1 hour.

2. Meanwhile, in a medium saucepan, boil the stock until reduced to ½ cup, 45 minutes.

3. Preheat the oven to 450°. In a large skillet, heat the remaining 2 tablespoons of oil. Cook the chicken in 2 batches over moderately high heat until browned on both sides, 5 minutes. Transfer the chicken, skin side up, to a rack set over a baking sheet and roast for 25 minutes, until golden and cooked through. Let rest for 10 minutes.

4. In a small saucepan, cook the butter over moderate heat until golden brown, 5 minutes; strain into a bowl. Rewarm the stock and whisk in the browned butter over moderate heat. Add the lemon juice, then stir in the herbs. Transfer the chicken to plates and top with the vinaigrette. Serve with lemon wedges. —*Viet Pham*

WINE Vibrant, full-bodied Austrian Riesling: 2013 Schloss Gobelsburg Gobelsburger.

CRISP CHICKEN THIGHS
WITH PEAS AND CARROTS

Butter-Roasted Chicken with Soy-Garlic Glaze

Active **40 min**; Total **1 hr 45 min**; Serves **4**

- **5** whole cloves
- **5** star anise pods
- **4** Tbsp. unsalted butter, at room temperature
- Kosher salt and pepper
- **½** cup low-sodium soy sauce
- **2** Tbsp. distilled white vinegar
- One 2-inch piece of ginger, thinly sliced
- **3** garlic cloves, crushed
- **1½** Tbsp. sugar
- One 3½- to 4-lb. chicken
- **2** Tbsp. canola oil
- **1** cup all-purpose flour
- **⅓** cup plus 1 Tbsp. boiling water
- Toasted sesame oil, for brushing
- Sliced cucumbers, sliced scallions and hoisin sauce, for serving

1. Preheat the oven to 450°. Finely grind the cloves and 3 of the star anise pods in a spice grinder; transfer to a small bowl. Mix in the butter; season with salt and pepper.

2. In a small saucepan, combine the soy sauce, vinegar, ginger, garlic, sugar and the remaining 2 star anise pods. Cook over moderate heat, stirring occasionally, until the glaze thickens, about 10 minutes.

3. Set the chicken on a rack over a baking sheet. Beginning at the top of the breast, gently separate the skin from the breast and thighs. Season the chicken cavity with salt and pepper. Rub the spiced butter under the skin, spreading it over the breast and thighs. Rub the canola oil all over the outside of the chicken and season with salt and pepper. Roast for 50 to 60 minutes, until golden brown and an instant-read thermometer inserted into the thickest part of a thigh registers 165°. Brush the chicken with the soy glaze and let rest for 15 minutes.

4. Meanwhile, in a small bowl, using a wooden spoon, stir the flour and boiling water until a shaggy dough forms. Turn out the dough onto a lightly floured surface and knead until smooth, about 5 minutes. Cut into 8 even pieces and roll into balls; keep covered with a damp paper towel. Using a lightly floured rolling pin, roll each piece of dough into an ⅛-inch-thick round.

5. Heat a griddle and brush it with sesame oil. Cook the pancakes, turning once, until golden in spots and cooked through, about 2 minutes. Transfer the pancakes to a plate and cover to keep warm.

6. Carve the chicken and serve with the warm pancakes, sliced cucumbers, sliced scallions and hoisin sauce. —*Kay Chun*

WINE Focused, full-bodied white Burgundy: 2013 Domaine Michel Barraud Mâcon-Villages.

Baja-Style Rosemary Chicken Skewers

Active **35 min**; Total **1 hr**; Serves **8**

- **½** small white onion, finely chopped
- **3** garlic cloves, minced
- **2** dried árbol chile peppers, crumbled (or ½ tsp. crushed red pepper)
- **1** tsp. minced rosemary
- **1** tsp. dried Mexican oregano, crumbled
- **¼** cup fresh lemon juice
- **¼** cup extra-virgin olive oil
- **2** lbs. boneless, skinless chicken thighs, cut into 1½-inch pieces
- Kosher salt and pepper
- **8** sturdy 12-inch rosemary sprigs, leaves on bottom half removed
- Lime wedges, for serving

1. In a large bowl, combine the onion, garlic, chiles, minced rosemary, oregano, lemon juice and olive oil; set aside ¼ cup of the marinade. Season the chicken with salt and pepper and add it to the bowl. Mix well, cover and marinate for 30 minutes.

2. Light a grill. Remove the chicken from the marinade and thread the pieces onto the rosemary skewers; discard the marinade. Oil the grate and grill the chicken over moderate heat, turning occasionally and basting with the reserved marinade, until golden and cooked through, 15 to 20 minutes. Serve with lime wedges. —*Marcela Valladolid*

WINE Ripe, full-bodied Chardonnay: 2012 Spring Seed Four O'Clock.

Butcher Shop Chicken

Active **25 min**; Total **45 min**; Serves **4**

This recipe from chef John Besh of August in New Orleans gives you everything you want in a roast chicken—juicy white and dark meat—without the trouble of carving at the table. He serves the chicken pieces with a warm, basil-flecked tomato salad.

- **2** shallots, chopped
- **1** carrot, chopped
- **1** celery rib, chopped
- **2** bone-in chicken breast halves with skin
- **2** whole chicken legs
- **3** Tbsp. extra-virgin olive oil
- Kosher salt and black pepper
- **1½** tsp. finely chopped rosemary
- **1** tsp. finely chopped thyme
- **3** Tbsp. finely chopped basil
- **1** garlic clove, thinly sliced
- **2** pints grape tomatoes, halved
- **¼** tsp. crushed red pepper
- **1** tsp. sherry vinegar

1. Preheat the oven to 450°. In a small roasting pan, scatter the shallots, carrot and celery in an even layer.

2. Rub the chicken with 2 tablespoons of the olive oil, then generously season with salt and black pepper. Arrange the chicken skin side up on top of the vegetables in the pan. Sprinkle the rosemary, thyme and 1 tablespoon of the basil over the chicken.

3. Roast for 35 minutes, until an instant-read thermometer inserted in an inner thigh registers 165°. The skin should be golden brown and the juices should run clear.

4. Meanwhile, in a small skillet, heat the remaining 1 tablespoon of olive oil over moderately high heat. Add the garlic and cook, stirring, for 45 seconds, until golden brown. Add the tomatoes, red pepper and vinegar; season with salt. Cook, stirring frequently, until the tomatoes are softened, about 3 minutes. Transfer to a serving bowl, stir in the remaining 2 tablespoons of basil and season with salt and pepper. Serve the tomatoes with the roast chicken. —*John Besh*

WINE Juicy Italian white: 2013 Fontana Candida Frascati.

BAJA-STYLE ROSEMARY
CHICKEN SKEWERS

Chicken-Tomatillo Fajitas

⏱ Total **45 min**; Serves **4**

For fajitas with a twist, toss shredded chicken in a spicy, tangy tomatillo sauce instead of grilling chicken with the usual bell pepper strips.

- **4 whole chicken legs (3 lbs.)**
- **¼ cup canola oil**
- **Kosher salt and freshly ground pepper**
- **1 pound tomatillos—husked, rinsed and chopped**
- **1 large jalapeño, chopped**
- **3 garlic cloves, crushed**
- **1 bunch of scallions, chopped**
- **2 cups low-sodium chicken broth**
- **1½ cups packed cilantro leaves and tender sprigs**
- **Warm flour tortillas, sliced radishes, pico de gallo and sour cream, for serving**

1. Preheat the oven to 450°. Set a rack over a baking sheet. Rub the chicken with 2 tablespoons of the oil and season with salt and pepper. Arrange the chicken on the rack and roast for 45 minutes, until golden and cooked through. Let cool slightly, then discard the chicken skin and shred the meat.

2. Meanwhile, in a large cast-iron skillet, heat the remaining 2 tablespoons of oil. Add the tomatillos, jalapeño, garlic and scallions. Cook over moderately high heat, stirring, until the tomatillos are softened, about 15 minutes. Add the broth and bring to a boil, then simmer over moderate heat, stirring occasionally, until thickened, 10 minutes.

3. Scrape the tomatillo mixture into a blender and add the cilantro; puree until smooth. Return the sauce to the skillet and add the shredded chicken. Simmer over moderate heat, stirring, until the chicken is heated through, 2 minutes; season with salt and pepper. Serve the chicken with tortillas, radishes, pico de gallo and sour cream. —*Kay Chun*

MAKE AHEAD The tomatillo sauce can be refrigerated overnight.

WINE Medium-bodied, citrusy Chilean Sauvignon Blanc: 2013 Root: 1.

Honey-Ginger Chicken with Lime

⏱ Total **45 min**; Serves **4**

Chef Suvir Saran gives pan-roasted chicken legs aromatic hints of ginger and Indian spices. He then sprinkles the chicken with lime zest and sugar for an appealingly sweet-tart glaze.

- **2 Tbsp. balsamic vinegar**
- **1 Tbsp. honey**
- **⅓ cup minced fresh ginger**
- **1 jalapeño, finely chopped**
- **2 tsp. garam masala**
- **1½ tsp. ground coriander**
- **1 tsp. ground cumin**
- **½ tsp. cayenne pepper**
- **1 Tbsp. plus 1 tsp. salt**
- **1 tsp. cracked black pepper**
- **3½ tsp. finely grated lime zest**
- **4 chicken legs, cut into drumsticks and thighs**
- **2 tsp. sugar**
- **4 Tbsp. unsalted butter**
- **2 Tbsp. canola oil**
- **2 Tbsp. fresh lime juice**
- **Rice, warm naan and lime wedges, for serving**

1. Preheat the oven to 400°. In a large bowl, whisk the vinegar, honey, ginger, jalapeño, garam masala, coriander, cumin, cayenne, salt, black pepper and 3 teaspoons of the lime zest. Prick the chicken legs with a fork, add them to the bowl and toss. In a small bowl, mix the sugar with the remaining ½ teaspoon of lime zest.

2. In a large ovenproof skillet, melt 2 tablespoons of the butter in the oil over moderately high heat. Add the chicken and cook, turning, until golden, 5 minutes. Sprinkle with the lime sugar and roast for 25 minutes, or until the chicken is cooked through.

3. Stir the lime juice and the remaining 2 tablespoons of butter into the skillet. Serve the chicken with the pan juices, rice or naan and lime wedges. —*Suvir Saran*

WINE Vibrant, lightly sweet Washington state Riesling: 2012 Eroica.

Chicken Cassoulet with Fennel and Sausage

Active **40 min**; Total **1 hr 30 min**
Serves **4**

- **Four 10- to 12-oz. whole chicken legs**
- **1 Tbsp. extra-virgin olive oil, plus more for brushing**
- **Kosher salt and freshly ground pepper**
- **½ lb. sweet Italian sausage, casings removed**
- **1 medium onion, finely chopped**
- **1 medium fennel bulb—halved, cored and cut into ½-inch dice**
- **1 carrot, cut into ½-inch dice**
- **4 garlic cloves, minced**
- **2 tsp. minced rosemary**
- **2 tsp. minced thyme**
- **2 tsp. ground fennel**
- **2½ cups chicken stock or low-sodium broth**
- **One 15-oz. can cannellini beans, rinsed and drained**
- **½ cup panko**
- **⅓ cup freshly grated Parmigiano-Reggiano cheese**

1. Preheat the oven to 450°. On a rimmed baking sheet, brush the chicken legs with olive oil and season with salt and pepper. Roast for 35 to 40 minutes, until browned and cooked through. Leave the oven on.

2. Meanwhile, in a large, deep ovenproof skillet, heat the 1 tablespoon of olive oil. Add the sausage and cook over moderately high heat, breaking up the meat with a wooden spoon, until nearly cooked through, about 8 minutes. Add the onion, fennel and carrot and cook, stirring occasionally, until the vegetables are softened, about 8 minutes. Add the garlic, rosemary, thyme and ground fennel and cook, stirring, until fragrant, about 3 minutes. Stir in the stock and beans and bring to a boil.

3. Nestle the chicken legs in the stew and sprinkle the panko and cheese evenly on top. Bake the cassoulet in the upper third of the oven for 20 to 25 minutes, until bubbling and crisp on top. Let stand for 15 minutes before serving. —*Curtis Stone*

WINE Herbal, medium-bodied Pinot Noir: 2012 Banshee Sonoma County.

CHICKEN-TOMATILLO FAJITA

Beer-Braised Chicken Wings with Clams and Chickpeas

⏱ Total **40 min**; Serves **4**

This dish was a "wicked lucky success" for chef Jamie Bissonnette of Toro in Boston and Manhattan. When he had some unexpected dinner guests one evening, he took a pound of chicken wings out of the fridge and came up with this hybrid recipe, inspired by beer-steamed clams.

- 1 lb. chicken wings
- 1 Tbsp. Old Bay seasoning
  Kosher salt and pepper
- 4 Tbsp. unsalted butter
- 1 medium onion, finely chopped
- 5 garlic cloves, minced
- 1 fresh bay leaf
- 1 Tbsp. tomato paste
- 12 littleneck clams, scrubbed
- 1 cup beer, such as lager
- 2 cups chicken stock or low-sodium broth
  One 15-oz. can chickpeas, rinsed and drained
- 2 Tbsp. chopped flat-leaf parsley

1. Preheat the oven to 350°. On a rimmed baking sheet, toss the chicken wings with the Old Bay and season with salt and pepper. Spread out the wings and roast for 10 minutes, until the skin looks tight.

2. Meanwhile, in a large, deep skillet, melt the butter over moderate heat. Add the onion, garlic, bay leaf and a pinch each of salt and pepper. Cook, stirring occasionally, until the onion is softened but not browned, about 10 minutes.

3. Add the tomato paste and chicken wings to the skillet and stir until the wings are well coated, then stir in the clams. Add the beer and bring to a boil over high heat. Boil for 3 minutes, then add the stock and chickpeas. Season with salt and pepper. Cook, stirring occasionally, until the clams open, 5 to 10 minutes; as they open, transfer them to a serving bowl. Stir the parsley into the skillet, then spoon the chicken wings and broth over the clams and serve. —*Jamie Bissonnette*

WINE Ripe, fruity Spanish white: 2012 Torres Verdeo.

Spicy Fish Sauce Chicken Wings with Vermicelli Salad

Total **1 hr 15 min**; Serves **6 to 8**

- ½ lb. rice vermicelli
- 1½ cups coconut water
- ½ cup Asian fish sauce
- ⅓ cup fresh lime juice
- 3 Thai chiles, thinly sliced
- 1 lemongrass stalk, tender inner white bulb only, chopped
- 3 garlic cloves, finely grated
- 2 Tbsp. sugar
- 3 cups shredded red cabbage
- 3 cups shredded iceberg lettuce
- ½ cup roasted peanuts, crushed
- ½ cup each of mint, basil and cilantro leaves
- 2 Tbsp. chopped chives
- 4 shiso leaves, thinly sliced (optional)
  Canola oil, for greasing
- 2 lbs. chicken wings
  Kosher salt
  Thinly sliced scallions, for garnish

1. In a pot of boiling water, cook the vermicelli until al dente, 5 to 7 minutes. Drain, transfer to a bowl of ice water to cool and drain well.

2. In a medium bowl, whisk the coconut water with the fish sauce, lime juice, chiles, lemongrass, garlic and sugar. Refrigerate the fish sauce vinaigrette until chilled.

3. In a large bowl, toss the cabbage, lettuce, peanuts, mint, basil, cilantro, chives and shiso.

4. Light a grill and lightly brush the grate with canola oil. Season the chicken wings with salt and grill over moderate heat, turning once, until crisp and cooked through, about 15 minutes. Transfer to a large bowl and toss with ½ cup of the fish sauce vinaigrette until coated.

5. Pile the cabbage salad on a platter. Toss the vermicelli with some of the fish sauce vinaigrette and arrange on top of the salad. Top with the chicken wings and drizzle with more of the vinaigrette. Garnish the salad with sliced scallions and serve the wings warm, with the remaining fish sauce vinaigrette on the side. —*Danny Bowien*

BEER Crisp, cooling craft pilsner: North Coast Brewing Co. Scrimshaw.

Cambodian Red Curry Chicken Wings

Total **1 hr**; Serves **4 to 6**

- 3 Tbsp. canola oil
- 2 lbs. chicken wings, tips discarded
- 2 shallots, minced
- 4 garlic cloves, minced
- 2 lemongrass stalks, tender white inner bulbs only, finely chopped
- 2 Tbsp. minced ginger
- 2 small dried árbol chile peppers, stems discarded
- 2 Tbsp. soy sauce
- 1 Tbsp. Asian fish sauce
- 1 tsp. ground cumin
- 1 tsp. ground coriander
- ½ tsp. paprika
- ½ tsp. freshly grated nutmeg
- ½ tsp. ground turmeric
- 1 cup unsweetened coconut milk
  Kosher salt
  Lime wedges, for serving

1. In a large skillet, heat 2 tablespoons of the oil. In 2 batches, cook the wings over moderate heat, turning, until golden all over, 5 minutes per batch. Transfer to a paper towel–lined plate to drain.

2. Add the remaining 1 tablespoon of oil to the skillet with the shallots, garlic, lemongrass and ginger; cook over low heat, stirring, until softened, 3 minutes. Stir in the chiles, soy sauce, fish sauce, cumin, coriander, paprika, nutmeg and turmeric and cook, stirring, until fragrant, 3 minutes. Stir in the coconut milk. Transfer to a blender and puree the sauce until smooth.

3. Return the sauce to the skillet. Add the chicken wings and toss to coat. Cover and cook over low heat, stirring occasionally, until the wings are cooked through, 10 minutes. Uncover and cook, stirring, until the sauce is very thick, 5 minutes. Season with salt. Transfer the wings to a platter and serve with lime wedges. —*Edward Lee*

BEER Fresh, lightly spiced wheat beer: Allagash White.

BEER-BRAISED CHICKEN WINGS
WITH CLAMS AND CHICKPEAS

Honey-Butter-Grilled Chicken Thighs with Parsley Sauce

Total **1 hr**; Serves **4 to 6**

Chef Daniel Bojorquez of La Brasa in Somerville, Massachusetts, brushes chicken thighs with honey-horseradish butter while they grill, creating a wonderful glaze.

- **1 stick unsalted butter, at room temperature**
- **2 small garlic cloves, finely grated**
- **2 Tbsp. fresh lemon juice**
- **1½ Tbsp. honey**
- **1 Tbsp. finely grated horseradish**
- **2 Tbsp. finely chopped parsley, plus 1 cup packed parsley leaves**
- **Kosher salt and pepper**
- **⅓ cup extra-virgin olive oil, plus more for brushing**
- **12 bone-in chicken thighs with skin (about 7 oz. each)**

1. In a medium bowl, blend the butter with half of the garlic, 1 tablespoon of the lemon juice, the honey, horseradish and chopped parsley. Season the honey butter generously with salt and pepper.

2. In a small saucepan of salted boiling water, blanch the parsley leaves until bright green, about 1 minute. Drain and cool under running water. In a blender, puree the parsley with 2 tablespoons of water and the remaining garlic and 1 tablespoon of lemon juice until nearly smooth. With the machine on, gradually add the ⅓ cup of oil until incorporated. Season the parsley sauce with salt and pepper.

3. Light a grill. Brush the chicken thighs with oil and season with salt and pepper. Grill over moderate heat, turning occasionally, until charred in spots and just cooked through, 20 to 25 minutes. Brush the chicken all over with the honey butter and grill, turning and brushing, until glazed, about 2 minutes more. Transfer the chicken to a platter or plates and serve with the parsley sauce. —*Daniel Bojorquez*

MAKE AHEAD The honey butter can be refrigerated for up to 3 days. Bring to room temperature before using.

WINE Juicy South African Chenin Blanc: 2013 Ken Forrester Petit Chenin.

Lemon-Thyme Roast Chicken

Active **15 min**; Total **1 hr 15 min**; Serves **4**

Rubbing a simple lemon-and-herb butter all over a whole chicken before roasting serves a dual purpose: It gives the bird a fabulously crisp skin and flavors the pan sauce.

- **½ stick plus 1 Tbsp. unsalted butter, softened**
- **1½ Tbsp. thyme leaves**
- **3 Tbsp. fresh lemon juice**
- **Kosher salt and pepper**
- **One 3½-lb. whole chicken, patted dry**
- **1 lemon, quartered**

1. Preheat the oven to 450°. In a small bowl, blend the ½ stick of butter with the thyme and 2 tablespoons of the lemon juice. Season with salt and pepper.

2. Season the chicken cavity with salt and pepper and tuck the lemon inside. Spread one-third of the lemon-thyme butter under the skin of the breasts and thighs. Rub the remaining lemon-thyme butter all over the chicken and season with salt and pepper.

3. Set the chicken breast side up in a large cast-iron skillet. Roast for 40 to 45 minutes, until an instant-read thermometer inserted in an inner thigh registers 160°. Transfer the chicken to a carving board and let rest for 10 minutes.

4. Meanwhile, skim off all but 1 tablespoon of fat from the pan juices. Stir in the remaining 1 tablespoon of lemon juice and cook over moderate heat until hot, 1 to 2 minutes. Remove from the heat and stir in the remaining 1 tablespoon of butter. Season with salt and pepper.

5. Carve the chicken and transfer to a platter. Spoon the pan sauce on top and serve. —*Jamie McDaniel*

WINE Citrusy New Zealand Sauvignon Blanc: 2012 Craggy Range.

Roast Chicken with Bread Salad

Active **25 min**; Total **1 hr 30 min**; Serves **4**

Megachef Mario Batali dresses up his smoky, spice-rubbed roast chicken with his version of a classic Italian bread salad.

CHICKEN

- **1 Tbsp. smoked paprika**
- **2 tsp. dried rubbed sage**
- **1 tsp. ground cumin**
- **2 tsp. kosher salt**
- **2 tsp. pepper**
- **One 3½- to 4-lb. chicken**
- **½ lemon**
- **2 Tbsp. extra-virgin olive oil**
- **3 bunches of wine grapes (optional)**

BREAD SALAD

- **½ cup extra-virgin olive oil**
- **¼ cup red wine vinegar**
- **Kosher salt and pepper**
- **9 oz. day-old peasant bread, cut into ¾-inch cubes (6 cups)**
- **3 tomatoes, chopped**
- **2 Kirby cucumbers, sliced**
- **1 small red onion, sliced**
- **½ cup torn basil leaves**

1. Prepare the chicken Preheat the oven to 450°. In a small bowl, mix the paprika, sage, cumin, salt and pepper. Set a rack over a baking sheet and place the chicken on the rack. Rub the chicken with the lemon, then rub 2 teaspoons of the spice mix all around the cavity and stuff the lemon in it. Tie the legs together with kitchen twine. Rub the chicken with the oil, then massage with the remaining spice mix. Roast until an instant-read thermometer inserted in the thickest part of a thigh registers 165°, about 50 minutes. Let rest for 15 minutes.

2. Meanwhile, make the bread salad In a large bowl, whisk the oil with the vinegar and season with salt and pepper. Add the bread, tomatoes, cucumbers, onion and basil, season with salt and pepper and toss.

3. Carve the chicken and transfer it to a platter. Serve with the bread salad and wine grapes on the side. —*Mario Batali*

WINE Cherry-rich Sangiovese: 2011 Fattoria Le Pupille Morellino di Scansano.

ROAST CHICKEN
WITH BREAD SALAD

Fried Chicken with Honey Mustard
Total **2 hr** plus **4 hr marinating**
Serves **6 to 8**

Star chef Bobby Flay has two techniques for achieving tender and juicy fried chicken: First, he marinates the chicken in yogurt for four hours; second, he roasts the bird before deep-frying it. "The problem with fried chicken is scorching the crust before the meat's fully cooked," he says. "I bake it three-quarters of the way, so when you fry, the focus is getting a perfect, golden, crispy crust."

- **1 quart plain fat-free Greek yogurt**
- **1½ cups whole milk**
- **2 tsp. crushed árbol chile pepper or crushed red pepper**
- **Kosher salt and ground pepper**
- **Two 3-lb. chickens, cut into 8 pieces each**
- **Canola oil, for brushing and frying**
- **4 cups all-purpose flour**
- **½ Tbsp. garlic powder**
- **½ Tbsp. onion powder**
- **Honey Mustard (recipe follows), for serving**

1. In a large bowl, whisk 2 cups of the yogurt with ¾ cup of the milk, 1 teaspoon of the crushed chile, 2 teaspoons of salt and ½ teaspoon of ground pepper. Add the chicken and turn to coat. Cover and refrigerate for at least 4 hours or overnight.

2. Preheat the oven to 400°. Remove the chicken from the marinade and rinse under cold water; discard the marinade. Pat the chicken dry and arrange on 2 large rimmed baking sheets.

COOKBOOK TIP

Better Basting
Swirl melted butter into heated lime juice for an all-purpose basting liquid.

Ruhlman's How to Roast
Michael Ruhlman

---

3. In a small bowl, mix the remaining 1 teaspoon of crushed chile with 2 teaspoons of salt and 1 teaspoon of ground pepper. Brush the chicken with oil and season with the chile salt. Bake for 20 to 25 minutes, until an instant-read thermometer inserted in the thickest part of each piece registers 145°. Let the chicken cool slightly.

4. Meanwhile, in a large baking dish, whisk the remaining 2 cups of yogurt and ¾ cup of milk with 1 teaspoon of salt and a pinch of ground pepper. In another large baking dish, whisk the flour with 1 tablespoon of salt, ½ teaspoon of ground pepper and the garlic and onion powders.

5. Set a rack over a baking sheet and line another baking sheet with wax paper. Working in batches, coat the chicken pieces in the yogurt, then dredge in the seasoned flour and shake off the excess. Transfer the chicken to the wax paper–lined baking sheet.

6. In a large enameled cast-iron casserole, heat 2 inches of oil to 365°. Add half of the chicken and fry over moderately high heat, turning, until deep golden brown and cooked through, about 7 minutes. Transfer to the rack to drain and fry the remaining chicken. Serve with Honey Mustard. —*Bobby Flay*

WINE Fruit-forward Oregon Pinot Gris: 2013 Raptor Ridge.

HONEY MUSTARD
Active **5 min**; Total **50 min**
Makes **about 2 cups**

This sweet and spicy condiment from Bobby Flay is excellent on both chicken and pork.

- **¾ cup Dijon mustard**
- **¾ cup whole-grain mustard**
- **¼ cup prepared horseradish**
- **¼ cup honey**
- **Salt and pepper**

In a medium bowl, whisk both mustards with the horseradish and honey and season with salt and pepper. Cover and refrigerate until well chilled, about 45 minutes. —*BF*

MAKE AHEAD The Honey Mustard can be refrigerated for up to 3 days.

Roast Chicken Panzanella
⏱ Active **30 min;** Total **45 min**
Serves **4**

This main-course version of bread salad, interpreted through a California lens, includes shredded rotisserie chicken, strawberries, cilantro and toasted pumpkin seeds. "My husband, Evan, and I make wild fennel levain at our restaurant, Rich Table, and this is a delicious way to use up day-old bread," says San Francisco chef Sarah Rich.

- **¾ lb. country bread, torn into 1-inch pieces (8 cups)**
- **¼ cup plus 2 Tbsp. extra-virgin olive oil**
- **Kosher salt and pepper**
- **½ small red onion, chopped**
- **¼ cup Champagne vinegar**
- **¼ cup sherry vinegar**
- **2 romaine hearts, torn into bite-size pieces**
- **1 large tomato, chopped**
- **2 Persian cucumbers, chopped**
- **1 cup strawberries, hulled and chopped**
- **1 cup cilantro leaves**
- **2 Tbsp. chopped dill**
- **One 2½- to 3-lb. rotisserie chicken, meat shredded (about 4 cups)**
- **¼ cup salted roasted pumpkin seeds**

1. Preheat the oven to 350°. On a large baking sheet, toss the bread with 2 tablespoons of the olive oil and season with salt and pepper. Bake for 15 minutes, until crisp. Let cool.

2. Meanwhile, in a large bowl, toss the onion with both vinegars and let stand for 10 minutes. Whisk in the remaining ¼ cup of olive oil and season with salt and pepper. Add the romaine, tomato, cucumbers, strawberries, cilantro, dill, chicken and the toasted bread and toss well. Transfer the salad to a platter, sprinkle with the pumpkin seeds and serve. —*Evan and Sarah Rich*

WINE Bright, fragrant Napa white: 2013 Massican Annia.

ROAST CHICKEN
PANZANELLA

Grilled Chicken Thighs with Spicy Miso Mayo

Total **1 hr plus 3 hr marinating**
Serves **4**

Yuzo *kosho* (a spicy, citrusy Japanese condiment), roasted peppers, lemongrass and ginger create a fragrant, flavor-packed marinade for boneless chicken thighs.

- 1 **small yellow bell pepper**
- **One 1½-inch piece of ginger, peeled and chopped**
- 5 **garlic cloves, crushed**
- ¼ **cup yuzu *kosho* paste (see Note)**
- 2 **stalks of fresh lemongrass, tender inner white parts only, chopped**
- ¼ **cup yuzu juice**
- ⅓ **cup finely chopped cilantro**
- 1 **cup canola oil, plus more for greasing**
- 8 **boneless chicken thighs with skin (about 3 lbs.)**
- ⅓ **cup mayonnaise**
- 2 **tsp. *shiro* miso (see Note)**
- 2 **tsp. Sriracha**
- **Kosher salt**
- **Thinly sliced scallions, for garnish**

1. Roast the bell pepper directly over a gas flame or under the broiler, turning, until charred all over, 5 minutes. Place the bell pepper in a small bowl and cover with plastic wrap; let steam for 15 minutes. Peel, seed and chop the pepper.

2. In a blender, combine the bell pepper with the ginger, garlic, yuzu *kosho*, lemongrass, yuzu juice and cilantro and pulse a few times. With the blender on, slowly add the 1 cup of canola oil, scraping down the side, until well blended. Transfer ¼ cup of the marinade to a small bowl, cover and refrigerate.

3. Pour the remaining marinade into a large bowl. Add the chicken and massage the marinade into it. Cover and refrigerate for 3 hours.

4. Meanwhile, in a small bowl, combine the mayonnaise, miso and Sriracha. Season with salt and mix well.

5. Light a grill and brush the grate with oil. Remove the chicken from the marinade and season with salt. Grill over moderate heat, brushing with the reserved marinade and turning occasionally, until the skin is crispy and the chicken is cooked through, about 15 minutes. Transfer the chicken to a cutting board and let rest for 5 minutes. Slice the chicken and transfer to a platter. Garnish with scallions and serve with the spicy mayo. —*Ricardo Zarate*

NOTE Yuzu *kosho* is a Japanese condiment made from hot chiles and ultra-citrusy yuzu zest. *Shiro* miso is light yellow miso. Yuzu *kosho* and *shiro* miso are available at Asian markets and amazon.com.

WINE Zippy Vinho Verde from Portugal: 2012 Quinta da Raza Dom Diogo.

Curried Chicken Salad with Roasted Carrots

Total **1 hr**; Serves **6**

- ¾ **lb. carrots, peeled and cut into 1-inch pieces**
- ¼ **cup extra-virgin olive oil**
- **Kosher salt and black pepper**
- ½ **cup chopped walnuts**
- 2 **cups plain whole-milk Greek yogurt**
- 2 **Tbsp. honey**
- 1 **Tbsp. ground cumin**
- 2 **tsp. curry powder**
- 1 **tsp. ground turmeric**
- ½ **tsp. ground cardamom**
- 4 **cups shredded rotisserie chicken (1 lb.)**
- 1 **cup chopped prunes**
- ½ **cup chopped dried apricots**
- 1 **small Granny Smith apple—halved, cored and chopped**

1. Preheat the oven to 400°. On a rimmed baking sheet, toss the carrots with 2 tablespoons of the olive oil and season with salt and pepper. Roast for about 20 minutes, stirring occasionally, until the carrots are tender. Let cool to room temperature. While the carrots are roasting, spread the walnuts on a pie plate and toast for 3 to 5 minutes, until golden.

2. In a large bowl, mix the yogurt with the honey, cumin, curry powder, turmeric, cardamom and remaining 2 tablespoons of olive oil. Fold in the shredded chicken, carrots, walnuts, prunes, apricots and apple, season with salt and pepper and serve. —*Eli Sussman*

WINE Vibrant, medium-bodied Austrian Grüner Veltliner: 2012 Sepp.

Sweet and Spicy Roast Chicken with Chiles and Thyme

Active **35 min**; Total **2 hr 45 min plus overnight brining**; Serves **6**

- 6 **cups plus 3 Tbsp. pineapple juice**
- ¾ **cup packed light brown sugar**
- 3 **fresh hot red chiles—2 halved lengthwise, 1 thinly sliced**
- 2 **thyme sprigs, plus 1½ tsp. finely chopped thyme**
- 2 **garlic cloves, crushed**
- 1 **bay leaf**
- **Kosher salt**
- 5 **lbs. mixed bone-in chicken pieces with skin, such as whole legs and breast halves**
- **Pepper**

1. In a large saucepan, combine 6 cups of the pineapple juice with ½ cup of the brown sugar and bring just to a boil, stirring until the sugar is dissolved. Add the halved red chiles, thyme sprigs, crushed garlic, bay leaf and 2 tablespoons of salt and let cool completely.

2. Submerge the chicken in the brine, cover and refrigerate overnight. Let the chicken stand at room temperature in the brine for 1 hour before roasting.

3. Preheat the oven to 425° and line a large rimmed baking sheet with foil. In a medium bowl, whisk together the remaining 3 tablespoons of pineapple juice and ¼ cup of brown sugar. Stir in the sliced red chile and chopped thyme to make the glaze.

4. Remove the chicken from the brine and pat dry with paper towels; discard the brine. Season the chicken lightly with salt and pepper and arrange skin side up on the prepared baking sheet. Roast in the upper third of the oven for about 45 minutes, basting with the glaze every 15 minutes, until browned and an instant-read thermometer inserted near the bone registers 160°. Transfer the chicken pieces to a platter and let rest for 10 minutes before serving. —*Justin Chapple*

SERVE WITH Sautéed greens.

WINE Ripe, tropical fruit–inflected South African Chardonnay: 2012 Tokara.

GRILLED CHICKEN THIGHS
WITH SPICY MISO MAYO

Roast Chicken Cacciatore with Red Wine Butter

Active **1 hr**; Total **2 hr 45 min plus overnight curing**; Serves **4**

- One 3½-lb. chicken
- Kosher salt
- 5 thyme sprigs
- 1 cup red wine
- 2 Tbsp. tomato paste
- 2 Tbsp. unsalted butter, softened
- 4 basil sprigs, plus leaves for garnish
- 4 oregano sprigs
- 3 garlic cloves, crushed
- 1 small fennel bulb, cut into ¾-inch wedges through the core
- 1 cup cherry tomatoes
- ¾ cup pearl onions
- 8 jarred sweet Peppadew peppers, halved
- 6 baby bell peppers, halved lengthwise and seeded
- 1 Tbsp. extra-virgin olive oil
- ½ cup chicken stock or low-sodium broth
- ½ cup Castelvetrano olives, pitted and chopped

1. Season the chicken with 2 teaspoons of salt and stuff the thyme sprigs in the cavity. Transfer the chicken to a bowl, cover with plastic wrap and poke holes in the top; refrigerate overnight.

2. In a small saucepan, boil the wine over moderately high heat until reduced to 2 tablespoons, 7 minutes. Off the heat, whisk in the tomato paste, butter and 1 teaspoon of salt. Let cool slightly.

3. Preheat the oven to 400°. Loosen the breast and thigh skin of the chicken; spread three-fourths of the wine butter under the skin. Stuff the basil sprigs, oregano sprigs and garlic into the cavity and tie the legs with string. Rub the remaining butter over the chicken and let stand for 30 minutes.

4. Meanwhile, in a large, deep ovenproof skillet, toss the fennel, tomatoes, onions and both peppers with the olive oil; season with salt. Set the chicken in the center of the vegetables. Pour in the stock. Roast for 1 hour and 10 minutes, until an instant-read thermometer inserted in an inner thigh registers 155°. Transfer to a carving board and let rest for 15 minutes.

5. Simmer the broth over moderately high heat until slightly reduced, 3 minutes. Stir in the olives and transfer to a platter. Carve the chicken and arrange on the platter. Garnish with basil leaves and serve. —*Giada De Laurentiis*

WINE Bold, red berry–scented Barbera: 2012 G.B. Burlotto Barbera d'Alba.

Grilled Chicken with Spicy-Sweet Chile Oil

Active **30 min**; Total **1 hr plus overnight salting and marinating**; Serves **2 to 4**

- One 3½-lb. chicken, backbone removed and chicken cut in half
- 2 tsp. kosher salt
- 2½ Tbsp. fresh lemon juice
- ½ cup extra-virgin olive oil
- 1 Tbsp. piment d'Espelette
- 1 Fresno or red jalapeño chile, chopped
- 1½ Tbsp. light brown sugar
- 2 garlic cloves, thinly sliced
- ¼ tsp. black pepper

1. Place the chicken halves skin side up on a baking sheet. Season all over with the salt, cover and refrigerate overnight.

2. In a medium bowl, combine all of the remaining ingredients and mix well. Pour half of the chile oil into a large bowl, add the chicken and turn to coat; refrigerate for 4 hours. Reserve the remaining chile oil for serving.

3. Light a grill and set it up for indirect grilling. Alternatively, preheat the broiler and position the rack 8 to 10 inches from the heat. Remove the chicken from the bowl; reserve any chile oil remaining. Grill the chicken skin side down over indirect heat for 20 minutes, until lightly golden. Alternatively, broil the chicken skin side up on a rack set over a baking sheet for 20 minutes. Baste the chicken with any chile oil remaining in the large bowl and continue grilling or broiling for 15 minutes longer; if grilling, turn occasionally. The chicken is done when the skin is deep golden and an instant-read thermometer inserted in an inner thigh registers 165°. Let the chicken rest for 10 minutes. Carve into 8 pieces and serve with the reserved chile oil. —*Paul Kahan*

WINE Juicy, medium-bodied Garnacha from Spain: 2013 Lurra.

Grilled Chicken and Corn with Jalapeño-Lime Dressing

Total **1 hr**; Serves **4**

JALAPEÑO-LIME DRESSING

- ½ cup plus 2 Tbsp. fresh lime juice
- 5 Tbsp. extra-virgin olive oil
- 2 Tbsp. minced jalapeños (with seeds)
- 1¼ Tbsp. kosher salt
- ½ tsp. pepper

SALAD

- 4 ears of corn
- 2 bunches of scallions, halved
- ¼ cup extra-virgin olive oil
- Kosher salt and pepper
- Four 6-oz. boneless chicken breast halves with skin
- 1 Tbsp. rosemary leaves, chopped
- 1 pint Sun Gold tomatoes, halved
- ¼ cup thinly sliced basil
- Chopped chives and finely grated lime zest, for garnish

1. Make the dressing In a small bowl, whisk all of the ingredients.

2. Make the salad Light a grill. Remove all but the last layer of green husk from the corn. In a large bowl, soak the corn in water for 10 minutes, then drain.

3. In a large bowl, toss the scallions with 2 tablespoons of the oil; season with salt and pepper. In another large bowl, coat the chicken with the remaining 2 tablespoons of oil and the rosemary; season with salt and pepper.

4. Grill the corn, scallions and chicken over moderate heat, turning occasionally, until the corn and scallions are lightly charred and the chicken is cooked through, 5 minutes for the scallions and 15 minutes for the corn and chicken. Let the chicken rest for 5 minutes, then thinly slice across the grain.

5. Chop the scallions into 1-inch pieces. Remove the husks and cut the corn kernels off the cobs. In a large bowl, combine the scallions, corn, tomatoes, basil and half of the dressing and toss. Transfer the salad to a platter. Top with the chicken and garnish with chives and lime zest. Serve the remaining dressing at the table. —*Dan Kluger*

WINE Dry, lime-scented Australian Riesling: 2013 Pewsey Vale Eden Valley.

ROAST CHICKEN CACCIATORE
WITH RED WINE BUTTER

Extra-Crispy Fried Chicken

Active **1 hr 15 min**; Total **4 hr 30 min**
Serves **6 to 8**

- ¼ cup plus 2 Tbsp. kosher salt
- ¼ cup freshly ground pepper
- ¼ cup extra-virgin olive oil
- 1½ Tbsp. minced rosemary, plus 4 medium sprigs
- 1½ Tbsp. minced thyme, plus 4 sprigs
- 1½ Tbsp. minced sage, plus 4 sprigs
- 5 minced bay leaves, preferably fresh, plus 5 whole leaves
- 3 garlic cloves, minced, plus 1 head broken into cloves
- Two 3-lb. chickens
- 1 quart buttermilk
- 1 Tbsp. hot sauce, such as Tabasco
- 1 tsp. sugar
- Grapeseed or vegetable oil, for frying
- 2 cups all-purpose flour
- ½ cup rice flour
- ¼ cup garlic powder
- ¼ cup onion powder
- Flaky sea salt, for sprinkling
- Lemon wedges, for serving

1. Preheat the oven to 200°. In a small bowl, whisk 3 tablespoons of the kosher salt with 2 tablespoons of the pepper, the olive oil and the minced rosemary, thyme, sage, bay leaves and garlic. Rub the mixture all over the chickens and set them in a roasting pan. Roast for about 2 hours and 30 minutes, until an instant-read thermometer inserted in the inner thighs registers 150°. Let the chickens cool, then cut each into 10 pieces. (You should have 4 drumsticks, 4 thighs, 4 wings and 8 breast quarters.)

2. In a very large bowl, whisk the buttermilk with the hot sauce and sugar. Add the chicken pieces and toss well. Cover and refrigerate for 1 hour.

3. In a large saucepan, heat 2 inches of grapeseed oil to 375° with the rosemary, thyme and sage sprigs, the 5 whole bay leaves and the head of garlic. When the herbs are crispy and the garlic is golden, transfer to a paper towel–lined plate.

4. Meanwhile, in a large bowl, whisk the all-purpose and rice flours with the garlic and onion powders. Whisk in the remaining 3 tablespoons of kosher salt and the remaining 2 tablespoons of pepper.

5. Remove half of the chicken pieces from the buttermilk, letting the excess drip back into the bowl. Dredge the chicken in the seasoned flour, patting it on lightly so it adheres. Fry the chicken over high heat, turning occasionally, until golden and an instant-read thermometer inserted in the thickest part of each piece registers 160°, about 6 minutes for the breasts and 8 minutes for the wings, thighs and drumsticks. Transfer the fried chicken to a paper towel–lined baking sheet to drain. Let the oil return to 375° before you coat and fry the remaining chicken. Transfer the fried chicken to a platter and garnish with the fried garlic and herbs. Sprinkle with flaky sea salt and serve right away, with lemon wedges. —*Tyler Florence*

WINE Dry, frothy Lambrusco: NV Cantina di Sorbara Amabile.

Arroz con Pollo with Avocado–Green Pea Salsa

Active **1 hr**; Total **1 hr 15 min**; Serves **4 to 6**

- 2 Tbsp. extra-virgin olive oil
- One 3½-lb. chicken, cut into 8 pieces
- Kosher salt and pepper
- 1 medium onion, minced
- 2 serrano chiles, seeded and minced
- 2 garlic cloves, minced
- 3 plum tomatoes (1 lb.), cored and finely diced
- 1 tsp. ground achiote (annatto)
- ½ tsp. ground cumin
- Small pinch of saffron threads
- 1 cup dry white wine
- 3 cups chicken stock or low-sodium broth
- 1 cup pilsner or light beer
- 2 cups Bomba or other short-grain rice
- ½ cup chopped parsley
- Avocado–Green Pea Salsa (recipe follows), for serving
- JE Hot Sauce (p. 363) or other hot sauce, for serving

1. Preheat the oven to 400°. In a very large, deep ovenproof skillet, heat the olive oil until shimmering. Season the chicken with salt and pepper and cook skin side down over moderate heat, turning once, until nicely browned, 10 to 12 minutes. Transfer to a plate.

2. Add the onion, serranos and garlic to the skillet and season with a generous pinch each of salt and pepper. Cook over moderately high heat, stirring occasionally, until softened, about 6 minutes. Add the tomatoes, achiote, cumin and saffron and cook, stirring, until the tomatoes start to break down, about 5 minutes. Add the wine and simmer until slightly reduced, about 3 minutes. Add the stock and beer and bring to a boil. Stir in the rice and return to a boil. Nestle the chicken into the rice and bake uncovered in the lower third of the oven for about 30 minutes, until the liquid is absorbed, the rice is tender and the chicken is cooked through.

3. Transfer the chicken to a plate. Fluff the rice with a fork, then gently fold in the parsley and season with salt and pepper. Return the chicken to the skillet and serve with Avocado–Green Pea Salsa and hot sauce. —*Jose Enrique*

WINE Medium-bodied, citrusy Spanish white: 2013 Finca Os Cobatos Godello.

AVOCADO–GREEN PEA SALSA
⏱ Total **25 min**; Serves **4 to 6**

This unusual, colorful salsa combines green peas and creamy avocado with a hit of lime. It's outstanding with baked rice dishes like arroz con pollo.

- 1 cup fresh or thawed frozen peas
- 1 small red onion, minced
- ¼ cup fresh lime juice
- Kosher salt
- 3 Hass avocados—peeled, pitted and finely diced
- ¼ cup extra-virgin olive oil

1. In a medium saucepan of salted boiling water, blanch the peas until crisp-tender, about 1 minute. Drain and cool under running water, then drain on paper towels.

2. In a bowl, mix the onion with the lime juice and ¾ teaspoon of salt; let stand for 10 minutes. Fold in the avocados, peas and oil, season with salt and serve. —*JE*

ARROZ CON POLLO WITH
AVOCADO-GREEN PEA SALSA

Red-Cooked Chicken with Potatoes and Eggs

Active **45 min**; Total **1 hr 10 min**; Serves **4**

- 2 Tbsp. canola oil
  One 3¾-lb. chicken, cut into 8 pieces
  Kosher salt and pepper
- 1 small onion, chopped
  One 1-inch piece of peeled fresh ginger, cut into ¼-inch rounds
- 3 star anise pods
- 2 dried hot red chiles
- 2 garlic cloves, crushed
- ½ cup Shaoxing wine or dry vermouth
- ¼ cup soy sauce
- 3 Tbsp. packed light brown sugar
- 1¼ cups chicken stock or low-sodium broth
- 2 Yukon Gold potatoes (1 lb.), peeled and cut into ¾-inch pieces
- 4 small carrots, cut into ¾-inch pieces
- 4 large eggs
  Chopped cilantro and scallions, for garnish
  Steamed rice, for serving

1. In a large, deep skillet, heat the oil until shimmering. Season the chicken lightly with salt and pepper and add to the skillet skin side down. Cook over moderately high heat, turning occasionally, until browned all over, 10 to 12 minutes. Transfer the chicken to a plate.

2. Add the onion to the skillet and cook over moderate heat, stirring occasionally, until softened and browned, about 7 minutes. Add the ginger, star anise, chiles and garlic and cook, stirring, until fragrant, about 1 minute. Add the wine, soy sauce, sugar and chicken stock and bring to a boil. Add the potatoes and carrots and return to a boil. Nestle the chicken in the skillet, cover and braise over moderately low heat, turning occasionally, until the vegetables are tender and the chicken is cooked through, 15 to 20 minutes. Discard the star anise and chiles.

3. Meanwhile, in a medium saucepan, cover the eggs with water and bring to a boil. Simmer over moderate heat for 8 minutes, then cool under running water. Peel the eggs and quarter lengthwise.

4. Gently submerge the eggs in the stew and spoon into shallow bowls. Garnish with chopped cilantro and scallions and serve with rice. —*Cara and Cecile Stadler*

WINE Oregon Pinot Noir with spice notes: 2012 Ken Wright Cellars Willamette Valley.

Yogurt-Marinated Grilled Chicken

Active **20 min**; Total **1 hr 10 min plus 3 hr marinating**; Serves **4**

- 1 cup plain whole-milk Greek yogurt
- 1 cup lightly packed cilantro, finely chopped
- 2 Tbsp. fresh lemon juice
- 3 garlic cloves, minced
- 1 tsp. cayenne pepper
- 1 tsp. ground cumin
  Kosher salt and ground pepper
  One 3½-lb. chicken—halved, breast and rib bones removed, leg bones left intact (have your butcher do this)
  Vegetable oil, for brushing

1. In a large resealable plastic bag, mix the yogurt with the cilantro, lemon juice, garlic, cayenne, cumin, 2 teaspoons of salt and 1 teaspoon of ground pepper. Add the chicken halves and turn to coat. Seal the bag and transfer to a baking dish. Refrigerate for at least 3 hours or overnight. Bring the chicken to room temperature before grilling.

2. Set up a gas grill for indirect grilling, then heat to 400° and oil the grate. Remove the chicken from the marinade, scraping off any excess; discard the marinade. Season the chicken with salt and ground pepper. Set the chicken skin side up on the grate over indirect heat. Close the grill and cook, turning once, until the chicken is browned and nearly cooked through, about 25 minutes; use a spray bottle filled with water to stop flare-ups.

3. Reduce the heat to moderately low. Flip the chicken and grill it over direct heat, turning occasionally, until lightly charred and an instant-read thermometer inserted in an inner thigh registers 160°, about 15 minutes more. Transfer the chicken to a carving board and let rest for 10 minutes before carving. —*Tom Mylan*

WINE Citrusy California Sauvignon Blanc: 2012 Honig.

Coq au Vin

📷 PAGE 138

Active **45 min**; Total **1 hr 45 min**; Serves **6**

- 6 oz. meaty slab bacon, sliced ¼ inch thick and cut into 1-inch lardons
  One 4-lb. chicken, cut into 8 pieces
  Salt and freshly ground pepper
- 2 garlic cloves, smashed
- 1 medium onion, finely chopped
- 4 large carrots, sliced ¼ inch thick
- 2 cups dry red wine, such as Pinot Noir
- 2 cups chicken stock or low-sodium broth
  Bouquet garni (4 thyme sprigs, 8 parsley sprigs and 1 bay leaf tied with kitchen twine)
- 2 Tbsp. unsalted butter
- 2 Tbsp. extra-virgin olive oil
- 1 lb. shiitake mushrooms, stems discarded and caps thickly sliced
- 2 Tbsp. chopped parsley

1. In a very large, deep skillet, cook the bacon over moderately high heat, stirring frequently, until crisp, 6 minutes. Using a slotted spoon, transfer the bacon to a plate.

2. Pat the chicken dry and season generously with salt and pepper. Add the chicken to the skillet skin side down in a single layer and cook over moderately high heat, turning once, until browned all over, 10 minutes. Transfer the chicken to a plate and pour off all but 2 tablespoons of the fat in the skillet.

3. Add the garlic, onion and carrots to the pan. Cover and cook over moderate heat, stirring occasionally, until barely softened, about 2 minutes. Uncover and cook until nearly tender, 3 minutes. Add the wine and cook over high heat, scraping up any browned bits, until reduced by half, about 5 minutes. Add the stock, bouquet garni and bacon and bring to a simmer. Nestle the chicken in the broth, cover partially and simmer over moderately low heat until the chicken is white throughout, 45 minutes.

4. In a large skillet, melt the butter in the oil over high heat. When the foam subsides, add the mushrooms and season with salt and pepper. Cook over moderate heat, stirring occasionally, until browned and tender, 7 to 8 minutes. Add the mushrooms to the chicken and simmer for 5 minutes. Discard the bouquet garni. Garnish with the parsley and serve. —*Marjorie Taylor*

WINE Earthy, raspberry-scented red Burgundy: 2011 Domaine Faiveley Mercurey Rouge.

Turmeric Chicken and Rice

Active **35 min**; Total **1 hr 10 min**; Serves **4**

- One 4½-lb. chicken, cut into 8 pieces
- Kosher salt and pepper
- 2 Tbsp. unsalted butter
- 1½ tsp. ground turmeric
- 1 small onion, chopped
- 1 Tbsp. finely chopped peeled fresh ginger
- 4 garlic cloves, minced
- 2 plum tomatoes, chopped
- 2 tsp. curry powder
- ½ tsp. ground cinnamon
- ½ tsp. ground cumin
- 2 cups jasmine rice
- 3 bay leaves
- 1½ Tbsp. Asian fish sauce
- 3 cups chicken stock or low-sodium broth
- Plain whole yogurt, sliced cucumbers, mint leaves and lime wedges, for serving

1. Season the chicken with salt and pepper. In a large enameled cast-iron casserole or Dutch oven, melt the butter and sprinkle with the turmeric. Add the chicken skin side down and cook over moderately high heat, turning once, until browned on both sides, 8 minutes total. Transfer the chicken to a plate.

2. Add the onion, ginger and garlic to the casserole and cook, stirring occasionally, until starting to brown, about 5 minutes. Add the tomatoes, curry powder, cinnamon, cumin and rice and stir constantly until fragrant, about 1 minute. Return the chicken to the pot, skin side up. Add the bay leaves, fish sauce and chicken stock and bring to a boil over high heat.

3. Cover and simmer over low heat for 10 minutes. Adjust the lid to cover partially and simmer until the rice is cooked, 10 to 15 minutes longer. Remove from the heat, uncover and let stand for 5 minutes. Serve with yogurt, cucumbers, mint and lime wedges. —*Edward Lee*

BEER Fresh, floral American pilsner: Victory Prima Pils.

Slow-Cooker Chicken "Potpie" with Stuffing Crust

Active **1 hr**; Total **5 hr 30 min**; Serves **6**

CHICKEN STEW

- 5 thyme sprigs
- 3 sage sprigs
- 1½ sticks unsalted butter
- 2 cups all-purpose flour
- 3 cups chicken stock or low-sodium broth
- 2 cups half-and-half
- 4 carrots, cut into ½-inch-thick rounds
- 1 leek, white and light green parts only, finely chopped
- 1 onion, finely chopped
- 2 celery ribs, cut into ½-inch pieces
- ½ lb. cremini mushrooms, quartered
- 6 garlic cloves, minced
- 1 lb. fingerling potatoes, halved
- 4 bay leaves
- 2 tsp. kosher salt
- 3 lbs. boneless, skinless chicken thighs, cut into 1-inch pieces
- 1 cup fresh or frozen peas
- 1 cup fresh or frozen corn kernels
- Pepper

CRUST

- ¼ cup extra-virgin olive oil, plus more for greasing
- 11 oz. light multigrain bread, cut into 1-inch cubes (6 cups)
- 4 oz. potato chips (7 cups), broken into pieces
- 33 Ritz crackers, broken into pieces
- 1 onion, finely chopped
- 3 garlic cloves, minced
- 1 Tbsp. thyme leaves
- 2 Tbsp. chopped sage
- ¼ cup chopped parsley
- 1 tsp. kosher salt
- ½ tsp. pepper
- 6 Tbsp. unsalted butter, melted and cooled
- ½ cup chicken stock or low-sodium broth
- ½ cup half-and-half
- 2 large eggs, beaten
- Poached eggs, chopped thyme and parsley, and grated lemon zest, for serving and garnish

1. Make the chicken stew Using kitchen twine, tie the thyme and sage sprigs into a bundle. Turn a 6- to 6½-quart slow cooker to low and set the timer for 5 hours and 15 minutes.

2. Add the butter and cover until the butter melts. Stir in the flour and mix with a wooden spoon until well incorporated and a paste forms. Stir in the chicken stock and half-and-half, cover and cook for 5 minutes. Whisk the mixture until smooth. Add the herb bundle, then add the vegetables, bay leaves and salt. Cover and cook for 4 hours, stirring after 2 hours.

3. Stir in the chicken, peas and corn. Cover and cook until the chicken is white throughout, about 1 hour and 15 minutes. Discard the herb bundle. Season the stew with pepper.

4. Meanwhile, make the crust Preheat the oven to 375°. Lightly oil a baking sheet. In a food processor, pulse the bread cubes until coarse crumbs form. Transfer to a large bowl. Add the potato chips and Ritz crackers to the processor and pulse until coarse crumbs form; add to the bowl. Stir in the ¼ cup of oil and all of the remaining ingredients except the poached eggs and garnishes. Spread the mixture on the prepared baking sheet and pat it out to an even ¼-inch layer with your fingertips. Bake until golden and crisp, about 45 minutes. Transfer to a rack and let cool. Break into 3-by-3-inch pieces.

5. Serve the chicken stew in bowls, each topped with a poached egg and a piece of crust. Garnish with thyme, parsley and lemon zest. —*Grant Achatz*

MAKE AHEAD The crust can be stored in an airtight container at room temperature for 1 day. Rewarm in a 350° oven until crisp.

WINE Ripe, apple-inflected Chardonnay: 2012 Lafond Santa Rita Hills.

Arroz con Pollo

Active **1 hr 30 min**; Total **2 hr 30 min**
Serves **6**

"I poured all of my culinary knowledge into this peasant one-pot meal," says Iron Chef Jose Garces.

- ½ cup canola oil
- 3 Tbsp. annatto seeds
- 7 parsley sprigs
- 3 thyme sprigs
- 2 bay leaves
- ¼ cup fresh orange juice
- 7 garlic cloves
- 1 Tbsp. dried oregano
  Kosher salt and ground pepper
- 2 boneless chicken breasts with skin (1¼ lbs.)
- 4 chicken legs (2½ lbs.)
- 1 carrot, chopped
- 1 celery rib, chopped
- 1 small shallot, thinly sliced
- 1 leek, white and light green parts, thinly sliced
- 1 onion, finely chopped
- 1½ cups dry white wine
- 2 Tbsp. tomato paste
- 5 cups chicken stock or low-sodium broth
- ½ green bell pepper, sliced
- 1 Anaheim or poblano chile, seeded and thinly sliced
- 2 cups long-grain white rice
- ½ cup canned chickpeas
- 4 jarred piquillo peppers (2 oz.), thinly sliced
- ⅓ cup pitted green olives

1. In a small saucepan, simmer the oil and annatto seeds over low heat for 2 minutes. Let the oil cool to room temperature, 15 minutes. Strain the oil and reserve the seeds.

2. Wrap and tie the reserved annatto seeds with the parsley, thyme and 1 bay leaf in a double layer of cheesecloth.

3. In a medium bowl, combine the orange juice, 3 tablespoons of the annatto oil, 2 minced garlic cloves and 2 teaspoons of the dried oregano. Season with salt and pepper. Add the chicken breasts and turn to coat. Let marinate for 1 hour.

4. Meanwhile, preheat the oven to 350°. In a large enameled cast-iron casserole, heat 2 tablespoons of the annatto oil. Season the chicken legs with salt and pepper, add to the casserole and cook over moderate heat, turning, until browned all over; transfer to a plate. Add the carrot, celery, shallot, leek, 2 sliced garlic cloves and half of the chopped onion to the casserole and cook, stirring, until softened. Add the wine, bring to a boil and cook until reduced by half. Add the tomato paste and cook, stirring, for 2 minutes. Stir in the stock, chicken legs and herb bundle and bring to a boil.

5. Cover and transfer the casserole to the oven. Bake for 1 hour, until the chicken is very tender. Transfer the chicken to a baking sheet. Strain the braising liquid; you should have 4 cups (if necessary, add water). Clean out the casserole. Shred the chicken meat; discard the skin.

6. Increase the oven temperature to 425°. In the casserole, heat 1 tablespoon of the annatto oil. Add the bell pepper, chile and remaining 3 minced garlic cloves, 1 teaspoon of oregano, 1 bay leaf and chopped onion. Cook over moderate heat, stirring, until the vegetables are softened. Add the shredded chicken and braising liquid, season with salt and pepper and bring to a boil. Add the rice and chickpeas and stir once; arrange the piquillos and olives on top. Press a 9-inch square of parchment paper on the rice. Cover and cook over low heat for 25 minutes, until the rice is tender. Let stand off the heat for 5 minutes. Remove the paper.

7. Meanwhile, in an ovenproof cast-iron skillet, heat the remaining 2 tablespoons of annatto oil. Pat dry the chicken breasts. Cook in the skillet, skin side down, over moderately high heat until well browned. Turn the chicken, transfer the skillet to the oven and roast for 20 minutes, until the juices run clear when a knife is inserted. Transfer to a plate and let rest for 5 minutes, then slice ¼ inch thick. Top the rice with the chicken breast. —*Jose Garces*

SERVE WITH Plantain chips and hot sauce.

WINE Balanced, fruit-forward California Chardonnay: 2012 Luli.

Grilled Mango Chicken with Cabbage Salad

Active **25 min**; Total **45 min plus 4 hr marinating**; Serves **6**

Jeni Britton Bauer of Jeni's Splendid Ice Creams cleverly uses melted mango sorbet as a marinade for chicken and in the dressing for her crunchy cabbage slaw.

- 1½ cups mango sorbet, melted
  Four 6-oz. skinless, boneless chicken breast halves, butterflied
- ¼ cup fresh lime juice
- 2 Tbsp. toasted sesame oil
- 2 Tbsp. soy sauce
- 1 tsp. Asian fish sauce
- ¾ lb. red cabbage, cored and very thinly sliced (4 cups)
- ¾ lb. green cabbage, cored and very thinly sliced (4 cups)
- ½ cup chopped cilantro
- 6 scallions, thinly sliced
  Kosher salt
  Vegetable oil, for brushing
  Pepper
  Dry-roasted peanuts, for serving

1. In a large, resealable plastic bag, combine 1¼ cups of the sorbet with the chicken and turn to coat. Seal and set the bag in a large baking dish. Refrigerate for at least 4 hours or overnight.

2. In a large bowl, whisk the remaining ¼ cup of sorbet with the lime juice, sesame oil, soy sauce and fish sauce. Add the red and green cabbage, cilantro and scallions, season with salt and toss well.

3. Heat a grill pan. Remove the chicken from the marinade and pat dry. Brush with vegetable oil and season with salt and pepper. Grill over moderately high heat, turning once, until cooked through, about 6 minutes. Transfer the chicken to a carving board and let cool, about 10 minutes. Cut the chicken crosswise into ½-inch-thick slices. Spoon the slaw onto plates, top with the chicken and peanuts and serve. —*Jeni Britton Bauer*

WINE Ripe, tropical-fruit-scented Chardonnay: 2012 Talbott Kali Hart.

Market Math: Turkey

1 Turkey Curry Soup

In a saucepan, heat 2 Tbsp. **canola oil**. Add 2 Tbsp. **Thai red curry paste** and 4 cups **kabocha squash** (1½-inch pieces); cook over high heat, stirring, for 3 minutes. Add 1 cup **unsweetened coconut milk**, 1 Tbsp. **Asian fish sauce** and 4 cups **water**; bring to a boil. Cover and simmer until the squash is tender, 15 minutes. Stir in 3 cups shredded **roast turkey**, 3 Tbsp. **lime juice** and ½ cup chopped mixed **cilantro** and **basil**; season with **salt** and **pepper**.

2 Turkey Tonnato

In a food processor, combine one 6½-oz. can drained **tuna**, ½ cup cooked **chickpeas** and ¼ cup **plain yogurt**. With the machine on, drizzle in ½ cup **olive oil**. Transfer to a bowl; stir in ¼ cup chopped **capers** and ½ cup chopped mixed **tarragon**, **dill** and **chives**; season with **salt** and **pepper**. Serve with **roast turkey breast**.

3 Turkey Reuben Hash

In a cast-iron skillet, heat 3 Tbsp. **olive oil**. Add ½ small chopped **onion** and 1 coarsely grated peeled **baking potato** and cook over moderately high heat, stirring, for 8 minutes. Add 1 cup drained **sauerkraut**, 2 cups shredded **roast turkey**, 2 chopped **scallions** and ⅛ tsp. **caraway seeds**. Cook until golden, 3 minutes.

4 Turkey-Stuffing Salad

In a bowl, whisk 1 Tbsp. each of **Dijon mustard** and **lemon juice** with ½ cup **olive oil**. Add 3 cups chopped **roast turkey**, 3 sliced **celery ribs**, 1 sliced **fennel bulb**, 1 chopped **apple** and 1 cup **parsley**. Season with **salt** and **pepper**; toss. Top with **croutons**. *–Kay Chun*

Arroz con Pollo with Mushrooms

Active **50 min**; Total **1 hr 15 min**; Serves **4**

- **3** plum tomatoes, halved lengthwise
- **¼** cup extra-virgin olive oil
- One 3½-lb. chicken, cut into 8 pieces
- Kosher salt and pepper
- **1** medium Spanish onion, finely chopped
- **1** medium green bell pepper, finely chopped
- **5** garlic cloves, minced
- **4** thyme sprigs
- **1** bay leaf
- **½** tsp. sweet pimentón de la Vera (smoked Spanish paprika)
- **½** lb. oyster or cremini mushrooms, cut into 1-inch pieces
- **1** cup Bomba or Calasparra rice
- Small pinch of saffron threads
- Hot sauce, for serving

1. Working over a bowl, grate the cut sides of the tomatoes on the large holes of a box grater; discard the skins.

2. In a very large, deep skillet, heat the olive oil until shimmering. Season the chicken with salt and pepper, add it to the skillet skin side down and cook over moderate heat, turning once, until nicely browned on both sides; transfer the chicken to a plate.

3. Pour off all but 2 tablespoons of the fat from the skillet. Add the onion and green pepper, season with salt and cook over moderate heat, stirring occasionally, until just starting to brown, 10 minutes. Add the garlic, thyme sprigs, bay leaf and pimentón and cook, stirring, until fragrant, 2 minutes. Add the grated tomatoes and cook, stirring, until the liquid has evaporated, about 5 minutes. Stir in the mushrooms and cook over moderately high heat until they start to soften, 3 minutes.

4. Add 3 cups of water to the skillet and bring to a boil. Stir in the rice, saffron and a generous pinch of salt and return to a boil. Nestle the chicken in the rice and cook over moderately low heat, without stirring, until the rice is tender and the chicken is cooked through, 20 to 25 minutes. Discard the thyme sprigs and bay leaf.

5. Season the dish with salt and pepper and serve with hot sauce. —*José Andrés*

WINE Intense Virginia Cabernet-based red: 2010 RdV Lost Mountain.

Spicy Barbecued Chicken with Miso Corn

⏲ Total **45 min**; Serves **4**

CHICKEN

- **⅓** cup packed light brown sugar
- **3** Tbsp. soy sauce
- **1** Tbsp. toasted sesame oil
- **1** Tbsp. finely grated peeled fresh ginger
- **2** tsp. crushed red pepper
- **1** tsp. kosher salt
- **4** garlic cloves, minced
- **1** scallion, thinly sliced, plus more for garnish
- **8** boneless, skinless chicken thighs (about 2½ lbs.)

CORN

- **4** Tbsp. unsalted butter, at room temperature
- **1** Tbsp. white miso or *doenjang* (Korean fermented bean paste)
- **½** scallion, thinly sliced
- Canola oil, for brushing
- **4** ears of corn, shucked

1. Make the chicken In a large bowl, stir together all of the ingredients except the chicken. Add the chicken thighs and toss to coat. Let stand at room temperature for 20 minutes.

2. Meanwhile, make the corn In a small bowl, mix the butter with the miso and scallion.

3. Light a grill and brush the grate with canola oil. Grill the corn and chicken over moderate heat, turning, until charred in spots and the chicken is cooked through, about 10 minutes for the corn and 12 to 15 minutes for the chicken. Transfer the corn to a large platter and slather with the seasoned butter. Arrange the chicken alongside, garnish with sliced scallion and serve warm. —*Judy Joo*

BEER Fruity German wheat beer: Paulaner Hefe-Weizen.

Honey-Roasted Duck Breasts with Toasted Red Quinoa and Asian Pears

Active **40 min**; Total **1 hr 10 min**; Serves **4**

- **1** Tbsp. extra-virgin olive oil
- **½** cup finely chopped onion
- Kosher salt
- **1½** cups red quinoa, rinsed and drained
- **2¼** cups chicken stock
- **¼** cup chopped parsley
- **½** cup pecans
- Two 1-lb. Moulard duck breast halves
- Finely ground pepper
- **1** Tbsp. honey
- **2** small Asian pears, peeled and diced
- **2** Tbsp. unsalted butter
- **1** Tbsp. dry sherry
- **1** tsp. chopped rosemary

1. Preheat the oven to 350°. In a large ovenproof saucepan, heat the oil. Add the onion and cook over moderate heat, stirring, until softened, about 3 minutes. Season with salt. Add the quinoa and cook, stirring, until lightly toasted, 2 minutes. Add 2 cups of the stock and bring to a simmer. Cover and bake for about 20 minutes, until all of the liquid is absorbed and the quinoa is tender. Let stand, covered, for 10 minutes, then fluff with a fork and fold in the parsley; keep warm.

2. Spread the pecans on a baking sheet and toast for 4 minutes, until lightly golden; coarsely chop and transfer to a bowl. Increase the oven temperature to 400°.

3. Score the duck skin in a crosshatch pattern and season with salt and pepper. In a large cast-iron skillet, cook the duck skin side down over low heat until most of the fat has rendered, 10 minutes. Pour off all but 2 tablespoons of the fat. Turn the duck breasts skin side up and add the honey to the pan. Baste the duck with the honey and roast in the oven for 6 to 7 minutes, until medium-rare. Transfer the duck to a cutting board and let rest for 10 minutes.

4. Meanwhile, in the same skillet, cook the pears over moderately high heat, stirring, until golden, 2 minutes. Add the butter, sherry and remaining ¼ cup of chicken stock and cook until thickened, stirring to loosen any browned bits, about 3 minutes. Stir in the rosemary.

5. Thinly slice the duck breasts crosswise. Spoon the quinoa onto 4 plates and top with the duck and pecans. Spoon on the pear sauce and serve. —*Kyle Bailey*

BEER Deep, intense sour beer: Duchesse de Bourgogne Flanders red ale.

Spice-Roasted Duck

Active **30 min;** Total **2 hr 30 min plus overnight drying; Serves 4**

- 1 tsp. coriander seeds
- 1 tsp. fennel seeds
- ½ tsp. caraway seeds
- 1 tsp. sweet pimentón de la Vera
  Kosher salt and ground pepper
  One 5½-lb. Pekin duck, excess fat from cavity and neck removed
- 1 small onion, quartered
- 2 thyme sprigs
- 1 sage sprig

1. In a small skillet, toast the coriander, fennel and caraway seeds over moderate heat, tossing, until fragrant, about 2 minutes. Transfer to a spice grinder and let cool, then grind to a powder. Transfer the spice mix to a small bowl and stir in the pimentón de la Vera, 2 teaspoons of salt and ½ teaspoon of pepper.

2. Prick the duck all over with a sharp paring knife. Season all over with the spice mixture and transfer it to a large plate. Refrigerate the duck uncovered overnight.

3. Preheat the oven to 300°. Rinse the duck under cool water and pat dry. Season the duck and cavity lightly with salt and stuff it with the onion, thyme and sage. Tie the legs together and transfer the duck breast side up to a rack set in a roasting pan.

4. Roast the duck for 1 hour, until an instant-read thermometer inserted in an inner thigh registers 140°. Increase the oven temperature to 425° and roast for 20 to 30 minutes, until the skin is crisp and an instant-read thermometer inserted in an inner thigh registers 160°. Tip any juices from the cavity into the roasting pan and transfer the duck to a carving board. Spoon off as much fat as possible from the pan juices. Carve the duck and serve with any pan juices. —*Hugh Acheson*

WINE Peppery, red-berried southern Rhône red: 2010 Mas Carlot Costières de Nîmes Rouge.

Jamaican Jerk Duck

Active **30 min;** Total **2 hr plus overnight drying; Serves 4**

- One 4½- to 5-lb. Pekin duck
- 3 Tbsp. dried thyme leaves
- 2 Tbsp. ground allspice
- 1 Tbsp. garlic powder
- 2 tsp. black pepper
- 2 tsp. crushed red pepper
- 1 tsp. onion powder
- 1 tsp. light brown sugar
  Kosher salt
- 2 carrots, chopped
- 1 head of garlic, halved crosswise
- 1 onion, chopped
- 2 cups chicken stock or low-sodium broth
- 1 Tbsp. unsalted butter
- 1 Tbsp. chopped parsley

1. Gently prick the duck skin all over with a sharp paring knife (without piercing the meat) and place it on a rack set in the sink.

2. Bring a small pot of water to a boil. Slowly pour the water all over the duck to render some of the fat; tilt the duck to drain the cavity. Transfer the rack with the duck to a baking sheet; pat the duck dry with paper towels.

3. In a bowl, combine the thyme, allspice, garlic powder, black pepper, crushed red pepper, onion powder and sugar. Rub the spice mix inside the cavity and all over the duck. Refrigerate uncovered for 1 to 2 days.

4. Preheat the oven to 300°. Season the duck with salt and stuff the cavity with half of the carrots and garlic. Transfer the duck to a rack (preferably V-shaped) set in a roasting pan and add the onion, stock and the remaining carrots and garlic to the pan.

5. Roast the duck until lightly golden and an instant-read thermometer inserted in the thickest part of a thigh registers 140°, about 1 hour. Increase the oven temperature to 450° and roast for 15 minutes longer, until the skin is deep golden and crispy and an instant-read thermometer inserted in the thickest part of a thigh registers 160°. Let the duck rest for 20 minutes.

6. Tilt the duck to release the juices into the roasting pan, then strain the pan juices into a medium saucepan and degrease with a spoon. Bring to a boil. Whisk in the butter and simmer until slightly thickened, 5 minutes. Stir in the parsley and season with salt and pepper. Carve the duck and serve with the pan sauce. —*Kay Chun*

WINE Spiced, strawberry-rich Australian Pinot Noir: 2013 Innocent Bystander.

Simplest Roast Turkey

Active **20 min;** Total **5 hr plus overnight refrigerating; Serves 10 to 12**

The trick to this two-ingredient roast turkey from F&W editor in chief Dana Cowin is allowing it to air-dry overnight in the refrigerator, resulting in supercrispy skin.

- One 13- to 15-lb. turkey
  Kosher salt
- ¼ cup extra-virgin olive oil
- 1½ tsp. freshly ground pepper

1. Rinse the turkey inside and out under cold water and pat it thoroughly dry with paper towels. Season the cavity with ½ tablespoon of salt, then season the outside with another 1½ tablespoons of salt. Put the turkey on a large plate and refrigerate, uncovered, for 8 to 24 hours. Let the turkey stand at room temperature for 1 hour before roasting.

2. Preheat the oven to 425°. Rub the turkey all over with the olive oil, season with salt and the pepper and transfer to a large roasting pan. Roast for about 1 hour, until lightly golden. Reduce the oven temperature to 375° and roast for 2 to 2¼ hours longer, until an instant-read thermometer inserted in an inner thigh registers 165°. Cover the breast with foil if it browns too quickly. Transfer the turkey to a carving board and let rest for at least 45 minutes before carving and serving. —*Dana Cowin*

WINE Lively, floral Oregon Pinot Noir: 2012 Evesham Wood Willamette Valley.

Moroccan-Spiced Turkey

Active **30 min**; Total **4 hr 45 min**
Serves **8 to 10**

Marcus Samuelsson, the chef at Red Rooster in New York City, bastes this spiced turkey with a vibrant mix of four citrus juices, then serves it with a chutney or savory jam.

> **One 12-lb. turkey, patted dry**
> **Kosher salt and pepper**
> 1 **lemon, quartered**
> 4 **sage sprigs, plus 1½ tsp. finely chopped sage leaves**
> 1 **head of garlic, halved crosswise**
> ⅓ **cup fresh grapefruit juice**
> ¼ **cup fresh orange juice**
> 2 **Tbsp. fresh lemon juice**
> 2 **Tbsp. fresh lime juice**
> 2 **Tbsp. *ras el hanout* (see Note)**
> **Chutney or onion jam, for serving**

1. Put the turkey on the rack of a roasting pan. Season the turkey cavity with salt and pepper and stuff the lemon quarters and sage sprigs inside. Tie the legs together, season the turkey all over with salt and pepper and let stand at room temperature for about 1 hour.

2. Meanwhile, preheat the oven to 400°. Wrap the garlic in foil and roast for 1 hour, until very tender. Let cool completely, then squeeze the cloves into a medium bowl. Whisk in the citrus juices along with the *ras el hanout* and chopped sage.

3. Brush the turkey all over with the citrus-garlic mixture. Roast in the lower third of the oven for 30 minutes, then baste with the citrus-garlic mixture. Reduce the oven temperature to 325° and continue to roast, basting every 30 minutes, for 2 hours and 15 minutes longer, until an instant-read thermometer inserted in an inner thigh registers 165°. Transfer the turkey to a board; let rest for 30 minutes to 1 hour. Carve the turkey, drizzle with any pan juices and serve with chutney. —*Marcus Samuelsson*

NOTE *Ras el hanout* is a North African spice mixture that usually includes ginger and anise. It's available at some grocery stores (McCormick makes a version) and from kalustyans.com.

WINE Cranberry-inflected Italian red: 2012 J. Hofstätter Meczan Pinot Nero.

Ancho-Rubbed Turkey Breast with Vegetables

Active **30 min**; Total **2 hr 45 min**; Serves **6**

> 1½ **Tbsp. ancho chile powder**
> 1 **tsp. ground coriander**
> 1 **tsp. onion powder**
> ½ **tsp. sugar**
> 1½ **tsp. chopped oregano, plus 6 oregano sprigs**
> **One 3¾-lb. boneless whole turkey breast with skin, patted dry**
> ¼ **cup plus 2 Tbsp. extra-virgin olive oil**
> **Kosher salt and pepper**
> 3 **large baking potatoes, cut lengthwise into 1-inch wedges**
> 3 **poblano chiles, halved lengthwise**
> 3 **medium red onions, peeled and cut into 1-inch wedges through the core**

1. In a small bowl, whisk the chile powder with the coriander, onion powder, sugar and chopped oregano. Set the turkey breast skin side down on a work surface. Drizzle with 1 tablespoon of the olive oil and season generously with salt and pepper, then rub with half of the spice mixture. Fold in the sides and tie up the turkey breast with twine to make a neat roast. Season the outside of the turkey breast with salt and pepper, then rub with the remaining spice mix. Drizzle with 1 tablespoon of the olive oil and let stand at room temperature for 1 hour.

2. Preheat the oven to 425°. On a large rimmed baking sheet, toss the potatoes, poblanos, onions and oregano sprigs with the remaining ¼ cup of olive oil. Season the vegetables with salt and pepper and spread in an even layer. Set the turkey breast skin side up on the vegetables. Roast for about 1 hour, until an instant-read thermometer inserted in the thickest part of the turkey registers 155°; tent with foil if it browns too quickly. Transfer the turkey breast to a carving board and let stand for 20 minutes. Untie the roast and thinly slice crosswise. Serve with the roasted vegetables. —*Justin Chapple*

WINE Smoky, meaty Syrah from Washington state: 2012 Corvidae Lenore.

Roast Turkey with Pepperoni

Active **30 min**; Total **5 hr plus overnight dry brining**; Serves **8**

Chef Alex Pope of The Local Pig in Kansas City, Missouri, adds lots of flavor to his roast turkey by stuffing thin slices of pepperoni and preserved lemon rind under the skin.

> **One 12- to 14-lb. turkey**
> 2 **Tbsp. kosher salt**
> ½ **lb. thinly sliced pepperoni**
> 1 **preserved lemon—halved lengthwise, pulp discarded and rind sliced ½ inch thick, plus 2 tsp. minced rind**
> 12 **large sage leaves, plus 2 sage sprigs**
> 2 **rosemary sprigs**
> 2 **sticks unsalted butter, softened**
> 2 **Tbsp. finely chopped thyme**
> ½ **tsp. ground fennel**
> **Pepper**

1. Rinse the turkey inside and out with cold water and pat it thoroughly dry with paper towels. Season the turkey inside and out with the salt and transfer to a rack set in a roasting pan. Refrigerate uncovered overnight. Let the turkey return to room temperature before cooking.

2. Preheat the oven to 300°. Carefully run your fingers under the turkey breast and thigh skin to loosen; tuck the pepperoni, sliced preserved lemon rind and sage leaves under the skin. Stuff the sage and rosemary sprigs in the cavity. Tie the legs together with kitchen string.

3. In a medium bowl, blend the butter with the thyme, ground fennel and minced lemon rind. Rub the butter all over the turkey and season with pepper.

4. Roast the turkey in the lower third of the oven for 2½ hours. Increase the oven temperature to 425° and continue to roast for 30 minutes longer, until the skin is well browned and an instant-read thermometer inserted in an inner thigh registers 165°. Transfer the turkey to a carving board and let rest in a warm place for 30 minutes to 1 hour. Strain the pan juices into a bowl. Carve the turkey and serve with the pan juices. —*Alex Pope*

WINE Peppery, medium-bodied Spanish Tempranillo: 2012 Protocolo Tinto.

MOROCCAN-SPICED TURKEY

Greek-Style Quail with Yogurt Sauce

Total **30 min plus overnight marinating**
Serves **8**

- ¾ cup extra-virgin olive oil
- 1 Tbsp. fresh lemon juice
- 1 large shallot, finely chopped
- 6 garlic cloves—5 finely chopped, 1 grated
- 1½ tsp. dried oregano
- 1½ tsp. ground cumin
- ½ tsp. freshly grated nutmeg
  Freshly ground pepper
- 8 quail (3¼ lbs.), backbones removed and quail flattened
  Kosher salt
- ¾ cup plain low-fat Greek yogurt
- 1 scallion, finely chopped
  Warm pita bread, for serving

1. In a large bowl, combine ½ cup of the olive oil with the lemon juice, shallot, chopped garlic, oregano, cumin, nutmeg and ½ teaspoon of pepper. Add the quail and toss to coat. Cover and marinate in the refrigerator overnight.

2. Preheat the oven to 475°. Arrange the quail skin side up on a baking sheet in a single layer. Season with salt and pepper and roast for 9 to 10 minutes, until golden and just cooked through. Transfer the quail to a platter and let rest for 5 minutes.

3. Meanwhile, in a small bowl, stir the yogurt with the scallion, grated garlic and the remaining ¼ cup of olive oil and season with salt and pepper. Serve the quail with the yogurt sauce and warm pita bread. —*Kay Chun*

WINE Citrusy Sauvignon Blanc from Chile: 2013 Casas del Bosque Reserva.

PAIRING TIP

Best Wines for Roasted Birds

Roasting intensifies the savory qualities of poultry. Earthy, umami-driven wines like Chardonnay, Pinot Noir and Syrah are a natural match.

Grilled Squab Breasts with Creamy Orzo

Active **1 hr**; Total **2 hr 40 min**
Serves **4 as a main dish, 8 as a starter**

At Le Pigeon in Portland, Oregon, chef Gabriel Rucker cooks all kinds of game birds. Here, he pairs squab with a fresh tomato vinaigrette and orzo in a spiced-yogurt dressing.

SQUAB

- ¼ cup lightly packed cilantro leaves
- ¼ cup lightly packed mint leaves
- 1 tsp. ground cumin
- 1 tsp. ground coriander
- 1 tsp. paprika
- 1 tsp. finely grated orange zest
- ½ cup extra-virgin olive oil
- 8 boneless squab breast halves with skin, first wing joints left intact (see Note)
  Kosher salt

TOMATO VINAIGRETTE

- One ¾-lb. heirloom tomato
- ¼ cup extra-virgin olive oil
- 1 small shallot, minced
- 2 Tbsp. fresh lemon juice
- 1 Tbsp. brine from a jar of green olives
- ¾ tsp. ground cumin
- 1 small garlic clove, minced
  Kosher salt

ORZO

- 1 cup orzo
- ¼ cup extra-virgin olive oil
- ½ cup plain yogurt
- 2 Tbsp. fresh lemon juice
- ½ tsp. ground coriander
- ¼ tsp. ground cumin
- ¼ tsp. piment d'Espelette
- ½ cup lightly packed cilantro leaves
- ½ cup lightly packed mint leaves
- ½ cup crumbled feta cheese, preferably French
  Kosher salt
- ¼ cup halved pitted Castelvetrano olives, ¼ cup halved grape tomatoes and very thinly sliced red onion, for garnish

1. Marinate the squab In a food processor, combine all of the ingredients except the squab and salt and puree until nearly smooth. Scrape the marinade into a large baking dish. Season the squab breasts with salt and add to the marinade, turning to coat. Cover and refrigerate for 1 hour. Let the squab stand at room temperature for 30 minutes before grilling.

2. Meanwhile, make the tomato vinaigrette In a medium bowl, grate the tomato on the large holes of a box grater; discard the skin. Whisk the grated tomato pulp with the remaining ingredients and season with salt.

3. Prepare the orzo In a medium saucepan of salted boiling water, cook the orzo until al dente; drain well. Toss the orzo with 1 tablespoon of the olive oil and spread it out on a large plate to cool. In a medium bowl, whisk the yogurt with the lemon juice, coriander, cumin, piment d'Espelette and the remaining 3 tablespoons of olive oil. Fold in the orzo, cilantro, mint and feta and season with salt.

4. Light a grill and brush the grate with oil or heat a grill pan. Remove the squab from the marinade, scraping off the excess; discard the marinade. Grill the squab breasts skin side down over moderate heat until lightly charred, 3 to 4 minutes. Flip the squab breasts and cook until medium within, 2 to 3 minutes longer. Transfer to a plate and let rest for 5 minutes.

5. Spoon the creamy orzo onto plates and arrange the squab on top. Scatter the olives, tomatoes and onion around the squab and drizzle some of the tomato vinaigrette around the plate. Serve, passing the remaining vinaigrette at the table. —*Gabriel Rucker*

NOTE You will have to order the boneless squab breasts from your butcher.

MAKE AHEAD The tomato vinaigrette can be refrigerated overnight.

WINE Toasty, berried Côtes du Rhône: 2012 J.L. Chave Selection Mon Coeur.

GRILLED SQUAB BREAST
WITH CREAMY ORZO

GRILLED BRATS AND ONIONS
WITH PARSLEY SAUCE
Recipe, page 188

Pork & Veal

Grilled Pork Chops with Concord Grapes

Active **20 min**; Total **1 hr plus 4 hr brining**
Serves **4**

Star chef Mario Batali's fantastic savory-sweet dish will convert anyone skeptical about combining meat and fruit. He uses Concord grapes but says that pretty little Champagne grapes or even blueberries work well in the recipe, too.

- ½ cup kosher salt, plus more for seasoning
- ¼ cup sugar
- 2 cups boiling water
  Four 10-oz. bone-in pork rib chops, 1¼ inches thick
- 1 head of garlic
- 5 Tbsp. extra-virgin olive oil
  Pepper
- 1 lb. seedless purple grapes, stemmed (3 cups), preferably Concord
  Aged balsamic vinegar, for drizzling

1. In a large bowl, stir the ½ cup of salt with the sugar and boiling water until the sugar dissolves. Let cool until lukewarm. Add the chops and refrigerate for 4 hours.

2. Meanwhile, preheat the oven to 400°. Place the garlic on a sheet of foil and drizzle with 1 tablespoon of the oil. Wrap tightly and roast until very soft, 45 minutes. Let cool, then squeeze the cloves from the skins and mash.

3. Light a grill and oil the grate. Remove the pork chops from the brine and pat dry. Rub all over with 2 tablespoons of the oil and season with salt and pepper. Grill over moderate heat, turning once, until lightly charred and just cooked through, 10 minutes. Transfer to plates; keep warm.

4. In a large skillet, heat 1 tablespoon of the oil. Add the grapes and cook over moderately high heat, stirring, until they start to burst, 3 to 4 minutes. Add the remaining 1 tablespoon of oil and half of the mashed garlic and cook, stirring, until incorporated, 1 minute. Reserve the remaining garlic for another use. Transfer the grapes to the plates. Drizzle the chops and grapes with vinegar and serve. —*Mario Batali*

WINE Dark, cherry-scented Italian red: 2011 Masciarelli Montepulciano d'Abruzzo.

Brined Pork Chops with Fennel

Active **45 min**; Total **1 hr 10 min plus overnight brining**; Serves **8 to 10**

- 1 cup kosher salt, plus more for seasoning
- 1 cup packed light brown sugar
- 12 whole black peppercorns
- 4 bay leaves
  Six 1-lb. pork rib chops, 1¼ inches thick
- ½ cup extra-virgin olive oil
- 3 medium fennel bulbs—halved, cored and thinly sliced (8 cups), 2 Tbsp. fronds chopped and reserved
- 2 sweet onions, halved and sliced
- 1 tsp. crushed red pepper
- 1 Tbsp. fennel pollen or 1 tsp. ground fennel
  Black pepper
- ¾ cup dry white wine
- 1 cup all-purpose flour

1. In a small saucepan, combine the 1 cup of salt with the sugar, peppercorns, bay leaves and 2 cups of water; bring to a simmer, stirring to dissolve the salt and sugar. Pour the brine into a large pot and add 4 cups of cold water. Let cool. Add the pork chops, cover and refrigerate overnight.

2. Remove the pork from the brine; discard the brine. Pat the chops dry and let stand at room temperature for 30 minutes.

3. Preheat the oven to 450°. In a large, deep skillet, heat ¼ cup of the oil until shimmering. Add the sliced fennel, onions, crushed red pepper and fennel pollen, season with salt and black pepper and cook over moderate heat, stirring occasionally, until lightly golden and tender, 15 minutes. Add the wine and simmer until almost evaporated, about 2 minutes. Scrape into a large roasting pan. Wipe out the skillet.

4. Pour the flour in a shallow baking dish. Season the chops on both sides with salt and black pepper, then dredge in the flour, tapping off the excess. Heat 2 tablespoons of the oil in the skillet. Add 3 of the chops and cook over moderately high heat until deep golden, 4 to 5 minutes per side. Transfer the chops to the roasting pan. Repeat with the remaining 2 tablespoons of olive oil and 3 pork chops.

5. Roast the chops for 18 to 20 minutes, until an instant-read thermometer inserted in the center registers 135°. Transfer to a platter and let rest for 5 minutes. Season the vegetables with salt and black pepper and stir in the fennel fronds. Serve the chops with the vegetables. —*Benno and Leo Batali*

WINE Red-fruit-and-spice-inflected Pinot Noir: 2012 Drew Fog-Eater.

Grilled Pork Chops with Fried-Sage Salsa Verde

⏱ Total **45 min**; Serves **4**

  Grapeseed oil, for frying
- ½ cup sage leaves
- ½ medium shallot, minced
- 1 Tbsp. red wine vinegar
- ¾ cup extra-virgin olive oil, plus more for brushing
- 1 cup lightly packed parsley leaves, finely chopped
- 2 Tbsp. minced celery heart with leaves
- 1 Tbsp. capers—rinsed, drained and minced
- 1½ tsp. minced thyme
  Kosher salt and pepper
  Four ¾-lb. bone-in pork rib chops, about 1 inch thick

1. In a small saucepan, heat ¼ inch of grapeseed oil until shimmering. Add the sage and fry over moderate heat, stirring, until the sizzling stops and the leaves are crisp, 2 minutes. Using a slotted spoon, transfer to paper towels to drain.

2. In a medium bowl, whisk the shallot with the vinegar and let stand for 5 minutes. Whisk in the ¾ cup of olive oil, the parsley, celery, capers and thyme and season with salt and pepper.

3. Light a grill or heat a grill pan. Brush the pork chops with olive oil and season generously with salt and pepper. Grill over moderate heat, turning once, until lightly charred and an instant-read thermometer inserted near the bone registers 135°, 12 to 14 minutes. Transfer the chops to a platter and let rest for 5 minutes. Stir the fried sage leaves into the salsa verde and serve with the pork chops. —*Charlie Hallowell*

WINE Herbal Cabernet Franc from France's Loire Valley: 2011 J.M. Raffault Les Galuches Chinon.

GRILLED PORK CHOPS WITH
CONCORD GRAPES

Cider-Brined Pork Tenderloins with Roasted Apples

Active **1 hr**; Total **1 hr 30 min plus overnight brining**; Serves **4 to 6**

- 2 cups apple cider
- 1 cinnamon stick
- 2 tsp. black peppercorns
- 2 tsp. coriander seeds
- 1 teaspoon crushed red pepper
- 2 garlic cloves, crushed
  Kosher salt
- 4 cups ice
  Two 1- to 1¼-lb. pork tenderloins
- ¼ cup plus 2 Tbsp. cider vinegar
- 1 large shallot, minced
- 2 thyme sprigs
- 3 Tbsp. sorghum syrup or pure maple syrup
- ¾ cup chicken stock
- 2 Tbsp. unsalted butter
- 1 lb. medium carrots, cut crosswise ¼ inch thick
- 2 Honeycrisp or Pink Lady apples—peeled, cored and cut into ½-inch pieces
- 2 Tbsp. fresh orange juice
- 1½ Tbsp. extra-virgin olive oil
- 2 Tbsp. canola oil

1. In a large saucepan, combine the cider, cinnamon, peppercorns, coriander, crushed red pepper, garlic and 3 tablespoons of kosher salt and bring to a boil, stirring to dissolve the salt. Remove from the heat, add the ice and let cool completely. Pour the brine into a large bowl, add the pork tenderloins, cover and refrigerate overnight.

2. Preheat the oven to 450°. In a small saucepan, combine the vinegar with the shallot, thyme and sorghum syrup and bring to a boil. Simmer over moderately high heat until reduced to ¼ cup, about 3 minutes. Add the stock and simmer until reduced to ½ cup, about 5 minutes; discard the thyme sprigs. Whisk in the butter and season lightly with salt; keep warm.

3. On a large rimmed baking sheet, toss the carrots with the apples, orange juice and olive oil; season with salt. Roast in the lower third of the oven, stirring once, until tender and browned in spots, about 25 minutes.

4. Meanwhile, drain the pork tenderloins and cut them in half crosswise; discard the brine. Pat the pork dry and season lightly with salt. In a large cast-iron skillet, heat 1 tablespoon of the canola oil until shimmering. Add half the pork and cook over moderately high heat, turning, until browned all over, about 10 minutes. Transfer the pork to a rimmed baking sheet. Wipe out the skillet and repeat with the remaining 1 tablespoon of canola oil and pork. Roast the pork in the upper third of the oven for about 12 minutes, until an instant-read thermometer inserted in the thickest part of the meat registers 140°. Transfer the pork to a work surface and let rest for 10 minutes.

5. Slice the pork and transfer to plates. Drizzle the sauce on top and serve with the roasted carrots and apples.
—*Hugh Acheson*

WINE Medium-bodied Spanish red: 2012 Algueira Ribeira Sacra Mencía.

Adobo Pork Chops

Total **50 min**; Serves **4**

- 2 Tbsp. canola oil
- 1 small white onion, chopped
- 2 garlic cloves, chopped
- 1½ oz. dried guajillo chiles—stemmed, seeded and cut into 2-inch pieces
- 1½ cups low-sodium chicken broth
  Pinch of sugar
  Kosher salt and pepper
  Four 1-inch-thick bone-in pork rib chops
  Corn salad, for serving

1. In a medium saucepan, heat the oil. Add the onion and cook over moderate heat, stirring occasionally, until softened, 5 minutes. Add the garlic and chiles and cook, stirring, until well toasted and fragrant, 2 minutes. Add the broth and bring to a boil. Simmer the sauce over moderate heat, stirring occasionally, until the chiles are softened, 5 minutes.

2. Transfer the mixture to a blender, add the sugar and puree until smooth. Transfer the adobo sauce to a bowl. Season with salt and pepper.

3. Light a grill and oil the grate. Season the chops with salt and pepper and rub with ¾ cup of the adobo sauce. Grill over moderate heat, turning every 5 minutes and basting with the remaining ¾ cup of sauce, until cooked through, 20 minutes. Transfer the chops to plates and let rest for 5 minutes. Serve with corn salad.
—*Marcela Valladolid*

WINE Medium-bodied, red-berried Italian red: NV Casamatta Toscana Rosso.

Grilled Double-Cut Pork Chops

Active **45 min**; Total **2 hr 15 min plus 2 days brining**; Serves **10**

- ⅓ cup sugar
- 1 medium carrot, thinly sliced
- 1 small onion, halved and thinly sliced
- 1 medium celery rib, thinly sliced
- 3 whole cloves
- 3 juniper berries
  Kosher salt
- 8 cups ice cubes (2 lbs.)
  Five 1½-lb. double-cut bone-in pork rib chops
  Canola oil, for brushing
  Freshly ground pepper

1. In a large pot, combine 4 cups of water with the sugar, carrot, onion, celery, cloves, juniper berries and ¼ cup plus 2 tablespoons of salt. Bring just to a boil, stirring to dissolve the salt and sugar. Remove from the heat and add the ice; let cool completely. Submerge the pork chops in the brine, cover and refrigerate for 2 days.

2. Remove the pork chops from the brine and pat dry with paper towels. Let stand at room temperature for 1 to 2 hours.

3. Light a grill. Brush the chops with oil and season lightly with salt and pepper. Grill the chops over moderate heat, turning occasionally, until lightly charred all over and an instant-read thermometer inserted in the thickest part of each chop registers 130°, 25 to 30 minutes. Transfer the chops to a carving board and let rest for 15 minutes. Cut between the rib bones into individual chops. —*Paul Berglund*

SERVE WITH Berglund's Pickled Garden Vegetables (p. 358).

WINE Bold, fruit-forward Pinot Noir from Sonoma County: 2013 Banshee.

Pork Schnitzel with Plum, Parsley and Radicchio Salad

Total **1 hr**; Serves **6**

- 3 large eggs
- ½ cup sour cream
- 1 cup all-purpose flour
- 1 tsp. ground ginger
- 1 tsp. dried dill
- 1 tsp. garlic powder
- 1 tsp. onion powder
- 1 tsp. dried oregano
- 1 tsp. sweet paprika
- 2 cups panko
- One 1¼-lb. pork tenderloin, cut crosswise into 6 medallions and pounded ¼ inch thick
- Kosher salt and freshly ground pepper
- 3 Tbsp. grapeseed or vegetable oil, plus more for frying
- 3 firm, ripe plums, cut into ⅓-inch wedges
- One 10-oz. head of radicchio—halved, cored and thinly sliced
- 2 cups packed parsley, chopped
- 1 Tbsp. fresh lemon juice
- 1 tsp. Dijon mustard
- Freshly shaved Parmigiano-Reggiano cheese, for garnish

1. In a shallow bowl, beat the eggs with the sour cream. In another shallow bowl, whisk the flour, ginger, dill, garlic powder, onion powder, oregano and paprika. Spread the panko in a third shallow bowl.

2. Season the pork with salt and pepper. Dredge the cutlets in the flour mixture, dip them in the egg mixture and coat with panko; transfer to a baking sheet.

3. In a very large skillet, heat ¼ inch of oil until shimmering. Add half of the cutlets and fry over moderately high heat, turning once, until golden and just cooked through, 4 minutes total; transfer to paper towels. Repeat with the remaining cutlets.

4. In a large bowl, toss the plums, radicchio, parsley, lemon juice and mustard with the 3 tablespoons of oil. Season with salt and pepper and garnish with the cheese. Serve the pork schnitzel with the salad. —*Jason Vincent*

WINE Fruity red with soft tannins: 2013 Allegrini Valpolicella.

Garlicky Roast Pork Shoulder

Active **45 min**; Total **7 hr plus overnight marinating**; Serves **10 to 12**

San Juan chef Jose Enrique's version of the Puerto Rican classic *pernil* is extra-flavorful because he marinates the pork overnight in lime and orange juices, plus plenty of garlic, before roasting. It can be carved, shredded or pulled into pieces for serving.

- 1 cup coarsely chopped cilantro leaves
- ½ cup fresh orange juice
- ½ cup fresh lime juice
- 9 garlic cloves, finely chopped
- 3 Tbsp. finely chopped oregano
- 1½ Tbsp. extra-virgin olive oil
- Kosher salt and pepper
- One 5-lb. boneless pork shoulder roast with fat cap
- Lime wedges, for serving

1. In a large, sturdy resealable plastic bag, combine the cilantro, orange and lime juices, garlic, oregano, olive oil, 2 tablespoons of kosher salt and ½ teaspoon of pepper. Add the pork shoulder, seal the bag and turn to coat. Transfer the bag to a large baking dish and refrigerate the pork overnight, turning the bag once or twice.

2. Remove the pork from the marinade and scrape off the garlic and herbs; discard the marinade. Season the pork all over with salt and pepper and transfer to a large enameled cast-iron casserole. Let stand at room temperature for 1 hour.

3. Preheat the oven to 400°. Roast the pork fat side up for 1 hour, until lightly browned. Reduce the oven temperature to 300° and roast for 4 hours longer, until the pork is very tender and the fat cap is crispy; transfer to a carving board and let rest for 30 minutes. Chop the fat cap into bite-size pieces. Carve, shred or pull apart the pork and garnish with the crispy cap pieces. Serve with lime wedges. —*Jose Enrique*

SERVE WITH Black beans and rice.

MAKE AHEAD The roast pork can be refrigerated overnight; rewarm in a 300° oven.

BEER Fruity, high-acid Belgian saison: Saison Dupont.

Herb-Rubbed Porchetta

Active **30 min**; Total **3 hr 50 min**; Serves **8**

- 3 Tbsp. dried rosemary
- 2 Tbsp. dried lavender
- 10 garlic cloves, peeled
- ½ cup plus 2 Tbsp. extra-virgin olive oil
- One 1-lb. pork tenderloin
- Kosher salt and pepper
- One 5-lb. meaty pork belly with skin, about 1½ inches thick
- 4 carrots, cut into ½-inch pieces
- 2 medium onions, cut into ½-inch pieces
- 1 medium fennel bulb, cored and cut into ½-inch pieces, 2 Tbsp. fronds chopped and reserved
- 1½ cups dry Marsala wine

1. Preheat the oven to 350°. In a blender, combine the rosemary and lavender with 6 of the garlic cloves and ½ cup of the olive oil; puree until smooth.

2. Season the tenderloin with salt and pepper. Make 4 evenly spaced 1-inch-deep slits in the tenderloin and insert the remaining 4 garlic cloves. Rub 2 tablespoons of the herb oil over the tenderloin.

3. Place the pork belly skin side down on a work surface, season with salt and pepper and rub with the remaining herb oil. Place the pork tenderloin on top of the pork belly and roll the belly tightly around the tenderloin. Tie with kitchen twine at 1-inch intervals. Rub the outside of the pork belly with the remaining 2 tablespoons of olive oil.

4. Combine the carrots, onions, fennel pieces and Marsala in a large roasting pan. Top with the pork and roast for 2½ to 3 hours, basting occasionally, until the skin is deeply golden and crispy and an instant-read thermometer inserted in the thickest part of the pork registers 150°. Transfer the pork to a cutting board and let rest for 20 minutes. Stir the fennel fronds into the vegetables. Using a serrated knife, slice the porchetta crosswise about 1 inch thick and serve with the vegetables. —*Armandino Batali*

WINE Bold red with a firm tannic structure: 2008 Arnaldo Caprai Collepiano.

Roman-Style Pork Roast

Active **30 min**; Total **3 hr 30 min**; Serves **8**

¼ cup extra-virgin olive oil

1 yellow onion, thinly sliced

1 fennel bulb, cored and thinly sliced, 2 Tbsp. fronds chopped and reserved

2 lbs. sweet Italian sausage, casings discarded

2 Tbsp. fennel seeds

2 Tbsp. chopped rosemary

6 garlic cloves, thinly sliced

1 Tbsp. pepper, plus more for seasoning

Kosher salt

2 eggs, beaten

4 medium red onions, peeled and halved

One 5-lb. boneless pork shoulder, butterflied 1 inch thick (roughly a 10-by-14-inch rectangle—have your butcher do this)

1. In a large skillet, heat 2 tablespoons of the oil until shimmering. Add the yellow onion and sliced fennel and cook over moderate heat, stirring occasionally, until softened, 10 minutes. Add the sausage, fennel seeds, rosemary, garlic and the 1 tablespoon of pepper and cook, breaking up the meat, until the sausage is browned, about 5 minutes. Season with salt. Transfer the mixture to a bowl and let cool. Stir in the eggs and chopped fennel fronds.

2. Preheat the oven to 350°. Place the red onions in a large roasting pan. Arrange the pork shoulder on a work surface and season with salt and pepper. Spread the sausage mixture over the pork, leaving a 1-inch border all around. Starting at a long side, roll up the pork and tie with kitchen twine at 1-inch intervals. Rub with the remaining 2 tablespoons of oil and place on top of the red onions. Roast the pork for about 2½ hours, basting occasionally with any pan juices, until an instant-read thermometer inserted in the center of the meat registers 160°. Transfer to a cutting board and let rest for 15 minutes.

3. Discard the strings, cut the pork into 1-inch-thick slices and serve with the red onions. —*Mario Batali*

WINE Italian red with concentrated fruit and high acidity: 2011 Foradori Teroldego.

Paprika-Spiced Pork and Sauerkraut Stew

Active **40 min**; Total **2 hr 40 min plus overnight marinating**; Serves **10 to 12**

6 garlic cloves, thinly sliced

4 red bell peppers, chopped

2 medium yellow onions, chopped

Kosher salt

2 lbs. trimmed pork shoulder, cut into 1½-inch cubes

2 Tbsp. canola oil

2 Tbsp. tomato paste

½ cup Hungarian sweet paprika

2 tsp. Hungarian hot paprika

1 lb. sauerkraut, drained

One 750-ml bottle red wine

1 quart low-sodium beef broth

1 tsp. dried marjoram

2 bay leaves

2 Hungarian wax, banana or Cubanelle peppers, thinly sliced

1 tsp. black pepper

Cooked egg noodles and crème fraîche, for serving

1. In a food processor, puree half of the garlic, bell peppers and onions with 1 tablespoon of salt until smooth. Pour the puree into a large bowl, add the pork and stir to coat. Cover with plastic wrap and refrigerate overnight.

2. Drain the pork, wipe off any marinade and pat dry with paper towels. In a large Dutch oven, heat the canola oil. Working in batches, add the pork and brown over moderate heat, turning once, about 4 minutes per batch. Transfer the browned pork to a plate. Add the tomato paste to the pot and cook, stirring, until lightly caramelized, about 2 minutes. Add both paprikas and cook, stirring constantly, for 1 minute. Return the pork to the pot and add the sauerkraut, wine, broth, marjoram, bay leaves and 4 cups of water. Bring to a boil. Reduce the heat and simmer, uncovered, until the pork is nearly tender, about 1½ hours.

3. Stir in the Hungarian wax peppers along with the remaining garlic, bell peppers and onion and cook until the pork and vegetables are tender, about 30 minutes longer. Discard the bay leaves. Stir in the black pepper and season with salt. Serve in bowls over egg noodles with a dollop of crème fraîche. —*Jeremy Nolen*

WINE Lightly off-dry German Riesling: 2013 Weiser-Künstler Feinherb.

Shio Koji–Marinated Pork Shoulder Steaks

Total **20 min plus overnight marinating**
Serves **6**

Two 1¼- to 1½-lb. boneless pork shoulder steaks, 1½ inches thick (see Note)

½ cup *shio koji* (see Note)

Salt

2 tsp. canola oil, preferably cold-pressed

1. In a very large resealable plastic bag, coat the pork steaks with the *shio koji*. Seal the bag, pressing out the air. Set the bag in a baking dish and refrigerate overnight. Let the pork stand at room temperature for 30 minutes before cooking.

2. Remove the pork from the marinade; scrape off any excess. Season the pork with salt. In a cast-iron skillet, heat the canola oil until shimmering. Add the pork steaks and cook over moderately high heat, turning once, until lightly charred, 2 minutes per side. Cover the skillet and cook over low heat, turning once and wiping the moisture from the bottom of the lid, until an instant-read thermometer inserted in the thickest part of the steaks registers 135°, 10 minutes. Transfer the steaks to a carving board and let rest for 5 minutes. Slice the steaks across the grain and serve. —*Nancy Singleton Hachisu*

NOTE Order the thick-cut pork shoulder steaks from your butcher. *Shio koji*, a seasoning paste made from fermented rice soaked in salt water, is available at Japanese groceries.

SAKE Rich and fruity, but dry, junmai ginjo: Rihaku Wandering Poet.

ROMAN-STYLE PORK ROAST

Mojo Pork Cubanos

⏲ Total **30 min**; Makes **6 sandwiches**

6 oz. thinly sliced boiled ham

   Softened butter, for brushing

   Six 6-inch soft baguettes, split

   Yellow mustard, for brushing

¾ lb. thinly sliced Mojo-Marinated Pork Shoulder (recipe follows), or store-bought roast pork

½ lb. thinly sliced Swiss cheese

3 half-sour dill pickles, thinly sliced lengthwise

1. Heat a large cast-iron griddle or panini press. Add the ham slices to the griddle and cook over moderate heat, turning once, until browned in spots, about 1 minute. Transfer the ham to a plate.

2. Generously butter the cut sides of each baguette and toast on the griddle over moderate heat until lightly browned, 1 to 2 minutes; transfer to a work surface and generously brush the cut sides with mustard. Layer the ham, pork, cheese and pickles on the sandwiches and close.

3. Generously brush the outsides of the sandwiches with butter and set them on the griddle or press; if using a griddle, top the sandwiches with a large baking sheet and weigh it down with heavy cans or a cast-iron skillet. Cook the sandwiches over moderate heat until the bread is browned and crisp and the cheese is melted, 3 minutes per side on a griddle or 3 minutes total in a press. Cut the *cubanos* in half and serve hot. —*Roy Choi*

BEER Fresh, nicely hoppy pale ale: Dale's from Oskar Blues.

MOJO-MARINATED PORK SHOULDER

Active **45 min**; Total **3 hr 15 min plus overnight marinating**; Serves **6 to 8**

¾ cup extra-virgin olive oil

1 cup cilantro, finely chopped

1 Tbsp. finely grated orange zest

¾ cup fresh orange juice

½ cup fresh lime juice

¼ cup mint leaves, finely chopped

8 garlic cloves, minced

1 Tbsp. minced oregano

2 tsp. ground cumin

   Kosher salt and pepper

3½ lbs. boneless pork shoulder

1. In a bowl, whisk together all of the ingredients except salt, pepper and the pork. Whisk in 1 teaspoon each of salt and pepper. Transfer the marinade to a large resealable plastic bag and add the pork. Seal the bag and turn to coat; set in a baking dish and refrigerate overnight.

2. Preheat the oven to 425° and set a rack over a rimmed baking sheet. Transfer the pork to a work surface; discard the marinade. Fold the pork under itself, into thirds if necessary, and tie with string to form a neat roll. Season all over with salt and pepper and set it on the rack.

3. Roast the pork for 30 minutes, until lightly browned. Reduce the oven temperature to 375° and roast for 1 hour and 30 minutes longer, until an instant-read thermometer inserted in the center registers 160°; transfer to a carving board and let rest for 30 minutes. Discard the string before slicing across the grain. —*RC*

Cherry-Pork Meat Loaf

Active **25 min**; Total **1 hr 15 min**
Makes **one 12-by-4-inch loaf**

12 saltine crackers, finely crushed (about ½ cup)

2 large eggs, beaten

1½ lbs. ground pork

½ lb. loose breakfast sausage, crumbled

1½ cups cherries, pitted and chopped

1 tsp. kosher salt

½ tsp. pepper

¼ cup Dijon mustard

   Chopped parsley, for garnish

1. Preheat the oven to 375°. Line a baking sheet with parchment paper.

2. In a large bowl, combine the saltines, eggs, pork, sausage, cherries, salt, pepper and ½ cup of water. Mix gently. Transfer the meat to the baking sheet and form it into a 12-by-4-inch oval loaf. Bake for about 50 minutes, until browned and cooked through. Spread the mustard on top, sprinkle with parsley and serve. —*Kay Chun*

WINE Cherry-scented Austrian red: 2012 Moric Blaufränkisch.

Fresh Ham Steak with Pineapple and Sesame

Total **50 min plus overnight marinating**
Serves **6**

Tom Mylan, owner of The Meat Hook artisanal butcher shop in Brooklyn, loves grilling fresh ham steaks because, he says, "They're huge, cheap and great for feeding many people while staying epic and getting oohs and aahs." The key in this recipe is pineapple juice, which tenderizes the meat.

1½ cups pineapple juice

½ cup dark beer

¼ cup red wine vinegar

¼ cup soy sauce

¼ cup finely chopped peeled fresh ginger

2 Tbsp. toasted sesame oil

1½ Tbsp. kosher salt

   One 3- to 3¼-lb. bone-in fresh ham steak, about 1½ inches thick

   Toasted sesame seeds, for garnish

1. In a large resealable plastic bag, combine all of the ingredients except the ham steak and sesame seeds and shake to mix. Add the ham steak and seal the bag, pressing out the air. Set the bag in a large baking dish and refrigerate overnight.

2. Light a gas grill. Remove the ham from the marinade and let stand at room temperature for 30 minutes.

3. Pat the ham dry with paper towels. Grill over high heat, turning once, until lightly charred, about 3 minutes per side. Flip again and grill over low heat, turning occasionally, until an instant-read thermometer inserted in the thickest part registers 140°, 20 to 25 minutes.

4. Transfer the ham steak to a carving board and let rest for 10 minutes. Cut the meat off the bone and slice against the grain. Garnish with toasted sesame seeds and serve. —*Tom Mylan*

WINE Juicy California Grenache: 2012 Dashe Les Enfants Terribles.

Market Math: Ham

1 Muffuletta Calzone

Roll out ½ lb. of **pizza dough** to a 10-inch round. On half of the dough, layer 4 oz. each of thinly sliced **provolone** and **ham**. Top with 2 oz. sliced **Genoa salami**, 2 **roasted bell peppers** and ½ cup chopped **pimiento-stuffed olives**. Fold over the dough; crimp to seal. Brush with **olive oil** and bake at 450° for 25 minutes.

2 Spring Ham Steaks

In a large skillet, cook four ¼-inch-thick **ham steaks** in 2 Tbsp. **butter** over moderate heat, turning once, until golden; transfer to plates. Add 1 thinly sliced **leek** and 1½ cups **water** to the skillet and cook 3 minutes. Stir in 10 oz. thawed **peas**, 3 Tbsp. chopped **tarragon** and 2 Tbsp. **butter**; season and serve over the ham.

3 Open-Face Ham Monte Cristos

Melt 4 Tbsp. **butter** on a griddle. Cook ½ lb. very thinly sliced **ham** until golden and crispy. In a bowl, whisk 2 large **eggs** with 2 Tbsp. **milk**. Dip four 1-inch-thick slices of **bakery white bread** in the eggs, then griddle until golden; flip and top with 8 slices of **Gruyère cheese** and the ham. Cover and cook until the cheese melts. Top with **basil**.

4 Country Ham Flapjacks

In a large bowl, whisk 1½ cups **corn muffin mix** with ¾ cup **buttermilk**, 1 large **egg**, 1 cup chopped **ham** and 1 sliced **scallion**. Scoop ¼-cup mounds into a buttered nonstick skillet and cook, flipping once, until golden. Serve with **maple syrup**. –*Kay Chun*

Tiki Ribs with Pineapple Pickles

Active **45 min**; Total **3 hr plus overnight pickling**; Serves **4 to 6**

Danny Bowien—the Korean-born, alt-Chinese-inspired chef who cofounded Mission Chinese Food in San Francisco and New York—gives barbecued ribs the tiki treatment with shredded coconut, pineapple and maraschino cherries.

PINEAPPLE PICKLES

- **1** quart distilled white vinegar
- **1½** cups sugar
- **3** árbol chile peppers
- **2** garlic cloves, crushed
- **1** small pineapple—peeled, quartered, cored and sliced crosswise ¼ inch thick

RIBS

- **¼** cup chopped macadamia nuts
- One 3-lb. rack baby back ribs
- **2** Tbsp. canola oil
- Kosher salt and pepper
- **1½** cups packed light brown sugar
- **1** cinnamon stick
- **3** star anise pods
- **1** Tbsp. fennel seeds
- **½** cup soy sauce
- **¼** cup Asian fish sauce
- **1** mandarin orange
- Maraschino cherries and toasted unsweetened shredded coconut, for garnish (optional)

1. Make the pineapple pickles In a large saucepan, combine the vinegar with 1½ cups of water and the sugar, chiles and garlic. Cook over moderate heat, stirring, until the sugar dissolves, about 3 minutes. Transfer the pickling liquid to a large heatproof bowl and let cool to lukewarm. Add the pineapple and let cool completely, then cover and chill overnight.

2. Prepare the ribs Preheat the oven to 375°. Toast the macadamia nuts in a pie plate for 5 minutes, until golden. Let cool. Leave the oven on.

3. Set the ribs on a rack over a rimmed baking sheet and rub them all over with the oil; season with salt and pepper. Roast for 2 hours, until golden brown and very tender. Let cool, then cut the rack into single ribs.

4. Meanwhile, in a saucepan, cook the sugar with ¼ cup of water over moderate heat, stirring, until the sugar dissolves. Add the cinnamon stick, star anise, fennel seeds and ¼ teaspoon of pepper. Cook, without stirring, until a frothy, deep-amber caramel forms, 7 minutes. Off the heat, whisk in the soy sauce and fish sauce. Strain the caramel into a bowl; keep warm.

5. Using a small, sharp knife, peel the orange, removing any bitter white pith. Working over a bowl, cut between the membranes to release the sections.

6. In a large skillet, combine the ribs with 1 cup of the caramel. Cook over moderately high heat, tossing frequently, until the ribs are well glazed, 6 minutes; transfer to a platter. Garnish with some of the pineapple pickles and the mandarin sections, maraschino cherries, macadamia nuts and shredded coconut and serve with the remaining pineapple pickles.
—*Danny Bowien*

MAKE AHEAD The pineapple pickles can be refrigerated for up to 1 week.

WINE Bold California Zinfandel: 2011 St. Francis Old Vines.

Roast Pork with Buttermilk-Onion Puree

Active **1 hr 15 min**; Total **2 hr 45 min** Serves **4**

- **1** stick plus 3 Tbsp. unsalted butter
- **¼** cup extra-virgin olive oil
- One 2-lb. pork shoulder roast, tied
- Salt and freshly ground pepper
- **3** thyme sprigs
- **3** garlic cloves, unpeeled
- **2** sweet onions (1½ lbs.), chopped
- **1** cup buttermilk
- **7** small endives—6 halved lengthwise, 1 thinly sliced crosswise
- **¼** cup pitted and halved kalamata olives
- **1** Tbsp. fresh lemon juice

1. Preheat the oven to 400°. In a large ovenproof skillet, melt 1 tablespoon of the butter in 1 tablespoon of the olive oil. Season the pork roast all over with salt and pepper. Add the pork, thyme and garlic to the skillet and cook over moderate heat, turning occasionally, until the pork is browned on all sides, about 10 minutes. Transfer the skillet to the oven and roast the pork for about 1 hour, turning the meat and basting it with the pan juices every 15 minutes, until an instant-read thermometer inserted in the thickest part of the meat registers 165°. Transfer the pork to a rack set over a baking sheet and let rest for 30 minutes.

2. Meanwhile, in a large saucepan, melt 2 tablespoons of the butter in 1 tablespoon of the olive oil. Add the onions and cook over moderately low heat, stirring occasionally, until they are very soft but not browned, about 30 minutes. Add the buttermilk, bring to a simmer and cook, stirring occasionally, until the liquid is reduced and the onions are very tender, about 20 minutes. Transfer the onion-buttermilk mixture to a blender and add 4 tablespoons of the butter. Puree the mixture until very smooth and season with salt and pepper.

3. In a large skillet, melt 2 tablespoons of the butter. Arrange 6 of the endive halves cut side down in the skillet; season with salt and pepper. Cook over moderately high heat, turning, until nicely browned on both sides and crisp-tender, about 5 minutes. Repeat with the remaining 2 tablespoons of butter and endive halves.

4. In a medium bowl, combine the sliced raw endive with the olives, lemon juice and the remaining 2 tablespoons of olive oil and season with salt and pepper. Toss the endive to coat with the dressing.

5. Transfer the pork to a cutting board. Remove the strings and discard. Cut the meat crosswise into 4 thick slices. Spread the onion puree on plates. Arrange the endive halves on the puree and set a slice of pork on top. Scatter the endive salad over all and serve. —*Louis-Philippe Riel*

MAKE AHEAD The onion puree can be refrigerated for up to 2 days.

WINE Fruity, medium-bodied red: 2012 J.L. Chave Mon Coeur Côtes du Rhône.

Pork Roast with Garlic-Parmesan Cream

Active **30 min**; Total **4 hr 45 min**; Serves **8**

Poaching pork in garlic-and-Parmesan-infused cream helps it develop a savory glaze while it roasts; reduced, the cream becomes a lovely sauce.

- **1** quart heavy cream
- **2** cups buttermilk
- **4** Tbsp. unsalted butter
- **3** heads of garlic, top ½ inch cut off
  One 3-oz. Parmigiano-Reggiano cheese rind
- **2** small sage sprigs
  One 5-lb. boneless pork shoulder roast
  Kosher salt and pepper
- **¼** cup fresh lemon juice
- **4** medium fennel bulbs (3 lbs.), trimmed and cut into wedges
- **¼** cup extra-virgin olive oil
  Chopped parsley, for garnish

1. In a pot just large enough to hold the pork, combine the cream with the buttermilk, butter, garlic, cheese rind and 1 sage sprig. Season the pork with salt and pepper and add to the pot. Bring just to a simmer. Cover, leaving it open just a crack, and cook over low heat for about 3½ hours, until very tender. Transfer the pork and garlic to a large plate; discard the cheese rind.

2. Boil the poaching liquid over moderately high heat, whisking occasionally, until thickened, 20 minutes. Strain the sauce into a bowl. Whisk in the lemon juice and season with salt and pepper; keep warm.

3. Meanwhile, preheat the oven to 450°. On a large baking sheet, toss the fennel and the remaining sage sprig with the olive oil and season with salt and pepper. Arrange the fennel in a single layer. Place the pork on top of the fennel and roast until the pork is deeply golden and the fennel is tender, about 20 minutes. Transfer the pork to a cutting board and let rest for 15 minutes.

4. Thinly slice the pork. Arrange the fennel and garlic on a platter and top with the pork. Garnish with parsley and serve the sauce on the side. —*Kay Chun*

WINE Slightly herbal Tuscan red: 2012 Tenuta Campo di Sasso Insoglio del Cinghiale.

Wine-Braised Pork with Chestnuts and Sweet Potatoes

Active **30 min**; Total **3 hr 40 min**; Serves **8**

- One 4-lb. boneless pork shoulder
  Kosher salt and pepper
- **1** onion, finely chopped
- **5** garlic cloves, crushed
- **3** cups chicken stock or low-sodium broth
- **½** cup dry white wine
- **5** parsley sprigs, plus chopped parsley for garnish
- **3** thyme sprigs
- **1½** lbs. sweet potatoes (about 3 medium), peeled and cut into 2-inch pieces
- **1** lb. vacuum-packed roasted peeled chestnuts (3 cups)

1. Season the pork with 2 teaspoons of salt and 1 teaspoon of pepper. Heat a large cast-iron casserole over moderately high heat. Add the pork, fat side down, and pour in ½ cup of water. Cook until all of the water has evaporated, about 5 minutes. Continue to cook over moderate heat until the pork is golden brown, about 8 minutes. Flip the pork and cook, turning occasionally, until browned all over, about 5 minutes longer.

2. Add the onion and garlic to the casserole and cook, stirring occasionally, until lightly golden, about 5 minutes. Add the stock, wine and parsley and thyme sprigs and bring to a simmer. Cover and cook over low heat, turning once, until the pork is just tender, 2½ hours. Add the sweet potatoes and chestnuts, cover and cook until the pork and sweet potatoes are very tender, about 30 minutes.

3. Transfer the pork to a cutting board and let rest for 10 minutes. Using a slotted spoon, transfer the sweet potatoes and chestnuts to a platter. Strain the jus into a bowl and degrease with a spoon; season with salt and pepper.

4. Slice the pork and arrange it on top of the vegetables. Garnish with parsley and serve with the jus. —*Jacques Pépin*

WINE Medium-bodied Côtes du Rhône: 2012 Château Pesquié Terrasses Rouge.

Chicken-Fried Ribs with Red Eye Gravy

Active **45 min**; Total **2 hr 30 min**
Serves **4 to 6**

- One 3-lb. rack baby back ribs
- **2** Tbsp. canola oil, plus more for frying
  Kosher salt and pepper
- **4** oz. bacon, chopped
- **2¾** cups plus 3 Tbsp. all-purpose flour
- **1** cup heavy cream
- **¼** cup whole milk
- **¼** cup brewed espresso
- **2** large eggs
- **¼** cup fine yellow cornmeal
- **½** tsp. sweet paprika
  Poached eggs, for serving (optional)
  Arugula and thinly sliced scallions, for garnish

1. Preheat the oven to 375°. Set a rack over a rimmed baking sheet. Set the ribs on the rack, rub them all over with the 2 tablespoons of canola oil and season with salt and pepper. Roast for about 2 hours, until golden brown and very tender. Let cool slightly, then cut the rack into single ribs.

2. Meanwhile, in a medium saucepan, cook the bacon over moderately low heat, stirring occasionally, until crispy and all the fat has rendered, about 10 minutes. Using a slotted spoon, transfer the bacon to a paper towel–lined plate. If necessary, add enough canola oil to the saucepan to make 3 tablespoons of fat. Add 3 tablespoons of the flour and whisk over moderately low heat until the mixture turns tawny brown, about 5 minutes. Whisk in the cream, milk, espresso and bacon and cook, whisking, until the gravy thickens, about 2 minutes. Season the red eye gravy with salt and pepper and keep warm.

3. Spread 1 cup of the flour in a shallow bowl. In another shallow bowl, beat the eggs. In a third shallow bowl, combine the remaining 1¾ cups of flour with the cornmeal and paprika and season with salt and pepper. Dredge the ribs in the plain flour, dip them in the beaten egg, letting any excess drip off, then dredge them in the seasoned flour. Transfer to a rack.

4. In a large cast-iron skillet or enameled cast-iron casserole, heat 2 inches of oil to 350°. Add half of the ribs to the hot oil and fry over moderately high heat, turning occasionally, until golden and crispy, 5 minutes. Transfer the ribs to a clean rack and season lightly with salt. Repeat with the remaining ribs.

5. Spoon some red eye gravy onto plates. Top with the ribs and poached eggs, if using. Garnish with arugula and sliced scallions and serve. —*Danny Bowien*

WINE Subtly coffee-inflected Washington Syrah: 2013 Charles Smith Boom Boom!.

Spiced Pork Ribs

Active **30 min**; Total **4 hr**; Serves **6 to 8**

A simple rub and meaty ribs are all it takes to make this Mexican classic. Have the butcher cut the ribs in half for you—they absorb more flavor that way, and they're easier to eat, too.

- **4 garlic cloves, crushed**
- **3 Tbsp. coriander seeds**
- **3 Tbsp. cumin seeds**
- **1 tsp. crushed red pepper**
- **Kosher salt and black pepper**
- **⅓ cup fresh lime juice**
- **2 racks meaty baby back ribs (6 lbs.), halved through the bones**
- **Chopped cilantro and lime wedges, for serving**

1. In a mortar, mash the garlic with the coriander, cumin, crushed red pepper, 2 tablespoons of salt and 1½ tablespoons of black pepper. Add the lime juice and pound to a coarse paste.

2. Rub the paste all over the ribs and transfer to a large roasting pan; refrigerate for 2 hours or overnight. Let the ribs come to room temperature before roasting.

3. Preheat the oven to 325°. Cover the pan with foil and roast the ribs for about 1½ hours, until the meat is very tender but not falling apart.

4. Light a grill. Season the ribs lightly with salt and pepper. Grill over moderately high heat, turning, until lightly charred all over, 8 to 10 minutes. Transfer the ribs to a platter, scatter chopped cilantro on top and serve with lime wedges. —*Jane Coxwell*

WINE Fragrant, juicy Malbec: 2012 Maipe.

Pork Burgers with Bread-and-Butter Zucchini Pickles

Total **30 min**; Serves **6**

- **1 lb. ground pork**
- **1 lb. fresh chorizo, casings discarded and sausage broken up**
- **½ cup fresh ricotta cheese**
- **3 Tbsp. capers—drained, rinsed and finely chopped**
- **Kosher salt and pepper**
- **6 thin slices of sharp cheddar cheese**
- **Mayonnaise and ketchup**
- **6 brioche burger buns, split and toasted**
- **Bread-and-Butter Zucchini Pickles (recipe follows) and butter lettuce, for serving**

1. Light a grill or heat a grill pan. In a large bowl, gently mix the ground pork with the chorizo, ricotta and capers. Form the meat into six ¾-inch-thick patties and season lightly with salt and pepper.

2. Grill the burgers over moderately high heat, turning once, until lightly charred and cooked through, 10 minutes; top the burgers with the cheddar during the last minute of grilling and let melt. Transfer the burgers to a work surface and let rest for 5 minutes.

3. Spread mayonnaise and ketchup on the buns and set the burgers on the bottom halves. Top with the pickles and lettuce, close the burgers and serve right away. —*Tara Derr Webb*

WINE Bold, fruit-forward Rhône-style red: 2010 Red Car Sonoma Coast Syrah.

BREAD-AND-BUTTER ZUCCHINI PICKLES

Active **30 min**; Total **1 hr 30 min plus overnight pickling**; Makes **about 1 quart**

- **1 lb. very firm medium zucchini, sliced crosswise ⅛ inch thick**
- **½ cup thinly sliced onion**
- **3 Tbsp. kosher salt**
- **Ice water**
- **1½ cups unfiltered apple cider vinegar**
- **⅓ cup sugar**
- **2 tsp. brown or yellow mustard seeds, crushed**
- **1½ tsp. mustard powder**
- **1 tsp. ground turmeric**

1. In a large bowl, toss the zucchini and onion with 2 tablespoons of the kosher salt. Cover with ice water and let stand until just softened, about 45 minutes. Drain the zucchini and onion well and pat dry.

2. Meanwhile, in a medium saucepan, combine the remaining 1 tablespoon of salt with the vinegar, sugar, mustard seeds, mustard powder, turmeric and ½ cup of water. Bring to a boil, stirring to dissolve the sugar; let the brine cool completely.

3. Transfer the zucchini and onion to a 1-quart glass jar and pour in enough brine to cover. Seal with the lid and refrigerate overnight before serving. —*TDW*

Sweet-and-Sour Pork in Lettuce Cups

Total **30 min**; Serves **4**

- **2 Tbsp. canola oil**
- **1 small onion, finely chopped**
- **2 garlic cloves, minced**
- **1 lb. ground pork**
- **2 Tbsp. honey**
- **1 Tbsp. Asian fish sauce**
- **½ tsp. toasted sesame oil**
- **1 tsp. finely grated lime zest**
- **2 Tbsp. fresh lime juice**
- **Kosher salt and freshly ground pepper**
- **1 head of butter lettuce (6 oz.), leaves separated**
- **Thinly sliced scallions, for garnish**
- **Lime wedges, for serving**

1. In a large skillet, heat the canola oil. Add the onion and stir-fry over moderate heat until softened and golden, 5 minutes. Stir in the garlic and cook for 1 minute. Add the pork and cook, stirring occasionally and breaking up the meat, until browned, about 3 minutes. Stir in the honey, fish sauce and sesame oil and cook, stirring, until no traces of pink remain in the pork, about 2 minutes. Remove the skillet from the heat. Stir the lime zest and lime juice into the pork and season with salt and pepper.

2. Arrange the lettuce cups on a serving platter. Fill with the pork and garnish with scallions. Serve with lime wedges. —*Diane Cu and Todd Porter*

WINE Fragrant, fruit-forward Austrian Riesling: 2012 Salomon Steinterrassen.

Nut-and-Seed-Crusted Sausage Meatballs with Mustard Sauce

Total **50 min**; Serves **6 to 8**

- ¼ cup blanched hazelnuts
- ¼ cup raw almonds
- ¼ cup raw shelled pistachios
- ¼ cup raw pumpkin seeds
- 2 Tbsp. sesame seeds
- 1½ tsp. each of fennel seeds, coriander seeds and cumin seeds

  Kosher salt
- 2 lbs. sweet Italian pork sausage, casings removed

  Extra-virgin olive oil, for brushing
- 1 cup crème fraîche
- 1 Tbsp. whole-grain mustard
- ½ cup minced mixed fresh herbs, such as parsley, chives, tarragon and chervil, plus more chervil for garnish
- 1 Tbsp. fresh lemon juice

  Freshly ground pepper

1. Preheat the oven to 400°. On a rimmed baking sheet, toss the hazelnuts, almonds and pistachios. Add the pumpkin, sesame, fennel, coriander and cumin seeds and bake for about 10 minutes, stirring once, until lightly toasted. Transfer the nuts and seeds to a food processor and let cool completely. Add a pinch of salt and pulse to coarse crumbs. Spread the spice-and-nut crumbs in a shallow bowl.

2. Shape the sausage meat into 1½-inch balls and transfer to the baking sheet. Brush the meatballs with olive oil and dredge in the crumbs, pressing lightly to help them adhere. Return the meatballs to the baking sheet and bake for about 15 minutes, until firm and cooked through.

3. In a medium bowl, mix the crème fraîche with the mustard, minced herbs and lemon juice and season with salt and pepper. Arrange the meatballs on a platter and garnish with chervil. Serve with the mustard sauce alongside. —*Stuart Brioza*

MAKE AHEAD The uncooked meatballs and the sauce can be refrigerated overnight.

WINE Ripe, off-dry German Riesling: 2012 Maximin Grünhäuser Herrenberg Kabinett.

Mapo Tofu

⊙ Total **15 min**; Serves **4**

- 1 tsp. canola oil
- ½ lb. ground beef chuck (85 percent lean)
- ½ lb. ground pork

  Kosher salt
- 2 Tbsp. chile-bean sauce, preferably *toban djan*
- 2 Tbsp. hoisin sauce or *tenmenjan* (soybean paste)
- 1 Tbsp. soy sauce

  One 14-oz. package soft tofu, finely diced
- 1½ tsp. cornstarch
- 3 scallions, finely chopped

  White rice, for serving

1. Heat a large skillet until hot. Add the oil, followed by the beef and pork. Season with salt and cook over high heat, stirring and breaking up the meat, until crumbly and lightly browned, about 3 minutes.

2. Stir in the chile-bean sauce, hoisin and soy sauce and cook, stirring, for 3 minutes. Gently fold in the tofu. In a small bowl, whisk the cornstarch into ½ cup of water. Add to the skillet and simmer until the sauce thickens, 2 minutes. Stir in the scallions and serve with rice. —*Kuniko Yagi*

BEER Citrusy blond Belgian ale: Brasserie Lefebvre Blanche de Bruxelles.

Pork and Eggplant Stir-Fry

⊙ Total **30 min**; Serves **4**

- ¼ cup canola oil
- 2 baby eggplants (¾ lb.), preferably white, cut into ¾-inch dice
- ¼ lb. baby pattypan squash, thinly sliced

  Kosher salt and pepper
- ¾ lb. ground pork
- 5 garlic cloves, thinly sliced
- 3 scallions, thinly sliced

  Lime wedges, for serving

1. In a large nonstick skillet, heat the oil. Add the eggplants and squash and season with salt and pepper. Cook over moderate heat, stirring, until the vegetables are tender, about 10 minutes.

2. Add the pork and garlic to the skillet and cook, breaking up the meat with a spoon, until the pork is browned and cooked through, 3 minutes. Stir in the scallions and serve with lime wedges. —*Kay Chun*

WINE Juicy Spanish Garnacha: 2011 Bodegas Nekeas El Chaparral de Vega Sindoa.

Pork Satay with Sweet Coconut-Milk Glaze

Active **30 min**; Total **1 hr 30 min**
Serves **6**

- One 14-oz. can unsweetened coconut milk
- 2 Tbsp. Asian fish sauce
- 2 Tbsp. soy sauce
- 2 Tbsp. sugar
- 1½ tsp. curry powder
- 1 tsp. kosher salt
- 1 tsp. freshly ground white pepper
- ⅓ cup sweetened condensed milk
- 2 lbs. boneless pork shoulder, sliced ¼ inch thick and cut into 4-inch strips

  6-inch wooden skewers, soaked in water for 30 minutes

  Cucumber sticks and lime wedges, for serving

1. In a medium saucepan, combine the coconut milk, fish sauce, soy sauce, sugar, curry powder, salt and white pepper and whisk over moderate heat until the sugar is dissolved, 5 minutes. Pour the marinade into a large bowl and let cool completely.

2. Whisk the condensed milk into the marinade. Mix in the pork. Cover with plastic wrap and refrigerate for 1 hour.

3. Light a grill. Skewer the pork and brush lightly with the marinade; discard any remaining marinade. Grill the skewers over moderately high heat, turning, until the pork is lightly charred and just cooked through, about 6 minutes. Transfer the skewers to a platter and serve with cucumber sticks and lime wedges. —*Kris Yenbamroong*

MAKE AHEAD The marinade can be refrigerated overnight.

WINE Lively, berry-scented Italian red: 2012 La Kiuva Arnad-Montjovet.

MAPO TOFU

Pork Belly Carnitas with Tomatillo Salsa

Active **40 min**; Total **3 hr** plus overnight brining; Serves **8**

- 1 head of garlic, halved crosswise, plus 3 garlic cloves, crushed
- 1 shallot, quartered
- 5 thyme sprigs
- 1 bay leaf
- 1 tsp. whole black peppercorns
  Kosher salt
- 1 Tbsp. sugar
- 2 lbs. meaty pork belly with skin
- 1 lb. tomatillos, husked and rinsed
- 2 Tbsp. canola oil
- ¼ cup minced pineapple
- ¼ cup cup minced onion
- 2 serrano chiles, seeded and chopped
- ½ habanero chile, seeded and chopped
- 1 cup cilantro leaves, plus more for serving
  Warm flour tortillas, chopped white onion, and Petty Cash Guacamole (p. 12), for serving

1. In a large ovenproof pot, combine 4 quarts of water with the garlic head, shallot, thyme, bay leaf, peppercorns, 1 tablespoon of salt and 2 teaspoons of sugar and stir until the salt and sugar are dissolved. Add the pork and refrigerate overnight.

2. Preheat the broiler. On a rimmed baking sheet, toss the tomatillos with the canola oil and broil, stirring occasionally, until softened and nicely charred, about 20 minutes. Scrape the charred tomatillos into a blender. Add the pineapple, crushed garlic cloves, onion, serrano and habanero chiles, 1 cup of cilantro and the remaining 1 teaspoon of sugar; puree until smooth. Season the tomatillo salsa with salt.

3. Reduce the oven to 350°. Bring the pot with the pork to a boil over moderate heat. Cover and braise in the oven until the pork is very tender, 2 hours and 30 minutes.

4. Transfer the pork to a work surface and let cool slightly; discard the liquid. Thinly slice the pork and serve with the salsa, tortillas, chopped white onion, cilantro and guacamole. —*Walter Manzke*

BEER Southern California lower-alcohol beer: Ballast Point Longfin Lager.

Grilled Brats and Onions with Parsley Sauce

📷 PAGE 172
Total **1 hr 10 min**; Serves **10**

- 4 cups lightly packed parsley leaves, plus more for garnish
- 1 cup lightly packed dill sprigs
- 1 garlic clove
- 3½ Tbsp. fresh lemon juice
- ½ cup extra-virgin olive oil, plus more for brushing
  Kosher salt and pepper
- 4 red onions (2 lbs.), each peeled and cut into 6 wedges through the core
- ½ tsp. finely grated lemon zest
- ½ tsp. finely chopped thyme
- 20 bratwursts (4 lbs.)
  Dijon mustard and Torn Garlic Bread (recipe follows), for serving

1. Fill a large bowl with ice water. In a large saucepan of salted boiling water, blanch the 4 cups of parsley until bright green, about 45 seconds. Drain and immediately transfer the parsley to the ice bath. Drain well and transfer to a food processor. Add the dill, garlic, 1 cup of water and 2½ tablespoons of the lemon juice and puree until nearly smooth. With the machine on, gradually add the ½ cup of olive oil until smooth. Season the sauce with salt and pepper and transfer to a bowl.

2. Light a grill and brush the grate with olive oil. Brush the onion wedges with oil and season with salt and pepper. Grill over moderate heat, turning once, until lightly charred and softened, 7 minutes total. Transfer the onions to a bowl and toss with the lemon zest, thyme and remaining 1 tablespoon of lemon juice.

3. Grill the bratwursts over moderately low heat, turning, until an instant-read thermometer inserted into each sausage registers 165°, 15 minutes. Spoon some of the parsley sauce onto a platter and top with the bratwursts and onions. Garnish with parsley and serve with mustard and Torn Garlic Bread, passing the rest of the parsley sauce at the table. —*Mehdi Brunet-Benkritly and Gabriel Stulman*

BEER Lively Wisconsin wheat beer: Sprecher Hefe Weiss.

TORN GARLIC BREAD
⏱ Active **10 min**; Total **25 min**; Serves **10**

- 1 small shallot
- 2 garlic cloves
- 1 stick unsalted butter, softened
  Kosher salt and pepper
  One 1¼-lb. sourdough boule, torn into 2-inch pieces
  Chopped flat-leaf parsley, for garnish

1. Preheat the oven to 400°. In a food processor, pulse the shallot and garlic until finely chopped. Add the butter and puree until nearly smooth. Season the garlic butter with salt and pepper and scrape into a large bowl.

2. Add the bread to the bowl and toss until coated, then spread on 2 large rimmed baking sheets. Bake for 15 minutes, until crisp on the outside but chewy in the middle. Season with salt and pepper and transfer to a shallow bowl. Garnish with chopped parsley and serve warm. —*MBB and GS*

Campfire Bacon with Maple-Citrus Glaze

⏱ Total **30 min**; Serves **4**

Maple syrup, sherry vinegar and citrus combine to make a terrific coating for thick slices of slab bacon. This six-ingredient recipe is from chef Noah Blöm at Arc in Costa Mesa, California.

- ¼ cup pure maple syrup
- 2 Tbsp. sherry vinegar
- 1 tsp. finely grated orange zest
- 1 tsp. finely grated lime zest
  Four ¾-inch-thick slices of skinless slab bacon, halved crosswise
  Freshly snipped chives, for garnish

Light a grill or heat a grill pan. In a small bowl, whisk the maple syrup with the vinegar and orange and lime zests. Grill the bacon over moderately low heat, turning occasionally, until lightly browned and tender, about 12 minutes. Brush with the maple-citrus syrup and continue grilling, turning occasionally, until glazed, 2 to 3 minutes longer. Transfer the bacon to a platter, garnish with snipped chives and serve. —*Noah Blöm*

CAMPFIRE BACON WITH
MAPLE-CITRUS GLAZE

Veal Meatballs with Mustard Greens

⏱ Total **45 min**; Serves **4**

For this incredible one-skillet meal, Georgia chef Hugh Acheson flavors tender veal meatballs with fennel and smoked chile, then pan-fries them with stock to keep them moist.

- ¼ cup extra-virgin olive oil
- 1 cup minced onion
- 2 garlic cloves, minced
- ½ tsp. ground fennel seeds
- ¼ tsp. mustard powder
- ¼ tsp. crushed red pepper
- ¼ tsp. ground coriander
- ¼ tsp. chipotle chile powder
- 1 lb. ground veal
- ½ cup fresh bread crumbs (2 oz.)
- ¼ cup heavy cream
- 1 large egg, lightly beaten
- ½ tsp. kosher salt
- ½ lb. mustard greens, thick stems discarded and leaves chopped
- ⅓ cup chicken stock

1. In a medium skillet, heat 2 tablespoons of the olive oil until shimmering. Add the minced onion and cook over moderately high heat, stirring occasionally, until softened and starting to brown, 5 minutes. Stir in the minced garlic, the fennel seeds, mustard powder, crushed red pepper, coriander and chile powder and cook, stirring, until fragrant, about 2 minutes; let cool.

2. In a large bowl, mix the cooled onion mixture with the veal, bread crumbs, cream, egg and salt. Form into 1½-inch meatballs and transfer to a rimmed baking sheet.

3. In a large skillet, heat the remaining 2 tablespoons of olive oil until shimmering. Add the meatballs and cook over moderately high heat, turning, until browned all over, 5 minutes. Gently push the meatballs to one side of the skillet. Spoon off all but 2 tablespoons of the fat from the pan, then add the mustard greens and stock. Cover and cook over moderate heat until the greens are wilted, 4 minutes. Spoon the meatballs and greens into bowls and serve. —*Hugh Acheson*

WINE Rich, red fruit–driven, Pinot Noir–based Champagne: NV Champagne Geoffroy Expression Brut.

Blanquette de Veau

Active **30 min**; Total **2 hr 15 min**; Serves **6**

Marjorie Taylor, co-owner of the Cook's Atelier in Beaune, Burgundy, adapted this creamy veal stew from Julia Child's *Mastering the Art of French Cooking*. She emphasizes to students that it's important not to brown anything in the dish. "The end result should be completely white," she says.

- 3 lbs. trimmed veal shoulder, cut into 2-inch pieces
- 8½ cups chicken stock
- 1 large onion studded with 1 clove
- 1 garlic clove, minced
  Bouquet garni (4 thyme sprigs, 8 parsley sprigs and 1 bay leaf tied with kitchen twine)
  Salt
- 2 cups pearl onions
- 5 Tbsp. unsalted butter
- ½ lb. small white button mushrooms, halved
- 1 Tbsp. fresh lemon juice
- ⅓ cup all-purpose flour
  Freshly ground white pepper
- ½ cup plus 2 Tbsp. heavy cream
- 3 large egg yolks
- 2 Tbsp. chopped parsley
  Potatoes, rice or noodles, for serving

1. In a large enameled cast-iron casserole, cover the veal with cold water. Bring to a simmer and cook for 2 minutes. Drain the veal and rinse it under cold water.

2. Wash out the casserole and return the meat to it. Add 8 cups of the stock, the large onion, the garlic and the bouquet garni and season with salt. Bring to a simmer, cover partially and simmer over moderate heat until the veal is very tender, about 1 hour and 15 minutes. Drain the veal; reserve the broth. Discard the onion, garlic and bouquet garni. Rinse out the casserole and return the meat to it.

3. Meanwhile, in a saucepan of boiling water, blanch the pearl onions for 30 seconds. Drain and transfer the onions to a bowl of ice water. Drain again. Trim the roots and peel the onions.

4. In a medium skillet, melt 1 tablespoon of the butter. Add the pearl onions and remaining ½ cup of stock. Season with salt, cover and cook over low heat until the onions are tender, 30 minutes. Scatter the onions over the veal.

5. In a medium bowl, toss the mushrooms with the lemon juice. In a large saucepan, melt the remaining 4 tablespoons of butter over low heat. Add the flour and whisk until bubbling. Add 3½ cups of the reserved veal broth and bring to a simmer, whisking constantly. Simmer over low heat, whisking frequently, until thickened, 10 minutes. Add the mushrooms, season with salt and white pepper and simmer over low heat for 10 minutes. Pour the mushrooms and sauce over the veal and add 2 tablespoons of the cream. Cover and simmer for 5 minutes, stirring occasionally.

6. In a medium heatproof bowl, whisk the yolks with the remaining ½ cup of cream; season with salt and white pepper. Gradually ladle in about 1 cup of the hot sauce from the stew, whisking. Pour the enriched sauce into the casserole and warm the stew over low heat, stirring gently, until thickened; do not let the sauce simmer. Stir in the parsley and serve with potatoes, rice or noodles. —*Marjorie Taylor*

WINE Earthy, red-berried red Burgundy: 2010 Joseph Drouhin Santenay.

COOKWARE TIP

Cast-Iron Pan

Food & Wine's new collection uses a lighter version of cast iron; it still has fantastic heat distribution but is easier to handle. *$102; amazon.com.*

VEAL MEATBALLS WITH
MUSTARD GREENS

CUMIN-AND-CORIANDER-GRILLED
LAMB RIBS
Recipe, page 214

Beef & Lamb

Minute Steak Stack with Herbed Anchovy Butter

⏱ Total **30 min**; Serves **2**

In this ode to minute steaks, chef Hugue Dufour of M. Wells Steakhouse in Long Island City, New York, pounds top round steaks thin, so they cook in about 60 seconds, then serves them in a stack, sandwiched with pats of anchovy-herb butter.

- **2** Tbsp. chopped anchovy fillets in oil, drained
- **1** shallot, minced
- **2** Tbsp. red wine vinegar
- **1** stick unsalted butter, at room temperature
- **¼** cup equal parts chopped parsley, tarragon and chives
- **½** tsp. coarsely ground pepper
- **2** Tbsp. canola oil

  12 to 16 oz. top round steak, cut crosswise into 4 slices, each slice pounded to a ¼-inch thickness

  Montreal steak spice (see Note), for seasoning

1. In a small skillet, cook the anchovies, shallot and vinegar over moderate heat, stirring, until the anchovies break down and the vinegar evaporates, 5 minutes. Mash the anchovies with a wooden spoon. Transfer the mixture to a small bowl and let cool to room temperature. Add the butter, herbs and pepper and mix well. Scrape the butter onto a sheet of parchment paper and roll into a log or pack into an airtight container.

2. In a large cast-iron skillet, heat the canola oil until smoking. Season the steaks on both sides with the Montreal steak spice. Working in 2 batches, sear the steaks over high heat for 30 to 40 seconds per side, until well browned outside but rare within. Transfer the steaks to a rack set over a baking sheet.

3. On a platter, stack the steaks with a big pat of the anchovy butter between each one. Top with a big pat of butter and serve immediately, dividing the stack at the table. —*Hugue Dufour*

NOTE Montreal steak spice, which includes garlic, coriander and cayenne, is based on the spices used in Montreal smoked meat. It's available at supermarkets.

WINE Cabernet Sauvignon–based Bordeaux: 2011 Peyredon Lagravette.

California Steak Salad

⏱ Total **45 min**; Serves **4**

Food Network star Tyler Florence says this main-course salad can include whatever seasonal vegetables you like. He prefers crisp ones like snap peas, green beans and radishes.

- **2** Tbsp. grapeseed or vegetable oil

  One 2-lb. trimmed and tied beef tenderloin roast, at room temperature

  Salt and freshly ground pepper

- **½** small red onion, finely chopped
- **¼** cup fresh lemon juice
- **¼** cup red wine vinegar
- **2** Tbsp. Dijon mustard
- **¾** cup extra-virgin olive oil
- **2** Tbsp. chopped tarragon
- **½** cup crumbled blue cheese (about 2 oz.)
- **½** lb. green beans
- **½** lb. sugar snap peas, split open
- **1** small bunch of watercress, thick stems discarded
- **4** small radishes, thinly sliced
- **½** cup cherry tomatoes, halved
- **1** small head of iceberg lettuce, cut crosswise into 4 slabs
- **2** Tbsp. snipped chives

1. Preheat the oven to 350°. In an ovenproof skillet just large enough to hold the roast, heat the grapeseed oil until shimmering. Season the meat with salt and pepper and cook over moderately high heat until browned all over, about 5 minutes. Transfer the skillet to the oven and roast the meat for about 25 minutes, turning it a few times, until an instant-read thermometer inserted in the center registers 125° for medium-rare. Transfer the roast to a carving board to rest for 10 minutes. Remove the string and slice the roast 1 inch thick.

2. Meanwhile, in a medium bowl, whisk the onion with the lemon juice, vinegar and mustard. Whisk in the olive oil in a thin stream until emulsified. Stir in the tarragon and blue cheese and season the dressing with salt and pepper.

3. In a medium saucepan of salted boiling water, cook the green beans until crisptender, about 2 minutes. Drain and cool under running water. Pat the beans dry and transfer them to a large bowl. Add the snap peas, watercress, radishes and tomatoes and toss to mix.

4. Arrange the lettuce slabs on a large platter, scatter the vegetables over the lettuce and drizzle the dressing on top. Arrange the sliced roast beef on the salad, sprinkle with the chives and serve. —*Tyler Florence*

WINE Juicy, medium-bodied Pinot Noir: 2012 Domaine Eden Santa Cruz Mountains.

Grilled Strip Steaks with Onion Wedges

⏱ Total **35 min**; Serves **4**

This juicy strip steak is great for parties: Cook to medium-rare, then let it rest. Reheat just before serving.

  Two 12- to 14-oz. New York strip steaks, about 1¼ inches thick, at room temperature for 30 minutes

- **1** white onion, cut into 8 wedges through the core

  Canola oil, for brushing

  Kosher salt and freshly ground pepper

1. Light a grill or heat a grill pan. Brush the steaks and onion wedges with oil and season with salt and pepper. Using tongs, rub 1 of the onion wedges all over the grate or grill pan. Add the steaks and remaining onion wedges to the grill, cover and cook over moderately high heat, turning once, until the steaks are just medium-rare and the onion is tender, 6 to 7 minutes total. Transfer the steaks and onion to a cutting board and let rest for at least 10 minutes.

2. Return the steaks to the grill and cook, turning once, until the surfaces are just hot, about 2 minutes total. Transfer the strip steaks to the cutting board, slice them across the grain and serve with the grilled onions. —*Tim Love*

WINE Cherry-rich, not-too-tannic Merlot: 2012 Nelms Road.

GRILLED STRIP STEAKS WITH
ONION WEDGES

Throwback Porterhouse Steaks

Active **10 min**; Total **50 min**; Serves **4**

This is Brooklyn meat guru Tom Mylan's tribute to his father, who made the dead-simple steaks in the 1980s on a rusty, falling-apart grill. Mylan's advice for doctoring bottled barbecue sauce: "Use cheap beer!"

Two 1¼-lb. porterhouse steaks, 1¼ inches thick

Salt and pepper

½ cup bottled barbecue sauce

¼ cup beer, preferably American lager

Vegetable oil, for brushing

1. Light a gas grill. Season the steaks generously with salt and pepper and let stand at room temperature for 30 minutes. In a small bowl, whisk the barbecue sauce with the beer.

2. Oil the grill grate. Grill the steaks over high heat, turning once, until lightly charred on both sides, about 6 minutes total. Baste the steaks with the barbecue sauce and grill, turning and basting occasionally, until glazed and an instant-read thermometer inserted in the thickest part registers 120° for medium-rare meat, 3 to 5 minutes more. Transfer the steaks to a carving board and let rest for 10 minutes before serving. —*Tom Mylan*

WINE Spiced, concentrated Rioja Reserva: 2009 Muga Reserva.

Skirt Steak with Anchovy-Caper Sauce

Active **30 min**; Total **1 hr 25 min**; Serves **6**

¾ cup extra-virgin olive oil

½ cup finely chopped parsley

1 small shallot, minced

6 anchovy fillets, minced

2 Tbsp. finely chopped tarragon

2 Tbsp. finely chopped chives

2 Tbsp. fresh lemon juice

1 Tbsp. salt-packed capers, rinsed and minced

1 Tbsp. red wine vinegar

1 small garlic clove, minced

1 tsp. finely chopped thyme

Kosher salt and pepper

2 lbs. skirt steak, cut into 5-inch lengths

1. In a medium bowl, combine all of the ingredients except the steak and season with salt and pepper. Let stand at room temperature for 1 hour. Season the steak with salt and pepper and let come to room temperature, about 45 minutes.

2. Heat a grill pan. Grill the steak over high heat, turning once, until lightly charred on the outside and medium-rare within, 5 to 6 minutes total. Transfer to a cutting board and let rest for 5 minutes. Thinly slice the steak against the grain and transfer to a platter. Spoon some of the sauce on top and serve, passing the remaining sauce at the table. —*Sashi Moorman*

WINE Focused California Syrah: 2012 Moorman Piedrasassi Santa Barbara County.

Pepper-and-Spice-Rubbed Rib Eye Steaks

Active **30 min**; Total **1 hr 45 min** Serves **4**

¼ cup coarsely ground pepper

2 Tbsp. ground coriander

1½ tsp. light brown sugar

1½ tsp. sweet paprika

1 tsp. mustard powder

1 tsp. onion powder

1 tsp. garlic powder

Two 1¼-lb. bone-in rib eye steaks

Kosher salt

2 Tbsp. canola oil

1. In a small bowl, whisk together everything except the steaks, salt and oil. Rub 1 tablespoon of the spice mix on each side of the steaks and let stand at room temperature for 1 hour.

2. Season the steaks with salt. In a large cast-iron skillet, heat the oil until shimmering. Add the steaks and cook over moderate heat, turning once, until medium-rare, 6 to 7 minutes per side. Transfer the steaks to a cutting board and let rest for 10 minutes. Cut the steak off the bone, slice across the grain and serve. —*Marc Forgione*

MAKE AHEAD The spice rub can be stored in an airtight container for up to 1 month.

WINE Spicy California Syrah: 2011 Beckmen Vineyards Purisima Mountain.

Flat Iron Steaks with Blue Cheese Butter

⏱ Total **40 min**; Serves **4 to 6**

John Gorham, the chef at Tasty n Alder in Portland, Oregon, loves to make these easy steaks at home. The key is the blue cheese butter, which he brushes on the steak and serves alongside. It's seasoned with tarragon and shallot as well as Gorgonzola dolce, a young blue cheese that's milder and creamier than more aged Gorgonzolas.

1 stick unsalted butter, softened

4 oz. Gorgonzola dolce, at room temperature

2 Tbsp. minced shallot

1 Tbsp. finely chopped tarragon

Dash of Worcestershire sauce

Kosher salt and freshly ground pepper

Two 1- to 1¼-lb. beef flat iron steaks

Canola oil, for brushing

1. In a small bowl, blend the butter with the Gorgonzola, shallot, tarragon and Worcestershire sauce. Season the blue cheese butter with salt and pepper.

2. Light a grill or heat a grill pan. Brush the steaks with oil, season with salt and pepper and grill over high heat until lightly charred on the bottom, about 4 minutes. Flip the steaks, brush with 1 tablespoon of the blue cheese butter and grill until medium-rare, 3 to 4 minutes more. Let the steaks rest on a cutting board for 10 minutes, then thinly slice them across the grain. Serve with the remaining blue cheese butter on the side. —*John Gorham*

MAKE AHEAD The blue cheese butter can be refrigerated for up to 2 days. Let return to room temperature before serving.

WINE Fruit-forward Malbec: 2011 Renacer Punto Final.

Griddled Gaucho Steak with Bread-and-Basil Salad

Active **30 min**; Total **1 hr**; Serves **4**

- 1 **head of garlic**
- ½ **cup plus 2 Tbsp. extra-virgin olive oil, plus more for drizzling**
- 2 **Tbsp. red wine vinegar**
  Sea salt and freshly ground pepper
- ½ **lb. rustic bread, cut or torn into 1½-inch pieces**
- 1 **lb. center-cut filet mignon**
- 1 **large bunch of chives (1 oz.)**
- ¼ **cup basil leaves**
- 1 **cup microgreens**

1. Preheat the oven to 425°. Cut ½ inch off the top of the garlic head and set the head on a piece of foil. Drizzle the garlic with olive oil, wrap tightly and roast until tender, about 45 minutes. Unwrap the garlic and let cool slightly, then squeeze the cloves from their skins into a small bowl. Mash with a fork until smooth. Whisk in ¼ cup of the olive oil and the vinegar and season the dressing with sea salt and pepper.

2. Meanwhile, in a large nonstick skillet, heat ¼ cup of the olive oil. Add the bread and cook over moderate heat, tossing, until golden and crisp all over, about 5 minutes. Arrange the croutons on plates.

3. Using a sharp knife, make a ¼-inch-deep cut down the length of the filet mignon. Turning the filet and rolling it out as you go, spiral-cut the meat until you have a long, rectangular piece that's about ¼ inch thick; alternatively, have your butcher butterfly the steak for you. Make ½-inch-deep slits every 2 inches along the grain all over the steak. Rub the steak with 1 tablespoon of the olive oil. Season with sea salt and pepper and arrange the chives on top, tucking them into the slits.

4. Preheat a cast-iron skillet. Add the remaining 1 tablespoon of olive oil to the skillet and cook the steak, chive side up, over moderate heat until browned, about 3 minutes. Flip the steak and cook until the chives are charred and the steak is medium-rare inside, 2 to 3 minutes longer. Transfer the steak to a cutting board and let rest for 5 minutes.

5. Arrange the basil and microgreens on the croutons and spoon the roasted garlic dressing on top. Slice the steak against the grain and serve alongside.
—*Francis Mallmann*

WINE Robust, black cherry–rich Mendoza Malbec: 2012 Recuerdo.

London Broil with Horseradish Sauce

Active **25 min**; Total **1 hr 15 min**; Serves **4**

Tom Mylan, owner of The Meat Hook butcher shop in Brooklyn, says the trick to tenderizing an inexpensive cut like London broil is piercing it in several places with a knife or fork. (He uses a multi-bladed Jaccard tenderizer.) "Stab the meat mercilessly for one minute," he says.

- **One 2- to 2¼-lb. top round steak (for London broil), 2 inches thick**
  Kosher salt and pepper
- 1 **cup sour cream**
- ½ **cup lightly packed drained horseradish**
  Vegetable oil, for brushing

1. Put the steak on a work surface and, using a Jaccard knife or a fork, poke the steak all over until it's well tenderized. Season the steak with 1 tablespoon of salt and 1 teaspoon of pepper. Let stand at room temperature for 45 minutes.

2. Meanwhile, light a gas grill. In a medium bowl, whisk the sour cream with the horseradish and season with 2 teaspoons of salt and 1 teaspoon of pepper.

3. Oil the grill grate. Pat the steak dry and brush it lightly with oil. Grill over high heat, turning once, until lightly charred on both sides, about 6 minutes. Continue to grill the steak over moderate heat, turning occasionally, until an instant-read thermometer inserted in the center registers 120°, about 5 minutes longer. Transfer the steak to a carving board and let rest for 10 minutes. Thinly slice the steak against the grain and serve with the horseradish sauce.
—*Tom Mylan*

WINE Rich, fruit-forward Napa Cabernet: 2011 Oberon.

Seared Sous Vide–Style Tri-Tip

Active **40 min**; Total **2 hr 30 min**
Serves **4 to 6**

Nick Kokonas, co-owner of Alinea in Chicago, loves his home sous vide station, but for people who don't own one, he offers a clever hack using a resealable bag and a thermometer. The only bit of work is making sure the water temperature stays constant as the tri-tip cooks gently. To finish, the roast gets a crusty sear over very high heat. Kokonas stresses: "However hot you think it needs to be isn't enough. It has to be hotter than that."

- **One 2-lb. tri-tip roast**
  Kosher salt and pepper
- 2 **Tbsp. thyme leaves**
- 3 **large garlic cloves, minced**
- 4 **Tbsp. unsalted butter, cubed**
  Extra-virgin olive oil, for brushing

1. Heat a large pot of water until it registers 134° on a digital probe or candy thermometer. Season the roast generously with salt and pepper. Rub all over with the thyme and garlic and transfer to a large, BPA-free resealable freezer bag. Add the butter and seal all but 1 corner. Gradually lower into a large bowl of water until nearly all of the air is pressed out, then seal.

2. Add the bag with the roast to the pot and cook at 134° until an instant-read thermometer inserted in the thickest part registers 130°, about 1 hour and 45 minutes; reseal the bag using the same procedure as above, if necessary. Adjust the heat as needed to maintain the water temperature.

3. Transfer the roast to a cutting board and let rest for 5 minutes. Scrape off and discard the thyme and garlic.

4. Light a grill or heat a skillet. Pat the roast dry with paper towels, then brush with oil and season lightly with salt and pepper. Cook the roast over very high heat, turning once, until nicely browned all over, 5 to 7 minutes. Return the roast to the cutting board and let rest for another 10 minutes. Thinly slice the meat against the grain and serve. —*Nick Kokonas*

WINE Earthy, structured Sangiovese: 2009 Col d'Orcia Brunello di Montalcino.

Rib Eye with Brussels Sprouts and Stout Cream Sauce

Total **1 hr 15 min**; Serves **4**

The intense sauce for this steak is thickened with bread and enriched with dark stout. It's great on any steak, particularly a thick cut like rib eye.

STOUT SAUCE

- **2** Tbsp. vegetable oil
- **1** cup thinly sliced Spanish onion
- **½** cup dark stout
- **½** cup heavy cream
-    One ½-inch-thick slice of sourdough bread, crusts removed, bread diced
-    Kosher salt and pepper

VEGETABLES

- **1** Tbsp. extra-virgin olive oil
- **½** lb. brussels sprouts, halved or quartered if large
- **8** medium cipollini onions, peeled and halved lengthwise
- **4** medium spring onions, quartered lengthwise, or 12 large scallions, cut into 2-inch lengths
-    Kosher salt and pepper

RIB EYE

-    One 1½-lb. boneless rib eye steak, about 1½ inches thick
-    Vegetable oil, for brushing
-    Kosher salt and pepper

1. Make the sauce In a medium saucepan, heat the vegetable oil until shimmering. Add the onion and cook over moderate heat, stirring occasionally, until softened and golden, about 7 minutes. Add the stout, cream and bread and bring just to a boil. Simmer over moderately low heat, stirring occasionally, until the bread is very soft, about 10 minutes. Transfer to a blender and puree until smooth. Season the sauce with salt and pepper and keep warm over very low heat.

2. Make the vegetables In a large, deep skillet, heat the olive oil until shimmering. Add the brussels sprouts and cipollinis and cook over moderate heat, stirring, until just starting to brown, 5 minutes. Add the spring onions and 1 cup of water and cook, stirring, until the vegetables are crisp-tender and the water is absorbed, 5 minutes. Season with salt and pepper; keep warm.

3. Grill the rib eye Light a grill. Brush the steak with vegetable oil and season with salt and pepper. Grill over moderately high heat, turning once, until charred outside and medium-rare within, 5 minutes per side. Transfer to a carving board and let rest for 5 minutes. Slice the steak against the grain and serve with the vegetables and stout sauce. —*Mark Liberman*

BEER Dark, malty American craft beer: Left Hand Milk Stout.

Rib Eye and Radishes in Bagna Cauda Butter

Total **1 hr**; Serves **4**

- **1** stick unsalted butter, at room temperature
- **5** oil-packed anchovies, minced
- **1** large garlic clove, minced
- **¼** cup chopped parsley
-    Kosher salt and pepper
- **1** Tbsp. extra-virgin olive oil
-    One 1¾-lb. bone-in rib eye steak (2 inches thick), at room temperature for 1 hour
- **2** rosemary sprigs
- **2** bunches of radishes

1. Preheat the oven to 450°. In a medium bowl, stir the butter with the anchovies, garlic and 2 tablespoons of the parsley. Season with salt and pepper and mix well.

2. In a large cast-iron skillet, heat the oil until shimmering. Season the steak with salt and pepper. Add the steak and rosemary to the skillet and sear over moderately high heat until the steak is browned, 2 minutes per side. Add the radishes and half of the butter and roast in the oven for 18 to 20 minutes, basting every 3 minutes, until an instant-read thermometer inserted in the meat registers 125° for medium-rare; transfer to a board to rest for 15 minutes. Discard the rosemary.

3. Thinly slice the steak and transfer to a platter along with the radishes. Sprinkle with the remaining parsley and serve with the remaining butter. —*Kay Chun*

WINE Herby, cassis-scented Cabernet Franc: 2011 Couly-Dutheil La Baronnie Madeleine Chinon.

Tuscan Steak with "Sandy" Potatoes

Active **30 min**; Total **2 hr**; Serves **4**

The irresistible potatoes here are salt-roasted and then sautéed with bread crumbs and herbs. "Sandy" is a playful reference to their crunch.

-    Kosher salt
- **1½** lbs. new potatoes
-    One 1¾-lb. sirloin steak, about 1½ inches thick
-    Extra-virgin olive oil
-    Pepper
- **2** tsp. minced garlic
- **3** tsp. each of minced sage, rosemary and thyme
- **½** cup plain dried bread crumbs
-    Maldon salt

1. Preheat the oven to 350°. In a large bowl, mix 4 cups of kosher salt with ½ cup of water. Spread half of the salt in a 9-by-9-inch baking dish. Arrange the potatoes in the dish and pack the remaining salt on top.

2. Bake the potatoes for 45 minutes, until tender. Let cool slightly. Crack the salt crust and carefully remove it. Transfer the potatoes to a work surface and cut them into 1-inch pieces.

3. Lower the oven temperature to 200°. Light a grill or heat a grill pan. Brush the steak with oil, season with kosher salt and pepper and rub with the garlic and 2 teaspoons each of the herbs.

4. Grill the steak over high heat, turning once, until nicely charred, 5 minutes total. Transfer to a rimmed baking sheet and bake for 12 to 15 minutes, until an instant-read thermometer inserted in the thickest part registers 125° for medium-rare. Transfer to a board and let rest for 15 minutes.

5. In a large skillet, heat ¼ cup of oil. Cook the potatoes over moderately high heat, tossing, until browned. Add the bread crumbs and remaining 1 teaspoon each of the herbs and cook, tossing, until the bread crumbs are toasted, 4 minutes. Season with kosher salt and pepper. Slice the steak, spoon any juices on top and sprinkle with Maldon salt. Serve with the potatoes. —*Enrico Bartolini*

WINE Rich, dark-berried Brunello: 2008 La Poderina.

RIB EYE AND RADISHES IN
BAGNA CAUDA BUTTER

Beef Involtini with Artichokes

Total **1 hr**; Serves **6**

Ylenia Sambati, a cooking-school instructor at Cantele winery in Puglia, Italy, stuffs thin slices of beef with mozzarella, Parmigiano and parsley, then rolls them into pinwheels to braise in wine with artichokes.

- **12** thin slices of beef round (about 1½ lbs. total), pounded ⅛ inch thick
- **6** cherry tomatoes, halved
- **4** oz. fresh mozzarella, cut into ½-inch dice
- **¼** cup freshly grated Parmigiano-Reggiano cheese
- **24** parsley leaves, plus minced parsley for garnish
  Kosher salt and black pepper
- **1** lemon, halved
- **6** medium artichokes
- **3** Tbsp. extra-virgin olive oil
- **½** tsp. crushed red pepper
- **2** garlic cloves, minced
- **1½** cups dry white wine
- **6** sun-dried tomatoes in oil, cut into thin strips
- **1** Tbsp. pine nuts, toasted

1. Spread out the slices of beef on a work surface and place a cherry tomato half, 4 pieces of mozzarella, 1 teaspoon of Parmigiano and 2 parsley leaves in the center of each. Fold in the sides, roll into a packet and secure with toothpicks. Season the involtini with salt and black pepper.

2. Squeeze the juice from 1 lemon half into a bowl of water. Working with 1 artichoke at a time, discard the dark green outer leaves. Cut off the top inch of the artichoke and discard, then peel and trim the bottom and stem. Halve the artichoke lengthwise and scoop out the furry choke. Cut each half in half again, then rub the quarters with the remaining lemon half and add them to the lemon water.

3. In a large skillet, heat the olive oil. Cook the involtini over moderately high heat, turning, until browned on both sides, 9 minutes. Transfer to a plate.

4. Add the crushed red pepper and garlic to the skillet and cook until fragrant. Stir in the wine, ½ cup of water and the sun-dried tomatoes. Add the artichokes and bring to a boil. Cover and cook until almost tender,

20 minutes. Return the involtini to the skillet, reduce the heat and simmer until the artichokes are tender, 10 minutes. Transfer the involtini and artichokes to plates. Season the sauce and pour it on top. Sprinkle with the pine nuts and minced parsley and serve. —*Ylenia Sambati*

WINE Robust, fruity Italian red: 2010 Cantele Primitivo.

Grilled Hanger Steak with Kimchi-Apple Slaw

Total **45 min**; Serves **4**

- **2** Tbsp. canola oil, plus more for oiling the grate
- **3** Tbsp. plus 1 tsp. sugar
- **3** Tbsp. soy sauce
- **2** Tbsp. toasted sesame oil
- **1** Tbsp. finely grated fresh ginger
- **3** garlic cloves, minced
- **1** shallot, minced
  Kosher salt and pepper
- **2** lbs. hanger steak
- **⅓** cup mayonnaise
- **2** tsp. apple cider vinegar
- **1** small Granny Smith apple, peeled and julienned
- **1** small cucumber, julienned
- **1** cup kimchi with juices, chopped
  Sesame seeds and sliced scallion, for garnish

1. In a large bowl, combine the 2 tablespoons of canola oil and 3 tablespoons of the sugar with the soy sauce, sesame oil, ginger, garlic and shallot; season with salt and pepper. Add the steak and let stand for 15 minutes.

2. Meanwhile, in a medium bowl, combine the mayonnaise with the vinegar and remaining 1 teaspoon of sugar. Stir in the apple, cucumber and kimchi; season the slaw with salt and refrigerate.

3. Light a grill and oil the grate. Grill the steak over moderate heat until charred outside and medium-rare within, 4 to 5 minutes per side. Transfer to a cutting board and let rest for 5 minutes.

4. Thinly slice the steak, top with sesame seeds and scallion and serve with the slaw. —*Judy Joo*

WINE Spicy Australian red: 2012 Turkey Flat Butchers Block.

Grilled Skirt Steak with Fruit-and-Green-Tomato Salsa

Total **30 min**; Serves **4 to 6**

- **3** Tbsp. plus 2 tsp. extra-virgin olive oil, plus more for brushing
- **1½** Tbsp. red wine vinegar
- **1** Tbsp. soy sauce
- **1** tsp. *sambal oelek*
- **1** small spring onion or 2 scallions, thinly sliced
- **1** large green tomato, cored and cut into ⅓-inch dice
- **1** black plum, cut into ⅓-inch dice
- **½** cup fresh sweet cherries, pitted and quartered
- **¼** cup pitted Niçoise olives, chopped
- **2** Tbsp. finely chopped basil
- **2** Tbsp. finely chopped parsley
- **2** Tbsp. finely chopped cilantro
- **2** Tbsp. finely chopped sorrel (optional)
  Kosher salt and pepper
- **2** lbs. skirt steak, cut into 5-inch lengths

1. In a large bowl, whisk 3 tablespoons of the olive oil with the vinegar, soy sauce and *sambal oelek*.

2. In a small skillet, heat the remaining 2 teaspoons of olive oil. Add the onion and cook over moderate heat, stirring, until softened, about 3 minutes. Scrape the onion into the vinaigrette and let the mixture cool. Add the green tomato, plum, cherries, olives, basil, parsley, cilantro and sorrel, if using. Toss well and season the salsa with salt and pepper.

3. Light a grill or heat a grill pan. Brush the steak with olive oil and season with salt and pepper. Grill over high heat, turning once, until lightly charred outside and medium-rare within, about 6 minutes. Transfer the steak to a carving board and let rest for 5 minutes, then thinly slice across the grain. Serve with the fruit salsa. —*Stephanie Izard*

WINE Vivid, juicy California Grenache: 2012 Dashe Cellars Les Enfants Terribles.

Skirt Steak with Roasted Tomato Chimichurri and Potatoes

Active **45 min**; Total **1 hr 15 min**; Serves **4**

Classic chimichurri gets pumped up with sweet roasted tomatoes. The condiment is great with fish and poultry as well as steak.

CHIMICHURRI

- 4 **medium tomatoes (1½ lbs.), quartered**
- ½ **cup extra-virgin olive oil**
  Kosher salt
- 1 **cup lightly packed parsley leaves**
- 1½ **Tbsp. unseasoned rice vinegar**
- ¾ **tsp. crushed red pepper**

POTATOES AND STEAK

- 1 **lb. fingerling potatoes**
  Kosher salt
- 2 **Tbsp. extra-virgin olive oil**
- 1 **onion, very thinly sliced**
- 1 **Tbsp. unsalted butter**
- ¼ **cup finely chopped parsley**
- 2 **lbs. skirt steak, cut into 5-inch lengths**
  Black pepper

1. Make the chimichurri Preheat the oven to 400°. On a large rimmed baking sheet, toss the tomatoes with ¼ cup of the olive oil and season with salt. Roast for about 20 minutes, until softened and browned in spots; let cool slightly. Transfer the tomatoes to a food processor. Add the parsley, vinegar, crushed pepper and the remaining ¼ cup of oil. Pulse until almost smooth. Season with salt and transfer to a bowl.

2. Make the potatoes and steak In a saucepan, cover the potatoes with water and bring to a boil. Add a generous pinch of salt and simmer over moderate heat until tender, about 15 minutes. Drain the potatoes and let cool, then halve lengthwise.

3. In a large skillet, heat the olive oil until shimmering. Add the onion and cook over moderately high heat, stirring, until just softened, about 3 minutes. Add the potatoes cut side down and cook until browned on the bottom, about 5 minutes. Flip the potatoes and onion and cook, stirring, until well browned, about 4 minutes. Stir in the butter and parsley and season with salt. Transfer to a platter and keep warm.

4. Light a grill or heat a grill pan. Season the steak with salt and black pepper. Grill over high heat, turning once, until medium-rare, about 7 minutes total. Transfer to a carving board and let rest for 10 minutes. Thinly slice the steak across the grain and transfer to the platter with the potatoes. Serve with the tomato chimichurri. —*Jose Enrique*

WINE Slightly chilled, medium-bodied red: 2013 Domaine Dupeuble Beaujolais.

Butter-Basted Rib Eye Steaks

Active **20 min**; Total **1 hr**; Serves **4**

- **Two 1¼-lb. bone-in rib eye steaks**
  Kosher salt and freshly ground pepper
- 2 **Tbsp. canola oil**
- 4 **Tbsp. unsalted butter**
- 4 **thyme sprigs**
- 3 **garlic cloves**
- 1 **rosemary sprig**

1. Season the rib eye steaks all over with salt and ground pepper and let stand at room temperature for 30 minutes.

2. In a large cast-iron skillet, heat the canola oil until shimmering. Add the steaks and cook over high heat until crusty on the bottom, about 5 minutes. Turn the steaks and add the butter, thyme, garlic and rosemary to the skillet. Cook over high heat, basting the steaks with the melted butter, garlic and herbs, until the steaks are medium-rare, 5 to 7 minutes longer. Transfer the steaks to a cutting board and let rest for 10 minutes. Cut the steaks off the bone, then slice the meat across the grain and serve. —*Christopher Coombs*

WINE Boldly tannic Cabernet Sauvignon: 2011 Beaulieu Vineyard Rutherford.

Skirt Steak with Eggplant-and-Pepper Relish

Total **15 min**; Makes **3 cups of relish**

- 1 **medium eggplant**
- 4 **jarred roasted red bell peppers (12 oz.), drained**
- 1 **garlic clove, peeled**
- ½ **cup extra-virgin olive oil**
- 3 **Tbsp. fresh lemon juice**
- 2 **Tbsp. chopped flat-leaf parsley**
  Kosher salt and pepper
  Grilled skirt or flank steak

1. Roast the eggplant over a gas flame, turning, until charred all over and tender within, 6 minutes. Discard the skin.

2. In a food processor, pulse the eggplant with the peppers, garlic, olive oil, lemon juice and parsley until chunky. Transfer to a bowl and season with salt and pepper. Serve with steak. —*Jessica Koslow*

WINE Smoky, deeply flavorful Australian Shiraz: 2013 Paringa.

THREE GRILLING MARINADES

Each of these makes enough for 1 pound of beef or lamb. Coat with the marinade, refrigerate for 3 hours, then grill.

LEMONGRASS-COCONUT In a bowl, mix 2 finely chopped lemongrass stalks (tender inner bulbs only), ½ cup vegetable oil, ¼ cup unsweetened coconut milk, ¼ cup Asian fish sauce, 2 Tbsp. fresh lime juice, 3 crushed garlic cloves, 2 Tbsp. light brown sugar and 1 thinly sliced Thai chile.

CITRUS, FENNEL AND HERB In a bowl, thoroughly mix 1 thinly sliced lemon, 1 thinly sliced small fennel bulb, 3 crushed garlic cloves, ½ cup extra-virgin olive oil and 5 sprigs each of rosemary and sage.

GARLICKY PIMENTÓN-OREGANO In a bowl, mix ½ cup canola oil, 1 Tbsp. fresh lemon juice, 1 Tbsp. pimentón de la Vera, 7 crushed garlic cloves and 2 Tbsp. chopped oregano. –*Kay Chun*

Grilled Skirt Steak with Green Bean Salad and Citrus Vinaigrette

Active **1 hr**; Total **2 hr 30 min**; Serves **4 to 6**

STEAK

- ½ small red onion, chopped
- 2 garlic cloves, crushed
- ½ cup extra-virgin olive oil, plus more for oiling the grate
  Kosher salt and freshly ground pepper
- 2 lbs. skirt steak, cut into 3 equal pieces

SALAD

- ¾ lb. haricots verts or green beans, trimmed
- 1 pint cherry tomatoes, halved
- ½ small red onion, thinly sliced
- 1 jalapeño or serrano chile, thinly sliced
- ½ cup lightly packed cilantro leaves
- ¼ cup chopped roasted peanuts

VINAIGRETTE

- ½ cup extra-virgin olive oil
- ¼ cup fresh orange juice
- 1 Tbsp. Sriracha
- ⅛ tsp. pepper
- 2 Tbsp. Asian fish sauce
- 2 Tbsp. sherry vinegar
- 2 Tbsp. fresh lime juice
- 1 tsp. finely grated orange zest
- 1 tsp. kosher salt

1. Marinate the steak In a blender, combine the onion, garlic, ½ cup of olive oil and 1 tablespoon of water and season with salt and pepper. Puree until smooth, then pour into a large resealable plastic bag. Add the steak, seal the bag and rub the steak with the marinade. Refrigerate for at least 2 hours or overnight.

2. Make the salad Fill a medium bowl with ice water. In a medium saucepan of salted boiling water, cook the beans until crisp-tender, 2 to 3 minutes. Drain, then transfer the beans to the ice bath to cool. Drain well and pat dry. Halve the beans lengthwise and transfer to a large bowl. Add the remaining salad ingredients.

3. Make the vinaigrette In a small bowl, whisk all of the ingredients.

4. Light a grill and oil the grate. Remove the steak from the marinade and season with salt and pepper. Grill over moderately high heat until lightly charred outside and medium-rare within, about 3 minutes per side. Transfer the steak to a cutting board and let rest for 5 minutes. Thinly slice the steak across the grain.

5. Add two-thirds of the vinaigrette to the bean salad, season with salt and pepper and toss. Serve the steak with the salad, passing the extra vinaigrette at the table. —*Greg Denton and Gabrielle Quiñónez Denton*

MAKE AHEAD The vinaigrette can be refrigerated overnight.

WINE Vibrant, spiced Argentinean Malbec: 2012 Catena Zapata Vista Flores.

Skirt Steak with Pinto Beans and Pasilla Chile Vinaigrette

Active **40 min**; Total **1 hr 10 min**; Serves **4**

Tangy, smoky and sweet, chef Hugh Acheson's pasilla chile vinaigrette is a zippier alternative to the usual steak sauce. It's perfect with a rich, juicy cut like skirt steak.

- 1 pasilla chile, stemmed and seeded (see Note)
  Boiling water
- 1 Tbsp. apple cider vinegar
- 1 Tbsp. fresh lime juice
- 1 tsp. honey
- 1 tsp. Dijon mustard
- ¼ cup plus 2 Tbsp. extra-virgin olive oil, plus more for brushing
  Kosher salt and freshly ground pepper
- 1 medium onion, minced
  Two 15-oz. cans pinto beans, rinsed and drained
- ½ tsp. achiote seeds, finely ground (optional)
- ½ cup chicken stock or low-sodium broth
- 2 Tbsp. chopped cilantro
- 1½ lbs. skirt steak, cut into 5-inch lengths
- 8 large scallions

1. Heat a grill pan. Add the pasilla and toast over high heat, pressing down with a spatula and turning once, until pliable and fragrant, about 1 minute. Transfer the pasilla to a heatproof bowl and cover with boiling water. Let stand until softened, about 30 minutes.

2. Transfer the pasilla to a blender along with 2 tablespoons of the soaking liquid. Add the vinegar, lime juice, honey and mustard and puree until smooth. With the blender on, gradually add ¼ cup of the olive oil until incorporated. Season the vinaigrette with salt and pepper.

3. In a large skillet, heat the remaining 2 tablespoons of olive oil until shimmering. Add the onion and cook over moderately high heat, stirring occasionally, until softened, about 5 minutes. Add the beans and achiote and cook, stirring, until fragrant, about 2 minutes. Add the stock and cook until the beans are hot and glazed, about 3 minutes. Stir in half of the vinaigrette and the chopped cilantro. Season with salt and pepper and keep warm.

4. Heat the grill pan. Brush the steak with oil and season with salt and pepper. Grill over high heat, turning once, until lightly charred, about 6 minutes. Transfer to a carving board and let rest for 5 minutes.

5. Meanwhile, brush the scallions with oil and season with salt and pepper. Grill over high heat, turning, until lightly charred, 1 to 2 minutes. Thinly slice the steak against the grain and serve with the beans and scallions, passing the remaining vinaigrette at the table. —*Hugh Acheson*

NOTE Pasillas are long, black dried chiles with a fruity, herbaceous flavor. They are available at Latin markets.

WINE Blackberry-rich Argentinean red: 2012 Ruca Malen Malbec Reserva.

SKIRT STEAK WITH PINTO BEANS AND
PASILLA CHILE VINAIGRETTE

Sir Winston's Favorite Short Ribs

Total **45 min** plus overnight marinating
Serves **4**

MARINADE

½ cup Coca-Cola

½ cup fresh orange juice

½ cup shoyu (Japanese soy sauce)

½ cup Guinness

⅓ cup sake

⅓ cup packed light brown sugar

¼ cup soy sauce

¼ cup red miso paste

2 Tbsp. bourbon

2 Tbsp. pure maple syrup

1½ Tbsp. finely grated fresh ginger

1 Tbsp. toasted sesame oil

1 Tbsp. toasted sesame seeds

1½ tsp. Asian chile oil

2 garlic cloves, finely grated

RIBS

2¾ lbs. flanken-style beef short ribs (see Note), about ¼ inch thick

Canola oil, for brushing

Lemon wedges, for serving

1. Make the marinade In a medium saucepan, combine all of the marinade ingredients; bring just to a boil, stirring to dissolve the sugar. Let cool completely. Transfer the marinade to a large, sturdy resealable plastic bag.

2. Prepare the ribs Add the short ribs to the marinade and seal the bag. Set the bag in a baking dish and refrigerate overnight. Bring the short ribs to room temperature before cooking.

3. Light a grill and brush with oil. Remove the ribs from the bag and discard the marinade. Working in batches, grill the short ribs over high heat, turning once, until nicely browned and charred in spots, about 2 minutes per side. Transfer the ribs to a platter and serve with lemon wedges. —*Jayson Woodbridge*

NOTE Flanken-cut short ribs are cut across the bone, so they appear to have a row of small bones dotting a thick strip of meat.

WINE Robust Argentinean Malbec: 2011 Layer Cake Malbec.

Grilled Short Ribs with Smoky Blackberry Barbecue Sauce

Active **45 min**; Total **1 hr 30 min**; Serves **4**

This delicious barbecue sauce gets its smoky flavor from berries that are grilled in a perforated pan; you can use sturdy foil or a foil pan with punched holes instead. Chipotle chiles amplify the smokiness.

1 lb. blackberries

2 tsp. sweet pimentón de la Vera (sweet smoked paprika)

3 Tbsp. vegetable oil, plus more for oiling the grate

1 Tbsp. minced garlic

1 medium onion, finely chopped, plus ¼ cup minced

¼ cup tomato paste

1 cup apple cider vinegar

1 cup packed light brown sugar

¼ cup soy sauce

3 Tbsp. seeded and minced chipotles in adobo sauce

2 Tbsp. Dijon mustard

1 tsp. ground cumin

Kosher salt and pepper

2 Tbsp. extra-virgin olive oil

2 Tbsp. finely chopped oregano, plus more for garnish

4½ lbs. flanken-style beef short ribs, ⅓ inch thick

Thinly sliced radishes, for garnish

1. Light a grill. In a large bowl, toss the blackberries with the pimentón. Spread the berries in a perforated grill pan or in a foil pan with holes poked in it. Grill over moderately high heat, tossing, until the berries just start to burst, 3 to 5 minutes.

2. In a large saucepan, heat the 3 tablespoons of vegetable oil. Add the garlic and cook over moderately low heat, stirring, until just golden. Add the chopped onion and cook over moderate heat, stirring, until softened and just starting to brown, about 7 minutes. Stir in the tomato paste and cook until glossy, about 2 minutes. Add the blackberries, vinegar, brown sugar, soy sauce, chipotles, mustard and cumin and bring just to a boil. Simmer over moderately low heat, stirring, until the sauce is slightly thickened and the berries are very tender, about 20 minutes.

3. Transfer the sauce to a blender and let cool slightly, then puree until smooth. Strain through a fine sieve into a bowl, discarding the solids. Season the sauce with salt and pepper and let cool completely. Spoon 1 cup of the sauce into a bowl and stir in the minced onion, the olive oil and the 2 tablespoons of oregano. Reserve the remaining sauce for grilled chicken or pork.

4. Light the grill and oil the grate. Season the ribs with salt and pepper and brush with the blackberry sauce. Grill over high heat, turning once, until nicely charred, 3 minutes. Continue to grill for 2 minutes more, turning and basting with more sauce, until glazed. Garnish the ribs with radishes and chopped oregano; serve hot. —*Greg Denton and Gabrielle Quiñónez Denton*

WINE Peppery, blackberry-rich California Petite Sirah: 2012 Bogle.

Grilled Apple-Marinated Short Ribs

Total **1 hr** plus 4 hr marinating; Serves **4**

RIBS

1¼ cups apple juice

⅓ cup soy sauce

¼ cup fresh lemon juice

4 scallions, thinly sliced

3 garlic cloves, minced

1 Tbsp. minced peeled fresh ginger

1 Tbsp. toasted sesame oil

4 meaty, boneless beef short ribs

SAUCE

1 tsp. canola oil

2 shallots, thinly sliced

Salt

3 garlic cloves, crushed

2 scallions, thinly sliced

⅓ cup red miso

2½ Tbsp. *gochujang* (spicy Korean chile paste)

2 Tbsp. unseasoned rice vinegar

2 Tbsp. toasted sesame oil

2 Tbsp. sugar

1 Granny Smith apple, cored and very thinly sliced

1. Marinate the ribs In a medium bowl, combine the apple juice, soy sauce, lemon juice, scallions, garlic, ginger and sesame oil. Put the short ribs in a large, sturdy resealable plastic bag and pour in the marinade. Seal the bag, set it in a baking dish and refrigerate for at least 4 hours and up to 24 hours. An hour before cooking, remove the marinated ribs from the refrigerator and let stand at room temperature.

2. Make the sauce In a small skillet, heat the canola oil. Add the shallots, season with salt and cook over moderately high heat, stirring a few times, until lightly golden and softened, 5 minutes. Transfer to a blender or mini food processor and let cool slightly. Add the garlic, scallions, miso, *gochujang*, vinegar, sesame oil and sugar and process to a smooth puree. Season the sauce with salt and transfer to a small bowl.

3. Light a grill or heat a grill pan. Remove the ribs from the marinade, scraping off any excess. Grill the ribs over moderately high heat, turning occasionally, until medium-rare, about 20 minutes. Let rest for 10 minutes, then thinly slice across the grain. Serve the ribs with the sauce and the sliced apple. —*Kuniko Yagi*

WINE Generously fruity Santa Barbara Syrah: 2011 Martian Ranch Red Shift.

Dry-Aged Roast Beef with Fresh Hot Sauce
Active **30 min**; Total **1 hr 45 min plus 1 day curing**; Serves **6 to 8**

"I love this dish," says chef Stuart Brioza of The Progress in San Francisco. "It's a pretty traditional roast beef, but then you shake it up by serving it with crispy garlic chips and a fresh-chile hot sauce." The beef is salt-cured, so it's extra-juicy.

ROAST BEEF

One 4-lb. dry-aged sirloin roast

2 **tsp. kosher salt**

1 **tsp. freshly ground pepper**

HOT SAUCE

½ **lb. red Fresno or red jalapeño chiles—stemmed, seeded and coarsely chopped**

1 **garlic clove, crushed**

½ **cup fresh lime juice**

¼ **cup water**

2 **Tbsp. kosher salt**

GARNISHES

½ **cup whole milk**

½ **cup very thinly sliced garlic cloves (sliced on a mandoline)**

Canola oil, for frying

Kosher salt

2 **cups baby arugula**

Extra-virgin olive oil, for drizzling

2 **scallions, thinly sliced**

Freshly ground pepper

1. Prepare the roast On a baking sheet, rub the roast all over with the salt and pepper. Refrigerate, uncovered, for 1 day.

2. Preheat the oven to 400°. Heat a large cast-iron skillet, add the roast fat side down and cook over moderately high heat until well browned, about 3 minutes. Continue cooking, turning, until the meat is browned all over, about 5 minutes. Turn the meat fat side up and roast in the oven for 40 to 45 minutes, until an instant-read thermometer inserted in the center registers 125° for medium-rare. Transfer the roast to a cutting board and let rest for 15 minutes.

3. Meanwhile, make the hot sauce In a blender, combine all of the ingredients and puree until smooth. Strain into a bowl.

4. Make the garnishes In a small saucepan, bring the milk and garlic just to a boil. Drain the garlic and pat the slices dry on paper towels. In a small saucepan, heat ½ inch of canola oil to 275°. Working in 2 batches, fry the garlic, stirring, until light golden, 1 to 2 minutes. Using a slotted spoon, transfer the garlic to paper towels to drain. Season with salt and let cool.

5. Spread the arugula on a platter. Thinly slice the roast and arrange on the arugula. Drizzle a little hot sauce and olive oil over the meat and garnish with the garlic chips and scallions. Season with salt and pepper and serve with the remaining hot sauce at the table. —*Stuart Brioza*

WINE Juicy, medium-bodied Spanish red: 2012 Descendientes de J. Palacios Pétalos.

Orzo-and-Ricotta Meatballs with Marinara
⏱ Total **45 min**; Serves **4 to 6**

The addition of orzo and fresh ricotta helps lighten these little cinnamon-spiced meatballs.

¼ **cup orzo**

1 **large egg**

1 **large shallot, minced**

2 **garlic cloves, minced**

⅛ **tsp. cinnamon**

⅛ **tsp. freshly grated nutmeg**

1 **lb. ground chuck (preferably 20 percent fat)**

½ **cup fresh ricotta cheese**

1 **tsp. kosher salt**

¼ **tsp. pepper**

¼ **cup chopped basil, plus more for garnish**

2 **Tbsp. extra-virgin olive oil**

24 **oz. jar marinara sauce**

Freshly shaved Parmigiano-Reggiano cheese, for serving

1. In a medium saucepan of salted boiling water, cook the orzo until al dente. Drain and let cool.

2. In a large bowl, beat the egg, shallot, garlic, cinnamon and nutmeg. Add the orzo, ground beef, ricotta, salt, pepper, ¼ cup of water and the ¼ cup of basil and mix well. Shape into 1¼-inch meatballs and transfer to a rimmed baking sheet.

3. In a large, deep skillet, heat the olive oil. Cook the meatballs over moderately high heat, turning, until just cooked through, 7 minutes. Transfer to a plate.

4. Add the marinara sauce to the skillet and cook over moderate heat until hot, 5 minutes. Add the meatballs and simmer until hot, 3 minutes. Spoon the meatballs and sauce into shallow bowls, garnish with basil and serve with shaved cheese. —*Giada De Laurentiis*

SERVE WITH Grilled bread.

WINE Red-berried, earthy Sangiovese: 2010 Nozzole Chianti Classico Riserva.

Oven-Braised Short Ribs with Pasilla-Tomato Mole

Active **1 hr**; Total **5 hr**; Serves **6**

- 4 oz. pasilla chiles—stemmed, seeded and rinsed
- 3 cups boiling water
- 2 unripe medium green tomatoes, cored
- ½ cup plus 1 Tbsp. extra-virgin olive oil
- 1 onion, finely chopped
- 5 garlic cloves, minced
- 1 Tbsp. minced oregano
- ½ cinnamon stick (1½ inches)
- 5 allspice berries
- 3 whole cloves
  Kosher salt and pepper
- 1½ Tbsp. white vinegar
  Eight 10-oz. English-cut beef short ribs (cut between the ribs)
- 1½ cups beef stock or low-sodium broth

1. In a medium heatproof bowl, cover the chiles with the boiling water and let stand until softened, 20 minutes.

2. Meanwhile, roast the tomatoes directly over an open flame or under a broiler, turning occasionally, until charred in spots and just starting to soften, 5 to 8 minutes. Transfer to a work surface and let cool slightly, then coarsely chop.

3. In a large saucepan, heat ¼ cup of the oil until shimmering. Add the chopped tomatoes, onion, garlic, oregano, cinnamon stick, allspice, cloves and a generous pinch each of salt and pepper. Cook over moderate heat, stirring occasionally, until softened and saucy, 8 to 10 minutes. Let cool slightly; discard the cinnamon.

4. Drain the chiles, reserving 2 cups of the soaking liquid. Add them to a blender along with the reserved soaking liquid and the tomato mixture and puree until the mole sauce is smooth. In a large saucepan, heat ¼ cup of the oil. Add the sauce and bring to a boil. Cover and simmer over moderate heat, stirring occasionally, until reduced to 3½ cups, about 30 minutes. Stir in the vinegar and season the mole with salt and pepper.

5. Preheat the oven to 350°. In a large skillet, heat the remaining 1 tablespoon of oil until shimmering. Season the short ribs all over with salt and pepper. Cook half of the ribs over moderately high heat, turning occasionally, until browned all over, about 10 minutes. Transfer to a small roasting pan. Pour off all but 2 tablespoons of fat from the skillet and brown the remaining ribs.

6. Spread 2 tablespoons of the mole sauce on each rib and arrange them bone side up in the roasting pan. Add the stock to the roasting pan and cover tightly with foil. Braise the ribs in the oven for about 3 hours and 30 minutes, until very tender. Transfer the ribs to a platter and serve, passing the remaining mole at the table. —*Hugo Ortega*

SERVE WITH Quinoa pilaf and roasted squash and root vegetables.

WINE Flavorful Argentinean Malbec: 2012 Achával-Ferrer Mendoza.

Barbacoa Beef Tacos with Two Sauces

Active **40 min**; Total **4 hr**; Serves **6**

Chef Roberto Santibañez of the Fonda restaurants in New York City serves his tacos with both a chile sauce made from the braising liquid and an uncooked (*cruda*) salsa verde. This recipe makes extra chile sauce, which is terrific tossed with pasta or poured over fried or poached eggs.

- 4 large ancho chiles, stemmed and seeded
- 4 dried chipotle chiles, stemmed
- 3 celery ribs, chopped
- 2 medium carrots, chopped
- 1 large onion, halved and thinly sliced
- 15 garlic cloves, crushed and peeled
- 8 bay leaves
  Six 1-lb. English-cut beef short ribs
- 2 Tbsp. dried oregano
- ½ tsp. ground cumin
  Kosher salt and pepper
  Warm corn tortillas, cilantro sprigs, finely chopped white onion and lime wedges, for serving
  Salsa Verde Cruda (recipe follows), for serving

1. Preheat the oven to 325°. In a medium skillet, toast the ancho chiles over moderate heat, turning, until pliable and charred in spots, about 2 minutes; let cool slightly, then tear into pieces.

2. In a large roasting pan, toss the ancho and chipotle chiles with the celery, carrots, onion, garlic and bay leaves. In a large bowl, toss the short ribs with the oregano, cumin and 2 tablespoons of salt. Arrange the ribs over the vegetables in the roasting pan. Add 2 cups of water to the pan, cover tightly with foil and braise in the oven for about 3½ hours, until the meat is very tender.

3. Transfer the ribs to a baking sheet. Strain the braising liquid through a colander set over a heatproof bowl; skim off any fat. Discard the bay leaves and return the vegetables and chiles to the braising liquid. Working in batches, puree the vegetables and liquid in a blender until smooth. Season the sauce with salt and pepper.

4. Light a grill or heat a grill pan. Working in batches if necessary, grill the ribs over high heat, turning occasionally, until charred and crisp, about 5 minutes total. Transfer to a platter and, using 2 forks, shred the meat; discard the bones. Serve the *barbacoa* in warm corn tortillas with the sauce, cilantro, chopped onion, lime wedges and Salsa Verde Cruda. —*Roberto Santibañez*

MAKE AHEAD The braised short ribs and sauce can be refrigerated separately for up to 3 days. Warm the ribs in a low oven before grilling.

BEER Crisp Mexican pilsner: Pacifico.

SALSA VERDE CRUDA
Total **15 min**; Makes **1¼ cups**

- ½ pound tomatillos—husked, rinsed and quartered
- ½ cup coarsely chopped cilantro
- 1 jalapeño, stemmed and chopped
- 1 garlic clove, crushed and peeled
  Kosher salt and pepper

In a blender, combine the tomatillos, cilantro, jalapeño and garlic and puree until smooth. Season with salt and pepper and serve. —*RS*

BARBACOA BEEF TACOS
WITH TWO SAUCES

Pot-au-Feu

Active **45 min**; Total **4 hr 30 min**
Serves **8 to 10**

- 2 lbs. beef marrowbones in 2-inch lengths (have your butcher cut them)

  Kosher salt

- 3 lbs. English-cut beef short ribs

  One 2-lb. beef rump roast, tied

  One 1½-lb. beef shank, about 1½ inches thick

- 2 parsley sprigs
- 3 thyme sprigs
- 1 garlic clove
- 1 bay leaf
- 1 tsp. black peppercorns
- 2 whole cloves
- 4 medium unpeeled turnips, quartered
- 1 celery root (1¼ lbs.)—peeled, quartered and cut into ¾-inch-thick slices
- 1 rutabaga (1¼ lbs.)—peeled, quartered and cut into ¾-inch-thick slices
- 4 large carrots, peeled and quartered crosswise
- 2 medium leeks—halved lengthwise, cleaned and cut crosswise into 4-inch lengths
- 1 large onion, quartered

  Freshly ground pepper

  Dijon mustard, cornichons and fleur de sel, for serving

1. Rub both sides of each piece of marrowbone with ½ teaspoon of salt and transfer to a large pot; let stand for 10 minutes. Add the short ribs, rump roast and beef shank. Wrap the parsley, thyme, garlic, bay leaf, black peppercorns and cloves in a piece of moistened cheesecloth and tie into a bundle. Add the bundle to the pot along with 8 quarts of water and bring to a boil over high heat. Reduce the heat to moderate and simmer, skimming occasionally, until the rump roast is very tender, about 2 hours and 45 minutes.

2. Add the turnips, celery root, rutabaga, carrots, leeks and onion to the pot. Simmer over moderate heat until the vegetables are just tender, 30 minutes.

3. Transfer the roast to a carving board. Using a slotted spoon, transfer the marrowbones, ribs, shank and vegetables to a platter and tent with foil. Untie the roast and slice it across the grain ¾ inch thick; arrange on the platter.

4. Strain the broth into another pot, discarding the solids and herb bundle. Skim off the fat and season with salt and pepper. Serve the meat, vegetables and broth separately or together with Dijon mustard, cornichons and fleur de sel. —*Ludo Lefebvre*

MAKE AHEAD The pot-au-feu can be refrigerated for up to 5 days. Reheat gently.

WINE Earthy, dense red Burgundy: 2011 Louis Latour.

Tender Oven-Roasted Beef-and-Quinoa Meatballs

⏱ Active **15 min**; Total **45 min**; Serves **4**

- **Extra-virgin olive oil, for greasing**
- 1½ lbs. ground beef chuck
- 1½ cups cooked quinoa
- ¾ cup freshly grated Parmigiano-Reggiano cheese, plus more for garnish
- 2 large eggs, lightly beaten
- ½ cup finely chopped flat-leaf parsley, plus more for garnish
- 1 large garlic clove, minced
- 1¾ tsp. kosher salt
- ¾ tsp. freshly ground pepper
- 1½ cups jarred marinara sauce

1. Preheat the oven to 400° and grease a large baking dish with olive oil. In a large bowl, using your hands, gently mix all of the remaining ingredients except the marinara sauce. Form the ground beef mixture into twelve 2½-inch meatballs.

2. Arrange the meatballs in the baking dish and roast for 20 to 25 minutes, until just cooked through. Spoon the marinara sauce on top and bake until the sauce is hot, about 5 minutes. Garnish with grated cheese and chopped parsley and serve. —*Justin Chapple*

WINE Red-berried Oregon Pinot Noir: 2012 Brooks Willamette Valley.

Beef-Ricotta Meatballs with Braised Beet Greens

Total **1 hr 30 min**; Serves **6**

GREENS

- ½ cup extra-virgin olive oil
- 1 carrot, chopped into ½-inch pieces
- 1 small yellow onion, chopped into ½-inch pieces
- 1 celery rib, chopped into ½-inch pieces

  Kosher salt and freshly ground pepper

- 3 anchovy fillets in oil, drained and chopped
- ½ cup tomato paste
- 1 lb. beet greens, coarsely chopped

MEATBALLS

- 2 oz. day-old bread (one 1-inch-thick slice)
- ¼ cup whole milk
- 1 lb. ground beef (25 percent fat)
- ½ cup fresh ricotta cheese
- ⅓ cup freshly grated Parmigiano-Reggiano cheese, plus more for garnish
- 1 large egg
- 1 tsp. finely grated lemon zest
- 1 tsp. crushed red pepper
- 1 Tbsp. finely chopped parsley
- ½ Tbsp. ground fennel
- 1 tsp. kosher salt
- ½ tsp. freshly ground black pepper
- ¼ cup canola oil

  Chopped oregano and flaky sea salt, for garnish

1. Prepare the greens In a large pot, heat the olive oil. Add the carrot, onion and celery, season with salt and pepper and cook over moderately low heat, stirring, until the vegetables are very tender and caramelized, 20 minutes. Add the anchovies and tomato paste and cook, stirring, until the anchovies dissolve and the tomato paste is deep red, 5 minutes. Add the beet greens, season with salt and pepper, and cook, tossing occasionally, until wilted, 7 minutes.

2. Meanwhile, make the meatballs In a small bowl, soak the bread in the milk until the milk is absorbed, about 5 minutes.

3. In a large bowl, combine the beef, ricotta, Parmigiano, egg, lemon zest, crushed red pepper, parsley, fennel, kosher salt and black pepper. Squeeze any excess milk from the bread and add the bread to the bowl. Mix the meat mixture well, then roll it into eighteen 1½-inch balls; transfer to a baking sheet.

4. In a large cast-iron skillet, heat 2 tablespoons of the canola oil. Cook half of the meatballs over moderate heat, turning, until golden brown outside and no longer pink within, about 15 minutes. Repeat with the remaining oil and meatballs.

5. Rewarm the beet greens and transfer to a platter; top with the meatballs. Garnish with Parmigiano, chopped oregano and sea salt and serve. —*Ori Menashe*

WINE Vibrant, medium-bodied Barbera d'Alba: 2012 Elio Altare.

Golden Onion Cheeseburgers with Caper Mayonnaise

Total **45 min plus 8 hr curing**; Serves **10**

- **3 lbs. beef chuck roast, cut into 1-inch cubes**
  Kosher salt
- **1 lb. boneless short rib, cut into 1-inch cubes**
- **¼ cup plus 2 Tbsp. canola oil**
- **2 large onions (2 lbs.), thinly sliced**
- **10 English muffins or hamburger buns, split**
- **10 slices of Monterey Jack cheese**
  Caper Mayonnaise (recipe follows)

1. Set a rack over a rimmed baking sheet. In a large bowl, toss the beef chuck with 2 teaspoons of salt to evenly coat. Spread in a single layer on half of the rack. Add the short rib to the bowl and toss with 1 teaspoon of salt to evenly coat. Spread in a single layer alongside the chuck. Refrigerate the meat uncovered for 8 hours. Store the meat grinder attachment—including the blade and coarse grinding plate—in the freezer.

2. In a large nonstick skillet, heat 2 tablespoons of the oil. Add the onions and cook over moderate heat, stirring frequently, until deep golden, 25 minutes. Season with salt and keep warm.

3. Working over a large bowl, gently pass the short rib through the grinder. Gently press the beef chuck through the grinder, gradually adding the ground short rib as you go so they are ground together. Gently shape the ground beef into ten 1-inch-thick patties, packing them just enough so they hold together.

4. Preheat the oven to 425°. Arrange the English muffins on 2 baking sheets. Set a cheese slice on each top half. Toast until the muffins are crusty and the cheese is melted, about 5 minutes. Spread some Caper Mayonnaise on the bottom halves.

5. Preheat a cast-iron griddle. Add 2 tablespoons of the canola oil and cook half of the burgers over moderately high heat until browned, 2 to 3 minutes. Flip the burgers and top with half of the caramelized onions, lightly pressing them into the burgers. Cook until browned and pink within, about 2 minutes for medium-rare. Repeat with the remaining oil, burgers and caramelized onions. Set the onion burgers on the English muffins and serve. —*Danny Bowien*

BEER Hoppy American India pale ale: Peak Organic IPA.

CAPER MAYONNAISE
Total **10 min**; Makes **2 cups**

This simple, tangy mayonnaise is great on almost any burger as well as grilled chicken and fish.

- **¼ cup capers, drained**
- **¾ cup mayonnaise**
- **1 Tbsp. Dijon mustard**
- **1 Tbsp. fresh lemon juice**
- **1 cup plus 2 Tbsp. canola oil**
  Kosher salt

In a food processor, pulse the capers with the mayonnaise, mustard, lemon juice and 2 tablespoons of water until combined. With the machine on, slowly drizzle in the canola oil until a thick sauce forms. Season with salt and scrape into a medium bowl. —*DB*

Bacon Burgers with Cilantro-Yogurt Sauce

Total **45 min**; Serves **8**

- **1 cup plain Greek yogurt**
- **2 jalapeños, chopped**
- **1 cup cilantro, chopped**
- **¼ cup minced fresh ginger**
- **½ small red onion, chopped**
- **1 tsp. sugar**
- **2½ tsp. kosher salt**
- **2½ lbs. ground beef chuck**
- **½ lb. bacon, minced (1 cup)**
- **6 scallions, white and light green parts only, minced**
- **½ cup chopped mint**
- **¾ cup freshly grated Parmigiano-Reggiano cheese**
- **1 Tbsp. finely grated lemon zest**
- **2 Tbsp. fresh lemon juice**
- **½ tsp. black pepper**
- **¼ tsp. cayenne pepper**
  Canola oil, for brushing
- **8 toasted hamburger buns**
  Sliced tomatoes and onions, lettuce, ketchup, mustard and Sriracha, for serving

1. In a food processor, puree the yogurt, jalapeños, cilantro, ginger, onion, sugar and 1 teaspoon of the salt until smooth. Transfer to a bowl.

2. In another bowl, mix the ground beef with the bacon, scallions, mint, cheese, lemon zest, lemon juice, black pepper, cayenne and the remaining 1½ teaspoons of salt. Form into eight 1-inch-thick patties.

3. Heat a cast-iron griddle and brush with oil. Cook the burgers over moderate heat, turning once, until charred outside and medium within, 6 to 8 minutes.

4. Spread some of the yogurt sauce on the bottom buns, top with the burgers and layer with toppings. Close the burgers and serve. —*Suvir Saran*

BEER Herb-scented, citrusy IPA: Brooklyn Brewery.

Chianti Burgers with Caramelized Onions

Total **1 hr 30 min**; Serves **4**

- ½ cup white wine vinegar
- ¼ cup sugar
- One 14-oz. can diced tomatoes
- 1 small red bell pepper, finely chopped
- 1 tsp. finely grated fresh ginger
- Kosher salt and freshly ground pepper
- 2 Tbsp. extra-virgin olive oil, plus more for brushing
- 2 medium onions (1 lb.), thinly sliced
- 1 Tbsp. minced sage
- Four 4-inch focaccia squares, split horizontally
- 1½ lbs. ground beef chuck
- 4 slices of young pecorino cheese (4 oz.)

1. In a small saucepan, combine the vinegar and sugar and cook over moderate heat, stirring occasionally, until a medium amber caramel forms, 8 to 10 minutes. Carefully add the tomatoes and red pepper and cook, stirring occasionally, until the mixture is very thick, about 20 minutes. Transfer to a blender and puree. Strain the ketchup through a sieve into a small bowl. Stir in the ginger and season with salt and pepper.

2. In a large skillet, heat the 2 tablespoons of olive oil. Add the onions and cook over moderately low heat, stirring, until golden, 15 minutes. Stir in the sage and keep warm.

3. Preheat the oven to 475°. Heat a griddle, lightly brush it with oil and toast the focaccia until lightly golden, 1 to 2 minutes per side. Transfer the focaccia to plates.

4. Gently shape the ground beef into four ½-inch-thick patties and season with salt and pepper. Griddle the burgers over high heat until browned, 1 minute per side. Transfer to a baking sheet and top each one with a slice of cheese. Bake for 5 minutes for medium-rare. Set the burgers on the focaccia and top with the onions and a dollop of the ketchup. Close the burgers and serve. —*Matteo Gambi*

WINE Herb-scented Chianti: 2011 Fèlsina Chianti Classico.

Spicy 50/50 Burgers

Total **30 min**; Serves **4**

Mixing seasonings into ground beef can make burgers tough if the meat gets overworked. But this burger recipe, adapted from chef Michael Symon's *5 in 5* cookbook, ingeniously solves the problem by incorporating the seasonings in the form of hot Italian sausage. The sausages give these cheeseburgers great texture as well as flavor.

- ¾ lb. ground beef chuck
- ¾ lb. hot Italian sausage, casing removed
- Salt and pepper
- 2 Tbsp. extra-virgin olive oil
- 8 slices of Monterey Jack cheese (½ lb.)
- 4 brioche hamburger buns, split and toasted
- 1 cup cilantro leaves
- Thickly sliced hot or sweet pickled peppers, for serving

1. In a medium bowl, combine the ground chuck with the sausage just until they are thoroughly mixed. Form the meat into four 4-inch patties, about ¾ inch thick. Season the patties with salt and pepper.

2. In a large cast-iron skillet, heat the olive oil until shimmering. Add the patties to the skillet and press down slightly with a spatula to flatten them to a ½-inch thickness. Cook the patties over moderately high heat until very crusty on the bottom, 2 to 3 minutes. Flip the patties and cook until well browned, about 2 minutes more. Top each patty with 2 slices of the cheese and add 2 tablespoons of water to the skillet. Cover the skillet and cook over moderate heat until the cheese is melted and the burgers are cooked through, 1 to 2 minutes.

3. Set the cheeseburgers on the toasted buns and top with the cilantro and pickled peppers. Close the burgers and serve right away. —*Michael Symon*

BEER Fresh, malty Colorado amber ale: New Belgium Fat Tire.

Fire-and-Ice Ohio Chili

Active **30 min**; Total **1 hr 45 min**; Serves **8**

Jeni Britton Bauer, the founder of Jeni's Splendid Ice Creams in Columbus, Ohio, adds richness to chili with a surprise ingredient: dark chocolate ice cream. She loves serving the saucy chili over spaghetti, Cincinnati-style.

- 1 Tbsp. vegetable oil
- 2 lbs. ground beef
- 2 large onions, minced
- Kosher salt and pepper
- ¼ cup chile powder
- 1 Tbsp. ground cumin
- 1 tsp. cinnamon
- 1 tsp. ground coriander
- ¼ tsp. ground cloves
- One 15-oz. can tomato puree
- One 15-oz. can diced tomatoes
- 1 cup dark chocolate ice cream
- Cooked spaghetti, shredded Monterey Jack cheese and thinly sliced scallions, for serving

1. In a large saucepan, heat the oil. Add the ground beef and cook over moderately high heat, breaking up the meat with a wooden spoon, until browned, about 8 minutes. Add the onions, season with salt and pepper and cook, stirring occasionally, until softened, about 8 minutes. Add the chile powder, cumin, cinnamon, coriander and cloves and cook, stirring occasionally, until fragrant, about 2 minutes.

2. Stir the tomato puree, diced tomatoes and 6 cups of water into the beef and bring to a boil. Simmer over moderately low heat for 1 hour and 15 minutes, stirring occasionally. Stir in the ice cream and cook until hot, about 5 minutes. Season with salt and pepper. Serve the chili in bowls over spaghetti, passing shredded Monterey Jack and thinly sliced scallions at the table. —*Jeni Britton Bauer*

MAKE AHEAD The chili can be refrigerated for up to 3 days. Reheat gently.

WINE Peppery, berry-rich Zinfandel: 2011 Ravenswood Vintners Blend.

CHIANTI BURGER WITH CARAMELIZED ONIONS

Ode to the KronnerBurger

Active **45 min**; Total **2 hr**; Serves **4**

Inspired by chef Chris Kronner's popular hamburger at KronnerBurger in San Francisco, writer Daniel Duane created this streamlined version at home. It features from-scratch supertart pickles and a thick, creamy white-cheddar mayonnaise. Duane has advice on ground beef: "If possible, ask your butcher to grind fresh chuck mixed with short rib fat; have the meat ground once only, through a medium die." He swears the extra effort is worth it.

- **2 cups distilled white vinegar**
- **½ small yellow onion, thinly sliced**
- **3 garlic cloves, crushed and peeled**
- **2 whole cloves**
- **1 star anise pod**
- **½ tsp. each of coriander seeds and caraway seeds**
- **Kosher salt**
- **1 English cucumber, sliced ¼ inch thick**
- **4 dill sprigs**
- **2 large egg yolks**
- **1½ Tbsp. apple cider vinegar**
- **1 cup vegetable oil**
- **½ cup finely grated aged white cheddar, such as Cabot Clothbound**
- **1 tsp. hot mustard powder**
- **Pepper**
- **4 medium white or brioche burger buns**
- **Softened unsalted butter, for brushing**
- **1 red onion, sliced ¼ inch thick**
- **1½ lbs. ground beef chuck (25 percent fat)**
- **Sliced beefsteak tomato and iceberg lettuce, for serving**

1. In a medium saucepan, combine the white vinegar, yellow onion, garlic, whole cloves, star anise, coriander and caraway seeds and 2½ tablespoons of salt and bring just to a boil, stirring to dissolve the salt. Add the cucumber slices and dill, remove from the heat and let cool completely. Transfer the cucumbers and brine to a jar and refrigerate for at least 1 hour or up to 3 days.

2. Meanwhile, in a blender or mini food processor, combine the egg yolks with the cider vinegar and 2 tablespoons of water and puree until smooth. With the machine on, add the oil a few drops at a time until the mayonnaise starts to thicken, then add the remaining oil in a very thin stream until emulsified. Add the cheese and mustard powder and puree until smooth. Season the mayonnaise with salt and pepper and scrape into a bowl. Refrigerate until chilled, about 30 minutes.

3. Heat a cast-iron grill pan until very hot. Brush the cut sides of the buns with butter and grill over moderately high heat until lightly browned, about 1 minute; transfer to a platter. Add the red onion slices to the pan and grill until lightly charred on the bottom, about 2 minutes; transfer to a plate.

4. Gently form the ground beef into four ¾-inch-thick patties, packing them as loosely as possible. Season generously with salt and pepper and grill over moderately high heat, turning once, until lightly charred outside and medium-rare within, about 4 minutes total. On each bun, set 3 pickle rounds, 1 slice of tomato and 1 slice of grilled onion and top with the burger and an iceberg leaf. Generously brush the bun tops with the cheddar mayonnaise, close the burgers and serve right away. —*Daniel Duane*

MAKE AHEAD The mayonnaise can be refrigerated overnight.

BEER Crisp, refreshing lager: Anchor California Lager.

Merguez-Spiced Colorado Lamb

⏱ Total **45 min**; Serves **6**

Chef Jennifer Jasinski of Rioja in Denver, a breakout star on *Top Chef Masters*, makes a simple, fragrant spice rub for lamb chops. She serves the chops with a delectable garlic-and-sherry pan sauce.

- **1 tsp. sweet smoked Spanish paprika**
- **1 tsp. ground cumin**
- **1 tsp. ground fennel**
- **½ tsp. ground coriander**
- **½ tsp. cinnamon**
- **½ tsp. ground allspice**
- **¼ tsp. cayenne pepper**
- **Six 5-oz. lamb loin chops**
- **¼ cup extra-virgin olive oil**
- **Kosher salt**
- **4 garlic cloves, minced**
- **2 Tbsp. sherry**
- **Freshly ground pepper**
- **Parsley, for garnish**

1. In a small bowl, combine all of the spices. Set aside 2 teaspoons of the spice mixture for the pan sauce. Rub the lamb chops with the remaining spice mixture and let stand at room temperature for 15 minutes.

2. In a large cast-iron skillet, heat 2 tablespoons of the oil. Season the lamb with salt and cook over moderate heat until golden and an instant-read thermometer inserted in the center of a chop registers 125°, 3 to 4 minutes per side. Transfer to plates; let rest for 5 minutes.

3. Meanwhile, pour off all but 1 tablespoon of oil from the skillet. Add the garlic and cook over low heat, stirring, for 1 minute. Add the reserved 2 teaspoons of spice mixture and cook, stirring, for 1 minute. Add the sherry and whisk in the remaining 2 tablespoons of oil. Season the sauce with salt and pepper and spoon over the lamb. Garnish with parsley and serve. —*Jennifer Jasinski*

WINE Peppery Spanish red: 2012 Casa Castillo Monastrell.

Spiced Moroccan Meat Patties

⏱ Total **45 min**; Serves **4 to 6**

These skewerless kebabs are seasoned generously with *ras el hanout,* a distinctive Moroccan spice blend that varies by shop. It usually includes cumin, coriander, turmeric, ginger, cardamom, nutmeg and dried rose petals. Look for McCormick's *ras el hanout* at the supermarket.

1½ cups Israeli couscous

2 Tbsp. fresh lemon juice, plus lemon wedges for serving

¾ tsp. pimentón de la Vera (smoked paprika)

6 Tbsp. extra-virgin olive oil

½ cup minced red onion

6 Tbsp. chopped parsley

6 Tbsp. chopped cilantro

Kosher salt and pepper

1½ lbs. ground lamb or beef

4 garlic cloves, minced

2 Tbsp. *ras el hanout*

1. Preheat the oven to 425°. In a large saucepan of salted boiling water, cook the couscous until al dente, about 8 minutes. Drain, then transfer to a large bowl. Add the lemon juice, paprika, ¼ cup each of the olive oil and onion and 2 tablespoons each of the chopped parsley and cilantro. Season with salt and pepper and toss to coat. Transfer to a platter, cover and keep warm.

2. Meanwhile, in another large bowl, combine the meat, garlic and *ras el hanout* with 1½ teaspoons of salt and the remaining onion, parsley and cilantro. Season with pepper and gently mix until well combined. Form the meat into 12 ovals about 3 inches long.

3. In a large cast-iron skillet, heat the remaining 2 tablespoons of olive oil. Add the kebabs and cook over moderately high heat, turning, until browned all over, 3 to 4 minutes. Transfer to the oven and bake for about 8 minutes, until cooked through. Arrange the kebabs on the couscous and serve with lemon wedges. —*Eli Sussman*

WINE Berry-rich Malbec: 2012 Pulenta Estate La Flor.

Grilled Lamb Chops with Cucumber Relish

⏱ Active **20 min**; Total **45 min**; Serves **4**

Chef Renee Erickson of Boat Street Café in Seattle has an easy trick for extra-juicy chops: She rubs the lamb with a little oil and seasoning and lets it sit for a bit before grilling. While the chops come to room temperature, you can prepare the sweet-savory Mediterranean-inspired cucumber relish.

3 Tbsp. extra-virgin olive oil

8 double-cut lamb chops (about 4¼ lbs.)

Kosher salt and pepper

1 English cucumber, peeled and cut into ¼-inch dice

½ tsp. finely grated lemon zest

1 tsp. fresh lemon juice

¼ cup golden raisins

¼ cup pine nuts, toasted

2 Tbsp. mint leaves, torn

Flaky sea salt, such as Maldon, for serving

1. Rub 1 tablespoon of the oil all over the lamb chops and season generously with kosher salt and pepper. Let stand at room temperature for 30 minutes.

2. Meanwhile, in a medium bowl, stir the cucumber with the lemon zest, lemon juice, raisins, pine nuts, mint and 1 tablespoon of the oil. Season with kosher salt and pepper.

3. Heat 2 large grill pans or cast-iron skillets over high heat. Divide the remaining 1 tablespoon of oil between the pans. Add the lamb and cook until nicely browned on both sides and an instant-read thermometer inserted in the center of a chop registers 125°for medium-rare, 12 minutes. Transfer the chops to plates; let rest for 5 minutes.

4. Sprinkle the lamb chops with flaky sea salt, spoon the cucumber relish on top and serve. —*Renee Erickson*

WINE Fragrant, medium-bodied Cabernet Franc: 2011 Catherine & Pierre Breton Trinch!.

Roast Leg of Lamb with Rosemary

Active **45 min**; Total **2 hr 30 min** Serves **6 to 8**

One 4½-lb. semi-boneless leg of lamb, at room temperature (shank end, hip bone removed)

Kosher salt and ground pepper

3 Tbsp. extra-virgin olive oil

2 Tbsp. finely grated lemon zest

4 garlic cloves, minced

20 large rosemary sprigs

½ cup red wine vinegar

2 Tbsp. turbinado sugar

1 cup lightly packed mint leaves

1. Preheat the oven to 350°. Season the lamb all over with salt and pepper. In a very large, deep skillet, heat 2 tablespoons of the olive oil until shimmering. Add the lamb and cook over moderately high heat, turning occasionally, until browned all over, about 12 minutes. Transfer to a plate.

2. In a small bowl, whisk the lemon zest with the garlic and remaining 1 tablespoon of olive oil. Rub the mixture all over the lamb.

3. Arrange 9 long pieces of kitchen string crosswise on a large rimmed baking sheet, 1 inch apart. Arrange 10 rosemary sprigs across the strings and set the lamb on top. Cover the lamb with the remaining rosemary, then pull up each piece of string and tie tightly to secure the rosemary and form a neat roast.

4. Roast the lamb on the baking sheet for about 1 hour and 20 minutes, until an instant-read thermometer inserted in the thickest part of the meat registers 130°. Transfer the lamb to a carving board and let rest for 30 minutes.

5. Meanwhile, in a small saucepan, bring the vinegar, sugar and ½ cup of water just to a simmer, stirring to dissolve the sugar. Remove from the heat, add the mint leaves and let stand for 30 minutes. Season the sauce with salt.

6. Untie the lamb and discard the rosemary sprigs. Carve the lamb and serve with the mint sauce. —*Curtis Stone*

WINE Powerful Australian Shiraz: 2010 Henry's Drive Dead Letter Office.

Roast Leg of Lamb with Rosemary and Lavender

Active **35 min**; Total **2 hr**; Serves **6 to 8**

- ¼ cup plus 2 Tbsp. extra-virgin olive oil
- ¼ cup minced rosemary
- 3 Tbsp. minced fresh lavender leaves (see Note)
- 4 garlic cloves, grated
- One 3½-lb. boneless leg of lamb
- Kosher salt and freshly ground black pepper
- 6 medium shallots, thinly sliced
- ½ cup pitted Medjool dates, thinly sliced
- 1 tsp. honey
- ¼ cup apple cider vinegar

1. Preheat the oven to 450°. In a small bowl, whisk ¼ cup of the olive oil with the rosemary, lavender and garlic. Season the lamb all over with salt and pepper. Rub half of the herb oil all over the inside of the lamb, then roll up the meat and tie with kitchen string to form a neat roast. Spread the remaining herb oil all over the roast and set it on a rimmed baking sheet.

2. Roast the lamb for about 15 minutes, until just starting to brown. Reduce the oven temperature to 375° and roast the lamb for about 1 hour longer, until an instant-read thermometer inserted in the thickest part registers 130° for rare meat. Transfer the lamb to a carving board and let rest for 30 minutes.

3. Meanwhile, in a medium saucepan, heat the remaining 2 tablespoons of olive oil until shimmering. Add the shallots, dates, honey and a pinch of salt and cook over moderate heat, stirring occasionally, until the shallots are softened, about 7 minutes. Add the vinegar and cook, stirring occasionally, until most of the liquid has evaporated and the jam is thick, 3 to 5 minutes; season with salt and let cool.

4. Untie the lamb roast and slice the meat against the grain. Serve with the shallot-date jam. —*Melia Marden*

NOTE Fresh lavender is sold at farmers' markets. If it's unavailable, substitute 1½ tablespoons herbes de Provence.

MAKE AHEAD The shallot-date jam can be refrigerated for up to 5 days. Bring to room temperature before serving with the roast leg of lamb.

WINE Bold, fruit-forward red: 2012 Bradford Mountain Dry Creek Valley Zinfandel.

Cumin-and-Coriander-Grilled Lamb Ribs

📷 PAGE 192

Active **1 hr 30 min**; Total **3 hr**; Serves **4 to 6**

Lamb ribs are the least expensive and utilized part of the lamb, says Brooklyn butcher Tom Mylan, who compares them to pork spare ribs. Here he combines the sweet and tangy flavors of American barbecue with Middle Eastern seasonings like pomegranate molasses.

- ¼ cup kosher salt
- 2 Tbsp. light brown sugar
- 1 Tbsp. ground cumin
- 1 Tbsp. ground coriander
- 1 tsp. freshly ground pepper
- ½ tsp. ground cinnamon
- Two 2½- to 3-lb. racks of lamb ribs
- 1 cup apple cider vinegar
- 2 Tbsp. pomegranate molasses

1. In a small bowl, mix the salt with the sugar, cumin, coriander, pepper and cinnamon. Transfer 2 tablespoons of the rub to a medium bowl. In a large, shallow baking dish, sprinkle the remaining rub over the lamb ribs, massaging it into the meat. Let stand at room temperature for 1 hour.

2. Light a gas grill. Whisk the apple cider vinegar and pomegranate molasses into the reserved 2 tablespoons of rub.

3. Transfer the lamb ribs meaty side down to the grill and cook over moderately low heat, turning once, until lightly charred all over, 7 to 10 minutes. Reduce the heat to low and grill, turning and basting with the sauce every 10 minutes, until the meat is very tender and nicely charred, 1 hour and 30 minutes. Transfer the ribs to a carving board, tent with foil and let rest for 10 minutes. Cut the ribs between the bones and serve. —*Tom Mylan*

WINE Spicy, robust red: 2012 Domaine d'Andezon Côtes du Rhône.

Braised Lamb Neck with Turnip

Active **45 min**; Total **3 hr**; Serves **6**

Lamb neck, an underappreciated cut, is fantastic when braised, as in this homey stew from Boston chef Tony Maws. The meat gets succulent as it cooks in the slightly sweet braising liquid, while the neck bones intensify the broth's flavor.

- Six 1½-inch-thick bone-in lamb necks
- Kosher salt and freshly ground pepper
- 2 Tbsp. canola oil
- 2 celery ribs, chopped
- 1 carrot, chopped
- 1 large onion, chopped
- 1 turnip, peeled and chopped
- 1 Tbsp. tomato paste
- 1 anchovy fillet
- 2 cups dry white wine
- 2 cups chicken stock
- 1 cup raisins
- 1 bay leaf and 1 sprig of parsley, cilantro and rosemary, tied in cheesecloth

1. Preheat the oven to 300°. Season the lamb with salt and pepper. In a large enameled cast-iron casserole, heat the oil until shimmering. Add the lamb and cook over moderately high heat, turning, until browned, 10 minutes; transfer to a plate.

2. Pour off all but 2 tablespoons of fat from the casserole. Add the celery, carrot, onion, turnip, tomato paste and anchovy and cook, stirring, until the vegetables just start to soften, 5 minutes. Stir in the wine, scraping up any browned bits, and simmer for 3 minutes. Add the stock, raisins and herb bundle and bring to a boil.

3. Return the lamb to the casserole, cover and braise in the oven for 2 hours, until the meat is very tender. Discard the herb bundle and season with salt and pepper. Serve. —*Tony Maws*

SERVE WITH Buttered noodles.

WINE Juicy Oregon Pinot Noir: 2012 Willamette Valley Vineyards Whole Cluster.

ROAST LEG OF LAMB WITH
ROSEMARY AND LAVENDER

Red Wine–Braised Lamb with Saffron Rice

Active **1 hr 15 min;** Total **6 hr 30 min plus overnight brining;** Serves **4 to 6**

- 1 Tbsp. paprika
- 1 Tbsp. kosher salt
- 1 Tbsp. freshly ground black pepper
  One 5-lb. bone-in lamb shoulder roast
- 3 Tbsp. extra-virgin olive oil
- 1 large onion, quartered through the core
- 2 carrots, quartered crosswise
- 11 garlic cloves
- 2 cups chopped tomatoes (2 large)
  One 750-ml bottle dry red wine, such as Syrah
- 1 quart chicken stock or low-sodium broth
- 12 parsley stems
- 5 thyme sprigs
- 3 bay leaves
  Oven-Baked Saffron Rice (recipe follows), for serving

1. In a small bowl, mix the paprika with the salt and black pepper. Rub the lamb all over with the spice mixture and let stand at room temperature for 2 to 4 hours.

2. Meanwhile, in a large enameled cast-iron casserole, heat the oil until shimmering. Add the onion, carrots and garlic and cook over moderately high heat, stirring occasionally, until starting to brown, 3 to 5 minutes. Add the tomatoes and cook, stirring occasionally, until starting to soften, about 5 minutes. Add the wine and bring to a boil, then simmer over moderately high heat until reduced by half, about 5 minutes. Remove the casserole from the heat and add the stock, parsley, thyme and bay leaves; let cool completely. Set the lamb meat side down in the brine, cover and refrigerate overnight. Bring the lamb and brine to room temperature before proceeding.

3. Preheat the oven to 350°. Bring the lamb and brine to a simmer over moderate heat. Cover and braise in the oven for about 3 hours, until very tender. Transfer the lamb to a carving board, tent with foil and let rest for 20 minutes. Discard the bones and any visible fat and cut the meat into 8 pieces.

4. Spoon off all the fat from the braising liquid and discard the herbs. Transfer the braising liquid and vegetables to a blender and puree until smooth. Return the sauce to the casserole and boil until slightly thickened, about 5 minutes. Season the sauce with salt and black pepper. Add the meat and turn to coat. Cook over moderately low heat just until warmed through. Serve the lamb and sauce over saffron rice. —*Linton Hopkins*

SERVE WITH Hopkins's Mint Pistou and Persian-Spiced Pickled Peaches (both on p. 365).

WINE Raspberry-rich Spanish Garnacha: 2013 Bernabeleva Camino de Navaherreros.

OVEN-BAKED SAFFRON RICE
Active **20 min;** Total **1 hr;** Serves **8**

- 4 Tbsp. unsalted butter
- 1 medium onion, minced
- 1 bay leaf
  Kosher salt
- 2 Tbsp. fresh lemon juice
- ½ tsp. ground coriander
  Small pinch of saffron threads
- 2 cups Carolina Gold or Carolina extra-long-grain white rice
- ½ cup dry white wine
- 3½ cups chicken stock or low-sodium broth

1. Preheat the oven to 375°. In a large ovenproof saucepan, melt the butter. Add the onion, bay leaf and a generous pinch of salt and cook over moderate heat, stirring occasionally, until the onion is softened but not browned, 5 to 7 minutes. Add the lemon juice, coriander and saffron and cook until fragrant, about 1 minute. Add the rice and cook, stirring, until translucent, about 3 minutes. Add the wine and simmer over moderately high heat until nearly absorbed, about 3 minutes. Stir in the stock and a generous pinch of salt and bring to a boil.

2. Cover the saucepan and bake in the oven until all of the liquid is absorbed and the rice is tender, 20 minutes. Let stand for 15 minutes; fluff with a fork and serve. —*LH*

Smoked Lamb with Sorghum Barbecue Sauce

Active **1 hr;** Total **9 hr plus 8 hr marinating** Serves **8**

- 1½ Tbsp. ancho chile powder
- ½ Tbsp. each of garlic powder, dried oregano, celery salt, smoked sweet paprika, ground coriander, mustard powder and ground allspice
  Kosher salt and pepper
  One 7-lb. boneless lamb shoulder, excess fat trimmed
  Canola oil, for brushing
- 4 cups applewood chips, soaked in water for 1 hour and drained
  Sorghum Barbecue Sauce (recipe follows)

1. In a medium bowl, whisk the chile and garlic powders with the oregano, celery salt, paprika, coriander, mustard powder, allspice, 1 tablespoon of salt and ½ tablespoon of pepper.

2. On a rimmed baking sheet, open up the lamb shoulder and rub the spice mix into the meat. Roll up the meat and tie at 1-inch intervals with kitchen string. Cover the lamb shoulder and refrigerate for at least 8 hours or overnight.

3. Remove the seasoned lamb shoulder from the refrigerator. Brush it all over with oil and season with salt and pepper; let the meat stand at room temperature for 30 minutes. Meanwhile, light a hardwood charcoal fire in a smoker. When the coals are ready, scatter the wood chips evenly over them. Attach the indirect cooking plate and heat the smoker to 225°.

4. Smoke the lamb fat side up for 6 to 7 hours, basting with some of the Sorghum Barbecue Sauce during the last 30 minutes. The lamb is done when an instant-read thermometer inserted in the center registers 185° and the meat is very tender; monitor the temperature throughout the cooking process and adjust the air valves as needed.

5. Transfer the lamb to a carving board and let rest for 20 minutes. Discard the kitchen string. Thinly slice the lamb across the grain and serve with the barbecue sauce. —*Bobby Flay*

WINE Concentrated California Syrah: 2012 Tensley Santa Barbara County.

SORGHUM BARBECUE SAUCE
Total **30 min plus cooling and chilling**
Makes **1 quart**

Star chef Bobby Flay makes his barbecue sauce with sorghum syrup, a traditional Southern sweetener that comes from sorghum grass. Buy it at Whole Foods or online from zingermans.com.

- **3 cups ketchup**
- **1 cup pure cane sorghum syrup or sorghum molasses**
- **½ cup apple cider vinegar**
- **3 garlic cloves**
- **1 habanero chile, pierced with a knife**
  Salt and pepper

In a medium saucepan, combine all of the ingredients except the salt and pepper. Bring to a boil and simmer over moderate heat, stirring frequently, until thickened and reduced to 4 cups, about 20 minutes. Discard the garlic and habanero and season the barbecue sauce with salt and pepper. Let cool completely, then refrigerate until well chilled, about 45 minutes. —*BF*

Vadouvan-Spiced Lamb Ribs
Active **10 min**; Total **3 hr plus 8 hr curing**
Serves **4**

- **1½ Tbsp. *vadouvan* (see Note)**
- **1 Tbsp. kosher salt**
- **1 Tbsp. sugar**
  One 3½-lb. rack of lamb ribs (see Note)

1. In a small bowl, whisk the *vadouvan*, salt and sugar. Set the ribs on a rimmed baking sheet and rub the spice mixture all over them; refrigerate, covered, for 8 hours or overnight.

2. Preheat the oven to 300°. Roast the ribs for 2½ hours, until browned and tender; transfer to a carving board and let rest for 10 minutes. Cut into 2-rib pieces and serve. —*Tony Maws*

NOTE *Vadouvan*, a French curry spice blend flavored with shallots and garlic, is available at specialty food stores and laboiteny.com. Lamb ribs can be fatty, so it's best to get them from small farms, where the animals tend to be younger and leaner.

WINE Spicy southern French red: 2009 Domaine Rimbert Le Mas au Schiste.

Lamb Steak Frites
Total **30 min**; Serves **4**

Whole and butterflied legs of lamb are familiar cuts; steaks cut from the leg are much less common. They're worth trying, though, because they cook quickly. Here, the steaks are pan-roasted and basted with an herbed butter, then served with fries as a fun variation on steak frites.

- **Two 1¼-lb. lamb leg steaks, about 1¼ inches thick**
- **½ tsp. ground cumin**
- **½ tsp. ground fennel seeds**
  Kosher salt and freshly ground pepper
- **2 Tbsp. canola oil**
- **4 small thyme sprigs**
- **2 garlic cloves**
- **6 Tbsp. unsalted butter, cubed**
- **1 shallot, minced**
- **1 cup dry red wine**
- **1 cup chicken stock**
  French fries, for serving

1. Rub the lamb with the cumin and fennel; season with salt and pepper. In a large cast-iron skillet, heat the oil until smoking. Add the lamb and cook over high heat, turning once, until browned, 3 minutes. Reduce the heat to moderate. Add the thyme, garlic and 4 tablespoons of the butter and cook for 5 minutes, basting the lamb with the butter. Turn the steaks and cook, basting, until an instant-read thermometer inserted in the thickest part registers 130°, 5 minutes; transfer to a carving board and let rest for 10 minutes. Thickly slice against the grain.

2. Pour off all but 1 tablespoon of the fat from the skillet. Add the shallot and cook over moderately high heat until softened, 1 minute. Add the wine and simmer until syrupy, 4 minutes. Add the stock and simmer until slightly reduced, 3 minutes. Off the heat, whisk in the remaining 2 tablespoons of butter; season with salt and pepper. Serve with the lamb and french fries. —*Tony Maws*

WINE Earthy, peppery Sangiovese: 2009 Il Molino di Grace Chianti Classico.

Lamb-and-Eggplant-Stuffed Plantains with Feta
Active **40 min**; Total **1 hr**; Serves **8**

- **Eight ¾-lb. very ripe yellow plantains**
- **2 Tbsp. extra-virgin olive oil, plus more for brushing**
  Kosher salt
- **1 large tomato, cored and finely chopped**
- **1½ cups finely diced eggplant**
- **1 small onion, finely chopped**
- **¼ cup finely chopped green bell pepper**
- **2 garlic cloves, minced**
- **1 lb. ground lamb**
- **½ tsp. ground cumin**
- **2 Tbsp. each of finely chopped parsley and cilantro, plus more for garnish**
- **4 oz. feta cheese, crumbled**
  Plain yogurt, preferably goat, for serving

1. Preheat the oven to 350°. Using a sharp knife, shave ¼ inch lengthwise off the bottom of each plantain so they sit flat. Slit the tops lengthwise; gently open the peels to expose the fruit. Using a spoon, scoop about 2 tablespoons of the fruit out of each plantain to make room for the stuffing.

2. Brush the plantains all over with olive oil and season with salt. Arrange them slit side up on a rimmed baking sheet. Bake for about 35 minutes, until very tender; let cool slightly. Leave the oven on.

3. Meanwhile, in a large skillet, heat the 2 tablespoons of olive oil. Add the tomato, eggplant, onion, pepper, garlic and a large pinch of salt and cook over moderately high heat, stirring occasionally, until softened, about 8 minutes. Add the lamb and cumin and cook, stirring to break up the meat, until no pink remains, about 7 minutes. Stir in the 2 tablespoons each of parsley and cilantro and season with salt.

4. Spoon the filling into the plantains and sprinkle the feta on top. Bake the stuffed plantains for about 10 minutes, until heated through and the cheese just starts to melt. Transfer the plantains to a platter and garnish with chopped parsley and cilantro. Serve with yogurt. —*Jose Enrique*

COCKTAIL Fruity, white rum–based drink: Enrique's Pineapple Mojitos (p. 374).

Herbed Lamb Meatballs with Rich Tomato Sauce and Ricotta
Total **1 hr 30 min**; Serves **6 to 8**

New York chef Seamus Mullen loads these Spanish-style lamb meatballs with almonds, basil, parsley, mint, oregano and thyme, then serves them in a savory tomato sauce spiked with anchovies and dolloped with ricotta cheese.

SAUCE

- ¼ cup extra-virgin olive oil
- 4 large garlic cloves, minced
- 1 cup lightly packed basil leaves, torn
- 2 Tbsp. oregano leaves
- 2 bay leaves
- ½ tsp. crushed red pepper
  Two 28-oz. cans whole Italian tomatoes with their juices, crushed
- 6 large anchovy fillets, chopped
  Kosher salt and ground black pepper

MEATBALLS

- ½ cup raw almonds, finely chopped
- ½ cup milk
- 2½ lbs. ground lamb
- 2 large eggs, lightly beaten
- ¼ cup finely chopped basil, plus whole basil leaves for garnish
- ¼ cup finely chopped flat-leaf parsley
- 2 Tbsp. finely chopped mint
- 1 Tbsp. finely chopped oregano
- 1½ tsp. finely chopped thyme
- 2 large garlic cloves, minced
- 1 Tbsp. dry red wine
- 1½ tsp. ground cumin
- 1½ tsp. ground coriander
- ½ tsp. ground fennel
- 1½ Tbsp. kosher salt
- ½ tsp. ground black pepper
- ¼ cup extra-virgin olive oil
  Ricotta cheese, for serving

1. Make the sauce In a large saucepan, heat the olive oil until shimmering. Add the garlic, basil, oregano, bay leaves and crushed red pepper and cook over moderately high heat, stirring, until the herbs are wilted, about 30 seconds. Add the tomatoes and bring to a boil, then simmer over moderately low heat, stirring, until the tomatoes are saucy, 1 hour. Stir in the anchovies and season the sauce with salt and black pepper.

2. Meanwhile, make the meatballs In a large bowl, cover the almonds with the milk; let stand until most of the milk has been absorbed, about 30 minutes. Add all of the remaining ingredients except the whole basil leaves, olive oil and ricotta; mix well. Form into 1½-inch meatballs and transfer to a rimmed baking sheet.

3. In a large skillet, heat the olive oil until shimmering. Working in batches, cook the meatballs over moderately high heat, turning occasionally, until browned all over and nearly cooked through, about 7 minutes per batch.

4. Add the meatballs to the sauce and simmer until the meatballs are cooked through, about 8 minutes. Spoon the meatballs and sauce into bowls, top with ricotta and garnish with basil. —*Seamus Mullen*

SERVE WITH Crusty bread.

WINE Traditional Sangiovese-based Chianti Classico: 2011 Fèlsina Berardenga.

Cumin-Spiced Lamb Tacos
Active **30 min**; Total **1 hr 45 min plus overnight marinating**; Serves **8 to 10**

Marinated in Greek yogurt and spiced with cumin, this lamb from F&W's Kay Chun roasts in just 30 minutes. Instead of serving the meat in the traditional pita, try it in warm tortillas with avocado, cilantro and lime.

- One 4½- to 5-lb. butterflied boneless leg of lamb
- 1 cup plain Greek yogurt
- ¼ cup extra-virgin olive oil
- 9 garlic cloves, minced
- 3 Tbsp. ground cumin
- 1 tsp. crushed red pepper
- 1 tsp. black pepper
- ½ tsp. kosher salt
- ½ cup fresh orange juice
  Corn tortillas, avocado slices, cilantro sprigs and lime wedges, for serving

1. On a baking sheet, lay out the lamb. In a small bowl, whisk the yogurt with the oil, garlic, cumin, crushed red pepper, black pepper, salt and ¼ cup of the orange juice and rub all over the lamb. Wrap in plastic and refrigerate overnight.

2. Preheat the oven to 450°. Lay the lamb on a rack set over a baking sheet and let stand for 30 minutes. Roast for 30 to 35 minutes, basting occasionally with the remaining ¼ cup of orange juice, until an instant-read thermometer inserted in the meat registers 130° for medium-rare. Let rest for 15 minutes.

3. Thinly slice the lamb and serve with corn tortillas, avocado, cilantro and lime. —*Kay Chun*

WINE Spicy Australian red: 2012 The Chook Shiraz-Viognier.

HERBED LAMB MEATBALLS WITH
RICH TOMATO SAUCE AND RICOTTA

MISO-ROASTED EGGPLANTS
WITH TOMATOES, DILL, SHISO
AND BLACK VINEGAR
Recipe, page 224

Vegetables & Tofu

PAGE NUMBERS IN RED INDICATE F&W STAFF FAVORITES

Pan-Roasted Asparagus in Asparagus Sauce

Total **25 min**; Serves **6**

In this ingenious dish, chef David Chang of the Momofuku empire uses asparagus in two ways: First he makes a delicate, sweet sauce from asparagus trimmings, then he sautés the spears to serve with the sauce.

- **2 lbs. asparagus, trimmed and trimmings reserved**
- **1 Tbsp. canola oil**
  Kosher salt
- **4 Tbsp. unsalted butter**
- **1 Tbsp. pure maple syrup**
- **1 tsp. sherry vinegar**
  Chopped smoked almonds, for garnish

1. Peel 1½ pounds of the asparagus; reserve the peelings. In a blender, combine the trimmings and peelings with the remaining ½ pound of unpeeled asparagus and ½ cup of water and puree until smooth. Strain the asparagus juice through a sieve into a medium bowl.

2. In a large skillet, heat the oil. Add the peeled asparagus and season with salt. Cook over moderate heat until lightly golden on the bottom, about 2 minutes. Turn the asparagus and add the butter and asparagus juice. Cover and cook over moderate heat until the asparagus are just tender, 2 to 3 minutes. Using tongs, transfer to a platter.

3. Whisk the maple syrup and sherry vinegar into the juice in the skillet and season with salt. Spoon the sauce over the asparagus, top with almonds and serve. —*David Chang*

Haricots Verts with Chanterelles

Total **45 min**; Serves **6**

- **1 lb. haricots verts, trimmed**
- **3 Tbsp. unsalted butter, cubed**
- **2 Tbsp. extra-virgin olive oil**
- **1 lb. chanterelle mushrooms, halved lengthwise**
- **3 medium shallots, thinly sliced**
- **2 tsp. Salted Herbs (p. 226), or kosher salt for seasoning**

1. In a large pot of salted boiling water, blanch the haricots verts for 2 minutes. Drain and transfer the beans to a baking sheet to cool. Using a sharp knife, split the beans lengthwise down the middle.

2. In a large skillet, melt 1 tablespoon of the butter in 1 tablespoon of the oil. Add the mushrooms and cook over high heat, stirring occasionally, until tender and golden, 5 to 7 minutes. Add the shallots and the remaining 1 tablespoon of olive oil and cook, stirring, until softened, 2 to 3 minutes longer. Stir in the haricots verts, then gradually add the remaining 2 tablespoons of butter, stirring constantly. Stir in the Salted Herbs and serve immediately. —*Hugue Dufour*

Sautéed Haricots Verts and Morels with Scallions

Total **45 min**; Serves **6 to 8**

Fresh morels are wonderful simply sautéed in butter and oil. When they're not in season, dried morels can be used instead: Soak 1 cup (1 ounce) of them in boiling water for about 20 minutes; drain well before sautéing.

- **1½ lbs. haricots verts, ends trimmed**
- **3 Tbsp. unsalted butter**
- **2 Tbsp. extra-virgin olive oil**
- **8 scallions, white and light green parts only, thinly sliced crosswise**
- **½ lb. fresh morels—halved lengthwise, rinsed and dried**
  Kosher salt and freshly ground pepper
- **½ cup chervil sprigs**

1. Fill a large bowl with ice water. In a large saucepan of salted boiling water, cook the haricots verts until crisp-tender, about 3 minutes. Drain the beans and let cool in the ice bath; drain and pat dry.

2. In a large skillet, melt the butter in the oil. Add the scallions and cook over moderate heat, stirring, until softened, 1 minute. Add the morels and season with salt and pepper. Cook over moderately high heat, stirring occasionally, until softened, 5 minutes. Add the haricots verts and cook, tossing, until hot, 3 minutes. Fold in the chervil and season with salt and pepper. Transfer the beans and morels to a platter and serve. —*Melia Marden*

Warm Yellow Wax Beans in Bacon Vinaigrette

Total **30 min**; Serves **6 to 8**

A cross between a salad and a side, these warm wax beans are loaded with fresh tomatoes and basil.

- **2 lbs. yellow wax beans, trimmed**
- **3 Tbsp. extra-virgin olive oil**
- **4 oz. thickly sliced bacon, cut into lardons (1 cup)**
- **2 Tbsp. sherry vinegar**
- **10 oz. cherry tomatoes, halved**
- **1 small shallot, very finely chopped**
- **2 garlic cloves, very finely chopped**
- **⅓ cup chopped basil**
  Kosher salt and freshly ground pepper

1. In a large pot of salted boiling water, cook the beans until crisp-tender, about 5 minutes. Drain the beans and cool them under cold running water. Drain well and pat dry; transfer the beans to a large bowl.

2. In a large skillet, heat the olive oil. Add the bacon and cook over moderate heat, stirring, until golden, 7 to 8 minutes. Remove the skillet from the heat and stir in the vinegar, tomatoes, shallot, garlic and basil. Scrape the bacon vinaigrette over the beans, season with salt and pepper and toss to coat. Serve warm. —*Jody Williams*

Quick Soy-Pickled Zucchini

Total **40 min**; Serves **6 as part of a multicourse meal**

Umami-packed *shoyu koji*, a sweet-salty condiment made from fermented rice soaked in soy sauce, gives zucchini a Japanese accent in this zingy pickle. Look for the Marukome brand at Japanese markets.

- **3 medium zucchini (about 1 lb.), cut crosswise ¼ inch thick**
- **¼ cup *shoyu koji***

In a medium bowl, toss the zucchini with the *shoyu koji* and let stand for 30 minutes; serve. —*Nancy Singleton Hachisu*

PAN-ROASTED ASPARAGUS IN ASPARAGUS SAUCE

End-of-Summer Eggplant Bake

⏱ Total **45 min**; Serves **4**

- 2 large eggplants, cut into 1-inch cubes
- ½ cup plus 1 Tbsp. extra-virgin olive oil, plus more for greasing
- Kosher salt and pepper
- 2 spring onions or 6 scallions, thinly sliced
- 2 Tbsp. unsalted butter, cubed
- 1¼ cups fresh ricotta cheese
- ¼ cup heavy cream
- 1 tsp. finely grated lemon zest
- 2 tsp. fresh lemon juice
- 1 Tbsp. finely chopped flat-leaf parsley
- 4 oz. country white bread, crusts removed and bread torn into ½-inch pieces (2 cups)

1. Preheat the oven to 450°. On 2 rimmed baking sheets, spread the eggplant in an even layer. Drizzle with 6 tablespoons of the olive oil, season with salt and pepper and toss. Roast for 10 minutes.

2. In a small bowl, toss the spring onions with 2 tablespoons of the olive oil. Add the onions to the eggplant and dot with the butter. Roast for 15 minutes longer, stirring, until the eggplant is tender.

3. In a medium bowl, stir the ricotta with the cream, lemon zest, lemon juice and parsley and season with salt and pepper. In a small bowl, toss the bread with the remaining 1 tablespoon of olive oil.

4. Lightly grease a 2-quart, 2-inch-deep baking dish. Transfer the eggplant and onions to the baking dish. Dollop with the ricotta mixture and scatter the bread on top. Bake for about 10 minutes, until the bread is golden. —*Jessica Koslow*

WINE Fragrant, medium-bodied Sicilian white: 2013 Tami Grillo.

Miso-Roasted Eggplants with Tomatoes, Dill, Shiso and Black Vinegar

📷 PAGE 220

Total **1 hr**; Serves **4**

For this stunning vegetarian dish, F&W Best New Chef 2014 Cara Stadler of Tao Yuan in Brunswick, Maine, tops long, skinny Asian eggplants with a bright salad drizzled with Chinese black vinegar. Typically made from fermented rice, wheat, barley and sorghum, black vinegar is slightly sweet, with a rich, malty flavor. It's available at Asian markets and from amazon.com.

DRESSING

- 1 Tbsp. sugar
- 6 Tbsp. black vinegar
- 6 Tbsp. canola oil
- 1 Tbsp. soy sauce

EGGPLANTS

- 3 Tbsp. *shiro* (white) miso
- 1½ Tbsp. mirin
- 6 Tbsp. canola oil
- 1 lb. Asian eggplants, halved lengthwise

SALAD

- 1 heirloom tomato, cut into ½-inch dice
- ½ pint cherry tomatoes, halved
- ⅓ cup chopped dill, plus more for garnish
- ¼ cup chopped shiso, plus more for garnish
- 1 Tbsp. minced scallions
- Kosher salt

1. Make the dressing Preheat the oven to 350°. In a small saucepan, combine the sugar with 1 teaspoon of water. Cook over low heat, swirling the pan, until the sugar melts and an amber caramel forms, 4 minutes. Whisk in the black vinegar. Remove from the heat and let cool to room temperature. Whisk in the oil and soy sauce.

2. Prepare the eggplants In a small bowl, mix the miso with the mirin. In a large nonstick skillet, heat 3 tablespoons of the canola oil. Add 1 eggplant half, cut side down, and cook over moderate heat until deep golden, 3 to 4 minutes. Transfer the eggplant cut side up to a baking sheet.

Repeat with the remaining 3 tablespoons of canola oil and eggplants.

3. Spread the miso mixture on the cut sides of the eggplants and roast for 15 minutes, until the eggplants are very tender. Transfer to a platter.

4. Meanwhile, make the salad In a large bowl, toss the tomatoes with the ⅓ cup of dill, ¼ cup of shiso, the scallions and two-thirds of the dressing; season with salt.

5. Spoon the salad over the warm eggplants and drizzle with the remaining dressing. Garnish with dill and shiso and serve. —*Cara Stadler*

WINE Lively Beaujolais: 2012 Georges Descombes Morgon Vieilles Vignes.

Japanese Cucumbers with Bonito and Umeboshi

⏱ Total **20 min**; Serves **6 as part of a multicourse meal**

Cookbook author Nancy Singleton Hachisu first tasted these salty, crisp cucumbers at a restaurant in Japan. They were served with sashimi and *tamago dofu* (egg custard) before a course of soba noodles. Hachisu suggests snacking on them before dinner with drinks or alongside grilled pork, chicken or fish.

- 4 Japanese cucumbers (1 lb.), cut crosswise ¼ inch thick
- 1½ tsp. sea salt
- 1 Tbsp. pitted and finely chopped *umeboshi* (see Note)
- ½ tsp. organic soy sauce
- ⅓ cup lightly packed bonito flakes (see Note)

In a medium bowl, toss the cucumbers with the salt and let stand for 10 minutes. Gently squeeze out any liquid from the cucumbers and transfer them to a serving bowl. Add the *umeboshi* and soy sauce and toss to coat. Add the bonito flakes and toss again; serve right away. —*Nancy Singleton Hachisu*

VARIATION Swap 8 thinly sliced shiso leaves for the *umeboshi*.

NOTE *Umeboshi* are intensely sour plums that have been pickled and dried. Bonito flakes are shavings of a dried tuna-like fish. Both are available at Japanese markets and from edenfoods.com.

Market Math: Cucumbers

1 Cucumber Gazpacho

Puree 4 peeled, seeded and chopped **cucumbers** with 1½ cups **green grapes**, 1 **garlic clove**, ⅓ cup **olive oil**, 2 tsp. **white vinegar** and 1 cup **water**. Season with **salt**. Serve chilled with **shrimp** and **almonds**.

2 Grilled Cucumbers and Eggplant

In a bowl, whisk ¼ cup each of **olive oil** and **red wine vinegar** with 5 minced **garlic cloves** and 5 minced **anchovies**; season with **salt** and **pepper**. In another bowl, toss 4 quartered **Kirby cucumbers** with 1 small **eggplant**, cut into wedges; toss with 3 Tbsp. of the dressing, then grill until tender. Add the grilled vegetables to the remaining dressing, toss with **basil** and serve with **bread**.

3 Cucumber–Snap Pea Salad

In a bowl, whisk 6 Tbsp. **olive oil**, 6 Tbsp. fat-free plain **Greek yogurt** and 2 Tbsp. **water**. Add 2 julienned hothouse **cucumbers** and ½ lb. thinly sliced **sugar snap peas**. Season and top with **granola**.

4 Cucumber Fried Rice

Toss 4 thinly sliced **Kirby cucumbers** with 2 tsp. **salt** in a colander. Let stand 30 minutes; rinse and dry. In a large nonstick skillet, heat 2 Tbsp. **canola oil**. Add the cucumbers, 3 minced **garlic cloves** and 3 oz. slivered, thinly sliced **salami**. Stir-fry 3 minutes. Add 4 cups **cooked rice**, 2 sliced **scallions**, 1 minced **serrano chile** and 4 cups chopped **arugula** and stir-fry until hot. –*Kay Chun*

Creamed Spinach with Montreal Salted Herbs

Active **1 hr 15 min; Total 1 hr 40 min**
Serves **6 to 8**

At M. Wells Steakhouse in Long Island City, New York, Canadian-born chef Hugue Dufour has reimagined the American steak house. To reinvent classics like creamed spinach, he uses seaweed-like sea spinach (this recipe calls for regular spinach). He also flavors the dish with salted herbs, a Montreal condiment that's easy to re-create at home.

- **4 Tbsp. unsalted butter, plus more for greasing**
- **2 Tbsp. extra-virgin olive oil**
- **2½ lbs. trimmed spinach (not baby spinach)**
- **4 shallots, finely chopped (1 cup)**
- **1 cup dry white wine**
- **2 cups heavy cream**
- **2 tsp. Salted Herbs (recipe follows)**
- **Freshly ground pepper**

1. Preheat the oven to 425°. In a large saucepan, melt 2 tablespoons of the butter in 1 tablespoon of the olive oil. Add the spinach in large handfuls, letting each batch wilt slightly before adding more. Cook the spinach over high heat, stirring occasionally, until wilted, about 7 minutes. Transfer the spinach to a strainer set over a large bowl to drain. Let the cooked spinach cool slightly, then squeeze out all of the excess water from the leaves.

2. Wipe out the saucepan, then use it to melt the remaining 2 tablespoons of butter in the remaining 1 tablespoon of olive oil. Add the shallots and cook over moderately high heat, stirring, until softened, about 3 minutes. Add the wine and cook, stirring, until absorbed, about 3 minutes. Add the cream and bring just to a boil. Simmer over moderate heat, stirring occasionally, until reduced by half, about 7 minutes. Stir in the Salted Herbs and season lightly with pepper.

3. Fold the spinach into the cream sauce and scrape the mixture into a buttered 1½-quart baking dish. Bake the creamed spinach for about 15 minutes, until bubbling and the sauce is thickened. Let stand for 5 minutes before serving. —*Hugue Dufour*

SALTED HERBS

Total **25 min plus overnight salting**
Makes **about 1½ cups**

This magic salt transforms everything from steak, chicken and fish to vegetables, soups and stews.

- **1 medium carrot, coarsely chopped**
- **1 small parsnip, coarsely chopped**
- **1 celery rib, coarsely chopped**
- **½ medium onion, coarsely chopped**
- **1 cup packed parsley leaves**
- **1 cup snipped chives**
- **1 cup packed spinach (not baby spinach)**
- **⅓ cup coarse sea salt**

In a food processor, combine the carrot, parsnip, celery and onion. Pulse the vegetables until they are finely chopped. Add the parsley, chives and spinach and pulse until the mixture is very finely minced. Transfer the mixture to a bowl and stir in the salt. Cover and refrigerate the salted herbs at least overnight and up to 1 month in an airtight jar. —*HD*

Steamed Mustard Greens with Balinese Sambal

Total **20 min; Serves 4**

Sambal matah is a fragrant Balinese sauce made with lime, shallots and lemongrass. It's delicious on the steamed mustard greens here as well as on chicken or fish.

- **2 Tbsp. minced shallots**
- **1 stalk of fresh lemongrass, tender inner white part only, minced (1 Tbsp.)**
- **1 kaffir lime leaf, minced (¼ tsp.) or ¼ tsp. finely grated lime zest**
- **1 Tbsp. fresh lime juice**
- **1 Tbsp. coconut oil**
- **1 tsp. soy sauce**
- **Kosher salt**
- **1 bunch of mustard greens (12 oz.), stemmed, leaves coarsely chopped**
- **1 Tbsp. extra-virgin olive oil**
- **Sweet potato chips, broken into small pieces, for garnish (optional)**

1. In a large bowl, combine the shallots, lemongrass, kaffir lime leaf, lime juice, coconut oil and soy sauce. Season the *sambal matah* with salt.

2. Bring an inch of water to a boil in a large pot fitted with a steamer. Steam the greens until wilted and tender, about 3 minutes. Transfer the greens to the large bowl, add the olive oil and toss to coat. Season with salt.

3. Arrange the greens on a platter, garnish with sweet potato chips and serve.
—*Kuniko Yagi*

MAKE AHEAD The *sambal matah* can be refrigerated for up to 2 days.

Blistered Shishito Peppers with Miso

Total **15 min; Serves 6 as part of a multicourse meal**

Nicely bitter, finger-long shishito peppers are sautéed, simmered or grilled all over Japan in the summer. This charred version gets a salty, earthy, spicy hit from brown rice miso and fresh ginger.

- **1½ Tbsp. brown rice miso**
- **1½ Tbsp. sake**
- **1 Tbsp. canola oil, preferably cold-pressed**
- **1 small dried red chile**
- **¾ lb. shishito peppers**
- **1 Tbsp. minced peeled fresh ginger**

In a small bowl, stir the miso and sake until smooth. In a large skillet, heat the oil with the chile until shimmering. Add the shishitos and ginger and cook over high heat, tossing, until tender and blistered in spots, 2 to 3 minutes. Remove from the heat, add the miso sake and toss well. Transfer to a plate and serve.
—*Tadaaki Hachisu*

BLISTERED SHISHITO
PEPPERS WITH MISO

Spicy Sautéed Kale with Shredded Cheese

Total **35 min**; Serves **4 to 6**

¼ cup extra-virgin olive oil

4 garlic cloves, thinly sliced

1 Fresno chile—halved, seeded and thinly sliced

¼ tsp. crushed red pepper

2½ lbs. Tuscan kale, stems discarded and leaves coarsely chopped

2 Tbsp. fresh lemon juice

Kosher salt

Shredded *ricotta salata* cheese, for serving

In a deep skillet, heat the oil. Add the garlic, chile and crushed pepper and cook over moderately high heat, stirring, until fragrant, 1 minute. Add the kale in large handfuls; let wilt slightly before adding more. Cook, tossing, until the kale is barely tender, 3 to 5 minutes. Stir in the lemon juice; season with salt. Transfer to a platter, sprinkle with cheese and serve. —*Isaac Becker*

Sautéed Kale and Radishes in Tomato Bagna Cauda

Total **30 min**; Serves **4**

¼ cup extra-virgin olive oil

5 garlic cloves, finely chopped

7 anchovy fillets in oil, drained and chopped

3 Tbsp. tomato paste

1½ lbs. curly kale, stems discarded and leaves chopped

6 oz. radishes (about 8 small radishes), halved if large

3 Tbsp. fresh lemon juice

2 Tbsp. chopped chives

Kosher salt and freshly ground pepper

In a large saucepan, heat the olive oil. Add the garlic, anchovies and tomato paste and cook over moderately low heat, stirring frequently, until the tomato paste is deep red, about 7 minutes. Add the kale, radishes and ½ cup of water and cook, stirring, until the kale is softened, about 5 minutes. Stir in the lemon juice and chives, season with salt and pepper and serve warm. —*Kay Chun*

Roasted Sunchokes with Brown Butter–Cider Vinaigrette

Active **20 min**; Total **1 hr**; Serves **4 to 6**

2 lbs. sunchokes (Jerusalem artichokes), scrubbed and cut into 1-inch pieces

¼ cup extra-virgin olive oil

4 thyme sprigs

8 garlic cloves, crushed

Kosher salt

¼ cup apple cider vinegar

2 Tbsp. minced shallots

½ tsp. crushed red pepper

1 tsp. honey

2 Tbsp. unsalted butter

Black pepper

2 cups fresh spinach leaves

¼ cup chopped chives

1. Preheat the oven to 375°. On a rimmed baking sheet, toss the sunchokes with the oil, thyme sprigs and garlic and season with salt. Roast for about 1 hour, stirring occasionally, until golden and tender. Discard the thyme sprigs and garlic. Transfer the sunchokes to a large bowl.

2. Meanwhile, in a small saucepan, cook the vinegar over moderate heat until reduced to 2 tablespoons, 3 minutes. Transfer to a bowl. Stir in the shallots, crushed red pepper and honey.

3. Wipe out the saucepan. Add the butter and cook over moderate heat until golden brown, 2 to 3 minutes. Whisk the butter into the vinegar mixture and season with salt and black pepper.

4. Add the spinach, chives and vinaigrette to the sunchokes; season with salt and black pepper and toss to coat. Serve warm. —*Jamie Malone*

Nonna's Artichokes

Total **1 hr 15 min**; Serves **4**

TV personality Giada De Laurentiis, the chef at Las Vegas's new Giada restaurant, loves her *nonna* Luna's artichokes. They're an old-school Italian-American classic amped up with anchovies, olives and capers.

1 lemon, halved

4 medium artichokes

½ cup extra-virgin olive oil, plus more for greasing

3 garlic cloves

6 anchovy fillets, minced

½ cup plain dried bread crumbs

⅓ cup freshly grated Parmigiano-Reggiano cheese

Salt and pepper

½ cup pitted kalamata olives, minced

½ Tbsp. capers, rinsed and minced

1. Squeeze the juice from 1 lemon half into a bowl of water. Working with 1 artichoke at a time, discard the dark green outer leaves. Cut off the top 1 inch of the artichoke, then peel and trim the bottom and stem. Halve the artichoke lengthwise and scoop out the furry choke. Rub with the remaining lemon half and add to the bowl of lemon water.

2. Preheat the oven to 400°. In a large saucepan of simmering water, cook the artichoke halves until barely tender, 7 minutes. Drain well and pat dry.

3. Lightly oil a large ceramic baking dish. In a large skillet, heat the ½ cup of oil. Add the garlic and cook over moderately high heat until golden, 4 minutes; discard the garlic. Add the anchovies and stir until dissolved. Add the artichokes cut side down and cook until crusty on the bottom. Flip them and cook until lightly browned, 3 minutes longer; transfer the artichokes cut side up to the baking dish. Let the garlic-anchovy oil cool slightly.

4. In a bowl, mix the bread crumbs and cheese. Stir in the garlic-anchovy oil and season very lightly with salt and pepper. In another bowl, mix the olives and capers with a pinch of pepper. Fill the artichoke halves with the olive mixture and top with the bread crumbs. Bake for 12 minutes, until the topping is browned and crisp and the artichokes are tender. Let stand for 5 minutes, then serve. —*Giada De Laurentiis*

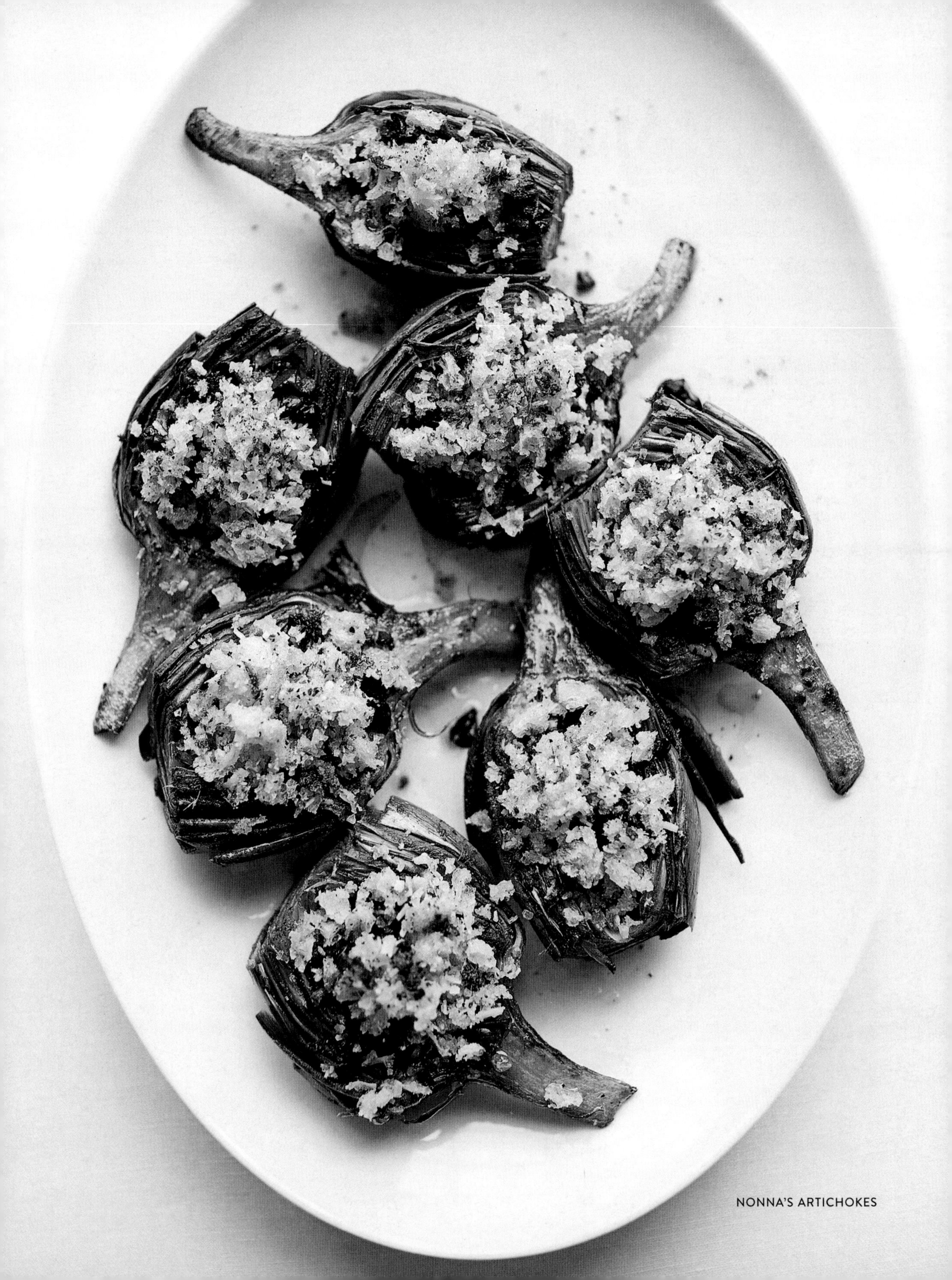

NONNA'S ARTICHOKES

Market Math: Kale

Kale is as versatile as it is nutritious. F&W's **KAY CHUN** uses four types—baby, red, green and Tuscan—transforming the superfood into a healthy snack, a side dish, an entree and a melty, cheesy sandwich filling.

Nutty Baby Kale Chips
Total **30 min plus cooling**
Makes **4 cups**

- ½ cup raw almond butter
- ¼ cup canola oil
  Kosher salt
- 4 cups baby kale leaves

Preheat the oven to 325°. Set 2 racks on 2 large baking sheets. In a large bowl, whisk the almond butter with the oil and season with salt. Add the kale leaves and massage to coat. Arrange on the racks in single layers. Bake for about 20 minutes, rotating the baking sheets, until the kale is golden and almost crisp. Let cool completely before serving (the leaves will crisp up as they cool).

KALE THREE MORE WAYS

Kale Rice Bowl
Total **30 min**; Serves **4**

- 2 **Tbsp. canola oil**
- 5 **garlic cloves, thinly sliced**
- 2 **Tbsp. chopped peeled fresh ginger**
- ¾ **lb. ground pork**
- 1 **lb. red kale (2 bunches), stemmed and leaves torn into large pieces (16 cups)**
- 1 **Tbsp. Asian fish sauce**
- 1 **cup mixed chopped basil and cilantro**
- **Kosher salt and pepper**
- **Steamed rice and Sriracha, for serving**

In a large nonstick skillet, heat the canola oil. Add the garlic, ginger and pork and cook over moderate heat, stirring, until the pork is just cooked through, 3 minutes. In batches, add the kale and stir-fry until tender, about 5 minutes. Stir in the fish sauce and herbs and season with salt and pepper. Serve with rice and Sriracha.

Garlicky Kale-and-Provolone Grinders
Active **20 min**; Total **40 min**; Serves **4**

- 2 **Tbsp. extra-virgin olive oil**
- 7 **oil-packed anchovy fillets**
- 5 **garlic cloves, minced**
- 1 **lb. green kale (2 bunches), stemmed and leaves torn into large pieces (about 18 cups)**
- ½ **lb. thinly sliced provolone cheese**
- **One 12-inch ciabatta loaf, halved horizontally**
- **Sliced radishes, chopped green olives and mayonnaise, for serving**

In a large nonstick skillet, heat the olive oil. Add the anchovies and garlic, then add the kale in batches and cook over moderate heat, stirring, until the kale is wilted, 3 minutes. Add 1 cup of water, cover and cook until tender, 15 minutes. Top the kale with the cheese in an even layer. Cover and cook until the cheese melts, 2 minutes. Using a large slotted spoon, transfer the kale and cheese to the bottom half of the ciabatta. Top with radishes, olives and the top half of the ciabatta spread with mayonnaise. Close the sandwich and cut into 4 pieces.

Cacio e Pepe–Style Braised Kale
Active **10 min**; Total **25 min**; Serves **4**

- 2 **Tbsp. unsalted butter**
- 2 **Tbsp. extra-virgin olive oil**
- 1 **lb. Tuscan kale (2 bunches), stemmed and leaves torn into large pieces (16 cups)**
- 2 **cups low-sodium chicken broth**
- **Kosher salt**
- **Pinch of crushed red pepper**
- **Cracked black pepper**
- ⅓ **cup freshly grated Parmigiano-Reggiano cheese**

In a large pot, melt the butter in the olive oil. Add the kale in batches and cook over moderate heat, stirring, until wilted, about 3 minutes. Add the chicken broth and bring to a simmer. Cover and cook until the kale is tender and almost all of the broth is absorbed, about 10 minutes. Season with salt. Transfer the kale to a platter and top with the crushed red pepper, lots of black pepper and the cheese.

Cauliflower Steaks with Herb Salsa Verde

⏲ Total **25 min**; Serves **2 to 4**

"It's amazing how meaty cauliflower can be," says Alex Guarnaschelli, the chef at Butter in Manhattan. She treats the vegetable like steak, searing thick slabs and topping them with a tangy salsa verde.

- ¼ cup chopped flat-leaf parsley
- 2 Tbsp. chopped cilantro
- 2 Tbsp. chopped tarragon
- 1½ Tbsp. drained capers, coarsely chopped
- 6 cornichons, finely chopped
- 1 small garlic clove, minced
- 1 Tbsp. Dijon mustard
- 1 Tbsp. grainy mustard
- ⅓ cup extra-virgin olive oil
- 1 large head of cauliflower
  Kosher salt and pepper
- 2 Tbsp. canola oil
- ½ cup dry white wine
- ½ tsp. finely grated lemon zest
- 4½ Tbsp. fresh lemon juice
- 1 tsp. red wine vinegar

1. In a large bowl, whisk the parsley with the cilantro, tarragon, capers, cornichons, garlic, mustards and olive oil.

2. Cut the cauliflower from top to bottom into four ½-inch-thick steaks. Generously season them with salt and pepper. In a very large skillet, heat the canola oil until very hot. Add the cauliflower in a single layer and cook over high heat until browned, 2 to 3 minutes. Carefully flip the steaks, add the wine and cook until it has evaporated and the cauliflower is easily pierced with a knife, 3 to 5 minutes.

3. Transfer the cauliflower to a platter and sprinkle with the lemon zest. Stir the lemon juice and vinegar into the salsa verde and season with salt and pepper. Spoon the sauce on the cauliflower and serve.
—*Alex Guarnaschelli*

WINE Vibrant, ripe Alsace white: 2010 Zind-Humbrecht Calcaire Pinot Gris.

Maple-Glazed Carrots

⏲ Total **30 min**; Serves **4**

- 1½ lbs. trimmed baby carrots, preferably heirloom
- 2 cups chicken stock
  Kosher salt and ground pepper
- ½ cup pure maple syrup
- 1 anchovy fillet, drained and chopped
- 2 Tbsp. unsalted butter, cut into ½-inch cubes
- 2 Tbsp. chopped dill

In a deep skillet, combine the carrots and chicken stock and season with salt and pepper. Bring to a boil. Cover and cook over moderate heat until the stock is reduced to ⅔ cup, about 10 minutes. Add the maple syrup and simmer, stirring occasionally, until the sauce is sticky and the carrots are tender and well coated, 7 to 8 minutes. Stir in the anchovy until dissolved. Remove the skillet from the heat and whisk in the butter 1 cube at a time. Stir in the dill, season with salt and serve.
—*Hugue Dufour*

Brussels Sprouts with Prosciutto and Juniper

⏲ Total **45 min**; Serves **6 to 8**

- ½ cup extra-virgin olive oil
- 8 large garlic cloves, halved lengthwise
- 6 thin slices of prosciutto (3 oz.), torn in half crosswise
- 1¾ lbs. brussels sprouts, halved lengthwise or quartered if large
  Flaky sea salt, such as Maldon
- 2 Tbsp. fresh lemon juice
  Generous pinch of crushed red pepper
- 8 juniper berries, crushed and minced
- 1 tsp. finely chopped thyme
  Lemon wedges, for serving

1. In a very large skillet, heat the olive oil until shimmering. Add the garlic and cook over moderately high heat, turning once, until golden, 3 minutes. Transfer the garlic to a plate. In batches, add the prosciutto to the skillet in a single layer and cook over moderately high heat, turning, until browned and just crisp, 3 minutes per batch. Transfer the crispy prosciutto to paper towels to drain.

2. Add the brussels sprouts to the skillet and arrange them cut side down. Add a generous pinch of salt and cook over moderately high heat until browned on the bottom, about 5 minutes. Turn the brussels sprouts and cook over moderate heat, tossing occasionally, until just tender, about 10 minutes longer. Remove from the heat and stir in the lemon juice, crushed red pepper, juniper berries and thyme.

3. Coarsely chop the garlic and tear the prosciutto into bite-size pieces, then fold them into the brussels sprouts. Season with salt and serve with lemon wedges.
—*April Bloomfield*

Collard Greens with Black-Eyed Peas

Active **30 min**; Total **1 hr 15 min**; Serves **6**

- 2½ cups chicken stock or low-sodium broth
- 2 chipotles in adobo sauce
- 1 small Spanish onion, halved
  Salt and pepper
- 2½ lbs. collard greens, ribs discarded and leaves chopped
  One 15-oz. can black-eyed peas, drained and rinsed
- 2 Tbsp. white wine vinegar

1. In a large saucepan or stockpot, combine 1½ cups of the stock with the chipotles, onion and a generous pinch each of salt and pepper and bring to a boil. Add the collards in large handfuls, letting each batch wilt slightly before adding more.

2. Cover and cook over moderate heat, stirring occasionally, until the collards are just tender, about 25 minutes. Uncover and cook, stirring occasionally, until the broth is slightly reduced, about 7 minutes; discard the chipotles and onion.

3. Meanwhile, in a small saucepan, combine the black-eyed peas with the remaining 1 cup of stock and bring to a boil. Simmer over moderate heat for 8 minutes; season with salt and pepper. Using a slotted spoon, add the black-eyed peas to the collards; reserve the bean broth for another use. Add the vinegar to the collard greens, season with salt and pepper and serve. —*Bobby Flay*

CAULIFLOWER STEAKS WITH
HERB SALSA VERDE

Mix-and-Match Pickles

With one master brine and four herb-and-spice combinations, **KENDRA COGGIN** and **BARON CONWAY** of Pernicious Pickling Co. in Costa Mesa, California, make dozens of different pickles—sometimes roasting them to delicious effect.

Pickled and Roasted Cauliflower with Curry

Active **20 min**; Total **2 hr 45 min**; Serves **8**

Instead of simply roasting cauliflower, try quick-pickling it first in a tangy curry brine for extra layers of flavor.

- 3½ lbs. cauliflower, cut into 1-inch florets
- 1 quart distilled white vinegar
- ½ cup plus 2 Tbsp. dark brown sugar
- 1 Tbsp. curry powder
- Salt
- ¼ cup extra-virgin olive oil
- Pepper

1. Fill a large bowl with ice water. In a large saucepan of salted boiling water, blanch the cauliflower until just starting to soften, 1 to 2 minutes. Drain and transfer to the ice bath to cool. Drain again.

2. In a large saucepan, combine 2½ cups of water with the vinegar, sugar, curry powder and 1 tablespoon of salt and bring to a boil, stirring to dissolve the sugar. Remove from the heat, stir in the cauliflower and let cool completely. Refrigerate for 1 hour. Drain the cauliflower; reserve the brine to pickle more vegetables, if desired.

3. Preheat the oven to 375°. On a large rimmed baking sheet, toss the cauliflower with the olive oil and season with salt and pepper. Roast for about 35 minutes, stirring once or twice, until tender and browned in spots. Transfer the cauliflower to a platter and serve.

MAKE AHEAD The drained pickled cauliflower can be refrigerated overnight before roasting. Bring to room temperature before proceeding with the recipe.

INDIAN-STYLE
Cumin, coriander, curry powder, mustard seeds, chile, raisins

ITALIAN-STYLE
Oregano, rosemary, bay leaf, fennel, black peppercorns

FRENCH-STYLE
Rosemary, thyme, bay leaf, black peppercorns, chile, garlic, white wine vinegar

CLASSIC
Dill, garlic, black peppercorns

Coggin and Conway's master brine can pickle almost anything. Try it with one of the four herb-and-spice combinations above.

Master Brine

In a large saucepan, combine 1½ cups **distilled white vinegar** and 2 cups **water** with 1 Tbsp. **sugar** and ¼ tsp. **salt**. Bring just to a simmer to dissolve the sugar. Pour the warm brine over whole or sliced **vegetables** and refrigerate for at least 3 days before serving.

PICK ANY VEGETABLE
- **Carrots**
- **Pearl Onions**
- **Parsnips**
- **Cauliflower**
- **Shallots**
- **Brussels Sprouts**
- **Celery**
- **Rutabaga**
- **Fennel**
- **Cucumbers**
- **Turnips**
- **Radishes**

Cauliflower and Gruyère Soufflé

Active **30 min**; Total **1 hr 45 min**
Serves **6 to 8**

- ½ **lb. cauliflower florets,
  cut into 1-inch pieces**
- 1 **stick unsalted butter**
- ⅓ **cup all-purpose flour**
- 2 **cups whole milk**
  Kosher salt and pepper
- 6 **oz. Gruyère cheese, shredded
  (2 lightly packed cups)**
- 2 **Tbsp. finely chopped chives**
- 6 **large eggs**

1. In a medium saucepan of salted boiling water, cook the cauliflower until very tender, about 7 minutes. Drain well and pat dry. In a medium bowl, puree the cauliflower with a potato masher or fork. Transfer the cauliflower to a colander and let drain until cooled completely.

2. Meanwhile, preheat the oven to 350°. Grease a 6-cup soufflé dish with 1 tablespoon of the butter and set it on a rimmed baking sheet. In a medium saucepan, melt the remaining 7 tablespoons of butter. Add the flour and whisk over moderate heat until bubbling, about 3 minutes. Gradually whisk in the milk and bring to a boil. Simmer over moderately low heat, whisking, until thickened and no floury taste remains, about 7 minutes. Season the béchamel with salt and pepper. Scrape into a large bowl and let cool, stirring occasionally.

3. Stir the cauliflower puree into the béchamel, then fold in the cheese and chives. In a medium bowl, beat the eggs until frothy, then gently fold them into the cauliflower béchamel. Scrape the soufflé base into the prepared dish and bake for about 1 hour and 10 minutes, until puffed and browned; serve right away.
—*Claudine Pépin*

WINE Lively Spanish sparkling wine: NV Avinyó Brut Reserva Cava.

Giardiniera-Style Roasted Vegetables

Active **30 min**; Total **1 hr 30 min**; Serves **6**

This salad unites the elements of Italian giardiniera—red peppers, olives, celery—with pickled-and-roasted carrots and fennel. Roasting the vegetables adds an appealing caramelized flavor.

- 1 **lb. carrots, halved lengthwise and
  cut into 3-inch pieces**
- 1 **fennel bulb, trimmed and
  cut into thin wedges**
- 1 **quart distilled white vinegar**
- 5 **garlic cloves, crushed**
- 2 **Tbsp. yellow mustard seeds**
- ¼ **cup sugar**
- ¼ **cup kosher salt, plus more
  for seasoning**
- 1 **jalapeño, halved lengthwise**
- ¼ **cup extra-virgin olive oil**
- 2 **jarred roasted red bell peppers,
  thinly sliced**
- 3 **celery ribs, chopped, plus celery
  leaves for garnish**
- ½ **cup chopped pitted green olives**

1. In a large heatproof bowl, combine the carrots and fennel. In a medium saucepan, combine 2 cups of water with the vinegar, garlic, mustard seeds, sugar, the ¼ cup of salt and half of the jalapeño. Warm over low heat, stirring to dissolve the sugar. Pour the brine over the carrots and fennel and let stand for 30 minutes. Drain the carrots and fennel; reserve the brine for another use.

2. Preheat the oven to 450°. Arrange the carrots and fennel on a rimmed baking sheet. Drizzle with the olive oil and roast for about 30 minutes, stirring occasionally, until tender and caramelized. Transfer the vegetables to a large bowl. Finely chop the remaining jalapeño and add to the bowl along with the bell peppers, chopped celery and olives. Season with salt, mix well and transfer to a platter. Garnish with celery leaves and serve. —*Kay Chun*

WINE Ripe, citrusy California Chenin Blanc: 2013 Dry Creek Vineyard.

Sautéed Cauliflower Wedges with Bagna Cauda

Total **40 min**; Serves **6**

Chef Chad Colby of Chi Spacca in L.A. brilliantly turns the classic Piedmontese dip bagna cauda into a savory side: He spoons the "hot bath" of olive oil, anchovies and garlic over pan-seared cauliflower.

- 4 **Tbsp. unsalted butter**
- 5 **garlic cloves, finely chopped**
- 10 **anchovy fillets in oil, drained
  and finely chopped**
- ¼ **cup plus 2 Tbsp.
  extra-virgin olive oil**
- 2 **tsp. finely grated lemon zest**
  Salt and freshly ground black pepper
- 1 **head of cauliflower (2½ lbs.),
  halved lengthwise and sliced
  through the core into 6 wedges**
- 1 **tablespoon chopped parsley**

1. In a small saucepan, melt the butter. Add the garlic, anchovies, ¼ cup of the olive oil and 1 teaspoon of the lemon zest and cook over moderately low heat, stirring occasionally, until the garlic is softened and the anchovies are melted, about 10 minutes. Season with salt and pepper. Remove the bagna cauda from the heat and keep warm.

2. Meanwhile, in a large pot of boiling salted water, blanch the cauliflower wedges until crisp-tender, about 3 minutes. Drain the cauliflower and transfer it to a paper towel–lined plate; pat thoroughly to dry.

3. In a large skillet, heat the remaining 2 tablespoons of olive oil until shimmering. Add the cauliflower and cook over moderately high heat, turning once, until cooked through and golden brown on both sides, 10 minutes. Season with salt and pepper. Transfer the cauliflower to plates and spoon some of the bagna cauda on top. Top with the parsley and the remaining 1 teaspoon of lemon zest and serve with the remaining bagna cauda. —*Chad Colby*

Grilled Radishes with Rosemary Brown Butter

⏱ Total **45 min**; Serves **6 to 8**

At Miller's Guild, his modern steak house in Seattle, chef Jason Wilson emphasizes whole grains and vegetables. His lovely appetizers include grilled radishes and radish greens—both tossed with fresh mint and nutty brown butter.

- 1 stick unsalted butter, softened
- 3 Tbsp. heavy cream
- 1 Tbsp. fresh lemon juice
- 1 tsp. finely chopped rosemary
  Sea salt
- 3 bunches of radishes (about 2¼ lbs.), 2 cups of the greens reserved
- 1 cup lightly packed mint
  Grilled rustic bread, for serving

1. In a small skillet, cook 4 tablespoons of the butter over moderate heat, swirling, until browned, 3 to 5 minutes; let the browned butter cool completely.

2. In a small bowl, blend the cooled brown butter with the remaining 4 tablespoons of butter and the cream, lemon juice and rosemary. Season with salt.

3. Light a grill or heat a grill pan. In a large bowl, toss the radishes with 2 tablespoons of the rosemary brown butter and season with salt. Grill on a perforated grill pan (if using a grill) over high heat, tossing occasionally, until lightly charred and crisp-tender, about 5 minutes. Return the radishes to the bowl. Add the 2 cups of radish greens and the mint; toss well. Pile the radishes and greens on a platter and serve with grilled bread, sea salt and the remaining brown butter. —*Jason Wilson*

MAKE AHEAD The rosemary brown butter can be refrigerated for up to 3 days.

PAIRING TIP

Best Wines for Roasted Vegetables

Match the sweetness of caramelized vegetables with wines that have ripe fruit: whites like Chenin Blanc and not-too-tannic reds like Grenache.

Blistered Diced Radishes with Parsley

⏱ Total **20 min**; Serves **4**

In this recipe from her cookbook *The Nourished Kitchen*, Jennifer McGruther shows how easy it is to turn radishes into an unexpected side dish just by sautéing them in butter.

- 1 tablespoon unsalted butter
- 16 radishes (1 lb.), cut into ⅓-inch dice
- ¼ cup finely chopped flat-leaf parsley
  Sea salt

In a large skillet, melt the butter. Add the radishes and cook over moderately high heat, tossing occasionally, until browned in spots, about 8 minutes. Stir in the parsley, season with salt and serve right away. —*Jennifer McGruther*

Roasted Root Vegetables with Tamari

Active **30 min**; Total **1 hr**; Serves **8**

- 10 small white Japanese turnips, halved lengthwise
- 3 medium parsnips, quartered lengthwise
- 6 medium carrots, preferably mixed colors, halved lengthwise
- 10 small golden beets, scrubbed and quartered lengthwise
- ¼ cup extra-virgin olive oil
- 1 Tbsp. finely chopped thyme
- 1 Tbsp. finely chopped sage
- 1 Tbsp. finely chopped rosemary
  Salt and pepper
- 2½ Tbsp. distilled white vinegar
- 2 Tbsp. tamari

1. Preheat the oven to 425°. In a large saucepan of salted boiling water, blanch the turnips until barely tender, about 1 minute. Using a slotted spoon, transfer the turnips to a baking sheet to cool slightly. Add the parsnips and carrots to the saucepan and bring to a boil, then simmer until barely tender, about 2 minutes; transfer the carrots and parsnips to the baking sheet. Add the beets to the saucepan and simmer until just tender, about 5 minutes; transfer to the baking sheet and let cool slightly.

2. In a large bowl, toss the vegetables with the olive oil, thyme, sage and rosemary and season with salt and pepper. Spread the vegetables in an even layer on 2 large rimmed baking sheets. Roast for 20 to 25 minutes, until browned in spots. Transfer the vegetables to a platter. Drizzle with the vinegar and tamari, season with salt and pepper and toss to coat. Serve. —*Nevia No*

Roasted Butternut Squash with Spiced Pecans

⏱ Total **45 min**; Serves **8 to 10**

Marcus Samuelsson, the Ethiopian-born, Swedish-bred chef at Red Rooster in New York City, seasons roasted butternut squash and toasted pecans with berbere, an intriguing spice blend that includes chiles, allspice and ginger. Berbere is available at specialty food shops and from kalustyans.com.

- One 3-lb. butternut squash—peeled, seeded and cut into 1½-inch pieces
- ¼ cup plus 1 tsp. extra-virgin olive oil
- 1½ tsp. berbere
  Kosher salt and pepper
- 1 tsp. finely grated orange zest
- ¼ cup fresh orange juice
- ½ cup pecans
- ¼ tsp. sugar
- ¼ cup dried cranberries, chopped

1. Preheat the oven to 450°. On a parchment paper–lined baking sheet, toss the squash with 2 tablespoons of the olive oil and 1 teaspoon of the berbere; season with salt and pepper. Roast for 30 minutes, stirring occasionally, until golden and tender.

2. Meanwhile, in a small bowl, whisk 2 tablespoons of the olive oil with the orange zest and juice. Season the dressing with salt and pepper.

3. In a skillet, heat the remaining 1 teaspoon of olive oil. Add the pecans and toast over moderately low heat, stirring, until fragrant, 3 minutes. Transfer the nuts to a bowl and stir in the sugar, ¼ teaspoon of salt and remaining ½ teaspoon of berbere.

4. Arrange the squash on a platter and drizzle the dressing on top. Scatter the cranberries and spiced nuts over the squash and serve warm or at room temperature. —*Marcus Samuelsson*

GRILLED RADISHES WITH
ROSEMARY BROWN BUTTER

Fried Squash with Sage Honey, Parmesan and Pickled Chiles

Active **1 hr 15 min**; Total **1 hr 45 min**
Serves **8**

PICKLED CHILES

½ cup apple cider vinegar

2 Tbsp. sugar

2 tsp. kosher salt

4 sage leaves

Pinch of freshly grated nutmeg

3 Fresno or red jalapeño chiles, seeded and thinly sliced crosswise

SAGE HONEY

¼ cup honey

2 tsp. finely chopped sage

Pinch of freshly grated nutmeg

Kosher salt

SQUASH

One 3¼-lb. butternut squash or sugar pumpkin—peeled, seeded and cut into 1-inch dice

2 Tbsp. unsalted butter, melted

¼ tsp. piment d'Espelette

Kosher salt and ground pepper

1¼ cups rice flour

¾ cup all-purpose flour

1½ Tbsp. cornstarch

2 cups cold sparkling water

1½ Tbsp. vodka

Canola oil, for frying

½ cup lightly packed sage leaves

Freshly grated Parmigiano-Reggiano cheese and lemon wedges, for serving

1. Make the pickled chiles In a small saucepan, bring the vinegar, sugar, salt, sage and nutmeg just to a boil, stirring to dissolve the sugar. Add the chiles and let cool completely; refrigerate until chilled.

2. Make the sage honey In another small saucepan, warm the honey, sage, nutmeg and a pinch of salt over moderately low heat for 3 minutes. Let steep off the heat for 30 minutes.

3. Meanwhile, prepare the squash Preheat the oven to 375°. On a large rimmed baking sheet, toss the squash with the butter and piment d'Espelette and season with salt and pepper. Roast for about 20 minutes, until just tender; let cool.

4. Spread ½ cup of the rice flour in a shallow bowl. In a large bowl, whisk the all-purpose flour with the cornstarch and remaining ¾ cup of rice flour, then whisk in the sparkling water, vodka and a pinch of salt until the batter is smooth.

5. Line 2 large baking sheets with paper towels. In a large saucepan, heat 2 inches of oil over moderately high heat to 350°. Add the sage leaves and fry until crisp, 1 minute. Using a slotted spoon, transfer the crispy sage to the paper towels to drain.

6. Working in 3 batches, dust the squash with the rice flour, then coat in the batter and fry until golden, 4 to 5 minutes per batch. Transfer to the paper towels to drain. Arrange the fried squash and sage leaves on a platter. Drizzle with some of the sage honey and garnish with Parmigiano and some of the pickled chiles. Serve with lemon wedges, passing additional sage honey and pickled chiles at the table. —*Gabriel Rucker*

WINE Toasty sparkling wine: NV Louis Bouillot Grande Réserve Crémant de Bourgogne.

Roasted Leeks with Yogurt and Shaved Toasted Walnuts

⏱ Total **45 min**; Serves **6**

1 cup plain Greek yogurt

1½ tsp. finely grated lemon zest

1 tsp. minced marjoram

1 tsp. sugar

Kosher salt and freshly ground pepper

¼ cup walnut halves

6 very fresh leeks, white and light green parts only, trimmed and halved lengthwise

Extra-virgin olive oil, for drizzling

2 Tbsp. fresh lemon juice

1. Preheat the oven to 375°. In a small bowl, blend the yogurt with the lemon zest, marjoram and sugar. Season with salt and pepper and mix well.

2. Spread the walnuts in a small cake pan and toast in the oven for 7 to 8 minutes, until browned and fragrant. Transfer to a plate to cool.

3. Spread the leeks on a baking sheet in a single layer. Drizzle with 3 tablespoons of olive oil and the lemon juice and season with salt and pepper; rub to coat the leeks

thoroughly. Roast for about 20 minutes, tossing occasionally, until the leeks are tender, golden and crispy in spots.

4. Transfer the leeks to a platter. Coarsely chop half of the walnuts and sprinkle them over the leeks. Using a Microplane, finely shave the rest of the walnuts over the leeks. Drizzle with olive oil and serve with the yogurt sauce. —*Viet Pham*

Grilled Leeks with Shishito Romesco

Total **1 hr 15 min**; Serves **4**

Shishitos and crushed red pepper add layers of heat to this spicy twist on *romesco,* the classic Spanish almond sauce. It's terrific with the lightly charred leeks.

8 large leeks, white and light green parts only

¾ cup extra-virgin olive oil, plus more for brushing

Kosher salt and ground pepper

1 garlic clove, finely grated

¼ tsp. crushed red pepper

12 shishito peppers, stemmed

1 cup lightly packed parsley

½ cup toasted marcona almonds

2 Tbsp. fresh bread crumbs

½ tsp. finely grated lemon zest

1 Tbsp. fresh lemon juice

1. Light a grill. Halve the leeks lengthwise through the light green part; leave the white parts and root attached. Rinse under cold water. Brush with oil and season with salt and ground pepper. Grill over moderately low heat, turning, until charred outside, 25 minutes. Transfer to a platter and cover with plastic; let steam for 15 minutes.

2. Discard the charred outsides and return the leeks to the platter. Toss with the garlic, red pepper and ¼ cup of the oil and season with salt and ground pepper; let stand for 30 minutes.

3. Meanwhile, grill the shishitos over high heat, turning, until lightly charred, 2 minutes. Transfer to a food processor and let cool slightly. Add the parsley, almonds, bread crumbs and lemon zest and juice and pulse until minced. With the machine on, add the remaining ½ cup of oil. Season with salt and ground pepper. Serve the leeks with the shishito *romesco.* —*Eli Kulp*

Market Math: Corn

1 Skillet Corn with Bulgur

In a large skillet, heat ¼ cup **olive oil**. Add 3 cups **fresh corn kernels** and 3 thinly sliced garlic cloves and cook over high heat until the corn is charred, 5 minutes. Scrape into a bowl. Add 1 cup each of **cooked bulgur**, chopped **tomatoes** and **parsley**. Add 1 Tbsp. **lemon juice**; season with **salt** and **pepper**.

2 Corn-Shrimp Dumplings

In a medium bowl, mix 1 cup **fresh corn kernels** with ½ lb. chopped **raw shrimp**, 2 minced **scallions** and 2 tsp. each of minced **garlic** and **ginger**; season with **salt**. Brush the edges of 20 **small round gyoza wrappers** with **water** and fill each with 1 Tbsp. filling; fold and seal. Steam for 3 to 4 minutes and serve with **soy sauce**.

3 Parmesan-Corn Butter

In a cast-iron skillet, cook 1 ear **shucked corn** over high heat until charred in spots, 10 minutes; let cool. Cut the kernels off the cob and transfer to a bowl. Stir in 1 stick **softened butter**, ¼ cup **Parmesan cheese**, 1 tsp. grated **lime zest** and 1 Tbsp. **lime juice**; season with **salt** and **pepper**; serve with grilled fish.

4 Thai-Glazed Corn

In a small saucepan, cook ½ cup **unsweetened coconut milk** with ¼ cup **soy sauce**, 2 Tbsp. **light brown sugar** and 1 Tbsp. each of **fish sauce** and **lime juice** until syrupy, 10 minutes. Light a grill. Grill 4 ears **shucked corn**, turning, for 15 minutes; brush with the glaze for the last 5 minutes. Sprinkle with chopped **cilantro** and grated **Cotija cheese** and serve with **lime wedges**. –*Kay Chun*

Bacon-Wrapped Vegetable Skewers with Dill Pickle Relish

⏱ Total **40 min**; Serves **10**

Ordinary pickles become flavor bombs, as both a seasoning and a dipping sauce for smoky mushrooms and cherry tomatoes.

- ¾ **cup minced dill pickles (from 2 large pickles)**
- ¾ **cup minced parsley**
- ¾ **cup extra-virgin olive oil, plus more for brushing**
  Kosher salt
- ¾ **lb. oyster mushrooms, sliced and arranged in 2-inch clusters**
- 20 **large cherry tomatoes**
- 20 **thin strips of bacon (1 lb.), halved crosswise**
  Lemon wedges, for serving

1. In a medium bowl, toss the pickles with the parsley and the ¾ cup of olive oil. Season the relish with salt.

2. Light a grill. Wrap each mushroom cluster and cherry tomato in a bacon slice. Thread the bacon-wrapped vegetables onto skewers, brush with olive oil and season lightly with salt.

3. Grill the skewers over moderate heat, turning, until the bacon is cooked and the vegetables are tender, 8 minutes; brush with a little pickle relish during the last minute of grilling. Transfer to a platter and serve with lemon wedges and the remaining pickle relish. —*Paul Berglund*

Roasted Maitake Mushrooms with Seaweed Butter

Active **20 min**; Total **1 hr 15 min**; Serves **4**

This recipe is a vegetarian surf-and-turf that's loaded with umami.

- ½ **cup dried wakame seaweed (½ oz.)**
- 1 **cup boiling water**
- 1 **stick unsalted butter, at room temperature**
  Kosher salt and pepper
- 1¼ **lbs. whole heads of maitake (hen-of-the-woods) mushrooms**
- ¼ **cup extra-virgin olive oil**
- 2 **Tbsp. chopped chives**
  Lemon wedges, for serving

1. In a small bowl, cover the seaweed with the boiling water and let stand until pliable, about 30 minutes. Drain and chop the seaweed; transfer to a bowl. Stir in the butter and season with salt and pepper.

2. Preheat the oven to 425°. On a rimmed baking sheet, drizzle the mushrooms with the olive oil, season generously with salt and pepper and toss to coat. Arrange the mushrooms in a single layer, dollop with three-fourths of the seaweed butter and roast for about 30 minutes, basting occasionally, until tender, deeply golden and crispy in spots.

3. Scrape the mushrooms and crispy seaweed onto a serving platter and top with the chives. Serve with lemon wedges and pass the remaining seaweed butter at the table. —*Kay Chun*

WINE Minerally, savory white Burgundy: 2012 Savary Chablis.

Mushrooms with Pickle-Brine Butter

⏱ Total **45 min**; Serves **6 to 8**

- 1 **stick plus 1 Tbsp. unsalted butter**
- 6 **Tbsp. extra-virgin olive oil**
- 3 **medium shallots, thinly sliced (1½ cups)**
- 3 **lbs. mixed mushrooms, such as cremini, oyster and stemmed shiitake, thickly sliced or quartered**
- ¾ **cup brine, strained from a jar of dill pickles**
  Kosher salt and pepper

1. In a very large skillet, melt 3 tablespoons of the butter in 2 tablespoons of the olive oil over moderately high heat, swirling, until the butter is golden, about 2 minutes. Add one-third of the shallots to the skillet and cook, stirring, until softened, about 1 minute. Add one-third of the mushrooms and cook, stirring occasionally, until tender and golden, 5 to 7 minutes. Add one-third of the pickle brine and cook until absorbed, about 1 minute. Transfer the mushrooms to a serving bowl and keep warm.

2. Repeat the process twice more with the remaining butter, olive oil, shallots, mushrooms and pickle brine. Season the mushrooms with salt and pepper and serve. —*Stuart Brioza*

Tomato-Portobello Stacks with Cheater's Béarnaise

⏱ Total **30 min**; Serves **6**

This vegetarian dish is triple-grilled: The portobello mushroom steaks and thick tomato slices are grilled separately, then they're stacked and covered with a five-minute béarnaise and grilled once more.

- 2 **Tbsp. minced shallot**
- 1½ **Tbsp. tarragon vinegar or white wine vinegar**
  Kosher salt and pepper
- ¾ **cup mayonnaise**
- 1 **Tbsp. minced tarragon**
  Extra-virgin olive oil, for brushing
- 6 **large portobello mushrooms, stems discarded**
  One 1-lb. beefsteak tomato, cored and cut crosswise into six ½-inch-thick slices
  Thinly sliced scallions, for garnish

1. In a medium bowl, whisk the shallot and vinegar with a generous pinch each of salt and pepper; let stand for 5 minutes. Whisk in the mayonnaise, tarragon and 1½ tablespoons of water. Season the béarnaise sauce with salt and pepper.

2. Light a grill and brush with oil. Brush the portobello caps with oil and season with salt and pepper. Grill over moderately high heat, turning once, until lightly charred, 6 minutes. Transfer to a plate. Brush the tomato slices with oil and season with salt and pepper. Grill, turning once, until lightly charred, 3 minutes total. Set the tomato slices on the portobellos.

3. Spoon the béarnaise on the tomato slices. Transfer the stacks to the grill and close the grill. Cook over moderate heat until the sauce is just hot, 3 minutes. Transfer to plates, garnish with scallions and serve. —*Greg Denton and Gabrielle Quiñónez Denton*

WINE Light, dark-berried Piedmontese red: 2012 Roagna Dolcetto.

BACON-WRAPPED VEGETABLE
SKEWERS WITH DILL PICKLE RELISH

Garden Salad Tacos
⏱ Total **30 min**; Serves **4**

"I've been making this garden salad taco with my daughter, Fanny, since she was young," says Alice Waters, founder of Berkeley, California's legendary Chez Panisse and The Edible Schoolyard Project. "It was a good way to add fresh vegetables to her meals without hiding the fact that she was eating a salad." Waters likes to make these tacos for a group. "Prepare the salad a little in advance and add handfuls of it to the tortillas as they come out from under the broiler," she recommends.

- 2 Tbsp. extra-virgin olive oil
- 1 Tbsp. red wine vinegar
- ½ small garlic clove, finely grated
  Pinch of ground cumin
  Kosher salt
- 2 cups lightly packed mixed baby greens
- ½ small fennel bulb, very thinly sliced on a mandoline
- 1 medium carrot, very thinly sliced crosswise
- 4 radishes, very thinly sliced
- ½ cup lightly packed cilantro leaves
- 8 corn tortillas, warmed
- 3 oz. Monterey Jack cheese, shredded (1 cup)

1. Preheat a broiler. In a large bowl, whisk the olive oil with the vinegar, garlic, cumin and a pinch of salt. Add the baby greens, fennel, carrot, radishes and cilantro and toss to coat. Season the salad with salt.

2. Arrange the warm corn tortillas on a large baking sheet in a single layer. Sprinkle the shredded Jack cheese on the tortillas and broil 6 inches from the heat until the cheese is melted, about 1 minute. Pile the salad on the tortillas, fold them in half and serve right away. —*Alice Waters*

WINE Lively, fragrant Provençal rosé: 2013 Domaine Houchart.

Zucchini Quesadilla with Spicy Salsa Roja
⏱ Active **20 min**; Total **45 min**
Serves **2**

- 1 lb. tomatoes, cored and quartered
- 1 small onion, peeled and quartered
- 4 garlic cloves
- ¼ cup canola oil
- 6 dried árbol chiles, stemmed
- 1 chipotle chile in adobo
- 2 Tbsp. apple cider vinegar
- 1 tsp. sugar
  Kosher salt
  Two 10-inch flour tortillas
- ½ cup shredded Monterey Jack cheese
- 2 small zucchinis, thinly sliced crosswise
  Chopped cilantro and thinly sliced Fresno chiles, for garnish

1. Preheat the broiler. On a rimmed baking sheet, toss the tomatoes, onion and garlic with 2 tablespoons of the oil. Broil 6 inches from the heat for 20 minutes, or until the tomatoes and onion are softened and nicely charred.

2. In a small skillet, toast the árbol chiles over moderately low heat, stirring, until lightly charred, 3 minutes; transfer to a blender. Add the broiled tomatoes, onion and garlic along with the chipotle chile, vinegar and sugar and puree until smooth. Season the *salsa roja* with salt.

3. In a large cast-iron skillet, heat 1 tablespoon of the oil. Place 1 tortilla in the skillet and scatter the cheese and zucchini evenly on top. Drizzle over some of the *salsa roja* and top with the second tortilla. Cook over moderately high heat until crisp on the bottom, 3 minutes. Flip the quesadilla, add the remaining 1 tablespoon of canola oil and cook until the cheese is melted, 2 minutes. Slice the quesadilla into wedges, transfer to a plate, garnish with the cilantro and Fresno chiles and serve with the remaining *salsa roja*. —*Walter Manzke*

COCKTAIL Simple tequila drink: Limey margarita or a Paloma (made with grapefruit juice and soda).

Shredded-Tofu Stir-Fry
⏱ Total **20 min**; Serves **4**

Shredding extra-firm tofu before stir-frying gives it a chewier texture that's fantastic in this superquick stir-fry tossed with a spicy, creamy dressing.

- 1 Tbsp. white wine vinegar
- 1 tsp. honey
- 1 small serrano chile, seeded and minced
- ¼ cup extra-virgin olive oil
- 1 Tbsp. crème fraîche, buttermilk or sour cream
  Salt
- ½ cup raw *pepitas* (hulled pumpkin seeds)
- 4 oz. pea shoots (2 cups)
- 8 oz. extra-firm tofu, drained well and shredded on the large holes of a box grater
- 2 Tbsp. black sesame seeds

1. In a small bowl, whisk the vinegar with the honey, serrano and 3 tablespoons of the olive oil; whisk in the crème fraîche and season the dressing with salt.

2. In a large skillet, toast the *pepitas* over moderate heat, stirring, until golden, about 5 minutes. Transfer the *pepitas* to a small bowl. In the skillet, heat the remaining 1 tablespoon of olive oil. Add the pea shoots and stir-fry over high heat just until wilted, about 30 seconds; transfer to a plate.

3. Add the tofu and two-thirds each of the *pepitas*, sesame seeds and dressing to the skillet. Stir-fry over moderate heat until the tofu is warmed through. Season with salt and transfer to a platter. Top with the pea shoots and the remaining *pepitas*, sesame seeds and dressing and serve. —*Heidi Swanson*

MAKE AHEAD The dressing can be refrigerated overnight.

WINE Zippy, lemon-scented Grüner Veltliner: 2012 Sepp Moser.

Market Math: Peppers

1 Spicy Pickled Peppers

Put 12 oz. chopped **peppers** and **chiles** into a 1-quart jar. In a saucepan, heat ½ cup **water** with 1½ cups distilled **white vinegar**, 1 Tbsp. **kosher salt**, 2 tsp. **caraway seeds** and 1 tsp. **sugar** until the sugar dissolves. Pour over the peppers and let stand until cool.

2 Grilled Pepper-and-Steak Sandwiches

In a bowl, whisk ¼ cup **canola oil**, ½ cup **soy sauce**, 7 minced **garlic cloves** and 1 Tbsp. minced **ginger**. Add 2 thinly sliced **green bell peppers**, 2 bunches of halved **scallions** and 1 lb. thinly sliced **rib eye steak** and toss. Grill over moderately high heat, 2 minutes for steak, 3 minutes for scallions and 8 minutes for peppers. Pile onto **buns** with **mayo** and **pickles**.

3 Mixed-Pepper Pasta

In a skillet, heat 2 Tbsp. **olive oil**. Add 1 chopped **onion**, 5 minced **garlic cloves** and 1½ lbs. chopped **bell peppers**. Season with **salt** and **pepper**. Cook over moderate heat until soft. Add 1 cup halved **cherry tomatoes**, ¼ cup chopped **parsley** and 1 lb. cooked **spaghetti** along with 1 cup of its **cooking water**. Cook, tossing, for 1 minute.

4 Peppers and Tuna

In a baking dish, combine 2 cups **olive oil** with 1 head peeled and crushed **garlic cloves**, 4 thinly sliced **poblanos** and ⅓ cup drained **capers** and roast at 450° for 20 minutes. Let cool to warm, then stir in two 8-oz. jars good-quality drained **tuna** and ½ cup **basil**.
–Kay Chun

GRILLED POTATO SALAD
WITH SCALLION VINAIGRETTE
Recipe, page 250

Potatoes, Grains & Beans

PAGE NUMBERS IN RED INDICATE F&W STAFF FAVORITES

Granny's Roasted Spuds

Active **20 min**; Total **1 hr**
Serves **6 to 8**

TV chef Curtis Stone likes using baking potatoes for their light, fluffy texture, but Yukon Golds, which are slightly creamy, are quite good here too.

- **3 lbs. large Yukon Gold or medium baking potatoes—peeled, halved lengthwise and cut in half crosswise on the diagonal**
- **5 large unpeeled shallots, quartered lengthwise**
- **3 large unpeeled garlic cloves, lightly smashed**
- **4 medium rosemary sprigs**
- **1 Tbsp. thyme leaves**
- **¼ cup extra-virgin olive oil**
- **2 Tbsp. unsalted butter, melted**
  Kosher salt and freshly ground pepper

1. Preheat the oven to 425°. Set a large rimmed baking sheet on the lowest rack of the oven. In a large bowl, toss the potatoes with the shallots, garlic, rosemary sprigs, thyme, olive oil and butter. Season with salt and pepper.

2. Remove the hot baking sheet from the oven and scrape the potatoes onto it, spreading them in an even layer. Roast on the bottom rack for 40 to 45 minutes, turning occasionally, until the potatoes are golden and crisp. Transfer to a platter and serve. —*Curtis Stone*

Fingerling Potatoes with Kale Pesto

Total **35 min**; Serves **6**

- **2 lbs. fingerling potatoes**
  Kosher salt
- **2 cups packed chopped kale**
- **½ cup toasted almonds**
- **2 Tbsp. fresh lemon juice**
- **1 small garlic clove**
- **¾ cup extra-virgin olive oil**
  Freshly ground pepper

1. In a medium saucepan, cover the potatoes with water and bring to a boil. Add a generous pinch of salt and simmer over moderate heat until tender, about 20 minutes. Drain and let cool slightly, then cut the potatoes in half lengthwise.

2. Meanwhile, in a food processor, combine the kale with the almonds, lemon juice and garlic and pulse until the kale and nuts are very finely chopped. With the machine on, drizzle in the olive oil and process until incorporated. Season with salt and pepper.

3. In a large bowl, toss the warm fingerlings with the pesto and serve. —*Justin Chapple*

Tornado Hash Brown

Active **30 min**; Total **1 hr**; Serves **10**

This skillet-size hash brown was inspired by a dish at the beloved Tornado Steakhouse in Madison, Wisconsin. Slicing potatoes lengthwise on a mandoline makes for long, dramatic-looking strands. (You can also julienne them in a food processor.)

- **2½ lbs. baking potatoes, peeled and cut into medium julienne**
  Kosher salt and pepper
- **½ cup canola oil**
- **1 cup thinly sliced scallions, whites and light green parts only, plus sliced scallion greens for garnish**
  Sour cream, for serving

1. Preheat the oven to 400°. In a colander, rinse the julienned potatoes until the water runs clear; drain well and pat very dry. In a large bowl, toss the potatoes with 2 teaspoons of salt and ½ teaspoon of pepper.

2. In a 10-inch ovenproof skillet, heat the canola oil until shimmering. Remove the pan from the heat and add half of the potatoes. Return the skillet to the heat and, using a spatula, spread the potatoes in an even layer. Scatter the 1 cup of thinly sliced scallions evenly over the potatoes, then scatter the remaining potatoes on top. Using the spatula, shape the potatoes into a neat cake.

3. Cook the potatoes over moderately high heat until well browned on the bottom, 9 minutes. Using a metal spatula, flip the cake, then cook over moderately high heat until lightly browned on the bottom, 5 minutes. Transfer the skillet to the oven and bake for 12 minutes, until cooked through. Slide the hash brown onto paper towels to drain. Transfer to a plate and season with salt and pepper. Garnish with sliced scallion greens and serve with sour cream. —*Mehdi Brunet-Benkritly and Gabriel Stulman*

Best-Ever Potato Latkes

Total **50 min**; Serves **6**

Niki Russ Federman of New York City's Russ & Daughters makes the tastiest, crispiest latkes with both scallions and onion. "These latkes are very traditional—my favorite way to eat them is with crème fraîche, smoked salmon and salmon roe on top," she says.

- **2½ lbs. baking potatoes, peeled and coarsely shredded on a box grater**
- **1 medium onion, coarsely shredded on a box grater**
- **2 large eggs, beaten**
- **½ cup finely chopped scallions**
- **¼ cup matzo meal**
- **3 Tbsp. unsalted butter, melted and cooled slightly**
- **2 tsp. kosher salt**
- **½ tsp. black pepper**
- **½ tsp. baking powder**
  Vegetable oil, for frying
  Applesauce, sour cream, smoked salmon and salmon roe, for serving

1. In a colander set over a large bowl, toss the potatoes with the onion and squeeze dry. Let the potatoes and onion drain for 2 to 3 minutes, then pour off the liquid in the bowl, leaving the starchy paste at the bottom. Add the potatoes, onion, eggs, scallions, matzo meal, butter, salt, pepper and baking powder to the bowl and mix well.

2. In a large skillet, heat an ⅛-inch layer of oil until shimmering. Spoon ¼-cup mounds of the latke batter into the skillet about 2 inches apart and flatten slightly with a spatula. Fry the latkes over moderately high heat, turning once, until golden and crisp, 5 to 7 minutes. Transfer the latkes to paper towels to drain, then transfer to a platter. Repeat to make the remaining latkes, adding more oil to the skillet as needed. Serve with applesauce, sour cream, smoked salmon and salmon roe. —*Niki Russ Federman*

MAKE AHEAD The latkes can be fried early in the day; recrisp on a baking sheet in a 350° oven.

WINE Refreshing, frothy sparkling wine from Spain: NV Vilarnau Brut Cava.

TORNADO HASH BROWN AND, TOP, TORN GARLIC BREAD (P. 188)

Smashed Potatoes with Wagon Wheel Fondue

Active **30 min**; Total **1 hr 20 min**; Serves **8**

For his over-the-top roasted potatoes with creamy cheese sauce, San Francisco chef Stuart Brioza uses the semi-firm cow-milk cheese Wagon Wheel from Cowgirl Creamery in the Bay Area; you can substitute another good melting cheese, like raclette.

POTATOES

3½ lbs. small Yukon Gold or fingerling potatoes, scrubbed

Kosher salt

½ cup extra-virgin olive oil

Freshly ground pepper

2 Tbsp. chopped thyme

1 Tbsp. chopped rosemary

12 garlic cloves, smashed

FONDUE

1½ cups heavy cream

9 oz. Cowgirl Creamery Wagon Wheel, raclette or imported Fontina cheese, shredded (3 cups)

3 large egg yolks, beaten

2 Tbsp. unsalted butter

¼ cup crème fraîche

Small parsley leaves, for garnish

1. Cook the potatoes Preheat the oven to 400°. In a small pot, cover the potatoes with water. Add salt, bring to a simmer and cook until the potatoes are tender, about 10 minutes. Drain the potatoes and spread them out on 2 baking sheets to cool slightly. Lightly crush the potatoes so that they split at the sides but remain intact.

2. Drizzle the oil over the potatoes and season with salt and pepper, carefully turning to coat. Sprinkle the thyme, rosemary and garlic on top. Roast the potatoes for about 30 minutes, flipping them halfway through, until golden and crisp; discard the garlic.

3. Meanwhile, make the fondue In a saucepan, bring the cream just to a boil. Put the cheese in a heatproof bowl set over a saucepan of simmering water (the bowl should be larger than the pan). Stir in the hot cream until the cheese is melted and smooth. Stir in the egg yolks, butter and crème fraîche and cook over low heat, stirring, until thickened, about 10 minutes. Let cool slightly.

4. Arrange the potatoes on a platter and drizzle with a little of the cheese fondue. Garnish with parsley and serve with the remaining fondue. —*Stuart Brioza*

Poutine-Style Twice-Baked Potatoes

Active **1 hr**; Total **2 hr 30 min**
Serves **6**

At Boston Chops, chef Christopher Coombs takes inspiration from the Canadian french fry classic *poutine*, topping stuffed baked potatoes with rich gravy, melted mozzarella and bits of crisp bacon.

GRAVY

2 Tbsp. unsalted butter

2 Tbsp. all-purpose flour

2 cups chicken stock or low-sodium broth

1 Tbsp. veal demiglace (optional)

½ tsp. finely chopped sage

½ tsp. finely chopped thyme

1 Tbsp. fresh lemon juice

1 Tbsp. heavy cream

Kosher salt and freshly ground black pepper

STUFFED POTATOES

6 baked potatoes (about ½ lb. each)

6 Tbsp. unsalted butter, cubed and chilled

1 cup milk, warmed

½ cup sour cream

3 oz. freshly grated Parmigiano-Reggiano cheese (1 cup)

1 Tbsp. Dijon mustard

Pinch of cayenne pepper

⅓ cup chopped chives

Kosher salt and freshly ground black pepper

Vegetable oil, for frying

6 oz. thick-sliced bacon, cut crosswise ½ inch thick

1 cup shredded mozzarella cheese

Sour cream, thinly sliced scallions, parsley leaves and celery leaves, for garnish

1. Make the gravy In a small saucepan, melt the butter. Add the flour and cook over moderate heat, stirring, until deep golden brown, about 5 minutes. Add the stock, demiglace, sage and thyme and cook until thickened to a gravy-like consistency, 15 to 20 minutes. Stir in the lemon juice and heavy cream and season with salt and black pepper. Keep warm.

2. Prepare the stuffed potatoes Cut one ½-inch-wide strip off the top of each baked potato and reserve. Scoop the potato flesh into a large bowl. Place the potato shells on a baking sheet. Using a ricer, mash the potato flesh with the butter into another large bowl; add the warm milk and mix until blended. Stir in the sour cream, Parmigiano, mustard, cayenne and chives and season with salt and black pepper.

3. In a small saucepan, heat the vegetable oil to 350°. Scrape the flesh off the reserved strips of the potato tops. Cut the skins into wedges and fry until golden and crisp, about 2 minutes. Drain the potato skins on a paper towel–lined plate.

4. Preheat the oven to 450°. In a small non-stick skillet, cook the bacon over moderate heat, stirring occasionally, until golden and crisp, 5 to 7 minutes. Drain the bacon on paper towels.

5. Spoon about ⅔ cup of the mashed potato mixture into each potato shell and make a well in the center. Bake for about 20 minutes, until heated through and golden on top. Spoon some gravy into the well of each potato, then top with the shredded mozzarella. Bake the potatoes for about 5 minutes, until the cheese is melted. Transfer the potatoes to a serving platter and top with the bacon. Garnish with sour cream, scallions, parsley and celery leaves and the crispy potato skins and serve. —*Christopher Coombs*

MAKE AHEAD The gravy can be refrigerated for up to 3 days.

Market Math: Potatoes

1 Potato-Apple Pancakes

In a bowl, grate 2 peeled **baking potatoes** and 1 peeled **green apple**; mix and squeeze dry. Add ¼ cup chopped **dill** and 3 Tbsp. **flour**; season with **salt** and **pepper**. In a nonstick skillet, heat **canola oil**. Fry flattened ¼-cup mounds of the potato mixture over moderately high heat until golden on both sides. Serve with sour cream.

2 Crispy Buffalo Potatoes

On a baking sheet, toss 3 **baking potatoes**, cut into ½-inch wedges, with 2 Tbsp. **olive oil**; season with **salt** and **pepper**. Roast at 450° for 40 minutes, turning once, until golden. In a bowl, mix 3 Tbsp. **melted butter** with 2 Tbsp. **hot sauce**; season with **salt** and **pepper**. Toss with the potatoes. Serve with **blue cheese dressing**.

3 Stuffed Baked Potatoes

Bake 4 **potatoes** and slice halfway down the centers. In a skillet, cook 1¼ lbs. **mixed mushrooms** in 1 Tbsp. **butter** and 2 Tbsp. **olive oil** until tender; season with **salt** and **pepper**. Stuff each potato with 1 Tbsp. **butter** and 2 Tbsp. shredded **Fontina**. Top with the mushrooms and more cheese. Bake at 450° for 3 minutes, until the cheese melts. Garnish with chopped **parsley**.

4 Potato–Green Bean Salad

In a bowl, whisk ½ cup **olive oil**, 2 Tbsp. minced **shallot**, ¼ cup chopped **tarragon** and 3 Tbsp. each of **lemon juice** and **Dijon mustard**. Stir in ½ lb. blanched **haricots verts**. Boil 2 lbs. peeled **baking potatoes**, cut into 1-inch pieces, until tender. Drain, toss with the beans and season with **salt** and **pepper**. –*Kay Chun*

Grill-Baked Potatoes with Chive Butter

Active **25 min**; Total **2 hr 10 min**; Serves **4**

- 1 **stick unsalted butter, softened**
- ¾ **cup finely chopped chives, plus more for garnish**
- ½ **cup sour cream, plus more for serving**
- 1½ **tsp. kosher salt**
- 1 **tsp. freshly ground pepper**
  Four 10-oz. baking potatoes

1. In a medium bowl, combine the butter, ¾ cup of chives, ½ cup of sour cream and the salt and pepper; mix until smooth. Transfer the butter to a large sheet of plastic wrap and form into a log. Wrap and refrigerate until firm, about 1 hour.

2. Light a gas grill. Slice each potato crosswise at ⅓-inch intervals, cutting down but not all the way through the potato. Cut the chive butter into thin slices, then carefully tuck the butter in between the potato slices. Wrap each potato tightly in foil.

3. Set the potatoes on the grill over low heat, cover and cook, turning occasionally, until tender, 45 to 50 minutes. Unwrap the potatoes, garnish with chives and serve with sour cream. —*Tom Mylan*

MAKE AHEAD The chive butter can be wrapped in plastic and refrigerated for up to 2 days.

Grilled Potato Salad with Scallion Vinaigrette

📷 PAGE 244

Active **20 min**; Total **40 min**; Serves **6**

- 1½ lbs. fingerling potatoes
  Kosher salt
- 10 scallions, trimmed
- ⅓ cup extra-virgin olive oil, plus more for brushing
  Ground black pepper
- 2 Tbsp. unseasoned rice vinegar
- 2 tsp. fresh lemon juice
  Piment d'Espelette (see Note)
- 1 small jalapeño—stemmed, seeded and thinly sliced

1. In a large saucepan, cover the potatoes with water and bring to a boil. Add a generous pinch of salt and simmer over moderate heat until just tender, 15 minutes. Drain and let cool slightly, then halve lengthwise.

2. Meanwhile, light a grill or heat a grill pan. Brush the scallions with oil and season with salt and black pepper. Grill over high heat, turning, until lightly charred, about 2 minutes. Transfer to a plate, cover with plastic wrap and let steam for 10 minutes. Cut the scallions into 1-inch lengths.

3. Brush the potatoes with oil and season with salt and pepper. Grill cut side down over high heat until lightly charred, 3 to 5 minutes. Transfer to a plate.

4. In a large bowl, whisk the ⅓ cup of olive oil with the vinegar and lemon juice. Add the scallions and potatoes and toss well. Season with salt and piment d'Espelette and toss again. Scatter the jalapeño slices on top, garnish with a large pinch of piment d'Espelette and serve warm or at room temperature. —*Mark Liberman*

NOTE Piment d'Espelette, a mildly spicy ground red pepper from the Basque region of France, is available at specialty food shops and lepicerie.com.

Eggplant Potato Salad

Total **30 min**; Serves **4**

In this mayo-free potato salad, F&W's Kay Chun combines thick-cut bacon and baby red potatoes with silky eggplant. Dill and lemon add a bright, refreshing hit of flavor.

- 4 oz. thick-cut bacon, cut into lardons
- 2 Tbsp. extra-virgin olive oil
- ½ lb. baby red potatoes, quartered
- 1 small red onion, thinly sliced
- 2 Japanese eggplants (¾ lb.), quartered lengthwise and thinly sliced crosswise
  Kosher salt and pepper
- 1 Tbsp. fresh lemon juice
- 2 Tbsp. chopped dill

In a large, deep skillet, cook the bacon over moderate heat, stirring, until lightly golden, about 5 minutes. Add the olive oil, potatoes, onion and eggplants and season with salt and pepper. Cover and cook over moderately low heat, stirring occasionally, until the eggplants and potatoes are tender and golden, 12 to 15 minutes. Stir in the lemon juice and dill and serve warm. —*Kay Chun*

Potato and Roasted Cauliflower Salad

Active **40 min**; Total **1 hr 15 min**; Serves **10**

Cauliflower florets are a sly substitute for half of the baby potatoes in this creamy salad. The white-on-white combo gets a zingy lift from capers, Dijon mustard and grated fresh horseradish.

- 3 lbs. cauliflower, cut into 1-inch florets
- ¼ cup grapeseed oil
  Kosher salt
- 1¼ lbs. fingerling potatoes, halved lengthwise and sliced crosswise ¼ inch thick
- 2 Tbsp. Champagne vinegar
- 1¼ lbs. baby red potatoes, halved and sliced ¼ inch thick
- 1 cup mayonnaise
- 2 small shallots, minced
- 2 Tbsp. Dijon mustard
- ¼ cup brined capers—drained, rinsed and finely chopped
- ¼ cup finely chopped parsley, plus more for garnish
  Finely grated fresh horseradish, for serving

1. Preheat the oven to 400°. On a large rimmed baking sheet, toss the cauliflower with the oil and season with salt. Roast for 25 to 30 minutes, stirring once, until just tender and lightly browned; let cool.

2. Meanwhile, in a large saucepan of salted boiling water, cook the fingerlings just until tender, about 8 minutes. Using a slotted spoon, spread the fingerlings on a large baking sheet and sprinkle with 1 tablespoon of the vinegar. Repeat with the baby red potatoes and remaining 1 tablespoon of vinegar; let cool.

3. In a large bowl, whisk the mayonnaise, shallots, mustard, capers and the ¼ cup of parsley. Add the cauliflower and potatoes and toss. Season with salt and garnish with parsley. Serve with horseradish. —*Paul Berglund*

MAKE AHEAD The potato salad can be refrigerated in an airtight container for up to 4 hours. Bring to room temperature and garnish just before serving.

POTATO AND ROASTED
CAULIFLOWER SALAD

Sweet Potatoes with Crispy Rice Topping

Active **45 min**; Total **1 hr 30 min**; Serves **12**

Instead of marshmallows, these sweet potatoes get a crunchy topping inspired by Rice Krispies Treats.

- **5 lbs. medium sweet potatoes**
- **Nonstick cooking spray**
- **3 cups Rice Krispies**
- **¼ tsp. baking soda**
- **Kosher salt**
- **⅛ tsp. cayenne pepper, plus more for seasoning**
- **½ cup plus 2 Tbsp. sugar**
- **6½ Tbsp. unsalted butter, plus more for serving**
- **¼ cup heavy cream**
- **½ tsp. finely grated orange zest**
- **Freshly ground black pepper**

1. Preheat the oven to 350° and line a large rimmed baking sheet with foil. Prick each sweet potato all over with a fork and transfer to the baking sheet. Bake the sweet potatoes until tender, about 1 hour, turning them over halfway through baking. Let cool slightly.

2. Meanwhile, lightly coat a large rimmed baking sheet, 2 large spoons and a large heatproof bowl with nonstick cooking spray. Pour the Rice Krispies into the bowl. In a small bowl, mix the baking soda with ¼ teaspoon of salt and ⅛ teaspoon of cayenne.

3. In a medium saucepan, combine the sugar with ½ tablespoon of the butter and ¼ cup of water and bring to a boil, stirring until the sugar dissolves. Boil over moderately high heat, swirling the pan occasionally, until a golden caramel forms, about 7 minutes. Remove from the heat and stir in the baking soda mixture; the caramel will foam. Immediately drizzle all of the hot caramel over the cereal and, using the 2 greased spoons, quickly toss to coat. Spread the topping on the prepared baking sheet in an even layer and let cool completely, then break into pieces.

4. Scoop the sweet potato flesh into a food processor. Add the remaining 6 tablespoons of butter and the cream, orange zest and a generous pinch of cayenne and puree until smooth. Season with salt and black pepper. Transfer the sweet potatoes to a serving bowl and dollop with additional butter. Serve, passing the crispy rice topping at the table. —*Dana Cowin*

Potato and Radicchio Salad with Montasio Cheese

Total **45 min**; Serves **8 as a starter**

- **1½ lbs. German butterball or baby Yukon Gold potatoes**
- **Kosher salt**
- **¼ cup extra-virgin olive oil**
- **Pepper**
- **One ½-lb. head of radicchio—halved lengthwise, cored and coarsely chopped**
- **1 Tbsp. red wine vinegar**
- **½ cup finely shredded young Montasio cheese (1½ oz.)**
- **½ Golden Delicious apple, peeled and shredded**
- **Fresh horseradish, for serving**

1. In a medium saucepan, cover the potatoes with water and bring to a boil. Add a generous pinch of salt and simmer over moderate heat until tender, about 15 minutes. Drain and spread the potatoes on a plate to cool slightly, then peel and cut into ⅓-inch-thick slices. Transfer the potatoes to a medium bowl and toss with 2 tablespoons of the olive oil; season generously with salt and pepper.

2. Meanwhile, in a large skillet, heat the remaining 2 tablespoons of olive oil. Add the radicchio and cook over moderately high heat, tossing, until just wilted, about 3 minutes. Stir in the vinegar and season with salt and pepper.

3. Arrange the sliced potatoes on a platter or plates and spoon the radicchio on top. Scatter the cheese and apple over the salad, then finely grate fresh horseradish on top. Serve, passing additional freshly grated horseradish at the table.
—*Lachlan Mackinnon-Patterson*

Sautéed Golden Potato Salad with Leek and Black Olives

Total **40 min**; Serves **4**

"I love opposites: raw and cooked, hot and cold," says renowned Argentinean chef Francis Mallmann. "I don't believe in harmony; that's for children." Here, he redefines potato salad by tossing contrasting ingredients together in unusual combinations, like warm, crisp potatoes and sautéed leek with fresh mixed salad greens.

- **3 small baking potatoes (1¼ lbs.), peeled and halved**
- **1 quart low-sodium chicken broth**
- **2 Tbsp. extra-virgin olive oil, plus more for drizzling**
- **1 leek, white and tender green parts only, sliced crosswise ¼ inch thick**
- **4 cups mixed lettuces, such as arugula, mesclun and sunflower sprouts**
- **12 pitted black olives, chopped**
- **6 anchovies, thinly sliced**
- **Kosher salt and pepper**
- **Red wine vinegar, for drizzling**

1. In a medium saucepan, cover the potatoes with the broth and bring to a simmer. Cook over moderate heat until the potatoes are tender when pierced with a fork, 20 minutes. Using a slotted spoon, transfer the potatoes to a plate. Discard the broth, or strain and reserve for making soup later.

2. Meanwhile, in a large skillet, heat 1 tablespoon of the olive oil. Add the leek and cook over moderate heat, stirring occasionally, until softened and golden, about 3 minutes. Transfer to a plate.

3. Heat the remaining 1 tablespoon of olive oil in the skillet. Add the potatoes and cook over moderately high heat, turning, until golden and crisp, 2 minutes per side.

4. Arrange the lettuces on plates. Using your hands, break the potatoes into large chunks and arrange them on top of the lettuces. Scatter the leek, olives and anchovies on top. Season the salad with salt and pepper, drizzle with vinegar and olive oil and serve. —*Francis Mallmann*

MAKE AHEAD The boiled potatoes can be refrigerated overnight; let return to room temperature before crisping.

SWEET POTATOES WITH
CRISPY RICE TOPPING

Collard Greens, Blue Potato and Bacon Salad

Active **45 min; Total 1 hr 30 min**
Serves **8**

- 6 oz. thick-cut bacon, cut into ¼-inch dice
- 1 lb. baby blue potatoes, quartered
  Kosher salt and freshly ground pepper
- ½ cup chopped walnuts
- 8 quail eggs (see Note)
- ¼ cup plus 2 Tbsp. extra-virgin olive oil
- 2 Tbsp. apple cider vinegar
- 1 Tbsp. Dijon mustard
  Pinch of sugar
- 1½ lbs. young collard greens—stems discarded, leaves halved lengthwise and cut into ½-inch-wide ribbons
- 4 oz. Stilton cheese, crumbled

1. Preheat the oven to 400°. In a large skillet, cook the bacon over moderate heat, stirring occasionally, until crisp, about 8 minutes. Using a slotted spoon, transfer the bacon to paper towels.

2. On a large rimmed baking sheet, toss the quartered potatoes with the rendered bacon fat and season with salt and pepper. Roast for about 40 minutes, stirring once, until the potatoes are tender and browned. Let cool.

3. Meanwhile, spread the walnuts in a pie plate. Bake for about 12 minutes, until golden and fragrant. Let cool slightly, then roughly chop the walnuts.

4. In a small saucepan, cover the quail eggs with water. Bring to a boil and cook for 2 minutes. Drain the eggs and cool them under cold running water. Peel the eggs and cut them in half lengthwise.

5. In a very large bowl, whisk the olive oil with the vinegar, mustard and sugar. Season the dressing with salt and pepper. Add the collards, bacon and potatoes and toss well. Scatter the walnuts, eggs and Stilton on top and serve. —*Melia Marden*

NOTE Hard-boiled chicken eggs cut into smaller pieces would be a fine substitute for quail eggs.

WINE Robust, juicy California rosé: 2012 La Clarine Farm.

Grilled Sweet Potatoes with Jerk Vinaigrette

Total **1 hr 45 min; Serves 6**

- ½ cup Pepsi
- ¼ cup soy sauce
- 2 Tbsp. unsulfured molasses
- 2 Tbsp. minced peeled fresh ginger
- 1 Tbsp. dark brown sugar
- 2 tsp. red wine vinegar
- 1 tsp. minced thyme
- 1 small garlic clove, minced
- ¼ tsp. *vadouvan* (see Note) or curry powder
- ⅛ tsp. ground allspice
- ⅛ tsp. ground cinnamon
  Kosher salt and pepper
- ½ cup mayonnaise
- 2 tsp. extra-virgin olive oil, plus more for brushing
  Six 6-oz. sweet potatoes, baked and peeled
- 1½ cups torn escarole, light green leaves only
- ½ cup finely diced fresh pineapple
- ½ cup each of finely diced red and orange bell pepper

1. In a saucepan, boil the Pepsi over moderately high heat until reduced to ¼ cup, about 3 minutes. Transfer to a blender. Add the soy sauce, molasses, ginger, brown sugar, vinegar, thyme, garlic, *vadouvan*, allspice and cinnamon and puree. Season the jerk vinaigrette with salt and pepper.

2. In a small bowl, whisk the mayonnaise with 2 tablespoons of the jerk vinaigrette and season with salt and pepper.

3. Light a grill or heat a grill pan; brush with oil. In a bowl, gently toss the sweet potatoes with half of the remaining jerk vinaigrette and season with salt and pepper. Grill the potatoes over moderately high heat, turning and basting with the remaining vinaigrette, until lightly charred all over, 6 to 8 minutes. Transfer to a platter and lightly break them apart with a fork.

4. In a bowl, toss the escarole, pineapple and bell peppers with the 2 teaspoons of oil; season with salt and pepper. Scatter the salad over the grilled potatoes and serve right away, with the jerk mayonnaise. —*John Fraser*

NOTE *Vadouvan*—a French spice blend with Indian flavors that can include fried onion, garlic, curry leaves, fenugreek and mustard seeds—is available online from thespicehouse.com.

Curried Fried Rice with Smoked Trout

Total **30 min; Serves 4**

You can use any kind of smoked white fish (grouper, snapper, flounder) for this fragrant rice. For a milder dish, seed and de-rib the chile before mincing.

- 2 Tbsp. unsalted butter
- ¾ cup diced tomatoes
- 1 Tbsp. curry powder
- 1 Tbsp. peeled and minced fresh ginger
- 1 tsp. minced Thai bird chile
- 4 garlic cloves, minced
- 2 shallots, minced
- 3 cups leftover or cooked and cooled basmati rice
- 1 cup flaked smoked trout (about 8 oz.)
- 1 Tbsp. extra-virgin olive oil
- 2 large eggs, lightly beaten
- ½ cup coarsely chopped basil
- ½ cup coarsely chopped cilantro
- ½ cup coarsely chopped mint
- ½ cup thinly sliced scallions, green and light green parts only
  Kosher salt and pepper
- ¼ cup chopped unsalted roasted peanuts

In a large skillet, melt the butter over moderately high heat. Add the tomatoes, curry powder, ginger, chile, garlic and shallots and cook, stirring, until the tomatoes are beginning to brown, about 4 minutes. Stir in the rice and trout and cook, stirring once or twice, until the rice is toasted and crisped, 3 minutes. Using a spoon, make a hole in the middle of the rice and pour in the olive oil. Add the eggs and let them cook, undisturbed, until the bottom starts to set. Stir in the herbs and scallions and season with salt and pepper. Transfer the fried rice to a platter, sprinkle with the peanuts and serve immediately. —*Adam Evans*

WINE Citrusy, lightly sweet Loire Valley Chenin Blanc: 2012 La Craie Vouvray.

CURRIED FRIED RICE WITH
SMOKED TROUT

Japanese Pizza

📷 PAGE 4

⏱ Total **45 min**; Serves **4**

"Think fried rice meets pizza," says avant-garde Chicago chef Grant Achatz, who makes this crazy-fun dish for dinner with his kids. You can pick your toppings, he says, but the most important one is the Manchego cheese, which has a flavor that's similar to miso.

- 2½ oz. shiitake mushrooms, stemmed and caps thinly sliced
- 2 Tbsp. soy sauce
- 2 Tbsp. canola oil
- ½ tsp. toasted sesame oil
- 3 cups cooked sushi rice
- 5 oz. firm tofu, sliced
- 2 tsp. *unagi* sauce (optional; see Note)
- ⅓ cup shelled edamame
- 5 oz. Manchego cheese, shredded (about 1½ cups)
- ½ cup soy bean sprouts
- Kosher salt
- *Togarashi* and toasted white and black sesame seeds, for sprinkling
- 1 cup large bonito flakes
- 6 shiso leaves, thinly sliced
- ¼ cup cilantro leaves

1. Preheat the oven to 375°. In a small bowl, toss the mushrooms with the soy sauce. Let stand for 5 minutes, tossing frequently; drain, discarding the liquid.

2. In a 9-inch ovenproof nonstick skillet, heat both oils. Press the rice into the skillet in an even layer about ¼ inch thick. Cook over moderately high heat until the bottom is golden and crisp, 10 to 12 minutes. Top with the tofu slices in a single layer and drizzle with *unagi* sauce. Top with the shiitake, edamame, shredded cheese and bean sprouts and season with salt. Sprinkle with *togarashi* and sesame seeds.

3. Transfer the skillet to the oven and bake the pizza on the top shelf for 15 to 17 minutes, until the top is golden. Slide the pizza onto a platter; top with the bonito, shiso and cilantro and serve. —*Grant Achatz*

NOTE Sweet-salty *unagi* sauce is available at Japanese markets.

BEER Citrusy Belgian-style wheat beer: Hitachino Nest White Ale.

Shrimp-Asparagus Risotto

Total **1 hr 10 min**; Serves **6**

- 1 lb. asparagus, trimmed
- ¾ lb. medium shrimp, shelled and deveined
- Salt and pepper
- 1 Tbsp. extra-virgin olive oil
- 2 cups vegetable stock
- 6 Tbsp. unsalted butter
- 1 small onion, minced
- 12 oz. carnaroli rice
- 1 cup dry white wine
- Pinch of saffron threads
- ¼ cup freshly grated Parmigiano-Reggiano cheese

1. Cook the asparagus in a medium saucepan of salted boiling water until they are crisp-tender, 1 to 2 minutes. Drain and cool under running water, then cut into 1-inch pieces.

2. Season the shrimp with salt and pepper. In a large skillet, heat the olive oil until shimmering. Add the shrimp and cook over moderately high heat, turning once, until just white throughout, about 3 minutes. Transfer to a plate.

3. In the medium saucepan, bring 4 cups of water and the stock to a boil. Cover and keep warm.

4. In a large saucepan, melt 4 tablespoons of the butter. Add the onion and a generous pinch of salt and cook over moderate heat, stirring, until softened, about 5 minutes. Add the rice and cook, stirring, until the grains are evenly coated with butter, 2 minutes. Add the wine and simmer until almost evaporated. Add enough stock to just cover the rice and cook, stirring, until the stock has been absorbed. Stir in the saffron and continue stirring in stock, ½ cup at a time, until nearly absorbed between additions. The risotto is done when the rice is al dente and suspended in a creamy sauce, about 25 minutes. Stir in the cheese and remaining 2 tablespoons of butter. Fold in the asparagus and shrimp. Season the risotto with salt and pepper and serve. —*Daniele Sera*

WINE Lemony Tuscan white: 2012 San Quirico Vernaccia di San Gimignano.

Broccoli Rabe Risotto with Grilled Lemon

Total **1 hr 15 min**; Serves **6**

Lightly charred lemon and mascarpone cheese enhance this luscious vegetarian risotto, which is made with broccoli rabe puree and vegetable stock.

- ½ lemon, thinly sliced crosswise
- Olive oil, for brushing
- ½ lb. broccoli rabe, trimmed and cut into large pieces
- 2 cups vegetable stock or low-sodium broth
- 6 Tbsp. unsalted butter
- 1 small onion, finely chopped
- 1 garlic clove, minced
- Kosher salt
- 1½ cups arborio rice (about ¾ lb.)
- 1 cup dry white wine
- ½ cup freshly grated Parmigiano-Reggiano cheese
- 2 Tbsp. finely chopped tarragon
- 2 Tbsp. finely chopped flat-leaf parsley
- Freshly ground pepper
- Mascarpone cheese, for serving

1. Light a grill or heat a grill pan. Brush the lemon slices with oil and grill over high heat, turning once, until lightly charred, 2 to 3 minutes total. Transfer to a cutting board and let cool. Finely dice the lemon.

2. Meanwhile, in a large saucepan of salted boiling water, blanch the broccoli rabe until tender, about 3 minutes. Drain and cool under running water; drain again. Transfer the broccoli rabe to a food processor and puree until smooth. Scrape the puree into a measuring cup (you should have about 1 cup).

3. In a medium saucepan, bring the vegetable stock and 2 cups of water just to a boil; keep warm. In a large saucepan, melt 4 tablespoons of the butter. Add the onion, garlic and a generous pinch of salt and cook over moderate heat, stirring occasionally, until softened, about 5 minutes. Add the rice and cook, stirring, until coated and opaque, about 3 minutes. Add the wine and cook, stirring, until absorbed, about 7 minutes. Add half of the warm vegetable stock and cook over moderately low heat, stirring, until nearly absorbed, about

7 minutes. Add the remaining vegetable stock and cook, stirring, until the stock is nearly absorbed and the rice is al dente, 8 to 10 minutes longer.

4. Stir the broccoli rabe puree into the risotto along with the grated Parmigiano-Reggiano cheese, tarragon, parsley and the remaining 2 tablespoons of butter. Cook, stirring, until the risotto is creamy and heated through, about 3 minutes. Season with salt and pepper. Spoon the risotto into shallow bowls, top with the chopped grilled lemon and dollops of mascarpone and serve. —*Isaac Becker*

MAKE AHEAD The broccoli rabe puree can be refrigerated overnight.

WINE Bright northern Italian white: 2011 Terlan Müller-Thurgau.

Giant Grilled Rice Balls

Active **30 min**; Total **1 hr plus overnight soaking**; Serves **8**

½ cup sweet white rice (3½ oz.) (see Note)

2 cups white or brown short-grain rice (about 1 lb.)

1 Tbsp. red miso paste

2 Tbsp. canola oil

Soy sauce, for drizzling

1. In a small bowl, cover the sweet rice with water and refrigerate overnight. Drain and transfer to a medium bowl.

2. Wash the white or brown rice in a bowl or a sieve until the water is no longer cloudy. Drain well, then add to the sweet rice and mix well. Transfer to a rice cooker and add the miso and 2½ cups of water. Close the lid securely. Cook the rice according to the manufacturer's instructions.

3. Stir the rice so the miso is well incorporated, then gently pack the rice into 8 balls (about ¾ cup each).

4. In a large grill pan, heat the canola oil. Cook the rice balls, turning frequently, until golden and crispy on the outside, 7 to 8 minutes. Serve the rice balls drizzled with soy sauce. —*Kuniko Yagi*

NOTE Sweet white rice is also called glutinous or sticky rice. Look for it at large supermarkets and Asian markets.

Quinoa Risotto with Lemon and Roasted Tomatoes

Total **1 hr**; Serves **4**

1½ cups white quinoa, rinsed
   Kosher salt

½ cup panko

6 Tbsp. extra-virgin olive oil

1½ tsp. minced rosemary

2 garlic cloves, minced
   Freshly ground pepper

4 whole canned Italian tomatoes, drained and halved lengthwise

1 lemon

1 large shallot, finely chopped

2 cups chicken stock

¼ cup crème fraîche, plus more for garnish

1 tsp. finely grated lemon zest

⅓ cup freshly grated Parmigiano-Reggiano cheese, plus more for garnish
   Chopped flat-leaf parsley, for garnish

1. Preheat the oven to 375°. In a saucepan, combine the quinoa with 2½ cups of water and a large pinch of salt and bring to a boil. Cover and cook over low heat until the water is absorbed and the quinoa is tender, 20 minutes. Let stand, covered, for 15 minutes, then fluff with a fork.

2. Meanwhile, in a bowl, mix the panko with 2 tablespoons of the olive oil, ½ teaspoon of the rosemary, half of the garlic and a generous pinch each of salt and pepper. Arrange the tomatoes cut side up on a rimmed baking sheet and top with the panko mixture. Bake for 25 minutes, until the crumbs are lightly browned and the tomatoes are softened; keep warm.

3. Peel the lemon with a sharp knife, being sure to remove all of the bitter white pith. Working over a bowl, cut in between the membranes to release the sections. Cut the lemon sections into ¼-inch pieces.

4. In a medium saucepan, heat the remaining ¼ cup of olive oil until shimmering. Add the shallot and remaining garlic and cook over moderate heat, stirring, until softened, about 4 minutes. Add the remaining 1 teaspoon of rosemary and cook for 1 minute.

5. Stir in the quinoa and stock and bring just to a boil. Simmer over moderate heat,

stirring, until the quinoa is suspended in a thickened sauce, about 5 minutes. Stir in the ¼ cup of crème fraîche, lemon zest, lemon sections and ⅓ cup of grated cheese. Season with salt and pepper. Spoon the risotto into bowls and top with the tomatoes. Garnish with crème fraîche, grated cheese and chopped parsley and serve. —*Ricardo Zarate*

WINE California Sauvignon Blanc: 2012 Yellow + Blue.

Quinoa Salad with Spring Vegetables

Total **30 min**; Serves **4**

1 Tbsp. unsalted butter

1 cup red quinoa, rinsed and drained

½ cup white wine

2 tarragon sprigs

2 thyme sprigs

1 cup frozen lima beans

1 cup frozen peas

3 Tbsp. fresh lemon juice

3 Tbsp. extra-virgin olive oil

2 tsp. Dijon mustard

2 tsp. honey
   Kosher salt and pepper

5 radishes, thinly sliced (2 cups)

1. In a medium saucepan, melt the butter over moderate heat. Add the quinoa and cook, stirring, until toasted, about 2 minutes. Add the wine, herb sprigs and 1½ cups of water and bring to a boil. Cover and simmer over low heat for 20 minutes, until the quinoa is tender; drain any extra liquid if necessary. Discard the herb sprigs. Spread the quinoa on a large rimmed baking sheet to cool to room temperature.

2. Meanwhile, fill a large bowl with ice water. In a small saucepan of salted boiling water, cook the lima beans for 2 minutes. Add the peas and cook for 1 minute longer. Drain and immediately transfer the lima beans and peas to the ice water. When cool, drain again.

3. In a large bowl, whisk the lemon juice with the olive oil, mustard and honey and season with salt and pepper. Stir in the quinoa, lima beans, peas and radishes and season with salt and pepper. Serve. —*Carla Hall*

MAKE AHEAD The salad can be refrigerated overnight.

Toasted Quinoa, Charred Onion and Brussels Sprout Salad

Total **1 hr 30 min**; Serves **6**

"I stopped eating meat when I was researching the vegan menu we did at Next," says Chicago chef Dave Beran. For his amped-up vegan salad, he adds both boiled quinoa and crunchy roasted quinoa.

QUINOA

- ½ cup white or red quinoa, rinsed
- 1 large garlic clove, thinly sliced
- 2 tsp. finely chopped peeled fresh ginger
- ½ small shallot, thinly sliced
- ¼ tsp. kosher salt

CHARRED ONION MIX

- 3 red onions, sliced ¼ inch thick
- ½ cup white quinoa, rinsed and dried
- 1 small shallot, thinly sliced
- 3 garlic cloves, minced
- ¼ cup chopped mint
- 2 tsp. kosher salt

DRESSING

- 1¼ cups grapeseed or canola oil
- ⅔ cup fresh lime juice
- 2 tsp. Dijon mustard
- 2 tsp. crushed red pepper
- 1 tsp. kosher salt

SALAD

- ½ lb. brussels sprouts, shaved on a mandoline
- 3 scallions, thinly sliced
- 1½ cups loosely packed cilantro leaves, coarsely chopped
- 1 cup loosely packed basil leaves, torn
- 1 cup loosely packed mint leaves, torn
- 1 small red onion, thinly sliced
- 1 large tomato, cut into ¼-inch dice
  Kosher salt
  Basil and mint leaves, mung bean sprouts and thinly sliced Fresno chiles, for garnish

1. Make the quinoa In a medium saucepan, combine all of the ingredients with 1 cup of water and bring to a boil. Cover and cook over low heat until the quinoa is tender and all of the water has been absorbed, about 25 minutes. Spread the quinoa out on a baking sheet to cool.

2. Meanwhile, make the charred onion mix Heat a large cast-iron skillet. In 2 batches, cook the onions over moderately low heat, turning occasionally, until well charred, 18 to 20 minutes. Chop the onions; reserve ⅓ cup for the dressing. Transfer the remaining onions to a medium bowl.

3. In a small skillet, toast the quinoa over low heat, stirring frequently, until it's crunchy and starts to pop, about 5 minutes. Add the toasted quinoa to the charred onions in the bowl, then add all of the remaining ingredients and mix well.

4. Make the dressing In a blender, combine all of the ingredients along with the reserved ⅓ cup of charred onions. Puree until smooth. Strain the dressing into a small bowl.

5. Make the salad In a large bowl, combine all of the ingredients except the salt and garnishes. Add the cooled quinoa, charred onion mix and half of the dressing; season with salt and toss. Transfer the salad to a platter and top with the garnishes. Serve the remaining dressing on the side. —*Dave Beran*

MAKE AHEAD The quinoa, charred onion mix and dressing can be refrigerated separately overnight.

Roasted Cauliflower and Quinoa Salad with Pepitas

⏱ Active **15 min**; Total **45 min**; Serves **6**

- One 2-lb. head of cauliflower, cut into bite-size florets
- ½ cup extra-virgin olive oil
- ¼ tsp. crushed red pepper
  Kosher salt and freshly ground black pepper
- 1½ cups cooked quinoa
- 1 cup chopped flat-leaf parsley
- ½ cup salted roasted hulled pumpkin seeds (*pepitas*)
- ¼ cup fresh lemon juice

Preheat the oven to 425°. On a rimmed baking sheet, toss the cauliflower with the olive oil and crushed red pepper; season with salt and black pepper. Roast for 30 minutes, until the cauliflower is softened and browned in spots; toss with the remaining ingredients and serve warm. —*Justin Chapple*

Wheat Berries with Roasted Vegetables

Active **30 min**; Total **1 hr**; Serves **6 to 8**

Miller Nan Kohler grinds wheat into extraordinary flours at Grist & Toll in Pasadena, California. At home she uses hearty, chewy whole wheat berries (wheat kernels minus the hull) in salads.

- 6 Tbsp. extra-virgin olive oil, plus more for drizzling
- 2 cups (12 oz.) soft white wheat berries (see Note)
- ½ cup dried cranberries
- 2 thyme sprigs
  Kosher salt
- 2 medium carrots, cut into ½-inch pieces
- 1 leek, white and light green parts only, cut into ¼-inch slices
- ½ lb. cremini mushrooms, halved
  Pepper
- 4 oz. soft goat cheese, crumbled
  Flaky sea salt, for sprinkling

1. In a large saucepan, heat 2 tablespoons of the oil. Add the wheat berries and cook over moderate heat, stirring, until lightly toasted, 5 minutes. Add 6 cups of water, the cranberries and thyme and bring to a boil. Cover and simmer, stirring occasionally, until the wheat berries are tender, 50 minutes. Off the heat, add 1 teaspoon of kosher salt and let stand for 5 minutes, then drain; discard the thyme.

2. Meanwhile, preheat the oven to 375°. In a large bowl, toss the carrots, leek and mushrooms with the remaining ¼ cup of oil and season with kosher salt and pepper. Spread the vegetables on 2 large rimmed baking sheets and bake for 30 to 35 minutes, until tender and browned in spots; transfer to a serving bowl. Stir in the wheat berries and cranberries. Fold in the cheese and season with kosher salt and pepper. Drizzle with oil, sprinkle with sea salt and serve. —*Nan Kohler*

NOTE Soft white wheat berries are more tender than their red counterparts. They're available at specialty food shops and from bobsredmill.com.

WINE Fruit-forward, spiced California Pinot Noir: 2012 Foxen Santa Maria Valley.

TOASTED QUINOA, CHARRED ONION
AND BRUSSELS SPROUT SALAD

Rye Berry Salad with Cranberries and Sausage

Active **45 min**; Total **2 hr**; Serves **6**

10 oz. rye berries (1½ cups); see Note

¼ cup plus 2 Tbsp. extra-virgin olive oil

½ cup finely chopped onion

5¾ cups chicken stock

Kosher salt

½ butternut squash—peeled, seeded and cut into 1-inch pieces

Freshly ground white pepper

¾ cup apple cider

1 Tbsp. unsalted butter

2 allspice berries

⅓ cup fresh or frozen cranberries

½ cup fresh orange juice

¼ cup ruby port

1 lb. loose, uncooked garlic-pork sausage (removed from casings)

2 cups packed baby arugula

2 Tbsp. chopped tarragon

2 Tbsp. white balsamic vinegar

1. In a large, dry saucepan, toast the rye berries over moderate heat, stirring, until they start to pop and are lightly toasted, 5 minutes. Transfer to a medium bowl. In the same saucepan, heat 1 tablespoon of the olive oil. Add the onion and cook over moderate heat, stirring, until softened, 3 minutes. Add the toasted rye berries and 5 cups of the stock and season with salt. Bring to a simmer, cover and cook over moderate heat until tender, 1 hour and 45 minutes. Drain and spread on a baking sheet to cool to room temperature.

2. Meanwhile, preheat the oven to 350°. Spread the squash on a rimmed baking sheet and season with salt and white pepper. Add the cider, butter, allspice, and the remaining ¾ cup of stock. Roast for 1 hour, stirring, until the liquid has evaporated and the squash is tender. Discard the allspice. Transfer the squash to a large serving bowl.

3. In a small saucepan, combine the cranberries, orange juice and port and bring to a simmer. Cook over moderate heat, stirring, until the cranberries start to pop, about 5 minutes. Using a slotted spoon, transfer the cranberries to a bowl. Continue to simmer the liquid until syrupy, about 10 minutes. Cool the syrup to room temperature, then stir in the cranberries.

4. In a large nonstick skillet, heat 1 tablespoon of the olive oil. Add the sausage and cook over moderately high heat, stirring to break up the meat, until lightly golden and cooked through, 4 to 5 minutes. Add the sausage, rye berries, cranberries, arugula and tarragon to the bowl with the squash.

5. In a small bowl, whisk the remaining ¼ cup of olive oil with the balsamic vinegar; season with salt. Toss the vinaigrette with the salad in the bowl and serve. —*Kyle Bailey*

NOTE Rye berries are available from bobsredmill.com.

BEER Mildly sour beer from Belgium: Boon Oude Geuze.

Farro with Spanish Chorizo, Feta and Dill

Total **45 min**; Serves **4**

2 cups farro (12 oz.)

Kosher salt

2 tsp. extra-virgin olive oil

8 oz. dry Spanish chorizo, very thinly sliced

2 medium shallots, minced

½ cup minced celery

1 cup chicken stock or low-sodium broth

2 Tbsp. unsalted butter

½ cup chopped parsley

4 oz. feta cheese, crumbled (½ cup)

¼ cup chopped dill

1. In a medium saucepan, cover the farro with water and bring to a boil. Add a generous pinch of salt and simmer over moderate heat, stirring occasionally, until al dente, about 25 minutes; drain well.

2. In a large, deep skillet, heat the olive oil. Add the chorizo and cook over moderate heat, stirring occasionally, until just starting to brown, about 5 minutes. Add the shallots and celery and cook, stirring, until softened, about 4 minutes. Stir in the drained farro and the chicken stock and cook, stirring, until most of the stock is absorbed, about 3 minutes. Stir in the butter and parsley and season lightly with salt. Transfer the farro to shallow bowls, scatter the feta and dill on top and serve. —*Hugh Acheson*

WINE Light northern Spanish white: 2012 Granbazán Ámbar Albariño.

Double-Nutty Farro with Radishes

Total **30 min**; Serves **4**

5 Tbsp. extra-virgin olive oil

1 cup mixed chopped nuts, such as walnuts and almonds

3 cups cooked farro

Kosher salt and pepper

3 Tbsp. fresh lemon juice

4 radishes, thinly sliced

3 Tbsp. snipped chives

1. In a nonstick skillet, heat 1 tablespoon of the oil. Add the nuts and toast over low heat, stirring frequently, until golden and fragrant, 7 to 8 minutes. Stir in the farro and 2 tablespoons of the oil and season with salt and pepper. Cook, stirring frequently, until the farro is lightly toasted, about 5 minutes.

2. Transfer the farro to a bowl. Stir in the lemon juice, radishes, chives and the remaining 2 tablespoons of oil; season with salt and pepper and serve. —*Kay Chun*

Thai Chicken and Wheat Berry Salad

Total **20 min**; Serves **4**

2 Tbsp. canola oil

1 lb. ground chicken, preferably dark meat

Kosher salt and pepper

½ cup cooked wheat berries or spelt

2 Tbsp. Asian fish sauce

1 Tbsp. fresh lime juice, plus lime wedges for serving

⅓ cup chopped basil, plus whole basil leaves for serving

Lettuce cups, for serving

In a nonstick skillet, heat the oil. Add the chicken, season with salt and pepper and cook over moderately high heat, stirring, until cooked through, 3 to 4 minutes. Stir in the wheat berries, fish sauce and lime juice. Remove the skillet from the heat; stir in the chopped basil. Serve the salad warm with lettuce cups, lime wedges and basil leaves. —*Kay Chun*

WINE Lively, limey Albariño: 2013 La Caña.

THAI CHICKEN AND WHEAT BERRY SALAD

Bulgur-Pomegranate Salad

⏱ Total **45 min**; Serves **4 to 6**

- 1½ cups medium-grind bulgur
- 1 pomegranate
- 3 Tbsp. fresh lemon juice
- 2 Tbsp. honey
- 1 garlic clove, minced
  Pinch of ground cinnamon
- ¼ cup extra-virgin olive oil
  Fine sea salt and pepper
- 1 endive—halved lengthwise,
  cored and chopped
- 1 cup chopped parsley,
  plus more for garnish
- ½ cup chopped mint,
  plus more for garnish
- 2 tsp. finely chopped preserved lemon
  (optional; see Note) or 1 tsp. finely
  grated lemon zest
- 3 Tbsp. chopped pistachios

1. In a large saucepan of salted boiling water, cook the bulgur until just tender, about 15 minutes. Drain well, then spread out on a baking sheet to cool.

2. Meanwhile, working over a bowl to catch any juice, remove the seeds from the pomegranate. In a small bowl, combine the lemon juice, honey, garlic and cinnamon. Add 1 tablespoon of the reserved pomegranate juice. Whisking constantly, drizzle in the olive oil until emulsified. Season the dressing with salt and pepper.

GENIUS TIP

Supereasy Grain Swaps

WHEAT BERRIES Add them cooked to stir-fried vegetables for a twist on fried rice.

FARRO Simmer it in a combo of water and milk for creamy oatmeal. Stir in honey and chopped nuts at the end for crunch.

3. In a medium bowl, combine the bulgur, endive, 1 cup of parsley, ½ cup of mint, the preserved lemon, if using, and the pomegranate seeds. Add the dressing and toss to coat. Season with salt and pepper. Transfer the salad to a platter and top with the pistachios. Garnish with parsley and mint and serve. —*Athena Calderone*

NOTE Preserved lemons, common in Moroccan cooking, have been soaked in brine for about a month, which makes their skins tender and delicious.

Cranberry Bean and Squid Salad

Active **45 min**; Total **1 hr 45 min**
Serves **6 to 8**

- 3½ lbs. fresh cranberry beans,
  shelled (3¾ cups)
- 1 small carrot
  Bouquet garni: 3 thyme sprigs,
  3 parsley sprigs, 1 bay leaf,
  ½ celery rib
- 8 garlic cloves, peeled and smashed
- 2 medium yellow onions—1 halved,
  1 diced
- 3 medium tomatoes—1 halved;
  2 peeled, seeded and diced
  Kosher salt
- ¼ cup extra-virgin olive oil
- 1 lb. cleaned squid, bodies cut
  into ½-inch rings
  Piment d'Espelette or
  cayenne pepper
- 1 small fennel bulb, diced
- 2 Tbsp. finely chopped parsley
- 2 Tbsp. finely chopped chives
- 2 Tbsp. red wine vinegar
- 12 basil leaves, thinly sliced crosswise
- 1 jarred roasted red pepper,
  drained and julienned
  Black pepper

1. In a medium saucepan, cover the beans with 8 cups of water. Add the carrot, bouquet garni, 4 of the garlic cloves and the halved onion and tomato and bring to a boil. Reduce the heat and simmer until the beans are tender, about 40 minutes. Remove from the heat, stir in 1 teaspoon of salt and let cool. Drain the beans. Discard the garlic cloves, onion, tomato, carrot and bouquet garni.

2. Meanwhile, in a skillet, heat 1 tablespoon of the olive oil. Season the squid with salt

and piment d'Espelette and cook over high heat until just white, 2 minutes. With a slotted spoon, transfer the squid to a bowl.

3. Add 1 tablespoon of the olive oil to the skillet along with the diced onion and fennel and the remaining 4 garlic cloves. Cook over moderately low heat until softened, about 5 minutes. Stir in the diced tomatoes and cook until softened, about 5 minutes. Return the squid to the skillet and cook until warmed through, about 5 minutes. Transfer the squid and vegetables to a large serving bowl and let cool.

4. Add the beans to the bowl along with the parsley, chives, vinegar, basil, roasted red pepper and remaining 2 tablespoons of olive oil. Season with salt and black pepper and serve. —*Denise Lurton Moullé and Jean-Pierre Moullé*

WINE Crisp white Bordeaux: 2013 Château Graville-Lacoste.

Lemony Barley Salad with Kale Pesto

⏱ Total **35 min**; Serves **4**

- 1 cup pearled barley (about 8 oz.)
- 2 Tbsp. pine nuts
- ½ cup plus 2 Tbsp. extra-virgin olive oil
- ½ cup currants
- 1 Tbsp. minced shallot
- 6 oz. kale, stems discarded and leaves
  torn into small pieces (4 cups)
- 1 Tbsp. fresh lemon juice
  Kosher salt
- 2 Tbsp. chopped preserved lemon
  (optional)

1. In a medium saucepan of salted boiling water, cook the barley until al dente, about 30 minutes. Drain well and transfer to a large bowl. Let cool slightly.

2. Meanwhile, in a small skillet, toast the pine nuts over low heat, stirring, until lightly golden, 3 to 5 minutes. Transfer to a plate.

3. In the small skillet, heat 2 tablespoons of the olive oil. Add the currants and shallot and cook over moderate heat, stirring, until the shallot is golden, about 3 minutes. Scrape into the barley along with the pine nuts.

4. In a food processor, pulse two-thirds of the kale with the lemon juice until chopped. With the machine on, slowly drizzle in the remaining ½ cup of olive oil until smooth. Season with salt. Scrape the pesto into the barley. Add the preserved lemon, if using, and the remaining kale leaves; season with salt and toss well. Serve. —Jessica Koslow

Sprouted Rye Berry and Shallot Salad

Active **10 min**; Total **1 hr plus 3 days soaking and sprouting**; Serves **8**

- 1½ cups whole rye berries or hulled barley
- Kosher salt
- 1 Tbsp. extra-virgin olive oil
- 1 Tbsp. sherry vinegar
- 1 tsp. minced shallot
- Pepper

1. In a large bowl, cover the rye berries with 2 inches of water. Cover and let stand at room temperature overnight; drain and pat dry. Spread the rye berries in an even layer in a large, shallow container. Cover and let stand at room temperature until the rye berries sprout, about 48 hours.

2. In a medium saucepan, combine the rye with 2 quarts of water. Bring to a simmer and stir in 1 teaspoon of salt. Cover and cook until just tender, about 30 minutes. Remove from the heat and let cool in the water. Drain well and transfer to a large bowl. Add the olive oil, sherry vinegar and shallot and toss to coat. Season with salt and pepper. —Dan Barber

Pimento Cheese Grits

Total **50 min**; Serves **6 to 8**

- 3 cups whole milk
- 1½ cups medium-grind stone-ground corn grits
- Salt
- 4 oz. sharp yellow cheddar cheese, shredded (1¼ cups)
- 4 oz. sharp white cheddar cheese, shredded (1¼ cups)
- 3 oz. cream cheese, at room temperature
- ⅓ cup finely diced jarred piquillo peppers, patted dry
- ⅛ tsp. cayenne pepper
- Freshly ground black pepper
- Thinly sliced scallions, for garnish

1. In a large saucepan, bring the milk and 5 cups of water to a boil. Whisk in the grits in a slow, steady stream. Add a generous pinch of salt and cook over moderately low heat, whisking frequently, until the grits are thickened and tender, about 30 minutes.

2. Remove the saucepan from the heat and whisk both cheddar cheeses into the grits along with the cream cheese, piquillo peppers and cayenne; season with salt and black pepper. Scrape the grits into a serving bowl, garnish with thinly sliced scallions and serve. —Bobby Flay

Green Pea and Bean Salad with Seeds and Nuts

Active **25 min**; Total **1 hr 20 min plus overnight soaking**; Serves **8**

- 1 cup dried navy beans (6 oz.), soaked overnight in water and drained
- Kosher salt and pepper
- 1½ lbs. fresh English peas, shelled (2 cups)
- 2 Tbsp. flaxseeds
- 2 Tbsp. sesame seeds
- 2 tsp. yellow mustard seeds
- ½ cup unsalted roasted peanuts, chopped
- 1 Tbsp. minced shallot
- 1 Tbsp. Champagne vinegar
- 2 tsp. toasted sesame oil
- 2 tsp. peanut oil, preferably toasted

1. In a large saucepan, cover the navy beans with 8 cups of water. Bring to a simmer and cook until the beans are tender, about 30 minutes. Season the beans with salt and pepper and let cool in the cooking liquid. Drain the beans.

2. Fill a medium bowl with ice water. In a medium saucepan of salted boiling water, cook the peas until just tender, about 2 minutes. Drain and cool the peas in the ice bath; drain well.

3. In a small skillet, toast all the seeds over low heat until golden and starting to pop, about 2 minutes. Scrape the seeds into a large bowl. Add the beans, peas, peanuts, shallot, vinegar, sesame oil and peanut oil and toss to coat evenly. Season with salt and pepper. Let marinate for 10 minutes or overnight before serving. —Dan Barber

Beans and Bacon on Buttered Toasts

Total **30 min**; Serves **2 to 4**

Star chef Hugh Acheson says, "Toast deserves a place at the table." Here he tops it with hearty beans and chewy bits of bacon sprinkled with Parmesan. The toasts can serve four as a starter or two as a meal.

- 1 tsp. extra-virgin olive oil
- ¼ lb. thickly sliced bacon, cut crosswise into ¼-inch-wide lardons
- One 15-oz. can navy beans, rinsed and drained
- ½ cup chicken stock or low-sodium broth
- 2 small turnips (½ lb.)—peeled, quartered and very thinly sliced crosswise
- 1 Tbsp. fresh lemon juice
- ¼ cup chopped parsley, plus more for garnish
- Kosher salt and freshly ground pepper
- Softened unsalted butter, for spreading
- Four ½-inch-thick, diagonal slices of baguette, lightly toasted
- Freshly shaved Parmigiano-Reggiano cheese, for serving

1. In a large skillet, heat the olive oil. Add the bacon and cook over moderately high heat, stirring occasionally, until browned but not crisp, about 5 minutes. Add the beans and stock and cook over moderate heat, stirring occasionally, until the stock is nearly absorbed, about 5 minutes. Add the turnips, lemon juice and ¼ cup of parsley and cook, stirring, until the turnips are crisp-tender, about 2 minutes. Season with salt and pepper.

2. Butter the toasts and arrange on plates. Spoon the turnips, beans and bacon over the toasts and top with shaved cheese and chopped parsley. —Hugh Acheson

WINE Ripe, full-bodied white: 2012 Triennes Sainte Fleur Viognier.

Black-Eyed Pea Salad with Corn Bread Croutons

Active **20 min**; Total **1 hr**; Serves **6**

This Southern main-course salad is from Sean Brock, the chef at Husk in Nashville and Charleston, South Carolina. He seasons his black-eyed peas with hot sauce, lemon and vinaigrette before tossing them with crackling corn bread and watercress.

- 1 Tbsp. canola oil
- 2 oz. bacon, cut into ¼-inch-dice
- 2¼ cups dried black-eyed peas (15 oz.)
- 2 quarts chicken stock or low-sodium broth
- 5 thyme sprigs
- 1 bay leaf
- ¼ cup apple cider vinegar
- ¼ cup chopped parsley
- ¼ tsp. Aleppo pepper
  Pinch of sugar
- ⅓ cup extra-virgin olive oil
  Kosher salt
- 2 Tbsp. unsalted butter, melted
- 2 Tbsp. fresh lemon juice
- 1 Tbsp. hot sauce
- 1 bunch of watercress, tough stems discarded
  Freshly ground white pepper
- ½ lb. corn bread, cut into ½-inch cubes and lightly toasted

1. In a large pot, heat the canola oil. Add the bacon and cook over moderate heat for 3 minutes, stirring occasionally. Add the peas, stock, thyme and bay leaf and bring to a boil. Cover and cook over low heat until the peas are tender, about 45 minutes. Drain the peas and discard the thyme sprigs and bay leaf; reserve the cooking liquid for another use.

2. Meanwhile, in a small bowl, whisk the vinegar with the parsley, Aleppo pepper and sugar, then whisk in the olive oil; season with salt. Let stand for at least 30 minutes.

3. In a large bowl, toss the black-eyed peas with the melted butter, lemon juice and hot sauce and season with some of the vinaigrette. Add the watercress, season with salt and white pepper and toss. Transfer the salad to plates and garnish with the corn bread croutons. Serve the extra vinaigrette on the side. —*Sean Brock*

Black-Eyed Peas with Coconut Milk and Ethiopian Spices

Total **55 min**; Serves **8 to 10**

- 2 cups dried black-eyed peas (12 oz.)
  Kosher salt
- 4 Tbsp. unsalted butter
- 1 large red onion, minced
- 1½ Tbsp. minced peeled fresh ginger
- 3 garlic cloves, minced
- 1 habanero chile, seeded and minced
- 2 tsp. berbere seasoning (see Note)
- 1 tsp. ground turmeric
- 3 medium tomatoes, chopped
- 1 cup unsweetened coconut milk
- 1 cup chicken stock or low-sodium broth
- ⅓ cup chopped cilantro
- 2 scallions, thinly sliced

1. In a large saucepan, cover the peas with water and bring to a boil. Simmer over moderately low heat until tender, about 40 minutes. Add a generous pinch of salt and let stand for 5 minutes, then drain well.

2. Meanwhile, in another large saucepan, melt the butter. Add the onion, ginger, garlic and chile and cook over moderate heat, stirring occasionally, until softened and just starting to brown, about 10 minutes. Add the berbere and turmeric and cook, stirring, until fragrant, about 2 minutes. Add the tomatoes and cook, stirring, until softened, about 5 minutes. Stir in the coconut milk and stock and bring to a boil. Simmer over moderately low heat, stirring occasionally, until the tomatoes break down and the sauce is thickened, about 20 minutes.

3. Add the peas to the sauce and cook over moderately low heat, stirring, until the peas are lightly coated, about 10 minutes. Fold in the cilantro and scallions and serve. —*Marcus Samuelsson*

NOTE Berbere is an Ethiopian ground red chile spice mix. It's available at specialty food shops and from kalustyans.com.

Green Pea and Fava Bean Salad with Sliced Speck

Total **1 hr**; Serves **10**

Sliced *speck*, the prosciutto-like ham, adds smokiness to this bean and herb salad, while *ricotta salata* gives it a pleasant milky flavor.

- 3 cups shelled fresh English peas (about ¾ lb.)
- 4 lbs. fava beans, shelled (4 cups)
- 1 large shallot, halved and thinly sliced
- ¼ cup sherry vinegar
- ¼ cup extra-virgin olive oil, plus more for drizzling
  Kosher salt and pepper
- ⅓ cup snipped dill sprigs
- ⅓ cup lightly packed flat-leaf parsley leaves
- ⅓ cup snipped chives
- ⅓ cup small basil leaves or torn basil
- 2 Tbsp. finely chopped sage
- 20 thin slices of *speck* (½ lb.)
- 4 oz. *ricotta salata*, crumbled (1 cup)

1. Fill a large bowl with ice water. In a large saucepan of salted boiling water, blanch the peas until crisp-tender, about 3 minutes. Using a slotted spoon, transfer the peas to the ice bath to cool. Drain well, pat dry and transfer to a large bowl.

2. Add the fava beans to the boiling water and cook just until the skins start to loosen, about 3 minutes. Using a slotted spoon, transfer the favas to the ice bath to cool. Squeeze the favas from their skins and add them to the peas. Add the shallot, sherry vinegar and the ¼ cup of oil; season with salt and pepper and toss well. In a small bowl, toss the dill with the parsley, chives, basil and sage.

3. Spoon the pea and fava bean salad onto a large platter. Arrange the *speck* slices on the salad and sprinkle the *ricotta salata* and herbs on top. Lightly drizzle with olive oil, season with salt and pepper and serve. —*Mehdi Brunet-Benkritly and Gabriel Stulman*

MAKE AHEAD The blanched peas and favas can be chilled 1 day ahead. Let the vegetables return to room temperature before serving.

BLACK-EYED PEAS WITH COCONUT
MILK AND ETHIOPIAN SPICES

Breads, Pizzas & Sandwiches

Focaccia with Roasted Squash

Active **1 hr**; Total **4 hr plus overnight fermenting**; Makes **two 8-inch round loaves**

STARTER

1¼ cups all-purpose flour

¾ cup tepid water

1⅛ tsp. active dry yeast

DOUGH

Extra-virgin olive oil, for greasing and brushing

2½ cups all-purpose flour

¾ cup tepid water

2¼ tsp. active dry yeast (from one ¼-oz. packet)

1 Tbsp. plus 1 tsp. kosher salt

TOPPING

One 1¾-lb. butternut squash or pumpkin—peeled, halved lengthwise, seeded and cut crosswise into ⅛-inch-thick slices

2 Tbsp. extra-virgin olive oil, plus more for brushing

Kosher salt and pepper

Honey, for drizzling

Thyme leaves and Maldon salt, for sprinkling

COOKBOOK TIP

A Solution for Sticky Fingers

If dough sticks to your fingers when making bread, don't run them under water. Instead, put a little flour on your hands and rub them together.

Della Fattoria Bread
Kathleen Weber

---

1. Make the starter In a large bowl, mix the flour with the water and yeast. Cover the bowl and let stand at room temperature overnight.

2. Make the dough Grease a large bowl with olive oil. In the bowl of a standing mixer fitted with the dough hook, combine the starter with the flour, water and yeast; mix at medium speed for 8 minutes. Let rest for 20 minutes, then add the salt; mix at medium speed until smooth and tacky, 8 minutes. Scrape the dough into the greased bowl and shape it into a ball. Cover and let stand in a warm place until doubled in bulk, 1 hour.

3. Transfer the dough to a lightly floured work surface and cut it in half. Shape the dough into 2 balls and transfer to a parchment-lined baking sheet. Brush the balls with olive oil, cover with plastic wrap and let stand until doubled in bulk, about 1 hour.

4. Meanwhile, prepare the topping Preheat the oven to 400°. In a large bowl, toss the squash with the 2 tablespoons of olive oil and season with salt and pepper. Spread the slices in a single layer on 2 large rimmed baking sheets and roast for about 15 minutes, until tender; let cool completely. Increase the oven temperature to 450°.

5. Gently curl the cooled squash slices and press them into the dough. Brush the focaccia with olive oil and bake for 25 to 30 minutes, until risen and browned on top. Transfer to a rack and let cool for 5 minutes. Drizzle honey on top and sprinkle with thyme leaves and Maldon salt. Serve warm. —*Michelle Gayer*

MAKE AHEAD The focaccia can be baked and cooled, then rewarmed before serving.

WINE Citrusy, focused Alsace Riesling: 2012 Trimbach Riesling.

Tomato Ciabatta with Olives and Onions

Active **25 min**; Total **2 hr 30 min plus cooling**; Makes **2 loaves**

These substantial loaves, called *pizzi Leccese*, come from the region around the Puglian city of Lecce in the far south of Italy. Tomato paste, tomatoes, onions and olives are blended right into the dough, which comes together easily and requires no kneading.

5 Tbsp. extra-virgin olive oil

2 large yellow onions, coarsely chopped

2 Tbsp. tomato paste

½ tsp. crushed red pepper

½ cup pitted kalamata olives, quartered

½ cup cherry or grape tomatoes, quartered

Kosher salt and black pepper

Three ¼-oz. packages active dry yeast

1 tsp. sugar

1¾ cups warm water

2½ cups all-purpose flour, plus more for shaping

¾ cup fine semolina

1. In a large skillet, heat 3 tablespoons of the olive oil. Add the onions and cook over moderately high heat until lightly caramelized, 8 minutes. Add the tomato paste and crushed red pepper and cook for 2 minutes. Stir in the olives and tomatoes, season with salt and black pepper and let cool.

2. In a large bowl, whisk the yeast, sugar and water; let stand until foamy, 10 minutes. Whisk in the remaining 2 tablespoons of oil and 1 teaspoon of salt. Stir in the 2½ cups of flour and the semolina until the dough comes together; it will be quite wet. Stir in the cooled olive mixture. Cover the dough with a damp kitchen towel and let stand in a warm spot until doubled in bulk, about 1½ hours.

3. Preheat the oven to 450°. Scrape the dough out onto a well-floured work surface. Shape it into 2 rough 14-by-3½-inch loaves and transfer to a parchment paper–lined baking sheet. Bake for 25 minutes, until the loaves are lightly browned and risen; transfer to a rack and let cool completely, then serve. —*Ylenia Sambati*

FOCACCIA WITH ROASTED SQUASH

Ultimate Parker House Rolls

ACTIVE: 35 MIN; TOTAL: 2 HR 55 MIN; MAKES 3 DOZEN ROLLS

Tender, buttery and sweet, with a sprinkling of crunchy salt on top, these rolls from chef **ALEX GUARNASCHELLI** of Butter in New York City are uncommonly good.

One ¼-oz. package active dry yeast

½ cup warm water

½ cup sugar

2 sticks unsalted butter, melted and cooled (1 cup)

2 cups whole milk, at room temperature

2 large eggs, lightly beaten

1 Tbsp. kosher salt

7½ to 8 cups all-purpose flour, plus more for shaping

Flaky sea salt, for sprinkling

HOW TO SHAPE THE ROLLS

1 Turn the risen dough out onto a lightly floured work surface.

2 Form a large rectangle, then cut the dough into strips.

3 Fold each strip unevenly so the top half slightly overlaps the bottom half.

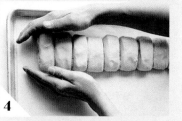

4 Place the rolls snugly in 2 rows, 4 inches apart, on baking sheets.

HOW TO FINISH THE ROLLS

1 After baking, brush the rolls with melted butter and season with crunchy sea salt.

2 Let the rolls cool slightly on a wire rack before serving.

STEP 1 MAKE THE DOUGH

In a stand mixer fitted with the dough hook, mix the yeast with the water and 1 teaspoon of the sugar. Let stand until foamy, 10 minutes. Beat in the remaining sugar, ¾ cup of the butter and the milk, eggs and kosher salt. At low speed, stir in the 7½ cups of flour until the dough comes together; add more flour by the tablespoon, if necessary. Mix at medium speed until the dough is smooth and forms a loose ball around the hook, 3 minutes. Brush a large bowl with some of the melted butter. Transfer the dough to the bowl and cover with plastic wrap. Let stand in a warm spot until nearly doubled in bulk, 1½ to 2 hours.

STEP 2 FORM THE ROLLS

Preheat the oven to 375° and line 2 baking sheets with parchment paper. Scrape the dough out onto a lightly floured work surface; shape it into a 9-by-16-inch rectangle. Using a floured knife, cut the dough lengthwise into 3 strips, then cut each strip crosswise into 12 small strips. Working with 1 piece at a time, fold it unevenly so the top half slightly overlaps the bottom half. Tuck the overhang under and place the roll seam side down on a baking sheet. Repeat with the remaining dough, forming 2 rows of 9 rolls on each baking sheet. Each roll should just touch its neighbors, but leave about 4 inches between the rows.

STEP 3 BAKE THE ROLLS

Bake the rolls for about 18 minutes, until browned; rotate the baking sheets from top to bottom and front to back halfway through baking. Immediately brush the rolls with the remaining melted butter and sprinkle with sea salt. Transfer the rolls to a rack and let cool for 15 minutes before serving. To reheat, toast in a 350° oven for about 10 minutes.

MAKE AHEAD The fully formed unbaked rolls can be frozen for up to 1 month. Bake from frozen.

Multigrain Bread Stuffing with Sausage and Herbs

Active **1 hr**; Total **3 hr**; Serves **12**

- **4 Tbsp. unsalted butter, plus more for greasing**
- **1¼ lbs. soft multigrain bread, cut into 1-inch pieces**
- **2 Tbsp. extra-virgin olive oil**
- **1 lb. sweet Italian sausage, casings removed**
- **2 cups finely chopped onion (1 medium onion)**
- **1 cup finely diced celery (2 large ribs)**
- **Kosher salt**
- **2 garlic cloves, minced**
- **1 Tbsp. finely chopped sage**
- **1 Tbsp. finely chopped thyme**
- **½ tsp. crushed red pepper**
- **½ cup dry white wine**
- **4 large eggs**
- **2½ cups chicken stock or low-sodium broth**
- **½ tsp. black pepper**
- **1 cup coarsely chopped flat-leaf parsley**

1. Preheat the oven to 375°. Lightly butter a 9-by-13-inch baking dish. On a large rimmed baking sheet, toast the bread for about 15 minutes, tossing halfway through, until lightly golden and dry. Transfer the bread to a large bowl.

2. In a large skillet, heat the olive oil until shimmering. Add the sausage and cook over moderately high heat, breaking up the meat with the back of a spoon, until browned and just cooked through, about 7 minutes. Scrape the sausage and any fat into the bowl with the bread.

3. In the same skillet, melt the 4 table-spoons of butter. Add the onion, celery and a generous pinch of salt and cook over moderately high heat, stirring occasionally, until the onion and celery are softened and just starting to brown, about 8 minutes. Stir in the garlic, sage, thyme and crushed red pepper and cook, stirring, until fragrant, about 1 minute. Add the wine and simmer until nearly absorbed, about 2 minutes. Scrape the vegetables into the bowl with the bread and sausage.

4. In a medium bowl, beat the eggs with 1½ teaspoons of salt and the stock and black pepper. Pour over the bread, add the parsley and toss thoroughly until the bread soaks up all of the liquid.

5. Transfer the stuffing to the prepared baking dish and cover with foil. Refrigerate for at least 1 hour or overnight.

6. Preheat the oven to 375°. Bake the stuffing for 30 minutes. Uncover and bake for 30 minutes longer, until the top is lightly golden and crisp. Serve the stuffing hot or warm. —*Dana Cowin*

Rosemary-Scented Dinner Rolls

Active **30 min**; Total **2 hr**; Makes **18 rolls**

- **1 stick cold unsalted butter, cubed, plus melted butter for brushing**
- **1 cup warm water**
- **¼ cup sugar**
- **One ¼-oz. packet active dry yeast**
- **4 cups all-purpose flour**
- **1 Tbsp. baking powder**
- **1¾ tsp. kosher salt**
- **1½ cups plain yogurt**
- **Eighteen 1½-inch rosemary sprigs**

1. Brush 18 cups of 2 standard-size muffin pans with melted butter. In a small bowl, whisk the warm water with the sugar and yeast and let stand until foamy, about 5 minutes.

2. In a large bowl, whisk the flour, baking powder and salt. Using your fingers, pinch the cold butter into the flour until the mixture resembles coarse crumbs with some pea-size pieces of butter remaining. Stir in the yeast mixture until the dough is evenly moistened (it will be shaggy), then stir in the yogurt to form a sticky dough. Scoop ¼ cup of the dough into each buttered muffin cup and let stand in a warm place until risen, about 1 hour.

3. Preheat the oven to 400°. Brush the rolls with melted butter and stick a rosemary sprig in each one. Bake the rolls in the lower and upper thirds of the oven for 18 to 20 minutes, until golden; shift the pans from top to bottom and front to back halfway through baking. Transfer the rolls to a platter or basket and serve warm. —*Dana Cowin*

Garlic-Rosemary Flatbreads

Active **40 min**; Total **1 hr 40 min**
Makes **four 11-inch flatbreads**

OIL

- **⅔ cup extra-virgin olive oil**
- **1 shallot, finely chopped**
- **1 medium rosemary sprig**
- **1 large garlic clove**
- **Fine sea salt and freshly ground pepper**

FLATBREADS

- **½ cup warm water**
- **1¼ tsp. active dry yeast**
- **1 tsp. sugar**
- **1⅓ cups all-purpose flour**
- **1 tsp. fine sea salt**

1. Make the oil In a small saucepan, combine the olive oil, shallot, rosemary and garlic and cook over low heat until fragrant, about 10 minutes. Let cool completely, then season with salt and pepper.

2. Make the flatbreads Very lightly grease a small baking sheet with some of the garlic-rosemary oil. In a small bowl, whisk the warm water with the yeast and sugar. Let stand until foamy, about 5 minutes. Whisk 2 teaspoons of the garlic-rosemary oil into the yeast mixture.

3. In a food processor, pulse the flour with the salt. With the machine on, drizzle in the yeast mixture until the dough just starts to come together; scrape onto a work surface and knead until smooth. Cut the dough into 4 pieces and form into balls, then transfer to the prepared baking sheet. Brush lightly with some of the garlic-rosemary oil. Cover with a damp kitchen towel and let stand in a warm spot until nearly doubled in size, about 1 hour.

4. Meanwhile, preheat the oven to 500° and set a pizza stone on the lowest rack. On a lightly floured work surface, roll 2 of the dough balls out to 11-by-5-inch ovals and transfer to a lightly floured pizza peel. Lightly brush the dough with some of the garlic-rosemary oil and slide the breads onto the hot stone. Bake for about 3 minutes, until lightly golden and just risen. Transfer the breads to a towel to keep warm. Repeat with the remaining dough. Serve the flatbreads with the remaining garlic-rosemary oil. —*Curtis Stone*

Flatbreads with Herb-Roasted Tomatoes

Active **45 min**; Total **2 hr**; Serves **4**

These crisp, pizza-like flatbreads are topped with a rich, spicy, spreadable pork sausage called *nduja* (available at Italian markets and allepiasalume.com). Spicy salami or chorizo make fine substitutes.

- **1 bunch each of thyme, oregano and parsley**
- **6 garlic cloves, crushed**
- **6 tomatoes (1½ lbs.), sliced ⅓ inch thick**
- **Extra-virgin olive oil**
- **Salt and ground pepper**
- **3 Tbsp. unsalted butter**
- **1¼ lbs. onions, thinly sliced**
- **Pinch of sugar**
- **1 lb. pizza dough, divided into 4 equal pieces**
- **¼ lb. *nduja* or thinly sliced spicy salami or dry chorizo**
- **½ lb. firm aged sheep-milk cheese, shredded**
- **1 small bunch of arugula, thick stems discarded**
- **Red wine vinegar and fleur de sel, for sprinkling**

1. Preheat the oven to 375°. Line a rimmed baking sheet with parchment paper. Spread the herbs and garlic on the paper and arrange the tomatoes on top in a single layer. Drizzle with 3 tablespoons of olive oil and season with salt and pepper. Roast for 1½ hours, until the tomatoes are soft; discard the herbs. Increase the oven temperature to 450°.

2. Meanwhile, in a large skillet, melt the butter. Stir in the onions and sugar. Cover and cook over moderately low heat, stirring, until the onions are golden in spots, 10 minutes. Uncover and cook over moderate heat, stirring, until the onions are deep brown, 7 minutes longer. Season with salt and pepper and keep warm.

3. Light a grill. On a floured work surface, using a lightly floured rolling pin, roll out each piece of dough into an 8-inch round. Grill each round until bubbles appear on the surface, 2 minutes, then flip and cook until golden and slightly puffed, 2 minutes longer. Transfer the flatbreads to 2 baking sheets.

4. Spread the flatbreads with the *nduja*, then top with the tomatoes, onions and cheese. Bake for 7 minutes, until the cheese is melted. Top with the arugula, sprinkle with olive oil, vinegar and fleur de sel and serve. —*Will Torres*

WINE Spicy Paso Robles Cabernet Sauvignon: 2011 Justin.

Black Forest Ham and Cabbage Tarte Flambée

Active **30 min**; Total **1 hr**; Serves **4 to 6**

For his German riff on the classic Alsatian flatbread, F&W's Justin Chapple uses Black Forest ham instead of the more traditional lardons and adds thinly sliced cabbage to the usual scattering of onion.

- **All-purpose flour, for dusting**
- **1 lb. store-bought pizza dough, halved**
- **¾ cup sour cream**
- **2 oz. thinly sliced Black Forest ham, torn into bite-size pieces (½ cup)**
- **½ cup thinly sliced green cabbage**
- **½ cup thinly sliced red onion**
- **Kosher salt and pepper**

1. Put a pizza stone on the bottom rack of the oven and preheat to 500°, at least 30 minutes. On a lightly floured work surface, stretch each piece of dough out to an 8-by-12-inch oval.

2. Slide a piece of dough onto a lightly floured pizza peel. Spread half of the sour cream on the dough, then scatter half of the ham, cabbage and onion on top. Season with salt and pepper.

3. Slide the dough onto the hot pizza stone and bake until crisp, 8 minutes. Transfer the tarte to a work surface, cut into strips and serve. Repeat to make the second tarte flambée. —*Justin Chapple*

WINE Off-dry German Riesling: 2012 Hexamer Porphyr.

Pizza with Baked Meatballs

⏱ Total **45 min**; Serves **4**

- **1 Tbsp. extra-virgin olive oil, plus more for brushing**
- **1 large egg**
- **2 Tbsp. panko**
- **2 garlic cloves, minced**
- **¼ cup finely chopped flat-leaf parsley**
- **1 cup freshly grated Parmigiano-Reggiano cheese**
- **Kosher salt and pepper**
- **1 lb. ground beef chuck**
- **One 28-oz. can crushed tomatoes**
- **Two 8-oz. balls of pizza dough, at room temperature**
- **1 cup basil leaves**

1. Preheat the oven to 450°. Brush a large ceramic baking dish with oil or line 2 baking sheets with parchment paper. In a large bowl, whisk the egg. Stir in the panko, garlic, parsley, ¼ cup of the cheese, 1 teaspoon of salt and ½ teaspoon of pepper. Add the beef and gently knead to combine. Form the mixture into 1-inch meatballs and transfer to the baking dish. Bake for about 10 minutes, turning once, until browned.

2. Meanwhile, in a large saucepan, heat the 1 tablespoon of oil. Add the tomatoes; cook over moderately high heat until bubbling.

3. Add the meatballs to the tomato sauce, cover partially and simmer over moderately low heat until the meatballs are cooked through, about 10 minutes. With a large spoon, mash the meatballs into large chunks. Remove from the heat.

4. Meanwhile, brush 2 large baking sheets with oil and preheat in the upper and lower thirds of the oven. On a lightly floured work surface, cut each ball of dough in half. Roll each piece into a 10-inch oval. Arrange on the heated sheets; bake until lightly golden on top and browned on the bottom, shifting the pans halfway through, 7 minutes.

5. Spread the meatball sauce over the crusts, leaving a ½-inch border. Sprinkle with the remaining ¾ cup of cheese. Bake until the crust is crisp on the bottom and the cheese is melted, about 5 minutes. Scatter basil leaves over the pizzas and serve hot. —*Matt Jennings*

WINE Fruit-forward Sicilian Nero d'Avola: 2012 Colosi.

PIZZA WITH BAKED MEATBALLS

12 Minutes

DELHI MELTS

Mix ½ lb. shredded **mozzarella** with 1 small chopped **tomato**, 1 seeded and chopped **jalapeño**, ½ tsp. **Sriracha** and ¼ cup each of minced **red onion**, chopped **cilantro** and **mayonnaise**; season with **salt** and **pepper**. Spread on 4 slices of hearty **whole-wheat toast**; broil for 4 minutes, until the cheese melts. *–Suvir Saran*

Smoked Trout Flatbreads

Active **45 min**; Total **2 hr 45 min plus overnight resting**; Serves **4**

The dough for this supersavory flatbread gets an overnight proof to develop flavor, but once you're ready to bake, the bread comes together in minutes. (If you're short on time, you can use 1 pound of refrigerated pizza dough instead.) The finishing drizzle of good-quality olive oil is key.

DOUGH

- 1 lb. "00" flour (3 cups), plus more for rolling
- 1 Tbsp. extra-virgin olive oil
- 2 tsp. honey
- 1¼ tsp. packed fresh cake yeast
- 1½ tsp. kosher salt
- 1 cup room temperature water

FLATBREAD TOPPINGS

- ¼ cup pine nuts
- ¼ cup extra-virgin olive oil, plus more for drizzling
  Kosher salt
- 6 oz. skinless smoked trout fillet, flaked into 1-inch pieces (1 cup)
- 3 oz. pitted Picholine olives, chopped (½ cup)
- ¼ cup drained capers
- 1 cup grated Pecorino Sardo cheese, plus more for garnish
  Chopped parsley, for garnish

1. Make the dough Line a baking sheet with parchment paper. In a stand mixer fitted with the dough hook, combine the 1 pound of flour with the remaining ingredients and mix at medium-low speed until the dough is elastic, 10 minutes. Scrape the dough out onto a lightly floured work surface and divide into 4 equal pieces; roll into balls and arrange on the prepared baking sheet 3 inches apart. Let rest at room temperature for 1 hour, then cover and refrigerate overnight.

2. Make the flatbreads Let the dough stand at room temperature for 1 hour before baking. Preheat the oven to 400° and line 2 baking sheets with parchment paper. In a pie plate, toast the pine nuts in the oven until lightly golden, 6 minutes. Working on a lightly floured work surface and using a lightly floured rolling pin, roll out each ball of dough into an oblong shape about ⅛ inch thick. Transfer the flatbreads to the prepared baking sheets. Brush each flatbread with 1 tablespoon of olive oil and season lightly with salt. Top with the trout, olives, capers and the 1 cup of grated cheese. Bake the flatbreads in the upper and lower thirds of the oven for 15 minutes, until lightly golden around the edges and cooked through, rotating the sheets after 7 minutes. Sprinkle the pine nuts on top and garnish with parsley and more cheese. Drizzle with olive oil and serve. —*Kyle Bailey*

BEER Crisp, citrusy sour beer: Westbrook Brewing Company Gose.

Avocado, Feta and Cherry Tomato Salsa Flatbreads

⏱ Total **40 min**; Makes **four 8-inch flatbreads**

- 2 **cups cherry tomatoes, quartered**
- ½ **cup extra-virgin olive oil, plus more for brushing**
- 1 **small shallot, minced**
- ⅓ **cup chopped mint**
- ⅓ **cup chopped cilantro**
- 1½ **Tbsp. red wine vinegar**
- ¼ **tsp. crushed red pepper**
  Kosher salt and black pepper
  All-purpose flour, for dusting
- 1 **lb. store-bought pizza dough, cut into 4 pieces**
- 4 **oz. feta cheese, crumbled**
- 1 **Hass avocado—peeled, pitted and thinly sliced**

1. In a bowl, toss the cherry tomatoes with the ½ cup of olive oil, shallot, mint, cilantro, vinegar and crushed red pepper. Season the salsa with salt and black pepper.

2. Light a grill. On a lightly floured work surface, press and stretch each piece of dough to an 8-inch oval and brush with olive oil. Grill 2 dough ovals over moderately high heat, turning once, until puffed and lightly charred, 5 minutes. Transfer to a work surface. Repeat with the remaining dough. Spoon the salsa over the flatbreads and top with the feta and avocado. Cut the flatbreads into wedges and serve right away. —*Charlie Hallowell*

Tomato-Oregano Pizzas

Active **30 min**; Total **4 hr plus 1 day resting** Makes **nine 8-inch pizzas**

Pizza expert Nancy Silverton was not a fan of the Neapolitan style before she tried a pie made by Franco Pepe at Pepe in Grani in the old town of Caiazzo, outside Naples. She's been converted: "It feels almost as if Franco invented pizza and everyone else is copying him....He has this glow around him. It's probably the best pizza in the world," she says. Topped with only tomato sauce and oregano, this is her version of the one that Pepe makes for the crowds waiting for tables at his restaurant.

DOUGH

- 2 **Tbsp. plus ½ packed tsp. fresh cake yeast (not active dry yeast)**
- 3¾ **cups bread flour**
  Extra-virgin olive oil
- 1 **Tbsp. kosher salt**
  All-purpose flour, for dusting

TOMATO SAUCE

  One 28-oz. can whole tomatoes, drained
- 2 **Tbsp. extra-virgin olive oil, plus more for garnish**
- 2 **tsp. kosher salt**
- 2 **tsp. sugar**
  Sea salt and dried or fresh oregano, for garnish

1. Make the dough In a medium bowl, crumble ½ teaspoon of the yeast into ½ cup of lukewarm water. Let stand until the yeast dissolves, 3 minutes. Stir in ½ cup of the bread flour until incorporated. Cover the bowl tightly with plastic wrap and let stand at room temperature until the sponge is bubbly and thickened, 12 to 18 hours.

2. Lightly coat a large bowl with olive oil. In the bowl of a stand mixer fitted with the dough hook, combine the sponge with 1¼ cups plus 2 tablespoons of lukewarm water. With the mixer at low speed, add the remaining 2 tablespoons of yeast and 3¼ cups of bread flour and mix until combined, scraping down the side of the bowl, 2 minutes. Add the salt and mix at medium speed until the dough is smooth and pulls away from the side of the bowl, 7 minutes. Scrape the dough out onto a lightly floured work surface and knead

into a ball; transfer to the prepared bowl and turn to coat with oil. Cover the bowl tightly with plastic wrap and let stand at room temperature until the dough has doubled in bulk, about 1½ hours.

3. Turn out the dough onto a floured work surface. Fold the top and bottom of the dough toward the center, then fold in the right and left sides; flip the dough over and return it to the bowl, folded side down. Cover tightly with plastic wrap and let stand at room temperature until doubled in bulk, 1 hour.

4. Line a baking sheet with parchment paper. Turn out the dough onto a lightly floured work surface and divide into nine 4-ounce pieces. Shape each one into a ball and transfer to the baking sheet; brush the tops with oil. Loosely cover with a kitchen towel and let stand for 1 hour.

5. Meanwhile, make the tomato sauce In a food processor, puree the tomatoes until smooth. Transfer to a bowl and stir in the remaining ingredients except the garnishes.

6. Preheat the oven to 500°. Lightly grease four 8-inch cake pans with oil. Place 1 ball of dough in a cake pan and use your fingers to press and flatten the dough until it covers the bottom of the pan. Spread 3 tablespoons of the sauce all over the dough. Repeat with 3 more dough balls and more sauce. Bake the pizzas for about 10 minutes, until the bottoms are crisp and golden. Drizzle with oil and sprinkle with sea salt and oregano; serve hot. Repeat with the remaining dough and sauce. —*Nancy Silverton*

Smoky Vegetarian Beet Reubens

Active **30 min**; Total **1 hr 45 min**
Makes **4 sandwiches**

With this reimagined deli favorite, Atlanta chef Todd Ginsberg proves that vegetarian versions of classic meat dishes can be just as delicious. In place of corned beef, Ginsberg layers roasted beet slices on buttered rye toast with all the traditional Reuben fixings.

- 1 **large beet (about 14 oz.)**
- 1 **Tbsp. extra-virgin olive oil, plus more for brushing**
  Kosher salt and freshly ground pepper
- ½ **tsp. coriander seeds, finely crushed**
  Smoked salt, for sprinkling
- ¼ **cup mayonnaise**
- 1 **Tbsp. ketchup**
- 1 **Tbsp. sweet pickle relish**
- 1 **Tbsp. fresh lemon juice**
- 8 **slices of rye bread**
  Softened unsalted butter, for brushing
- ½ **cup sauerkraut, drained and warmed**
- 4 **slices of Swiss cheese**

1. Preheat the oven to 350°. Brush the beet with olive oil and season with kosher salt and pepper. Wrap the beet in foil and roast for about 1 hour and 15 minutes, until tender; let cool slightly. Peel the beet and slice crosswise ¼ inch thick. Transfer the slices to a plate and drizzle with the 1 tablespoon of olive oil, then sprinkle with the coriander and smoked salt.

2. In a bowl, whisk the mayonnaise with the ketchup, relish and lemon juice. Season the Russian dressing with salt and pepper.

3. Preheat the broiler. Arrange the bread on a large baking sheet and brush with butter. Broil 6 inches from the heat until lightly toasted, 1 to 2 minutes. Transfer 4 slices of the bread to a work surface. Flip the remaining 4 slices on the baking sheet and top with the Russian dressing, beet slices, sauerkraut and cheese. Broil 6 inches from the heat until the cheese is melted. Close the sandwiches, cut in half and serve. —*Todd Ginsberg*

Roasted Tomato Croques with Pickled Peppers

📷 PAGE 266

Active **45 min**; Total **1 hr 30 min**
Makes **6 open-face sandwiches**

When she's cooking for her family at home, L.A. restaurateur Zoe Nathan prepares the kind of satisfying food that makes her restaurants so good. "When you work as hard as we do, in the restaurant and with the kids, you need these indulgent, open-face sandwiches," she says. "They're so naughty, so soul-satisfying and so fun."

- 5 **Tbsp. unsalted butter**
- ½ **cup finely chopped onion**
- 2 **small thyme sprigs, plus 1 Tbsp. thyme leaves**
- 1 **Tbsp. rosemary leaves**
- ½ **tsp. mustard powder**
  Kosher salt and pepper
- ¼ **cup all-purpose flour**
- 2 **cups whole milk**
- 2 **lbs. heirloom medium and cherry tomatoes, sliced crosswise ¼ inch thick**
  Extra-virgin olive oil, for brushing
  Six ½-inch-thick slices of sourdough bread
- ½ **lb. Gruyère cheese, shredded**
  Pickled Peppers (recipe follows)

1. Preheat the oven to 400°. In a medium saucepan, melt the butter. Add the onion, thyme sprigs, rosemary, mustard and a generous pinch each of salt and pepper and cook over moderately high heat, stirring occasionally, until softened and just starting to brown, about 7 minutes. Add the flour and cook, stirring constantly, until light golden, about 3 minutes. Gradually whisk in the milk until incorporated and bring to a boil. Simmer over moderately low heat, stirring, until the sauce has thickened and no floury taste remains, 7 to 10 minutes. Strain the béchamel through a fine sieve set over a heatproof bowl; discard the onion and herbs.

2. On 2 large rimmed baking sheets, arrange the tomato slices in a single layer. Brush with olive oil and season with salt and pepper. Bake for about 15 minutes, until softened and just starting to brown.

3. Set a rack on another large rimmed baking sheet. Arrange the bread in a single layer on the rack and top the slices evenly with the béchamel. Using a spatula, lay the tomatoes on the béchamel. Sprinkle with the Gruyère and thyme leaves and bake for about 20 minutes, until the tops are browned and the bottoms are crisp. Transfer the croques to plates and garnish with Pickled Peppers. Serve hot. —*Zoe Nathan*

SERVE WITH Greens dressed with good balsamic vinegar and olive oil.

MAKE AHEAD The béchamel can be refrigerated overnight. Let stand at room temperature for 30 minutes, then stir.

WINE Robust, red-berried Italian rosé: 2013 La Kiuva.

PICKLED PEPPERS

Total **30 min plus overnight pickling**
Makes **2 cups**

These spicy pickled peppers are just the right accompaniment for cheesy sandwiches or grilled meats.

- 1 **cup white wine vinegar**
- 2 **Tbsp. sugar**
- 1 **tsp. kosher salt**
- ¼ **lb. sweet small red peppers, such as baby bell—stemmed, seeded and thinly sliced**
- ¼ **lb. hot red chiles, such as Fresno and cayenne, stemmed and thinly sliced**
- ¼ **cup thinly sliced onion**
- 1 **bay leaf**
- 1 **garlic clove**
- 1 **tsp. black peppercorns**
- ½ **tsp. crushed red pepper**

In a small saucepan, combine the vinegar, sugar and salt with ¾ cup of water and bring to a boil, stirring to dissolve the sugar. Remove from the heat and add all of the remaining ingredients; let cool completely. Transfer the peppers and brine to a heatproof 1-pint jar and refrigerate overnight before serving. —*ZN*

MAKE AHEAD The pickled peppers can be stored in the brine for up to 1 week.

SMOKY VEGETARIAN BEET REUBENS

Brat Reubens

⏱ Total **45 min**; Serves **6**

Consulting chef Viet Pham created this dish for Salt Lake City's Beer Bar, which is all about artisanal sausage and craft beer. The sandwich is stuffed with bratwurst, pastrami and Swiss cheese, then topped with homemade Russian dressing and pickled vegetables.

½ cup mayonnaise

2½ Tbsp. ketchup

2 Tbsp. sweet pickle relish

Dash of Worcestershire sauce

1 large hard-cooked egg, peeled and finely chopped

Kosher salt and freshly ground pepper

Six 4-oz. bratwursts

1 small onion, thinly sliced

One 12-oz. beer, such as Budweiser

Six 8-inch rye hoagie rolls, split and toasted

6 slices of pastrami or corned beef

6 slices of imported Swiss or provolone cheese

Confetti Giardiniera, for serving (recipe follows)

1. In a small bowl, whisk the mayonnaise with the ketchup, relish and Worcestershire sauce. Fold in the chopped egg and season the dressing with salt and pepper. Refrigerate until chilled.

2. Meanwhile, in a large saucepan, cover the bratwursts and onion with the beer and 3 cups of water and bring to a boil. Simmer over moderately low heat until an instant-read thermometer inserted in the center of each brat registers 165°, 8 to 10 minutes. Transfer the brats to a plate.

3. Heat a grill pan or large cast-iron skillet. Cook the bratwursts over moderately high heat until browned all over, about 5 minutes. Fill the rolls with the pastrami, cheese and brats. Top with some of the dressing and *giardiniera* and serve. —*Viet Pham*

BEER Nutty Belgian-style beer: amber Ommegang Rare Vos.

CONFETTI GIARDINIERA

Total **20 min plus 1 week pickling**
Makes **about 4½ cups**

Pham has fond memories of eating with his family at Portillo's, outside Chicago. He always ordered the beef hoagies, which were topped with a pickled vegetable relish like this one.

3 jalapeño peppers, 1 green bell pepper, 1 yellow bell pepper, 1 small onion, 1 celery rib and ½ medium carrot, all cut into ¼-inch dice

½ small cauliflower, cut into ¼-inch florets

¼ cup plus 2 Tbsp. kosher salt

¾ cup apple cider vinegar

½ cup grapeseed or canola oil

2 garlic cloves, minced

1 tsp. minced oregano leaves

½ tsp. crushed red pepper

¼ tsp. yellow mustard seeds

¼ tsp. celery seeds

¼ tsp. freshly ground pepper

1. In a large bowl, toss the jalapeños, bell peppers, onion, celery, carrot and cauliflower with the salt. Add cold water to cover the vegetables and refrigerate for 12 hours.

2. Drain the vegetables and rinse well; pat dry. Transfer the vegetables to a 2-quart jar.

3. In a medium bowl, whisk the vinegar with all of the remaining ingredients. Add the vinegar mixture to the jar and stir well. Cover and refrigerate the *giardiniera* for 1 to 2 weeks before serving. —*VP*

Grilled Philly Cheesesteaks

⏱ Total **45 min**; Serves **6**

"Unexpected and a little trashy" is how Tom Mylan of Brooklyn's Meat Hook butcher shop describes the cheesesteaks he prepares in a cast-iron griddle on his grill. "I make these more often than I'd like to admit," he says.

1½ lbs. top round or other lean beef, cut into very thin strips

Kosher salt and ground black pepper

3 Tbsp. canola oil

1 large onion, halved and thinly sliced

1 green bell pepper, thinly sliced

1 red bell pepper, thinly sliced

13 slices of American cheese (¾ lb.), 4 slices torn

Six 6-inch hoagie rolls or large hot dog buns, split and warmed

1. Light a gas grill. Set a large cast-iron griddle or very large cast-iron skillet directly on the grill grate and heat it for about 10 minutes, until very hot.

2. Meanwhile, in a large bowl, toss the meat with 1½ teaspoons of salt and 1 teaspoon of pepper.

3. Brush the griddle with 1 tablespoon of the oil. Add the onion and bell peppers, season with salt and black pepper and cook over high heat, stirring occasionally, until the vegetables are softened and browned in spots, about 8 minutes. Transfer the onion and peppers to a bowl.

4. Brush the griddle with the remaining 2 tablespoons of canola oil. Spread the meat strips in an even layer on the griddle and cook over high heat, undisturbed, until they are well browned on the bottom, 2 to 3 minutes. Flip the meat and return the vegetables to the griddle. Cook over high heat, stirring occasionally, until the meat is just cooked through, about 3 minutes. Add the torn cheese and cook, stirring, until just melted, 1 minute. Fill each roll with 1½ slices of cheese and the steak-vegetable filling and serve the cheesesteaks immediately. —*Tom Mylan*

BEER American craft beer: Anderson Valley Boont Amber from California.

BRAT REUBENS

French Dip with Onion Jus

Total **2 hr**; Serves **6**

"I like the idea of a French dip, mainly because of the name. It's the most inauthentic thing you can put on a French menu," says San Francisco chef Corey Lee. His juicy, cheesy, drippy French dip is an outrageous take on the Los Angeles classic.

JUS

- 2 **Tbsp. unsalted butter**
- 1 **large sweet onion, thinly sliced**
- 2 **Tbsp. sugar**
- 1 **garlic clove, crushed**
- 2 **each of thyme sprigs and bay leaves**
- ⅓ **cup ruby port**
- 5½ **cups low-sodium beef broth**
- 1 **Tbsp. Banyuls vinegar**
- 1 **Tbsp. Worcestershire sauce**
  Kosher salt and freshly ground pepper

ROAST BEEF

- 2 **Tbsp. canola oil**
- 2 **lbs. trimmed center-cut beef tenderloin, at room temperature**
  Kosher salt and freshly ground pepper
- 4 **Tbsp. unsalted butter**
- 4 **garlic cloves, crushed**
- 2 **thyme sprigs**
- ½ **cup low-sodium beef broth**

AIOLI

- 3 **large egg yolks**
- 2 **Tbsp. Champagne vinegar**
  Kosher salt and freshly ground pepper
- 1 **cup canola oil**
- 3 **Tbsp. drained horseradish**

SANDWICHES

- ½ **small shallot, minced**
- 1 **garlic clove, minced**
- 4 **Tbsp. unsalted butter, melted**
- ½ **lb. baby spinach**
  Kosher salt
  Three 12-inch baguettes, halved and split
- ¾ **lb. Gruyère cheese, shredded**

1. Make the jus In a large saucepan, melt the butter. Add the onion and cook over moderate heat, stirring, until starting to brown, 10 minutes. Add the sugar, garlic, thyme and bay leaves and cook over moderately low heat, stirring, until the onion is deep golden, about 20 minutes. Add the port and simmer over moderately high heat until nearly absorbed, 2 minutes. Add the broth, vinegar and Worcestershire and simmer over moderate heat until reduced to 2 cups, about 30 minutes. Strain the jus into a small saucepan and season with salt and pepper.

2. Meanwhile, roast the beef Preheat the oven to 325°. Heat the oil in a large, heavy ovenproof skillet. Season the meat with salt and pepper and sear until well browned all over. Add the butter, garlic and thyme and baste the meat for 1 minute. Transfer to the oven and roast for 30 minutes, basting every 5 minutes, until an instant-read thermometer inserted in the center of the meat registers 128°; transfer to a rack set over a baking sheet and let rest for 20 minutes. Add the broth to the skillet and scrape up any browned bits. Boil until reduced by half; strain into the jus and skim off any fat.

3. Make the aioli In a food processor, blend the egg yolks, vinegar and a large pinch each of salt and pepper for 90 seconds. With the machine on, add the oil in a slow stream. Transfer to a bowl, stir in the horseradish and season with salt and pepper.

4. Make the sandwiches In a large skillet, cook the shallot and garlic in 1 tablespoon of the butter until softened. Add the spinach and season with salt. Cook, tossing, until just wilted; drain on paper towels.

5. Preheat the broiler. Thinly slice the beef. Arrange the baguettes on 2 baking sheets and spread with the aioli. Spoon the spinach over the bottom halves and top with the beef and cheese. Broil 6 inches from the heat until the cheese melts.

6. Increase the oven temperature to 425°. Reheat the jus. Close the sandwiches, brush with the remaining melted butter and weight down with a baking sheet and heavy skillet. Bake for 10 minutes; remove the weighted baking sheet and bake for 5 minutes longer. Serve with the jus. —*Corey Lee*

WINE Juicy Spanish Garnacha: 2011 Retorno.

Grilled Eggplant Tortas

⏱ Total **40 min**; Serves **4**

This vegetarian torta (Mexican-style sandwich) is piled high with meaty slices of grilled eggplant, mashed avocado and zippy taco garnishes.

- ½ **cup canola oil**
- 1½ **Tbsp. ground cumin**
  Kosher salt and pepper
- 2 **medium Italian eggplants (2 lbs.), sliced crosswise ¼ inch thick**
- 1 **Hass avocado**
- 1 **Tbsp. fresh lime juice**
- 4 **soft buns, toasted**
  Shredded cabbage, cilantro leaves and jarred pickled jalapeños and carrots, for serving

1. Heat a grill pan. In a large bowl, whisk the oil with the cumin and season with salt and pepper. Add the eggplants to the bowl and toss to coat. Working in batches, grill the eggplants over moderate heat, turning, until tender, about 5 minutes per batch.

2. In a small bowl, mash the avocado with the lime juice. Spread the mashed avocado on the bottom buns. Top with the eggplants, cabbage, cilantro and pickled jalapeños and carrots, close the tortas and serve. —*Kay Chun*

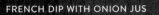
FRENCH DIP WITH ONION JUS

Five-Spice Chicken Banh Mi Sandwiches

Total **30 min plus 2 hr marinating; Serves 4**

Lemongrass is the classic seasoning for Vietnamese grilled pork or chicken, but Charles Phan of The Slanted Door in San Francisco uses fragrant Chinese five-spice powder instead. To replicate an airy Vietnamese baguette, Phan suggests hollowing out a soft roll and toasting it.

½ **cup Asian fish sauce**

3 **small shallots, minced**

¼ **cup light soy sauce**

2 **Tbsp. minced garlic**

1½ **tsp. red miso**

½ **tsp. Chinese five-spice powder**

1 **Thai bird chile, minced**

Four 5-oz. boneless chicken breasts with skin

¼ **cup sugar**

¼ **cup distilled white vinegar**

¼ **tsp. kosher salt**

1 **small carrot, julienned**

Canola oil, for greasing

Four 6-inch-long soft sandwich rolls, split lengthwise

¼ **cup mayonnaise**

½ **English cucumber, thinly sliced lengthwise**

12 **cilantro sprigs**

2 **jalapeños, thinly sliced**

1. In a large bowl, whisk the fish sauce, shallots, soy sauce, garlic, miso, five-spice powder and chile. Add the chicken and turn to coat. Cover with plastic wrap and refrigerate for 2 to 4 hours.

2. Meanwhile, in a medium bowl, whisk the sugar with the vinegar and salt until dissolved. Stir in the carrot and let stand at room temperature until lightly pickled, about 30 minutes.

3. Light a grill and oil the grate, or heat a grill pan. Remove the chicken from the marinade and grill over moderate heat, turning occasionally, until lightly charred and cooked through, 14 to 16 minutes. Transfer the chicken to a plate and let rest for 5 minutes.

4. Preheat the oven to 400°. Using your fingers, scoop out some of the bread from the insides of the rolls. Toast the rolls in the oven for 6 minutes, until golden. Let cool slightly. Thinly slice the chicken. Divide 1 tablespoon of mayonnaise between the top and bottom of each roll and arrange the cucumber slices and chicken on the bottoms. Top with the cilantro sprigs, jalapeños and pickled carrot. Close the sandwiches and serve. —*Charles Phan*

MAKE AHEAD The grilled chicken can be refrigerated for up to 1 day; bring it to room temperature before making the sandwiches.

WINE Bright, ripe California Chardonnay: 2011 Mount Eden Edna Valley.

Pulled Pork Sandwiches with Barbecue Sauce

Active **1 hr 15 min;** Total **8 hr 20 min** Serves **8**

PULLED PORK

2 **heads of garlic, halved crosswise**

¼ **cup extra-virgin olive oil, plus more for drizzling**

Kosher salt and pepper

1 **Tbsp. minced thyme**

2 **tsp. mustard powder**

2 **tsp. sweet paprika**

2 **tsp. finely grated peeled fresh ginger**

1 **tsp. finely grated orange zest**

One 5-lb. bone-in pork butt (shoulder roast)

¼ **cup light brown sugar**

¼ **cup distilled white vinegar**

¼ **cup apple cider vinegar**

BARBECUE SAUCE

1¼ **cups ketchup**

1 **cup cola**

¼ **cup apple cider vinegar**

¼ **cup cayenne pepper hot sauce, such as Frank's RedHot**

2 **Tbsp. unsulfured molasses**

2 **Tbsp. cornstarch**

Split potato buns, Red-and-Green Coleslaw (p. 48) and Habanero Vinegar (p. 365), for serving

1. Make the pork Preheat the oven to 350°. Set the garlic cut side up on a sheet of foil, drizzle with oil and season with salt and pepper. Wrap the garlic in the foil and roast for about 1 hour, until very soft. Let cool, then squeeze the garlic cloves out of the skins into a medium bowl. Add the thyme, mustard powder, paprika, ginger, orange zest and the ¼ cup of oil and mash into a paste.

2. Reduce the oven temperature to 300°. Set a rack in a flameproof medium roasting pan and put the pork on it. Season the pork with salt and pepper, then rub it all over with the garlic paste. Cover with foil and roast for 6 hours, until an instant-read thermometer inserted in the thickest part of the meat registers 200°; uncover for the last 45 minutes of cooking. Transfer to a work surface and let cool, then shred. Discard the fat and bones.

3. Spoon off all but 2 tablespoons of fat from the roasting pan. Add the sugar, both vinegars and ½ cup of water to the pan and cook over moderately high heat, whisking, until bubbling and the sugar dissolves, 5 minutes. Add the pork and toss to coat. Season the pork generously with salt and pepper and toss again; keep warm.

4. Meanwhile, make the barbecue sauce In a medium saucepan, whisk the ketchup, cola, vinegar, hot sauce, molasses and cornstarch and bring to a boil. Simmer over moderate heat, stirring, until glossy and thick, 8 minutes; keep warm.

5. Pile the pork on the buns and top with the barbecue sauce and coleslaw. Close the sandwiches and serve, passing the habanero vinegar at the table. —*Ruby Duke*

MAKE AHEAD The recipe can be prepared through Step 4 and refrigerated for up to 4 days. Reheat gently before serving.

BEER Easygoing beer from a can: Sierra Nevada Summerfest.

FIVE-SPICE CHICKEN
BANH MI SANDWICHES

GLUTEN-FREE BANANA-
COCONUT PANCAKES
Recipe, page 304

Breakfast & Brunch

Poached Eggs with Mustard Cream Sauce

Active **40 min**; Total **1 hr 15 min**; Serves **4**

This dish, inspired by Germany's Black Forest, is equally perfect served for brunch or as a hearty appetizer.

- 1 **lb. baking potatoes, peeled and cut into 2-inch pieces**
- **Kosher salt**
- **Pinch of freshly grated nutmeg**
- 1 **cup heavy cream**
- 1 **stick unsalted butter**
- **Pepper**
- 2 **Tbsp. extra-virgin olive oil**
- 1 **shallot, minced**
- ½ **cup vegetable broth**
- ⅓ **cup dry white wine**
- 3 **Tbsp. whole-grain mustard**
- 4 **large eggs**
- 2 **cups lightly packed baby spinach**
- 2 **tsp. fresh lemon juice**

1. In a medium saucepan, cover the potatoes with water and bring to a boil. Add a pinch of salt and simmer over moderate heat until tender, 20 minutes; drain well. Pass the potatoes through a ricer back into the saucepan. Stir in the nutmeg, ½ cup of the cream and 4 tablespoons of butter over low heat until incorporated. Season with salt and pepper; keep warm.

2. Meanwhile, in a small saucepan, heat 1 tablespoon of the oil. Add the shallot and cook over moderate heat until softened, 2 minutes. Add the broth and wine and simmer until reduced to ½ cup, 5 minutes. Whisk in the mustard and remaining ½ cup of cream and bring to a boil. Remove from the heat and whisk in the remaining 4 tablespoons of butter. Season with salt and pepper; keep warm.

3. Meanwhile, bring a large, deep skillet of water to a simmer and add a pinch of salt. One at a time, crack each egg into a small bowl and slide it into the water. Poach the eggs until the whites are firm and the yolks are runny, 3 minutes. Using a slotted spoon, transfer the eggs to a paper towel–lined plate to drain.

4. In a bowl, toss the spinach, lemon juice and remaining 1 tablespoon of oil and season with salt and pepper. Mound the potato puree on plates. Set the eggs on top and spoon the sauce over. Pile the spinach on the side and serve. *—Tim Mälzer*

WINE Full-bodied German Riesling: 2011 S.A. Prüm Wehlener Sonnenuhr Kabinett.

Meyer Lemon–Poached Eggs and Grilled Asparagus with Pecorino

Total **20 min**; Serves **4**

Philadelphia chef Nicholas Elmi and his family head outside to cook whenever they can. That means grilling the asparagus on the grate as well as poaching the eggs in a saucepan set on the grill.

- 2 **Tbsp. extra-virgin olive oil, plus more for oiling the grate**
- 1 **lb. thin asparagus**
- **Salt**
- 4 **large eggs**
- ¼ **cup plus 1 Tbsp. fresh Meyer lemon (or regular lemon) juice**
- 1 **tsp. finely grated Meyer lemon zest**
- ½ **cup freshly grated Locatelli Pecorino cheese**
- **Freshly ground pepper**

1. Light a grill and oil the grate. On a baking sheet, toss the asparagus with the 2 tablespoons of olive oil and season with salt. Grill over moderate heat, turning, until the asparagus are lightly charred and crisp-tender, 3 to 4 minutes. Transfer the asparagus to plates and keep warm.

2. Crack the eggs into 4 small bowls. Bring a medium saucepan of water to a simmer. Add the ¼ cup of lemon juice and season with salt. Stir the water to create a vortex. Add the eggs one at a time, stirring gently in the same direction so they do not settle. Poach over moderate heat until the whites are set and the yolks are runny, 3 minutes. Using a slotted spoon, transfer the eggs to paper towels to drain briefly.

3. Set the eggs on the asparagus. Drizzle with the remaining 1 tablespoon of lemon juice and sprinkle the lemon zest and cheese on top. Season generously with pepper and serve. *—Nicholas Elmi*

WINE Light, spritzy white from northern Spain: 2012 Uriondo Bizkaiko Txakolina.

Scallion Scrambled Eggs with Potato Chips

Total **15 min**; Serves **2**

- 4 **large eggs**
- ¼ **tsp. kosher salt**
- **Freshly ground pepper**
- 1 **Tbsp. unsalted butter**
- 4 **scallions, thinly sliced**
- **Kettle-cooked potato chips, for garnish**

In a medium bowl, beat the eggs with the salt, a generous pinch of pepper and 1 tablespoon of water. In a small nonstick skillet, melt the butter. Add the scallions and cook over moderate heat, stirring occasionally, until softened, about 4 minutes. Add the eggs and cook over moderately low heat, stirring to form small curds, about 2 minutes. Transfer the scrambled eggs to plates, garnish with potato chips and serve right away. *—Hugh Acheson*

WINE Refreshing, versatile sparkling wine: NV Nino Franco Rustico Prosecco.

Soft-Scrambled Eggs with Caviar and Toasted Challah

Total **15 min**; Serves **4**

According to Joshua Russ Tupper of the iconic Russ & Daughters store and café in New York City, "The best way to experience caviar is on eggs. It doesn't have to be superfancy caviar, either."

- 8 **large eggs, beaten**
- 2½ **Tbsp. cold unsalted butter, cubed**
- **Salt**
- **Paddlefish caviar and toasted challah, for serving**

In a large nonstick skillet, combine the eggs with 2 tablespoons of the butter and a pinch of salt. Cook over moderately low heat, stirring constantly, until small curds form and the eggs are creamy, about 8 minutes. Remove from the heat and stir in the remaining ½ tablespoon of butter until melted; season with salt. Transfer the eggs to plates and serve with caviar and toasted challah. *—Joshua Russ Tupper*

WINE Delicate, Chardonnay-based Champagne: NV Pierre Gimmonet Brut.

MEYER LEMON–POACHED EGGS AND
GRILLED ASPARAGUS WITH PECORINO

Poached Eggs in Red Wine Sauce

Total **1 hr 15 min**; Serves **4**

Like beef bourguignon, this French egg dish *oeufs en meurette* features a rich red wine sauce and a garnish of sautéed bacon, pearl onions and mushrooms.

    One 750-ml bottle Pinot Noir

1 **small onion, thinly sliced**

1 **medium carrot, thinly sliced**

3 **thyme sprigs**

1 **parsley sprig**

1 **bay leaf**

1 **garlic clove**

7 **Tbsp. unsalted butter, softened**

1 **Tbsp. all-purpose flour**

    Kosher salt and freshly ground pepper

½ **lb. white mushrooms, quartered**

2 **thick slices of bacon, cut crosswise ½ inch thick**

¾ **cup frozen pearl onions (4 oz.), thawed and patted dry**

8 **large eggs**

    Four ½-inch-thick slices of rustic country bread, halved crosswise and toasted

    Chervil sprigs or chopped parsley, for garnish

1. In a medium saucepan, combine the wine with the onion, carrot, thyme and parsley sprigs, bay leaf and garlic and bring to a boil. Simmer over moderately high heat until reduced by half, 12 to 15 minutes. Strain the wine through a fine sieve and return it to the saucepan; discard the vegetables and herbs.

2. In a small bowl, blend 4 tablespoons of the butter with the flour to form a paste. Bring the wine sauce to a boil and whisk in the flour paste. Simmer over moderate heat, whisking, until thickened, 2 minutes. Season the sauce with salt and pepper and keep warm.

3. In a large skillet, melt 2 tablespoons of the butter. Add the mushrooms and season with salt and pepper. Cook over moderately high heat, stirring occasionally, until tender and browned, about 7 minutes; transfer to a large plate. In the same skillet, melt the remaining 1 tablespoon of butter. Add the bacon and cook over moderately high heat, turning once, until browned but not crisp, about 3 minutes; transfer to the plate. Add the pearl onions to the skillet and season with salt and pepper. Cook over moderate heat, stirring occasionally, until tender and golden, about 5 minutes; transfer to the plate. Keep warm.

4. Bring a large, deep skillet of water to a simmer over moderate heat. One at a time, crack each egg into a small bowl and carefully slide it into the water. Poach the eggs over moderate heat until the whites are set and the yolks are slightly runny, about 4 minutes. Using a slotted spoon, gently transfer the poached eggs to paper towels to drain.

5. Arrange the toasts on plates, set the eggs on top and spoon the red wine sauce over the eggs. Scatter the mushrooms, bacon and pearl onions around the plate, garnish with chervil sprigs and serve right away. —*Marjorie Taylor*

MAKE AHEAD The red wine sauce can be refrigerated overnight. Reheat gently, adding a few tablespoons of water if it's too thick.

COOKBOOK TIP

How to Scramble Eggs

Scramble eggs in a double boiler to keep them moist.

Inside the Test Kitchen
Tyler Florence

Fried Eggs with Mustard Seed Oil and Kale

Total **25 min**; Serves **2 to 4**

2 **Tbsp. canola oil**

½ **tsp. mustard seeds**

4 **large eggs**

½ **lb. baby kale, chopped**

2 **Tbsp. sunflower seeds**

½ **tsp. cumin seeds**

    Kosher salt

¼ **cup grated Gruyère cheese (1 oz.)**

½ **cup plain yogurt, for serving**

1 **Hass avocado, peeled and cut into wedges**

1. In a large cast-iron skillet, heat 1 tablespoon of the oil. Add the mustard seeds and toast over low heat, stirring, until they just start to pop, 1 to 2 minutes. Using a small spoon, transfer the seeds to a small bowl. Add the remaining 1 tablespoon of oil to the skillet. Crack the eggs into the skillet and cook over moderate heat until the whites are set and the yolks are slightly runny, 4 to 5 minutes. Transfer to plates and keep warm.

2. Add the kale to the skillet and cook over moderate heat, stirring, until wilted, 3 minutes. Add the sunflower, cumin and mustard seeds and cook, stirring, until the sunflower seeds are toasted, 2 minutes. Season with salt. Remove from the heat and stir in the cheese.

3. Meanwhile, in a small bowl, stir the yogurt with salt. Top each egg with some kale, salted yogurt and avocado and serve. —*Heidi Swanson*

Reuben Benedict

Total **40 min**; Serves **4**

- 2 Tbsp. fresh lemon juice
- 3 Tbsp. ketchup
- 3 Tbsp. minced yellow onion
- 1½ Tbsp. Worcestershire sauce
- 1 Tbsp. sweet pickle relish
- 1 tsp. sugar
- ½ tsp. kosher salt
- ¼ tsp. cayenne pepper
- 3 large egg yolks
- 1 stick unsalted butter, melted and warmed
- 1 Tbsp. distilled white vinegar
- 4 large eggs
- 4 slices of rye bread
- ½ lb. sliced corned beef or pastrami
- 1 cup drained sauerkraut, warmed
  Finely chopped parsley, for garnish

1. In a heatproof medium bowl, whisk 1 tablespoon of the lemon juice with the ketchup, onion, Worcestershire sauce, pickle relish, sugar, salt and cayenne. Place the bowl over a small saucepan of just simmering water and keep warm.

2. In a blender, combine the remaining 1 tablespoon of lemon juice with the egg yolks and ½ tablespoon of water and blend until smooth. With the blender on, slowly drizzle in the melted butter until the sauce is emulsified. Gently fold the hollandaise into the ketchup mixture and keep warm.

3. Preheat the oven to 425°. Fill a high-sided skillet halfway with water. Add the vinegar and bring to a boil. Reduce the heat to maintain a steady simmer. Crack each egg into a ramekin and slide it into the water. Poach the eggs until the whites are set and the yolks are runny, about 3 minutes. Using a slotted spoon, gently transfer the eggs to a paper towel–lined plate to drain. Cover the poached eggs with foil to keep warm.

4. On a baking sheet, toast the rye bread for 8 minutes, turning once. Top with the corned beef and bake for 2 more minutes. Top each toast with sauerkraut, a poached egg and the Reuben hollandaise. Sprinkle with parsley and serve right away. —*Josh Habiger*

WINE Fruit-forward rosé cava: 2010 Llopart Brut Rosé.

Roasted Brussels Sprout and Gruyère Quiche

Active **30 min**; Total **3 hr 30 min**
Makes **one 9-inch quiche**

PASTRY

- 1 cup all-purpose flour
- 1 cup cake flour
- ½ tsp. kosher salt
- 2 sticks chilled unsalted butter, cut into ½-inch cubes
- 6 Tbsp. ice water

FILLING

- ¾ lb. brussels sprouts, quartered
- 2 Tbsp. extra-virgin olive oil
- 1½ cups milk
- 1½ cups heavy cream
- 4 large egg yolks
- 3 large eggs
- 1 tsp. salt
- ¾ tsp. freshly ground white pepper
- ⅛ tsp. freshly grated nutmeg
- ⅓ cup thinly sliced scallions
- 4 oz. Gruyère cheese, shredded (1⅓ cups)

1. Make the pastry In a food processor, pulse both flours with the salt. Add the butter and pulse until the mixture resembles coarse meal. Drizzle the ice water on top and pulse until the dough just comes together. Turn the dough out onto a work surface, gather up any crumbs and pat the dough into a disk. Wrap in plastic and refrigerate until well chilled, about 1 hour.

2. On a lightly floured work surface, roll out the dough to a 14-inch round, ¼ inch thick. Ease it into a 9-inch round, 2-inch-deep cake pan; do not trim the overhanging dough. Refrigerate until firm, 30 minutes.

3. Preheat the oven to 350°. Line the pastry with parchment paper and fill with pie weights. Bake for 20 minutes, until barely set. Remove the parchment and pie weights. Bake for 15 to 20 minutes, until lightly browned. Let cool on a rack. Increase the oven temperature to 425°.

4. Make the filling On a rimmed baking sheet, toss the brussels sprouts with the olive oil. Roast in the oven for about 20 minutes, tossing once, until browned and tender. Let cool, then coarsely chop. Reduce the oven temperature to 325°.

5. In a medium bowl, whisk the milk with the cream, egg yolks, eggs, salt, white pepper and nutmeg. Stir in the brussels sprouts and scallions. Sprinkle the Gruyère in the crust and pour the filling on top. Set the cake pan on a foil-lined baking sheet and bake the quiche for about 1½ hours, until set. Transfer to a rack and let cool for 30 minutes. Using a paring knife, trim the excess crust and discard. Cut the quiche into wedges and serve. —*Billy Allin*

MAKE AHEAD The quiche can be refrigerated overnight. Bring to room temperature or rewarm slightly before serving.

WINE Vibrant, full-bodied white: 2013 Adelsheim Pinot Gris.

Egg Tortilla with Cumin Sour Cream

Total **15 min**; Serves **1**

- 2 Tbsp. sour cream
  Pinch of ground cumin
  Kosher salt
- 1 tsp. extra-virgin olive oil
- 2 large eggs, beaten
- 1 corn tortilla
- 3 Tbsp. freshly grated Parmigiano-Reggiano cheese
  Chopped chives and chopped pitted green olives, for garnish

In a small bowl, mix the sour cream with the cumin and season with salt. In a 6-inch skillet, heat the olive oil. Add the eggs and cook over moderate heat, without stirring, until set at the edge, about 1 minute. Place the tortilla over the eggs, press gently and cook until the eggs are just set, about 2 minutes. Flip the eggs and tortilla and sprinkle on half of the cheese. Cook until the tortilla is golden on the bottom, about 2 minutes. Slide the tortilla onto a plate. Top with the remaining cheese and garnish with chives and olives. Serve with a dollop of the cumin sour cream. —*Heidi Swanson*

No–Fail Soufflé

ACTIVE: 25 MIN; TOTAL: 1 HR • SERVES 4

Editor Daniel Gritzer learns how to create both a sweet and a savory soufflé with a little guidance from master chef **JACQUES PÉPIN**.

A perfectly puffy soufflé can seem like a small miracle. To learn the basics of making one, I headed to The International Culinary Center in New York City for a lesson from the legendary master of French technique, F&W contributing editor Jacques Pépin. Pépin pulled out a copper bowl, explaining that the metal interacts with the egg whites to make them more stable as they take on air. Then he proceeded to whip up soufflé after soufflé, all the while describing in more detail than I thought possible the finer points of beating egg whites by hand. "Start fast to make them more liquid, then slow down–lifting them with the whisk, and not touching the bowl too much," he told me. But for Pépin, the most important thing when working with beaten egg whites is the timing: Use them right away, he warns, or they'll deflate. "It is relatively easy when you're serving two to four people; a party for 20, though, would be more difficult." Here, his tips for getting started.

RUNNY OR NOT?
"Some people like a soufflé that's wet in the center, others do not," says Jacques Pépin. "Both are perfectly fine."

GRUYÈRE SO

SAVORY SOUFFLÉ

Gruyère Soufflé

To get the most crust with the cheesiest flavor, Pépin uses a wide, shallow gratin dish, then creates a lattice on top with thin slices of American cheese. A soufflé ramekin would work too.

- 3 Tbsp. unsalted butter, plus more for greasing
- 2 Tbsp. freshly grated Parmigiano-Reggiano cheese
- 3½ Tbsp. all-purpose flour
- 1 cup cold whole milk
- 5 large eggs, separated
- ½ tsp. kosher salt
- ½ tsp. freshly ground pepper
- 3 oz. Gruyère cheese, shredded (1 cup)
- 2 Tbsp. chopped chives
- 2 slices of yellow American cheese, each cut into 6 strips

1. Preheat the oven to 400°. Grease a 1-quart gratin dish with butter and dust with the Parmigiano; refrigerate. In a saucepan, melt the 3 tablespoons of butter over moderate heat. Whisk in the flour and cook, whisking, for 1 minute. Whisk in the milk, bring to a boil and cook, whisking, until thickened, 1 minute. Remove the béchamel from the heat, then whisk in 4 egg yolks along with the salt and pepper; reserve the remaining yolk for another use.

2. In a clean bowl, beat the egg whites until firm peaks form. Whisk one-third of the whites into the béchamel, then fold in the remaining beaten whites. Fold in the Gruyère and chives; scrape the mixture into the prepared dish. Arrange the American cheese strips on top in a criss-cross pattern. Bake for 25 minutes, until puffed and golden. Serve.

WINE Toasty, full-bodied Champagne: NV Aubry Brut.

SWEET SOUFFLÉ

Rothschild Soufflé

This soufflé features preserved fruits and kirsch (cherry brandy). "The base for a sweet soufflé is traditionally pastry cream," says Pépin. He substitutes béchamel here—it's "basically the same thing, but easier."

- ½ cup candied and dried fruits, chopped into ¼-inch pieces
- 3 Tbsp. kirsch (cherry brandy)
- 3 Tbsp. unsalted butter, plus more for greasing
- ⅓ cup plus 2 Tbsp. sugar
- 3½ Tbsp. all-purpose flour
- 1 cup cold whole milk
- 1 tsp. pure vanilla extract
- 5 large eggs, separated
  Confectioners' sugar, for dusting

1. In a bowl, soak the fruits in the kirsch for 30 minutes or overnight. Preheat the oven to 400°. Butter a 1-quart soufflé dish and dust with 2 tablespoons of the sugar; refrigerate. In a saucepan, melt the 3 tablespoons of butter over moderate heat. Whisk in the flour to form a paste and cook, whisking, for 1 minute. Whisk in the milk, bring to a boil and cook, whisking constantly, until thickened, 1 minute. Remove the béchamel from the heat, then whisk in the vanilla and remaining ⅓ cup of sugar. Whisk in 4 egg yolks and reserve the remaining yolk for another use.

2. In a clean bowl, beat the whites until firm peaks form; whisk one-third into the béchamel, then fold in the remaining whites. Fold in the fruit and kirsch; scrape the mixture into the dish. Bake for 25 minutes, until puffed and lightly golden. Dust with confectioners' sugar and serve.

WINE Fruit-forward, off-dry Champagne: NV Veuve Clicquot Ponsardin Demi-Sec.

EGG TIP
Egg whites can yield different volumes when beaten. "Sometimes there's extra that won't fit in the dish–that's OK," says Jacques Pépin.

HOW TO START A SOUFFLÉ

MAKE ROUX Add flour to melted butter and whisk to form a paste.

MAKE BÉCHAMEL Whisk in milk and cook, whisking constantly, until thickened.

ADD YOLKS Blend egg yolks into the béchamel.

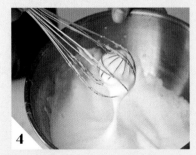

BEAT WHITES Whisk the egg whites until firm peaks form; fold into the béchamel.

Sunchoke Hash with Fried Eggs

Active **1 hr**; Total **1 hr 40 min**; Serves **4**

Adding nutty, slightly sweet roasted sunchokes and some well-aged cheddar cheese transforms a basic potato hash. Buy the smoothest, least knobby sunchokes you can find; they're easier to peel.

- **2½ lbs. sunchokes—scrubbed, peeled and cut into 1-inch pieces**
- **½ lb. German Butterball, baby Yukon or baby white potatoes, peeled and cut into 1-inch pieces**
- **5 Tbsp. extra-virgin olive oil**
  Kosher salt and freshly ground pepper
- **2 oz. sharp cheddar cheese, such as Beecher's or Bleu Mont Bandage Wrapped Cheddar, shredded (½ cup)**
- **4 small scallions, thinly sliced**
- **3 Tbsp. unsalted butter**
- **4 large eggs or duck eggs**

1. Preheat the oven to 400°. Spread the sunchokes and potatoes on 2 separate rimmed baking sheets. Toss the sunchokes with 2 tablespoons of the olive oil and season with salt and pepper. Toss the potatoes with 1 tablespoon of the olive oil and season with salt and pepper. Roast until fork-tender, 30 minutes for the potatoes and 35 minutes for the sunchokes.

2. Transfer the sunchokes and potatoes to a large bowl and mash with a wooden spoon or potato masher. Stir in the cheese and scallions and season the hash with salt and pepper.

3. In a large nonstick skillet, melt 1 tablespoon of the butter in 1 tablespoon of the olive oil over moderate heat. Scoop two ¾-cup measures of the hash into the skillet and flatten into 4-inch rounds. Cook over moderate heat until golden and crisp, 3 to 4 minutes per side. Transfer to plates and keep warm. Repeat with another 1 tablespoon each of the butter and olive oil and the remaining hash.

4. Wipe out the skillet and heat the remaining 1 tablespoon of butter in it. Add the eggs and cook over moderate heat until the whites are set and the yolks are slightly runny, about 3 minutes. Serve the hash topped with the eggs. —*Jessica Koslow*

Noodle Frittata with Smoky Paprika

Active **40 min**; Total **1 hr 10 min**; Serves **6**

Combining cooked egg noodles with smoky pimentón and eggs creates a fabulous dish that's a playful combination of noodle kugel and Spanish tortilla.

- **4 oz. wide egg noodles**
- **3 Tbsp. unsalted butter**
- **½ medium sweet onion, thinly sliced**
- **1 garlic clove, minced**
- **½ tsp. finely chopped thyme**
- **5½ oz. Idiazabal cheese, shredded (2 cups)**
- **1 tsp. sweet Pimentón de la Vera (smoked Spanish paprika), plus more for sprinkling**
- **8 large eggs**
- **½ cup fresh ricotta cheese**
- **¼ cup chicken stock or low-sodium broth**
- **¼ cup whole milk**
- **1 tsp. kosher salt**
- **½ tsp. freshly ground white pepper**

1. Preheat the oven to 375°. In a medium saucepan of salted boiling water, cook the noodles until al dente. Drain the noodles and cool under running water, then drain again.

2. In a 10-inch ovenproof nonstick skillet, melt the butter. Add the onion, garlic and thyme and cook over moderate heat, stirring occasionally, until the onion is softened and just starting to brown, about 7 minutes. Remove from the heat and stir in the noodles.

3. In a medium bowl, toss 1½ cups of the shredded cheese with the 1 teaspoon of paprika. In a blender, combine the eggs with the ricotta, chicken stock, milk, salt and white pepper and puree until smooth. Add the egg mixture and cheese to the skillet and mix well. Cover tightly with foil and bake for about 25 minutes, until the frittata is just set. Uncover and sprinkle the remaining ½ cup of cheese on top. Turn on the broiler and broil for about 2 minutes, until lightly browned on top. Let stand for 5 minutes. Sprinkle the frittata with paprika, cut into wedges and serve. —*Sherry Yard*

MAKE AHEAD The frittata can be kept at room temperature for up to 2 hours.

Brussels Sprout, Bacon and Gruyère Frittata

Total **30 min**; Serves **4 to 6**

Brussels sprouts have become one of America's favorite ingredients. Here, F&W's Justin Chapple comes up with a delicious way to use them: sautéed with shallots and bacon and baked into a cheesy frittata.

- **½ pound thick-cut bacon, diced**
- **2 shallots, halved and thinly sliced**
- **¾ lb. brussels sprouts, halved and sliced ¼ inch thick**
  Kosher salt and freshly ground pepper
- **8 large eggs**
- **2 Tbsp. whole milk**
- **1 cup shredded Gruyère cheese**
- **¼ cup snipped chives**

1. Preheat the broiler and position a rack 6 inches from the heat. In a 12-inch nonstick ovenproof skillet, cook the bacon over moderately high heat, stirring occasionally, until softened, 3 to 5 minutes. Add the shallots and cook, stirring occasionally, until softened, about 3 minutes. Add the brussels sprouts, season with salt and pepper and cook, tossing occasionally, until crisp-tender and lightly browned, about 5 minutes.

2. Meanwhile, in a large bowl, beat the eggs with the milk, 1 teaspoon of salt and ¼ teaspoon of pepper. Stir in the shredded cheese and snipped chives. Pour the egg mixture into the skillet and cook over moderate heat, stirring gently, until the eggs start to set and the bottom is lightly browned, about 5 minutes. Transfer the skillet to the oven and broil the frittata for about 3 minutes, until the center is just set. Run a rubber spatula around the edge of the frittata and slide it onto a serving plate. Cut into wedges and serve. —*Justin Chapple*

MAKE AHEAD The frittata can stand at room temperature for 1 hour.

BRUSSELS SPROUT, BACON AND
GRUYÈRE FRITTATA

Époisses, Ham and Apple Tart
Active **45 min**; Total **3 hr 45 min**
Serves **8 to 10**

For this savory tart, L.A. chef Ludo Lefebvre uses the pungent, soft cow-milk cheese Époisses, which is made in the Burgundy region of France near his hometown of Auxerre. He adds ham and apple to balance the richness of the cheese.

PASTRY

1¾ cups all-purpose flour, plus more for dusting

1¼ tsp. kosher salt

1 stick plus 1 Tbsp. cold butter, cubed

1 large egg yolk

FILLING

One 8-oz. wheel of chilled Époisses, cut into ½-inch pieces (with rind)

1 Pink Lady apple or other sweet cooking apple—peeled, cored and cut into ½-inch dice

¼ lb. piece of Parisian-style or boiled ham, cut into ⅓-inch dice

2 large eggs

1¼ cups heavy cream

1 tsp. kosher salt

¼ tsp. freshly ground white pepper

Pinch of freshly grated nutmeg

1. Make the pastry In a food processor, pulse the 1¾ cups of flour with the salt. Add the butter and pulse until it is the size of small peas. Add the egg yolk and ¼ cup of cold water and pulse until the pastry is moistened. Turn the pastry out onto a lightly floured work surface, gather any crumbs and pat into a disk. Wrap in plastic and refrigerate until firm, about 45 minutes.

2. Preheat the oven to 375°. On a lightly floured work surface, roll out the pastry to a 13-inch round. Ease the pastry into an 11-inch fluted tart pan with a removable bottom, pressing it into the corners and up the side. Trim the pastry ¼ inch above the rim of the tart pan and use the excess to patch any holes or thin parts. Refrigerate the tart shell until chilled, about 15 minutes.

3. Line the tart shell with parchment and fill with pie weights or dried beans. Bake for about 30 minutes, just until dry. Remove the parchment and weights and bake for 15 minutes longer, until golden. Let cool slightly, then transfer to a baking sheet.

4. Make the filling Scatter the Époisses, apple and ham evenly in the tart shell. In a bowl, beat the eggs with the heavy cream, salt, white pepper and nutmeg. Pour the custard into the tart shell and bake for about 45 minutes, rotating the sheet halfway through baking, until the custard is just set and lightly browned on top. Transfer the tart to a rack and let cool for 30 minutes. Remove the ring, cut the tart into wedges and serve. —*Ludo Lefebvre*

MAKE AHEAD The tart can be refrigerated overnight. Let come to room temperature before serving.

WINE Rich, minerally Chablis: 2012 Joseph Drouhin Réserve de Vaudon.

Sausage-and-Maple Bread Pudding
Active **30 min**; Total **1 hr 20 min**
Serves **6 to 8**

1 lb. bulk breakfast sausage

6 large eggs

1 pint vanilla or cinnamon ice cream, melted

2 tsp. thinly sliced sage leaves

2 tsp. kosher salt

1 cup pure maple syrup

¾ lb. brioche, crusts removed and bread torn into 1-inch pieces (10 cups)

¼ cup heavy cream

1. Preheat the oven to 350°. In a large skillet, cook the sausage over moderately high heat, breaking it up with a wooden spoon, until nicely browned and cooked through, 8 to 10 minutes. Using a slotted spoon, transfer the sausage to a bowl and let cool.

2. In a large bowl, beat the eggs with the ice cream, sage, salt, ½ cup of water and ½ cup of the maple syrup. Fold in the sausage and brioche. Scrape the mixture into a 9-inch square or 2-quart oval baking dish and let stand for 15 minutes. Bake for 35 minutes, or until the top is browned and the center is set.

3. Meanwhile, in a small saucepan, boil the remaining ½ cup of maple syrup over moderate heat, stirring, until reduced to ¼ cup, about 7 minutes. Remove from the heat; whisk in the cream. Serve the bread pudding with the maple cream.
—*Jeni Britton Bauer*

Christmas-Morning Casserole
Active **40 min**; Total **1 hr 40 min plus overnight soaking**; Serves **8**

Butter, for greasing

2 Tbsp. extra-virgin olive oil

2 oz. pepperoni, finely diced (½ cup)

½ lb. shiitake mushrooms, stems discarded and caps cut into ¾-inch pieces

1 medium onion, minced

1 red bell pepper, cut into ½-inch pieces

Kosher salt

8 large eggs

3 cups whole milk

1 Tbsp. Dijon mustard

1 Tbsp. soy sauce

½ tsp. pepper

¾ lb. day-old challah, sliced 1 inch thick and cut into 1-inch dice (10 cups)

6 oz. Black Forest ham, finely diced (1¼ cups)

¼ lb. Monterey Jack cheese, shredded (1 cup)

¼ lb. aged white cheddar cheese, shredded (1 cup)

½ cup finely chopped scallions, plus thinly sliced scallions for garnish

Hot sauce, for serving

1. Butter a 9-by-13-inch baking dish. In a large skillet, heat the olive oil. Add the pepperoni and cook over moderate heat until the fat is rendered, about 3 minutes. Add the shiitake and cook until lightly browned and tender, about 5 minutes. Add the onion, bell pepper and a generous pinch of salt and cook, stirring occasionally, until softened and browned, about 7 minutes; let cool completely.

2. In a large bowl, beat the eggs with the milk, mustard, soy sauce, pepper and 2 teaspoons of salt. Add the the cooled vegetable mixture, the challah, ham, both cheeses and the chopped scallions and mix well. Scrape the mixture into the prepared baking dish, cover with plastic wrap and refrigerate overnight.

3. Preheat the oven to 350°. Bake the casserole for about 50 minutes, until just set and browned on top. Let stand for 10 minutes, then garnish with sliced scallions and serve with hot sauce. —*Bryan Voltaggio*

Savory Oatmeal with Tomatoes, Parmesan and Eggs
⏱ Total **45 min**; Serves **4**

For this clever take on oatmeal, L.A. chef Sang Yoon cooks oats risotto-style with white wine and chicken stock. He tops the creamy mix with perfect poached eggs.

- **5 Tbsp. unsalted butter**
- **1 small shallot, minced**
- **1 garlic clove, very thinly sliced**
- **12 cherry tomatoes, halved**
- **½ Tbsp. tomato paste**
- **¾ cup dry white wine**
- **1 cup old-fashioned rolled oats**
- **2½ cups chicken stock or low-sodium broth**
- **¼ cup torn basil leaves, plus more for garnish**
- **¼ cup freshly grated Parmigiano-Reggiano cheese, plus more for serving**
- **Kosher salt and freshly ground pepper**
- **1 Tbsp. white vinegar**
- **4 large eggs**

1. In a medium saucepan, melt 4 tablespoons of the butter. Add the shallot and cook over moderate heat, stirring, until softened, about 2 minutes. Add the garlic, tomatoes, tomato paste and wine and bring to a boil. Simmer over moderately high heat, stirring, until nearly all the wine is absorbed and the tomatoes just start to pop, 4 to 5 minutes. Add the oats and chicken stock and cook over moderate heat, stirring occasionally, until the oats are just tender and suspended in a creamy sauce, 8 to 10 minutes. Stir in the ¼ cup of basil, ¼ cup of grated cheese and the remaining 1 tablespoon of butter. Season the oatmeal with salt and pepper and keep warm, adding tablespoons of water if it becomes too thick.

2. Meanwhile, bring a large, deep skillet of water to a simmer over moderate heat. Add the white vinegar and a generous pinch of salt. Crack the eggs into a small bowl, one at a time, and carefully slide them into the simmering water. Poach the eggs over moderate heat until the whites are set but the yolks are still slightly runny, about 4 minutes. Using a slotted spoon, transfer the poached eggs to paper towels to drain.

3. Spoon the oatmeal into shallow bowls. Top with the poached eggs, garnish with basil and serve right away, passing additional cheese at the table. —*Sang Yoon*

Pearl Barley Porridge with Ham and Eggs
Active **30 min**; Total **2 hr 20 min**
Serves **4 to 6**

Chef David Chang of the Momofuku empire first made this recipe at a food conference in Copenhagen. He simmered barley in local apple cider with chicken stock and kombu (an edible kelp available at natural food stores and Asian markets), creating a deliciously sweet and savory porridge.

- **1 cup apple cider**
- **3 cups low-sodium chicken broth**
- **One 4-by-6-inch piece of kombu**
- **4 Tbsp. unsalted butter**
- **2 onions, thinly sliced**
- **Kosher salt**
- **2 oz. cooked smoked ham, chopped (½ cup)**
- **2 cups pearled barley**
- **2 Tbsp. low-sodium soy sauce**
- **4 large eggs, poached**
- **Thinly sliced scallions, for serving**

1. In a large saucepan, combine the cider, broth, kombu and 2 cups of water. Bring just to a boil, then remove from the heat. Let steep for 40 minutes. Discard the kombu and transfer the cider broth to a bowl.

2. Wipe out the saucepan and melt the butter in it. Add the onions, season with salt and cook over moderate heat, stirring occasionally, until golden, about 20 minutes. Add the ham and cook for 3 minutes. Stir in the barley, soy sauce and cider broth and bring

to a boil. Cover and cook over low heat, stirring occasionally, until the barley is porridge-like, about 1 hour. Season with salt.

3. Spoon the porridge into bowls and top with the eggs. Garnish with scallions and serve. —*David Chang*

Ham and Deviled Egg Breakfast Sandwiches
⏱ Total **30 min**; Makes **4 sandwiches**

This irresistible breakfast is a hybrid of an egg salad sandwich and an Egg McMuffin. It combines spicy, pickle-laced egg salad with warm smoky ham and crisp frisée on a toasted English muffin.

- **8 large eggs**
- **¼ cup mayonnaise**
- **1 Tbsp. Dijon mustard**
- **1 tsp. hot sauce**
- **¾ tsp. hot paprika**
- **¼ cup finely chopped dill pickles, plus 1½ Tbsp. brine from the jar**
- **1 Tbsp. thinly sliced scallion**
- **Kosher salt and freshly ground black pepper**
- **1 cup torn frisée, light green parts only**
- **1½ tsp. extra-virgin olive oil**
- **Four 1-oz. slices of baked country ham**
- **4 English muffins, split and lightly toasted**

1. In a saucepan, cover the eggs with water and bring to a boil. Simmer over moderately high heat for 8 minutes. Drain and cool the eggs slightly under cold running water. Peel the eggs and coarsely chop them.

2. In a large bowl, whisk the mayonnaise with the mustard, hot sauce, paprika and 1 tablespoon of the pickle brine. Fold in the chopped eggs, pickles and scallion and season with salt and pepper.

3. In a medium bowl, toss the frisée with the olive oil and the remaining ½ tablespoon of pickle brine. Season the frisée with salt and pepper.

4. Preheat a large cast-iron skillet. Fry the ham slices, turning once, until lightly browned, about 2 minutes. Lay the ham slices on the muffin bottoms and top with the egg salad and frisée. Close the sandwiches and serve. —*Justin Chapple*

Ham-and-Cheddar Scallion Biscuit Sandwiches

Active **20 min**; Total **1 hr 30 min**
Makes **8 sandwiches**

"Scallions are so great with eggs," says Will Gilson, the chef at Puritan & Company in Cambridge, Massachusetts. He adds them to the biscuits he fills with ham, cheddar and fried eggs; they're one reason the breakfast sandwich is so good.

- **3** cups all-purpose flour, plus more for dusting
- **¼** cup sugar
- **1½** Tbsp. kosher salt
- **2** tsp. baking powder
- **1½** tsp. baking soda
- **1½** sticks chilled unsalted butter, cut into ½-inch cubes
- **1** cup chilled buttermilk
- **½** cup thinly sliced scallions
- **9** large eggs, 1 lightly beaten
- **16** slices of cheddar cheese (about 1 lb.)
- **16** slices of Virginia ham (about 1 lb.)
- **2** Tbsp. canola oil

1. In a large bowl, whisk the 3 cups of flour with the sugar, salt, baking powder and baking soda. Pinch the butter into the dry ingredients to form pea-size clumps. Stir in the buttermilk, scallions and the beaten egg just until a dry, shaggy dough forms. Turn the dough out onto a lightly floured work surface and knead gently just until it comes together. Pat the dough out to a ½-inch-thick rectangle. Using a 4-inch round cookie cutter, stamp out 6 biscuits. Gently press the scraps together and stamp out 2 more biscuits. Arrange the biscuits on a parchment paper–lined baking sheet and freeze for 30 minutes.

2. Preheat the oven to 375°. Bake the biscuits for about 20 minutes, until golden brown. Let cool slightly, then split in half, laying the halves cut side up on the baking sheet. Cover each biscuit half with 1 cheddar slice and 1 ham slice. Bake until the cheese is melted, about 8 minutes.

3. In a large nonstick skillet, heat the canola oil. Crack 4 eggs into the skillet and cook sunny side up over moderately high heat until the whites are set and the yolks are runny, 2 to 3 minutes. Set the fried eggs on 4 of the biscuit bottoms and keep warm while you fry the remaining eggs. Close the sandwiches and serve immediately.
—*Will Gilson*

Breakfast Banh Mi Sandwiches

Active **45 min**; Total **1 hr 30 min**
Makes **4 sandwiches**

Booty's Street Food in New Orleans offers dishes from around the world at brunch. Their Vietnamese banh mi includes duck pâté and spicy carrot and daikon pickles along with, less conventionally, five-spice-flavored bacon and a fried egg.

- **1½** cups unsweetened rice vinegar
- **½** cup granulated sugar
- **1½** Tbsp. Sriracha
- **½** tsp. kosher salt
- **1** cup carrot ribbons (shaved with a peeler from 1 medium carrot)
- **1** cup daikon ribbons (shaved with a peeler from 1 small peeled daikon)
- **8** thick-cut slices of bacon (about 1 lb.)
- **¼** cup light brown sugar
- **2** Tbsp. soy sauce
- **2** Tbsp. Shaoxing rice wine
- **1½** tsp. Chinese five-spice powder
- **½** tsp. garlic powder
- **¼** tsp. pepper
- **5** oz. liver pâté, preferably duck
   Four 8-inch soft baguette rolls, split and toasted
- **8** thin cucumber spears
- **2** jalapeños, seeded and julienned
- **8** cilantro sprigs
- **¼** cup mayonnaise
- **1** Tbsp. extra-virgin olive oil
- **4** large eggs

1. In a medium saucepan, stir the vinegar, granulated sugar, Sriracha and salt over high heat until the sugar is dissolved. Add the carrot and daikon ribbons and let cool to room temperature.

2. Preheat the oven to 400°. On a rack set over a rimmed baking sheet, sprinkle the bacon slices with the brown sugar. In a small saucepan, cook the soy sauce, rice wine, 1 teaspoon of the five-spice powder, ¼ teaspoon of the garlic powder and the pepper over high heat, stirring, for 1 minute. Drizzle the mixture over the bacon. Bake just until cooked through, about 15 minutes. Sprinkle the bacon with the remaining ½ teaspoon of five-spice powder and ¼ teaspoon of garlic powder and bake until browned and crisp, about 5 minutes.

3. Spread the pâté on the bottom halves of the toasted rolls and top with the bacon, cucumber, carrot and daikon pickles, jalapeños and cilantro. Spread the mayonnaise on the top halves of the rolls.

4. Heat the olive oil in a large nonstick skillet. Crack the eggs into the skillet and cook sunny side up until the whites are set and the yolks are runny, 2 to 3 minutes. Place a fried egg on each sandwich and serve.
—*Booty's Street Food • New Orleans*

HAM-AND-CHEDDAR SCALLION
BISCUIT SANDWICHES

Skillet Buttermilk Biscuits

Total **40 min**
Makes **about twenty 2-inch biscuits**

For these biscuits baked in a cast-iron skillet, Colleen Cruze Bhatti uses the excellent buttermilk from her dairy farm in Knoxville, Tennessee. She says there are three secrets to making a good biscuit: "Be sure your butter is nice and cold, use high-quality buttermilk and don't overwork your dough." She adds, "Being a proud biscuit-maker runs in my family. My mom says she has never tasted a biscuit better than her own. I haven't tasted a biscuit better than mine. My dad says my sister makes the best he's ever had."

- **1 stick cold unsalted butter, cubed, plus more for greasing**
- **2 cups all-purpose flour, plus more for dusting**
- **4 tsp. baking powder**
- **1 tsp. kosher salt**
- **¼ tsp. baking soda**
- **1¼ cups cold buttermilk**

1. Preheat the oven to 450° and butter a 12-inch cast-iron skillet. In a large bowl, whisk the 2 cups of flour with the baking powder, salt and baking soda. Add the cubed butter and, using your fingers, pinch the butter into the flour until the mixture resembles very coarse crumbs, with some of the butter the size of small peas. Gently stir in the buttermilk just until a soft dough forms.

2. Scrape the dough out onto a lightly floured work surface and pat it into a ¾-inch-thick round. Using a 2-inch round biscuit cutter, stamp out biscuits as close together as possible. Gently press the scraps together and stamp out more biscuits. Arrange the biscuits in the prepared skillet and bake for 12 to 14 minutes, until golden brown. Serve warm. —*Colleen Cruze Bhatti*

MAKE AHEAD The biscuits can be made earlier in the day and reheated in a 350° oven for 3 to 5 minutes.

Bannock Scones with Three Butters

Active **30 min**; Total **1 hr 50 min**
Makes **10 large scones**

Bannock is a traditional Scottish flat-bread. Chef Paul Berglund of The Bachelor Farmer in Minneapolis adds butter and cream to magically transform the bread into light and tender scones.

- **3½ cups all-purpose flour**
- **¼ cup sugar**
- **1 Tbsp. plus 1 tsp. baking powder**
- **2 tsp. kosher salt**
- **2 sticks plus 2 Tbsp. unsalted butter, diced and chilled**
- **2 cups heavy cream**
- **1 large egg**
- **1 large egg beaten with 1 Tbsp. of water**
- **Three butters (recipes follow), for serving**

1. In a medium bowl, sift the flour with the sugar, baking powder and salt. In a food processor, pulse the dry ingredients with the diced butter until the butter is the size of large peas. Transfer the mixture to a large bowl and refrigerate until well chilled, about 30 minutes.

2. Line 2 baking sheets with parchment paper. In a medium bowl, whisk the cream with the egg. Stir the cream mixture into the dry ingredients until a sticky dough forms. Using a ½-cup measure, scoop 5 mounds of dough onto each prepared baking sheet, spacing them well apart. Brush the mounds with the egg wash and refrigerate until chilled, about 20 minutes.

3. Preheat the oven to 400° and position racks in the upper and lower thirds. Bake the scones for about 30 minutes, until golden and cooked through; shift the sheets from front to back and top to bottom halfway through baking. Let the scones cool on the baking sheets. Serve with the three butters. —*Paul Berglund*

MAKE AHEAD The scones can be stored in an airtight container overnight.

BURNT BUTTER

Active **10 min**; Total **30 min**
Makes **about ½ cup**

The clever trick here is mixing melted and cooled browned butter with softened butter, giving the finished spread a creamy texture and a toasty, nutty flavor.

- **1 stick unsalted butter at room temperature, diced**
- **Kosher salt**

1. In a medium skillet, cook 4 tablespoons of the butter over moderately high heat, swirling the pan, until the milk solids are very dark brown, 3 to 5 minutes. Pour the brown butter into a bowl, leaving the dark solids behind; let cool to room temperature.

2. Gradually whisk the remaining 4 table-spoons of butter into the browned butter. Refrigerate until slightly thickened, 15 minutes. Season with salt and serve. —*PB*

HONEY BUTTER

Total **5 min**; Makes **½ cup**

- **1 stick unsalted butter at room temperature**
- **1 Tbsp. honey**
- **Kosher salt**

In a medium bowl, blend the softened butter with the honey until smooth. Season with salt and serve. —*PB*

THREE-HERB BUTTER

Total **15 min**; Makes **about ½ cup**

This simple flavor booster is great with pretty much everything: bread, steak, seafood, and corn and other vegetables.

- **1 stick unsalted butter at room temperature**
- **2 Tbsp. finely chopped tarragon**
- **2 Tbsp. finely chopped flat-leaf parsley**
- **½ tsp. finely chopped thyme**
- **½ Tbsp. fresh lemon juice**
- **Kosher salt and pepper**

In a medium bowl, blend the softened butter with the chopped tarragon, parsley and thyme. Stir in the lemon juice. Season with kosher salt and pepper and serve. —*PB*

MAKE AHEAD The herb butter can be wrapped in plastic and refrigerated for up to 3 days. Serve at room temperature.

SKILLET BUTTERMILK BISCUITS

Pimento Cheese Muffins

⏱ Total **45 min**; Makes **12 muffins**

2½ cups all-purpose flour

 1 Tbsp. plus 1 tsp. smoked paprika

 1 Tbsp. kosher salt

 1 Tbsp. baking powder

 1 tsp. baking soda

 1 tsp. freshly ground pepper

1½ cups buttermilk

 2 large eggs

 4 Tbsp. unsalted butter, melted and cooled

 ½ Tbsp. jarred harissa paste (see Note)

 ¼ cup finely chopped chives

 ½ small yellow onion, minced

 3 Tbsp. sliced scallions

 3 Tbsp. minced parsley

1½ Tbsp. Worcestershire sauce

 5 oz. extra-sharp cheddar cheese, shredded (1½ cups)

 3 oz. drained jarred pimientos, chopped (½ cup)

   Pimento cheese, for serving (optional)

1. Preheat the oven to 375°. In a medium bowl, whisk the flour with the paprika, salt, baking powder, baking soda and pepper. In a large bowl, whisk the buttermilk with the eggs, butter, harissa, chives, onion, scallions, parsley and Worcestershire until smooth. Whisk in the dry ingredients just until combined. Stir in the cheese and chopped pimientos.

2. Using a ⅓-cup measure, scoop the batter into 12 muffin cups. Bake for about 18 minutes, until golden brown on top and a toothpick inserted in the middle of a muffin comes out clean. Let cool for 5 minutes, then unmold and serve with pimento cheese. —*Lincoln Carson*

NOTE Harissa, the brick-red Tunisian chile paste, is available at specialty food stores and markets like Whole Foods.

MAKE AHEAD The muffins can be stored in an airtight container overnight.

Black Pepper Biscuits with Bourbon-Molasses Butter

Active **1 hr;** Total **2 hr 15 min**
Makes **8 to 10 biscuits**

"Once you add the buttermilk, quit mixing as soon as the dough comes together," star chef Bobby Flay advises. "Overmixing creates biscuits that aren't tender and flaky."

BOURBON-MOLASSES BUTTER

 2 Tbsp. unsulfured molasses

 1 Tbsp. bourbon

   Small pinch of cinnamon

1½ sticks unsalted butter, softened

   Salt

BISCUITS

 4 cups all-purpose flour

 1 Tbsp. plus 1 tsp. baking powder

 1 tsp. baking soda

   Kosher salt and coarsely ground black pepper

 1 stick plus 6 Tbsp. unsalted butter, cubed and chilled

 2 cups cold buttermilk, plus more for brushing

1. Make the bourbon-molasses butter In a small saucepan, whisk the molasses with the bourbon and cinnamon. Bring just to a boil, then cook over low heat for 2 minutes. Let cool completely.

2. In a food processor, combine the cooled molasses mixture with the butter and puree until smooth. Scrape the butter into a bowl and season with salt. Cover and refrigerate for 1 hour.

3. Make the biscuits Preheat the oven to 450° and line a baking sheet with parchment. In a large bowl, whisk the flour with the baking powder, baking soda, 2 teaspoons of salt and 1½ teaspoons of pepper. Scatter the cubed butter over the dry ingredients and, using your fingers, pinch the butter into the flour to form small sheets of butter, with some of the butter about the size of peas. Stir in the 2 cups of buttermilk just until a dry, shaggy dough forms.

4. Turn the dough out onto a work surface and knead gently, folding the dough over itself 2 or 3 times to form a layered dough. Pat the dough out to a 1-inch-thick rectangle. Using a large, sharp knife, cut out as many 3-inch-square biscuits as you can. Gently press the scraps together and cut out more biscuits.

5. Arrange the biscuits on the prepared baking sheet. Brush them with buttermilk and sprinkle with coarsely ground black pepper. Bake for about 15 minutes, until golden brown. Serve warm with the bourbon-molasses butter. —*Bobby Flay*

Jumbo Pancetta, Thyme and Gruyère Muffins

Active **35 min;** Total **1 hr 10 min**
Makes **6 jumbo muffins**

 1 cup finely diced pancetta (5 oz.)

 3 cups all-purpose flour

 2 Tbsp. fresh thyme leaves

 1 Tbsp. sugar

 1 Tbsp. baking powder

 ½ tsp. baking soda

 1 tsp. kosher salt

 ¼ tsp. finely grated orange zest

 4 Tbsp. unsalted butter, melted and cooled slightly

 2 large eggs

 2 cups buttermilk

 6 oz. Gruyère cheese, shredded (2 cups)

1. Preheat the oven to 375° and position the rack in the lower third. Coat 6 jumbo muffin cups with nonstick baking spray. In a medium skillet, cook the pancetta over moderate heat, stirring occasionally, until browned but not crisp, about 7 minutes. Using a slotted spoon, transfer the pancetta to a paper towel–lined plate to drain.

2. In a large bowl, whisk the flour with the thyme, sugar, baking powder, baking soda, salt and orange zest. In another large bowl, beat the butter with the eggs until well combined. Fold in the dry ingredients and the buttermilk in 2 alternating additions, then fold in the cheese and pancetta.

3. Spoon the batter into the prepared muffin cups. Bake for 30 to 35 minutes, until golden on top and a toothpick inserted in the center of a muffin comes out clean. Let cool for 5 minutes, then transfer the muffins to a rack to cool slightly before serving. —*Georgia Pellegrini*

Fresh Corn Muffins

Active **25 min**; Total **50 min plus cooling**
Makes **24 muffins**

Zoe Nathan of Huckleberry Bakery and Café in Los Angeles likes both sweet and savory breakfast foods. She bakes these muffins with fresh corn kernels, giving them a delicate, moist crumb.

- 1 **cup all-purpose flour**
- ¾ **cup fine stone-ground cornmeal**
- ¼ **cup plus 2 Tbsp. rye flour**
- 1 **Tbsp. baking powder**
- ½ **tsp. baking soda**
- 1½ **cups buttermilk**
- ½ **cup canola oil**
- ¼ **cup honey**
- 6 **Tbsp. unsalted butter**
- ¼ **cup sugar**
- 1¾ **tsp. kosher salt**
- 4 **large eggs**
- 1 **cup fresh corn kernels (from 2 ears)**

1. Preheat the oven to 400° and line two 12-cup muffin tins with paper or foil liners. In a medium bowl, whisk the all-purpose flour with the cornmeal, rye flour, baking powder and baking soda. In another medium bowl, whisk the buttermilk with the oil and honey.

2. In a stand mixer fitted with the paddle or using a handheld electric mixer, beat the butter, sugar and salt at medium-high speed until light and fluffy, 1 to 2 minutes. Beat in the eggs 1 at a time, scraping down the side of the bowl as needed. Add the dry ingredients and beat at medium speed until evenly combined. At low speed, gradually beat in the buttermilk mixture until just incorporated, then fold in the corn.

3. Spoon the batter into the prepared muffin cups. Bake for about 15 minutes, until a toothpick inserted in the center of the muffins comes out clean. Let the muffins cool in the pans for 10 minutes before turning them out onto a rack to cool completely. —*Zoe Nathan*

MAKE AHEAD The muffins can be stored in an airtight container for up to 3 days.

Pear and Sour Cream Coffee Cake

Active **50 min**; Total **1 hr 50 min plus cooling**; Serves **12**

TOPPING

- 1½ **cups all-purpose flour**
- 1 **cup rolled oats**
- 1 **cup pecans, coarsely chopped (optional)**
- 1 **cup light brown sugar**
- 2½ **tsp. cinnamon**
- 1 **tsp. ground ginger**
- 1 **tsp. kosher salt**
- 1 **stick plus 6 Tbsp. unsalted butter, softened**
- 2 **Bartlett pears—peeled, cored and cut into ½-inch pieces**

CAKE

- 2½ **cups all-purpose flour**
- 1 **tsp. baking powder**
- ¾ **tsp. baking soda**
- 1 **tsp. kosher salt**
- 2 **sticks unsalted butter, softened, plus more for greasing**
- 1½ **cups granulated sugar**
- 3 **large eggs**
- 1¼ **cups sour cream**
- 2 **tsp. pure vanilla extract**
  Confectioners' sugar, for dusting (optional)

1. Make the topping In a large bowl, whisk the flour with the oats, pecans (if using), brown sugar, cinnamon, ginger and salt. With your hands, rub the butter into the mixture until incorporated, pressing it into clumps. Add the pears and toss well. Refrigerate the topping until chilled, about 20 minutes.

2. Meanwhile, make the cake Preheat the oven to 350° and grease a 9-by-13-inch metal baking pan. In a medium bowl, whisk the flour, baking powder, baking soda and salt. In a stand mixer fitted with the paddle, beat the 2 sticks of butter with the sugar at medium speed until fluffy, 2 minutes. Beat in the eggs 1 at a time, then beat in the sour cream and vanilla. Scrape down the side of the bowl, then beat the dry ingredients into the batter in 3 additions until just incorporated.

3. Scrape the batter into the prepared pan, spreading it in an even layer. Cover with the streusel-pear topping. Bake for 1 hour and 15 minutes, until the crumb topping is browned and a toothpick inserted in the center of the cake comes out clean. Transfer the pan to a rack and let the cake cool completely, about 1 hour. Dust the cake with confectioners' sugar, cut into squares and serve. —*Justin Chapple*

Jumbo Strawberry and Rhubarb Muffins

Active **30 min**; Total **1 hr 20 min**
Makes **6 jumbo muffins**

- 3 **cups all-purpose flour**
- ¾ **cup turbinado sugar, plus more for sprinkling**
- 1 **Tbsp. baking powder**
- ½ **tsp. baking soda**
- 1 **tsp. kosher salt**
- 1 **stick plus 2 Tbsp. unsalted butter, melted and cooled slightly**
- 2 **large eggs**
- 1½ **cups buttermilk**
- 1¾ **cups diced strawberries**
- 1¾ **cups diced fresh rhubarb**
- 1 **tsp. finely grated lemon zest**

1. Preheat the oven to 375° and position the rack in the lower third of the oven. Coat 6 jumbo muffin cups with nonstick baking spray. In a large bowl, mix the flour with the ¾ cup of sugar, the baking powder, baking soda and salt. In another large bowl, beat the butter with the eggs until well combined. Fold in the dry ingredients and buttermilk in 2 alternating additions, then fold in the strawberries, rhubarb and lemon zest.

2. Spoon the batter into the prepared muffin cups and sprinkle the tops generously with sugar. Bake for 50 to 60 minutes, until golden on top and a toothpick inserted in the center of a muffin comes out clean. Transfer the muffins to a rack to cool before serving. —*Georgia Pellegrini*

MAKE AHEAD The muffins can be stored in an airtight container overnight. Reheat for 5 minutes in a 375° oven.

Glazed Maple-Walnut Kringle

Active **2 hr**; Total **7 hr 30 min**
Serves **12 to 16**

"An all-out Wisconsin classic," says New York City restaurateur (and Wisconsin native) Gabriel Stulman about the kringle. "It's like a giant toaster strudel filled with things like nuts, fruit and cheeses." Here, the tender pastry, made with sour cream and flavored with vanilla, is filled with a walnut mixture sweetened with brown sugar and maple syrup, then shaped into a giant round and baked.

DOUGH

- ½ cup whole milk
- One ¼-oz. package active dry yeast
- 2 Tbsp. granulated sugar
- ½ cup sour cream
- 1 large egg, lightly beaten
- 1 Tbsp. pure vanilla extract
- ½ tsp. kosher salt
- 3 cups all-purpose flour, plus more for dusting
- 2 sticks unsalted butter, at room temperature

FILLING

- 1½ cups walnuts
- ¾ cup all-purpose flour
- ½ cup packed dark brown sugar
- ½ cup pure maple syrup
- 1 stick unsalted butter, at room temperature, plus melted butter for brushing
- 1 tsp. pure vanilla extract
- ½ tsp. kosher salt
- Turbinado sugar, for sprinkling

GLAZE

- 2 cups confectioners' sugar
- 3½ Tbsp. milk
- Pinch of salt

1. Make the dough In a small saucepan, warm the milk over moderately low heat to 110°. Pour into a large bowl and stir in the yeast and 1 tablespoon of the sugar. Let stand until foamy, 10 minutes. Whisk in the sour cream, egg, vanilla, salt and the remaining 1 tablespoon of sugar. Add all but 2 tablespoons of the flour and stir until a shaggy dough forms.

2. Coat a large bowl with nonstick cooking spray. Scrape the dough out onto a lightly floured surface and knead until very smooth, 6 minutes. Form into a ball and transfer to the bowl. Cover tightly with plastic wrap and let stand in a warm place until doubled in bulk, 1½ hours.

3. In a bowl, blend the butter with the remaining 2 tablespoons of flour until smooth. Scrape the butter onto a large sheet of plastic wrap, shape it into a 6-inch square and wrap well. Refrigerate until barely firm, about 15 minutes.

4. On a lightly floured surface, roll out the dough to a 10-by-16-inch rectangle. Set the butter square in the center of the dough. Fold the short sides of the dough over the butter to enclose it; pinch the open ends of the packet to seal. Rotate the packet so that one pinched end is facing you. Roll out the dough to a 15-by-8-inch rectangle. (The butter should be pliable; chill the dough for 10 minutes if the butter is too soft.) Fold one-third of the dough into the center and the other third on top, like you would fold a letter. Turn the dough 90°. Roll out the dough again to a 15-by-8-inch rectangle and fold like a letter again. (This is 2 turns.) Wrap in plastic and refrigerate for 1 hour. Repeat the rolling, folding and chilling 2 more times for a total of 6 turns.

5. Meanwhile, make the filling Preheat the oven to 350°. On a rimmed baking sheet, toast the nuts for 12 minutes, until golden. Let cool, then finely chop. In a bowl, mix the nuts with the flour and brown sugar. Mix in the maple syrup, 1 stick of butter, vanilla and salt. Cover and refrigerate for 10 minutes. Leave the oven on.

6. On a lightly floured surface, roll out the dough to a 30-by-8-inch rectangle. Spread the filling down the length of the rectangle, leaving a 2-inch border of dough on each side. Fold one long side over the filling, then fold the other long side on top, overlapping by ½ inch; pinch to seal. Slide the dough onto a large sheet of parchment paper and roll it over so it's seam side down. Shape the dough into a ring: Moisten the inside of one end with water and place the other end inside, pinching to seal. Slide the parchment and kringle onto a rimmed baking sheet. Refrigerate until chilled, 30 minutes.

7. Brush the kringle all over with melted butter and sprinkle with turbinado sugar. Bake the kringle in the center of the oven for about 50 minutes, until puffed and golden; some of the filling may seep out. Let the kringle cool for 30 minutes.

8. Make the glaze In a medium bowl, whisk all of the ingredients together until smooth. Drizzle the glaze over the kringle and let stand for 15 minutes before cutting into wedges and serving. —*Mehdi Brunet-Benkritly and Gabriel Stulman*

MAKE AHEAD The glazed kringle can be kept at room temperature for up to 2 days.

GLAZED MAPLE-WALNUT KRINGLE

Coconut Pancakes

⏱ Total **35 min**; Serves **6**

2½ cups sweetened shredded coconut (10 oz.)

4 cups all-purpose flour

2 Tbsp. baking powder

2 tsp. kosher salt

2 cups buttermilk

1½ cups whole milk

3 large eggs

2 Tbsp. pure coconut extract

1½ tsp. honey

4 Tbsp. unsalted butter, melted and cooled, plus more for serving

Canola oil, for brushing

Confectioners' sugar, blueberries and pure maple syrup, for serving

1. Preheat the oven to 350°. Spread the coconut in an even layer on a parchment paper–lined baking sheet and toast until lightly browned, about 5 minutes. Let cool, then transfer to a bowl; reserve the baking sheet. Reduce the oven temperature to 200°.

2. In a large bowl, whisk the flour with the baking powder and salt. In a medium bowl, whisk the buttermilk, whole milk, eggs, coconut extract, honey and the 4 tablespoons of the butter until smooth. Whisk into the dry ingredients just until combined; there will be a few lumps. Let the batter stand for 10 minutes.

3. Heat a griddle or large nonstick skillet until hot, then brush with canola oil. Ladle ¼ cup of batter per pancake onto the griddle and spread into 4- to 5-inch rounds. Sprinkle each pancake with 1 tablespoon of the toasted coconut and cook over moderate heat, flipping once, about 1½ minutes per side. Transfer the pancakes to the reserved baking sheet, cover with a kitchen towel and keep warm in the oven. Repeat with the remaining batter and more toasted coconut to make 18 pancakes in all. To serve, stack the pancakes on plates, sprinkling additional toasted coconut between the layers. Dust with confectioners' sugar and top with blueberries. Serve immediately, with butter and maple syrup. —Adam Schop

Gluten-Free Banana-Coconut Pancakes

📷 PAGE 284

⏱ Total **30 min**; Serves **4**

The key to these easy pancakes is coconut flour, which contributes a delicate flavor and airy texture. It's available at specialty food shops and from amazon.com.

8 large eggs, at room temperature

1 cup mashed overripe banana

1½ tsp. pure vanilla extract

½ cup coconut flour, preferably Bob's Red Mill

2 tsp. baking powder

1 tsp. kosher salt

Coconut oil, for greasing

Warm pure maple syrup, fresh berries, crisp bacon and slivered almonds, for topping

1. In a medium bowl, beat the eggs with the banana, vanilla and ¼ cup of water. In another medium bowl, whisk the coconut flour with the baking powder and salt. Whisk in the egg mixture until incorporated.

2. Heat a griddle or large nonstick skillet and grease with coconut oil. For each pancake, scoop 3-tablespoon mounds of batter onto the griddle and cook over moderate heat until golden on the bottom and bubbles just appear on the surface, about 3 minutes. Flip and cook until risen and firm, about 3 minutes longer. Repeat with the remaining batter. Transfer the pancakes to plates and top with maple syrup, berries, bacon and almonds; serve right away. —Jamie McDaniel

Lemon-Ricotta Pancakes with Caramelized Apples

⏱ Total **40 min**; Serves **4**

Whipped egg whites make these ricotta pancakes especially fluffy. The apples piled on top are so luscious and buttery that you might not even need syrup.

2 Tbsp. unsalted butter, plus more for greasing

2 crisp red or pink apples, preferably Honeycrisp—peeled, cored and cut into ½-inch pieces

½ teaspoon cinnamon

¼ cup sugar

1¼ tsp. finely grated lemon zest

Kosher salt

1½ cups all-purpose flour

1 tsp. baking powder

1½ cups whole milk

3 large eggs, separated

½ cup fresh ricotta cheese

Warm pure maple syrup, for serving

1. In a large skillet, melt the 2 tablespoons of butter. Add the apples, cinnamon, 2 tablespoons of the sugar, ½ teaspoon of the lemon zest and a pinch of salt and cook over moderately high heat, stirring occasionally, until the apples are just tender and golden, about 5 minutes; keep warm.

2. In a large bowl, whisk the flour and baking powder with ½ teaspoon of salt and the remaining 2 tablespoons of sugar. In a medium bowl, whisk the milk with the egg yolks, ricotta and the remaining ¾ teaspoon of lemon zest. Whisk into the dry ingredients until just incorporated.

3. In a clean large stainless steel bowl, beat the egg whites until stiff peaks form; fold them into the batter.

4. Preheat a griddle and grease it with butter. Scoop ¼-cup mounds of batter onto the griddle. Cook the pancakes over moderately high heat until bubbles appear on the surface, 1 to 2 minutes. Flip and cook until the pancakes are risen and golden brown on the bottom, about 2 minutes longer. Transfer to plates, spoon the warm apples on top and serve with warm maple syrup. —Justin Chapple

12 Minutes

SPICED STRAWBERRIES WITH YOGURT

In a mortar, using a pestle, grind ³⁄₄ tsp. toasted **caraway seeds** with 1½ Tbsp. **light brown sugar** and a pinch of **sea salt**. Add 3 Tbsp. **olive oil** and grind until blended. Stir in ½ cup toasted sliced **almonds** and 2 tsp. finely grated **lemon zest**. In a large bowl, toss 1 lb. halved **strawberries** with the almond mixture and serve with **Greek-style yogurt**.
—*Heidi Swanson*

Caramelized Bananas Foster Crêpes with Whipped Cream

Active **30 min**; Total **1 hr 45 min**; Serves **4**

Caramelized bananas Foster originated at the legendary Brennan's in New Orleans. To transform it into a brunch dish, the restaurant's chef, Slade Rushing, bakes the bananas on tender crêpes.

- ²⁄₃ **cup all-purpose flour**
- ¼ **tsp. ground cinnamon**
- ¼ **tsp. kosher salt**
- ¾ **cup milk**
- 2 **large eggs**
- 1½ **tsp. dark rum**
- 5 **Tbsp. unsalted butter, melted and cooled, plus more for greasing**
- 3 **bananas, cut into ½-inch diagonal slices**
- ½ **cup light brown sugar**
- ¾ **cup heavy cream**
- 2 **tsp. confectioners' sugar**

1. In a medium bowl, whisk the flour with the cinnamon and salt. In a small bowl, whisk the milk with the eggs, dark rum and 3 tablespoons of the melted butter until smooth. Whisk the wet ingredients into the dry ingredients just until combined; there will be a few lumps. Refrigerate, covered, for 1 hour or overnight.

2. Preheat the oven to 425°; butter 2 foil-lined baking sheets. Heat an 8-inch nonstick skillet. Pour ½ cup of the batter into the skillet, swirl to distribute evenly and cook over moderate heat until set, about 2 minutes. Invert the crêpe onto a prepared baking sheet. Repeat with the remaining batter to make a total of 4 crêpes.

3. Heat the remaining 2 tablespoons of melted butter in the skillet. Add the bananas and cook over moderately high heat, stirring once, until lightly caramelized but not falling apart, about 2 minutes. Spoon the bananas over the crêpes and sprinkle with the brown sugar. Bake for 16 minutes, until the sugar is melted and bubbling.

4. In a bowl, beat the heavy cream with the confectioners' sugar until firm. Using 2 large spatulas, transfer the crêpes to plates. Top with a dollop of the whipped cream and serve at once. —*Slade Rushing*

WINE Creamy, lightly sweet sparkling Moscato d'Asti: 2013 Elio Perrone Sourgal.

Nutty Granola with Strawberry Compote and Greek Yogurt

Active **45 min**; Total **1 hr 30 min**; Makes **10 cups granola and 2 cups compote**

This granola from Zoe Nathan of L.A.'s Huckleberry Bakery and Café is toasty and crisp, and loaded with nuts, dried fruit and coconut. She serves it with plain Greek yogurt and a generous dollop of her garnet-hued strawberry compote.

GRANOLA

- **1 lb. old-fashioned rolled oats (4 cups)**
- **1 stick unsalted butter, melted and cooled**
- **½ cup honey**
- **1½ tsp. kosher salt**
- **¼ tsp. ground cinnamon**
- **1 cup unsweetened coconut flakes**
- **½ cup raw almonds**
- **½ cup raw walnuts**
- **⅓ cup raw *pepitas* (hulled pumpkin seeds)**
- **¼ cup flaxseeds**
- **1 cup dried cherries (4 oz.)**
- **1 cup dried apricots, chopped (5 oz.)**
- **Plain Greek yogurt, for serving**

COMPOTE

- **1½ lbs. strawberries, hulled**
- **¼ cup sugar**
- **2 Tbsp. water**
- **¼ tsp. kosher salt**

1. **Make the granola** Preheat the oven to 325°. In a large bowl, toss the oats, butter, honey, salt and cinnamon until evenly coated. Spread the oats on a rimmed baking sheet. Bake for 20 minutes, stirring once or twice, until just starting to brown. Add the coconut, almonds, walnuts, *pepitas* and flaxseeds and mix well. Bake for 25 minutes longer, stirring, until the granola is golden brown and nearly dry. Remove from the oven and toss in the dried cherries and apricots. Let the granola cool completely on the baking sheet, stirring occasionally.

2. **Meanwhile, make the compote** In a medium saucepan, combine all of the ingredients and bring to a boil. Cover and cook over moderate heat, stirring, until the strawberries soften, 8 minutes. Uncover and simmer over moderately low heat, stirring, until the compote is syrupy,

10 minutes. Let cool completely, then refrigerate until chilled, 30 minutes.

3. To serve, spoon some yogurt and granola into bowls and top with the strawberry compote. —*Zoe Nathan*

MAKE AHEAD The granola can be stored in an airtight container and the compote refrigerated for up to 1 week.

Candied Ginger, Coconut and Quinoa Granola

Active **15 min**; Total **45 min plus cooling** Makes **about 5½ cups**

- **¾ cup rolled oats**
- **½ cup quinoa, rinsed and drained**
- **⅓ cup pumpkin seeds**
- **⅓ cup sliced almonds**
- **⅓ cup sweetened shredded coconut**
- **¼ cup light brown sugar**
- **1 tsp. ground cinnamon**
- **1 tsp. ground ginger**
- **1 tsp. kosher salt**
- **½ cup applesauce**
- **¼ cup honey**
- **2 Tbsp. coconut oil**
- **¼ cup each of dried cranberries and halved dried cherries**
- **¼ cup crystallized ginger, finely chopped**
- **Mixed berries and fresh ricotta cheese or plain Greek yogurt, for serving**

1. Preheat the oven to 325°. In a medium bowl, combine the oats, quinoa, pumpkin seeds, almonds, coconut, brown sugar, cinnamon, ground ginger and salt. In a small bowl, whisk the applesauce with the honey and coconut oil. Add the applesauce mixture to the dry ingredients and toss to coat. Scatter the granola in an even layer on a parchment paper–lined baking sheet and bake for 30 minutes, stirring occasionally, until golden brown and crisp. Let cool completely.

2. Transfer the granola to a bowl and stir in the dried cranberries and cherries and the crystallized ginger. Serve with mixed berries and ricotta. —*Amanda Rockman*

Fresh Ricotta

Active **15 min**; Total **1 hr**; Makes **2 cups**

This recipe is from Dan Barber, the chef-owner of Blue Hill at Stone Barns in Pocantico Hills, New York, and author of *The Third Plate*. He makes his wonderful ricotta with buttermilk as well as whole milk, so it's slightly tart and creamy. It's terrific spread on toast with a little honey.

- **2 quarts whole milk**
- **2 cups buttermilk**
- **Kosher salt**

Line a colander with cheesecloth and set it over a large bowl. In a large saucepan, combine the milk and buttermilk. Cook over moderate heat, stirring occasionally, until the milk starts to separate and reaches 185° on a candy thermometer, about 5 minutes. Cook for 3 more minutes. Remove the saucepan from the heat and let stand for 10 minutes. Using a ladle, gently spoon the mixture into the prepared colander and let drain until the ricotta is thick, about 30 minutes. Transfer the ricotta to a medium bowl and season with salt; reserve the whey for another use. —*Dan Barber*

MAKE AHEAD The ricotta can be refrigerated for up to 2 days.

Blackberry Buttermilk Smoothies

Total **20 min**; Serves **2**

Colleen Cruze Bhatti, co-owner of Cruze Farm in Knoxville, Tennessee, thinks of her buttermilk smoothies as drinkable yogurt, with the same kind of healthy probiotic bacteria. She serves the extra-tangy smoothies at her farm stand in the hope of creating new buttermilk aficionados.

- **1 cup chilled blackberries**
- **1 cup chilled buttermilk**
- **2 Tbsp. honey**
- **Pinch of salt**

In a blender, combine all of the ingredients and puree until smooth. Refrigerate until well chilled, about 15 minutes. Pour the smoothies into tall glasses and serve. —*Colleen Cruze Bhatti*

CANDIED GINGER, COCONUT
AND QUINOA GRANOLA

ROASTED PEACH COBBLER
WITH VANILLA ICE CREAM AND
BALSAMIC SYRUP
Recipe, page 322

Tarts, Pies & Fruit Desserts

Spiced Apple Pie
with Cheddar Crust

Active **35 min**; Total **2 hr 55 min plus
4 hr cooling**; Makes **one 10-inch pie**

CRUST

- **2 cups all-purpose flour**
- **1 cup shredded sharp cheddar cheese
  (3 oz.)**
- **½ tsp. kosher salt**
- **1 stick cold unsalted butter, cubed**
- **7 Tbsp. ice water**

FILLING

- **1 cup packed light brown sugar**
- **3 Tbsp. all-purpose flour**
- **4 tsp. cornstarch**
- **2 tsp. ground cinnamon**
- **½ tsp. ground ginger**
- **½ tsp. ground cardamom**
- **½ tsp. salt**
- **Pinch of ground cloves**
- **6 tart apples, such as Granny Smith,
  peeled and sliced ½ inch thick**
- **Finely grated zest of 1½ lemons**
- **¼ cup fresh lemon juice**
- **3 Tbsp. cold unsalted butter, cubed**

1. Make the crust In a food processor,
pulse the flour with the cheddar and salt.
Add the butter and pulse until the mixture
resembles coarse meal, with some pea-
size pieces of butter still visible. Sprinkle
in the ice water and pulse until the dough
starts to come together; you should still see
small pieces of butter. Scrape the dough
out onto a work surface and pat into
a disk. Wrap in plastic and refrigerate until
chilled, at least 1 hour or up to 3 days.

2. Make the filling Preheat the oven to
400°. In a large bowl, combine the brown
sugar with the flour, cornstarch, cinnamon,
ginger, cardamom, salt and cloves. Stir
in the apples and the lemon zest and juice.

3. On a lightly floured work surface, roll
the dough out to a 16-inch round. Transfer
to a 10-inch glass or ceramic pie plate;
do not trim the overhang. Mound the filling
in the crust and dot with the butter. Fold
the overhanging dough over the filling,
leaving the apples in the center exposed.
Bake the pie for 15 minutes, then cover
with a sheet of aluminum foil and reduce
the oven temperature to 350°. Bake for
50 minutes. Remove the foil and bake for
15 to 20 minutes longer, until the filling is
bubbling in the center. Transfer the pie
to a rack and let cool completely, at least
4 hours. —*Marcus Samuelsson*

Apple-Plum Tarts
with Rye-Cornmeal Crust

Active **20 min**; Total **1 hr 45 min plus
30 min cooling**; Makes **four 5-inch tarts**

These beautiful, rustic tarts have a super-
tender, terrifically tasty crust made with
rye flour and cornmeal. They're extremely
easy to make ahead at any stage: The
dough can be refrigerated for up to 3 days;
the unbaked tarts can be refrigerated
overnight; or the baked tarts can be frozen, then reheated shortly before serving.

DOUGH

- **1 cup all-purpose flour**
- **¾ cup rye flour**
- **¼ cup cornmeal**
- **2 Tbsp. sugar**
- **1 tsp. salt**
- **14 Tbsp. cold unsalted butter, cubed**
- **½ cup ice water**

FILLING

- **3 Tbsp. unsalted butter**
- **⅓ cup plus 2 Tbsp. sugar, plus more
  for sprinkling**
- **½ vanilla bean, split and seeds scraped**
- **6 tart apples (2¾ lbs.), such as
  Granny Smith—peeled, cored
  and cut into 20 wedges each**
- **Juice of ½ lemon**
- **4 red or black plums (¾ lb.), pitted
  and cut into 16 wedges each**
- **2 Tbsp. all-purpose flour**
- **Crème fraîche or vanilla ice cream,
  for serving**

1. Make the dough In a food processor,
pulse both flours with the cornmeal, sugar
and salt. Add the butter and pulse until the
mixture resembles coarse meal with some
pea-size pieces of butter still visible. Sprinkle the ice water over the mixture and
pulse until the dough just starts to come
together; you should still see small pieces
of butter. Scrape the dough out onto a
work surface and gather it together. Quarter the dough and form into four ½-inch-
thick disks. Wrap the disks in plastic and
refrigerate until well chilled, at least 1 hour.

2. Meanwhile, make the filling In a large
saucepan, melt the butter. Add ⅓ cup of the
sugar and the vanilla seeds and cook over
moderately high heat, stirring constantly,
until the sugar turns light amber, about
1 minute. Add the apples and lemon juice
and cook, stirring occasionally, until all of
the liquid has evaporated and the apples
begin to caramelize, 11 minutes. Transfer
to a bowl to cool, then stir in the plums.

3. Preheat the oven to 400°. On a lightly
floured work surface, roll out each disk
of dough to a 6-inch round, a scant ¼ inch
thick. Transfer the rounds to 2 baking
sheets lined with parchment paper. Mix
the remaining 2 tablespoons of sugar
with the flour and sprinkle evenly in the
center of the dough rounds. Spoon the
apple-plum filling over the dough, leaving
a 1½-inch border. Fold the dough border
over the filling, leaving the centers exposed.
Lightly brush the tart rims with water and
liberally sprinkle them with sugar.

4. Bake the tarts for about 35 minutes,
until the crust is browned and the filling
is bubbling. Let cool slightly on the baking
sheets, then transfer the tarts to a rack
and let cool completely, at least 30 minutes. Serve with crème fraîche or vanilla
ice cream. —*Susan Spungen*

APPLE-PLUM TARTS WITH
RYE-CORNMEAL CRUST

Lemon Puddings with Granny Smith Apple Compote

Total **1 hr plus 6 hr chilling**; Serves **6**

These simple British puddings, called possets, are set with lemon juice, not gelatin. The lemon zest gives them an extra hit of tanginess.

PUDDING

2¼ cups heavy cream

⅔ cup sugar

2 tsp. finely grated lemon zest

½ cup fresh lemon juice

Kosher salt

COMPOTE

½ cup sugar

2 Granny Smith apples—peeled, cored and cut into ¼-inch dice

2 Tbsp. fresh orange juice

1 vanilla bean, split lengthwise and seeds scraped

1 Tbsp. Calvados or apple brandy

2 tsp. fresh lemon juice

1 tsp. finely grated orange zest

Salt

1. Make the pudding In a medium saucepan, combine the cream and sugar and cook over moderate heat, stirring with a wooden spoon, until the cream is hot and the sugar is dissolved, about 5 minutes. Let cool slightly, then whisk in the lemon zest, lemon juice and a generous pinch of salt. Pour the pudding into six 5- to 6-ounce glasses or ramekins; cover tightly with plastic wrap. Refrigerate the puddings until well chilled and set, at least 6 hours or overnight.

COOKBOOK TIP

How to Roast Fruit

Roast fruit such as pears on a bed of rock salt. The salt locks in the moisture and flavor while gently seasoning.

Bar Tartine
Nicolaus Balla and Cortney Burns

2. Meanwhile, make the compote In a medium saucepan, combine the sugar and 1 tablespoon of water and cook over moderate heat, swirling the pan, until the sugar dissolves, about 3 minutes. Continue to cook, brushing down the side of the pan with a wet pastry brush, until an amber caramel forms, 3 to 5 minutes. Add the apples, orange juice and the vanilla bean and seeds; the caramel will harden, but it will melt again. Cook over moderate heat, stirring occasionally, until the apples are crisp-tender and coated in a light caramel, about 8 minutes; discard the vanilla bean. Stir in the Calvados, lemon juice, orange zest and a pinch of salt. Let cool completely, then refrigerate until chilled.

3. Serve the puddings topped with the apple compote. —*Curtis Stone*

Pear Tart with Vanilla Cream and Black Tea Crust

Active **1 hr**; Total **2 hr 45 min plus cooling**
Serves **8**

The smart idea here: adding fragrant, smoky-flavored Lapsang souchong tea to a buttery crust. The filling: a delicate combo of vanilla cream and juicy pears.

VANILLA CREAM

3 large egg yolks

1 cup plus 2 Tbsp. whole milk

¼ cup plus 2 Tbsp. heavy cream

⅔ cup granulated sugar

3 Tbsp. plus 1 tsp. cornstarch

1 Tbsp. pure vanilla bean paste or 1 tsp. pure vanilla extract

3 Tbsp. unsalted butter

CRUST

1 cup plus 2 Tbsp. all-purpose flour

½ Tbsp. finely ground Lapsang souchong tea (from 1 tea bag)

½ tsp. kosher salt

1 stick unsalted butter, at room temperature

3 Tbsp. light brown sugar

TOPPING

2 Bosc pears (about 1 lb.)—halved, peeled, cored and sliced lengthwise ¼ inch thick

¼ cup light brown or turbinado sugar

1. Make the vanilla cream In a medium bowl, whisk the egg yolks until smooth. In a medium saucepan, combine the milk, cream, granulated sugar, cornstarch and vanilla bean paste and whisk until smooth. Cook over moderate heat, whisking constantly, until the mixture comes to a gentle simmer and thickens, about 5 minutes. While whisking constantly, drizzle one-third of the milk mixture into the egg yolks. Slowly drizzle the egg yolk mixture back into the saucepan, whisking constantly. Cook over moderately low heat, stirring occasionally, until the mixture is very thick, 2 to 3 minutes. Whisk in the butter, then strain the custard into a medium heatproof bowl. Press a piece of plastic wrap onto the surface of the vanilla cream and refrigerate until cold, about 2 hours.

2. Meanwhile, make the crust Preheat the oven to 350°. In a small bowl, whisk the flour with the tea and salt. In the bowl of a stand mixer fitted with the paddle, beat the butter and brown sugar at medium-high speed until light and fluffy, about 3 minutes. Add the dry ingredients and beat at medium speed until well combined, 2 minutes. Press the dough into the bottom and halfway up the side of a 9-inch tart pan with a removable bottom. Refrigerate until firm, at least 30 minutes.

3. Bake the crust for 20 to 25 minutes, until lightly golden. Transfer to a wire rack and let cool slightly.

4. Make the topping Set the crust on a baking sheet. Scrape the vanilla cream into the crust, spreading it evenly. In a medium bowl, toss the pears with the brown sugar. Arrange the pear slices in a slightly overlapping circular pattern over the cream. Bake the tart for about 30 minutes, until the pears are softened and golden. Transfer the tart to a rack to cool. Serve at room temperature or chilled. —*Valerie Gordon*

MAKE AHEAD The baked tart can be refrigerated overnight.

LEMON PUDDINGS WITH
GRANNY SMITH APPLE COMPOTE

Dark Chocolate–Pear Galette

Active **45 min**; Total **3 hr plus cooling**
Serves **6**

"The combination of chocolate and pears sounded weird to me when I first tried it on a trip to Milan, but now it's one of my favorites," says Athena Calderone, a New York designer turned blogger.

CRUST

- **2** cups all-purpose flour
- **1** Tbsp. granulated sugar
- **1** tsp. kosher salt
- **1** stick unsalted butter, cubed and chilled
- **½** Tbsp. heavy cream
- **¼** cup ice water

TOPPING

- **4** large Bosc pears (2 lbs.)—peeled, cored and cut into ½-inch dice
- **7** Tbsp. turbinado sugar
- **1** large egg
- **2** Tbsp. heavy cream
- **½** tsp. pure vanilla extract
- **⅓** cup coarsely chopped bittersweet or semisweet chocolate
- **3** Tbsp. toasted hazelnuts
- **½** tsp. flaky sea salt
  Vanilla ice cream or whipped cream, for serving

1. Make the crust In a food processor, pulse the flour with the granulated sugar and kosher salt. Add the butter and pulse until the mixture resembles coarse meal with some pea-size pieces of butter remaining. With the machine on, slowly drizzle in the cream, then the ice water, until the dough just holds together. Turn the dough out onto a lightly floured surface and knead 3 times, until it just comes together. Pat the dough into a 1-inch-thick disk. Wrap in plastic and refrigerate for at least 1 hour or overnight.

2. Preheat the oven to 375°. Line a work surface with a 12-by-14-inch sheet of parchment paper. Roll out the dough on the paper into a 12-inch round, about ⅛ inch thick. Transfer the paper and dough to a baking sheet and refrigerate until the dough is firm but still pliable, about 15 minutes.

3. Meanwhile, make the topping
In a large bowl, toss the pears with 4 tablespoons of the tubinado sugar. In a small bowl, whisk the egg, cream and vanilla.

4. Brush the dough with the egg wash, leaving a 2-inch border. Spread the pears over the dough, leaving a 2-inch border, and sprinkle the chocolate, hazelnuts, sea salt and 2 tablespoons of the turbinado sugar on top. Fold the edge of the dough up and over the pears, pinching the folds. Brush the folded edge with egg wash and sprinkle with the remaining 1 tablespoon of turbinado sugar.

5. Bake the galette for about 1 hour and 15 minutes, until the crust is golden brown. Slide a large spatula under the galette to release it from the parchment paper, then let cool to room temperature on the baking sheet. Transfer the galette to a platter and serve with ice cream or whipped cream. —Athena Calderone

MAKE AHEAD The baked galette can sit at room temperature for 1 day before serving.

Cherry Hand Pies

Active **25 min**; Total **1 hr**; Serves **8**

- One 14-oz. package all-butter puff pastry, thawed and chilled
- **2** cups cherries, pitted and coarsely chopped
- **¼** cup sugar
- **1** Tbsp. cornstarch
- **1** Tbsp. fresh lemon juice
- **⅛** tsp. ground cinnamon
- **1** large egg, beaten

1. Preheat the oven to 350°. Using a lightly floured rolling pin, roll out the puff pastry on parchment paper to a 14-by-12-inch rectangle and cut into eight 3-by-3½-inch pieces. Transfer the parchment paper to a baking sheet.

2. In a medium bowl, toss the cherries with the sugar, cornstarch, lemon juice and cinnamon. Brush the pastry edges with the beaten egg. Mound the filling in the center of each pastry and fold the dough over; press to seal and crimp decoratively. Brush the pies with beaten egg and make a small slit in the top of each one. Bake for 40 minutes, until golden. —Kay Chun

Apple Sharlotka

Active **30 min**; Total **2 hr**
Makes **one 8-inch cake**

Matt Danko, the self-taught chef at Trentina in Cleveland, makes his father's recipe for *sharlotka*, a light and fluffy Russian apple cake. It's perfect for dessert, brunch or an afternoon snack.

- **4** Granny Smith apples—peeled, cored, quartered and thinly sliced
- **1** Tbsp. fresh lemon juice
- **1** cup sugar
- **¾** cup plus 2 Tbsp. all-purpose flour
- **¼** tsp. ground cinnamon
- **¼** tsp. freshly grated nutmeg
  Pinch of kosher salt
- **3** large eggs
- **½** tsp. pure almond extract
  Confectioners' sugar, for dusting

1. Preheat the oven to 350°. Grease the bottom and side of an 8-inch springform pan.

2. In a large bowl, toss the apples with the lemon juice and 2 tablespoons of the sugar and let stand for 15 minutes.

3. Meanwhile, in a small bowl, whisk the flour with the cinnamon, nutmeg and salt. In a medium bowl, using an electric mixer, beat the eggs with the almond extract and the remaining ¾ cup plus 2 tablespoons of sugar at medium-high speed until thick and pale yellow and a ribbon forms when the beaters are lifted, 8 to 10 minutes. Gently fold in the dry ingredients just until incorporated.

4. Spread the apples in the prepared pan in an even layer, then pour the batter evenly over them. Let stand for 5 minutes to allow the batter to sink in a little.

5. Bake the *sharlotka* for about 1 hour, until it is golden and crisp on top and a cake tester inserted in the center comes out clean. Transfer to a rack and let rest for 15 minutes. Unmold and transfer to a serving platter. Dust with confectioners' sugar and serve warm. —Matt Danko

MAKE AHEAD The *sharlotka* can be made up to 4 hours ahead.

CHERRY HAND PIES

Raspberry–Brown Butter Custard Pie

Active **1 hr**; Total **4 hr plus 3 hr cooling**
Makes **one 9-inch pie**

PIECRUST

1¾ cups all-purpose flour

¼ cup fine cornmeal

½ tsp. kosher salt

½ tsp. sugar

14 Tbsp. unsalted butter, cubed and chilled

CUSTARD

2 Tbsp. unsalted butter

1 vanilla bean, split, seeds scraped

3 large eggs

2 large egg yolks

1½ cups sugar

½ tsp. finely grated lemon zest

½ tsp. freshly grated nutmeg

Pinch of kosher salt

¼ cup all-purpose flour

2 cups raspberries

Whipped cream, for serving

1. Make the piecrust In a food processor, combine the flour, cornmeal, salt and sugar. Add the butter and pulse until the mixture resembles coarse meal with some pea-size pieces. With the machine on, drizzle in ⅓ cup of ice water and pulse until the dough just comes together. Turn the dough out onto a lightly floured work surface. Gather up any crumbs and knead a few times until the dough holds together. Pat into a 1-inch-thick disk, wrap in plastic and chill until firm, 1 hour.

2. On a lightly floured work surface, roll out the dough to a 12-inch round, a scant ¼ inch thick. Ease the dough into a 9-inch glass pie plate. Trim the overhanging dough to 1 inch, fold it under itself and crimp the edge decoratively. Freeze the crust until firm, 30 minutes.

3. Preheat the oven to 425°. Line the crust with parchment paper and fill with pie weights or dried beans. Bake for 20 minutes, until the edge is lightly golden and just set. Remove the paper and pie weights. Cover the crust rim with strips of foil and bake for 15 minutes, until lightly browned on the bottom. Let cool on a rack. Reduce the oven temperature to 375°.

4. Meanwhile, make the custard In a small saucepan, melt the butter. Add the vanilla bean and seeds and cook over moderately low heat until the butter is golden brown, about 5 minutes. Remove from the heat and let cool; discard the vanilla bean.

5. In a medium bowl, using a handheld electric mixer, beat the eggs and egg yolks with the sugar until thick and fluffy, about 3 minutes. Beat in the browned butter, lemon zest, nutmeg and salt, then beat in the flour just until blended.

6. Spread the raspberries in the crust and pour the custard over them. Bake the pie for about 1 hour and 15 minutes, until the filling is set around the edge but slightly jiggly in the center. Transfer to a rack and let cool for 3 hours. Serve with whipped cream. —*Kir Jensen*

Pistachio-Date Turnovers with Coffee Cream

Active **40 min**; Total **2 hr plus overnight infusing**; Makes **15 turnovers**

These not-too-sweet turnovers are made with an exceptionally flaky rye flour pastry and a date-spiked pistachio filling.

COFFEE CREAM

2 Tbsp. coffee beans

1 cup heavy cream

RYE PASTRY

1½ cups all-purpose flour

⅓ cup rye flour

1 tsp. sugar

1 tsp. kosher salt

6 Tbsp. unsalted butter, at room temperature

3 Tbsp. vegetable shortening

⅓ cup ice water

FILLING

1 cup unsalted pistachios (about 5 oz.)

1 cup almond flour (about 4 oz.)

¾ cup sugar, plus more for sprinkling

4 Tbsp. cold unsalted butter, diced, plus 2 Tbsp. melted butter

2 large eggs

½ tsp. kosher salt

8 Medjool dates, pitted and quartered

2 Bosc or Bartlett pears—stemmed, cored and cut into 8 wedges each

1. Make the coffee cream In a small bowl, cover the coffee beans with the heavy cream. Cover the bowl with plastic wrap and refrigerate overnight.

2. Make the rye pastry In a food processor, combine the all-purpose and rye flours with the sugar and salt. Add the butter and vegetable shortening and pulse until pea-size crumbs form. Add the ice water and pulse just until the dough comes together. Transfer the dough to a work surface and press into a rectangle, about ½ inch thick. Wrap in plastic and refrigerate for 1 hour.

3. Make the filling Preheat the oven to 400°. Line a baking sheet with parchment paper. Spread the pistachios in a pie plate and bake until lightly toasted, about 8 minutes. Let the nuts cool completely. Leave the oven on.

4. In a food processor, process the pistachios just until very finely ground. Add the almond flour, ¾ cup of sugar, the diced butter, the eggs and salt and process until the mixture is smooth.

5. On a lightly floured work surface, roll out the dough to a 9-by-15-inch rectangle. Trim the edges so they are straight and even. Cut the rectangle into fifteen 3-inch squares. Place 1 tablespoon of the pistachio filling in the center of each square and top with 2 pieces of date. Brush the edge of each square with water and fold the dough diagonally over the filling to make triangles; press the edges to seal. Arrange the turnovers 1 inch apart on the prepared baking sheet. Freeze the pastries until chilled, about 10 minutes.

6. Brush the turnovers with the 2 tablespoons of melted butter and sprinkle generously with sugar. Bake for 18 minutes, until the pastry is golden brown and the filling is heated through when a knife is inserted in the center. Transfer to a rack and let cool for 10 minutes.

7. Strain the coffee cream into a bowl and beat to stiff peaks. Serve the turnovers warm or at room temperature with the whipped coffee cream and pear wedges. —*Nicole Krasinski*

MAKE AHEAD The unbaked pistachio-date turnovers can be frozen for up to 1 week.

This pie, with its prebaked crust, is ready to go into the oven.

RASPBERRY–BROWN BUTTER
CUSTARD PIE

French Lemon Tart

Active **45 min**; Total **2 hr plus 2 hr chilling**
Makes **one 9-inch tart**

PASTRY

- **2 Tbsp. heavy cream**
- **1 large egg yolk**
- **1¼ cups plus 2 Tbsp. all-purpose flour, plus more for dusting**
- **2 Tbsp. sugar**
- **Pinch of salt**
- **1 stick cold unsalted butter, cut into ¼-inch dice**

FILLING

- **4 large eggs**
- **4 large egg yolks**
- **1 cup sugar**
- **1 cup fresh lemon juice (from about 6 lemons)**
- **Pinch of salt**
- **1 stick plus 2 Tbsp. cold unsalted butter, cut into tablespoons**
- **Lightly sweetened whipped cream, for serving**

1. Make the pastry In a small bowl, whisk the cream with the egg yolk. In a large bowl, combine the 1¼ cups plus 2 tablespoons of flour with the sugar and salt. Using a pastry blender or 2 knives, cut the butter into the dry ingredients until the mixture resembles coarse meal. Using a rubber spatula, gently stir in the yolk mixture. Using your hands, gently knead the pastry just until it comes together. Wrap in plastic, flatten into a disk and refrigerate for at least 1 hour.

2. Preheat the oven to 375° and coat a 9-inch fluted tart pan with a removable bottom with vegetable oil spray. On a floured work surface, roll out the pastry to a 12-inch round and ease it into the pan, pressing it into the corners. Roll the rolling pin over the tart pan to cut off any excess pastry. Refrigerate for 10 minutes.

3. Line the tart shell with parchment paper and fill it with pie weights or dried beans. Bake in the center of the oven for 15 minutes. Carefully remove the paper and weights and bake the tart shell for 20 minutes longer, until golden brown. Let cool completely.

4. Meanwhile, make the filling In a large, heavy saucepan, combine the whole eggs, egg yolks, sugar, lemon juice and salt and whisk until smooth. Set a strainer over a bowl near the stove. Cook the custard over moderate heat, whisking constantly, until thickened enough to coat the back of a spoon, about 3 minutes. Remove from the heat and add the butter a few pieces at a time, gently whisking until incorporated. Immediately strain the filling into the bowl. Scrape the filling into the cooled tart shell and refrigerate until chilled, about 2 hours.

5. Remove the tart ring and cut the tart into wedges. Serve with whipped cream.
—*Marjorie Taylor*

WINE Fragrant, rich Alsace Gewürztraminer: 2011 Albert Mann.

Beet-and-Wine-Infused Poached Pears

Active **25 min**; Total **1 hr plus 30 min chilling**; Serves **4**

These poached pears get gorgeous color and earthy flavor from the beet-juice syrup they're poached in. It's an ingenious twist on the French classic.

- **2 cups dry red wine**
- **1 cup fresh beet juice**
- **⅓ cup sugar**
- **½ lemon**
- **1 small cinnamon stick**
- **½ cup crème de cassis**
- **4 ripe Bosc pears, peeled**

1. In a medium saucepan, bring the wine, beet juice, sugar, lemon, cinnamon stick and ¼ cup of the crème de cassis to a boil. Simmer over moderate heat for 5 minutes, stirring to dissolve the sugar. Add the pears, cover and simmer over moderately low heat, turning once, until just tender, 15 minutes. Using a slotted spoon, transfer the pears to a bowl.

2. Boil the poaching liquid over moderately high heat until reduced to 1 cup, 13 minutes. Stir in the remaining ¼ cup of crème de cassis. Pour the syrup over the pears and let cool completely, then refrigerate until chilled, 30 minutes; discard the cinnamon stick.

3. Serve the pears with the syrup on a platter or in shallow bowls. —*Ludo Lefebvre*

SERVE WITH Vanilla ice cream.

Sweet Corn Panna Cotta with Fresh Blueberry Compote

Total **45 min plus overnight chilling**
Serves **4**

PANNA COTTA

- **2 ears of corn, husked**
- **1½ tsp. unflavored powdered gelatin**
- **¾ cup plus 1 Tbsp. whole milk**
- **1 cup plus 2½ Tbsp. heavy cream**
- **¼ tsp. plus ⅛ tsp. kosher salt**
- **¼ cup plus 2 Tbsp. granulated sugar**
- **3 Tbsp. dark brown sugar**

BLUEBERRY COMPOTE

- **1 Tbsp. sugar**
- **½ tsp. finely grated lemon zest**
- **1½ tsp. fresh lemon juice**
- **Pinch of kosher salt**
- **1½ cups blueberries**

1. Make the panna cotta In a medium pot fitted with a steamer basket, steam the corn until tender, 15 minutes. Let cool, then cut the kernels from the cobs (you should have 1½ cups); discard the cobs. Transfer the kernels to a blender.

2. Meanwhile, in a heatproof medium bowl, sprinkle the gelatin over ¼ cup of the milk. Let stand for 5 minutes.

3. In a small skillet, combine the remaining ½ cup plus 1 tablespoon of milk with the cream, salt and both sugars and bring to a bare simmer, whisking to dissolve the sugars. Scrape the hot milk mixture into the gelatin and stir until the gelatin dissolves. Pour the mixture into the blender over the corn and puree until smooth. Fill a large bowl with ice water.

4. Strain the puree through a sieve into a medium bowl, pressing on the solids; discard the solids. Strain again without pressing; discard any solids in the sieve. Set the panna cotta in the ice bath until cool, stirring occasionally. Scrape the panna cotta into four 8-ounce ramekins. Cover and refrigerate overnight until firm.

5. Make the blueberry compote In a large bowl, combine all of the ingredients and mix until the sugar is dissolved. Let stand for at least 30 minutes, stirring occasionally. Serve the panna cotta in the ramekins with the compote. —*Tracy Obolsky*

SWEET CORN PANNA COTTA WITH
FRESH BLUEBERRY COMPOTE

Whole-Grain Cherry Crumble

Active **40 min**; Total **1 hr 45 min**
Serves **6 to 8**

At first glance, this appears to be a classic cherry crumble, but there are three genius ways that chef Melia Marden of The Smile in Manhattan adds layers of delicious flavor. First, she uses whole-wheat flour in the topping for a pleasantly hefty, rustic character; second, she adds just a touch of balsamic vinegar to the cherries for subtle complexity; third, she mixes grated pear into the filling, which not only rounds out the bright cherry flavor but also helps thicken the juices.

- 1 **cup whole-wheat flour**
- ½ **cup packed light brown sugar**
- ½ **cup rolled oats**
- ¼ **cup raw almonds, chopped**
- ½ **tsp. kosher salt**
- ¼ **tsp. freshly grated nutmeg**
- 1½ **sticks cold unsalted butter, cubed**
- 2 **lbs. fresh or frozen cherries, pitted (4 cups)**
- ½ **cup granulated sugar**
- 1 **tsp. balsamic vinegar**
- 1 **vanilla bean, split, seeds scraped**
- 1 **firm Bartlett pear—halved, cored and coarsely shredded on a box grater**
   Vanilla ice cream, for serving

1. Preheat the oven to 350°. In a large bowl, whisk the flour with the brown sugar, oats, almonds, salt and nutmeg. Using your fingers, work in the butter until large crumbs begin to form. Press the streusel into small clumps and refrigerate until chilled, about 15 minutes.

2. Meanwhile, in a large ovenproof skillet, combine the cherries, granulated sugar, vinegar and the vanilla bean and seeds. Cook over moderate heat, stirring, until the juices are bubbling, 5 to 7 minutes. Stir in the grated pear and let cool completely; discard the vanilla bean.

3. Scatter the streusel evenly over the cherries. Bake for about 1 hour, until the topping is golden and the cherries are bubbling. Let cool slightly. Serve with vanilla ice cream. —*Melia Marden*

Creamy Citrus Puddings with Fresh Berries

Total **30 min plus 4 hr chilling**; Serves **10**

- 1 **quart heavy cream**
- 1¼ **cups sugar**
- ¾ **tsp. kosher salt**
- ¾ **cup fresh lemon juice**
- ¼ **cup fresh orange juice**
- 1 **tsp. orange flower water**
   Fresh blueberries, raspberries and blackberries, for serving
   Swedish Butter Cookies (p. 344), for serving

1. In a medium saucepan, combine the cream, sugar and salt and cook over moderate heat, stirring, until the sugar dissolves and the mixture is slightly thickened, about 10 minutes. Remove from the heat and stir in the lemon juice, orange juice and orange flower water.

2. Pour the mixture into small glasses, jars or ramekins, cover and refrigerate until thickened, at least 4 hours or overnight. Serve with berries and Swedish Butter Cookies. —*Paul Berglund*

Cherry Pudding Cups

Total **15 min plus overnight setting**
Makes **6 puddings**

   One ¼-oz. package unflavored powdered gelatin
- 1 **cup buttermilk**
- 2 **cups whole milk**
- ½ **cup honey**
- 1 **Tbsp. fresh lime juice**
- 1½ **cups chopped pitted cherries**
- 2 **tsp. finely grated lime zest, for garnish**

1. In a small bowl, whisk the gelatin with ⅓ cup of the buttermilk. Let the mixture stand for 5 minutes.

2. In a small saucepan, combine the milk and honey and warm over low heat, stirring, just until the honey dissolves. Remove from the heat and whisk in the gelatin mixture until dissolved. Whisk in the lime juice and remaining ⅔ cup of buttermilk. Pour the pudding into six 6-ounce cups or ramekins, cover and chill overnight until set and firm. Top with the cherries and lime zest and serve. —*Kay Chun*

Lemony Yogurt Custards with Cranberry-Apple Salad

⏱ Total **45 min**; Serves **8**

San Francisco pastry chef Nicole Krasinski adores creating desserts with yogurt. "It adds a great, unexpected tang, and you can use it to make custard without eggs." She tops her light, panna cotta–like custards with a vivid mix of sweetened cranberries, chopped apple and fennel.

   One 14-oz. can sweetened condensed milk
   Finely grated zest and juice from 1 lemon, preferably Meyer lemon
- ½ **vanilla bean, split, seeds scraped**
- ⅛ **tsp. ground cloves**
   Kosher salt
- 3 **cups plain whole-milk Greek yogurt**
   Boiling water
- 1 **cup fresh or frozen cranberries, halved**
- ¼ **cup sugar**
- ½ **cup finely diced tart green apple, such as Granny Smith**
- ¼ **cup finely diced fennel**
- 1 **Tbsp. extra-virgin olive oil**

1. Preheat the oven to 325°. In a large bowl, whisk the condensed milk with the grated lemon zest, vanilla bean seeds, cloves and ¼ teaspoon of kosher salt. Whisk in the yogurt until smooth. Arrange eight 8-ounce ceramic or glass ramekins in a large roasting pan and pour about ½ cup of the yogurt mixture into each one. Add enough boiling water to the roasting pan to reach halfway up the sides of the ramekins. Bake for about 12 minutes, until the custards are set but slightly loose in the centers. Transfer the ramekins to a rack and let cool to room temperature.

2. Meanwhile, in a small saucepan, cook the lemon juice, cranberries, sugar and 1 cup of water over high heat until the cranberries are just tender, about 2 minutes. Transfer to a bowl and let cool to room temperature, about 20 minutes.

3. Drain the cranberries; save the syrup for another use. In a medium bowl, toss the apple and fennel with the olive oil and season lightly with salt. Spoon the cranberries and the apple salad over the custards and serve. —*Nicole Krasinski*

Coconut-Buttermilk Pie with Blackberry Caramel

Active **1 hr**; Total **3 hr 45 min plus cooling**
Serves **8**

This pie from star chef Bobby Flay is creamy and crispy, but what pushes it over the top is the incredible blackberry caramel made with fresh blackberries and blackberry liqueur.

CRUST

- **1¼ cups all-purpose flour**
- **2 tsp. sugar**
- **¼ tsp. fine sea salt**
- **1 stick cold unsalted butter, cubed**
- **¼ cup plus 2 Tbsp. buttermilk**

FILLING

- **3 large eggs**
- **¾ cup sugar**
- **1 cup buttermilk**
- **4 Tbsp. unsalted butter, melted and cooled slightly**
- **¼ cup unsweetened coconut milk**
- **2 Tbsp. all-purpose flour**
- **1 vanilla bean, split, seeds scraped**
- **1 tsp. pure vanilla extract**
- **1 tsp. pure coconut extract**
- **¼ cup sweetened shredded coconut**

BLACKBERRY CARAMEL

- **2 cups blackberries (8 oz.), halved**
- **¾ cup plus 2 Tbsp. sugar**
- **½ cup heavy cream, warmed**
- **2 tsp. blackberry liqueur**
- **½ tsp. pure vanilla extract**
- **Pinch of kosher salt**
- **Toasted sweetened shredded coconut, for garnish**

1. Make the crust In a food processor, pulse the flour with the sugar and sea salt. Add the butter and pulse until the mixture resembles coarse meal with some pea-size pieces remaining. Drizzle the buttermilk on top and pulse until the dough just comes together. Turn the dough out onto a work surface, gather up any crumbs and pat the dough into a disk. Wrap in plastic and refrigerate until well chilled, about 1 hour.

2. On a lightly floured work surface, roll out the dough to a 12-inch round, a scant ¼ inch thick. Ease the dough into a 9-inch glass pie plate. Trim the overhanging dough to 1 inch, fold it under itself and crimp decoratively. Refrigerate the crust until firm, about 30 minutes.

3. Preheat the oven to 400°. Line the crust with parchment paper and fill with pie weights or dried beans. Bake the crust in the lower third of the oven for about 20 minutes, until barely set. Remove the parchment paper and pie weights. Cover the edge of the crust with strips of foil and bake for 15 to 20 minutes longer, until the crust is lightly browned. Let cool on a rack. Leave the foil strips on the crust rim. Reduce the oven temperature to 325°.

4. Make the filling In a large bowl, whisk the eggs with the sugar until pale. Add the buttermilk, butter, coconut milk, flour, vanilla seeds and both extracts and whisk until smooth, then stir in the shredded coconut.

5. Set the pie plate on a baking sheet. Pour in the custard and bake for 40 to 45 minutes, until set around the edge but slightly jiggly in the center. Transfer to a rack and let the pie cool completely.

6. Meanwhile, make the blackberry caramel In a small saucepan, combine 1 cup of the blackberries with 2 tablespoons of the sugar and 1 tablespoon of water. Cook over moderate heat, stirring occasionally, until the berries start to burst. Transfer the berries and any juices to a blender and puree until nearly smooth. Transfer the puree to the saucepan and let cool slightly, then whisk in the cream, blackberry liqueur, vanilla and salt.

7. In a medium saucepan, combine the remaining ¾ cup of sugar with ¼ cup of water. Cook over moderate heat, swirling the pan and brushing down the side with a wet pastry brush, until the sugar dissolves. Cook undisturbed until an amber caramel forms, about 7 minutes. Add the blackberry cream (be careful, it may boil vigorously) and simmer, whisking, until the caramel is smooth, 1 to 2 minutes. Let cool slightly, then stir in the remaining 1 cup of blackberries; let cool to room temperature. Garnish the pie with toasted coconut, cut into wedges and serve with the blackberry caramel. —*Bobby Flay*

3-2-1 Hidden Ice Cream Strawberry Shortcakes

Total **45 min plus 3 hr macerating**
Serves **12**

As a clever shortcut, Jeni Britton Bauer, founder of Jeni's Splendid Ice Creams, uses melted vanilla ice cream in her flaky biscuits. It replaces the usual egg and cream in the dough and gives the biscuits a lovely vanilla flavor.

- **1 quart strawberries, hulled and quartered**
- **½ cup sugar**
- **1 pint vanilla ice cream**
- **3 cups self-rising flour**
- **2 sticks cold unsalted butter, cubed**
- **1 cup heavy cream**
- **1 Tbsp. honey**

1. In a medium bowl, toss the strawberries with the sugar. Let stand at room temperature, stirring, until very juicy, 3 hours.

2. Meanwhile, thaw the ice cream in the refrigerator until soft, about 1 hour. Spoon the ice cream into a large bowl.

3. Preheat the oven to 450°. In a food processor, pulse the flour and butter until the mixture resembles coarse meal; stir into the ice cream with a wooden spoon until incorporated. Using your hands, gently knead the dough until it starts to clump together. Drop clumps of the dough into a 9-by-13-inch metal baking pan in an even layer. Bake for 20 minutes, until golden on top. Let cool slightly, then cut into 12 squares.

4. Meanwhile, in a medium bowl, whip the heavy cream and honey until soft peaks form. Serve the shortcakes with the macerated strawberries and whipped cream. —*Jeni Britton Bauer*

Summer Fruit Soup

Total **45 min plus 45 min chilling**
Serves **6 to 8**

"I recently read that I was the first Soup Nazi," says master chef Jacques Pépin. "Serving a dessert like this with the word *soup* in the name was not done back then [in the 1970s], but people liked it."

½ cup dry white wine, such
   as Sauvignon Blanc

½ cup crème de cassis
   (black currant liqueur)

¼ cup pomegranate juice

2 Tbsp. strawberry preserves

1 tsp. finely grated orange zest

½ lb. small red plums—halved, pitted
   and cut into ½-inch wedges

½ lb. Bing cherries, pitted

2 basil sprigs

½ lb. seedless red grapes

½ lb. strawberries, hulled
   and quartered

6 oz. blueberries

1 cup sour cream

1 Tbsp. sugar

Mint leaves, for garnish

Toasted brioche slices, for serving
   (optional)

1. In a medium saucepan, combine the white wine with the crème de cassis, pomegranate juice, strawberry preserves and orange zest and bring to a boil, stirring to dissolve the preserves.

2. Add the plums, cherries and basil to the saucepan and return to a boil, then simmer over moderately high heat for 1 minute. Using a slotted spoon, transfer the fruit to a large glass or ceramic bowl. Add the grapes to the saucepan and simmer for 30 seconds; transfer the grapes to the bowl. Add the strawberries and blueberries to the saucepan and simmer for 2 minutes. Transfer the berries and cooking juices to the bowl and let cool completely; discard the basil sprigs. Cover and refrigerate the fruit soup until chilled, about 45 minutes.

3. In a small bowl, whisk the sour cream with the sugar. Spoon the fruit soup into shallow bowls and dollop the sweetened sour cream on top. Garnish the fruit soup with mint leaves and serve with toasted brioche, if you like. —*Jacques Pépin*

Roasted Fruit and Cheese Plate

Active **20 min**; Total **45 min**; Serves **6**

Boston chef Barbara Lynch loves roasting everything from grapefruit to watermelon. Her enthusiasm was the impetus for this reimagined cheese plate from F&W's Justin Chapple, which combines roasted figs, pears and quince with blue cheese and toasted hazelnuts.

⅓ cup hazelnuts

2 Bosc pears—halved lengthwise,
   cored and cut lengthwise into
   ¾-inch wedges

1 large quince (1 lb.)—peeled, cored
   and cut into ½-inch dice

¼ cup sugar

4 Tbsp. unsalted butter, melted

1 Tbsp. fresh lemon juice

Salt

8 figs, halved lengthwise

4 oz. blue cheese,
   thinly sliced or crumbled

1. Preheat the oven to 425°. Spread the hazelnuts in a pie plate and toast for 7 to 10 minutes, until golden. Transfer to a clean kitchen towel and rub off the skins. Let cool, then coarsely chop.

2. On a large rimmed baking sheet, toss the pears and quince with the sugar, butter, lemon juice and a generous pinch of salt and spread in an even layer. Roast for 20 to 25 minutes, until browned in spots; add the figs during the last 5 minutes. Transfer the fruit to a platter and let cool slightly.

3. Scatter the cheese and hazelnuts over the fruit and serve. —*Justin Chapple*

MAKE AHEAD The roasted fruit can be kept at room temperature for up to 3 hours.

WINE Sweet, sparkling red Italian dessert wine: 2013 Banfi Rosa Regale Brachetto.

Roasted Peach Cobbler with Vanilla Ice Cream and Balsamic Syrup

📷 PAGE 308

Active **15 min**; Total **50 min**; Serves **6**

"I'm no pastry chef, but I bake a killer cobbler," says Andrew Zimmern, host of *Bizarre Foods*. He tops the dessert with vanilla ice cream and thick, rich aged balsamic syrup. Two favorites: Malpighi Saporoso *condimento balsamico* and Noble Tonic 05:XO, which is aged in bourbon casks.

8 large ripe peaches (4 lbs.), peeled
   and cut into ½-inch-thick wedges

3 Tbsp. light brown sugar

½ cup all-purpose flour

¼ cup granulated sugar

¼ tsp. baking soda

¼ tsp. kosher salt

4 Tbsp. cold unsalted butter, cubed

1 large egg yolk

¼ tsp. pure vanilla extract

1 Tbsp. fresh lemon juice

1 pint vanilla ice cream, for serving

1 Tbsp. balsamic vinegar syrup

1. Preheat the broiler on high and position a rack about 6 inches from the heat. In a large bowl, toss the peaches with the brown sugar and scrape them onto a rimmed baking sheet. Broil the peaches for about 15 minutes, flipping them halfway through, until caramelized and juicy. Let the peaches cool slightly. Lower the oven temperature to 375°.

2. Meanwhile, in another large bowl, combine the flour, granulated sugar, baking soda and salt. Add the butter and, with your fingers, rub it into the mixture evenly. Stir in the egg yolk and vanilla. Refrigerate the crumb topping.

3. In a medium bowl, toss the cooled peaches with the lemon juice; divide among six 8-ounce ramekins. Sprinkle with the crumb topping, transfer the ramekins to a baking sheet and bake until the topping is golden and the fruit is bubbling, about 20 minutes. Let cool for 5 minutes, then serve with the vanilla ice cream and a drizzle of the balsamic syrup. —*Andrew Zimmern*

SUMMER FRUIT SOUP

Neo-Traditional Pecan Pie

ACTIVE: 25 MIN • TOTAL: 1 HR 40 MIN PLUS 4 HR COOLING • MAKES ONE 9-INCH PIE

Using old-fashioned, less-refined sweeteners, **CHERYL DAY** of Savannah, Georgia's Back in the Day Bakery adds flavor complexity to a holiday classic. Her master recipe works with honey, sorghum, cane syrup or dark corn syrup.

Pecan pie is terrific with Italian dessert wines like the 2012 Pellegrino Passito di Pantelleria.

Bourbon-Pecan Pie

PIECRUST

- **2 cups all-purpose flour**
- **⅓ cup packed light brown sugar**
- **¾ tsp. fine sea salt**
- **1 stick plus 7 Tbsp. unsalted butter, melted and cooled**

FILLING

- **½ cup granulated sugar**
- **¼ cup packed light brown sugar**
- **1½ tsp. all-purpose flour**
- **½ tsp. fine sea salt**
- **4 large eggs**
- **1½ cups cane, sorghum or dark corn syrup, or honey**
- **2 Tbsp. bourbon**
- **1½ Tbsp. unsalted butter, melted**
- **1½ tsp. pure vanilla extract**
- **1¾ cups unsalted pecan halves (½ lb.)**

STEP 1 MAKE THE PIECRUST

1. In a medium bowl, whisk the flour with the brown sugar and salt. Stir in the butter until the dough comes together into a ball. Transfer the dough to a deep 9-inch glass or ceramic pie plate. Using your fingers, press the dough over the bottom and up the side of the plate to the rim. Crimp the edge with your fingers or a fork. Refrigerate for at least 20 minutes or up to 3 days.

STEP 2 MAKE THE FILLING

2. Meanwhile, preheat the oven to 350°. In a large bowl, whisk both sugars with the flour, salt and eggs until smooth, then mix in the syrup or honey. Add the bourbon, butter and vanilla and fold in the pecans.

3. Pour the filling into the chilled crust and transfer the pie to a foil-lined baking sheet. Cover loosely with foil and bake for 1 hour, until the filling is nearly set. Transfer the pie to a rack and let cool completely, about 4 hours, before serving.

You can give a traditional look to this cheater press-in piecrust by crimping the top edge with your fingertips.

THE ALT SWEETENERS

Old-fashioned sweeteners like the ones Day uses for her pecan pie are having a revival as bakers look beyond white sugar. The versions below offer not just sweetness but also complex flavor.

1
SORGHUM SYRUP
Made from sorghum-grass juice; fruity, tangy and almost leathery, with the highest ratio of overall flavor to pure sweetness.

2
CANE SYRUP
Made by boiling sugarcane juice in open kettles until it thickens and begins to taste a bit like caramel; has a long history in the South.

3
DARK CORN SYRUP
Has much more character than light corn syrup, evoking brown sugar, though it's still relatively neutral in flavor compared to syrups like sorghum.

4
HONEY
Intensely floral as well as more sugary-sweet than the syrups at left.

Chocolate-Hazelnut Tart

📷 PAGE 378
Active **45 min**; Total **3 hr 30 min**
Makes **one 9-inch tart**

PASTRY

- ¼ cup plus 2 Tbsp. hazelnuts (2 oz.), toasted and skinned (see Note)
- ¼ cup sugar
- 1 cup all-purpose flour
  Pinch of salt
- 1 stick cold unsalted butter, cut into ½-inch cubes
- 1 large egg
- ½ tsp. pure vanilla extract

FILLING

- 12 oz. bittersweet chocolate (70 percent), chopped
- 1½ cups heavy cream
- 1 cup hazelnuts (5 oz.)—toasted, skinned and coarsely chopped (see Note)

1. Make the pastry In a food processor, process the hazelnuts and 1 tablespoon of the sugar until fine. Scrape into the bowl of a stand mixer fitted with the paddle. Add the flour, salt and remaining 3 tablespoons of sugar and mix until combined. Add the butter and mix at low speed until incorporated. Add the egg and vanilla and mix until a soft dough forms. Scrape the pastry onto a sheet of plastic wrap and flatten into a disk. Wrap and refrigerate for 1 hour.

2. Preheat the oven to 350° and coat a 9-inch fluted tart pan with a removable bottom with vegetable oil spray. Roll out the pastry between 2 sheets of wax paper to a 12-inch round. Ease the pastry into the tart pan, pressing it into the corners and patching any tears. Roll the rolling pin over the tart pan to cut off any excess pastry. Refrigerate the tart shell for 10 minutes.

3. Line the pastry with parchment and fill it with pie weights or dried beans. Bake in the center of the oven for 20 minutes. Carefully remove the parchment and weights and bake the shell for about 15 minutes longer, until golden brown. Let cool completely.

4. Make the filling Put the chocolate in a heatproof bowl. In a small saucepan, bring the cream just to a simmer. Pour the hot cream over the chocolate and let stand for

5 minutes; whisk until smooth. Pour the chocolate cream into the tart shell and scatter the hazelnuts on top. Refrigerate until firm, about 1 hour and 30 minutes. Remove the tart ring, cut the tart into wedges and serve. —*Marjorie Taylor*

NOTE To toast and skin hazelnuts, spread the nuts in a pie plate and toast in a 350° oven for about 12 minutes, until golden and the skins blister. Let cool slightly, then transfer to a clean kitchen towel and rub off the skins.

WINE Sweet, dried-fruit-scented Banyuls: 2010 Vial-Magnères Rimage.

Golden Caramel and Chocolate Tart

Active **40 min**; Total **3 hr 30 min plus chilling**; Makes **one 9-inch tart**

"I think of myself as a baking evangelist," says cookbook author Dorie Greenspan. She has perfected all the elements of this phenomenal tart, from the buttery pastry to the rich filling. She knows that caramel is intimidating for lots of people and has a tip: "This caramel is easy to make perfectly— it just shouldn't color too much. When the sugar turns the color of pale ale, it's ready."

PASTRY

- 1½ cups all-purpose flour
- ½ cup confectioners' sugar
- ¼ tsp. kosher salt
- 1 stick plus 1 Tbsp. cold unsalted butter, cut into ½-inch dice
- 1 large egg yolk

FILLING

- 2 oz. bittersweet chocolate, chopped
- ⅔ cup granulated sugar
- ¼ tsp. fresh lemon juice
- 4 Tbsp. unsalted butter, cut into 4 pieces
- 1¼ cups heavy cream, at room temperature
- ½ tsp. kosher salt
- 4 large egg yolks

1. Make the pastry In a food processor, pulse the flour with the confectioners' sugar and salt. Add the butter and pulse until it's the size of peas. Add the egg yolk and pulse in 10-second increments until incorporated, about 4 long pulses.

Transfer the pastry to a sheet of parchment, shape into a disk and cover with another sheet of parchment. Roll out the pastry to a 12-inch round. Slide the pastry on the parchment onto a baking sheet and refrigerate until firm, about 1 hour.

2. Let the pastry stand at room temperature for 5 minutes. Discard the top sheet of parchment paper and invert the pastry into a 9-inch fluted tart pan with a removable bottom; fit the pastry into the pan and trim the overhang. Prick the pastry all over with a fork and refrigerate for 30 minutes.

3. Preheat the oven to 400°. Line the tart shell with parchment paper and fill with pie weights or dried beans. Bake until the pastry is set and lightly browned at the edge, 20 minutes. Remove the parchment paper and weights and bake the pastry for 5 minutes more, until lightly browned on the bottom. Transfer to a rack to cool completely. Reduce the oven temperature to 325°.

4. Make the filling In a small microwave-safe bowl, microwave the chocolate at high power in 30-second bursts just until melted. Let cool slightly, then pour into the baked tart shell, spreading it evenly.

5. In a small skillet, stir ⅓ cup of the granulated sugar with the lemon juice and ¼ cup of water over moderately high heat until the sugar dissolves. Cook, without stirring, until the mixture starts to color, about 5 minutes. Continue cooking, stirring constantly with a heatproof spatula, until a light golden caramel forms, about 5 minutes. Remove the skillet from the heat and stir in the butter, 1 piece at a time. Stir in the cream and salt, then let the caramel cool to room temperature.

6. In a medium bowl, whisk the egg yolks with the remaining ⅓ cup of granulated sugar until smooth. Stir the caramel into the egg yolk mixture, then pour the custard evenly over the chocolate in the tart shell. Transfer the tart to a foil-lined baking sheet and bake until the crust is browned and the filling is still slightly wobbly in the middle, about 30 minutes. Transfer the tart to a rack and let cool to room temperature. Refrigerate until set and thoroughly chilled, at least 2 hours. Unmold the tart and serve. —*Dorie Greenspan*

WINE Nutty, caramelly Madeira: Broadbent Malmsey 10 Years Old.

Black-Bottom Peanut Pie

Active **20 min**; Total **1 hr 40 min plus 4 hr cooling**; Makes **one 10-inch pie**

New York chef Marcus Samuelsson bakes this sticky, gooey pie as an ode to his favorite candy bar, Snickers.

CRUST

- 1 stick unsalted butter
  One 11-oz. box vanilla wafer cookies
- ½ cup sugar
- 2 vanilla beans, split, seeds scraped

FILLING

- 8 oz. bittersweet chocolate, finely chopped
- 1 cup heavy cream
- 1 cup sugar
- ½ cup light corn syrup
- 6 Tbsp. unsalted butter, melted and cooled
- 4 tsp. molasses
- ¾ tsp. kosher salt
- 3 large eggs
- 2 cups unsalted roasted peanuts

1. Make the crust Preheat the oven to 350°. Melt the butter in a saucepan over moderately low heat and cook, swirling, until browned, 9 minutes; let cool. Process the cookies, sugar and vanilla seeds in a food processor until finely ground. Add the browned butter and pulse until the crumbs are evenly moistened; transfer to a 10-inch glass or ceramic pie plate and press the crumbs over the bottom and up the side to form the crust. Bake for 12 minutes, until lightly browned and set; let cool completely. Increase the oven temperature to 375°.

2. Make the filling Put the chocolate in a small heatproof bowl. In a small saucepan, bring the cream to a boil and pour it over the chocolate. Let stand for 1 minute, then stir until smooth; pour into the cooled crust and let sit for 10 minutes.

3. In a bowl, whisk the sugar, corn syrup, butter, molasses, salt and eggs, then stir in the peanuts. Pour the filling over the chocolate. Transfer the pie to a foil-lined baking sheet and bake for 10 minutes. Reduce the oven temperature to 325° and bake the pie for 50 minutes longer, until the filling is almost set. Transfer to a rack and let cool completely, 4 hours. —*Marcus Samuelsson*

Sweet Potato Pie with Cornmeal Crust

Active **1 hr 15 min**; Total **5 hr 15 min plus cooling**; Makes **one 9-inch pie**

CRUST

- 1¼ cups pastry flour
- ¼ cup fine cornmeal
- 1½ tsp. kosher salt
- 1 tsp. sugar
- 1 stick plus 2 Tbsp. unsalted butter, cubed and chilled

FILLING

- 2¾ lbs. sweet potatoes
- 4 Tbsp. unsalted butter, softened
- ⅓ cup granulated sugar
- 3 large eggs
- ⅓ cup unsweetened coconut milk
- 1¼ tsp. cinnamon
- ¾ tsp. ground ginger
- ¾ tsp. kosher salt
- ¼ tsp. ground cloves
- 1 large egg beaten with 1 Tbsp. water
  Turbinado sugar, for sprinkling
  Unsweetened whipped cream, for serving

1. Make the crust In a food processor, pulse the pastry flour with the cornmeal, salt and sugar. Add the butter and pulse until the mixture resembles coarse meal with some pea-size pieces of butter remaining. Sprinkle ⅓ cup ice water on top and pulse until the dough just starts to come together. Scrape the dough out onto a work surface, gather up the crumbs and pat the dough into a disk. Wrap in plastic and refrigerate until well chilled, 1 hour.

2. On a lightly floured work surface, roll out the dough to a 13-inch round, a scant ¼ inch thick. Ease the dough into a deep 9-inch glass pie plate. Trim the overhanging dough to 1 inch and fold it under itself. Crimp decoratively and chill the crust until firm, about 15 minutes.

3. Preheat the oven to 375°. Line the crust with parchment and fill with pie weights or dried beans. Bake in the lower third of the oven until the crust is barely set, about 20 minutes. Remove the parchment and pie weights and bake for 20 minutes longer, until the crust is lightly browned; let cool. Increase the oven temperature to 400°.

4. Make the filling Poke the sweet potatoes all over with a fork and bake them on a large foil-lined baking sheet for about 1 hour, until tender. Let cool completely, then peel and coarsely mash. Measure out 3 cups of mashed sweet potatoes; reserve the rest for another use.

5. In a food processor, combine the butter and sugar and puree. Add the 3 cups of sweet potato and puree until very smooth. With the machine on, add the eggs 1 at a time until each is just incorporated. Add the coconut milk, cinnamon, ginger, salt and cloves; pulse until no streaks remain.

6. Scrape the filling into the cooled piecrust. Brush the rim with the egg wash and sprinkle turbinado sugar over the crust and filling. Bake for 45 to 50 minutes, until the filling is just set but slightly jiggly in the center; cover the crust with strips of foil if it gets too dark. Let the pie cool completely, then cut into wedges and serve with whipped cream. —*Tara Jensen*

WINE Dried-fruit-and-honey-scented Italian vin santo: 2007 Castello di Meleto.

Caramelized White Chocolate Spread

Total **3 hr 20 min plus cooling**
Makes **1¼ cups**

Slow-roasting white chocolate makes the cocoa butter in it silky, rich and caramel-like. Valrhona's Ivoire white baking chocolate (available at specialty food stores and valrhona-chocolate.com) has just the right amount of cocoa butter for this spread.

- ½ lb. Valrhona Ivoire white baking chocolate, chopped
- ½ cup heavy cream, warmed
  Salt

Preheat the oven to 225°. In a medium stainless steel bowl, bake the chocolate for 3 hours, stirring every 15 minutes, until golden. Gradually whisk in the warm cream and a generous pinch of salt. Let cool completely, then refrigerate until just spreadable, about 10 minutes. —*Justin Chapple*

SERVE WITH Toasted rustic bread, sliced apples, sliced pears or strawberries.

MAKE AHEAD The spread can be refrigerated for up to 5 days. Soften in the microwave at 10-second intervals, stirring between intervals, until just spreadable.

FOUR-LAYER COCONUT CAKE
Recipe, page 333

Cakes, Cookies & More

PAGE NUMBERS IN RED INDICATE F&W STAFF FAVORITES

Chocolate and Coffee-Hazelnut Meringue Cake

Active **1 hr**; Total **2 hr plus 6 hr chilling**
Serves **8**

MERINGUE

- **2** tsp. pure coffee extract
- **¾** cup hazelnut meal/flour (we use Bob's Red Mill)
- **1** Tbsp. cornstarch
- Scant **½** tsp. ground cinnamon
- **4** large egg whites
- **1½** cups confectioners' sugar

FILLING

- **2** cups heavy cream
- **2** Tbsp. pure coffee extract
- **4** large egg yolks
- **½** lb. white chocolate, finely chopped
- **½** lb. bittersweet dark chocolate, finely chopped
- Salt
- Cocoa powder or confectioners' sugar, for dusting

1. Make the meringue Preheat the oven to 250° and line 2 large baking sheets with parchment paper. Using the bottom of a 9-inch springform pan, draw a circle in the center of each sheet of parchment paper.

2. In a small bowl, combine the coffee extract with 1 teaspoon of water. In another small bowl, whisk the hazelnut meal with the cornstarch and cinnamon. In the bowl of a stand mixer fitted with the whisk, beat the egg whites at medium-high speed until soft peaks form. Gradually add the confectioners' sugar and beat at high speed until the whites are stiff, 2 to 3 minutes. Gently fold in the hazelnut mixture, then the coffee extract.

3. Scrape half of the meringue into the center of each traced circle. Using an offset spatula, spread in an even layer, leaving a ½-inch border. Bake the meringues in the lower and upper thirds of the oven for about 1 hour, until lightly browned and crisp; shift the sheets halfway through baking. Transfer to racks to cool.

4. Meanwhile, make the filling In a large heatproof bowl set over a medium saucepan of simmering water, heat ½ cup of the cream with the coffee extract until hot. In a medium bowl, whisk the egg yolks. Very gradually whisk the hot cream into the

yolks, then return the mixture to the large bowl and cook over the simmering water, stirring constantly, until the custard is hot and slightly thickened, about 7 minutes. Fold in both chocolates and a generous pinch of salt and let stand over the simmering water until the chocolate is nearly melted, about 3 minutes. Remove from the heat and stir gently until smooth. Let cool.

5. In a large bowl, using an electric mixer, beat the remaining 1½ cups of cream until stiff peaks form. Using a spatula, very gently fold the whipped cream into the cooled chocolate custard until no streaks remain. Refrigerate until just chilled, 30 minutes.

6. Trim the meringues to fit into the 9-inch springform pan. Set 1 meringue in the pan. Spread the mousse evenly over the meringue and top with the remaining meringue. Refrigerate the cake for at least 6 hours or overnight. Unmold the cake and dust with cocoa powder or confectioners' sugar. Cut the cake into wedges with a hot knife and serve. —*Ruben Ortega*

WINE Nutty, toffee-inflected Madeira: Blandy Malmsey 5 Years Old.

German Chocolate Cake

Active **45 min**; Total **1 hr 30 min**
Serves **8 to 10**

Actress Ali Larter's cookbook, *Kitchen Revelry*, includes a German chocolate cupcake recipe. Here, she turns it into a cake with layers of the same rich chocolate and sweet coconut-pecan frosting. "It's a party on every level," she says.

CAKE

- **1½** sticks unsalted butter, at room temperature, plus more for the pans
- **7** oz. semisweet chocolate, finely chopped
- **2** cups all-purpose flour
- **2** Tbsp. unsweetened cocoa powder
- **1** tsp. baking soda
- **¾** tsp. fine sea salt
- **1¾** cups granulated sugar
- **3** large eggs, at room temperature
- **1** large egg yolk, at room temperature
- **2** tsp. pure vanilla extract
- **1** cup buttermilk

FROSTING

- **3½** cups pecan halves (14 oz.)
- **2** sticks plus 2 Tbsp. unsalted butter, at room temperature
- Two 14-oz. cans sweetened condensed milk
- **¾** cup packed light brown sugar
- **5** large egg yolks
- **10** oz. sweetened shredded coconut (3 cups)
- **1½** tsp. pure vanilla extract
- **¼** tsp. sea salt

1. Make the cake Preheat the oven to 350°. Butter two 9-inch baking pans and line them with parchment paper.

2. Set a heatproof bowl over (but not in) a saucepan of simmering water. Add the chopped chocolate and melt, stirring occasionally. Let cool slightly.

3. In a medium bowl, whisk the flour with the cocoa powder, baking soda and salt. In a large bowl, beat the 1½ sticks of butter with the granulated sugar until light and fluffy, 3 minutes. Beat in the eggs and egg yolk, 1 at a time, then beat in the vanilla. At low speed, beat in the buttermilk and the flour mixture in 3 alternating batches, ending with the flour mixture. Fold in the melted chocolate until incorporated.

4. Scrape the batter into the prepared pans. Bake until a cake tester inserted in the center of the cakes comes out clean, 30 minutes. Transfer the cakes to a rack; let cool completely. Turn the cakes out of the pans and peel off the parchment paper.

5. Meanwhile, make the frosting Toast the pecans on a rimmed baking sheet until golden, 8 to 10 minutes. Let cool slightly, then coarsely chop. In a large saucepan, combine the butter, condensed milk and brown sugar and cook over moderately low heat, whisking frequently, until smooth. Add the egg yolks and cook over moderately low heat, whisking frequently, until thickened, 8 to 10 minutes. Transfer the frosting to a large bowl and stir in 3 cups of the pecans and the coconut, vanilla and salt; let cool.

6. Using a spoon or offset spatula, spread half of the frosting evenly over one cake. Top with the second cake layer and spread the remaining frosting on top. Garnish with the remaining pecans. —*Ali Larter*

CHOCOLATE AND COFFEE-
HAZELNUT MERINGUE CAKE

Chocolate Cake with Chocolate Buttercream and Cocoa Nibs

Active **45 min**; Total **2 hr 30 min**
Makes **one 9-inch-square cake**

CAKE

- **3** oz. dark chocolate (60 to 70 percent), finely chopped
- **1¼** cups all-purpose flour
- **½** cup Dutch-process cocoa powder
- **¾** tsp. baking powder
- **¼** tsp. baking soda
- **¾** cup buttermilk
- **¾** cup brewed coffee, cooled slightly
- **¾** tsp. pure vanilla extract
- **1** stick unsalted butter, softened
- **1½** cups granulated sugar
- **¾** tsp. kosher salt
- **2** large eggs

BUTTERCREAM

- **6** oz. dark chocolate (60 to 70 percent), finely chopped
- **½** cup heavy cream
- **¼** cup confectioners' sugar
- **2** sticks unsalted butter, at room temperature, cut into tablespoons

  Cocoa nibs, for garnish

1. Make the cake Preheat the oven to 350° and line a 9-inch-square baking pan with foil, allowing 2 inches of overhang on 2 sides. In a medium glass bowl, microwave the chocolate on high power in 20-second intervals until melted; stir between intervals. Let cool slightly.

2. In a medium bowl, whisk the flour with the cocoa powder, baking powder and baking soda. In another medium bowl, whisk the buttermilk with the coffee and vanilla.

3. In a stand mixer fitted with the paddle or with a handheld electric mixer, beat the butter with the granulated sugar and salt at medium speed until fluffy, about 2 minutes. Beat in the eggs 1 at a time until incorporated. At low speed, in 3 alternating batches, beat in the dry ingredients and the buttermilk mixture, scraping down the side of the bowl as necessary. Fold in the melted chocolate.

4. Scrape the batter into the prepared pan. Bake for about 40 minutes, until a toothpick inserted in the center comes out clean. Let the cake cool in the pan for 45 minutes. Using the foil, transfer the cake to a rack to cool completely.

5. Meanwhile, make the buttercream In a glass bowl, microwave the chocolate on high power in 20-second intervals until melted; stir between intervals. Let cool slightly. Scrape the chocolate into the bowl of a stand mixer fitted with the whisk. At medium speed, beat in the cream and confectioners' sugar until smooth. At high speed, gradually add the butter and beat until the frosting is thick.

6. Transfer the chocolate cake to a platter and discard the foil. Spread the buttercream frosting evenly over the top and sprinkle with cocoa nibs. Cut the cake into squares and serve. —*Zoe Nathan*

Mexican Chocolate Chip–Pumpkin Seed Cake

Active **10 min**; Total **1 hr 10 min**
Makes **one 9-inch cake**

Every time Chicago chef Rick Bayless travels to Mexico, he buys *pepitorias*—a kind of pumpkin seed–packed brittle—immediately after he lands. He incorporates the flavor of that street food here in a fluffy cake and adds Mexican chocolate, which is spiced with cinnamon and vanilla.

- **1** stick unsalted butter, cut into ½-inch pieces and softened, plus more for greasing
- **1¾** cups salted roasted pumpkin seeds
- **1** cup plus 2 Tbsp. granulated sugar
- **3** large eggs, at room temperature
- **1** Tbsp. tequila
- **⅓** cup all-purpose flour
- **¼** tsp. baking powder
- **3** oz. Mexican chocolate, finely chopped (about ¾ cup)
- **2** tsp. confectioners' sugar

1. Preheat the oven to 350°. Butter a 9-inch cake pan and line the bottom with parchment paper. Butter the paper. Sprinkle ½ cup of the pumpkin seeds in the pan and dust with 2 tablespoons of the granulated sugar.

2. In a food processor, pulse the remaining 1¼ cups of pumpkin seeds and 1 cup of sugar until the mixture resembles wet sand. Add the eggs, tequila and 1 stick of butter and pulse until smooth. Add the flour and baking powder and pulse just until incorporated. Add the chocolate and pulse until mixed, about 4 pulses.

3. Scrape the batter into the prepared pan and bake in the lower third of the oven for about 50 minutes, until a toothpick inserted in the center of the cake comes out clean; rotate the pan halfway through baking. Let the cake cool in the pan for 10 minutes.

4. Invert the cake onto a plate and peel off the parchment paper. Dust the cake with the confectioners' sugar and serve warm or at room temperature. —*Rick Bayless*

Red Velvet Beet Cake with Crème Fraîche Icing

Active **1 hr 20 min**; Total **2 hr 40 min plus cooling**; Serves **12 to 16**

At M. Wells Steakhouse in New York City, pastry chef Bethany Costello eschews red food coloring in favor of beet puree for her take on red velvet cake. The puree keeps the layers nicely moist and tender.

CAKE

- **1** lb. medium beets
- **½** cup plus 2 Tbsp. whole milk
- **6** Tbsp. unsalted butter
- **2** cups plus 2 Tbsp. all-purpose flour
- **½** cup Dutch-process cocoa powder
- **1¼** tsp. salt
- **10** large eggs
- **¾** cup plus 3 Tbsp. granulated sugar
- **¾** cup plus 3 Tbsp. light brown sugar

ICING

- **2** sticks unsalted butter
- **2** cups crème fraîche
- **2** lbs. confectioners' sugar (8 cups), sifted
- **2** tsp. pure vanilla extract
- **4** oz. cream cheese, cut into tablespoons

1. **Make the cake** Preheat the oven to 350°. Wrap the beets in foil and bake for about 1 hour, until tender. Let cool slightly.

2. Peel the roasted beets and cut them into chunks. Transfer to a food processor and let cool completely. Puree until smooth. Measure out 1⅓ cups of the puree; reserve any remaining beet puree for another use.

3. In a medium saucepan, bring the milk just to a boil with the butter. Remove from the heat and whisk in the 1⅓ cups of beet puree. In a medium bowl, sift the flour with the cocoa powder and salt.

4. Line a large rimmed baking sheet with parchment paper, allowing 1 inch of overhang on the 2 long sides. Add the eggs and the granulated and brown sugars to the bowl of a stand mixer. Set the bowl 2 inches above a saucepan of simmering water and whisk until the sugars dissolve and the mixture is smooth and slightly warmed, about 4 minutes.

5. Transfer the bowl to the stand mixer fitted with the whisk. Beat the warm egg mixture at high speed until thickened and cooled, about 5 minutes. Scrape into a large bowl and, using a rubber spatula, gently fold in the dry ingredients just until no streaks remain. Fold one-third of the batter into the beet milk, then gently fold the beet mixture into the batter in 3 additions.

6. Scrape the batter onto the prepared baking sheet in an even layer. Bake for 20 to 25 minutes, until a toothpick inserted in the center comes out clean. Transfer the baking sheet to a rack to cool completely.

7. **Meanwhile, make the icing** In the bowl of the stand mixer fitted with the paddle, beat the butter at medium speed until fluffy, about 2 minutes. Beat in the crème fraîche just until incorporated. Add the confectioners' sugar in 2 batches and beat at low speed just until blended. Beat in the vanilla. With the machine at high speed, gradually add the cream cheese by tablespoons until the icing is smooth.

8. Using the parchment, slide the cooled cake onto a work surface. Trim the cake edges to make them neat, then cut the cake crosswise into 3 even rectangles. Transfer 1 layer to a rectangular cake cardboard or cake plate. Spread about 1 cup of the icing evenly on top, then cover with another layer of the cake and frost with

1 cup more of icing. Set the last cake layer on top and frost the top and sides with the remaining icing. Refrigerate the cake until well chilled, at least 2 hours or overnight. Let the cake stand at room temperature for 1 hour before serving. —*Bethany Costello*

MAKE AHEAD The cake can be covered and refrigerated for up to 3 days.

Four-Layer Coconut Cake

📷 PAGE 328
Active **1 hr**; Total **2 hr plus cooling**
Makes **one 8-inch cake**

Coconut oil and toasted ground coconut are baked into the batter of this dreamy cake, which is layered with bittersweet marmalade and fluffy white frosting.

CAKE

1½ **sticks unsalted butter, at room temperature, plus more for greasing**
24 **oz. unsweetened flaked coconut (about 10 cups)**
2¼ **cups cake flour**
2 **tsp. baking powder**
½ **tsp. baking soda**
¼ **cup virgin coconut oil**
1½ **cups sugar**
½ **tsp. kosher salt**
¼ **tsp. ground cardamom**
3 **large eggs**
1¼ **cups buttermilk**

FROSTING

2 **cups sugar**
3 **Tbsp. honey**
6 **large egg whites**
¼ **tsp. plus ⅛ tsp. kosher salt**
¼ **tsp. plus ⅛ tsp. cream of tartar**
One 12-oz. jar orange marmalade

1. **Make the cake** Preheat the oven to 350°. Grease two 8-inch round cake pans and line the bottoms with parchment paper.

2. Place 4 cups of the coconut in a blender; pulse until finely ground. Spread the ground coconut on a baking sheet. On a separate baking sheet, spread the remaining coconut. Toast both sheets for 7 to 8 minutes, stirring occasionally, until lightly golden; let cool.

3. Into a large bowl, sift the cake flour, baking powder and baking soda. In another large bowl, using an electric mixer, cream the 1½ sticks of butter with the coconut oil, sugar, salt and cardamom at medium-high speed until light, 3 minutes. Beat in the ground toasted coconut. Beat in the eggs, 1 at a time, until incorporated. At low speed, beat in the flour mixture and buttermilk in 3 alternating batches, starting and ending with the flour.

4. Divide the batter evenly between the prepared pans. Bake for 50 to 60 minutes, until the cakes are deep golden and springy. Transfer the cakes to a rack and let cool. Turn the cakes out and peel off the parchment. Cut each cake in half horizontally to create 4 layers.

5. **Make the frosting** In a large saucepan, boil the sugar, honey and ¾ cup of water over moderately high heat until the syrup registers 240° on a candy thermometer. Meanwhile, in the bowl of a stand mixer fitted with the whisk, beat the egg whites at medium speed until foamy; beat in the salt and cream of tartar until soft peaks form. With the mixer on, drizzle the hot syrup down the side of the bowl. Once all of the syrup has been added, beat the frosting at high speed until shiny and thick, 11 minutes. Let cool.

6. Set a cake layer cut side up on a plate. Spread one-third of the marmalade over the top, then spread with ½ cup of the frosting; repeat with 2 more cake layers. Top with the last layer. Coat the cake with the remaining frosting. Cover with the toasted coconut. —*Michelle Polzine*

COOKBOOK TIP

Cake Layer Shortcut

When making a layer cake, don't trim the domes off the bottom layers. When they come out of the oven, use a clean kitchen towel to press down on the tops to flatten them.

Hand Made Baking
Kamran Siddiqi

Honey Chiffon Cake

Active **20 min**; Total **1 hr 20 min plus cooling**
Makes **one 10-inch cake**

- ¾ **cup honey**
- ½ **cup warm strong black tea**
- 1½ **cups self-rising flour**
- ½ **tsp. baking soda**
- ¾ **cup granulated sugar**
- 6 **large eggs, separated**
- ¾ **cup light olive oil**
- 1 **cup confectioners' sugar**
- 4 **tsp. fresh lemon juice**

1. Preheat the oven to 350°. In a small bowl, stir together the honey and tea; let cool. In a medium bowl, stir together the flour and baking soda. In a large bowl, using a handheld mixer at medium-high speed, beat half of the granulated sugar with the egg yolks until thick and pale, about 2 minutes. Slowly drizzle in the olive oil, beating until thickened, then beat in the honey-tea mixture and the dry ingredients in alternating batches.

2. In another medium bowl, beat the egg whites until soft peaks form. While beating, gradually add the remaining granulated sugar and beat until stiff peaks form. Fold the egg whites into the batter until no streaks of white remain. Pour the batter into an ungreased 10-inch angel food cake pan. Smooth the top and bake for 45 to 50 minutes, until the top is dark golden brown and a toothpick inserted in the middle comes out clean. Immediately invert the cake pan onto a wire rack and let the cake cool completely.

3. Meanwhile, stir the confectioners' sugar with the lemon juice, adding 1 teaspoon at a time, to form a thick glaze. Once the cake has cooled, run a thin knife around the edge to release it from the pan. Lift out the cake by the central tube. Run a knife between the bottom of the cake and the pan, then transfer the cake to a serving plate. Drizzle with the lemon glaze and serve.
—Monday Morning Cooking Club

MAKE AHEAD The cake can be wrapped and stored at room temperature for 1 day before glazing and serving.

WINE Lightly floral, frothy Moscato d'Asti: 2012 Oddero.

Buttermilk Bundt Cake with Lemon Glaze

Active **30 min**; Total **1 hr 45 min plus cooling**; Serves **10 to 12**

Colleen Cruze Bhatti of Cruze Farm in Knoxville, Tennessee, makes the ultimate Bundt cake with superfresh buttermilk from her dairy. It gives the cake a wonderful tang and a soft, tender crumb.

CAKE

- 1½ **sticks unsalted butter, at room temperature, plus more for greasing**
- 3½ **cups all-purpose flour, plus more for dusting**
- ¾ **tsp. fine salt**
- ½ **tsp. baking soda**
- ¾ **cup vegetable shortening, at room temperature**
- 2½ **cups granulated sugar**
- 4 **large eggs, at room temperature**
- 2 **tsp. pure vanilla extract**
- 1 **cup buttermilk, at room temperature**
- 3 **Tbsp. fresh lemon juice**

GLAZE

- 1 **cup confectioners' sugar**
- ½ **tsp. finely grated lemon zest**
- 2½ **Tbsp. fresh lemon juice**
- 1 **tsp. unsalted butter, melted**
  Pinch of fine salt

1. Make the cake Preheat the oven to 325°. Generously butter a 10-inch Bundt pan and dust with flour. In a medium bowl, whisk the 3½ cups of flour with the salt and baking soda.

2. In a stand mixer fitted with the paddle, beat the 1½ sticks of butter with the shortening at medium-high speed until smooth. Add the granulated sugar and beat until light and fluffy, about 2 minutes. At medium speed, beat in the eggs 1 at a time until just incorporated, then beat in the vanilla; scrape down the side of the bowl. Beat in the dry ingredients and buttermilk in 3 alternating batches, starting and ending with the dry ingredients. At low speed, beat in the lemon juice.

3. Scrape the batter into the prepared Bundt pan and use a spatula to smooth the surface. Bake in the middle of the oven for about 1 hour and 15 minutes, rotating the pan halfway through baking, until a toothpick inserted in the center of the cake comes out clean. Let the cake cool on a rack for 30 minutes, then turn it out on a platter or cake stand to cool completely.

4. Make the glaze In a medium bowl, whisk the confectioners' sugar with the lemon zest, lemon juice, butter and salt until smooth. Drizzle the glaze over the top of the cake, letting it drip down the sides. Let stand for 20 minutes, until the glaze is set. Cut the cake into wedges and serve.
—Colleen Cruze Bhatti

MAKE AHEAD The glazed cake can be stored in an airtight container for up to 3 days.

Lemony Layered Cheesecake

Total **20 min plus 8 hr chilling**
Serves **8 to 10**

Instead of crushing graham crackers into a crust, F&W's Justin Chapple layers whole crackers in a lemon-curd cream for this easy, no-bake cheesecake.

- 1½ **cups mascarpone cheese**
- 1 **cup heavy cream**
- 1 **cup prepared lemon curd**
  Kosher salt
  About 20 whole graham crackers
  Blueberries, for serving

1. Line a 9-by-5-inch loaf pan with plastic wrap, allowing 4 inches of overhang. In a large bowl, using an electric mixer, beat the mascarpone with the heavy cream at medium speed until smooth and just firm; do not overbeat. Fold in the lemon curd and a pinch of salt.

2. Spread a ¼-inch-thick layer of the lemon cream on the bottom of the pan. Arrange a single layer of graham crackers on top, breaking them to fit. Repeat the layering with the remaining lemon cream and crackers, finishing with a final layer of cream. Cover the cake with plastic wrap and refrigerate for at least 8 hours or overnight.

3. Uncover and invert the cheesecake onto a platter. Remove the plastic wrap. Serve with blueberries. *—Justin Chapple*

LEMONY LAYERED CHEESECAKE

Tres Leches Cake

Active **30 min**; Total **1 hr 15 min** plus **overnight chilling**; Makes **one 9-inch cake**

Chef José Andrés makes a light, butter-free version of tres leches, the Latin American chilled cake soaked in three kinds of milk: evaporated milk, sweetened condensed milk and heavy cream.

Canola oil, for greasing
1 cup all-purpose flour, plus more for dusting
1½ cups heavy cream
1 cup sweetened condensed milk
¼ cup dark rum
2 cups evaporated milk
1 tsp. baking powder
6 large eggs
¾ cup sugar

1. Preheat the oven to 350°. Lightly grease a 9-inch-square baking pan and dust with flour. In a medium bowl, combine the cream, condensed milk, rum and 1½ cups of the evaporated milk and whisk until smooth. Cover and refrigerate.

2. In a small bowl, sift the 1 cup of flour with the baking powder. In the bowl of a stand mixer fitted with the whisk, beat the eggs at medium speed until frothy, 3 minutes. Add the sugar 1 tablespoon at a time and beat for 30 seconds after each addition. Continue beating until the mixture is thick and forms a ribbon when the whisk is lifted, 10 minutes. At low speed, gently add the flour mixture and the remaining evaporated milk in 3 alternating batches.

3. Scrape the batter into the prepared pan. Bake for about 30 minutes, until the cake is golden and a tester inserted in the center comes out clean. Transfer to a rack to cool for 15 minutes.

4. Using a cake tester or fork, poke holes all over the top of the cake; slowly pour ½ cup of the chilled milk mixture all over and let stand until the liquid is absorbed. Repeat with the remaining milk mixture in ½-cup increments. Cover and refrigerate the cake overnight before serving. —*José Andrés*

SERVE WITH Dulce de leche ice cream, whipped cream, chopped pineapple and finely grated lime zest.

MAKE AHEAD The soaked cake can be refrigerated for up to 2 days.

Ricotta-Orange Pound Cake with Prosecco Strawberries

Active **40 min**; Total **2 hr 15 min**; Serves **8**

1½ sticks unsalted butter, at room temperature, plus more for greasing
1½ cups cake flour
2½ tsp. baking powder
1 tsp. kosher salt
1½ cups fresh ricotta cheese
1½ cups plus 2 Tbsp. granulated sugar
3 large eggs
2 Tbsp. amaretto liqueur
1 tsp. pure vanilla extract
1 tsp. finely grated orange zest
1 lb. strawberries, hulled and quartered
2 Tbsp. Prosecco
Confectioners' sugar, for dusting
Lightly sweetened whipped cream, for serving

1. Preheat the oven to 350°. Butter a deep, 9-inch round cake pan. In a medium bowl, whisk the cake flour, baking powder and salt. In a large bowl, beat the ricotta, 1½ sticks of butter and 1½ cups of the granulated sugar at medium-high speed until smooth. Beat in the eggs 1 at a time until just incorporated, then beat in the amaretto, vanilla and orange zest. Beat in the dry ingredients in 3 batches just until incorporated.

2. Scrape the batter into the prepared pan and bake for 50 minutes, until a toothpick inserted in the center comes out with a few crumbs. Transfer to a rack to cool for 20 minutes; unmold and let cool completely.

3. Meanwhile, in a large bowl, toss the strawberries with the Prosecco and remaining 2 tablespoons of granulated sugar and let stand at room temperature until juicy, about 30 minutes.

4. Dust the pound cake with confectioners' sugar. Cut into wedges and serve with the strawberries and whipped cream.
—*Giada De Laurentiis*

MAKE AHEAD The cake can be stored in an airtight container for up to 3 days.

Crumb Cake with Pear Preserves

Active **30 min**; Total **1 hr 30 min** plus **cooling**; Serves **8 to 10**

Stacy Amble of the small-batch jam maker Quince & Apple makes this crumb cake using their excellent pear preserves with honey and ginger. The preserves are available at specialty food shops and online from quinceandapple.com.

STREUSEL

4 Tbsp. unsalted butter, cubed, plus more for greasing
½ cup packed light brown sugar
½ cup all-purpose flour
1 tsp. cinnamon
½ tsp. kosher salt

CAKE

2 cups all-purpose flour
2 tsp. baking powder
1 tsp. cinnamon
¾ tsp. kosher salt
1 stick unsalted butter, softened
1 cup granulated sugar
3 large eggs
¾ cup whole milk
½ cup pear preserves (4 oz.)
Confectioners' sugar, for dusting

1. **Make the streusel** Preheat the oven to 350° and butter a 9-inch-square metal baking pan. In a medium bowl, mix the brown sugar with the flour, cinnamon and salt. Add the 4 tablespoons of diced butter and, using your fingers, pinch the butter into the dry ingredients until evenly moistened, then press into clumps. Refrigerate the streusel until chilled, about 15 minutes.

2. **Meanwhile, make the cake** In a medium bowl, whisk the flour with the baking powder, cinnamon and salt. In a large bowl, using an electric mixer, beat the butter with the granulated sugar at medium speed until fluffy, 2 minutes. Beat in the eggs 1 at a time. Scrape down the side of the bowl, then beat in the dry ingredients and milk in 3 alternating batches, starting and ending with the dry ingredients, until just incorporated.

3. Scrape the batter into the prepared pan, spreading it in an even layer. Dollop the pear preserves evenly in the batter and sprinkle the streusel evenly on top. Bake for about 50 minutes, until a toothpick inserted in the center of the cake comes out clean. (Some of the streusel will sink into the cake.) Transfer the pan to a rack and let the cake cool completely, about 1 hour. Dust the cake with confectioners' sugar, cut into squares and serve. —Stacy Amble

MAKE AHEAD The crumb cake can be covered and stored at room temperature for up to 3 days.

COFFEE Yirgacheffe Dumerso from Los Angeles roaster Heartbreak.

Homemade Ricotta

Active **30 min**; Total **5 hr**; Makes **5½ cups**

Chef Allison Jenkins of LaV in Austin uses a combination of whole milk, buttermilk and cream to make her ricotta luscious and creamy. It's equally excellent in sweet and savory dishes.

- 1 **gallon whole milk**
- 2 **quarts buttermilk**
- 1 **quart heavy cream**
  Sea salt

Line a colander with a double layer of cheesecloth and set it over a large bowl. In a very large saucepan, combine the milk with the buttermilk and cream. Cook over moderate heat, stirring occasionally, until the milk starts to separate and reaches 185° on an instant-read thermometer, about 20 minutes. Remove the saucepan from the heat and let stand for 10 minutes. Using a ladle, gently spoon the mixture into the prepared colander and let drain at room temperature until the ricotta is thick, about 4 hours. Transfer the ricotta to a large bowl, season with salt and refrigerate; reserve the whey for another use. —Allison Jenkins

MAKE AHEAD The ricotta can be refrigerated for up to 4 days.

Lemon-Ricotta Cupcakes with Fluffy Lemon Frosting

Active **40 min**; Total **3 hr**
Makes **12 cupcakes**

These are the perfect grown-up cupcakes: Boston pastry chef Joanne Chang makes them with honey instead of refined sugar, which keeps the sweetness in check.

FROSTING

One 8-oz. package cream cheese, at room temperature
6 Tbsp. unsalted butter, at room temperature
1 Tbsp. finely grated lemon zest, plus more for garnish
⅓ cup honey
2 tsp. pure vanilla extract
⅛ tsp. kosher salt

CUPCAKES

2 cups all-purpose flour
2 tsp. baking powder
¼ tsp. baking soda
½ tsp. kosher salt
⅔ cup honey
½ cup fresh ricotta cheese
½ cup vegetable oil
2 Tbsp. finely grated lemon zest
1 Tbsp. pure vanilla extract
2 large eggs
1 large egg yolk
¾ cup crème fraîche

1. Make the frosting In a medium bowl, using a handheld electric mixer, beat the cream cheese at medium speed until light and creamy, about 3 minutes. Scrape down the side of the bowl. Add the butter and 1 tablespoon of lemon zest and beat until incorporated. Beat in the honey, vanilla and salt. Cover and refrigerate until firm and spreadable, about 3 hours.

2. Meanwhile, make the cupcakes Preheat the oven to 350°. Line a 12-cup muffin pan with paper liners. In a medium bowl, whisk the flour with the baking powder, baking soda and salt. In another medium bowl, whisk the honey with the ricotta, vegetable oil, lemon zest and vanilla; whisk in the eggs and egg yolk. Whisk in one-third of the flour mixture just until incorporated, then whisk in half of the crème fraîche until smooth, scraping down the side and

bottom of the bowl with a rubber spatula. Fold in the remaining flour mixture in 2 batches, alternating with the remaining crème fraîche until well incorporated.

3. Spoon the batter into the muffin cups and bake for about 25 minutes, until the cupcakes are lightly golden and a toothpick inserted in the center comes out clean. Transfer the cupcakes to a wire rack and let cool completely. Frost the cupcakes and garnish with lemon zest. —Joanne Chang

Double-Chocolate Cookie Crumble

Active **20 min**; Total **50 min**; Makes **9 cups**

This crisp chocolate crumble from San Francisco pastry chef Nicole Krasinski is deeply chocolaty, with a nice saltiness. It's fantastic on ice cream but also extremely good on its own.

½ lb. dark chocolate (72 percent), coarsely chopped
1¾ cups all-purpose flour
⅓ cup oat flour
¼ cup plus 2 Tbsp. unsweetened cocoa powder
2 tsp. baking soda
1¼ tsp. kosher salt
2 sticks unsalted butter, at room temperature
1 cup turbinado sugar
⅓ cup plus 1 Tbsp. granulated sugar
Vanilla ice cream, for serving

1. In a food processor, pulse the chocolate until it is the size of peas. Transfer to a plate and freeze for 30 minutes.

2. Preheat the oven to 325°. Line 2 rimmed baking sheets with parchment paper. Sift both flours with the cocoa powder, baking soda and salt. In a large bowl, using an electric mixer, beat the butter with both sugars at medium speed until very light and fluffy, 5 minutes. Beat in the flour mixture just until incorporated, then stir in the frozen chocolate.

3. Drop almond-size clumps of the dough in a single layer onto the prepared baking sheets; the dough will look crumbly and uneven. Bake for 8 to 10 minutes, until the top is dry but the crumble is still soft. Let cool completely. Serve over ice cream. —Nicole Krasinski

Pumpkin Tiramisu

Total **45 min** plus overnight chilling
Serves **12**

This spectacular tiramisu from F&W editor in chief Dana Cowin is a no-fail alternative to pumpkin pie. She assembles the dessert in a tall trifle dish so you can see the layers of silky pumpkin mousse and coffee-soaked ladyfingers.

One 15-oz. can pumpkin puree
½ cup light brown sugar
¾ tsp. ground ginger
¾ tsp. ground cinnamon
¼ tsp. kosher salt
Pinch of freshly grated nutmeg
¾ cup granulated sugar
1½ cups mascarpone cheese
2½ cups heavy cream
2 cups brewed coffee, cooled
Two 7-oz. packages dry ladyfingers
Chocolate shavings and candied ginger, for garnish

1. In a large bowl, whisk the pumpkin puree with the brown sugar, ginger, cinnamon, salt, nutmeg and ½ cup of the granulated sugar. Add the mascarpone and 1½ cups of the heavy cream. Using an electric mixer, beat the pumpkin mixture at medium speed until soft peaks form; do not overbeat.

2. In a medium bowl, whisk the brewed coffee with 2 tablespoons of the granulated sugar until it's dissolved. Dip both sides of 6 ladyfingers in the coffee and arrange them in a single layer in a 4-quart trifle dish. Spread 1 cup of the pumpkin mousse on top. Repeat the layering 5 more times, ending with a layer of the pumpkin mousse. Cover and refrigerate the tiramisu overnight.

3. In a large bowl, using an electric mixer, beat the remaining 1 cup of cream with the remaining 2 tablespoons of granulated sugar until soft peaks form. Dollop the whipped cream over the tiramisu, garnish with shaved chocolate and candied ginger and serve. —*Dana Cowin*

Gluten-Free Chocolate-Almond Thumbprint Cookies

Active **45 min**; Total **3 hr** plus cooling
Makes **6½ dozen cookies**

1½ cups honey
¼ cup unsweetened coconut milk
¾ cup coconut oil
½ tsp. kosher salt
1 Tbsp. plus ¼ tsp. pure vanilla extract
2½ cups almond flour
2 Tbsp. unsweetened Dutch-process cocoa powder
¼ tsp. baking soda
⅛ tsp. ground cinnamon
Pinch of cayenne pepper
6 oz. dark chocolate, finely chopped
1 large egg beaten with 1 egg yolk
Flaky sea salt, for garnish

1. Line an 8½-by-4½-inch loaf pan with parchment paper. In a small saucepan, heat 1 cup of the honey with the coconut milk, 2 tablespoons of the coconut oil and ¼ teaspoon of the salt over moderately high heat. Attach a candy thermometer to the pan and cook, stirring occasionally, until the mixture reaches 250°, 6 to 8 minutes. Stir in ¼ teaspoon of the vanilla, then pour the mixture into the prepared pan. Refrigerate until solid, at least 2 hours.

2. Lift the caramel out of the pan and quickly cut into ½-inch squares. Arrange the squares on a parchment paper–lined baking sheet and refrigerate.

3. Meanwhile, in a medium bowl, whisk the almond flour with the cocoa powder, baking soda, cinnamon, cayenne and the remaining ¼ teaspoon of salt. Stir in the dark chocolate. In a small saucepan, combine the remaining ½ cup plus 2 tablespoons of coconut oil and ½ cup of honey over moderate heat and cook until the coconut oil liquefies. Remove from the heat and stir in the beaten egg and the remaining 1 tablespoon of vanilla. Pour this mixture over the dry ingredients and stir until just combined.

4. Preheat the oven to 350°. Line 2 large rimmed baking sheets with parchment paper. Using 2 teaspoons, scoop the dough into ¾-inch balls. Working in 4 batches, arrange the balls on the prepared sheets at least 2 inches apart. Bake the cookies for

8 minutes, until lightly browned at the edges; rotate the baking sheets from top to bottom and front to back halfway through baking.

5. When the cookies come out of the oven, immediately make a well in the center of each one and press in a square of honey caramel. Sprinkle the caramel with a pinch of sea salt. Let the cookies cool for 10 minutes on the baking sheet, then transfer to a rack to cool completely. —*Gregory Gourdet*

Chunky Peanut Butter Cookies

Active **15 min**; Total **45 min**
Makes **3 dozen cookies**

Chunky natural peanut butter lends a salty-sweet crunch to these easy cookies. For a double dose of PB, sandwich creamy peanut butter between the cookies.

1½ cups all-purpose flour
1 tsp. kosher salt
½ tsp. baking soda
½ tsp. baking powder
1 stick unsalted butter, softened
½ cup chunky natural peanut butter
¾ cup granulated sugar
¼ cup packed dark brown sugar
1 large egg
½ tsp. pure vanilla extract

1. Preheat the oven to 350° and position racks in the upper and lower thirds. In a medium bowl, whisk the flour with the salt, baking soda and baking powder. In a large bowl, using an electric mixer, beat the butter, peanut butter and both sugars at high speed until pale and fluffy, about 2 minutes. Beat in the egg and vanilla. At low speed, gradually beat in the dry ingredients until they are just incorporated.

2. Form half of the dough into 1-inch balls and arrange them 2 inches apart on 2 large baking sheets. Using a fork, gently press the tops of the cookies to form a cross-hatch pattern. Bake the cookies for 12 to 15 minutes, until lightly browned; shift the baking sheets from top to bottom and front to back halfway through baking. Let the cookies cool on the baking sheets for 2 minutes before transferring them to a rack to cool completely. Let the baking sheets cool slightly, then repeat with the remaining dough. —*Emily Farris*

PUMPKIN TIRAMISU

Oatmeal-Cherry Cookies

Active **30 min**; Total **1 hr plus cooling**
Makes **18 cookies**

Megan Garrelts, the pastry chef at Bluestem in Kansas City, Missouri, grew up eating pies filled with cherries from her family's backyard tree. In this recipe, she combines the fruit with another classic American dessert, oatmeal cookies. She makes buttery oversize cookies with Amarena cherries or, for a more sophisticated recipe, brandied cherries.

¾ cup all-purpose flour

½ cup whole-wheat flour

½ tsp. baking soda

½ tsp. kosher salt

½ tsp. ground cinnamon

¼ tsp. freshly grated nutmeg

2 sticks unsalted butter, softened

1 cup granulated sugar

½ cup packed light brown sugar

2 large eggs

2 tsp. pure vanilla extract

2 cups old-fashioned rolled oats

1 cup Amarena or brandied sour cherries in syrup, drained

1 Tbsp. turbinado sugar

1. Preheat the oven to 350° and position racks in the upper and lower thirds. Line 2 large baking sheets with parchment paper. In a medium bowl, whisk the flours with the baking soda, salt, cinnamon and nutmeg. In a large bowl, using an electric mixer, beat the butter with the granulated and brown sugars at medium-high speed until light and fluffy, about 5 minutes. Add the eggs and vanilla and beat until smooth. Add the dry ingredients and beat at low speed until combined. Add the oats and cherries and beat until the cherries are slightly mashed and evenly distributed.

2. Working in batches, scoop 6 scant ¼-cup balls of dough onto each of the baking sheets and sprinkle with turbinado sugar. Bake for 16 minutes, shifting the sheets from top to bottom and front to back halfway through, until dark golden brown. Let the cookies cool on the baking sheets for 5 minutes, then transfer to a rack to cool completely. Bake the remaining 6 cookies *—Megan Garrelts*

Milk Chocolate–Dipped Hazelnut Sandies

Active **45 min**; Total **4 hr**
Makes **6½ dozen cookies**

1½ cups hazelnuts

¾ cup cocoa nibs (2.5 oz.)

2¾ cups all-purpose flour

1 tsp. unsweetened Dutch-process cocoa powder

1 tsp. kosher salt

½ tsp. ground cinnamon

3 sticks unsalted butter, at room temperature

1½ cups confectioners' sugar

1 tsp. vanilla bean paste or pure vanilla extract

12 oz. high-quality milk chocolate, finely chopped

1. In a food processor, pulse the hazelnuts and cocoa nibs until coarsely ground. Scrape into a medium bowl and whisk in the flour, cocoa powder, salt and cinnamon.

2. In the bowl of a stand mixer fitted with the paddle, beat the butter with the confectioners' sugar and vanilla bean paste at medium speed until light and fluffy, about 3 minutes. Add the dry ingredients and beat at low speed just until incorporated. Scrape the dough onto a work surface and form into a ball. Halve the dough, then shape each half into a 1½-inch square log and wrap in parchment paper. Freeze until firm, at least 2 hours or overnight.

3. Preheat the oven to 350°. Line 2 large rimmed baking sheets with parchment paper. Working in 2 batches, cut the cookie-dough logs into ¼-inch-thick slices and arrange on the prepared sheets at least 1 inch apart. Bake the cookies for about 15 minutes, until lightly browned on the bottom; rotate the baking sheets from top to bottom and front to back halfway through baking. Let the cookies cool on the baking sheets for 5 minutes, then transfer to a rack to cool completely.

4. In a medium saucepan, bring 1 inch of water to a simmer. Place the milk chocolate in a small heatproof bowl and set it over the saucepan. Stir the chocolate until melted and smooth. Remove the saucepan from the heat; leave the bowl of chocolate on top. Dip 1 corner of each cookie in the chocolate to coat halfway, letting the excess chocolate drip back into the bowl. Transfer the cookies to parchment paper–lined baking sheets and refrigerate until the chocolate is set, about 20 minutes. *—Sarah Hart*

Chocolate–Pine Nut Cookies

Active **40 min**; Total **1 hr 10 min plus cooling**; Makes **3 dozen cookies**

¾ cup pine nuts

½ lb. bittersweet chocolate, finely chopped

½ stick unsalted butter, cubed

¼ cup all-purpose flour

1 tsp. baking powder

¼ tsp. fine salt

2 large eggs

¾ cup superfine sugar

1. Preheat the oven to 325° and line 2 baking sheets with parchment paper. In a large skillet, toast the pine nuts over moderate heat, tossing occasionally, until golden, 5 to 7 minutes. Transfer to paper towels to drain and cool completely.

2. Meanwhile, in a large heatproof bowl set over a medium saucepan of simmering water, melt the chopped chocolate with the butter, stirring occasionally, until smooth, 5 minutes; let cool completely.

3. In a small bowl, mix the flour with the baking powder and salt. In a large bowl, using an electric mixer, beat the eggs with the sugar at medium-high speed until thick and pale, about 3 minutes. Using a rubber spatula, fold in the melted chocolate, then fold in the dry ingredients. Stir in the pine nuts.

4. Bake the cookies in 2 batches: Scoop 1-tablespoon mounds of dough onto the prepared baking sheets, about 2 inches apart. Bake for about 12 minutes, until the cookies are dry around the edges and cracked on top; shift the sheets halfway through baking. Repeat with the remaining cookie dough. Transfer the cookies to a rack to cool completely before serving. *—Tara Derr Webb*

MAKE AHEAD The cookies can be stored in an airtight container for up to 3 days.

CHOCOLATE-PINE NUT COOKIES

Billionaire's Shortbread

Active **1 hr**; Total **3 hr 15 min**; Makes **16 bars**

For her spin on the popular British confection known as Millionaire's Shortbread, New York pastry chef Jennifer Yee sprinkles the ganache with flaky sea salt. She encourages bakers to add other toppings, like pretzels, candied ginger and nuts.

SHORTBREAD

- **1** stick cold unsalted butter, cubed
- **¾** cup all-purpose flour
- **⅓** cup sugar
- **¼** cup fine cornmeal
- **½** tsp. kosher salt

CARAMEL

- **1** stick unsalted butter
- **½** cup heavy cream
- **½** tsp. kosher salt
- **1** cup sugar

GANACHE

- **9** oz. dark chocolate (70 percent)
- **¾** cup heavy cream
  Flaky sea salt, for garnish
  Mini marshmallows, toasted nuts, thinly sliced candied orange peel, thinly sliced candied ginger and/or crushed pretzels, for toppings

1. Make the shortbread Preheat the oven to 350° and line an 8-inch-square baking pan with aluminum foil, allowing 2 inches of overhang on 2 sides. In a food processor, combine all of the ingredients and pulse until a dough forms, 1 to 2 minutes. Press the dough into the prepared pan in an even layer. Bake for about 25 minutes, until the shortbread is firm and the edges are golden; let cool completely.

2. Make the caramel In a small saucepan, melt the butter with the cream and salt over moderate heat; keep warm. In a medium saucepan, combine the sugar and 2 tablespoons of water and cook over moderate heat, swirling without stirring, until a golden caramel forms, about 7 minutes. Carefully drizzle in the warm cream and cook over moderate heat, stirring constantly, until the temperature reaches 230° on a candy thermometer, 3 to 5 minutes. Immediately pour the caramel over the cooled shortbread and let cool completely, about 45 minutes.

3. Make the ganache Finely chop the chocolate and transfer it to a medium heatproof bowl. In a small saucepan, bring the cream just to a simmer. Immediately pour the hot cream over the chocolate and let stand until the chocolate starts to melt, 2 minutes; stir until thickened and smooth. Pour the ganache over the cooled caramel and spread it in an even layer with an offset spatula. Sprinkle with flaky sea salt and your choice of toppings and refrigerate until chilled, about 1 hour. Lift the square out of the pan using the long sides of the foil. Cut the shortbread into squares and serve slightly chilled. —*Jennifer Yee*

Old-Fashioned Oatmeal-Raisin Cookies

Active **15 min**; Total **45 min** Makes **3 dozen cookies**

- **¾** cup all-purpose flour
- **½** tsp. baking soda
- **½** tsp. cinnamon
- **¼** tsp. kosher salt
- **1** stick unsalted butter, softened
- **¾** cup granulated sugar
- **¼** cup packed dark brown sugar
- **1** large egg
- **½** tsp. pure vanilla extract
- **1½** cups quick-cooking oats
- **½** cup raisins

1. Preheat the oven to 375° and position racks in the upper and lower thirds. In a medium bowl, whisk the flour, baking soda, cinnamon and salt. In a large bowl, using an electric mixer, beat the butter with both sugars at high speed until pale and fluffy, 2 minutes. Beat in the egg and vanilla. At low speed, gradually add the flour mixture until just incorporated, then beat in the oats and raisins.

2. Form half of the dough into 1-inch balls and arrange them 2 inches apart on 2 large baking sheets. Bake for 12 to 15 minutes, until lightly browned; shift the baking sheets from top to bottom and front to back halfway through baking. Let the cookies cool on the baking sheets for 2 minutes before transferring them to a rack to cool completely. Let the baking sheets cool slightly, then repeat with the remaining dough. —*Jeff Akin*

White Chocolate Chip Macadamia Cookies with Dried Cherries

Active **15 min**; Total **30 min** Makes **2 dozen cookies**

- **1½** cups all-purpose flour
- **½** tsp. baking soda
- **½** tsp. kosher salt
- **1** stick unsalted butter, softened
- **½** cup granulated sugar
- **½** cup packed dark brown sugar
- **1** large egg
- **1** tsp. pure vanilla extract
- **1** cup white chocolate chips
- **¾** cup dried cherries, coarsely chopped
- **½** cup macadamia nuts, coarsely chopped

1. Preheat the oven to 375° and position racks in the upper and lower thirds. In a medium bowl, whisk the flour, baking soda and salt. In a large bowl, using an electric mixer, beat the butter with both sugars until pale and fluffy, 2 minutes. Beat in the egg and vanilla. At low speed, beat in the dry ingredients until just incorporated, then beat in the white chocolate, dried cherries and macadamias.

2. Form the dough into 1½-inch balls and arrange them 2 inches apart on 2 large baking sheets. Bake for 12 to 15 minutes, until lightly browned; shift the baking sheets from top to bottom and front to back halfway through baking. Let the cookies cool on the baking sheets for 2 minutes before transferring them to a rack to cool completely. —*Jeff Akin*

Cardamom-Oatmeal Cookie Ice Cream Sandwiches

Active **30 min**; Total **1 hr 30 min** Makes **10 ice cream sandwiches**

- **¾** cup all-purpose flour
- **1** tsp. ground cardamom
- **1** tsp. kosher salt
- **½** tsp. baking soda
- **1** stick unsalted butter, softened
- **¾** cup packed light brown sugar
- **1** large egg
- **¼** cup buttermilk
- **1** tsp. pure vanilla extract
- **1½** cups old-fashioned rolled oats
- **1** pint ice cream, for filling

1. Preheat the oven to 350° and line 2 large baking sheets with parchment paper.

2. In a medium bowl, whisk the flour, cardamom, salt and baking soda. In a large bowl, using an electric mixer, beat the butter with the sugar at medium-high speed until fluffy, 1 to 2 minutes. At medium speed, beat in the egg. Beat in the buttermilk and vanilla until just smooth, then beat in the dry ingredients. Fold in the oats.

3. Using a 2-tablespoon ice cream scoop, scoop 10 mounds of dough onto each baking sheet, about 2 inches apart. Bake in the lower and upper thirds of the oven until the cookies are puffy and set, 13 minutes; shift the sheets halfway through baking. Transfer the cookies to racks to cool completely.

4. For each ice cream sandwich, scoop 3 tablespoons of the ice cream onto the underside of a cookie and top with another cookie. Wrap in plastic and freeze until the ice cream is just firm, about 30 minutes, then serve. —Colleen Cruze Bhatti

Chewy Salted-Oatmeal Cookies
Active **30 min;** Total **2 hr**
Makes **3½ dozen cookies**

- 2 **cups rolled oats**
- 2 **cups all-purpose flour**
- ½ **cup whole-wheat pastry flour**
- 2 **tsp. baking soda**
- 1 **tsp. kosher salt**
- 1 **tsp. ground cinnamon**
- ¼ **tsp. freshly grated nutmeg**
- 2 **sticks unsalted butter, at room temperature**
- 1 **cup granulated sugar**
- 1 **cup dark brown sugar**
- 1 **tsp. pure vanilla extract**
- 3 **large eggs**
  Flaky sea salt, for garnish

1. Preheat the oven to 350°. In a large bowl, whisk the oats with the flours, baking soda, salt, cinnamon and nutmeg. In the bowl of a stand mixer fitted with the paddle, beat the butter with both sugars and the vanilla at medium speed until light and fluffy, about 3 minutes. Add the eggs 1 at a time and beat until incorporated. Add the dry ingredients and beat at low speed until just combined. Cover the bowl with plastic wrap and refrigerate the cookie dough until chilled, at least 1 hour.

2. Line 2 large rimmed baking sheets with parchment paper. Working in 2 batches, using a 1-ounce ice cream scoop or 2 tablespoons, scoop the dough onto the prepared sheets, spaced at least 2 inches apart. Flatten the cookies slightly and sprinkle each with a pinch of sea salt. Bake for 10 minutes, until golden brown at the edges; rotate the baking sheets from top to bottom and front to back halfway through baking. Let the cookies cool on the baking sheets for 5 minutes, then transfer to a rack to cool completely before serving. —Kir Jensen

MAKE AHEAD The cookies can be stored in an airtight container for up to 5 days.

Dark Chocolate–Cherry Shortbreads
Active **30 min;** Total **2 hr plus cooling**
Makes **about 1½ dozen cookies**

- ¾ **cup all-purpose flour**
- ¼ **cup unsweetened cocoa powder**
- 1 **Tbsp. unsweetened black cocoa powder**
- ½ **tsp. kosher salt**
- 1 **stick unsalted butter, softened**
- ¼ **cup sugar, plus more for sprinkling**
- 1½ **tsp. finely grated lime zest**
- ½ **cup dried cherries, chopped**

1. In a medium bowl, sift the flour with both cocoa powders and the salt. In a stand mixer fitted with the paddle, beat the butter with the ¼ cup of sugar at medium-high speed until fluffy. Beat in the lime zest. Beat in the flour mixture at low speed until the dough comes together. Add the cherries; beat until incorporated.

2. Scrape the dough onto a work surface and pat it into a disk; roll it between 2 sheets of parchment paper to a ¼-inch thickness and refrigerate on a baking sheet until firm, 1 hour.

3. Preheat the oven to 350° and line a baking sheet with parchment paper. Peel off the top sheet of parchment from the dough. Using a 2-inch round cookie cutter, stamp out cookies. Arrange the cookies 1 inch apart on the baking sheet. Reroll the scraps between parchment paper, stamp out more cookies and add to the baking sheet. Sprinkle with sugar.

4. Bake the cookies in the middle of the oven for 13 minutes, until just set. Let cool for 5 minutes. Transfer to a rack to cool completely. —Umber Ahmad

Oatella Cookies
Active **25 min;** Total **1 hr**
Makes **5 dozen cookies**

This dessert is a cross between an oatmeal cookie and a Nutella cookie.

- 1¾ **cups all-purpose flour**
- 1 **tsp. kosher salt**
- ½ **tsp. ground cinnamon**
- ¼ **tsp. baking soda**
- 1 **cup vegetable shortening**
- 1 **cup granulated sugar**
- ¾ **cup packed dark brown sugar**
- 2 **large eggs**
  One 13-oz. jar Nutella
- 2 **cups rolled oats**

1. Preheat the oven to 375° and line 2 large baking sheets with parchment paper. In a medium bowl, whisk the flour with the salt, cinnamon and baking soda. In a stand mixer fitted with the paddle, beat the shortening with both sugars at medium speed until light and fluffy, about 2 minutes. Beat in the eggs 1 at a time, scraping down the side of the bowl. Add the Nutella and beat until smooth. Reduce the speed to low and beat in the dry ingredients until just incorporated, then beat in the oats.

2. Working in batches, scoop 1-tablespoon mounds of dough 2 inches apart on the prepared baking sheets. Bake for 8 to 10 minutes, until the edges are lightly browned and the cookies are just set; shift the sheets from front to back and top to bottom halfway through baking. Immediately transfer the cookies from the sheets to racks to cool. Repeat with the remaining dough. —Dagmara Kokonas

MAKE AHEAD The cookies can be stored in an airtight container for up to 5 days.

Marcona Almond Blondies

Active **30 min**; Total **2 hr**; Makes **20 blondies**

2½ sticks unsalted butter,
  plus more for brushing

3½ cups light brown sugar

 5 large eggs, lightly beaten

 ½ cup roasted almond butter

 1 Tbsp. pure vanilla extract

1½ tsp. kosher salt

 ¼ tsp. ground cinnamon

 3 cups all-purpose flour

 2 cups marcona almonds,
  chopped (9 oz.)

1¾ cups chocolate chips (11 oz.)

1. Preheat the oven to 325°. Lightly brush a 9-by-13-inch metal baking pan with butter.

2. In a medium saucepan, cook the 2½ sticks of butter over moderate heat until golden brown, 5 minutes. Transfer to a large bowl and let cool to room temperature, 30 minutes.

3. Add the sugar, eggs, almond butter, vanilla, salt and cinnamon to the butter and whisk until smooth. Stir in the flour, then fold in 1½ cups of the almonds and 1½ cups of the chocolate chips. Scrape the batter into the prepared pan and spread it evenly with an offset or a nonstick spatula. Scatter the remaining ½ cup of almonds and ¼ cup of chocolate chips over the top. Bake for about 1 hour, until a toothpick inserted in the center comes out with a few moist crumbs attached. Transfer the pan to a rack and let the blondies cool completely before cutting. —*Jose Garces*

Swedish Butter Cookies

Active **25 min**; Total **1 hr plus cooling**
Makes **3 dozen cookies**

The recipe for these *smör bullar*—light, crumbly pecan cookies similar to Mexican wedding cakes—comes from home cook Marge Peterson of Fort Dodge, Iowa. "She's my wife's great-aunt and a terrific Swedish cook," says chef Paul Berglund of The Bachelor Farmer in Minneapolis.

 2 sticks unsalted butter, softened

 ¼ cup confectioners' sugar,
  plus more for dusting

 1 tsp. pure vanilla extract

 2 cups all-purpose flour, sifted

 1 cup pecans, coarsely chopped

1. Preheat the oven to 325° and line 2 baking sheets with parchment paper. In a stand mixer fitted with the paddle, cream the butter with the ¼ cup of confectioners' sugar and the vanilla at medium speed until smooth and pale, about 2 minutes. Mix in the flour and pecans at low speed. Cover the dough with plastic wrap and refrigerate until firm, at least 30 minutes.

2. Roll tablespoons of the dough into balls and arrange them on the prepared baking sheets 1 inch apart. Bake the cookies for about 20 minutes, until cooked through and lightly golden on the bottom. Transfer the cookies to a rack to cool slightly. Coat the warm cookies with confectioners' sugar and let cool completely. Sift more confectioners' sugar over them and serve. —*Paul Berglund*

MAKE AHEAD The cookies can be stored in an airtight container for up to 5 days.

Almost-Instant Soft-Serve

◌ Total **15 min**; Makes **3½ cups**

This superquick soft-serve is easy to make without an ice cream maker: Just puree frozen fruit with sweetened condensed milk. For an almost-instant pie, spread the soft-serve into a prepared graham cracker crust and top with whipped cream.

1½ lbs. frozen strawberries, mangoes
  or blueberries

 ¾ cup sweetened condensed milk

 ¼ tsp. pure vanilla extract
  Kosher salt

In a food processor, pulse the fruit with the sweetened condensed milk, vanilla and a generous pinch of salt until the fruit is finely chopped. Puree until smooth, 2 to 3 minutes; scrape down the side of the bowl as needed. Serve soft or transfer to a metal baking pan, cover and freeze until just firm. —*Justin Chapple*

MAKE AHEAD The soft-serve can be frozen for up to 3 days. Let stand at room temperature for 10 minutes before serving.

Lemony Butter Cookies

Active **30 min**; Total **1 hr 15 min**
Makes **3 dozen cookies**

Confectioners' sugar sweetens both the dough and the glaze in these cookies. It gives the finished cookies a delicate crumb and melt-in-your-mouth texture.

COOKIES

 2 sticks unsalted butter, softened

 1 cup confectioners' sugar

 1 Tbsp. finely grated lemon zest

1½ Tbsp. fresh lemon juice

 2 cups all-purpose flour

 ¾ tsp. kosher salt

GLAZE

 ½ cup plus 2 Tbsp. confectioners'
  sugar

 1 Tbsp. fresh lemon juice

 1 Tbsp. unsalted butter, softened
  Finely grated lemon zest, for garnish

1. Make the cookies Preheat the oven to 350° and position racks in the upper and lower thirds. In a large bowl, using a handheld electric mixer, beat the butter with the confectioners' sugar until very smooth, about 2 minutes. Beat in the lemon zest and juice, then beat in the flour and salt until just incorporated; scrape down the side of the bowl as necessary.

2. Roll half of the dough into 1-inch balls. Arrange the balls 1 inch apart on 2 baking sheets and, using your fingers, gently flatten each cookie. Bake for 12 to 14 minutes, until the cookies are lightly browned on the bottom and just firm; shift the baking sheets from top to bottom and front to back halfway through baking. Let the cookies cool on the baking sheets for 2 minutes, then transfer them to a rack to cool completely. Let the baking sheets cool slightly, then repeat with the remaining dough.

3. Meanwhile, make the glaze In a bowl, whisk the confectioners' sugar with the lemon juice and butter until smooth.

4. Spread the lemon glaze on the cooled cookies and garnish with finely grated lemon zest. Let stand until the glaze is set, about 15 minutes. —*Kristen Stevens*

LEMONY BUTTER COOKIES

Salted-Caramel Cream Puffs with Warm Chocolate Sauce

Active 45 min; Total 1 hr 15 min plus cooling
Serves 8

One secret to pastry chef David Lebovitz's spectacular cream puffs is the salted butter he uses to make the bittersweet caramel custard filling. For a savory hors d'oeuvre, fill the puffs with Boursin or salmon spread instead.

CARAMEL CUSTARD

- 1 large egg
- 2 large egg yolks
- ¼ cup cornstarch
- 2 cups whole milk
- 1½ cups sugar
- 2 Tbsp. salted butter
- 1 tsp. pure vanilla extract
- ½ tsp. flaky sea salt

CREAM PUFFS

- 6 Tbsp. unsalted butter, cubed, at room temperature
- 2 tsp. sugar
- ½ tsp. kosher salt
- ¾ cup all-purpose flour
- 3 large eggs, at room temperature

CHOCOLATE SAUCE

- ½ cup half-and-half
- 2 Tbsp. unsweetened Dutch-process cocoa powder
- 2 Tbsp. light corn syrup
- 2 Tbsp. sugar
- ½ Tbsp. salted butter, at room temperature
- 4 oz. bittersweet chocolate, finely chopped

  Sliced almonds, confectioners' sugar or flaky sea salt, for garnish (optional)

1. Make the caramel custard In a medium bowl, whisk the egg with the egg yolks, cornstarch and ½ cup of the milk until smooth. In a small saucepan, heat the remaining 1½ cups of milk over low heat; keep warm.

2. In a medium saucepan, combine the sugar with ¼ cup of water. Cook over moderate heat, swirling the pan and brushing down the side with a wet pastry brush, until the sugar dissolves. Cook undisturbed until a deep amber caramel forms, about 5 minutes. Remove the saucepan from the heat and carefully whisk in the butter; it will boil vigorously. While whisking constantly, slowly drizzle in the warm milk until blended; the mixture may separate a little. Slowly whisk in the egg mixture and bring to a boil, then cook over moderate heat, stirring, until thickened, about 2 minutes. Stir in the vanilla and sea salt. Strain the caramel custard through a fine sieve into a heatproof bowl. Press a piece of plastic wrap directly onto the surface of the custard and refrigerate until completely chilled.

3. Make the cream puffs Preheat the oven to 400°. Line a baking sheet with parchment paper or a silicone mat.

4. In a medium saucepan, combine the butter, sugar and kosher salt with ¾ cup of water. Cook over moderate heat for 1 minute, until the butter dissolves. Add all of the flour at once and stir vigorously with a wooden spoon, then cook until the dough pulls away from the side of the pan, 1 to 2 minutes. Remove from the heat and let stand for 2 minutes, stirring a few times to cool down the dough. Add the eggs 1 at a time, beating constantly and thoroughly with a wooden spoon between additions; the dough should be smooth and shiny.

5. Transfer the dough to a pastry bag fitted with a ½-inch plain tip. Pipe the dough into twenty-four 1½-inch mounds on the prepared baking sheet, spacing them 1 inch apart. Bake for about 25 minutes, until the tops and bottoms are golden. Transfer the baking sheet to a rack. Using a skewer, poke a small hole in the side of each cream puff to allow steam to escape; let cool completely.

6. Make the chocolate sauce In a medium saucepan, combine the half-and-half, cocoa, corn syrup and sugar. Bring to a boil over moderate heat, stirring occasionally. Remove from the heat. Stir in the butter and chocolate until melted and the sauce is smooth.

7. Scrape the custard into a piping bag fitted with a ¼-inch plain tip. Pipe the custard into the hole in the side of each cream puff until full. Drizzle with some of the chocolate sauce, sprinkle with garnishes and serve. —David Lebovitz

Raspberry Rugelach

Active 30 min; Total 2 hr 30 min
Makes 2 dozen rugelach

- 2 cups all-purpose flour
- ½ cup plus 2 Tbsp. sugar
- ¼ tsp. kosher salt
- 2 sticks chilled unsalted butter, cut into ½-inch dice
- 6 oz. chilled cream cheese, cut into 8 pieces
- ½ cup finely chopped almonds
- ¾ cup raspberry jam

1. In a food processor, pulse the flour with 2 tablespoons of the sugar and the salt. Add the butter and pulse until the mixture resembles coarse meal with some pea-size pieces of butter still visible. Add the cream cheese and pulse until the dough just starts to come together. Scrape the dough out onto a work surface and pat into a ball. Halve the dough and flatten each half into a disk. Wrap in plastic and refrigerate until well chilled, about 1 hour.

2. Preheat the oven to 350°. Spread the almonds on a baking sheet and toast until lightly browned, 5 minutes. Transfer to a bowl and let cool.

3. Line 2 large rimmed baking sheets with parchment paper. On a lightly floured work surface, roll out 1 dough disk into a 16-inch round, a scant ¼ inch thick. Spread half of the jam evenly over the dough in a thin layer and sprinkle evenly with half of the toasted almonds and ¼ cup of the sugar. Using a knife or pizza cutter, cut the dough round into 12 wedges. Starting at the wide end, roll up each wedge, ending with the tip on the bottom. Arrange the rolls on the prepared baking sheets at least 1 inch apart; freeze for 20 minutes or up to 3 days. Repeat with the remaining dough, jam, almonds and sugar.

4. Bake the rugelach for 25 minutes, until golden brown. Let cool for 10 minutes on the baking sheets, then transfer to a rack and let cool completely. —Jenn Louis

MAKE AHEAD The rugelach can be stored in an airtight container for up to 5 days.

SALTED-CARAMEL CREAM PUFFS WITH
WARM CHOCOLATE SAUCE

Lebkuchen

Active **45 min**; Total **2 hr**
Makes **1½ dozen cookies**

These German molasses-spice cookies are from star bartender Jeffrey Morgenthaler of Clyde Common in Portland, Oregon. The recipe was passed down from his great-grandmother to his grandmother to his uncle, who ships these festive cookies off to family members every year.

- 1 **cup heavy cream**
- 1 **Tbsp. white vinegar**
- 4 **cups all-purpose flour**
- ½ **cup almond flour**
- 2 **Tbsp. minced candied orange peel**
- 2 **Tbsp. minced candied lemon peel**
- 1 **Tbsp. ground cinnamon**
- 1 **tsp. ground cloves**
- 1 **tsp. ground allspice**
- 1 **tsp. baking soda**
- ½ **tsp. freshly grated nutmeg**
- ½ **tsp. kosher salt**
- 1 **cup dark brown sugar**
- ½ **cup vegetable shortening, at room temperature**
- ½ **cup unsulfured molasses**
- ⅓ **cup blanched whole almonds**
- 2½ **cups confectioners' sugar, sifted**
- 5 **Tbsp. whole milk**

1. In a small bowl, stir the cream and vinegar together and let stand until thickened, about 30 minutes.

2. Preheat the oven to 325°. In a medium bowl, whisk the all-purpose flour with the almond flour, candied orange and lemon peels, spices and salt. In the bowl of a stand mixer fitted with the paddle, beat the brown sugar with the shortening and molasses at medium speed until light and fluffy, about 3 minutes. Add the thickened cream and beat until smooth. Add the dry ingredients and beat at low speed just until combined.

3. Line 2 large rimmed baking sheets with parchment. Working in 2 batches, using a 2-ounce ice cream scoop or ¼-cup measure, scoop the dough into mounds on the prepared sheets, spacing them 3 inches apart. Place 3 almonds in a star pattern on each cookie and, with the palm of your hand, gently flatten each mound slightly.

4. Bake the cookies for about 15 minutes, until lightly browned; rotate the baking sheets from top to bottom and front to back halfway through baking. Let the cookies cool on the baking sheets for 10 minutes, then transfer to a rack and let cool completely.

5. In a small, wide bowl, whisk the confectioners' sugar with the milk until smooth. Dip the top of each cookie in the glaze, letting the excess drip back into the bowl. Transfer the cookies to a rack and let stand until the glaze hardens, about 10 minutes. —*Jeffrey Morgenthaler*

Gingersnap Sandwich Cookies

Active **1 hr**; Total **2 hr plus 8 hr chilling**
Makes **2½ dozen sandwich cookies**

Kir Jensen of The Sugar Cube bakery in Portland, Oregon, says her gingersnaps are like the best version of a Little Debbie gingerbread cookie.

COOKIES

- 3¾ **cups all-purpose flour**
- 2 **tsp. baking soda**
- 2 **tsp. ground cinnamon**
- 2 **tsp. ground ginger**
- 1 **tsp. freshly grated nutmeg**
- ¼ **tsp. ground cardamom**
- ½ **tsp. kosher salt**
- 3 **sticks unsalted butter, softened**
- 2½ **cups granulated sugar**
- 1 **Tbsp. finely grated ginger**
- 2 **tsp. finely grated orange zest**
- 1 **tsp. pure vanilla extract**
- 2 **large eggs**
- ½ **cup blackstrap molasses**

FILLING

- 1½ **sticks unsalted butter**
- ½ **vanilla bean, split and seeds scraped**
- ½ **tsp. kosher salt**
- 12 **oz. cream cheese, at room temperature**
- 1 **cup confectioners' sugar, sifted**

1. Make the cookies In a bowl, whisk the flour with the baking soda, cinnamon, ground ginger, nutmeg, cardamom and salt until evenly combined. In the bowl of a stand mixer fitted with the paddle, combine the butter and 2 cups of the granulated sugar with the grated ginger, orange zest and vanilla. Beat at medium speed until light and fluffy, about 3 minutes. Add the eggs 1 at a time and beat until incorporated. Beat in the molasses, then add the dry ingredients and beat at low speed until incorporated. Scrape the dough into a large bowl, cover with plastic wrap and refrigerate for at least 8 hours or overnight.

2. Make the filling In a small saucepan, cook the butter with the vanilla bean and seeds over moderately high heat, stirring occasionally, until the butter begins to brown and smell nutty, about 4 minutes. Pour into a metal bowl set over an ice bath, making sure to scrape the browned solids from the bottom of the pan into the bowl. Add the salt and stir the butter until cooled and beginning to solidify. Discard the vanilla bean and let the butter stand in the ice bath until completely solid. Remove from the ice bath.

3. In the bowl of a stand mixer fitted with the paddle, beat the cream cheese at medium speed until light and fluffy. Add the brown butter and confectioners' sugar and beat at low speed until smooth. Increase the speed to high and beat until fluffy, about 2 minutes. Scrape the frosting into a medium bowl, cover with plastic wrap and refrigerate for at least 1 hour.

4. Preheat the oven to 350°. Line 2 large rimmed baking sheets with parchment paper. Place the remaining ½ cup of granulated sugar in a small bowl. Working in 2 batches, using a 1-ounce ice cream scoop or 2 tablespoons, portion the dough into 1-inch balls. Roll the balls in the sugar and arrange on the prepared sheets at least 2 inches apart. Using the flat bottom of a glass or measuring cup, gently flatten each ball into a thick disk. Bake the cookies for 14 minutes, until set at the edges; rotate the baking sheets from top to bottom and front to back halfway through baking. Let the cookies cool for 10 minutes on the baking sheet, then transfer to a rack and let cool completely.

5. Stir the frosting until spreadable. Dollop 1 heaping tablespoon on one side of half the cookies, then sandwich with the remaining cookies. —*Kir Jensen*

Ricotta Crêpes with Honey, Walnuts and Rose

Active **45 min**; Total **1 hr 20 min**
Makes **12 crêpes**

"I look for 'drama in the mouth' when eating....I am always on the lookout for bursts of pronounced flavors," writes London chef Yotam Ottolenghi in his cookbook *Plenty More*. The floral, aromatic sweetness here come from rosewater and honey. Both ingredients are staples in the Middle East, where Ottolenghi grew up.

- ¼ **cup walnuts, finely chopped**
- 1 **cup all-purpose flour, sifted**
- ¼ **tsp. kosher salt**
- ⅔ **cup whole milk**
- 3 **large eggs**
- 1 **cup plus 2 Tbsp. mascarpone cheese**
- 1 **cup plus 2 Tbsp. ricotta cheese**
- 2 **tsp. finely grated lemon zest**
- ¼ **tsp. ground cinnamon**
- ¼ **tsp. ground allspice**
- ¼ **cup confectioners' sugar, plus more for dusting**
- 2¼ **tsp. rosewater**
- 6 **Tbsp. unsalted butter**
- 2 **Tbsp. extra-virgin olive oil**
- 3 **Tbsp. honey**
- 1 **tsp. fresh lemon juice**
- 2 **tsp. edible dried rose petals (see Note)**

1. Preheat the oven to 350°. Spread the walnuts on a baking sheet and toast in the oven for 7 to 8 minutes, until browned and fragrant. Transfer to a plate to cool.

2. In a medium bowl, whisk together the flour and salt. Whisk in the milk, 6 tablespoons of water and 2 eggs until a smooth batter forms. Set aside while you make the filling.

3. In a medium bowl, combine the mascarpone, ricotta, toasted walnuts, lemon zest, cinnamon and allspice. Stir in the ¼ cup of confectioners' sugar, 2 teaspoons of rosewater and the remaining egg until smooth. Refrigerate the filling while you make the crêpes.

4. In a 6-inch nonstick skillet, melt ½ tablespoon of the butter over moderately high heat. Pour 2 tablespoons of the batter into the skillet, immediately swirling the pan to evenly cover the bottom. Cook until set, about 45 seconds. Flip the crêpe and cook until lightly browned on the bottom, about 45 seconds more. Transfer the cooked crêpe to a work surface and repeat with the remaining butter and batter to make 11 more crêpes.

5. Brush a 12-by-8-inch baking dish with 1 tablespoon of the olive oil. Spoon 3 tablespoons of the filling into the center of a crêpe, fold in the sides and roll up into a tight tube. Transfer to the baking dish, seam side down. Repeat with the remaining crêpes and filling, fitting the crêpes in the baking dish snugly in a single layer. Brush with the remaining 1 tablespoon of olive oil and bake for 25 minutes, until the crêpes are light golden brown and the filling is warmed through.

6. Meanwhile, in a small saucepan, combine the honey and lemon juice with the remaining ¼ teaspoon of rosewater and warm over moderate heat. Drizzle the honey mixture evenly over the crêpes, then lightly dust with confectioners' sugar and sprinkle with the rose petals. Serve the crêpes warm or at room temperature. —*Yotam Ottolenghi*

NOTE Edible dried rose petals are available at specialty food shops and online from amazon.com.

MAKE AHEAD Refrigerate the crêpes and filling separately for up to 3 days before filling and baking the crêpes.

WINE Silky, peach-scented Sauternes: 2011 Petit Guiraud.

Dulce de Leche Crêpes

Total **1 hr**; Makes **8 crêpes**

This dessert of delicate crêpes filled with the Latin caramel sauce called dulce de leche and topped with whipped cream is from chef Francis Mallmann. "We Argentineans have a very sweet tooth," he says.

- 1 **stick unsalted butter— 6 Tbsp. at room temperature, 2 Tbsp. melted and cooled**
- ¾ **cup all-purpose flour**
- ¼ **tsp. kosher salt**
- 2 **large eggs**
- ½ **cup cold milk**
- ½ **cup dulce de leche**
    Unsweetened whipped cream, for serving

1. In a small saucepan, melt the 6 tablespoons of butter and cook over moderately low heat until the foam rises to the surface and the splattering stops, about 3 minutes. Remove the saucepan from the heat and spoon off the foam. Strain the butter through a cheesecloth-lined sieve into a small bowl; you should have about 4 tablespoons of clarified butter.

2. In a medium bowl, whisk the flour with the salt. In another medium bowl, beat the eggs, then whisk in the milk, ½ cup of cold water and the 2 tablespoons of melted butter. Sift the flour mixture over the egg mixture and whisk just to blend the batter; it's okay if there are some lumps.

3. Heat a crêpe pan or 8-inch nonstick skillet. Add ½ tablespoon of the clarified butter and swirl it in the pan. Ladle ¼ cup of batter into the pan, swirling to spread it in a thin, even 6-inch round. Cook the crêpe over moderate heat until lightly golden on the bottom, about 2 minutes. Flip the crêpe and cook until golden, 1 to 2 minutes longer. Turn the crêpe out onto a plate. Repeat with the remaining clarified butter and batter to make 8 crêpes, stacking them on the plate as you go.

4. Spread a tablespoon of dulce de leche onto each crêpe and fold it in half. Place 2 folded crêpes on each plate. Top with whipped cream and serve.
—*Francis Mallmann*

VARIATION Seasonal fresh fruit, such as mixed berries, could be served alongside.

Chocolate Whoopie Pies with Vanilla Cream Cheese Fluff
Active **45 min**; Total **1 hr 30 min plus cooling**; Makes **20 whoopie pies**

CAKES

2¼ cups all-purpose flour

¼ cup plus 2 Tbsp. unsweetened cocoa powder

1½ tsp. baking soda

½ tsp. kosher salt

¼ tsp. cream of tartar

1½ sticks unsalted butter, softened

1¼ cups sugar

2 large eggs

½ tsp. pure vanilla extract

1 cup whole milk

FILLING

1 lb. cream cheese, at room temperature

2 sticks unsalted butter, softened

2 cups confectioners' sugar

1 Tbsp. pure vanilla extract

Generous pinch of kosher salt

Crushed candy canes, for rolling (optional)

1. Make the cakes Preheat the oven to 350° and line 2 large baking sheets with parchment paper. In a medium bowl, whisk the flour with the cocoa powder, baking soda, salt and cream of tartar. In a large bowl, using a handheld electric mixer, beat the butter with the sugar at medium speed until fluffy, about 2 minutes. Beat in the eggs and vanilla. At low speed, beat in the dry ingredients and milk in 3 alternating additions; scrape down the side and bottom of the bowl as necessary.

2. Using a 2-tablespoon ice cream scoop, scoop 10 level mounds of batter onto each baking sheet, about 2 inches apart. Bake the cakes in the lower and upper thirds of the oven for about 12 minutes, until risen; shift the sheets from top to bottom and front to back halfway through baking. Transfer the cakes to racks and let cool completely. Repeat with the remaining batter, allowing the baking sheets to cool between batches.

3. Make the filling In a large bowl, using an electric mixer, beat all of the ingredients except the candy canes until the filling is thick and smooth, 1 to 2 minutes. Scoop 3 tablespoons of the filling onto the flat side of 20 cakes and close with the remaining cakes, pressing the filling to the edges. Roll the edges in crushed candy canes and serve. —*Michael Voltaggio*

German Chocolate and Cookie Icebox Cake
Total **1 hr plus 3 hr chilling**
Makes **one 9-by-5-inch cake**

Known as *kalter hund* ("cold dog") in Germany, this icebox-style cake is a classic Black Forest dessert that can be found in many a German grandmother's refrigerator. It's made with alternating layers of silky, super-chocolaty ganache and crisp, crunchy Leibniz butter cookies, which are available at most supermarkets.

1¼ lbs. bittersweet chocolate, finely chopped

1 cup coconut oil

2 Tbsp. unsweetened cocoa powder

1½ tsp. pure vanilla extract

½ tsp. kosher salt

1 cup heavy cream

One 7-oz. package Leibniz Butter Biscuits

Whipped cream, for serving (optional)

1. Line a 9-by-5-inch loaf pan with foil, allowing 2 inches of overhang on all sides. In a large stainless steel bowl set over (but not touching) a saucepan of simmering water, melt the chocolate in the coconut oil, stirring, 7 minutes. Whisk in the cocoa powder, vanilla and salt until incorporated, then whisk in the cream until smooth. Let the ganache cool slightly.

2. Pour a ¼-inch-thick layer of the ganache into the prepared pan. Arrange a layer of biscuits on the ganache, breaking them to fit and leaving a ¼-inch border of ganache around the edge. Repeat the layering with the remaining ganache and biscuits, ending with a layer of ganache.

3. Cover the pan with plastic wrap and refrigerate until chilled, 3 hours. Let stand at room temperature for 30 minutes. Using the foil, lift out the cake onto a cutting board. Discard the foil and slice the cake crosswise ¾ inch thick. Serve with whipped cream. —*Justin Chapple*

Popcorn Pudding
Total **30 min plus chilling**; Serves **6**

Jonathon Sawyer and his family love the sweet-salty contrast of chocolate-covered pretzels. That gave Sawyer, chef at Cleveland's Greenhouse Tavern, the idea to create this velvety dessert: He brilliantly combines the flavor of buttered popcorn with a sweet, creamy vanilla pudding.

2¼ cups whole milk

¾ cup heavy cream

½ cup sugar

¼ tsp. salt

1 tsp. vegetable oil

¼ cup plus 1 Tbsp. popcorn kernels

3 large egg yolks

4 tsp. cornstarch

3 Tbsp. unsalted butter, cubed

¼ tsp. pure vanilla extract

1. In a large saucepan, combine the milk, cream, sugar and salt and bring to a boil over moderate heat, stirring to dissolve the sugar. Remove from the heat.

2. In a medium pot, heat the oil. Add the popcorn kernels, cover and cook over moderate heat until they start popping. Cook, shaking the pot constantly, until the popping has almost stopped, 2 to 3 minutes. Pour all but 1 cup of the popcorn into the cream mixture, cover and let stand for 10 minutes. Reserve the remaining popcorn for garnish.

3. In a medium bowl, whisk the egg yolks with the cornstarch until smooth. Strain the hot cream mixture into a clean medium saucepan; discard the solids. Bring the cream to a boil over moderate heat. Gradually whisk 1 cup of the hot cream into the egg yolks, then scrape the mixture into the saucepan. Whisk the pudding over moderate heat until it just comes to a boil, about 2 minutes. Stir in the butter and vanilla.

4. Scrape the pudding into a medium baking dish. Press a piece of plastic wrap directly onto the surface of the pudding and refrigerate until chilled. Spoon the pudding into bowls, sprinkle with the reserved cup of popcorn and serve. —*Jonathon Sawyer*

MAKE AHEAD The pudding can be refrigerated for up to 2 days

CHOCOLATE WHOOPIE PIES WITH
VANILLA CREAM CHEESE FLUFF

DIY Marshmallows

TOTAL: 40 MIN PLUS 3 HR COOLING · MAKES ABOUT 25 MARSHMALLOWS

At his eponymous bakery in New York City, **DOMINIQUE ANSEL** creates two kinds of marshmallows: a French variety made fluffy with whipped egg whites and a chewier, egg-free version he discovered in the US. To learn which kind you like best, try both of his recipes and favorite add-ins.

SOFT AND CHEWY

  Canola oil, for greasing
2 Tbsp. unflavored powdered gelatin
2 cups sugar
⅔ cup plus 3 Tbsp. light corn syrup
3 Tbsp. honey
  Cornstarch, for dusting

1. Lightly grease an 8-inch-square cake pan with canola oil. In a medium heatproof bowl, mix the gelatin with ½ cup plus 2 tablespoons of cold water; let stand for 15 minutes. Set the bowl over a saucepan of simmering water and cook, stirring occasionally, until the gelatin dissolves and the mixture is smooth.

2. Meanwhile, in a medium saucepan, combine the sugar, corn syrup, honey and ⅓ cup plus 2 tablespoons of water and bring to a boil, stirring to dissolve the sugar. Cook the syrup over moderately high heat until it registers 250° on a candy thermometer. Immediately pour the hot syrup into the bowl of a stand mixer fitted with the whisk. Scrape in the gelatin mixture and beat at high speed until a smooth white foam forms, about 4 minutes.

3. Spread the marshmallow in the prepared pan and smooth the surface. Press a lightly greased sheet of parchment paper on the surface and let stand until set, 3 hours.

4. Run a sharp knife around the marshmallow. Very lightly dust a work surface with cornstarch and invert the cake pan onto it, tapping to release the marshmallow. Using a lightly greased sharp knife, cut the marshmallow into 1½-inch pieces.

LIGHT AND FLUFFY

1 Tbsp. plus 2 tsp. unflavored powdered gelatin
  Canola oil, for greasing
  Cornstarch, for dusting
1 cup sugar
2 Tbsp. light corn syrup
3 large egg whites

1. In a small bowl, mix the gelatin with ⅓ cup of water and let stand for 15 minutes. Meanwhile, grease an 8-inch-square cake pan with oil and dust lightly with cornstarch, tapping out the excess.

2. In a small saucepan, mix the sugar with ⅓ cup of water and bring to a boil, stirring to dissolve the sugar. Add the corn syrup and cook over moderately high heat, without stirring, until the syrup registers 260° on a candy thermometer. Off the heat, stir in the gelatin mixture until dissolved.

3. In a stand mixer fitted with the whisk, beat the egg whites at moderately high speed until soft peaks form. With the machine on, drizzle the hot syrup into the egg whites in a very thin stream down the side of the bowl. Scrape the marshmallow into the prepared pan, smoothing the surface. Let stand until set, at least 3 hours.

4. Run a sharp knife around the marshmallow. Very lightly dust a work surface with cornstarch and invert the cake pan onto it, tapping to release the marshmallow. Using a lightly greased sharp knife, cut the marshmallow into 1½-inch pieces.

FLAVOR BOOSTS

Cinnamon Marshmallows

Add ½ tsp. Vietnamese **cinnamon** during the last minute of beating the marshmallow; lightly dust the cut marshmallows with a sifted mixture of ⅔ cup **cornstarch,** ⅓ cup **confectioners' sugar** and 1 tsp. **cinnamon.**

Coconut-Lime Marshmallows

Add 1 tsp. **pure coconut extract** and 2 tsp. finely grated **lime zest** during the last minute of beating; coat the cut marshmallows with **toasted unsweetened shredded coconut.**

Hazelnut Marshmallows

Add ¼ cup **hazelnut praline paste** during the last minute of beating; coat the cut marshmallows in coarsely ground **roasted hazelnuts.**

Preserved Lemon Pudding with Basil Syrup

Active **45 min**; Total **4 hr**; Serves **4**

LEMON PUDDING

- 1 tsp. unflavored powdered gelatin
- 8 large egg yolks
- ⅓ cup sugar
- 1⅓ cups heavy cream
- 1 tsp. pure vanilla extract
- ¼ preserved lemon, pulp discarded and rind finely chopped (¼ cup)
- ⅓ cup fresh lemon juice or Meyer lemon juice

BASIL SYRUP

- 1 cup lightly packed basil leaves, plus small leaves for garnish
- 2 Tbsp. simple syrup (see Note)

1. Make the lemon pudding In a small bowl, sprinkle the gelatin over 1 tablespoon of water. In a medium bowl, whisk the egg yolks with the sugar.

2. In a medium, heavy saucepan, combine the cream and vanilla and bring to a simmer. While whisking constantly, slowly drizzle the cream into the egg yolk mixture. Pour the custard base into the saucepan and cook over moderately low heat, stirring constantly, until thickened enough to coat the back of a wooden spoon, 3 to 4 minutes. Strain the custard into a medium bowl. Add the softened gelatin and whisk until dissolved. Press a sheet of plastic wrap directly onto the surface of the pudding and let cool to room temperature.

3. In a blender, puree the preserved lemon and lemon juice until well combined. Stir the lemon puree into the pudding. Cover again with plastic wrap and refrigerate the pudding until cold and thick, at least 3 hours or overnight.

4. Make the basil syrup Fill a medium bowl with ice water. In a medium saucepan of boiling water, blanch the 1 cup of basil until very tender, about 3 minutes. Drain and transfer to the ice bath to cool. Drain well and squeeze dry. In the blender, combine the basil and simple syrup with 1 tablespoon of water and puree until smooth.

5. Spoon the preserved lemon pudding into bowls. Drizzle with the basil syrup, garnish with basil leaves and serve. —*Justin Yu*

NOTE To make the simple syrup: In a small saucepan, combine ¼ cup sugar and ¼ cup water and cook over low heat, stirring, until the sugar dissolves. Refrigerate the syrup until chilled.

Goo Goo Pie Parfaits

Total **1 hr plus 3 hr chilling**; Serves **8**

CRÉMEUX

- 14 oz. milk chocolate, finely chopped (3 cups)
- 3½ oz. dark chocolate, finely chopped (¾ cup)
- 2 large egg yolks
- ¼ cup sugar
- 1 cup whole milk
- 1 cup heavy cream

PEANUT-CARAMEL SAUCE

- ½ cup heavy cream
- 2 Tbsp. unsalted butter
- 1 cup sugar
- 1½ Tbsp. light corn syrup
- 2 Tbsp. whiskey
- 1 cup salted roasted peanuts (5 oz.)
  Flaky sea salt, whipped cream and grated chocolate, for garnish

1. Make the crémeux In a large bowl, combine the 2 chocolates. In a medium bowl, whisk the egg yolks with the sugar until well combined.

2. In a medium saucepan, bring the milk and heavy cream just to a simmer. Whisking constantly, slowly drizzle half of the hot milk into the egg mixture. Pour the milk-egg mixture into the saucepan and cook over low heat, stirring constantly, until the custard is thick enough to coat the back of a wooden spoon, 12 to 14 minutes. Strain the custard into the bowl of chocolate. Stir until the chocolate is melted and the *crémeux* is smooth. Spoon into eight 1-cup jars or ramekins. Refrigerate for 3 hours, or until set.

3. Meanwhile, make the sauce In a small saucepan, warm the cream and butter over moderate heat until the butter melts; remove from the heat. In a large saucepan, combine the sugar, light corn syrup and water and bring to a boil. Cook over moderate heat, swirling the pan occasionally, until the sugar dissolves and a golden amber caramel forms, 10 minutes.

Carefully pour in the cream mixture (it will bubble vigorously) and whisk until smooth. Let the sauce cool to room temperature, 1 hour. Stir in the whiskey and peanuts.

4. To serve, spoon the peanut-caramel sauce over the *crémeux* and garnish with sea salt, whipped cream and grated chocolate. —*Rebecca Masson*

Maude's Vanilla Fudge

Total **1 hr plus cooling**; Makes **2 pounds**

Celebrity chef Curtis Stone says his love for cooking began with his granny Maude's fudge. If there wasn't any in the fridge waiting for him when he came over after school, she'd make some with him.

- 1 stick plus 2 Tbsp. unsalted butter
- 3 whole graham crackers, broken into bite-size pieces
- 4 cups sugar
  One 14-oz. can sweetened condensed milk
- ½ cup whole milk
- 1 Tbsp. pure vanilla extract
  Kosher salt

1. Grease a 9-by-13-inch baking pan with 2 tablespoons of the butter and scatter the graham crackers evenly over the bottom.

2. In a large saucepan, combine the remaining stick of butter with the sugar, condensed milk and whole milk. Cook over moderately low heat, brushing down the side of the pan with a wet pastry brush, until the sugar is dissolved, about 12 minutes. Bring the mixture to a simmer, then cook over moderately low heat, stirring occasionally with a wooden spoon, until a pale caramel forms and the temperature reaches 240° on a candy thermometer, about 15 minutes.

3. Remove the saucepan from the heat. Add the vanilla and a generous pinch of salt and stir vigorously until the fudge thickens but is still pourable, 8 minutes. Immediately scrape the fudge into the prepared pan and spread it evenly with a spatula. Let cool completely, 1 hour.

4. Invert the pan onto a surface and tap out the fudge. Break the fudge into pieces and serve. —*Curtis Stone*

Granola-Chocolate Bark

Total **15 min plus 3 hr chilling**
Makes **one 15-by-11-inch sheet**

Top Chef Season 11 winner Nicholas Elmi makes this supersimple dark chocolate bark with his four-year-old daughter. In addition to mixing in pistachios and dried fruit, he adds granola; Early Bird's Farmhand's Choice is a terrific brand to look for.

- **1 lb. dark chocolate, finely chopped**
- **¾ cup golden raisins**
- **⅔ cup dried cranberries**
- **1 cup shelled pistachios**
- **1¼ cups granola (5 oz.)**

1. Line a 15-by-11-inch baking sheet with parchment paper. Place two-thirds of the chocolate in a large heatproof bowl set over a saucepan of simmering water; make sure that the bottom of the bowl does not touch the water. Stir over moderately low heat until the chocolate is melted. Remove the bowl from the heat and stir in the remaining chocolate until melted, then stir in the remaining ingredients.

2. Scrape the chocolate onto the baking sheet and spread it in a ½-inch-thick layer. Let the bark cool to room temperature, then refrigerate for at least 3 hours or up to 1 week. —*Nicholas Elmi*

INGREDIENT TIP

Three Ways to Use Chocolate

DIPPING Try wafer crackers, cornflakes or saltines.

IN BREAD Add cocoa powder and chocolate chips to brioche dough to make an unusual, rich, lightly sweet loaf.

ON BREAD For the world's simplest snack (and a favorite of megachef Ferran Adrià), melt chocolate on toast, drizzle with olive oil and sprinkle with sea salt.

Milk Chocolate, Nut and Raisin Clusters

Total **30 min plus firming**
Makes **32 clusters**

At Le Chocolat Alain Ducasse in Paris, Nicolas Berger folds melted chocolate into conflakes, nuts and raisins to create crispy clusters that collapse with each bite.

- **½ cup hazelnuts**
- **1¾ cup cornflakes**
- **¾ cup *feuilletine* flakes (see Note) or more cornflakes**
- **½ cup golden raisins, chopped**
- **¼ cup pistachios, chopped**
- **½ tsp. kosher salt**
- **11½ oz. milk chocolate, finely chopped (2 cups)**
- **1½ oz. white chocolate, finely chopped**

1. Preheat the oven to 375°. Toast the hazelnuts in a pie plate for 7 to 8 minutes. Let cool, rub in a clean kitchen towel to remove the skins, then coarsely chop. In a large bowl, combine them with the cornflakes, *feuilletine*, raisins, pistachios and salt.

2. In a microwave-safe bowl, combine two-thirds of the chopped milk and white chocolates. Microwave at medium-high power in 30-second bursts, stirring in between, until melted, 2 minutes. Stir in the remaining chocolate until smooth.

3. Pour half of the melted chocolate over the hazelnut mixture. Using a rubber spatula, quickly fold in the chocolate until evenly coated. Add the remaining chocolate and fold gently until all of the ingredients are generously coated with chocolate.

4. Scoop heaping tablespoons of the mixture onto a parchment-lined baking sheet; shape with a spoon. Let firm up before serving. —*Nicolas Berger*

NOTE Crunchy *feuilletine* flakes are available from chefshop.com.

Noel Balls

Active **35 min;** Total **1 hr 45 min**
Makes **4½ dozen cookies**

Duane Sorenson of Stumptown Coffee Roasters in Portland, Oregon, gets together with his mother and sister to bake these buttery date-studded cookies every year for the holidays.

- **1¼ cups pecan halves**
- **2⅓ cups all-purpose flour**
- **½ cup finely chopped plump Medjool dates**
- **½ tsp. kosher salt**
- **2 sticks unsalted butter, softened**
- **3¾ cups confectioners' sugar**
- **½ tsp. pure vanilla extract**

1. In a food processor, pulse the pecans until finely ground. In a medium bowl, whisk the ground pecans with the flour, dates and salt. In the bowl of a stand mixer fitted with the paddle, combine the butter with ¾ cup of the confectioners' sugar and the vanilla and beat at medium speed until light and fluffy, about 3 minutes. Add the flour mixture and beat at low speed until just combined.

2. Preheat the oven to 350°. Line 2 large rimmed baking sheets with parchment paper. Spread the remaining 3 cups of confectioners' sugar in a large pie pan. Working in 3 batches, using a 1-ounce ice cream scoop or a tablespoon, scoop the dough into 1-inch balls. Arrange the balls on the prepared sheets at least 1 inch apart. Bake the cookies for 15 minutes, until lightly browned on the bottom; rotate the baking sheets from top to bottom and front to back halfway through baking. Let the cookies cool for 5 minutes on the baking sheet, then roll them in the confectioners' sugar until completely coated. Let cool completely, then roll again in the confectioners' sugar. —*Duane Sorenson*

MAKE AHEAD The cookies can be stored in an airtight container for up to 5 days.

GRANOLA-CHOCOLATE BARK

CRACKERSNACKS
Recipe, page 358

Snacks, Sauces & Condiments

Yuca Fries with Banana Ketchup

Active **50 min**; Total **1 hr 20 min**
Serves **8 to 10**

To make his spiced banana ketchup, L.A. chef Roy Choi spikes regular tomato ketchup with ginger, Thai basil and bananas. It's excellent with these crispy, starchy fries, though plain ketchup is good with them, too.

KETCHUP

- **2 large ripe bananas, peeled and chopped**
- **1½ cups vegetable stock**
- **1 small onion, halved and thinly sliced**
- **4 whole pickled jalapeños, stems discarded, plus 2 Tbsp. pickling liquid from the jar**
- **¼ cup thinly sliced garlic**
- **3 Tbsp. finely chopped peeled fresh ginger**
- **1 cup ketchup**
- **1 cup lightly packed Thai basil**
- **Salt and pepper**

FRIES

- **3 lbs. yuca (about 4 yuca)**
- **Vegetable oil, for frying**
- **Salt**
- **Lime wedges, for serving**

1. Make the ketchup In a medium saucepan, combine the bananas, stock, onion, jalapeños, garlic, ginger and ½ cup of water and bring to a boil. Simmer over moderate heat, stirring, until the bananas and onion are very tender, 15 minutes. Transfer to a blender and let cool slightly. Add the ketchup, basil and the jalapeño pickling liquid and puree until smooth. Scrape the banana ketchup into a bowl and season with salt and pepper. Cover and refrigerate until chilled, about 30 minutes.

2. Meanwhile, make the fries Bring a large saucepan of salted water to a boil. Peel the yuca and cut into 3-inch lengths. Cut the lengths into ½-inch-thick wedges. Cook the yuca in the boiling water until tender, 10 to 15 minutes. Drain well and spread on a baking sheet to cool and dry; discard any stringy pieces of yuca.

3. In a large saucepan, heat 1½ inches of oil to 360°. Set a rack over a baking sheet. Working in batches, fry the yuca, stirring gently to separate the wedges, until golden brown and crisp, 5 to 7 minutes. Using a slotted spoon, transfer the wedges to the rack and season generously with salt. Serve right away, with the banana ketchup and lime wedges. —*Roy Choi*

Crackersnacks

📷 PAGE 356
⏲ Total **40 min**; Makes **7 cups**

This sweet-and-savory take on Cracker Jack is one of the whimsical snacks that chef Katie Button serves at Nightbell, her restaurant and lounge in Asheville, North Carolina.

- **¼ cup plus 2 Tbsp. canola oil**
- **¼ cup popcorn kernels**
- **1 cup salted roasted peanuts**
- **¼ tsp. ground cumin**
- **¼ tsp. ground cinnamon**
- **⅛ tsp. sweet smoked paprika**
- **Pinch of cayenne pepper**
- **1 cup plus 2 Tbsp. sugar**
- **1½ tsp. kosher salt**

1. In a medium saucepan, heat 2 tablespoons of the oil until shimmering. Add the popcorn kernels, cover and shake the saucepan to coat the kernels with oil. Cook over moderate heat until the popping slows to several seconds between pops. Remove from the heat and wait 30 seconds, then pour the popcorn into a large bowl. Add the peanuts, cumin, cinnamon, paprika and cayenne and toss well to coat the popcorn.

2. Line a baking sheet with parchment paper. In a medium saucepan, combine the remaining ¼ cup of oil with the sugar, salt and ¼ cup of water and bring to a boil, stirring to dissolve the sugar. Cook over moderately low heat, stirring occasionally, until a light amber caramel forms, about 10 minutes. Immediately pour the caramel over the popcorn and toss quickly with spoons to evenly coat the popcorn and peanuts. Spread the popcorn mixture on the baking sheet in an even layer and let cool completely. Break into bite-size pieces. —*Katie Button*

Pickled Garden Vegetables

Active **25 min**; Total **4 hr**; Makes **3½ cups**

- **¾ lb. tender young carrots, tops removed and carrots halved lengthwise**
- **12 radishes, thinly sliced**
- **2 large Kirby cucumbers, thinly sliced**
- **3½ Tbsp. kosher salt**
- **½ oz. dried porcini mushrooms**
- **1½ cups boiling water**
- **1½ cups apple cider vinegar**
- **1 garlic clove, crushed**
- **1 Tbsp. sugar**

1. In a large colander set in a bowl, toss the carrots, radishes and cucumbers with 2 tablespoons of the salt. Let stand for 30 minutes.

2. Meanwhile, in a heatproof medium bowl, cover the porcini with the boiling water and let cool completely, about 30 minutes.

3. Strain the porcini broth through a fine sieve into a large bowl. Squeeze the mushrooms dry and reserve them for another use. Add the vinegar, garlic, sugar and the remaining 1½ tablespoons of salt to the porcini broth and whisk until the sugar and salt dissolve. Rinse the vegetables and squeeze them dry, then add to the porcini brine. Cover and refrigerate for at least 3 hours or overnight. Drain the pickled vegetables and serve. —*Paul Berglund*

Buttermilk–Blue Cheese Dressing

⏲ Total **10 min**; Makes **about 1¼ cups**

San Francisco chef Ryan Cantwell puts an original spin on this dressing by adding tarragon and cumin. He uses it to dress sweet Little Gem lettuce, radishes, bacon and croutons.

- **2 oz. blue cheese, crumbled**
- **½ cup buttermilk**
- **1 Tbsp. Champagne vinegar**
- **1 Tbsp. chopped tarragon**
- **Scant ¼ tsp. ground cumin**
- **½ cup extra-virgin olive oil**
- **Kosher salt**

In a blender, blend the blue cheese, buttermilk, vinegar, tarragon and cumin until smooth. With the machine on, blend in the olive oil. Season with salt. —*Ryan Cantwell*

PICKLED GARDEN VEGETABLES

Most Efficient Kitchen Tool

Graters make some onerous cooking tasks shockingly easy. Here's a guide to the surprising things these multitasking gadgets can do, with recipes from F&W's **KAY CHUN** to match.

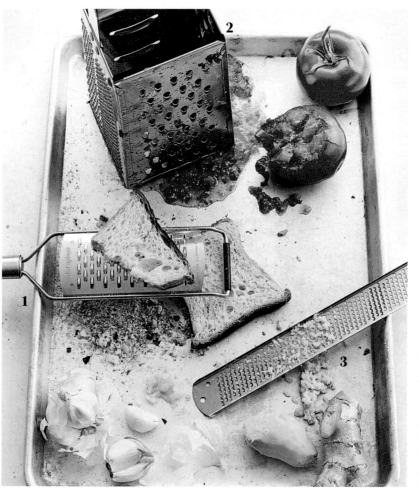

1

COARSE MICROPLANE
This handy little grater has small, sharp slits that cut in both directions, making it excellent for thinly shaving chocolate or cheese. A coarse Microplane is also good for making bread crumbs to top grilled vegetables or steaming bowls of pasta.

2

BOX GRATER
The broad work surface and large, sharp holes can quickly shred cheddar cheese and firm vegetables like cabbage and carrots. A less obvious use is pureeing corn kernels from a shucked ear and squishy vegetables like tomatoes (leaving the thin skin behind).

3

MICROPLANE
Its tiny, ultrasharp holes famously allow the Microplane to scrape the zest from citrus without cutting into the pith beneath. The Microplane can also quickly puree small, soft aromatics like garlic and ginger, or grate whole spices like cinnamon sticks and nutmeg.

THREE GRATER-FRIENDLY RECIPES

Tomato Jam

In a bowl, grate 1½ lbs. ripe **tomatoes** on the large holes of a box grater until only the skin remains; discard the skin. Cook ½ cup chopped **onion** in 1 tsp. **oil** until softened. Add ¼ cup **turbinado sugar,** 1 Tbsp. **cider vinegar** and the tomato pulp. Cook, stirring, until thick. Add 1½ tsp. **lime juice;** season with **salt** and **pepper.** Serve with grilled **chicken.** *Makes ¾ cup.*

Crisp Garlicky Bread Crumbs

Brush 1 thick slice of day-old **country bread** with **olive oil** and toast until golden. Rub all over with 1 cut **garlic clove;** let cool. Using a coarse Microplane, grate the bread into crumbs and serve sprinkled over 1½ lbs. grilled sliced **zucchini** that's been drizzled with **fresh lemon juice** and grated **Parmigiano-Reggiano cheese.** *Makes about ¾ cup of crumbs.*

Corn Chimichurri

Working over a bowl, grate 4 just-shucked ears of **fresh sweet corn** on the large holes of a grater; discard the corn cobs. Stir ½ cup minced **parsley,** 1 Tbsp. each of minced **shallot** and **fresh lemon juice,** 1 finely grated small **garlic clove** and ¼ cup **olive oil** into the corn puree and season with **salt** and **pepper.** Serve with grilled **shrimp.** *Makes 1 cup.*

Tostones with Chile Vinegar

⏱ Total **45 min**; Serves **6**

Savory fried plantains are especially good with this spicy, tangy vinegar sprinkled on top. The vinegar is great on anything you'd eat with hot sauce.

- ½ cup unseasoned rice vinegar
- 1 garlic clove, crushed
- 4 red jalapeños or Fresno chiles—stemmed, seeded and chopped
- 2 Thai chiles, stemmed
  Salt
  Vegetable oil, for frying
- 4 large green plantains, peeled and sliced ½ inch thick

1. In a blender, puree the vinegar, garlic, jalapeños and Thai chiles until smooth. Transfer the chile vinegar to a bowl and season with salt.

2. In a saucepan, heat 2 inches of oil to 350°. Working in batches, fry the plantains just until pale golden, 6 minutes. Using a slotted spoon, transfer the plantains to a paper towel–lined baking sheet. Using a meat pounder or ceramic mug, flatten the plantain slices until they're ¼ inch thick.

3. Reheat the oil to 375°. Working in batches, fry the plantains until crisp, 5 minutes. Drain on paper towels and season with salt. Serve with the chile vinegar. —*Roy Choi*

Dill-Parsley Sauce

⏱ Total **10 min**; Makes **1 cup**

This vibrant green sauce is terrific with fish or pasta, or drizzled over Caprese salad.

- ½ cup chopped dill
- ⅓ cup chopped parsley
- 2 Tbsp. minced shallot
- 2½ tsp. stone-ground mustard
- 2 tsp. malt vinegar
- 1 tsp. minced garlic
- ½ cup canola oil
  Kosher salt

In a blender, puree the dill, parsley, shallot, mustard, vinegar and garlic with ¼ cup of water. With the machine on, gradually add the canola oil and puree until smooth. Season with salt and serve. —*Gunnar Karl Gíslason*

Pancetta Cream Sauce

⏱ Total **40 min**; Makes **1¼ cups**

At his luxe Manhattan steak house Costata, chef Michael White offers this over-the-top cream sauce for steak; it would be equally wonderful on pasta.

- ¼ lb. pancetta, cut into ¼-inch dice
- ¼ cup vodka
- 2 cups heavy cream
- 1 Tbsp. veal demiglace
  Kosher salt and freshly ground pepper

1. In a medium saucepan, cook the pancetta over moderate heat, stirring occasionally, until golden but not crisp, 3 to 5 minutes. Using a slotted spoon, transfer the pancetta to a paper towel–lined plate. Pour off the fat in the saucepan, reserving 2 tablespoons.

2. Carefully add the vodka to the saucepan. Cook over moderate heat, scraping up any browned bits, until reduced to a glaze, 1 to 2 minutes. Add the cream, pancetta and the reserved 2 tablespoons of fat and bring to a boil. Simmer over moderate heat, stirring occasionally, until thickened and reduced to 1¼ cups, about 10 minutes. Stir in the demiglace and season the sauce with salt and pepper. Serve warm. —*Michael White*

Bacon-Shallot Gravy

⏱ Total **30 min**; Makes **3½ cups**

- 2 Tbsp. extra-virgin olive oil
- ¼ lb. thick-cut bacon, finely chopped
- 1 cup minced shallots (2 large)
- 1 large thyme sprig
  Kosher salt
- ⅓ cup all-purpose flour
- ½ cup dry white wine
- 4 cups turkey or chicken stock
- ¼ tsp. sweet paprika
- 2 Tbsp. unsalted butter
  Pepper

1. In a large skillet, heat the olive oil. Add the bacon, shallots, thyme and a generous pinch of salt and cook over moderate heat, stirring occasionally, until the shallots are browned and the bacon is nearly crisp, about 10 minutes.

2. Sift the flour into the skillet and stir until completely absorbed. Stir in the wine and cook until thick, 1 minute. Gradually stir in the stock, then stir in the paprika and bring to a boil. Simmer the gravy over moderate heat, stirring occasionally, until no floury taste remains and the gravy is reduced to 3½ cups, 10 minutes. Discard the thyme sprig. Remove from the heat and stir in the butter. Season the gravy generously with salt and pepper and serve hot. —*Dana Cowin*

Indonesian-Spiced Peanut Sauce

⏱ Total **20 min**; Makes **1½ cups**

This sweet, spicy and tangy peanut sauce is excellent tossed with warm noodles and as a dip for beef or chicken satay or grilled shrimp.

- 1 Tbsp. canola oil
- 1 shallot, finely chopped
- 1 garlic clove, minced
- 2 tsp. finely grated peeled fresh ginger
- ½ cup unsweetened coconut milk
- ½ cup all-natural creamy peanut butter
- ¼ cup fresh lime juice
- 1½ Tbsp. soy sauce
- 2 tsp. light brown sugar
- ½ tsp. crushed red pepper
- ½ tsp. ground coriander
- ⅛ tsp. ground cinnamon
- 3 dashes of Worcestershire sauce
  Kosher salt and black pepper

In a large skillet, heat the oil. Add the shallot, garlic and ginger and cook over moderately low heat, stirring occasionally, until softened, about 3 minutes. Reduce the heat to low. Add the coconut milk, peanut butter, lime juice, soy sauce and ¼ cup plus 2 tablespoons of water and whisk until blended. Whisk in the sugar, crushed red pepper, coriander, cinnamon and Worcestershire sauce; if a thinner sauce is desired, whisk in a little more water. Transfer the sauce to a medium bowl, season with salt and black pepper and serve. —*Edward Lee*

MAKE AHEAD The sauce can be refrigerated for up to 1 week.

Peanut Dipping Sauce

Total **1 hr plus cooling**; Makes **2¼ cups**

This fragrant peanut sauce is perfect as a dip for vegetables, but it is also terrific on grilled or poached chicken or shrimp.

- **2** small lemongrass stalks, tender inner bulbs only, chopped
- **1** medium shallot, chopped
- One 1-inch piece of fresh ginger, peeled and chopped
- **3** garlic cloves, chopped
- **2** small turmeric roots (about 2 inches), thinly sliced
- **1** dried guajillo chile—stemmed, seeded and torn
- **2** Thai chiles, stemmed and chopped
- Kosher salt
- **2** Tbsp. peanut oil
- **¼** cup turbinado sugar
- One 15-oz. can unsweetened coconut milk
- **1** cup natural peanut butter
- **2** Tbsp. finely chopped mint
- Assorted raw vegetables, for serving

1. In a food processor, combine the lemongrass, shallot, ginger, garlic, turmeric, guajillo, Thai chiles and 2 teaspoons of salt. Puree until a chunky paste forms; scrape down the side of the bowl as needed.

2. In a medium saucepan, heat the peanut oil until shimmering. Add the paste and cook over moderately low heat, stirring frequently, until browned, 10 minutes. Add the sugar and cook, stirring, until melted, 3 minutes. Stir in the coconut milk and bring to a simmer. Cook over moderately low heat, stirring occasionally, until slightly reduced, 10 minutes. Whisk in the peanut butter and cook, whisking occasionally, until thickened, 10 minutes. (The sauce may look broken.)

3. Remove the sauce from the heat and gradually whisk in ¼ cup plus 2 tablespoons of water until creamy and smooth. Season with salt and let cool completely. Garnish with the mint and serve with raw vegetables. —*Mark Overbay*

12
Minutes

YEMENI HOT SAUCE

In a food processor, mince 6 seeded **jalapeños**, 2 **garlic cloves** and 1 Tbsp. **fresh lemon juice**. Pulse in 10 Tbsp. **olive oil** and ½ Tbsp. **honey**. In batches, add 3 cups lightly packed **cilantro leaves** and puree until thick but pourable. Season with **salt** and lemon juice; serve with **roasted vegetables**. –*Eli Sussman*

Fresh Jalapeño Hot Sauce
⟳ Total **10 min**; Makes **1½ cups**

The inspiration for this sauce from Chicago chef Abraham Conlon is *cafreal*, an Indian braise with Portuguese roots. It's a sprightly sauce that's vividly flavored with cilantro, chiles, garlic and lime juice. (Seed and de-rib some or all of the chiles for a milder version.) Conlon recommends stirring the sauce into a green chile stew, using it as a marinade for chicken or sprinkling it on pork or fish tacos.

- 6 **oz. jalapeños (6 medium), stemmed and thinly sliced**
- 4 **cilantro sprigs, chopped**
- 2 **scallions, chopped**
- 2 **garlic cloves, crushed**
- ½ **cup distilled white vinegar**
- 2 **Tbsp. sugar**
- 1 **Tbsp. fresh lime juice**
- 1 **tsp. kosher salt**

In a blender, combine all of the ingredients and puree until smooth. —*Abraham Conlon*

Mozambique Hot Sauce
⟳ Total **10 min**; Makes **¾ cup**

Abraham Conlon, the chef at Fat Rice in Chicago, learned to make this lemony, *sambal oelek*–like sauce from a Mozambican chef in Lisbon. Any fresh red chiles will work, but Conlon uses piri piri chiles; small Thai bird chiles are closest in flavor to piri piris and will result in a blazingly hot sauce. (Seed and de-rib some or all of the chiles for a milder sauce.)

- 4 **oz. fresh red chiles, such as Thai bird, cayenne, red jalapeño, red serrano and/or piri piri, stemmed and chopped**
- 2 **garlic cloves, chopped**
- ⅓ **cup fresh lemon juice**
- 1½ **tsp. kosher salt**
- 1½ **tsp. sugar**

In a food processor, combine all of the ingredients and puree until smooth. —*Abraham Conlon*

MAKE AHEAD The hot sauce can be refrigerated for up to 2 weeks.

JE Hot Sauce
Active **30 min**; Total **5 hr 30 min**
Makes **3½ cups**

Chef Jose Enrique makes this wonderful hot sauce by confiting chiles, peppers and tomato, then pureeing them until creamy. The leftover braising oil is sensational with pasta or drizzled on chicken or vegetables.

- 1 **quart extra-virgin olive oil**
- 1 **large onion, cut into 2-inch pieces**
- 1 **large tomato, cut into 2-inch pieces**
- 1 **red bell pepper, seeded and cut into 2-inch pieces**
- 1 **Cubanelle pepper, seeded and cut into 2-inch pieces**
- 9 **serrano chiles, stemmed**
- 7 **garlic cloves**
- 5 **habanero chiles, stemmed**
  Kosher salt

1. In a large saucepan, combine all of the ingredients except the salt. Cook over low heat until all of the vegetables are falling-apart soft, about 4 hours; let cool slightly.

2. Drain the vegetables in a fine sieve set over a heatproof bowl; don't press on the solids. Transfer the vegetables to a blender, add ¼ cup of water and pulse until finely chopped. With the machine on, gradually drizzle in 2 cups of the cooking oil and puree until smooth and slightly thick (reserve the remaining cooking oil for another use). Season the hot sauce with salt and let cool completely before serving. —*Jose Enrique*

Portuguese-Style Brandied Chile Oil
Total **15 min plus 1 week steeping**
Makes **1 quart**

Steeping the chiles first in brandy and then in oil both extracts and enhances their flavor. Use the oil on bread, pizza, pasta or roasted meats or vegetables.

- 1 **oz. dried árbol chile peppers, stemmed and cut into ¼-inch pieces**
- 1 **cup brandy**
- 1 **lemon, halved**
- 2 **Tbsp. distilled white vinegar**
- 3 **garlic cloves, thinly sliced**
- 2 **thyme sprigs**
- 2 **rosemary sprigs**
  3 to 3½ cups extra-virgin olive oil

1. In a heatproof 1-quart jar, combine the chiles with the brandy. Cover and let stand at room temperature for at least 3 days and up to 1 week, until the chiles have absorbed most of the brandy.

2. In a small saucepan, combine the juice of half a lemon with the vinegar and garlic and bring to a boil; pour the vinegar mixture into the jar. Thinly slice the remaining lemon half and add to the jar. Rub the herbs between your fingertips to release their aromas and add them to the jar. Fill the jar with enough olive oil to submerge the chiles and lemon and shake to mix. Let stand at room temperature for 3 days, shaking the jar daily. —*Abraham Conlon*

Espresso Barbecue Sauce
Active **25 min**; Total **1 hr plus overnight chilling**; Makes **1½ cups**

Espresso gives this sauce a deeply rich, complex flavor. It's delicious with smoked or grilled pork, beef, lamb or duck.

- 1 **Tbsp. unsalted butter**
- 1 **Tbsp. vegetable oil**
- 1½ **cups chopped onion**
- 4 **garlic cloves, minced**
- 1 **serrano chile, minced**
- 1 **cup ketchup**
- 1 **cup brewed espresso**
- ¼ **cup distilled white vinegar**
- 3 **Tbsp. unsulfured molasses**
- 2 **tsp. chile powder**
- 1 **tsp. kosher salt**
- 1 **tsp. sugar**
- ¼ **tsp. Worcestershire sauce**

1. In a large saucepan, melt the butter in the oil. Add the onion, garlic and serrano and cook over moderately low heat, stirring occasionally, until the onion is softened, about 8 minutes. Stir in all of the remaining ingredients and bring to a simmer. Cover and cook the sauce over low heat for 30 minutes, stirring occasionally.

2. Scrape the sauce into a food processor and puree until smooth. Transfer to a bowl and let cool, then cover and refrigerate overnight to allow the sauce to mellow. —*Bill and Cheryl Jamison*

MAKE AHEAD The barbecue sauce can be refrigerated for up to 2 weeks.

DIY Cultured Butter

TOTAL: 1 HR PLUS 1 TO 2 DAYS CULTURING • MAKES ¾ POUND

European-style cultured butter is pleasingly tangy and nutty. **ADELINE DRUART,** dairy expert and general manager of the excellent Vermont Creamery, shows how to make it from scratch at home.

Cultured Butter

Since buttermilk and crème fraîche contain the same kind of "good" bacteria, use a little of either to culture the heavy cream.

- **1 quart heavy cream**
- **⅓ cup buttermilk or crème fraîche**
  Ice water

STEP 1 MAKE CULTURED CREAM

In a large bowl, whisk the cream with the buttermilk or crème fraîche. Cover with plastic wrap and let stand at room temperature until thickened, at least 12 hours and up to 48 hours.

STEP 2 CHURN, RINSE & KNEAD

1. Scrape the cultured cream into the bowl of a stand mixer, cover with plastic wrap and refrigerate the bowl until well chilled, about 45 minutes.

2. Cover the bowl rim well with plastic to catch any splatter, or use the pouring shield. Beat the cultured cream with the whisk at high speed until the butter solids start to form into a ball, about 4 minutes. Drain the butter solids in a fine sieve set over a medium bowl and reserve the buttermilk for another use.

3. Transfer the butter to a bowl and knead to expel any excess buttermilk. Pour ¼ cup of ice water over the butter, knead and drain. Repeat, adding ice water, kneading and draining 3 more times. Continue kneading the butter until it no longer expels any water.

4. Form the butter into a cylinder or block, wrap it in cheesecloth and gently squeeze to remove any remaining moisture. Discard the cheesecloth and wrap the butter tightly in plastic, followed by parchment paper. Refrigerate for up to 1 week.

STEP-BY-STEP

A stand mixer makes a great butter churner—but a messy one. Use a pouring shield or cover the bowl with plastic.

1

CULTURE Stir buttermilk or crème fraîche into cream and let stand.

2

CHURN Beat until the butterfat and buttermilk separate.

3

CHECK The butter is fully churned when it forms a ball on the whisk.

4

DRAIN Strain the butter in a sieve over a bowl; reserve the buttermilk.

5

RINSE In batches, pour ice water over the butter to wash it.

6

KNEAD Press the butter between rinsings to remove excess water.

Apricot Butter

Total **1 hr 30 min** plus cooling and chilling
Makes **2 cups**

Fresh apricots become a sweet-tart spread that's perfect as a snack with fresh ricotta and crackers or on buttered toast for breakfast.

3½ lbs. fresh apricots, halved and pitted
2 cups apricot juice or nectar
½ cup sugar
3 Tbsp. fresh lemon juice
Pinch of salt

1. Combine all of the ingredients in a large saucepan and bring to a boil. Cover partially and simmer over moderately high heat, stirring frequently, until the apricots are very tender, about 15 minutes. Uncover and continue to simmer over moderate heat, stirring frequently, until very thick, about 1 hour.

2. Scrape the apricot mixture into a food processor and let cool slightly, then puree until very smooth. Transfer the apricot butter to jars and let cool completely. Close the jars and refrigerate until chilled, about 1 hour. —*Molly Chester*

Habanero Vinegar

Total **30 min** plus cooling
Makes **about ⅔ cup**

This tangy, fiery condiment can stand in for any hot sauce. It's particularly delicious with fatty meat dishes like pulled pork.

3 habanero chiles, stemmed
⅔ cup distilled white vinegar
2 tsp. honey
1½ tsp. minced peeled fresh ginger
Kosher salt

1. Roast the chiles directly over a flame, turning, until lightly charred all over; transfer to a blender.

2. In a small saucepan, combine the vinegar with the honey, ginger and a pinch of salt and bring to a boil. Pour the vinegar into the blender and let cool completely, then puree until smooth. Transfer the habanero vinegar to a jar and season with salt. —*Ruby Duke*

MAKE AHEAD The habanero vinegar can be refrigerated for up to 2 weeks.

Mint Pistou

⏱ Total **15 min;** Makes **¾ cup**

2 Tbsp. pecans
1 cup lightly packed mint leaves
½ cup lightly packed flat-leaf parsley leaves
1 tsp. fresh lemon juice
½ tsp. finely grated lemon zest
¾ cup extra-virgin olive oil
Kosher salt

1. In a small skillet, toast the pecans over moderate heat, tossing occasionally, until lightly browned, about 4 minutes. Let cool, then chop.

2. In a food processor, combine the chopped pecans with the mint, parsley, lemon juice and lemon zest and puree until a paste forms. With the machine on, gradually add the olive oil until smooth. Season the *pistou* with salt. —*Linton Hopkins*

Persian-Spiced Pickled Peaches

Active **20 min;** Total **4 days;** Makes **3 cups**

These sweet-and-sour pickles are wonderful with all kinds of rich meat dishes.

1¼ lb. slightly underripe peaches— peeled, pitted and cut into thin wedges
1 Tbsp. coriander seeds
1 cup white wine vinegar
½ cup water
2 Tbsp. sorghum molasses
2 garlic cloves, crushed and peeled
1½ tsp. ground ginger
2 tsp. kosher salt
1 tsp. finely grated orange zest
½ tsp. piment d'Espelette

1. Pack the peach wedges into a 1-quart glass jar. In a small skillet, toast the coriander seeds over moderately high heat, tossing, until fragrant, 2 minutes. Let cool, then crush the seeds.

2. In a medium saucepan, bring the vinegar, water and molasses just to a boil. Stir in the garlic, ginger, salt, orange zest, piment d'Espelette and crushed coriander seeds. Pour the brine over the peaches and let cool completely. Cover and refrigerate for at least 4 days before serving. —*Linton Hopkins*

Five-Herb Salsa Verde

⏱ Total **20 min;** Makes **1 cup**

¾ cup extra-virgin olive oil
3 Tbsp minced flat-leaf parsley
3 Tbsp. minced mint
3 Tbsp. minced tarragon
2 Tbsp. minced chives
2 Tbsp. minced fennel fronds or dill
1 small shallot, minced
1 Tbsp. capers, rinsed and minced
1 Tbsp. red wine vinegar (optional)
Kosher salt

In a bowl, whisk together all of the ingredients and season with salt. —*John Gorham*

Turnip-Green Salsa Verde

⏱ Total **20 min;** Serves **8**

1 Tbsp. capers, drained and minced
4 anchovy fillets in oil, drained and minced
1 garlic clove, minced
¼ cup minced mint
¼ cup minced parsley
5 baby turnips with greens, turnips very thinly sliced on a mandoline, greens reserved
¼ cup fresh lemon juice
⅔ cup extra-virgin olive oil
Kosher salt and pepper

In a bowl, mash the capers, anchovies and garlic. Add the mint and parsley. Mince the turnip greens (you should have ¼ cup) and add them to the bowl. Whisk in the lemon juice and oil; season with salt and pepper. Serve with the turnips. —*Dan Barber*

COOKBOOK TIP

A Smoky Upgrade for Salsa

Add smoky flavor to salsa by blistering tomatoes under the broiler for about 8 minutes before chopping.

Richard Sandoval's New Latin Flavors
Richard Sandoval

Tomatillo-Avocado Sauce

Total **10 min**; Makes **1¾ cups**

This creamy sauce is outstanding as a dip for chips or spooned over egg dishes like huevos rancheros.

- **1 Hass avocado—peeled, pitted and diced**
- **4 fresh tomatillos—husked, rinsed and chopped**
- **¼ cup minced cilantro**
- **2 Tbsp. minced red onion**
- **2 Tbsp. fresh lime juice**
- **1 Tbsp. seeded and minced jalapeño**
  Kosher salt

In a bowl, using a fork, mash the avocado, tomatillos, cilantro, red onion, lime juice and jalapeño to form a chunky sauce. Season with salt. —*Geoffrey Zakarian*

Olive Tapenade

Total **45 min**; Makes **about 2 cups**

Typically spread on baguette toasts or crackers, this briny Provençal condiment is also fantastic on grilled fish or deviled eggs, or tossed in potato salad.

- **¾ lb. pitted kalamata olives, chopped**
- **1 cup extra-virgin olive oil**
- **¼ cup minced parsley**
- **2 Tbsp. each of minced basil and oregano**
- **2 Tbsp. fresh lemon juice**
  Kosher salt and pepper

In a medium bowl, combine all of the ingredients and season with salt and pepper; let stand for 30 minutes. —*Allison Jenkins*

Mango Jam

Total **15 min**; Makes **2 cups**

- **2 ripe mangoes—peeled, cut off the pit and cut into ½-inch pieces**
- **⅔ cup sugar**
- **1 Tbsp. fresh lemon juice**

In a food processor, puree the mangoes; scrape into a saucepan. Add the sugar and lemon juice and bring to a boil. Cover partially and cook over moderate heat, stirring to dissolve the sugar, 5 minutes. Transfer to a bowl and let cool to room temperature. —*Jeni Britton Bauer*

Balsamic Figs

Total **45 min**; Makes **about 4 cups**

Firm figs are best for this quick condiment. It's excellent on a cheese plate, with ricotta crostini or alongside pork chops.

- **1 lb. fresh Black Mission figs, stemmed and halved lengthwise**
- **2 Tbsp. extra-virgin olive oil, plus more for brushing**
- **6 basil leaves, thinly sliced**
- **2 Tbsp. balsamic vinegar**
  Kosher salt and pepper

Light a grill or heat a grill pan. Lightly brush the cut sides of the figs with olive oil and grill until lightly browned and warm, 2 minutes. Transfer the figs to a bowl and top with the basil, balsamic vinegar and the 2 tablespoons of olive oil. Season with salt and pepper. Toss to coat and let stand for 20 minutes. —*Allison Jenkins*

Cranberry Sauce with Dried Cherries

Total **25 min plus cooling**; Makes **3 cups**

F&W editor in chief Dana Cowin adds dried sour cherries to her quick cranberry sauce for an appealing tart-sweet flavor.

- **1 lb. fresh or thawed frozen cranberries (4 cups)**
- **1½ cups dried sour cherries (9 oz.)**
- **1½ cups sugar**
- **½ cup pure cranberry juice**
  Juice from ½ navel orange (¼ cup)
  Kosher salt

In a medium saucepan, combine all of the ingredients except the salt and bring to a simmer. Cook over moderate heat, stirring occasionally, until the cranberries burst and the sauce is jammy, about 15 minutes. Scrape the cranberry sauce into a heatproof bowl and let cool completely. Season with salt and refrigerate until chilled. Serve the sauce cold or at room temperature; stir in a few tablespoons of water if the sauce is too thick. —*Dana Cowin*

Cranberry Mostarda

Active **15 min**; Total **40 min plus cooling and overnight soaking**; Makes **2 cups**

This glossy, jammy *mostarda* (an Italian fruit and mustard condiment) is a great spin on traditional cranberry sauce.

- **2½ Tbsp. yellow mustard seeds**
- **¾ cup dry white wine**
- **1 small cinnamon stick**
  One ½-inch slice of fresh ginger
- **5 whole cloves**
- **1½ cups sugar**
- **1 cup Champagne vinegar**
- **¾ cup pure cranberry juice**
- **1 Tbsp. mustard powder**
- **2 cups dried cranberries (½ lb.)**
- **1 tsp. finely grated orange zest**
  Salt

1. In a small bowl, soak the mustard seeds in the wine at room temperature overnight.

2. Wrap the cinnamon stick, ginger and cloves in a piece of cheesecloth and tie it closed. In a medium saucepan, whisk the mustard seeds and wine with the sugar, vinegar, cranberry juice and mustard powder and bring to a boil. Add the spice bundle and cook over moderate heat, without stirring, until the syrup coats the back of a spoon, about 25 minutes. Discard the spice bundle. Stir in the dried cranberries and orange zest and let the *mostarda* cool completely. Season with salt and serve; stir in water by the tablespoon if it seems too thick. —*Chris Eley*

Dried-Fruit Compote

Total **45 min**; Makes **about 3 cups**

- **1 cup dry white wine**
- **¾ cup sugar**
- **½ cup water**
- **½ cup each of golden raisins, tart dried cherries, sliced dried apricots and stemmed and quartered dried figs**
- **2 thyme sprigs**

Combine all of the ingredients in a medium saucepan and bring to a boil. Cook over moderately low heat, stirring occasionally, until the liquid is syrupy, about 30 minutes. Transfer to a bowl and let cool for 5 minutes; discard the thyme sprigs. —*Allison Jenkins*

CRANBERRY MOSTARDA

PINEAPPLE MOJITOS
Recipe, page 374

Drinks

Low Approach

Total **5 min**; Makes **1 drink**

This beer cocktail is relatively low in alcohol (hence the name), making it a great aperitif. The wintry flavor comes from allspice dram, a fragrant liqueur originally produced in Jamaica.

- **1 oz. sweet vermouth**
- **½ oz. Lillet blanc**
- **½ oz. allspice dram**
- **1 dash of orange bitters**
  Ice
- **2 oz. chilled IPA**
- **1 lemon twist, for garnish**

In a cocktail shaker, combine the vermouth, Lillet, allspice dram and bitters; fill the shaker with ice and shake well. Strain into a chilled collins glass half-filled with ice. Stir in the beer and garnish with the twist. —*Duncan Burrell and Richard Noel*

Champagne with a Twist

Total **5 min**; Makes **8 drinks**

A lemon twist adds a dash of bitter and citrus to this festive Champagne cocktail.

- **One 750-ml bottle chilled dry Champagne or sparkling wine**
- **Eight 3-inch strips of lemon zest, for garnish**

Fill 8 chilled flutes with the Champagne. Twist the lemon zest strips over the drinks and drop them in. —*Ali Larter*

SIMPLE SYRUP

A quick combination of sugar and water, this clear syrup is used to sweeten countless cocktails.

In a small saucepan, simmer 1 cup sugar with 1 cup water over moderate heat, stirring, until the sugar dissolves. Let the syrup cool completely, then refrigerate for up to 1 month. Makes about 12 ounces.

Blood Orange–Rosemary Fizz

Active **10 min**; Total **45 min**
Makes **1 drink**

- **2 oz. fresh blood orange juice or pink grapefruit juice**
- **½ oz. Aperol or Campari**
- **½ oz. Rosemary Simple Syrup (recipe follows)**
  Ice
- **2 oz. Prosecco**
- **1 blood orange wheel and 1 rosemary sprig, for garnish**

In a cocktail shaker, combine the blood orange juice, Aperol and Rosemary Simple Syrup; fill the shaker with ice, shake well and strain into a chilled Champagne coupe or flute. Top with the Prosecco and garnish with the blood orange wheel and rosemary sprig. —*Athena Calderone*

ROSEMARY SIMPLE SYRUP

Total **35 min**; Makes **6 ounces**

- **½ cup sugar**
- **1 rosemary sprig**

In a small saucepan, combine the sugar and rosemary sprig with ½ cup of water. Warm over low heat, stirring, until the sugar dissolves. Remove from the heat and let stand for 30 minutes. Discard the rosemary and refrigerate the syrup in an airtight container for up to 1 month. —*AC*

Blood Orange Screwdrivers

Total **10 min**; Makes **8 drinks**

"I just want to make one drink for parties," says actress Ali Larter. This pretty version of the classic cocktail is dressed up with a splash of Aperol and a jewel-toned orange wheel.

- **12 oz. vodka**
- **2 oz. Aperol**
- **1 pint chilled blood orange juice**
  Ice
- **8 blood orange wheels, for garnish (optional)**

In a chilled pitcher, stir the vodka with the Aperol and blood orange juice. Pour into 8 chilled, ice-filled highball or collins glasses and garnish with the blood orange wheels. —*Ali Larter*

Green Lantern

Total **5 min**; Makes **1 drink**

Kiwi adds a lovely green hue to this floral, sweet-tart classic gin cocktail.

- **½ kiwi, peeled and diced, plus 1 or 2 kiwi slices skewered on a pick for garnish**
- **¼ oz. Simple Syrup (below left)**
- **1½ oz. gin, preferably Hendrick's**
- **1 oz. chilled Viognier**
- **½ oz. fresh lime juice**
  Ice

In a cocktail shaker, muddle the diced kiwi with the Simple Syrup. Add the gin, Viognier and lime juice, fill the shaker with ice and shake well. Strain into a chilled martini glass and garnish with the skewered kiwi slices. —*Thomas Waugh*

Roasted Lemon and Bay Leaf Hard Lemonade

Total **35 min plus chilling**; Makes **6 drinks**

The inspiration for this roasted citrus drink from F&W's Justin Chapple is an incredible cocktail at Monica Pope's Sparrow Bar + Cookshop in Houston. Roasting citrus makes it more intense and fragrant.

- **3 lemons, quartered lengthwise, plus 6 lemon wheels for garnish**
- **9 fresh bay leaves**
- **1 cup superfine sugar**
- **1 cup plus 2 Tbsp. vodka**
  Ice
- **1 cup plus 2 Tbsp. chilled club soda**

1. Preheat the oven to 400°. In a small roasting pan, roast the lemon quarters with 3 of the bay leaves for about 20 minutes, until the lemons are softened and browned in spots. Scrape the lemons, bay leaves and any pan juices into a large pitcher. Add the sugar, vodka and 3 cups of water and muddle with the lemons. Let cool completely, then refrigerate until chilled.

2. Strain the lemonade through a fine sieve into 6 chilled, ice-filled glasses. Stir 3 tablespoons of club soda into each drink and garnish with a lemon wheel and bay leaf. —*Justin Chapple*

MAKE AHEAD The strained hard lemonade can be refrigerated overnight.

GREEN LANTERN

Tomato Water Bloody Marys

Active **10 min**; Total **1 hr 10 min**; Serves **2**

Bloody Marys can be filling, but chef Gavin Kaysen makes an especially light and refreshing version by using fresh tomato water.

- 1½ lbs. sliced tomatoes
- 2 tsp. kosher salt
- ½ cup tomato juice
- ¼ cup plus 2 Tbsp. vodka
- 3 Tbsp. fresh lemon juice
- 2 Tbsp. dill pickle juice
- 1½ tsp. grated horseradish
- 1 pinch of pepper
- 2 dashes of Worcestershire sauce
- 2 dashes of Tabasco
  Ice
  Herb sprigs, for garnish

1. In a colander set over a bowl, sprinkle the tomatoes with the salt. Let stand for 1 hour. Press the tomatoes lightly; you should have about 1 cup of tomato water. Reserve the tomatoes for a salad.

2. In a cocktail shaker, combine ¾ cup of the tomato water with the tomato juice, vodka, lemon juice, dill pickle juice, horseradish, pepper, Worcestershire sauce and Tabasco. Stir and pour into 2 chilled, ice-filled glasses. Garnish with herb sprigs and serve. —*Gavin Kaysen*

Rosé All Day

Total **5 min**; Makes **1 drink**

- 1½ oz. Lillet rosé
- 1 oz. chilled rosé wine
- ¼ oz. vodka
- ¼ oz. mandarin liqueur
- ¼ oz. orange curaçao
- ¾ tsp. fresh lemon juice
- ¼ tsp. agave nectar
  Ice
  One 3-inch strip of orange peel, for garnish

In a chilled rocks glass, stir together all of the ingredients except the ice and orange peel. Fill with ice and stir again. Pinch the orange peel over the cocktail to release its oils, then rub the peel on the rim of the glass, drop it into the cocktail and serve. —*Trencherman • Chicago*

Vodka Micheladas

Total **15 min plus overnight infusing**
Makes **2 drinks**

In her take on the Michelada—the spicy Mexican cocktail—cookbook author and TV personality Georgia Pellegrini substitutes seltzer and homemade jalapeño-infused vodka for the usual beer. "Good things are meant to evolve," she says.

- Sea salt
- 1 lime wedge
  Ice
- ¼ cup fresh lime juice
- 3 oz. Jalapeño-and-Citrus-Infused Vodka (recipe follows)
- 4 dashes of Worcestershire sauce
- 2 dashes of soy sauce
- 2 dashes of hot sauce
- ⅛ tsp. freshly ground pepper
- 6 oz. chilled seltzer
- 2 strips of crispy bacon, for garnish

1. Spread the sea salt on a small plate. Moisten half the rims of 2 double old-fashioned glasses with the lime wedge, then roll the rims in the salt. Fill the glasses with ice.

2. In a cocktail shaker, combine all of the remaining ingredients except the seltzer and bacon and stir well. Strain the drink into the glasses. Stir in the seltzer, garnish with the bacon and serve.
—*Georgia Pellegrini*

JALAPEÑO-AND-CITRUS-INFUSED VODKA

Total **15 min plus overnight infusing**
Makes **32 ounces**

This vodka can be used in any number of cocktails, from martinis to Bloody Marys.

- 32 oz. vodka
- 1 jalapeño, halved lengthwise
  Zest of 2 lemons, peeled into large strips with a vegetable peeler

Combine all of the ingredients in a jar and let stand at room temperature overnight. Strain, discarding the jalapeño and lemon zest, and refrigerate the infused vodka for up to 1 month. —*GP*

Italian Berry Mule

Total **5 min**; Makes **1 drink**

- 6 raspberries
- 2 oz. vodka
- ½ oz. fresh lime juice
- ½ oz. Simple Syrup (p. 370)
- ½ tsp. aged balsamic vinegar
  Ice
- 2 oz. chilled ginger beer

In a cocktail shaker, muddle the raspberries. Add the vodka, lime juice, Simple Syrup and vinegar; fill the shaker with ice and shake well. Strain the drink into a chilled, ice-filled highball glass and stir in the ginger beer. —*Philip Duff*

Belgian 75

Total **5 min**; Makes **1 drink**

- 1 oz. gin
- ½ oz. fresh lemon juice
- ½ oz. Simple Syrup (p. 370)
  Ice
- 5 oz. chilled Orval beer or other Belgian ale
- 1 lemon twist, for garnish

In a cocktail shaker, combine the gin, lemon juice and Simple Syrup; fill the shaker with ice and shake well. Strain into a chilled stemmed beer glass, stir in the beer and garnish with the twist.
—*Duncan Burrell and Richard Noel*

Stone Wall

Total **5 min**; Makes **1 drink**

- One 1-inch piece of fresh ginger, peeled and thinly sliced
- 1½ tsp. Simple Syrup (p. 370)
- 1½ oz. aged rum
- 1½ oz. chilled unsweetened apple cider
  Ice
- 1½ oz. chilled ginger beer
- 1 lime wedge and 1 apple slice, for garnish

In a cocktail shaker, muddle the ginger with the Simple Syrup. Add the rum and cider, fill the shaker with ice and shake well. Strain into a chilled, ice-filled rocks glass, stir in the ginger beer and garnish with the lime wedge and apple slice. —*Dale DeGroff*

STONE WALL

Tom Terrific

⏱ Total **5 min**; Makes **1 drink**

This slightly spritzy cocktail features IPA and Old Tom, a style of gin popular in the 1800s that's a little sweeter and less juniper-forward than modern versions.

1½ oz. Old Tom gin

½ oz. Heering cherry liqueur

½ oz. fresh lemon juice

½ oz. Simple Syrup (p. 370)
   Ice

2 oz. chilled IPA

1 lemon wheel, for garnish

In a cocktail shaker, combine the gin, cherry liqueur, lemon juice and Simple Syrup. Fill the shaker with ice, shake well and strain into a chilled highball glass. Stir in the beer and garnish with the lemon wheel. —*Daren Swisher*

Better than Advil

⏱ Total **5 min**; Makes **1 drink**

This spicy margarita riff is a great hair-of-the-dog remedy at brunch.

1½ oz. blanco tequila

¾ oz. fresh lime juice

½ oz. agave nectar

¼ tsp. spicy pickle brine (from a jar of pickles)
   Dash of habanero hot sauce
   Ice

1 lime wedge and 1 green olive, for garnish

In a cocktail shaker, combine the tequila, lime juice, agave nectar, pickle brine and hot sauce; fill the shaker with ice and shake well. Strain into a chilled, ice-filled rocks glass, garnish with a lime wedge and an olive and serve. —*Trencherman • Chicago*

Pineapple Mojitos

📷 PAGE 368

Active **20 min**; Total **1 hr 30 min**
Makes **8 drinks**

Puerto Rican chef Jose Enrique's family comes from Cuba; their pineapple soda was the country's most popular soft drink after Coke. The flavors inspired this mojito, which combines a rich brown sugar–pineapple syrup with rum, mint and club soda.

PINEAPPLE SYRUP

1½ lbs. peeled fresh pineapple chunks

2 Tbsp. packed dark brown sugar

MOJITOS

½ lb. diced fresh pineapple (2 cups)

1 cup lightly packed mint leaves, plus mint sprigs for garnish

2 cups white rum

¾ cup fresh lime juice
   Ice

1¼ cups chilled club soda
   Lime wedges, for garnish

1. Make the pineapple syrup In a medium saucepan, bring the pineapple chunks, sugar and 4 cups of water to a boil. Simmer over moderately low heat, stirring, until the pineapple is very soft and the mixture is reduced to 2½ cups, 40 minutes. Strain the mixture into a heatproof bowl, pressing on the solids; discard the solids. Let the syrup cool; you should have about 1⅓ cups.

2. Make the mojitos In a pitcher, muddle the pineapple and mint leaves. Stir in the rum, lime juice and 1 cup of the pineapple syrup. Pour into 8 chilled, ice-filled glasses. Stir in the club soda and garnish with mint sprigs and lime wedges. —*Jose Enrique*

Manhattan

⏱ Total **5 min**; Makes **1 drink**

2 oz. bourbon or rye whiskey

1 oz. sweet vermouth

2 dashes of Angostura bitters
   Ice

1 orange twist, for garnish

In a mixing glass, combine the bourbon, vermouth and bitters; fill the glass with ice and stir well. Strain into a chilled martini glass and garnish with the twist.

Alpine Manhattan

Active **5 min**; Total **1 hr**; Makes **1 drink**

Herbalist Shae Whitney makes a lovely pine syrup from fresh pine needles. She uses it in this strong and wonderfully fragrant drink.

1½ oz. bourbon

1 oz. Pine Syrup (recipe follows)

2 dashes of Angostura bitters
   Ice

1 orange twist, for garnish

In a mixing glass, combine the bourbon, Pine Syrup and bitters; fill with ice and stir well. Strain into a chilled coupe and garnish with the orange twist. —*Shae Whitney*

PINE SYRUP

Active **5 min**; Total **50 min plus cooling**
Makes **about 12 ounces**

2 cups fresh pine or spruce needles on the branch

1 cup sugar

1. Pick the pine needles off the branch. Chop the branch into 1-inch pieces and smash lightly with a rolling pin.

2. In a medium saucepan, combine the needles, chopped branches and 6 cups of water; bring to a simmer. Cook until the liquid is reduced to 1 cup, 40 minutes. Stir in the sugar until completely dissolved. Remove from the heat and let cool.

3. In a blender, puree the pine needle mixture for 1 minute. Strain the syrup into a jar and refrigerate for up to 1 month. —*SW*

Ginger-Bourbon Creek Tea

⏱ Total **20 min**; Makes **4 drinks**

6 oz. bourbon or whiskey

4 oz. cold water

3 oz. fresh lemon juice

2 oz. ginger liqueur, such as Domaine de Canton

2 oz. Simple Syrup (p. 370)

6 dashes of orange bitters
   Ice

4 lemon wheels, for garnish

In a large pitcher, combine all of the ingredients except the ice and lemon wheels and stir well. Pour into chilled, ice-filled rocks glasses and stir again. Garnish with lemon wheels and serve. —*Nick Kokonas*

Memorial Union Old-Fashioned

⏱ Total **5 min**; Makes **1 drink**

½ tsp. maple syrup

1½ oz. rye whiskey

1 oz. brandy

¼ oz. Grand Marnier

3 drops of orange bitters

Ice

1 lemon twist and 1 orange twist,
for garnish

Pour the maple syrup into a chilled rocks glass and swirl to evenly coat the bottom. Add the rye, brandy, Grand Marnier and bitters. Fill the glass with ice and stir vigorously for 15 seconds. Garnish the drink with the lemon and orange twists.
—*Brian Bartels*

Ginger Julep

Active **5 min**; Total **1 hr 20 min**
Makes **1 drink**

1½ oz. bourbon

1½ oz. fresh orange juice

1 Tbsp. Ginger-Mint Syrup
(recipe follows)

Crushed ice

1 mint sprig, for garnish

In a chilled julep cup or glass, combine the bourbon with the orange juice and Ginger-Mint Syrup and stir well. Fill the cup with crushed ice, then spin a swizzle stick or bar spoon between your hands to mix the drink. Top with additional crushed ice and garnish with the mint sprig. —*Bobby Flay*

GINGER-MINT SYRUP
Active **15 min**; Total **1 hr 15 min**
Makes **1½ cups**

1¼ cups sugar

¼ lb. fresh ginger, peeled and
finely chopped

One 3-inch piece of orange peel

¼ cup lightly packed mint leaves

In a small saucepan, bring the sugar and 1¼ cups of water to a boil; simmer until the sugar is dissolved, 3 minutes. Remove from the heat and add the ginger, orange peel and mint. Let the syrup cool completely, 1 hour; strain through a fine sieve before using. —*BF*

Oaxaca Old-Fashioned

⏱ Total **5 min**; Makes **1 drink**

Mezcal gives an extra kick to tequila in this updated version of the old-fashioned.

1½ oz. reposado tequila

½ oz. mezcal

2 dashes of Angostura bitters

1 tsp. agave nectar

Ice

1 orange twist, for garnish

In a mixing glass, combine the tequila, mezcal, bitters and agave nectar; fill the glass with ice and stir well. Strain into a chilled, ice-filled double rocks glass. Over the glass, hold the orange twist between your thumb and two fingers; hold a lit match 1 inch away from the twist and pinch the twist sharply to release its oils. Garnish the drink with the flamed twist. —*Philip Ward*

Alma Mater

⏱ Total **5 min**; Makes **1 drink**

In Wisconsin, the locally produced Death's Door white whiskey is a bartender's favorite. Star mixologist Jim Meehan, who went to college in Wisconsin, features it in this delicious strawberry cocktail.

2 strawberries, hulled, plus
1 strawberry slice for garnish

1¾ oz. white (unaged) whiskey,
preferably Death's Door

½ oz. Aperol

½ oz. dry vermouth

2 dashes of aromatic bitters,
preferably Bitter Truth

½ tsp. fresh lemon juice

Ice

In a cocktail shaker, muddle the hulled strawberries. Add the whiskey, Aperol, vermouth, bitters and lemon juice; fill the shaker with ice and shake well. Strain into a chilled coupe and garnish with the strawberry slice. —*Jim Meehan*

Citrus, Brandy and Pineapple Punch

⏱ Total **45 min**; Serves **8**

"Punches are the cocktail version of a feast," says Chris Harrison, cofounder of Liber & Co., a craft cocktail syrup company in Austin. He uses Liber's pineapple gum syrup in this mildly sweet punch, but simple syrup mixed with pineapple juice is a good substitute.

12 oz. brandy

6 oz. chilled unsweetened
pineapple juice

3 oz. fresh lime juice

3 oz. Simple Syrup (p. 370)

Pinch of freshly grated nutmeg

9 oz. chilled club soda

Ice

8 lemon wheels, for garnish

1. In a pitcher, combine the brandy with the pineapple and lime juices, Simple Syrup and nutmeg. Refrigerate until well chilled, about 30 minutes.

2. Stir in the club soda and serve over ice, garnished with a lemon wheel.
—*Chris Harrison and Adam and Robert Higginbotham*

MAKE AHEAD The recipe can be prepared through Step 1 and refrigerated overnight.

Edna's Lunchbox

⏱ Total **5 min**; Makes **1 drink**

Edna's is a legendary bar in Oklahoma City with dollar bills stapled to the walls. Its signature drink is an unlikely mix of three ingredients: fresh orange juice, amaretto and light beer. Key to the surprisingly tasty cocktail: a frosty mug.

6 oz. chilled fresh orange juice

6 oz. chilled light beer

1 oz. amaretto

A couple of orange wheels,
for garnish

In a chilled beer mug or pint glass, combine the orange juice with the light beer and amaretto. Stir well, garnish the cocktail with orange wheels and serve right away.
—*Edna Scott*

Wine Punch with Melon Ice Cubes

Total **15 min plus 2 hr chilling**
Makes **6 drinks**

Derek Brown, whose Washington, DC, bar empire includes Eat the Rich and The Passenger, sweetens this Riesling-based punch with honey syrup. Keeping the drink cool are frozen melon balls, which are fun to eat as they start to thaw.

- **1** small cantaloupe or honeydew melon
- **¼** cup honey
- One 750-ml bottle chilled dry Riesling
- **5** oz. Cointreau or other triple sec
- **2** oz. fresh lemon juice
- Lemon basil sprigs, for garnish

1. Using a large melon baller, scoop balls from the cantaloupe or honeydew, or a mix of the two. Transfer the melon balls to a baking sheet and freeze until firm, at least 2 hours.

2. Meanwhile, in a small bowl, dissolve the honey in 2 tablespoons of warm water and refrigerate until chilled. In a small pitcher, stir the honey syrup with the Riesling, Cointreau and lemon juice. Put the frozen melon balls in 6 chilled wineglasses and pour in the punch. Garnish with lemon basil sprigs. —*Derek Brown*

Peach-Thyme Ice Cubes

Total **10 min plus overnight freezing**
Makes **24 cubes**

Chef Gavin Kaysen makes these ice cubes—delicious in white sangria or sparkling wine—with slightly overripe peaches.

- **1¼** lbs. ripe peaches, pitted and quartered
- **1** cup water
- **¼** cup sugar
- **2** Tbsp. fresh lemon juice
- **1** tsp. thyme leaves

In a food processor, combine all of the ingredients and puree. Pour into 2 standard ice cube trays and freeze overnight. Serve in white sangria or sparkling wine. —*Gavin Kaysen*

Glögg

Total **25 min plus 1 day steeping**; Serves **10**

To spike his Swedish mulled wine, New York chef Marcus Samuelsson infuses vodka with cardamom.

- **4** cinnamon sticks
- **2** tsp. green cardamom pods
- One 2-inch piece of peeled fresh ginger, chopped
- **4** tsp. finely grated orange zest
- **12** whole cloves
- **1** cup vodka
- Two 750-ml bottles dry white wine
- **2** cups dry rosé
- **2** cups sugar
- **2** Tbsp. vanilla sugar
- **½** cup blanched whole almonds
- **½** cup raisins

1. In a mortar, crush the cinnamon and cardamom. Transfer to a 1-quart jar. Add the ginger, orange zest, cloves and vodka. Cover and let stand for 24 hours.

2. Strain the vodka into a large saucepan; discard the solids. Add the remaining ingredients and stir over moderate heat until bubbles form around the edge; do not boil. Serve hot. —*Marcus Samuelsson*

Huber's Iced Spanish Coffee

Total **5 min**; Makes **1 drink**

Spanish coffee (made tableside with flames and fanfare) is a signature drink at Huber's in Portland, Oregon. It's so popular that Huber's is now the largest independent restaurant user of Kahlúa in the US.

- **¾** oz. overproof rum
- **¼** oz. triple sec
- **1½** oz. coffee liqueur, preferably Kahlúa
- Ice
- **4** oz. chilled strong coffee
- **¼** cup unsweetened whipped cream
- Freshly grated nutmeg, for garnish

In a small saucepan, combine the rum and triple sec and ignite with a long match. Carefully add the coffee liqueur, then pour the flaming mixture into a chilled, ice-filled pint glass. Stir in the coffee, top with the whipped cream and garnish with nutmeg. —*Huber's • Portland, OR*

Melted Ice Cream Hot Chocolate

Total **15 min**; Serves **4**

The melted vanilla ice cream in this recipe makes the hot chocolate so creamy, rich and thick that you could have it for dessert, says Jeni Britton Bauer of Jeni's Splendid Ice Creams. Sometimes she serves it with giant marshmallows and a knife and fork.

- **2** cups whole milk
- **½** cup sugar
- Flaky sea salt
- **1** cup unsweetened cocoa powder
- **1** pint vanilla ice cream, softened
- Large or small marshmallows, for serving (optional)

In a medium saucepan, combine the milk with the sugar and a pinch of salt and cook over moderate heat, whisking, until the sugar dissolves, about 3 minutes. Whisk in the cocoa powder until incorporated. Add the ice cream and cook over moderate heat, whisking, until smooth and hot, about 3 minutes. Ladle the chocolate into mugs and garnish with marshmallows, if desired, and flaky sea salt. —*Jeni Britton Bauer*

Wake 'n' Bake

Total **5 min**; Makes **1 drink**

This iced-coffee cocktail is fantastic at brunch or as an after-dinner drink. It's sweetened with Kringle Cream, a spiced-rum cream liqueur meant to evoke a kringle (a danish-like pastry with fruits, nuts and spices; see p. 302). If Kringle Cream isn't available, substitute Bailey's Irish cream.

- **1½** oz. cold brewed coffee
- **1** oz. Kringle Cream liqueur or Irish cream liqueur, such as Bailey's
- **1** oz. coffee liqueur, such as Kahlúa
- Ice

In a cocktail shaker, combine the coffee with the cream and coffee liqueurs; fill the shaker with ice and shake well. Strain into a chilled, ice-filled rocks glass and serve. —*Trencherman • Chicago*

HUBER'S ICED SPANISH COFFEE

CHOCOLATE-HAZELNUT TART
Recipe, page 326

Recipe Index

Page numbers in **bold** indicate photographs.

B

C

S

Contributors

RECIPES

MATTHEW ACCARRINO, an F&W Best New Chef 2014, is the chef at SPQR in San Francisco. His recipes are featured in *SPQR*.

GRANT ACHATZ, an F&W Chef-in-Residence and F&W Best New Chef 2002, is the chef and co-owner of Alinea, Next and The Aviary cocktail bar, all in Chicago. He is a co-author of *Alinea* and *Life, On the Line*.

HUGH ACHESON, an F&W Chef-in-Residence, is the chef and co-owner of Five & Ten and The National in Athens, Georgia; Empire State South in Atlanta; and The Florence in Savannah. He is a judge on Bravo's *Top Chef* and the author of two cookbooks.

REEM ACRA is a New York fashion designer known for hosting extraordinary dinner parties.

UMBER AHMAD is the pastry chef and owner of Mah-Ze-Dahr Bakery in New York City.

JEFF AKIN is one of the bloggers behind Feed Me Creative, a culinary marketing agency in Kansas City, Missouri.

BILLY ALLIN is the chef and co-owner of Cakes & Ale and the forthcoming Bread & Butterfly Café, both in Atlanta.

STACY AMBLE is a gifted home baker and the sales manager of Quince & Apple, a small-batch preserves company in Madison, Wisconsin.

ERIK ANDERSON, an F&W Best New Chef 2012, is a visiting chef at Chefs Club by Food & Wine in New York City. He is a co-chef and co-owner of the forthcoming Brut in Minneapolis.

JOSÉ ANDRÉS is the chef and owner of restaurants in Las Vegas, Washington, DC, Los Angeles, Miami Beach and Dorado, Puerto Rico. He has authored four cookbooks, including *Tapas* and *Made in Spain*, a companion to his PBS series of the same name.

DOMINIQUE ANSEL is a pastry chef and the owner of Dominique Ansel Bakery in Manhattan.

CATHAL ARMSTRONG, an F&W Best New Chef 2006, is the chef and owner of Restaurant Eve, Eamonn's and The Majestic, all in Alexandria, Virginia. He is also the author of the cookbook *My Irish Table*.

KYLE BAILEY is the chef at Birch & Barley, Churchkey, GDB and Bluejacket brewery's The Arsenal, all in Washington, DC.

ALI BANKS is a resident chef at Sur la Table in Chicago and a recipe contributor to Sitka Salmon Shares, a CSF (community-supported fishery).

JIMMY BANNOS, Jr., is the chef and co-owner of The Purple Pig in Chicago.

DAN BARBER, an F&W Best New Chef 2002, is the chef and co-owner of Blue Hill in New York City and Blue Hill at Stone Barns in Pocantico Hills, New York. He is the author of *The Third Plate*.

BRIAN BARTELS is the spirits director and co-owner of Happy Cooking Hospitality, which includes Fedora, Perla and Bar Sardine, all in New York City.

ENRICO BARTOLINI is the chef at Devero Ristorante near Milan.

ARMANDINO BATALI, father of star chef Mario Batali, is a co-owner of Salumi Artisan Cured Meats in Seattle.

BENNO BATALI and his brother **LEO BATALI,** teenage sons of Mario Batali, are co-authors of *The Batali Brothers Cookbook*.

MARIO BATALI is the chef and co-owner of more than a dozen restaurants in New York City, Las Vegas, L.A. and Singapore and a co-owner of Eataly, a market and restaurant complex in Manhattan and Chicago. He co-hosts *The Chew* and is the author of nine cookbooks; his most recent is *America Farm to Table*.

RICK BAYLESS is the chef and co-owner of several restaurants in the Chicago area and Philadelphia, including Frontera Grill, Xoco and Topolobampo. He hosts PBS's *Mexico—One Plate at a Time* and most recently wrote *Frontera: Margaritas, Guacamoles, and Snacks*.

ISAAC BECKER is the chef and co-owner of 112 Eatery, Bar La Grassa and Burch Steak & Pizza Bar, all in Minneapolis.

DAVE BERAN, an F&W Best New Chef 2014, is the chef at Next in Chicago.

NICOLAS BERGER is the chocolatier and co-owner of Le Chocolat Alain Ducasse in Paris.

PAUL BERGLUND is the chef at The Bachelor Farmer in Minneapolis.

JOHN BESH, an F&W Best New Chef 1999, is the chef and owner of the Besh Restaurant Group, which includes August, Domenica and The American Sector, all in New Orleans, and Lüke in San Antonio. He is the author of three cookbooks and hosts the TV shows *Chef John Besh's New Orleans*, *Chef John Besh's Family Table* and *Hungry Investors*.

JAMIE BISSONNETTE is a co-chef and co-owner of Coppa in Boston and Toro in Boston and New York City.

NOAH BLÖM is the chef at Arc Food & Libations and Shuck Oyster Bar, both in Costa Mesa, California.

APRIL BLOOMFIELD, an F&W Best New Chef 2007, is the chef and co-owner of The Spotted Pig, The Breslin, The John Dory Oyster Bar and Salvation Taco, all in New York City, and Tosca Cafe in San Francisco. She is the author of the cookbook *A Girl and Her Pig*.

DANIEL BOJORQUEZ is the chef and co-owner of La Brasa in Somerville, Massachusetts.

DANNY BOWIEN, an F&W Best New Chef 2013, is the chef and cofounder of Mission Cantina in New York City and Mission Chinese Food in New York and San Francisco.

STUART BRIOZA, an F&W Best New Chef 2003, is the chef and co-owner of State Bird Provisions and The Progress, both in San Francisco. He is a co-author of the cookbook *The Workshop*.

JENI BRITTON BAUER is the owner of Jeni's Splendid Ice Creams, with shops in Ohio, Tennessee, Illinois and Georgia. She is the author of two cookbooks.

SEAN BROCK is the chef and co-owner of McCrady's and Minero in Charleston, South Carolina, and Husk in Charleston and Nashville. He is the author of the cookbook *Heritage*.

DEREK BROWN is a spirits writer and the owner of several bars around Washington, DC, including Mockingbird Hill, The Passenger and Eat the Rich.

MEHDI BRUNET-BENKRITLY is the chef at Bar Sardine and Fedora, both in New York City.

DUNCAN BURRELL is the mixologist and co-owner of Bar-X and Beer Bar in Salt Lake City.

KATIE BUTTON is the chef and co-owner of Cúrate and Nightbell in Asheville, North Carolina. She is the author of the forthcoming *The Cúrate Cookbook*.

TIM BYRES is the chef and co-owner of Smoke, Chicken Scratch, Bar Belmont and The Foundry, all in Dallas, and the author of *Smoke: New Firewood Cooking*.

ATHENA CALDERONE is the creator of the food and lifestyle blog EyeSwoon and a co-owner of Rawlins Calderone Design.

RYAN CANTWELL is the chef at the forthcoming Black Cat in San Francisco.

LINCOLN CARSON is the pastry chef for restaurants in the Michael Mina restaurant group, including Michael Mina in San Francisco and Las Vegas and Arcadia in San Jose, California.

RICHARD CARSTENS is the chef at Tokara Restaurant in Stellenbosch, South Africa.

CHRIS CARTER is a co-owner of two Porter Road Butcher shops in Nashville.

DAVID CHANG, an F&W Chef-in-Residence and F&W Best New Chef 2006, is the chef and founder of the Momofuku restaurant group, with restaurants in New York City, Sydney and Toronto, including Momofuku Noodle Bar and Momofuku Milk Bar. He is a co-author of *Momofuku* cookbook and co-editor of the quarterly food journal *Lucky Peach*.

JOANNE CHANG is the pastry chef and co-owner of Flour Bakery + Café, with locations in the Boston area, a co-owner of Myers + Chang in Boston and the author of *Flour* and *Flour, Too*.

JUSTIN CHAPPLE is an F&W Test Kitchen senior editor and the talent behind the "Mad Genius Tips" videos on foodandwine.com.

RATHA CHAUPOLY is a co-chef and co-owner of the Num Pang sandwich shops in New York City.

MOLLY CHESTER is the farm manager and chef at Apricot Lane Farms in Moorpark, California, and a co-author of *Back to Butter: A Traditional Foods Cookbook*.

ROY CHOI, an F&W Best New Chef 2010, is the chef and co-owner of Kogi BBQ food trucks as well as several brick-and-mortar restaurants in the Los Angeles area. He is also the owner of The Line Hotel in L.A. and author of *L.A. Son*.

ASHLEY CHRISTENSEN is the chef and owner of Poole's Downtown Diner, Beasley's Chicken + Honey, Chuck's, Fox Liquor Bar and Joule Coffee, all in Raleigh, North Carolina.

KAY CHUN is an F&W Test Kitchen senior editor.

MICHAEL CIMARUSTI is the chef and co-owner of Providence and Connie & Ted's, both in Los Angeles.

KENDRA COGGIN is a co-owner of Pernicious Pickling Co. in Costa Mesa, California.

CHAD COLBY is the chef at Chi Spacca in L.A.

PAOLO COLUCCIO is a co-chef and manager of Oreade restaurant in the Monteverdi hotel in Castiglioncello del Trinoro, Italy.

ABRAHAM CONLON is the chef and co-owner of Fat Rice in Chicago.

BARON CONWAY is a co-owner of Pernicious Pickling Co. in Costa Mesa, California.

CHRISTOPHER COOMBS is the chef and co-owner of Deuxave, dbar and Boston Chops, all in Boston.

CHRIS COSENTINO, winner of Bravo's *Top Chef Masters* Season 4, is the chef and co-owner of Porcellino and a co-owner of Boccalone Salumeria, both in San Francisco. He is the author of *Beginnings: My Way to Start a Meal*.

BETHANY COSTELLO is the pastry chef at M. Wells Steakhouse and M. Wells Dinette in Long Island City, New York.

DANA COWIN is *Food & Wine*'s editor in chief and the author of *Mastering My Mistakes in the Kitchen: Learning to Cook with 65 Great Chefs and Over 100 Delicious Recipes*.

JANE COXWELL is fashion designer Diane von Furstenburg's personal chef and the author of the cookbook *Fresh Happy Tasty*.

GERARD CRAFT, an F&W Best New Chef 2008, is the chef and owner of Niche, Brasserie, Taste and Pastaria, all in the St. Louis area.

GRANT LEE CRILLY is a cofounder of ChefSteps, a Seattle-based cooks' collective, and a collaborator on *Modernist Cuisine*.

COLLEEN CRUZE BHATTI is the chef and co-owner of Cruze Farm near Knoxville, Tennessee.

DIANE CU is a co-publisher of the blog White on Rice Couple and co-author of *Bountiful*.

BEN DAITZ is a co-chef and co-owner of the Num Pang sandwich shops in New York City.

MATT DANKO is the chef at Trentina in Cleveland.

MATT DANZER is a co-chef and co-owner of Uncle Boons in New York City.

HOMA DASHTAKI and her father, **GOSHTASB DASHTAKI,** own The White Moustache yogurt company in Brooklyn.

CAMAS DAVIS is the founder of and an instructor for the Portland Meat Collective, a distributor of meat from small Oregon farms and a traveling butchery school.

CHERYL DAY is a co-baker and co-owner of Back in the Day Bakery in Savannah, Georgia, and a co-author of *The Back in the Day Bakery Cookbook*.

DALE DEGROFF, one of America's most legendary mixologists, is a cofounder of The Museum of the American Cocktail in New Orleans and the author of *The Essential Cocktail* and *The Craft of the Cocktail*.

GIADA DE LAURENTIIS is the chef and owner of Giada restaurant in The Cromwell hotel in Las Vegas and the host of several cooking shows, including *Everyday Italian* and *Giada at Home*. She is also the author of numerous cookbooks; her most recent is *Giada's Feel Good Food*.

GREG DENTON and his wife, **GABRIELLE QUIÑÓNEZ DENTON,** F&W Best New Chefs 2014, are the chefs and owners of Ox Restaurant in Portland, Oregon.

TARA DERR WEBB is the chef and co-owner of The Farmbar and Deux Puces Farm, both in Awendaw, South Carolina.

ROCCO DISPIRITO, an F&W Best New Chef 1999, is the host of Ion Life's *Now Eat This with Rocco DiSpirito* and the author of several cookbooks; his most recent is *The Pound a Day Diet*.

ADELINE DRUART is a dairy expert and the general manager at Vermont Creamery in Websterville, Vermont.

DANIEL DUANE is a San Francisco–based writer and regular contributor to F&W. He is the author of *How to Cook Like a Man: A Memoir of Cookbook Obsession*.

PHILIP DUFF is a co-owner and mixologist at Door 74 in Amsterdam, the director of education for the Tales of the Cocktail festival and the director of the consulting company Liquid Solutions.

HUGUE DUFOUR is the chef and co-owner of M. Wells Dinette in MoMA PS1 and M. Wells Steakhouse, both in Long Island City, New York.

RUBY DUKE is a co-owner of Raven & Boar, a heritage pig farm in East Chatham, New York.

CHRIS ELEY is a co-owner of Goose the Market and Smoking Goose, both in Indianapolis.

NICHOLAS ELMI, winner of Bravo's *Top Chef* Season 11, is the chef and co-owner of Laurel in Philadelphia.

JOSE ENRIQUE, an F&W Best New Chef 2013, is the chef and owner of Jose Enrique in San Juan, Capital and Miel in Guaynabo and El Blok on the island of Vieques, all in Puerto Rico.

RENEE ERICKSON is the chef and co-owner of several Seattle restaurants, including The Whale Wins, The Walrus and the Carpenter and Boat Street Café. She is the author of *A Boat, A Whale & A Walrus*.

ADAM EVANS is the chef at The Optimist in Atlanta.

EMILY FARRIS is the creative director and co-owner of Feed Me Creative and the author of *Casserole Crazy*.

SUSAN FENIGER is a chef and restaurateur. She co-owns Mud Hen Tavern in Los Angeles; Border Grill in Las Vegas, Los Angeles and Santa Monica, California; and Border Grill Truck in L.A. She is a co-author of several cookbooks, including *Cooking with Too Hot Tamales* and *Susan Feniger's Street Food*.

FRANCESCO FERRETTI is the chef at Il Rosmarino in Tenuta di Castelfalfi, Italy.

CONTRIBUTORS

BOBBY FLAY is the chef and owner of several restaurants in the US and Bahamas, among them Gato and Bar Americain in New York City, and the host of various cooking shows, including *Bobby Flay's Barbecue Addiction*. He has written many cookbooks; his most recent is *Bobby Flay's Barbecue Addiction*.

TYLER FLORENCE, the host of Food Network's *Tyler's Ultimate* and *The Great Food Truck Race*, is the owner of Wayfare Tavern in San Francisco and El Paseo in Mill Valley, California. He is the author of several cookbooks; his latest is *Inside the Test Kitchen*.

MARC FORGIONE, winner of Food Network's *The Next Iron Chef* Season 3, is the chef and co-owner of American Cut and the chef and owner of Marc Forgione, both in New York City. He is the author of *Marc Forgione*.

JOHN FRASER is the chef and owner of Dovetail and the chef and co-owner of Narcissa, both in New York City.

ERIC FRECHON is the chef at Epicure, 114 Faubourg, Le Jardin Français, Le Bar du Bristol, Le Mini Palais and Lazare, all in Paris. He is the author of several cookbooks; his most recent is *Pomme de Terre*.

DAVID FRENKIEL is a co-creator of the blog Green Kitchen Stories and a co-author of *Green Kitchen Travels* and *Vegetarian Everyday*. He is a magazine art director in Stockholm.

MARK FULLER, an F&W Best New Chef 2009, is the chef and co-owner of Ma'ono Fried Chicken & Whisky in Seattle.

DYLAN FULTINEER is the chef at Rappahannock in Richmond, Virginia.

MATTEO GAMBI is the chef at Rinuccio restaurant at Marchesi Antinori Chianti Classico Cellar in Bargino, Italy.

JOSE GARCES is the chef and owner of a food truck and 14 restaurants, including Amada, Distrito and Tinto, all in Philadelphia; Mercat in Chicago; and El Jefe in Palm Springs, California. His latest cookbook is *The Latin Road Home*.

MEGAN GARRELTS is the pastry chef and co-owner of Bluestem in Kansas City, Missouri, and Rye in Leawood, Kansas. She is a co-author of *Bluestem: The Cookbook*.

MICHELLE GAYER is the pastry chef and owner of Salty Tart Bakery in Minneapolis.

WESLEY GENOVART is the chef at SoLo Farm & Table in South Londonderry, Vermont, which he owns with his wife, **CHLOE GENOVART.**

KAREN GILLINGHAM is a food stylist based in Los Angeles.

SARA KATE GILLINGHAM is the founding editor of Apartment Therapy's The Kitchn, a daily web magazine devoted to cooking and kitchen design. She is the author of *Good Food to Share* and *The Greyston Bakery Cookbook* and a co-author of *The Kitchn Cookbook*.

WILL GILSON is the chef and co-owner of Puritan & Company in Cambridge, Massachusetts.

TODD GINSBERG is the chef and co-owner of The General Muir, Yalla and Fred's Meat & Bread, all in Atlanta.

GUNNAR KARL GÍSLASON is the chef and co-owner of Dill Restaurant in Reykjavík, Iceland, and a co-author of *North: The New Nordic Cuisine of Iceland*.

SPIKE GJERDE is the chef and co-owner of Woodberry Kitchen, Artifact Coffee, Shoo-Fly Diner and Parts and Labor, all in Baltimore.

VALERIE GORDON is the pastry chef and co-owner of Valerie Confections in Los Angeles and the author of *Sweet*.

JOHN GORHAM is the chef and co-owner of Toro Bravo, Tasty n Sons, Tasty n Alder and the Mediterranean Exploration Company, all in Portland, Oregon. He is a co-author of the cookbook *Toro Bravo*.

GREGORY GOURDET is the chef at Departure Restaurant + Lounge in Portland, Oregon.

DORIE GREENSPAN has authored and co-authored numerous cookbook and pastry books, including *Around My French Table* and *Baking Chez Moi*.

ALEX GUARNASCHELLI, a judge on Food Network's *Chopped* and winner of *The Next Iron Chef* Season 5, is the chef at Butter in New York City.

JOSH HABIGER, an F&W Best New Chef 2012, is the chef at Patterson House and Pinewood Social, both in Nashville.

TADAAKI HACHISU runs Hachisu Egg Farm in Saitama, Japan.

CARLA HALL is a co-host of ABC's *The Chew* and the owner of Carla Hall Petite Cookies, an artisan cookie company. She is the author of *Cooking with Love* and *Carla's Comfort Food*.

CHARLIE HALLOWELL is the chef and owner of Pizzaiolo, Boot & Shoe Service and Penrose, all in Oakland, California.

CHRIS HARRISON is a cofounder of Liber & Co., a craft cocktail syrup company in Austin.

SARAH HART is the chef and owner of Tiny Kitchen Catering in New York City.

CHRIS HASTINGS is the chef and co-owner of Hot and Hot Fish Club and the forthcoming Ovenbird, both in Birmingham, Alabama.

ADAM HIGGINBOTHAM and his brother **ROBERT HIGGINBOTHAM** are cofounders of Liber & Co., a craft cocktail syrup company in Austin.

LINTON HOPKINS, an F&W Best New Chef 2009 and visiting chef at Chefs Club by Food & Wine in New York City, is the chef and co-owner of Restaurant Eugene, Holeman & Finch Public House and H&F Bread Co., all in Atlanta.

STEPHANIE IZARD is a winner of Bravo's *Top Chef* Season 4 and the chef and co-owner of Girl & the Goat and Little Goat Diner, both in Chicago. She is a co-author of *Girl in the Kitchen*.

BILL JAMISON and his wife, **CHERYL JAMISON,** are the authors of more than a dozen cookbooks, including *Good Grilling* and *Born to Grill*. Cheryl is also a contributing culinary editor at *New Mexico Magazine* and writes for the blog Tasting NM.

JENNIFER JASINSKI is the chef and co-owner of Rioja, Bistro Vendôme and Euclid Hall Bar and Kitchen, all in Denver.

ALLISON JENKINS is the chef at LaV in Austin.

MATT JENNINGS is the chef and co-owner of the forthcoming Townsman in Boston.

KIR JENSEN is the pastry chef and owner of The Sugar Cube in Portland, Oregon, and the author of *50 Deliciously Twisted Treats from the Sweetest Little Food Cart on the Planet*.

TARA JENSEN is the baker and co-owner of Smoke Signals in Marshall, North Carolina.

AMANDA JOHNSON is the pastry chef and co-owner of Our Town Bakery in Hillsboro, North Dakota.

JUDY JOO is the first female winner of *Iron Chef UK* and the chef at The Playboy Club in London. She also hosts the Cooking Channel's *Korean Food Made Simple*.

PAUL KAHAN, an F&W Best New Chef 1999, is a co-chef and co-owner of several restaurants in Chicago, including Blackbird, Avec and The Publican.

KRISTOFER KALAS is a chocolatier and personal chef based in East Hampton, New York.

GAVIN KAYSEN, an F&W Best New Chef 2007, is the chef and owner of Spoon and Stable in Minneapolis.

BETH KIRBY is a photographer, stylist, writer and recipe developer. Her blog is called Local Milk.

DAN KLUGER, an F&W Best New Chef 2012, is a former chef at ABC Kitchen in New York City.

NAN KOHLER is the pastry chef and co-owner of Grist & Toll, a flour mill in Los Angeles.

DAGMARA KOKONAS, wife of restaurateur Nick Kokonas, is a milliner and an avid home cook in Chicago.

NICK KOKONAS is a co-owner of Alinea, Next and The Aviary cocktail bar, all in Chicago, and a co-author of *Alinea* and *Life, On the Line*.

JESSICA KOSLOW is the chef and owner of Sqirl in Los Angeles and an active member of Edible School Yard, Bakers Will Bake, Farm on Wheels and Sustainable Kitchen, all initiatives that aim to promote healthful eating habits.

NICOLE KRASINSKI is the pastry chef and co-owner of State Bird Provisions and The Progress, both in San Francisco, and co-author of the cookbook *The Workshop*.

ELI KULP, an F&W Best New Chef 2014, is the chef at Fork, High Street on Market, a.kitchen and a.bar, all in Philadelphia.

PAT LAFRIEDA is the chief executive officer of Pat LaFrieda Meat Purveyors, the star of Food Network's *Meat Men* and author of *Meat: Everything You Need to Know*.

MOURAD LAHLOU is the chef and owner of Aziza in San Francisco and author of the cookbook *Mourad: New Moroccan*.

ALI LARTER is an actress and author of the cookbook *Kitchen Revelry*.

DAVID LEBOVITZ is the author of the cookbooks *The Perfect Scoop* and *My Paris Kitchen* and the memoir *The Sweet Life in Paris*.

COREY LEE, an F&W Best New Chef 2012, is the chef and owner of Benu and Monsieur Benjamin, both in San Francisco.

DENNIS LEE is the chef and co-owner of Magnolia Brewing Company's Smokestack, Namu Gaji and the forthcoming Namu Noodles, all in San Francisco.

EDWARD LEE is the chef and co-owner of 610 Magnolia and MilkWood in Louisville, Kentucky. He is the author of *Smoke & Pickles*.

LUDO LEFEBVRE is the chef and co-owner of Trois Mec, Petit Trois and Ludo Bird, all in L.A.

YONI LEVY is the chef at Alta CA in San Francisco.

MARK LIBERMAN is the chef and co-owner of AQ in San Francisco; the chef at TBD and Mélange Market, also in San Francisco; and the chef at the forthcoming Trading Post Market and Bakery in Sonoma County.

DONALD LINK is the chef and owner of five restaurants in New Orleans, including Cochon and Herbsaint. He is the author of the cookbooks *Real Cajun* and *Down South*.

JENN LOUIS, an F&W Best New Chef 2012, is the chef and co-owner of Sunshine Tavern and Lincoln and the chef and owner of the catering company Culinary Artistry, all in Portland, Oregon.

TIM LOVE is the chef and owner of Lonesome Dove Western Bistro, Woodshed Smokehouse, Queenie's Steakhouse, Love Shack and White Elephant Saloon, all in the Fort Worth, Texas, area. He is also the host of CNBC's *Restaurant Startup*.

LACHLAN MACKINNON-PATTERSON, an F&W Best New Chef 2005 and visiting chef at Chefs Club by Food & Wine in New York City, is the chef and co-owner of Frasca Food and Wine in Boulder, Colorado.

SERGE MADIKIANS is the chef and owner of Serevan Restaurant in Amenia, New York.

FRANCIS MALLMANN is the chef and owner of 1884 Restaurante and Siete Fuegos at The Vines Resort & Spa in Mendoza and Patagonia Sur in Buenos Aires, all in Argentina, as well as Hotel & Restaurant Garzón in Uruguay. He is the author of the cookbook *Seven Fires*.

JAMIE MALONE, an F&W Best New Chef 2013, is the co-chef and cofounder of the forthcoming Brut in Minneapolis.

TIM MÄLZER is the chef and owner of Bullerei in Hamburg and the author of seven cookbooks; his most recent is *Green Box*.

WALTER MANZKE is the chef and co-owner of Wildflour Bakery and Café in Manila, Philippines, and Petty Cash and République, both in L.A.

MELIA MARDEN is the chef at The Smile and The Smile To Go, both in New York City, and the author of *Modern Mediterranean*.

REBECCA MASSON is the pastry chef and owner of the online shop Fluff Bake Bar and its brick-and-mortar location in Houston.

TONY MAWS is the chef and owner of Craigie on Main in Cambridge, Massachusetts, and The Kirkland Tap & Trotter in Somerville, Massachusetts.

MATT MCCALLISTER, an F&W Best New Chef 2014, is the chef and owner of FT33 in Dallas.

JAMIE MCDANIEL is a private chef in Temecula, California.

JENNIFER MCGRUTHER is the author of the cookbook and blog *The Nourished Kitchen*.

JIM MEEHAN is a co-owner of PDT in New York City, the deputy editor of *F&W Cocktails 2014* and the drinks editor of Tasting Table.

ORI MENASHE is the chef and owner of Bestia in Los Angeles.

GEORGE MENDES, an F&W Best New Chef 2011, is the chef and owner of two Aldea restaurants in New York City and the author of *My Portugal: Recipes and Stories*.

JOSÉ MANUEL MIGUEL is the chef at Goust in Paris.

FERNANDA MILANEZI is the chef at Maeve's Kitchen in London.

MASA MIYAKE is the chef and owner of Miyake and Pai Men Miyake, both in Portland, Maine.

MONDAY MORNING COOKING CLUB is a not-for-profit group in Sydney whose proceeds from the *Monday Morning Cooking Club* cookbook sales go to charity.

AKIKO MOORMAN, a restaurant consultant, is the director of operations for EI Ideas in Chicago.

SASHI MOORMAN is a co-owner of the bakery and wine-tasting room Piedrasassi in Lompoc, California, and a winemaker and consultant for wineries in California and Oregon.

JEFFREY MORGENTHALER is the bar manager at Clyde Common in Portland, Oregon, and a co-author of *The Bar Book*.

JEAN-PIERRE MOULLÉ, a former chef at Chez Panisse in Berkeley, California, and his wife, **DENISE LURTON MOULLÉ,** lead culinary tours and classes at Two Bordelais in Bordeaux, France. They are co-authors of *French Roots*.

SEAMUS MULLEN is the chef and owner of Tertulia and El Colmado, both in New York City, and the author of *Hero Food*.

TOM MYLAN is the butcher and co-owner of The Meat Hook in Brooklyn and author of *The Meat Hook Meat Book*.

ZOE NATHAN is the chef and co-owner of Rustic Canyon, Huckleberry Café, Sweet Rose Creamery and Milo and Olive, all in Santa Monica, California. She is the author of *Huckleberry*.

NEVIA NO is the owner of Bodhitree Farm in Pemberton Township, New Jersey.

RICHARD NOEL is a bartender and co-owner of Bar-X and Beer Bar, both in Salt Lake City.

JEREMY NOLEN is the chef at Brauhaus Schmitz and Wursthaus Schmitz, both in Philadelphia, and a co-author of *New German Cooking: Recipes for Classics Revisited*.

TRACY OBOLSKY is the pastry chef at North End Grill in New York City.

JOSEPH OGRODNEK, an F&W Best New Chef 2014, is a co-chef and co-owner of Battersby and Dover in Brooklyn and a co-author of *Battersby*.

HUGO ORTEGA is the chef and co-owner of Hugo's, Backstreet Café and Caracol Restaurant, all in Houston, and the author of *Hugo Ortega's Street Food of Mexico* and *Backstreet Kitchen*.

RUBEN ORTEGA is the pastry chef at Hugo's and Backstreet Café, both in Houston.

YOTAM OTTOLENGHI is the chef and co-owner of Ottolenghi, a restaurant and chain of prepared-food shops in London. A contributor to the *Guardian*, he is the author of five cookbooks, including *Plenty* and *Plenty More*.

MARK OVERBAY is the founder of Big Spoon Roasters, a nut butter company in Durham, North Carolina.

GRACE PARISI, a former F&W Test Kitchen senior editor, is the Oxmoor House executive food director, the author of *Get Saucy* and *Summer/Winter Pasta* and a recipe contributor to *The Portlandia Cookbook*.

JAMES PEISKER is a co-owner of two Porter Road Butcher shops in Nashville.

GEORGIA PELLEGRINI is a chef and the author of *Food Heroes*, *Girl Hunter* and *Modern Pioneering*.

CLAUDINE PÉPIN is a co-author, with her father, Jacques Pépin, of several cookbooks, including *Cooking with Claudine* and *Kids Cook French*.

JACQUES PÉPIN, master chef and F&W contributor, is the dean of special programs at Manhattan's International Culinary Center. His most recent cookbook is *Essential Pepin Desserts*.

VIET PHAM, an F&W Best New Chef 2011 and winner of Food Network's *Iron Chef America* Season 9, is the chef and co-owner of Ember + Ash, a co-owner of Forage and the consulting chef at Beer Bar, all in Salt Lake City.

CHARLES PHAN is the chef and owner of five restaurants in San Francisco, including The Slanted Door and Out the Door. He is the author of *The Slanted Door* and *Vietnamese Home Cooking*.

CONTRIBUTORS

MICHELLE POLZINE is the pastry chef and owner of 20th Century Cafe in San Francisco.

ALEX POPE is a co-owner of The Local Pig, a butcher shop in Kansas City, Missouri, and a cofounder and chef at Vagabond Pop Ups.

TODD PORTER is a co-publisher of the blog White on Rice Couple and a co-author of the cookbook *Bountiful*.

PAUL QUI, an F&W Best New Chef 2014 and winner of Bravo's *Top Chef* Season 9, is the chef and co-owner of Qui and the East Side King restaurants and food trucks in Austin.

ALICE QUILLET is a co-chef at Le Bal Café in Paris.

ANN REDDING is a co-chef and co-owner of Uncle Boons in New York City.

ANDREA REUSING is the chef and owner of Lantern in Chapel Hill, North Carolina, and author of *Cooking in the Moment*.

EVAN RICH and his wife, **SARAH RICH,** are the chefs and owners of Rich Table in San Francisco.

LOUIS-PHILIPPE RIEL is the chef at Le 6 Paul Bert in Paris.

ERIC RIPERT, an F&W Chef-in-Residence, is the chef and co-owner of Le Bernardin and its offshoot Aldo Sohm Wine Bar, both in New York City; Blue in Grand Cayman; Westend Bistro in Washington DC; and 10 Arts Bistro in Philadelphia. He is the host of PBS's *Avec Eric* and the author of four cookbooks; his most recent is *Avec Eric*.

AMANDA ROCKMAN is the pastry chef at Nico in Chicago.

ASHLEY RODRIGUEZ is a pastry chef and author of the blog Not Without Salt.

STÉPHANE ROSSILLON is the chef at Hôtel Restaurant Les Avisés in Avize, France.

GABRIEL RUCKER, an F&W Best New Chef 2007 and visiting chef at Chefs Club by Food & Wine in New York City, is the chef and co-owner of Le Pigeon and Little Bird in Portland, Oregon, and a co-author of *Le Pigeon*.

SLADE RUSHING is the chef at Brennan's in New Orleans.

JOSHUA RUSS TUPPER and his cousin **NIKI RUSS FEDERMAN** are fourth-generation co-owners of the smoked-fish purveyor Russ & Daughters in New York City. They recently opened Russ & Daughters Cafe.

YLENIA SAMBATI is a tour designer based in Puglia, Italy, and an instructor at Cantele winery's cooking school, iSensi.

MARCUS SAMUELSSON is the chef and co-owner of five restaurants, including Red Rooster and American Table, both in New York City, and Marc Burger in Chicago. He is also the creative food director and owner of three restaurants in Sweden. He is the author of several cookbooks, including *Marcus Off Duty*.

AARÓN SÁNCHEZ is the chef and owner of Mestizo in Leawood, Kansas, and the chef and co-owner of four restaurants, including Paloma in Stamford, Connecticut. He is also a judge on Food Network's *Chopped* and the author of *La Comida del Barrio* and *Simple Food, Big Flavor*.

ROBERTO SANTIBAÑEZ is the chef and owner of the Fonda restaurants in New York City and the author of *Rosa's New Mexican Table*, *Truly Mexican* and *Tacos, Tortas and Tamales*.

SUVIR SARAN is the chairman of the Asian Culinary Studies Center at the Culinary Institute of America and the author of *Indian Home Cooking*, *American Masala* and *Masala Farm*.

JONATHON SAWYER, an F&W Best New Chef 2010, is the chef and co-owner of The Greenhouse Tavern, Noodlecat and Trentina, all in Cleveland.

ADAM SCHOP is the chef at Miss Lily's and Miss Lily's 7A Cafe, both in New York City.

EDNA SCOTT was the owner of Edna's Club & Restaurant in Oklahoma City.

DANNY SEO, an eco-lifestyle expert, is the editor in chief of *Naturally, Danny Seo* magazine and the author of seven books, including *Generation React*.

DANIELE SERA is the chef at Castello di Casole in Siena, Italy.

ALON SHAYA is the chef and co-owner of Domenica in New Orleans.

NANCY SILVERTON, an F&W Best New Chef 1990, is the chef and co-owner of Osteria Mozza and Mozza2Go, both in Los Angeles, and the owner of Chi Spacca, also in L.A., and Pizzeria Mozza, with locations in L.A., Newport Beach and Singapore. She is the founder of La Brea Bakery and the author and co-author of nine books, including *The Mozza Cookbook*.

NANCY SINGLETON HACHISU is the author of the cookbook *Japanese Farm Food*. A Slow Food education leader, she teaches cooking classes and runs an English immersion program in Saitama, Japan, that promotes home-cooked meals.

MARK SLAWSON is a co-chef at Bunches & Bunches in Portland, Oregon.

DUANE SORENSON is the owner of Stumptown Coffee Roasters, with locations in Portland, Oregon, Los Angeles, Seattle and New York City; and Roman Candle, The Woodsman Tavern and Ava Gene's, all in Portland, Oregon.

SUSAN SPUNGEN is a food stylist, recipe developer, contributing food editor at *More* magazine and the author of *What's a Hostess to Do?* and *Recipes: A Collection for the Modern Cook*.

CARA STADLER, an F&W Best New Chef 2014, is the chef and co-owner of Tao Yuan in Brunswick, Maine.

CECILE STADLER, chef Cara Stadler's mother, is a co-owner of Tao Yuan in Brunswick, Maine.

TAMALPAIS STAR ROTH-MCCORMICK is the owner and co-chef at Bunches & Bunches in Portland, Oregon.

WALKER STERN, an F&W Best New Chef 2014, is a co-chef and co-owner of Battersby and Dover in Brooklyn and a co-author of *Battersby*.

KRISTEN STEVENS is the chef and owner of The Endless Meal, an underground supper club in Vancouver.

CURTIS STONE is the host of Food Network's *Kitchen Inferno* and the author of three cookbooks; his latest is *What's for Dinner?* He is the chef and owner of Maude in Beverly Hills.

GABRIEL STULMAN is the owner of Happy Cooking Hospitality, which includes Fedora, Perla and Bar Sardine, all in New York City.

MARK SULLIVAN, an F&W Best New Chef 2002, is the chef and co-owner of Spruce, The Village Pub, Café des Amis and Mayfield Bakery & Cafe, all in the San Francisco Bay Area.

ELI SUSSMAN is the chef at both Mile End Delicatessens in New York City and a co-author, with his brother Max, of *This Is a Cookbook*.

HEIDI SWANSON writes the blog 101 Cookbooks. She is the author of three cookbooks, including *Super Natural Every Day*.

DAREN SWISHER is the mixologist at JM Curley in Boston.

MICHAEL SYMON, an F&W Best New Chef 1998 and winner of Food Network's *The Next Iron Chef* Season 1, is the chef and co-owner of Lola and Lolita in Cleveland, Roast in Detroit and B Spot in Detroit, Cleveland and Columbus, Ohio. He is a co-host of ABC's *The Chew* and is the author and co-author of several books, including *Michael Symon's Carnivore*.

MARJORIE TAYLOR is the head instructor of the Cook's Atelier, a culinary center in Beaune, France.

ARI TAYMOR, an F&W Best New Chef 2014, is the chef and co-owner of Alma in Los Angeles.

MIMI THORISSON is the host of the French cooking show *La Table de Mimi* and author of *A Kitchen in France*.

KURT TIMMERMEISTER is the owner of Kurtwood Farms, a dairy farm on Vashon Island, Washington, and the author of *Growing a Feast: The Chronicle of a Farm-to-Table Meal* and *Growing a Farmer*.

WILL TORRES is the chef at Justin Vineyards & Winery in Paso Robles, California.

ANNA TRATTLES is a co-chef at Le Bal Café in Paris.

GERARDO VALENZUELA is the former chef at Vinobar Cipreses, a wine bar in the Casa Marín winery in Chile's San Antonio Valley.

MARCELA VALLADOLID is the host of Food Network's *Mexican Made Easy* and a co-host of *The Kitchen*. She is the author of *Mexican Made Easy* and *Fresh Mexico*.

JASON VINCENT, an F&W Best New Chef 2013, is the former chef at Nightwood in Chicago.

LUISE VINDAHL is a co-creator of the blog Green Kitchen Stories and a co-author of *Green Kitchen Travels* and *Vegetarian Everyday.*

BRYAN VOLTAGGIO is the chef and owner of five restaurants, including Volt in Frederick, Maryland, and Range in Washington, DC. He is the author of *Home: Recipes to Cook with Family and Friends* and a co-author of *Volt ink.*

MICHAEL VOLTAGGIO, an F&W Best New Chef 2013 and winner of *Top Chef* Season 6, is the chef and owner of ink. and ink.sack, both in Los Angeles, and a co-author of *Volt ink.*

JEAN-GEORGES VONGERICHTEN is the chef and co-owner of dozens of restaurants around the world, including Jean-Georges in New York City and Shanghai and ABC Kitchen in New York City. He is the author of many cookbooks; his most recent is *Home Cooking with Jean-Georges.*

JOSHUA WALKER is the chef and owner of Xiao Bao Biscuit in Charleston, South Carolina.

PHILIP WARD is the owner and beverage director of Mayahuel and the owner of Onward Spirits, both in New York City.

ALICE WATERS is the chef and owner of Chez Panisse in Berkeley, California, and the author of 12 books; her latest is *The Art of Simple Food II.* She is the founder of The Edible Schoolyard Project, a nonprofit program that aims to get an "edible education" into public schools.

THOMAS WAUGH is the director of bar operations for the Major Food Group hospitality company, which includes Carbone, ZZ's Clam Bar, Torrisi Italian Specialties and Dirty French, all in New York City.

JONATHAN WAXMAN is the chef and owner of Barbuto in New York City and Adele's in Nashville. He is a co-author of *A Great American Cook* and *Italian, My Way.*

CHARLES WEKSELBAUM is the owner of the salumi producer Charlito's Cocina in Long Island City, New York.

PATRICIA WELLS is the author of numerous books; her most recent is an updated version of her seminal book, *The Food Lover's Guide to Paris.* She also runs the culinary school At Home with Patricia Wells in Paris and Provence.

CATHY WHIMS is the chef and co-owner of Nostrana and Oven and Shaker in Portland, Oregon.

MICHAEL WHITE is the chef and co-owner of the Altamarea restaurant group, which includes Marea, The Butterfly and Ai Fiori in Manhattan and Al Molo in Hong Kong. He is a co-author of *Classico e Moderno* and *Fiamma.*

SHAE WHITNEY is the mixologist and owner of Dram Apothecary, a craft bitters production factory and tasting room in Silver Plume, Colorado.

TIM WIECHMANN is the chef and co-owner of T. W. Food in Cambridge and Bronwyn in Somerville, Massachusetts.

JODY WILLIAMS is the chef and owner of Buvette Gastrothèque in New York City and Paris and the chef and co-owner of Via Carota in New York City. She is also the author of *Buvette.*

JASON WILSON, an F&W Best New Chef 2006, is the chef and co-owner of Crush and Miller's Guild, both in Seattle.

JOEY WÖLFFER is a co-owner of Wölffer Estate Vineyard in Sagaponack, New York.

JAYSON WOODBRIDGE is the winemaker and owner of Hundred Acre in Rutherford, California, and Layer Cake Wines in St. Helena, California.

KUNIKO YAGI is the chef at Hinoki & the Bird and Comme Ça, both in Los Angeles.

SHERRY YARD is the pastry chef and co-owner of Helms Bakery in Los Angeles and the pastry chef for iPic Theaters in the U.S. She is the author of *The Secrets of Baking* and *Desserts by the Yard.*

JENNIFER YEE, an F&W Best New Pastry Chef 2014, works at Lafayette in New York City.

KRIS YENBAMROONG is the chef and owner of Night + Market Song and Night + Market Weho, both in Los Angeles.

SANG YOON is the chef and owner of Father's Office and Lukshon and the chef and co-owner of Helms Bakery, all in Los Angeles.

CHRIS YOUNG is a cofounder of ChefSteps, a Seattle-based cooks' collective, and a co-author of the six-volume *Modernist Cuisine.*

JUSTIN YU, an F&W Best New Chef 2014, is the chef and co-owner of Oxheart and Public Services Wine and Whiskey in Houston.

GEOFFREY ZAKARIAN is the chef and owner of The National and The Lambs Club, both in New York City, and the culinary director of The Plaza Hotel in New York City and The Water Club at Borgata in New Jersey. He is a judge on Food Network's *Chopped* and a co-host of *The Kitchen.* He is also the author of *My Perfect Pantry.*

RICARDO ZARATE is an F&W Best New Chef 2011 and former chef at Picca, Mo-Chica and Paiche in Los Angeles.

ANDREW ZIMMERN, an F&W Chef-in-Residence, is the writer of the Kitchen Adventures column on foodandwine.com, the host and creator of Travel Channel's *Bizarre Foods America* and the chef behind the AZ Canteen food truck in the Minneapolis area. He is the author of three books, including *The Bizarre Truth.*

IMAGES

EVI ABELER 323

CEDRIC ANGELES 29, 119, 171, 279

CHRIS CHEN 120, 121, 356

PAUL COSTELLO 47, 79, 169, 215, 265

CHRIS COURT 241, 251, 359

TARA FISHER 37, 138

BROOKE FITTS 133

PARKER FITZGERALD 172, 247, 303

CHRISTINA HOLMES 13, 25, 35, 43, 57, 73, 91, 103, 123, 125, 137, 141, 143, 149, 165, 179, 181, 189, 191, 203, 211, 230, 231, 244, 249, 255, 270, 277, 283, 290, 291, 293, 331, 347, 351, 352, 362

FRANCES JANISCH 371, 373, 377

KYLE JOHNSON 130, 131

JOHN KERNICK 11, 38, 53, 55, 61, 67, 87, 97, 104, 145, 147, 220, 223, 225, 239, 253, 259, 261, 315, 317, 328, 339, 364

LINE KLEIN 15, 49, 99, 305

JONATHAN LOVEKIN 274, 335

JOHNNY MILLER 23, 69, 311

AMY NEUNSINGER 19, 313

MARCUS NILSSON 192

CON POULOS 8, 27, 31, 41, 62, 65, 80, 92, 93, 100, 101, 107, 111, 115, 129, 153, 157, 159, 161, 175, 183, 195, 199, 207, 219, 229, 234, 237, 243, 269, 281, 284, 287, 297, 299, 307, 319, 324, 325, 341, 355, 360, 367, 368

BRIGITTE SIRE 266

KRISTEN STEVENS 345

FREDRIKA STJÄRNE 17, 51, 75, 83, 151, 155, 187, 227, 233, 273, 308

MOLLY YEH 71

PRODUCT IMAGES
From top to bottom: BBS/THE FOOD PASSIONATES/Corbis; courtesy of Crock-Pot; courtesy of Bantam Books, an imprint of Random House, a division of Random House, LLC, 2013, 2014; courtesy of Crock-Pot; courtesy of Crock-Pot (77); Ryan Clark for Marxfoods.com (85); courtesy of Potager Inc. (94)

Measurement Guide

BASIC MEASUREMENTS

GALLON	QUART	PINT	CUP	OUNCE	TBSP	TSP	DROPS
1 gal	4 qt	8 pt	16 c	128 fl oz			
½ gal	2 qt	4 pt	8 c	64 fl oz			
¼ gal	1 qt	2 pt	4 c	32 fl oz			
	½ qt	1 pt	2 c	16 fl oz			
	¼ qt	½ pt	1 c	8 fl oz	16 Tbsp		
			⅞ c	7 fl oz	14 Tbsp		
			¾ c	6 fl oz	12 Tbsp		
			⅔ c	5⅓ fl oz	10⅔ Tbsp		
			⅝ c	5 fl oz	10 Tbsp		
			½ c	4 fl oz	8 Tbsp		
			⅜ c	3 fl oz	6 Tbsp		
			⅓ c	2⅔ fl oz	5⅓ Tbsp	16 tsp	
			¼ c	2 fl oz	4 Tbsp	12 tsp	
			⅛ c	1 fl oz	2 Tbsp	6 tsp	
				½ fl oz	1 Tbsp	3 tsp	
					½ Tbsp	1½ tsp	
						1 tsp	60 drops
						½ tsp	30 drops

US TO METRIC CONVERSIONS

THE CONVERSIONS SHOWN HERE ARE APPROXIMATIONS. FOR MORE PRECISE CONVERSIONS, USE THE FORMULAS TO THE RIGHT.

VOLUME			WEIGHT			TEMPERATURE			CONVERSION FORMULAS
1 tsp	=	5 mL	1 oz	=	28 g	475°F	=	246°C	tsp × 4.929 = mL
1 Tbsp	=	15 mL	¼ lb (4 oz)	=	113 g	450°F	=	232°C	Tbsp × 14.787 = mL
1 fl oz	=	30 mL	½ lb (8 oz)	=	227 g	425°F	=	218°C	fl oz × 29.574 = mL
¼ c	=	59 mL	¾ lb (12 oz)	=	340 g	400°F	=	204°C	c × 236.588 = mL
½ c	=	118 mL	1 lb (16 oz)	=	½ kg	375°F	=	191°C	pt × 0.473 = L
¾ c	=	177 mL				350°F	=	177°C	qt × 0.946 = L
1 c	=	237 mL	**LENGTH**			325°F	=	163°C	oz × 28.35 = g
1 pt	=	½ L	1 in	=	2.5 cm	300°F	=	149°C	lb × 0.453 = kg
1 qt	=	1 L	5 in	=	12.7 cm	275°F	=	135°C	in × 2.54 = cm
1 gal	=	4.4 L	9 in	=	23 cm	250°F	=	121°C	(°F − 32) × 0.556 = °C